RESTATEMENT OF THE LAW THIRD

———

THE AMERICAN LAW INSTITUTE

———

RESTATEMENT OF THE LAW
THE
FOREIGN RELATIONS LAW
OF THE
UNITED STATES

Volume 2

§§ 501–End

TABLES and INDEX

As Adopted and Promulgated

BY

THE AMERICAN LAW INSTITUTE

AT WASHINGTON, D.C.

May 14, 1986

ST. PAUL, MINN.

AMERICAN LAW INSTITUTE PUBLISHERS

1987

This project has been supported by funds from the Andrew W. Mellon Foundation, the Department of State, the Ford Foundation, the German Marshall Fund of the United States, and the Rockefeller Foundation. In addition, the preparation of this volume was made possible in part by a grant from the Program for Research Tools and Reference Works of the National Endowment for the Humanities, an independent federal agency.

Library of Congress Cataloging-in-Publication Data

Main entry under title:

American Law Institute

Restatement of the law, third. foreign relations law of the United States
  Includes index.
  1. United States—Foreign relations—Law and legislation. I. American Law Institute
KF4051.R47   1987   342.73'0412   86-20665
ISBN 0-314-30138-0   347.302412

    Vol. 2 Restatement Foreign Rel.Law 3rd
    1st Reprint—1990

The American Law Institute

OFFICERS *

Roswell B. Perkins, *President*
Edward T. Gignoux, *1st Vice President*
Charles Alan Wright, *2nd Vice President*
Bennett Boskey, *Treasurer*
Geoffrey C. Hazard, Jr., *Director*
Paul A. Wolkin, *Executive Vice President*

COUNCIL *

Shirley S. Abrahamson	Madison	Wisconsin
Philip S. Anderson	Little Rock	Arkansas
Richard Sheppard Arnold	Little Rock	Arkansas
Frederick A. Ballard	Alexandria	Virginia
Bennett Boskey	Washington	District of Columbia
Michael Boudin	Washington	District of Columbia
Hugh Calkins	Cleveland	Ohio
Gerhard Casper	Chicago	Illinois
William T. Coleman, Jr.	Washington	District of Columbia
Roger C. Cramton	Ithaca	New York
Lloyd N. Cutler	Washington	District of Columbia
R. Ammi Cutter**	Cambridge	Massachusetts
William H. Erickson	Denver	Colorado
Thomas E. Fairchild	Madison	Wisconsin
Jefferson B. Fordham	Salt Lake City	Utah
John P. Frank	Phoenix	Arizona
George Clemon Freeman, Jr.	Richmond	Virginia
Edward T. Gignoux	Portland	Maine
Ruth Bader Ginsburg	Washington	District of Columbia
Erwin N. Griswold	Washington	District of Columbia
Conrad K. Harper	New York	New York
Clement F. Haynsworth, Jr.	Greenville	South Carolina
Vester T. Hughes, Jr.	Dallas	Texas
Joseph F. Johnston	Birmingham	Alabama
Nicholas deB. Katzenbach	Morristown	New Jersey
Herma Hill Kay	Berkeley	California
Pierre N. Leval	New York	New York
Edward Hirsch Levi	Chicago	Illinois
Betsy Levin	Washington	District of Columbia
Hans A. Linde	Salem	Oregon
Martin Lipton	New York	New York

---

* As of December 1, 1987

** *Chairman Emeritus*

III

IV

CHIEF REPORTER

LOUIS HENKIN, Columbia University School of Law, New York, New York [as of 1979]

ASSOCIATE REPORTERS

ANDREAS F. LOWENFELD, New York University School of Law, New York, New York

LOUIS B. SOHN, University of Georgia School of Law, Athens, Georgia

DETLEV F. VAGTS, Harvard Law School, Cambridge, Massachusetts

ADVISERS *

RICHARD R. BAXTER, Harvard Law School, Cambridge, Massachusetts [Deceased 1980]**

BENNETT BOSKEY, Washington, District of Columbia

ROBERT R. BOWIE, Washington, District of Columbia [as of 1980]

CHARLES N. BROWER, Judge, Iran—United States Claims Tribunal, The Hague, The Netherlands [as of 1982]

THOMAS BUERGENTHAL, Emory University School of Law, Atlanta, Georgia

HARDY C. DILLARD, Charlottesville, Virginia [Deceased 1982]

THOMAS EHRLICH, Provost, University of Pennsylvania, Philadelphia, Pennsylvania

ALONA E. EVANS, Wellesley College, Wellesley, Massachusetts [Deceased 1980]

ADRIAN S. FISHER, Georgetown University Law Center, Washington, District of Columbia [Deceased 1983]

HERBERT J. HANSELL, Washington, District of Columbia

MONROE LEIGH, Washington, District of Columbia

ROBERT MacCRATE, New York, New York

---

* As of May 14, 1986.

** Professor Baxter was Chief Reporter until his election to the International Court of Justice, at which time he became an Adviser.

V

INTERNATIONAL ADVISORY PANEL *

EDUARDO JIMENEZ DE ARÉCHAGA, Montevideo, Uruguay; formerly Judge, International Court of Justice

DEREK W. BOWETT, Whewell Professor of International Law, Cambridge University, Cambridge, England

MANFRED LACHS, Poland; Judge, International Court of Justice, The Hague, The Netherlands

SHIGERU ODA, Japan; Judge, International Court of Justice, The Hague, The Netherlands

MICHEL VIRALLY, Professor of Public Law, University of Law, Economics and Social Sciences, University of Paris II, Paris, France

Special Consultant on International Economic Law

KARL M. MEESSEN, Professor of Law, University of Augsburg, Augsburg, Federal Republic of Germany, and Professor of International Trade Law, Graduate Institute of International Studies, Geneva, Switzerland

*

---

* As of May 14, 1986.

SUMMARY OF CONTENTS

Volume 1

PART I

INTERNATIONAL LAW AND ITS RELATION TO UNITED STATES LAW

PART II

PERSONS IN INTERNATIONAL LAW

PART III

INTERNATIONAL AGREEMENTS

PART IV

JURISDICTION AND JUDGMENTS

SUMMARY OF CONTENTS

Volume 2

PART V

THE LAW OF THE SEA

PART VI

THE LAW OF THE ENVIRONMENT (99)

PART VII

PROTECTION OF PERSONS (NATURAL AND JURIDICAL)

SUMMARY OF CONTENTS

*

TABLE OF CONTENTS

Volume 1

PART I

INTERNATIONAL LAW AND ITS RELATION TO UNITED STATES LAW

CHAPTER 1

INTERNATIONAL LAW: CHARACTER AND SOURCES

CHAPTER 2

STATUS OF INTERNATIONAL LAW AND AGREEMENTS IN UNITED STATES LAW

TABLE OF CONTENTS

PART II

PERSONS IN INTERNATIONAL LAW

TABLE OF CONTENTS

PART III

INTERNATIONAL AGREEMENTS

CHAPTER 1

INTERNATIONAL AGREEMENTS: DEFINITION, NATURE, AND SCOPE

CHAPTER 2

THE MAKING OF INTERNATIONAL AGREEMENTS

CHAPTER 3

EFFECT AND INTERPRETATION OF INTERNATIONAL AGREEMENTS

CHAPTER 4

INVALIDITY AND TERMINATION OF INTERNATIONAL AGREEMENTS

TABLE OF CONTENTS

PART IV

JURISDICTION AND JUDGMENTS

CHAPTER 1

JURISDICTION TO PRESCRIBE

Subchapter A. Principles of Jurisdiction to Prescribe

Subchapter B. Principles of Jurisdiction Applied

Subchapter C. Principles of Jurisdiction:
United States Applications

CHAPTER 2

JURISDICTION TO ADJUDICATE

CHAPTER 3

JURISDICTION TO ENFORCE

CHAPTER 4

JURISDICTION AND THE LAW OF OTHER STATES

Subchapter A. Foreign State Compulsion

Subchapter B. The Act of State Doctrine

TABLE OF CONTENTS

CHAPTER 5

IMMUNITY OF STATES FROM JURISDICTION

Subchapter A. Immunity of Foreign States from Jurisdiction to Adjudicate

Subchapter B. Immunity of Foreign States from Jurisdiction to Prescribe

Subchapter C. Immunity of Foreign States from Jurisdiction to Enforce

CHAPTER 6

IMMUNITIES OF DIPLOMATS, CONSULS, AND INTERNATIONAL ORGANIZATIONS

Subchapter A. Diplomatic and Consular Immunities

TABLE OF CONTENTS

CHAPTER 7

INTERNATIONAL COOPERATION IN ADJUDICATION AND ENFORCEMENT

Subchapter A. Judicial Assistance

Subchapter B. Extradition

CHAPTER 8

FOREIGN JUDGMENTS AND AWARDS

Subchapter A. Foreign Judgments: Law of the United States

XIX

TABLE OF CONTENTS

Volume 2

PART V

THE LAW OF THE SEA

CHAPTER 1

SHIPS

CHAPTER 2

RIGHTS AND DUTIES OF COASTAL AND PORT STATES

TABLE OF CONTENTS

CHAPTER 3

HIGH SEAS

PART VI

THE LAW OF THE ENVIRONMENT

PART VII

PROTECTION OF PERSONS (NATURAL AND JURIDICAL)

CHAPTER 1

INTERNATIONAL LAW OF HUMAN RIGHTS

CHAPTER 2

INJURY TO NATIONALS OF OTHER STATES

TABLE OF CONTENTS

CHAPTER 3

INDIVIDUAL RIGHTS IN FOREIGN RELATIONS: LAW OF THE UNITED STATES

PART VIII

SELECTED LAW OF INTERNATIONAL ECONOMIC RELATIONS

CHAPTER 1

LAW OF INTERNATIONAL TRADE

CHAPTER 2

INTERNATIONAL MONETARY LAW

TABLE OF CONTENTS

PART IX

REMEDIES FOR VIOLATIONS OF INTERNATIONAL LAW

Cite thus:

Rest. 3rd, Restatement of the Foreign Relations Law
of the United States § ___

RESTATEMENT OF THE LAW THIRD

———

THE AMERICAN LAW INSTITUTE

———

RESTATEMENT OF THE LAW
THE
FOREIGN RELATIONS LAW
OF THE
UNITED STATES
Volume 2

*

Part V

THE LAW OF THE SEA

Introductory Note:

The law of the sea, as used in this Restatement, is that part of international law that deals with relations, activities, and interests involving the sea.[1] It includes the law applicable between coastal states and other states (or international organizations)[2] with regard to areas of the sea subject to coastal state jurisdiction, as well as that applicable among states generally with regard to the areas of the sea and the sea-bed beyond national jurisdiction.

The history of the law of the sea reflects a constant struggle between states that asserted special rights with respect to areas of the sea and other states that insisted on the freedom to navigate and fish in all the ocean spaces. In the 18th and 19th centuries the principle of freedom of the seas became established, but pressure by coastal states for special rights continued. Chapter 2 of this Part reflects the successful encroachment on the seas by the coastal states. Large areas, however, remain "beyond national jurisdiction" and subject to "the regime of the high seas," and are open to all for reasonable use, with due consideration for the rights of other states to use them similarly. See Chapter 3.

The previous Restatement set forth the law as reflected in the four conventions adopted by the First United Nations Law of the

---

[1] To be distinguished is admiralty law (in common law countries) or maritime law (in civil law countries), which deals primarily with relations between private persons involved in transport of passengers or goods. Various aspects of maritime law are now regulated by international conventions. The International Maritime Organization (IMO), formerly the Inter-Governmental Maritime Consultative Organization (IMCO), has been dealing with both public and private international law issues with emphasis on maritime safety and prevention of marine pollution, preparing both international conventions and guidelines (often in the form of "codes") for the maritime industry. The law of the sea, as embodied in the 1958 Conventions and in the 1982 Convention, *infra*, contains some rules of maritime law, *e.g.*, those concerning penal jurisdiction in the event of a collision between ships on the high seas. (See 1958 Convention on the High Seas, Art. 11; 1982 Convention on the Law of the Sea, Art. 97.) Rules relating to naval warfare have been codified by several Hague Conventions of 1907. 1 Bevans, Treaties and Other International Agreements of the United States of America, 1776–1949, at 669–738 (1968). It is not clear to what extent these rules apply to modern warfare. Neither is it clear whether the rules stated in this Restatement will apply, and with what modifications, in case of a war.

[2] The United Nations and its agencies have asserted the right to fly the United Nations flag on vessels temporarily owned or operated by them. See, *e.g.*, [1963] U.N. Juridical Y.B. 180; [1971] *id.* 186. *Cf.* 1958 Convention on the High Seas, Art. 7, and LOS Convention, Art. 93. The European Economic Community has asserted jurisdiction with respect to fisheries. See 15 Int'l Leg.Mat. 1425 (1976).

Sea Conference in 1958. The United States is a party to all of these conventions.[3] They codified the law as it had grown up over two centuries, including also the law of the continental shelf (§ 515), which had developed since 1945. Since those conventions came into effect, however, pressures for further extension of coastal state jurisdiction, notably by states in Latin America and Africa, became more insistent. In addition, the United Nations began, in 1967, to address the law governing mining for resources of the sea-bed beyond national jurisdiction. That initiative, combined with demands by coastal states for wider authority, especially to control fishing and marine pollution, and with the determination of the maritime states to maintain maritime freedoms, especially unimpeded transit through international straits, led to the Third United Nations Conference on the Law of the Sea (UNCLOS III), with a mandate to review all aspects of the law of the sea.

After eight years, the Conference completed the comprehensive United Nations Convention on the Law of the Sea (LOS Convention). The Convention contains 320 articles and 9 annexes (with 119 additional articles). Its 17 parts are entitled: (1) use of terms and scope; (2) territorial sea and contiguous zone; (3) straits used for international navigation; (4) archipelagic states; (5) exclusive economic zone; (6) continental shelf; (7) high seas; (8) regime of islands; (9) enclosed or semi-enclosed seas; (10) right of access of land-locked states to and from the sea and freedom of transit; (11) the [deep sea-bed] area; (12) protection and preservation of the marine environment; (13) marine scientific research; (14) development and transfer of marine technology; (15) settlement of disputes; (16) general provisions; and (17) final provisions.

In 1981, when the Convention was almost completed, a new Administration in the United States made a number of proposals for changes in Part XI of the Convention, dealing with deep sea-bed mining, but the Convention was completed without most of these

---

[3] The conventions adopted in 1958 were: Convention on the Territorial Sea and the Contiguous Zone, 15 U.S.T. 1606, T.I.A.S. No. 5639, 516 U.N.T.S. 205; Convention on the High Seas, 13 U.S.T. 2312, T.I.A.S. No. 5200, 450 U.N.T.S. 82; Convention on Fishing and Conservation of the Living Resources of the High Seas, 17 U.S.T. 138, T.I.A.S. No. 5969, 559 U.N.T.S. 285; Convention on the Continental Shelf, 15 U.S.T. 471, T.I.A.S. No. 5578, 499 U.N.T.S. 311. The United States is a party to all these conventions, but has not ratified the 1958 optional protocol concerning the compulsory settlement of disputes arising out of the interpretation and application of these conventions. 450 U.N.T.S. 169.

The Second Law of the Sea Conference was held in Geneva in 1960 to discuss the breadth of the territorial sea. It failed, by one vote, to approve a compromise proposal for a six-mile wide territorial sea and an additional six-mile exclusive fishing zone. 4 Whiteman, Digest of International Law 122–35 (1965).

changes. The final text [4] of the Convention was approved on April 30, 1982, by 130 votes in favor, four against (including the United States), and 17 abstentions. It was signed at Montego Bay, Jamaica, on December 10, 1982, by 119 states, and by 40 states thereafter; the United States refrained from signing. The Convention provides that it will enter into force 12 months after ratification or accession by 60 states. As of 1987, the Convention was not yet in force, and, after its entry into force, it will apply as such to the United States only if the United States becomes a party to it.

For purposes of this Restatement, therefore, the Convention as such is not law of the United States. However, many of the provisions of the Convention follow closely provisions in the 1958 conventions to which the United States is a party and which largely restated customary law as of that time. Other provisions in the LOS Convention set forth rules that, if not law in 1958, became customary law since that time, as they were accepted at the Conference by consensus and have influenced, and came to reflect, the practice of states. See § 102, Reporters' Note 2. In particular, in March 1983 President Reagan proclaimed a 200-nautical-mile exclusive economic zone for the United States and issued a policy statement in which the United States in effect agreed to accept the substantive provisions of the Convention, other than those dealing with deep sea-bed mining, in relation to all states that do so with respect to the United States.[5] Thus, by express or tacit agreement accompanied by consistent practice, the United States, and states generally, have accepted the substantive provisions of the Convention, other than those addressing deep sea-bed mining, as statements of customary law binding upon them apart from the Convention. See Case Concerning Delimitation of the Maritime Boundary of the Gulf of Maine (Canada/United States), [1984] I.C.J. Rep. 246, 294 (the provisions of the LOS Convention concerning the continental shelf and the exclusive economic zone "were adopted without any objections" and may "be regarded as consonant at present with general international law on the question"). In a few instances, however, there is disagreement whether a provision of the Convention reflects customary law. See, *e.g.*, § 514, Reporters' Note 4, and § 515, Comment *b*. Some provisions of the Convention, notably those accepting particular arrangements for settling disputes, clear-

---

[4] United Nations, The Law of the Sea: United Nations Convention on the Law of the Sea, U.N.Pub. No. E.83.V.5 (1983).

[5] 19 Weekly Comp. of Pres. Docs. 383 (1983), 83 Dep't State Bull., No. 2075, at 70–71 (1983), 22 Int'l Leg.Mat. 464 (1983).

ly are not customary law and have not been accepted by express or tacit agreement.[6]

Where the Convention reflects customary law, this Restatement generally uses the language of the Convention as a "black-letter" statement of international law. A source note after each section indicates its relation to the Convention and to the four conventions of 1958 which remain the law of the United States

---

[6] Some provisions of the LOS Convention either would have no application to the United States or their applicability is in doubt. See, *e.g.*, the following Comments and Reporters' Notes:

Substantive provisions:

> Section 514, Reporters' Note 4. Special rules apply to fishing for certain stocks and species of fish and to marine mammals. There is some disagreement whether all the details of these provisions are customary law. (Arts. 64–67.)

> Section 515, Comments *a, b.* Parties to the Convention that exploit nonliving resources of the continental shelf beyond 200 miles will have to make payments to the International Sea-Bed Authority. (Art. 82.)

> Section 515, Reporters' Note 1. On the basis of the 1958 Convention on the Continental Shelf, some states have claimed as continental shelf sea-bed areas extending beyond 200 miles. Some developing countries have taken the view that the consensus on the definition of the continental shelf is contingent on payments to the international fund from the area beyond 200 miles. Thus, whether as a matter of customary law a state can claim such an area as continental shelf without making such payments is in dispute. (Arts. 76, 82.)

> Section 523. This section departs from Part XI of the LOS Convention, which establishes a regime for deep sea-bed exploration and exploitation, much of which is not customary law.

Institutions and Procedures:

The provisions of the LOS Convention establishing new institutions and a system for the settlement of disputes arising under the Convention are not customary international law and will not become law for the United States unless the United States becomes a party to the Convention. See, *e.g.*:

> Section 502, Comment *f.* Where a state suffers a loss due to the failure of the flag state to exercise proper control, a special dispute settlement mechanism is provided in Part XV of the Convention.

> Section 511, Reporters' Note 8. A special procedure to resolve continental shelf issues is to be established. (Art. 73(8).)

> Section 514, Comments *b, j,* and Reporters' Note 2; § 515, Reporters' Note 2. Under the Convention there will be a special procedure for settling certain disputes between coastal and other states as to their respective rights and duties in the exclusive economic zone. (Art. 297.)

> Section 517, Comment *e,* and Reporters' Note 3. The Convention provides for submission of certain maritime boundary disputes to a conciliation commission. (Art. 298(1)(a).)

> In addition to effecting changes in the substantive rules governing mining in the deep sea-bed, the Convention would establish institutions and procedures that are binding only on parties to the Convention. See § 523, Comment *e,* and Reporters' Note 3.

except to the extent that they have been superseded. Where the Convention does not reflect customary law or where a provision of the Convention is at variance with a provision of domestic United States law, this Restatement sets forth the customary law or the applicable United States domestic law. In a few instances, the difference between the Convention and customary law is subtle, being a matter of emphasis and degree, and this Restatement follows the text of the Convention with appropriate indications of deviation in Comments and Reporters' Notes.

As regards the exploitation of the minerals of the sea-bed beyond national jurisdiction, the Convention clearly does not reflect customary law and does not state the law of the United States as long as the Convention is not in force for the United States. In respect of such mining, therefore, this Restatement (§ 523) restates the customary international law that applies before the Convention goes into effect, and would apply thereafter to nonparties.

If the Convention comes into effect for the United States, those of its provisions that are self-executing will supersede any inconsistent United States law. See § 115, Comment c.

Apart from the 1958 conventions, many other international agreements deal with law of the sea matters; the United States is a party to several of them.[7] Where applicable, these agreements are reflected in this Restatement.

United States domestic law also contains provisions relating to the law of the sea. In some instances this law incorporates principles of international law. Thus, the Marine Sanctuaries Act

---

[7] Among those to which the United States is a party are: the International Conventions for the Safety of Life at Sea, London, 1960, 16 U.S.T. 185, T.I.A.S. No. 5780, 536 U.N.T.S. 27, and London, 1974, 32 U.S.T. 47, T.I.A.S. No. 9700, and a Protocol, London, 1978, 32 U.S.T. 5577, T.I.A.S. No. 10009; the International Convention for the Prevention of Pollution of the Sea by Oil, London, 1954, amended 1962, and 1969, 12 U.S.T 2989, T.I.A.S. No. 4900, 327 U.N.T.S. 3, amendments, 17 U.S.T. 1523, T.I.A.S. No. 6109, 600 U.N.T.S. 332, and 28 U.S.T. 1205, T.I.A.S. No. 8505; the International Convention Relating to Intervention on the High Seas in Cases of Oil Pollution Casualties, Brussels, 1969, 26 U.S.T. 765, T.I.A.S. No. 8068; Protocol Relating to Intervention on the High Seas in Cases of Pollution by Substances Other than Oil, London, 1973, T.I.A.S. No. 10561; the Convention on the Prevention of Marine Pollution by Dumping of Wastes and Other Matter, Washington, London, Mexico City, and Moscow, 1972, 26 U.S.T. 2403, T.I.A.S. No. 8165; London Protocol, 1978, replacing the nonratified 1973 Convention for the Prevention of Pollution from Ships, 17 Int'l Leg.Mat. 546 (1978); the Convention on the Facilitation of International Maritime Traffic, London, 1965, 18 U.S.T. 410, T.I.A.S. No. 6251, 591 U.N.T.S. 265; the International Convention on Load Lines, London, 1966, 18 U.S.T. 1857, T.I.A.S. No. 6331, 640 U.N.T.S. 133, corrections, 20 U.S.T. 17, T.I.A.S. No. 6629, and 20 U.S.T. 2577, T.I.A.S. No. 6720; the Convention on International Regulations for Preventing Collisions at Sea, London, 1972, 28 U.S.T. 3459, T.I.A.S. No. 8587. But, as of 1986, the United States was not yet a party to the United Nations Convention on Conditions for Registration of Ships, adopted on February 7, 1986 (U.N. Doc. TD/RS/CONF/23 (1986); 7 U.N. LOS Bull. 87 (1986)).

of 1972, as amended in 1984, provides that sanctuary regulations "shall be applied in accordance with generally recognized principles of international law." [8] In several respects the United States has anticipated the LOS Convention by legislation enacted while the United Nations Conference was in progress. The United States has adopted a 200-nautical-mile fishing zone, anticipating the 200-nautical-mile exclusive economic zone provided in the LOS Convention (this Restatement, § 514).[9] The United States also adopted interim sea-bed mining legislation, which was intended to apply pending the then-expected coming into force for the United States of a comprehensive law of the sea convention.[10] Earlier, the Outer Continental Shelf Lands Act of 1953 [11] anticipated the provisions in the 1958 Convention on the Continental Shelf. That legislation was amended and supplemented by the Outer Continental Shelf Resources Management Act of 1978.[12]

REPORTERS' NOTES

1. *Bibliography.*

C. Colombos, The International Law of the Sea (6th ed. 1967).

M. McDougal and W. Burke, The Public Order of the Oceans (1962).

O'Connell, The Law of the Sea (Shearer, ed. 1982).

L. B. Sohn & K. Gustafson, The Law of the Sea in a Nutshell (1984).

The literature on the law of the sea is voluminous. For a guide to that literature, see N. Papadakis and M. Glassner, eds., International Law of the Sea: A Bibliography (1984). The United Nations Office of the Special Representative of the Secretary-General for the Law of the Sea has published bibliographies on the subject since 1974; as of 1986, the latest was Law of the Sea: A Select Bibliography, U.N. Pub. No. E.85.V.2 (1985). In 1985, the Center for Oceans Law and Policy at the University of Virginia started publishing the United Nations Convention on the Law of the Sea, 1982: A Commentary, a multi-volume work that provides the legislative history of the Convention, article by article. For an unofficial systematic collection of the documents, formal and informal, relating to the preparation of the LOS Convention, see R. Platzöder, Third United Nations Conference on the Law of the Sea: Documents (12 vols., 1982–87; additional volumes forthcoming). See also, Nordquist *et al.* eds., New Directions in the Law of the Sea (11 volumes, 1973–81).

2. *Previous Restatement.* This Part follows the previous Restate-

---

[8] 16 U.S.C. § 1435.

[9] Fishery Conservation and Management Act of 1976, 16 U.S.C. § 1801.

[10] Deep Seabed Hard Mineral Resources Act of 1980, 30 U.S.C. § 1401; see this Restatement, § 523.

[11] 43 U.S.C. § 1331.

[12] 43 U.S.C. § 1801.

ment but reflects clarifications of and changes in the law since the 1958 conventions, notably as reflected in the 1982 LOS Convention.

Chapter One

SHIPS

§ 501. Nationality of Ships

A ship has the nationality of the state that registered it and authorized it to fly the state's flag, but a state may properly register a ship and authorize it to fly the state's flag only if there is a genuine link between the state and the ship.

Source Note:

This section follows Articles 5 and 6 of the 1958 Convention on the High Seas, and Articles 91 and 92 of the LOS Convention.

Comment:

a. Flag and registration. Each state is entitled to determine the conditions for granting its nationality to ships, for the registration of ships in its territory, and for the right to fly its flag. 1958 Convention on the High Seas, Article 5(1); LOS Convention, Article 91(1). Each state has the obligation to maintain a register containing the names and particulars of ships flying its flag. LOS Convention, Article 94(2)(a).

Ordinarily a state confers its nationality on a ship by registering it; then, the state provides the ship with basic documents and authorizes it to fly the state's flag. The conditions for registration of ships are set out in the 1986 United Nations Convention on that subject. See Reporters' Notes 3 and 4. Occasionally, a state will authorize temporary use of its flag by a ship not registered anywhere or, in exceptional cases, by a ship registered in another state. Some national laws and international agreements refer to the place of registry rather than the nationality or flag. See Reporters' Notes 4 and 6.

b. "Genuine link." In general, a state has a "genuine link" entitling it to register a ship and to authorize the ship to use its flag if the ship is owned by nationals of the state, whether natural or juridical persons, and the state exercises effective control over the

10

ship. In most cases a ship is owned by a corporation created by the state of registry. However, in determining whether a "genuine link" with the state of registry exists, the following additional factors are to be taken into account: whether the company owning the ship is owned by nationals of the state; whether the officers and crew of the ship are nationals of the state; how often the ship stops in the ports of the state; and how extensive and effective is the control that the state exercises over the ship.

Although international law requires a genuine link between the ship and the registering state, the lack of a genuine link does not justify another state in refusing to recognize the flag or in interfering with the ship. A state may, however, reject diplomatic protection by the flag state when the flag state has no genuine link with the ship. If another state doubts the existence of a genuine link, for instance, because there is evidence that the flag state has not been exercising its duties to control and regulate the ship (see § 502), it may request that the flag state "investigate the matter and, if appropriate, take any action necessary to remedy the situation." LOS Convention, Article 94(6); § 502, Comment *f.*

c. Registration and right to navigate. A ship may not navigate without being registered in, and flying the flag of, some state; it may navigate only under the flag of the state in which it is registered and must carry documents certifying its registration. A ship that is not registered in any state and is not entitled to fly the flag of any state is considered "a ship without nationality"; it may be boarded by a warship or other clearly marked law enforcement ship of any state, for the purpose of checking documents and such further examination as may be necessary. See § 522(2)(b); LOS Convention, Articles 92(2), 110(1)(d). If a ship sails under the flag of a state without that state's authorization, a warship or other law enforcement ship of the state may detain the ship and the state may institute proceedings against the ship, confiscate it, and punish the responsible individuals. See § 522(2)(b); LOS Convention, Article 110(1)(e).

A ship may sail under the flag of one state only. A state may not grant the right to use its flag to a ship that is already sailing under another flag except pursuant to arrangements for transferring the ship from one state's registry to another. A ship may not change its flag during voyage or in a port of call except in the case of a genuine transfer of ownership or change of registry. A ship that sails under the flags of two or more states, using each of them as convenient, may not claim the nationality of either of the states in question in relation to any other state, and may be treated as a ship without flag or nationality. 1958 Convention on the High Seas, Article 6; LOS Convention, Article 92.

REPORTERS' NOTES

1. *"Ships" and "vessels"*. The Drafting Committee of UNCLOS III concluded that the words "ship" and "vessel" should be interpreted as equivalent. U.N. Doc. A/CONF. 62/91 at 87 (1979).

Within the meaning of the 1986 United Nations Convention on Conditions for Registration of Ships, Introductory Note to this Part, n. 7, a ship is "any self-propelled sea-going vessel used in international seaborne trade for the transport of goods, passengers, or both with the exception of vessels less than 500 gross registered tons." Art. 2, U.N.Doc. TD/RS/CONF/23, at 2 (1986), 7 U.N. LOS Bull. 87, 90 (1986); see Reporters' Note 4. "Ship" has been defined also as meaning "a vessel of any type whatsoever operating in the marine environment," including "hydrofoil boats, air-cushion vehicles, submersibles, floating craft and fixed or floating platforms." International Convention for the Prevention of Pollution from Ships, London, 1973, Art. 2(4), 12 Int'l Leg.Mat. 1319 (1973). According to another definition, "ship" means "any sea-going vessel of any type whatsoever, including floating craft, whether self-propelled or towed by another vessel, making a sea voyage." 1962 Amendments to the 1954 International Convention for the Prevention of Pollution of the Sea by Oil, London, 1962, Art. 1(1), 17 U.S.T. 1523, T.I.A.S. No. 6109, 600 U.N. T.S. 332. In the United States Deepwater Port Act of 1974, "vessel" means "every description of watercraft or other artificial contri-

vance used as a means of transportation on or through the water." Section 3(19), 33 U.S.C. § 1502(19). See also the Whaling Convention Act of 1949, Section 2(e), 16 U.S.C. § 916(e). Oil drilling platforms and similar fixed installations are in some respects subject to the law of the sea and maritime law as if they were ships. See the International Convention for the Prevention of Pollution from Ships, London, 1973, Art. 2(4) and Annex I, Reg. 21, 12 Int'l Leg.Mat. 1319 (1973); Convention on Civil Liability for Oil Pollution Damage Resulting from Exploration for and Exploitation of Seabed Mineral Resources, London, 1977, Art. 1(2), 6 Churchill, Nordquist and Lay, New Directions in the Law of the Sea 535 (1977). On the other hand, the definition of "ship" in some conventions expressly excludes "an installation or device engaged in the exploration and exploitation of the resources of the sea-bed and the ocean floor and the subsoil thereof." See International Convention Relating to Intervention on the High Seas in Cases of Oil Pollution Casualties, Brussels, 1969, Art. II(2)(b), 26 U.S.T. 765, T.I.A.S. No. 8068. See also the Intervention on the High Seas Act of 1974, Section 2(1), 33 U.S.C. § 1471(5).

According to the LOS Convention, a "warship" is "a ship belonging to the armed forces of a State bearing the external marks distinguishing such ships of its nationality, under the command of an officer duly commissioned by the government of the State and whose name appears in the appropriate service list or its equivalent and is manned by a crew which is under regular armed forces discipline." Art. 29. See also 1958 Convention on the High Seas, Art. 8. For the status of warships, see § 513, Comment *h*, and § 522(1) and Comment *a* thereto; and as to law enforcement ships and aircraft, see § 513, Comment *g*; § 522, Comment *a*.

2. *Land-locked states as flag states.* By the Treaty of Versailles, land-locked states, though without a sea-coast or a maritime port, were permitted to confer their nationality on sea-going ships. Treaty of Peace with Germany, Versailles, 1919, Art. 273, 2 Bevans 43, at 167. According to Article 90 of the LOS Convention, "[e]very State, whether coastal or land-locked, has the right to sail ships flying its flag on the high seas." There is a similar provision in Article 4 of the 1958 Convention on the High Seas, and in Article 4(1) of the 1986 Convention on Conditions for Registration of Ships (Reporters' Note 1).

3. *Ships' documents.* A ship usually carries a certificate of registry, a log book, a cargo manifest, and other appropriate documents. For a list of such documents, see, *e.g.*, 1 Oppenheim, International Law 596 (8th ed. by Lauterpacht, 1955); United Nations, Economic and Social Commission for Asia and the Pacific, Guide-Lines for Maritime Legislation 55–60 (2d ed. 1986) (U.N. Doc. ST/ESCAP/180). For documents required under the 1965 Convention on Facilitation of International Maritime Traffic, see Annex to the Convention, Section 2, 18 U.S.T. 410, T.I.A.S. No. 6251, 591 U.N.T.S. 265. (As of 1986, the United States and 54 other states were parties to this Convention.)

4. *Conditions for registration of ships.* In 1986, after three years of intensive negotiations, the developed countries, the "open registry" countries (see Reporters' Note 7), and the developing countries concluded the United Nations Convention on Conditions for Registration of Ships (Reporters' Note 1). That Convention established the details of registration as well as special rules for enabling the state of registration to exercise effective control over ships flying its flag by ensuring that "those who are responsible for the management and operation of a ship on its register are readily identifiable and accountable" (preamble and Arts. 6 and 10). The Convention contains provisions relating to ship ownership, management, and manning (Arts. 8–10), including measures to protect the interests of labor-supplying countries (Art. 14). The Convention was adopted by consensus (U.N.Doc. A/41/301, para. 3 (1986)); it will enter into force when ratified by not less than 40 states having registered vessels with combined tonnage amounting to at least 25 percent of world tonnage. (The tonnage condition would be fulfilled if the Convention were ratified, for example, by just two countries, Liberia and Panama, but the Convention would not go into force unless ratified also by 38 other states).

The laws of most states authorize only vessels owned by nationals to fly the state's flag; sometimes it is also required that the vessel be constructed in the state or that it employ national crews. Some states require total national ownership, others require only that a 75 percent interest be owned by nationals, and some even less than 50 percent. When a vessel is owned by a corporation, the right to fly a state's flag usually depends upon the amount of capital of the corporation owned by the state's nationals, the required percentage ranging from 50 percent to 100 percent. In many states it is sufficient that the corporation be incorporated under the law of the state; in others it is required that the principal place of business be located in the state or that the corporation be managed, in whole or in part, by nationals of that state.

The laws of various states concerning the conditions for granting nationality to ships have been collected by the Secretariat of the United Nations in Laws Concerning the Nationality of Ships, 5 U.N. Legislative Series (U.N.Pub. 56.V.1); for a supplement, see 8 *id.* 113–34 (U.N.Pub. 59.V.2). For a brief survey of these laws, see Boczek, Flags of Convenience 41–44 (1962).

5. *Documentation of vessels: Law of the United States.* The law of the United States concerning documentation of vessels was codified in the Vessel Documentation Act of 1980, and recodified during a partial revision of Title 46 (Shipping) of the United States Code in 1983, 46 U.S.C. §§ 2101, 12101–12309. Under that law, the term "vessel of the United States" means "a vessel documented or numbered under the laws of the United States." *Id.* § 2101(46). A vessel of at least five net tons, not registered under the laws of a foreign country, is eligible for United States documentation if the vessel is owned by an individual who is a citizen of the United States or by an entity having strong links with the United States. *Id.* § 12102. A certificate of documentation, which is conclusive evidence

of nationality for international purposes, is not conclusive evidence of ownership in a proceeding conducted under the laws of the United States. *Id.* § 12104. A vessel may be issued a "registry" entitling it to be employed in foreign trade and in trade with outlying United States possessions. *Id.* § 12105. Vessels having additional qualifications (*e.g.,* a vessel built in the United States or captured in war and lawfully condemned as a prize) may be issued a coastwise license, a Great Lakes license or a fishery license, or any one of them. *Id.* §§ 12106– 12108. An undocumented vessel, if "equipped with propulsion machinery of any kind," may obtain a certificate or number from an appropriate authority of a State in which the vessel is principally operated. *Id.* §§ 12301, 12304. As to temporary documentation for vessels procured outside the United States, see § 12112.

6. *International agreements relating to nationality of ships.* Since the beginning of the 19th century, the nationality of ships has been dealt with in treaties of friendship, commerce, and navigation. Rienow, The Test of the Nationality of a Merchant Vessel 19–21, 165–70 (1937). For instance, in Article IV of the treaty between the United States and the Netherlands of January 19, 1839, the parties agreed "to consider and treat as vessels of the United States and of the Netherlands, all such as, being furnished by the competent authority with a passport or sealetter, shall, under the then existing laws and regulations, be recognized as national vessels by the country to which they respectively belong." 10 Bevans 22, at 23. Similar provisions are included in recent treaties. See,

e.g., United States-Netherlands, Treaty of Friendship, Commerce and Navigation, 1956, 8 U.S.T. 2043, T.I.A.S. No. 3942, 285 U.N.T.S. 231, Art. XIX(1); Federal Republic of Germany-Italy, Treaty of Friendship, Commerce and Navigation, 1957, Art. 24(1), reprinted in National Legislation and Treaties Relating to the Territorial Sea, *etc.*, 15 U.N. Legislative Series 747 (U.N.Pub. E/ F.70.V.9). An agreement between Japan and the United Kingdom provides differing criteria for determining the nationality of their respective vessels: United Kingdom vessels are those "registered at a port in any territory" of the United Kingdom to which the agreement applies, while Japanese vessels are those that carry "the papers required by the law of Japan in proof of Japanese nationality." United Kingdom-Japan, Treaty of Commerce, Establishment and Navigation, 1962, Art. 2(3), 478 U.N.T.S. 29, 88. An inter-American agreement, to which the United States is not a party, provides that the "nationality of ships is proved by the navigation license and the certificate of registration and has the flag as an apparent distinctive symbol." The Bustamante Code of Private International Law, Havana, 1928, Art. 274, 86 L.N.T.S. III, 326, 4 Hudson, International Legislation 2279, 2320 (1931).

7. *Genuine link and flags of convenience.* In Lauritzen v. Larsen, 345 U.S. 571, 584, 73 S.Ct. 921, 929, 97 L.Ed. 1254 (1953), the Supreme Court said:

Each state under international law may determine for itself the conditions on which it will grant its nationality to a merchant ship, thereby accepting responsibility for it and acquiring authority over it. Nationality is evidenced to the world by the ship's papers and its flag. The United States has firmly and successfully maintained that the regularity and validity of a registration can be questioned only by the registering state.

In McQuade v. Compania de Vapores San Antonio, S.A., 131 F.Supp. 365, 367 (S.D.N.Y.1955), the court pointed out that "a State, under international law, may be permitted to grant its nationality to a ship owned by foreigners and is considered to have done so when it authorizes the use of its maritime flag." The Attorney General, in an *amicus curiae* brief presented to the National Labor Relations Board in 1961 at the request of the Departments of State and Defense, submitted that "the flag, as a ready, recognizable, and accepted standard must be preferred pragmatically to any other and that in accordance with that standard, the indirect financial interest of American citizens in a foreign registered ship may not deprive a vessel of its status as a national of the country whose flag is flown." Cited in Empresa Hondurena de Vapores, S.A. v. McLeod, 300 F.2d 222, 225 (2d Cir.1962), *judgment vacated*, 372 U.S. 10, 83 S.Ct. 671, 9 L.Ed.2d 547 (1963); Reporters' Note 8. See also 1 Hyde, International Law Chiefly as Interpreted and Applied by the United States 809–13 (2d ed. 1945); 1 Oppenheim, International Law 595 (8th ed. by Lauterpacht, 1955).

In view of the rise of flag of convenience shipping in the 1950s, the 1958 Convention on the High Seas introduced the limitation that "[t]here must exist a genuine link between the State and the ship." Art. 5(1). An analogous requirement had been applied earlier to the nationality of an individual. The International Court of Justice in the Nottebohm Case (Liechtenstein v. Guatemala), [1955] I.C.J. Rep. 4, ruled that because of the absence of a genuine link between Nottebohm and Liechtenstein, Guatemala could refuse to recognize Nottebohm's acquisition of Liechtenstein nationality and Liechtenstein could not bring a proceeding on his behalf against Guatemala. See § 211, Reporters' Note 1.

Complaints about the lack of genuine link are directed primarily against "flags of convenience." Such flags benefit both the states granting them and the owners and users of the ships sailing under these flags. The United Kingdom Committee of Inquiry into Shipping (the "Rochdale Committee") listed six major features of flags of convenience:

(i) The country of registry allows ownership and/or control of its merchant vessels by noncitizens;

(ii) Access to the registry is easy. A ship may usually be registered at a consul's office abroad. Equally important, transfer from the registry at the owner's option is not restricted;

(iii) Taxes on the income from the ships are not levied by the flag state or are low. A registry fee and an annual fee, based on tonnage, are normally the only charges made. A guarantee or acceptable understanding regarding future freedom from taxation may also be given;

(iv) The country of registry is a small power with no national requirement under any foreseeable circumstances for all the shipping registered, but receipts from very small charges on a large tonnage may produce a substantial effect on its national income and balance of payments;

(v) Manning of ships by nonnationals is freely permitted; and

(vi) The country of registry has neither the power nor the administrative machinery effectively to impose any government or international regulations; nor has the country the wish or the power to control the companies themselves.

Cmnd. 4337, at 51 (1970); see also Osieke, "Flags of Convenience Vessels: Recent Developments," 73 Am.J.Int'l L. 604 (1979).

In order to tighten the conditions under which the "open-registry countries" (the new name for states granting "flags of convenience") would be allowed to register ships, the United Nations General Assembly arranged in 1982 for a conference on the subject, which led to the adoption of the United Nations Convention on Conditions for Registration of Ships (Reporters' Notes 1 and 4). The Convention provides, *inter alia*, that each state concerned shall establish "a competent and adequate national maritime administration," able to ensure compliance with international rules and standards concerning "the safety of ships and persons on board and the prevention of pollution of the marine environment"; provide for periodical surveying of ships; and require ships to carry documents evidencing the right of the ship to fly the state's flag, and other documents required by international conventions. Art. 5.

8. *Effects of lack of genuine link.* Another state is not entitled to decide unilaterally that there is no genuine link between a ship and the flag state or to refuse on that basis to recognize the flag.

> The existence of a "genuine link" between the state and the ship is not a condition of recognition of the nationality of a ship; that is, no state can claim the right to determine unilaterally that no genuine link exists between a ship and the flag state. Nevertheless there is a possibility that a state, with respect to a particular ship, may assert before an agreed tribunal, such as the International Court of Justice, that no genuine link exists. In such event, it would be for the Court to decide whether or not a "genuine link" existed.

S.Exec.Rep. No. 5 (Law of the Sea Conventions), 106 Cong.Rec. 1189, 1190 (86th Cong.2d sess., 1960), 9 Whiteman, Digest of International Law 14–15 (1968).

Moreover, as the court of appeals for the Second Circuit pointed out, "it would be unreasonable to conclude that . . . other states do not owe some obligations of respect" so long as the flag state effectively exercises its "jurisdiction and control in administrative, technical and social matters over ships flying its flag." Empresa Hondurena de Vapores, S.A. v. McLeod, 300 F.2d 222, 235–36 (2d Cir.1962), *reversed on other grounds, sub nom.* McCulloch v. Sociedad Nacional de Marineros de Honduras, 372 U.S. 10, 83 S.Ct. 671, 9 L.Ed.2d 547 (1962), citing the 1958 Convention on the High Seas, Art. 5(1) (followed

with minor changes in LOS Convention, Art. 94(1)). The court of appeals had held in that case that the National Labor Relations Act should be interpreted as not intended to apply to maritime operations of foreign-flag ships employing alien seamen. 300 F.2d 222 at 231. In vacating the court of appeals judgment, and upholding a district court judgment in a related case, the Supreme Court referred to the "well-established rule of international law that the law of the flag state ordinarily governs the internal affairs of a ship." McCulloch v. Sociedad Nacional de Marineros de Honduras, 372 U.S. at 21, 83 S.Ct. at 677. For United Kingdom decisions relating to attempts by an international labor union to induce port workers to withdraw services from a ship navigating under a flag of convenience in order to compel owners to pay standard union wages to the crew, see N.W.L. Ltd. v. Woods, [1979] 3 All E.R. 614 (H.L.) (injunction against labor union rejected); Merkur Island Shipping Co. v. Laughton, [1983] 2 All E.R. 189 (H.L.) (injunction against labor union upheld).

International law probably does not permit a state to assert authority with respect to a vessel owned by its nationals but registered in another state merely on the ground that there is no genuine link between the vessel and the flag state.

9. *Imposition of nationality on ships owned by nationals.* A state cannot impose its nationality on a ship owned by its nationals if the ship is already registered elsewhere and is flying the flag of the state of registration. McDougal, Burke, and Vlasic, "The Maintenance of Public Order at Sea and the Nation-

ality of Ships," 54 Am.J.Int'l L. 25, 57 (1960); Rienow, The Test of the Nationality of a Merchant Vessel 218–19 (1937). When Honduras enacted a law providing that a vessel owned by an individual residing in Honduras would be considered as Honduran, the United States protested that imposition of Honduran nationality upon vessels registered in the United States would constitute a violation of international law. As a result of the protest, Honduras did not enforce the law. [1909] U. S. Foreign Relations 366–75; Rienow, *supra* 106–107.

Some states, including the United States, have asserted the right to mobilize ships for purposes of national defense if they are owned by nationals or by a corporation controlled by nationals, or are under construction within the state. See Act of June 29, 1936, as amended, 46 U.S.C. § 1242; statement by the Legal Adviser (Hager), Dep't of State, May 4, 1960, I.C.J. Pleadings, Constitution of the Maritime Safety Committee of the Inter-Governmental Maritime Consultative Organization 427–28 (1960).

10. *Nationality of aircraft.* The rules as to nationality of ships have been followed, with some modifications, in developing the rules as to aircraft. According to the 1944 Chicago Convention on International Civil Aviation, aircraft have the nationality of the state in which they are registered. An aircraft cannot be validly registered in more than one state, but its registration may be changed from one state to another. The registration of an aircraft in a state is to be made in accordance with the laws and regulations of the state. Any aircraft engaged in international civil aviation must display appropriate nationality and registration marks and carry documents specified in the Convention. Arts. 17–20, 29–34, T.I.A.S. No. 1591, 3 Bevans 944, 15 U.N.T.S. 295. (As of 1986, this Convention was in force for 156 states, including the United States.) A state party to the Chicago Convention is apparently precluded from contesting the nationality of an aircraft registered in another state party. Cheng, The Law of International Air Transport 130–31 (1962). See also Honig, The Legal Status of Aircraft 34–37 (1956).

§ 502. Rights and Duties of Flag State

(1) The flag state is required

(a) to exercise effective authority and control over the ship in administrative, technical, and labor matters; and

(b) (i) to take such measures as are necessary to ensure safety at sea, avoid collisions, and prevent, reduce, and control pollution of the marine environment, and

(ii) to adopt laws and regulations and take such other steps as are needed to conform these measures to generally accepted internation-

al standards, regulations, procedures, and practices, and to secure their implementation and observance.

(2) The flag state may exercise jurisdiction to prescribe, to adjudicate, and to enforce, with respect to the ship or any conduct that takes place on the ship.

Source Note:

This section is drawn from Articles 5(1), 10, 11, 24, and 25 of the Convention on the High Seas, and Articles 94, 192, 194, 211, 217, and 219 of the LOS Convention.

Comment:

a. Flag state responsibility for control of ship. Under international law, the flag state is responsible for adopting and enforcing laws to protect the welfare of the crew and passengers aboard a ship and to maintain good order thereon, and for ensuring that activities aboard the ship do not endanger other ships or the marine environment. This responsibility continues at all times, wherever the ship is located. As to the concurrent jurisdiction of the coastal state over matters that are within the flag state's responsibility under this section, see § 512, Reporters' Notes 5 and 7.

b. Principal duties of flag state. The 1958 Convention on the High Seas, Article 5(a), contains only the general language set forth in Subsection (1)(a); the LOS Convention spells out the duties of the flag state in detail. According to Article 94, in particular, the flag state has the duty to take such measures as are necessary to ensure safety at sea with regard to, *inter alia:*

(i) the construction, equipment, and seaworthiness of ships;

(ii) the manning of ships, labor conditions, and the training of crews, taking into account the applicable international instruments;

(iii) the use of signals, the maintenance of communications, and the prevention of collisions; and

(iv) the qualifications of the ships' masters and their officers.

c. International standards for safety and environmental protection. The standards, regulations, procedures, and practices to which the flag state is required to conform, Subsection (1)(b)(ii), are principally those developed under the auspices of the International Maritime Organization (IMO) and to some extent the International Labor Organization (ILO). They are "generally accepted" if the convention or instrument setting them forth is widely approved, even if it is not formally adhered to. Under present customary law (§ 102, Comments *f* and *i*), a flag state has an obligation to conform to them even if it has not ratified such convention or instrument. Once a standard has been generally accepted, a state is obligated, in particular, to apply it to all ships flying its flag and to adopt any necessary laws, regulations, and penalties.

d. Jurisdiction of flag state. The flag state has jurisdiction to prescribe law with respect to the conduct of a ship. LOS Convention, Article 94. For the basis of that jurisdiction, see § 402(2). The flag state has jurisdiction to prescribe with respect to any activity aboard the ship (see § 402, Comment *h*), but such jurisdiction is not exclusive when the ship is in a port or internal waters of another state. The flag state's jurisdiction also overlaps in some respects with the jurisdiction of the coastal state when the ship is in the territorial sea, contiguous zone, or a deepwater port of that state. The flag state has exclusive jurisdiction to enforce regulations in respect of its warships and activities aboard them, even in the ports of another state, but the port state may ask a warship refusing to comply with port regulations to leave the port. See § 512, Reporters' Note 6.

In case of a collision on the high seas, no penal or disciplinary proceedings may be instituted against the master or crew member of the ship except before the judicial or administrative authorities of the flag state or of the state of which such person is a national; the ship itself may be detained for purposes of investigation, or arrested, only by the authorities of the flag state. 1958 Convention on the High Seas, Article 11; LOS Convention, Article 97.

e. Other rights and duties of flag state. In addition to the principal duties set forth in this section, the flag state has the specific duties: (i) to prescribe that a master of the ship, insofar as he can do so without serious danger to the ship, shall render assistance to any person in danger of being lost at sea, especially in case of a collision (1958 Convention on the High Seas, Article 12; LOS Convention, Article 98); (ii) to take effective measures to prevent and punish the transport of slaves in its ships (1958 Convention on the High Seas, Article 13; LOS Convention, Article 99); (iii) to adopt laws and regulations to prohibit and punish the breaking of or injury to a submarine telegraphic, telecommunication, or high-voltage power cable or a submarine pipeline (1958 Convention on the High Seas, Article 27; LOS Convention, Article 113); (iv) to ensure, in compliance, with applicable international rules and standards, the prevention, reduction, and control of pollution of the marine environment (§ 603; LOS Convention, Article 217).

The flag state also has the general duty to ensure that any person on board a ship respects the international law of the sea standards, and to punish any such person who fails to do so. See 1958 Convention on the High Seas, Articles 10, 12–13, 24–25, 27–28; LOS Convention, Articles 94(5), 98–99, 109, 113–14, 117, 216–17.

For the rights and duties of states as to the conservation of the living resources of the high seas, and the protection of the marine environment, see §§ 521 and 603.

f. Complaints by other states. A state that has clear grounds to believe that authorities of the flag state have not exercised proper jurisdiction and control with respect to a ship may report the facts to the flag state. Upon receiving such a report, the flag state is required to investigate the matter and take any action necessary to remedy the situation. LOS Convention, Article 94(6). Any state that has, or whose nationals have, suffered a loss as a result of the failure of the flag state to exercise proper jurisdiction and control may present an international claim for damages against the flag state. See, *e.g.*, LOS Convention, Article 235. For states parties to the Convention, Part XV provides a mechanism for resolving disputes on these issues.

g. Flag state failures as evidence of lack of "genuine link." Failure of a flag state to exercise effective authority and control, as called for by Subsection (1)(a), or to take the necessary measures, as called for by Subsection (1)(b), may be a factor in determining a lack of a "genuine link" between the flag state and the ship. See § 501, Comment *b* and Reporters' Notes 7 and 8.

h. Protection of merchant ships by flag states. The flag state has the same right to exercise diplomatic protection with respect to its ships as a state has with respect to its nationals or companies (see § 713, Comment *f*), and is entitled to make claims against other states in case of damage to its ship or injury to the seamen manning it, regardless of their nationality.

REPORTERS' NOTES

1. *Measures to ensure safety.* In carrying out its obligations under Subsection (1)(b)(i), the flag state is obligated to assure:

(a) that each ship, before registration and thereafter at appropriate intervals, is surveyed by a qualified surveyor of ships, and has on board such charts, nautical publications, and navigational equipment and instruments as are appropriate for the safe navigation of the ship;

(b) that each ship is in the charge of a master and officers who possess appropriate qualifications, in particular in seamanship, navigation, communications, and marine engineering, and that the crew is appropriate in qualification and numbers for the type, size, machinery, and equipment of the ship; and

(c) that the master, officers, and, to the extent appropriate, the crew are fully conversant with and required to observe the applicable international regulations concerning the safety of life at sea, the prevention of collisions, the prevention, reduction, and control of marine pollution, and the maintenance of communications by radio.

LOS Convention, Art. 94(4).

2. *Generally accepted international standards.* The obligation of the flag state under Subsection (1)(b)(ii) to conform to "generally accepted international standards" is provided in Article 10(2) of the 1958 Convention on the High Seas. Article 94(5) of the LOS Convention requires, more broadly, conformity with "generally accepted international regulations, procedures and practices," such as those laid down in the 1974 Safety of Life at Sea Convention (entered into force for the United States in 1980, and amended; see Introductory Note to this Part, n. 7). The broader obligation has become binding on all flag states as a matter of customary international law.

3. *Jurisdiction of flag state.* The notion that a ship is a floating part of the territory of the flag state is generally recognized as fiction, but the law of the flag state is applied to the ship "on the pragmat-

ic basis that there must be some law on shipboard, that it cannot change at every change of waters, and no experience shows a better rule than that of the state that owns her." Lauritzen v. Larsen, 345 U.S. 571, 585, 73 S.Ct. 921, 930, 97 L.Ed. 1254 (1953). The flag state may thus apply its laws to such events as birth of a child, marriage, a will or contract made, or a crime committed, aboard ship. 1 Oppenheim, International Law 597 (8th ed. by Lauterpacht, 1955). Compare The S.S. Lotus, P.C.I.J. ser. A, No. 10 at 25 (1927) ("a ship on the high seas is assimilated to the territory of the State of the flag of which it flies . . . what occurs on board a vessel on the high seas must be regarded as if it occurred on the territory of the State whose flag the ship flies"), and the statement of Judge Moore, *id.* at 69. Under United States law, however, a person born on board a United States ship is not born "in the United States" for purposes of citizenship under the Fourteenth Amendment. Lam Mow v. Nagle, 24 F.2d 316 (9th Cir.1928).

In United States v. Flores, 289 U.S. 137, 53 S.Ct. 580, 77 L.Ed. 1086 (1933), the Supreme Court held that United States law applied to an act done on a United States vessel on the river Congo in Africa. See also United States v. Ross, 439 F.2d 1355 (9th Cir.1971), *certiorari denied,* 404 U.S. 1015, 92 S.Ct. 686, 30 L.Ed. 2d 661 (1972) (act done in the harbor of Nha Trang, South Vietnam, held to be committed on the high seas and therefore within special maritime and territorial jurisdiction of United States); United States v. Warren, 578 F.2d 1058, 1064–65, n. 4 (5th Cir.1978), *modified,* 612 F.2d 887 (5th Cir.1980), *certiorari de-*

nied, 446 U.S. 956, 100 S.Ct. 2928, 64 L.2d.2d 815 (1980); Harvard Research in International Law, Jurisdiction with respect to Crime, 29 Am.J.Int'l L., Supp. 508–15 (1935).

In a case involving a collision between a French and a Turkish vessel on the high seas, as a result of which the Turkish vessel sank and several members of its crew drowned, the Permanent Court of International Justice held that Turkey's trial of an officer of the French ship was not contrary to international law, as the state of the flag was entitled to exercise jurisdiction over an offense that had an effect aboard its vessel. The *S.S. Lotus, supra*, at 32. In view of the delays in maritime transport that might result from the general application of that decision, the rule was changed by several international agreements limiting jurisdiction in such circumstances to the flag state of the vessel alleged to be responsible for the collision and the state of nationality of the accused person. This excludes the jurisdiction of the flag state of the damaged ship, which had been accepted in the Lotus case. See 1952 Brussels Convention for the Unification of Certain Rules relating to Penal Jurisdiction in Matters of Collision or Other Incidents of Navigation, 439 U.N.T.S. 233. See also 1958 Convention on the High Seas, Art. 11; LOS Convention, Art. 97.

For discussion of the jurisdiction of a consul over merchant ships flying the flag of his state that arrive in his district, see Lee, Consular Law and Practice 80–115 (1961).

4. *Exercise by United States of criminal jurisdiction over certain foreign vessels.* The United States Criminal Code, 18 U.S.C. § 7(1) in-cludes in the term "special maritime and territorial jurisdiction of the United States," the "high seas, any other waters within the admiralty and maritime jurisdiction of the United States and out of the jurisdiction of any particular State [of the United States]"; §§ 7(1) and 7(5) extend United States criminal jurisdiction to acts committed on "any vessel [or aircraft] belonging in whole or in part to the United States or any citizen thereof, . . . when such vessel is within the admiralty and maritime jurisdiction of the United States and out of the jurisdiction of any particular State [of the United States]." This language does not seem to exclude acts committed on the high seas on board foreign vessels owned in whole or in part by United States nationals, but courts have applied the statute only to vessels having either United States registry or no registry at all. See § 403, Reporters' Note 9; § 433, Reporters' Note 4; previous Restatement § 28, Reporters' Note 2. In United States v. Keller, 451 F.Supp. 631, 636–37 (D. Puerto Rico 1978), the court held that it had jurisdiction over defendants arrested on the high seas on board a ship flying no flag, on the ground that the ship appeared to be owned at least in part by United States citizens and was thus subject to the special maritime jurisdiction of the United States. The court indicated that it could have assumed jurisdiction as well on the basis that the vessel was registered in the United States and that "it was the American flag and no other, which this vessel was 'entitled to fly.'"

It is doubtful whether 18 U.S.C. § 7(1) was intended to apply where a United States corporation does not own the ship outright but merely owns in whole or in part a foreign corporation that in turn owns the ship flying a foreign flag. See previous Restatement § 28, Reporters' Note 2.

An act done on a ship in navigable waters of a State of the United States is subject to the laws of that State. The United States has not enacted federal law applicable to such acts. See United States v. Harvey, 54 F.Supp. 910 (D.Ore. 1943). For the meaning of "navigable waters," see cases collected in 52 A.L.R.Fed. 788 (1980).

5. *Protection of ship by flag state.* Whether diplomatic protection should be provided to a ship by the state of registration and flag or the state whose nationals own the ship, see Watts, "The Protection of Merchant Ships," 33 Brit.Y.B.Int'l L. 52 (1957). See also § 902, Comment *j.*

6. *Exercise of jurisdiction by state other than flag state.* In the rare case where the state of registry and the flag state are temporarily different (see § 501, Comment *a*), both states may exercise jurisdiction over the vessel in some respects, but in case of conflict of jurisdiction the state of registry prevails. Katrantsios v. Bulgaria, Greco-Bulgarian Mixed Arbitral Tribunal, 7 Recueil des décisions des

Tribunaux Arbitraux Mixtes 39, 42 (1928). See 9 Whiteman, Digest of International Law 23 (1968); Jenks, "Nationality, the Flag, and Registration as Criteria for Demarcating the Scope of Maritime Conventions," 19 J. of the Soc. of Comp. Leg. & Int'l L. (3d ser.) 245 (1937); Mugerwa, "Subjects of International Law," in Sørensen, ed., Manual of Public International Law 247, 259–60 (1968) (ships flying the flag of an international organization but registered in a state).

A foreign vessel present in the port, the internal waters or the territorial sea of a state is subject to the jurisdiction of that state for various purposes. See § 512, Comment *c* and Reporters' Note 5. When a vessel is owned, directly or indirectly, by a person not a national of the flag state, the state of nationality of the owner has no jurisdiction over the vessel but may affect the vessel by virtue of its jurisdiction to prescribe law in respect of the owner. See §§ 402–403.

7. *Previous Restatement.* Subsection (1)(a) follows § 28(2) of the previous Restatement; the other provisions of this section were not covered in the previous Restatement.

Chapter Two

RIGHTS AND DUTIES OF COASTAL AND PORT STATES

§ 511. Coastal State Authority in Zones of Adjacent Sea

Subject to §§ 512–15, a coastal state may exercise jurisdiction over the following coastal zones:

(a) **The territorial sea:** a belt of sea that may not exceed 12 nautical miles, measured from a baseline that is either the low-water line along the coast or the seaward limit of the internal waters of the coastal state or, in the case of an archipelagic state, the seaward limit of the archipelagic waters;

(b) **The contiguous zone:** a belt of sea contiguous to the territorial sea, which may not extend beyond 24 nautical miles from the baseline from which the breadth of the territorial sea is measured;

(c) **The continental shelf:** the sea-bed and subsoil of the submarine areas that extend beyond the coastal state's territorial sea

    (i) throughout the natural prolongation of the state's land territory to the outer edge of the continental margin, subject to certain limitations based on geological and geographical factors; or

    (ii) to a distance of 200 nautical miles from the baseline from which the breadth of the territorial sea is measured, where there is no continental margin off the coast or where

25

the continental margin does not extend to that distance;

(d) **The exclusive economic zone: a belt of sea beyond the territorial sea that may not exceed 200 nautical miles from the baseline from which the breadth of the territorial sea is measured.**

Source Note:

Subsections (a) and (b) combine elements of Articles 1(1), 3, and 5 of the 1958 Convention on the Territorial Sea and the Contiguous Zone, and of Articles 2(1), 3, 5, and 8(1) of the LOS Convention. Subsection (c) follows Article 76 of the LOS Convention (modifying considerably Article 1 of the 1958 Convention on the Continental Shelf). Subsection (d) follows Articles 55 and 57 of the LOS Convention; there was no such provision in the 1958 Conventions.

Comment:

a. Different coastal state authority in different zones. The authority of the coastal state is different in the different zones defined in this section. The coastal state exercises sovereignty in the territorial sea; limited policing rights in the contiguous zone; sovereign rights over the natural resources of the continental shelf and over economic exploitation of the exclusive economic zone; and limited jurisdiction within the exclusive economic zone with regard to marine scientific research, the protection and preservation of the marine environment, and artificial islands and certain installations and structures. *Compare* § 512 and § 513 *with* § 514 and § 515. With respect to matters falling within its authority in the particular zone, the coastal state generally has jurisdiction to prescribe, to adjudicate, and to enforce by nonjudicial measures, but such jurisdiction is not necessarily exclusive. See Introductory Note to Part IV.

b. "Sovereignty" and "sovereign rights." A state has complete sovereignty over the territorial sea, analogous to that which it possesses over its land territory, internal waters, and archipelagic waters. See § 512; LOS Convention, Article 2(1). See also the 1958 Convention on the Territorial Sea and the Contiguous Zone, Article 1(1). The sovereignty over the territorial sea is subject, however, to the right of innocent passage for foreign vessels (*id.* Articles 1(2) and 14(1); LOS Convention, Articles 2(3) and 17; see § 513(1) and (2)). The territorial sea within a strait or adjacent to archipelagic waters is also subject to the right of transit passage or archipelagic sea lanes passage (LOS Convention, Articles 38 and 53(1); see § 513(3) and (4)).

"Sovereign rights," which a coastal state enjoys in its exclusive economic zone and on its continental shelf, are functional in character, limited to specified activities. In the continental shelf, the coastal state exercises sovereign rights only "for the purpose of exploring it and exploiting its natural resources," both living and nonliving. See § 515; 1958 Convention on the Continental Shelf, Article 2; LOS Convention, Article 77. In the exclusive economic zone, a coastal state has sovereign rights "for the purpose of exploring and exploiting, conserving and managing the natural resources, whether living or nonliving, of the waters superjacent to the sea-bed and its subsoil," as well as "with regard to other activities for the economic exploitation and exploration of the zone, such as the production of energy from the water, currents and winds." See § 514; LOS Convention, Article 56(1)(a). In addition, international law confers on the coastal state limited jurisdiction in that zone for some other purposes, *e.g.*, with respect to marine scientific research and the protection and preservation of the marine environment, and artificial islands and certain installations and structures. *Id.* Articles 56(1)(b) and 60.

c. Overlap of continental shelf and exclusive economic zone. The exclusive economic zone and the continental shelf overlap to a large extent, as both extend to 200 nautical miles. However, the continental shelf may extend beyond 200 nautical miles where the outer edge of the continental margin extends farther. See Comment *j*. See also § 515, Comment *a*.

d. Exercise of coastal state jurisdiction optional. Under international law, every coastal state is entitled to exercise authority in areas of the sea adjacent to its coast, as indicated in this chapter. There is, however, no duty for a state to assert or exercise such authority or to do so to the fullest extent permissible. The United States, for instance, has refused to extend its territorial sea beyond three miles, to claim certain areas as historic waters, or to draw straight baselines in certain areas where its coast is deeply indented or where there is a fringe of islands along the coast, thus diminishing the sea areas to which its jurisdiction could have been extended. See United States v. California, 381 U.S. 139, 167–68, 175, 85 S.Ct. 1401, 1416–17, 1421, 14 L.Ed.2d 296 (1965); United States v. Louisiana, 394 U.S. 11, 72–73, 89 S.Ct. 773, 806–807, 22 L.Ed.2d 44 (1969). See also Reporters' Notes 3, 4, and 5.

In respect of coastal zones other than the continental shelf, the jurisdiction of the coastal state and the limits and content of that jurisdiction depend on a proclamation or other express act by the state, but the rights of the coastal state in the continental shelf are automatic and do not depend on exercise or assertion of authority.

Compare Article 77(3) of the LOS Convention *with* Articles 3, 33, 47, and 57.

    e. Internal waters and ports. Internal waters are waters wholly or largely surrounded by a state's land territory, as well as sea waters on the landward side of the baseline of the territorial sea or of the archipelagic waters. 1958 Convention on the Territorial Sea and the Contiguous Zone, Article 5(1); LOS Convention, Articles 8(1) and 50. Under international law, a coastal state's sovereignty over its land territory extends to its internal waters, including bays. See Comment *f.* A state also has complete sovereignty over its seaports, but there are special rules for roadsteads and offshore terminals. 1958 Convention on the Territorial Sea, Article 9; LOS Convention, Articles 12, 60, 218, and 220.

    f. Bays. A coastal state may designate a bay as its internal waters if it has prescribed characteristics. It must be a well-marked indentation in the coast, not a mere curvature. Its area must be as large as, or larger than, that of the semicircle whose diameter is a line drawn across the mouth of the indentation. The closing line of a bay is drawn between its natural entrance points; the line may not exceed 24 nautical miles, but a 24-mile line may be drawn within the bay in such manner as to enclose the maximum area of water that is possible with a line of that length. 1958 Convention on the Territorial Sea and the Contiguous Zone, Article 7; LOS Convention, Article 10.

    In addition, international law recognizes "historic" bays that have been considered internal waters even though they do not satisfy criteria for a bay. 1958 Convention on the Territorial Sea and the Contiguous Zone, Article 7(6); LOS Convention, Article 10(6).

    g. Islands. An island is "a naturally formed area of land, surrounded by water, which is above water at high tide." 1958 Convention on the Territorial Sea and the Contiguous Zone, Article 10(1); LOS Convention, Article 121(1). In this Restatement, the term "coast" includes not only the shore of the mainland but also of islands; all islands are entitled to a territorial sea, a contiguous zone, an exclusive economic zone, and a continental shelf. LOS Convention, Article 121(2). But rocks that cannot sustain human habitation or economic life of their own have only a territorial sea and a contiguous zone, not an exclusive economic zone or a continental shelf. *Id.* Article 121(3). See also *id.* Article 6 with respect to reefs.

    h. Baseline from which territorial sea is measured. The normal baseline for measuring the breadth of the territorial sea is the low-water line along the coast as marked on large-scale charts officially recognized by the coastal state. 1958 Convention on the Territorial Sea and the Contiguous Zone, Article 3; LOS Convention, Article 5. Where internal waters border the territorial sea, the line of demarcation between internal waters and the territorial sea forms the baseline for measuring the breadth of the territorial sea, the contiguous zone, and the exclusive economic zone. This line may be relevant also to determine the extent of the continental shelf under Subsection (c). 1958 Convention on the Territorial Sea and the Contiguous Zone, Articles 4–8; LOS Convention, Articles 3–11, 57 and 76.

In localities where the coastline is "deeply indented and cut into," or where there is a fringe of islands along the coast in its immediate vicinity, straight lines joining appropriate points may be drawn to form the baseline from which the breadth of the territorial sea is measured, provided that these baselines do not depart to any appreciable extent from the general direction of the coast. 1958 Convention on the Territorial Sea and the Contiguous Zone, Article 4; LOS Convention, Article 7.

i. Archipelagic states. An archipelagic state is one consisting of one or more archipelagoes, and perhaps other islands, and forming "an intrinsic geographical, economic and political" (or historic) entity (*e.g.*, the Philippines, and Indonesia). A state composed of both mainland territory and one or more archipelagoes (*e.g.*, Greece, India, or the United States) is not an archipelagic state for purposes of the law of the sea. An archipelagic state may "draw straight archipelagic baselines joining the outermost points of the outermost islands" and measure its territorial sea from these baselines, provided that the baselines do not exceed 100 nautical miles (with some exceptions), and that the area thus encompassed includes the main islands and has a ratio of water-area to land-area between 1 to 1 and 9 to 1. LOS Convention, Articles 46–47. The waters enclosed by the archipelagic baselines are "archipelagic waters." *Id.* Article 49(1). As to passage through such waters, see § 513(4).

j. Extent of continental shelf. The 1958 Convention on the Continental Shelf defined the continental shelf as referring "to the seabed and subsoil of the submarine areas adjacent to the coast [of mainland or islands] but outside the area of the territorial sea to a depth of 200 metres or, beyond that limit, to where the depth of the superjacent waters admits of the exploitation of the natural resources of the said areas." Article 1. After difficult negotiations, the Third United Nations Conference on the Law of the Sea adopted by consensus a more complex definition based on a combination of the concept of natural prolongation with a specified distance from the shore. The new definition broadens the area under the jurisdiction of the coastal state by extending it to the entire continental margin (*i.e.*, the continuation of the land mass until it reaches the abyssal plain), subject to some limitations where the margin is unusually large. LOS Convention, Article 76. The new definition also gives the coastal state authority over the sea-bed to a distance of 200 nautical miles even if that sea-bed is not the natural prolongation of the coastal land mass. In that area, the coastal state has jurisdiction over sea-bed resources both under the doctrine of the continental shelf and as one of its rights in the exclusive economic zone. This complex definition for the continental shelf has been accepted implicitly by the United States. See the 1983 Oceans Policy Statement, Introductory Note to this Part.

　　k. Contiguous zone and other special coastal zones. International law recognizes special rights for a coastal state to take measures to enforce specified laws in a zone contiguous to the territorial sea, extending up to 24 nautical miles from the baselines from which the breadth of the territorial sea is measured. See this section, clause (b), and § 513, Comment *f.* International law has not recognized coastal state assertions of special zones to protect security or environment. As to air defense identification zones asserted by some states, see § 521, Reporters' Note 2.

REPORTERS' NOTES

　　1. *Authority of coastal state.* Traditional international law accepted coastal state sovereignty only over internal waters, ports, historic bays, and territorial sea, and enforcement authority for the coastal state in a zone contiguous to its territorial sea. The 1958 Convention on the Continental Shelf recognized the exclusive jurisdiction of the coastal state over the sea-bed resources of the continental shelf. The LOS Convention added sovereignty over archipelagic waters, extended the definition of the continental shelf, and gave the coastal state exclusive rights to resources and other limited rights in the exclusive economic zone. The authority of the coastal state in the different zones is subject to navigational and overflight rights of other states and their right to use the sea for other purposes lawful under international law. These rights differ in the different coastal areas. See §§ 512–15.

　　2. *Internal waters, ports, roadsteads, and offshore terminals.* "Internal waters" include waters of lakes, rivers, and bays that are on the landward side of the baseline of the territorial sea or of archipelagic waters. For rivers, this baseline is a straight line across the mouth of the river between points on the low-tide line of its banks. See 1958 Convention on the Territorial Sea and the Contiguous Zone, Arts. 5 and 13; LOS Convention, Arts. 8–9.

A "port" is "a place where ships are in the habit of coming for the purpose of loading or unloading, embarking or disembarking." The Möwe, [1915] P. 1, 2 Lloyds Prize Cas. 70. According to Article 1 of the 1923 Statute on the International Regime of Maritime Ports, a "maritime port" is a port that is "normally frequented by sea-going vessels and used for foreign trade." 58 L.N.T.S. 285, 301, 2 Hudson, International Legislation 1162 (1931).

For the purpose of delimiting the territorial sea, the outermost permanent harbor works that form an integral part of the harbor system are regarded as forming part of the coast, but offshore installations are not considered permanent harbor works for this purpose. See 1958 Convention on the Territorial Sea and the Contiguous Zone, Art. 8; LOS Convention, Art. 11. The United States Supreme Court has stated that "harbor works" connote "structures" and "installations" that are "part of the land," that in some sense enclose and shelter the waters within, and that are "connected with the coast." Therefore, the Court held that "dredged channels leading to ports and harbors" are not "harbor works." United States v. Louisiana, 394 U.S. 11, 36–38, 89 S.Ct. 773, 787–789, 22 L.Ed.2d 44 (1969). See also United States v. California, 432 U.S. 40, 97 S.Ct. 2915, 53 L.Ed.2d 94 (1977), modified, 449 U.S. 408, 101 S.Ct. 912, 66 L.Ed.2d 619 (1981) (treating certain artificial extensions as part of the coastline for baseline purposes). Compare another proceeding in the same case, 447 U.S. 1, 100 S.Ct. 1994, 64 L.Ed.2d 681 (1980) (refusing such treatment to a different type of extension).

"Roadsteads" are places at a distance from the coast that are used for the loading, unloading, and anchoring of ships. Even when they are situated wholly or partly outside the outer limit of the territorial sea, they are considered part of the territorial sea for purposes of the law of the sea. 1958 Convention on the Territorial Sea and the Contiguous Zone, Art. 9; LOS Convention, Art. 12. As they are considered part of the territorial sea and not of the internal waters, their delimitation does not influence the baseline from which the areas of coastal jurisdiction are measured. See McDougal and Burke, The Public Order of the Oceans 423–27 (1962).

"Offshore terminals" or "deepwater ports" are "any fixed or floating man-made structures other than a vessel, or any group of such structures, located beyond the territorial sea . . . and which are used or intended for use as a port or terminal for the loading or unloading and further handling of oil for transportation to any State." Deepwater Port Act of 1974, as amended, 33 U.S.C. §§ 1501, 1502(10). See Get Oil Out! Inc. v. Exxon Corp., 586 F.2d 726 (9th Cir. 1978). For United States agreements with other countries as to the use of deepwater ports by foreign ships, see [1978] Digest of U.S. Practice in Int'l L. 826–27; [1979] id. 1082–83.

A coastal state may establish reasonable safety zones around an offshore terminal, in which it may take reasonable measures to ensure the safety both of navigation and of the installations themselves. In determining the breadth of the safety zone, the coastal state must take into account applicable international standards; ordinarily the zones may not exceed 500 meters in radius. See LOS Convention, Art. 60(4) and (5).

3. *Line of demarcation between internal waters and territorial sea.* Except for the normal baseline (Comment *h*), the rules for drawing baselines are complex. See 1958 Convention on the Territorial Sea and the Contiguous Zone, Arts. 4–13; LOS Convention, Arts. 6–14. These rules have led to considerable litigation between the United States and several States of the United States. See United States v. California, 381 U.S. 139, 85 S.Ct. 1401, 14 L.Ed.2d 296 (1965); United States v. Louisiana, Reporters' Note 2; United States v. Alaska, 422 U.S. 184; 95 S.Ct. 2240, 45 L.Ed.2d 109 (1975), *on remand,* 519 F.2d 1376 (9th Cir.1975); United States v. California, Reporters' Note 2; § 512, Comment *b.* The right of a coastal state, in special cases, to draw straight lines instead of following the sinuosities of the coast was confirmed in the Fisheries Case (United Kingdom v. Norway), [1951] I.C.J. Rep. 116.

4. *Extent of territorial sea.* Under clause (a) of this section, a coastal state may extend its territorial sea to 12 nautical miles. More than 80 states have already done so. United States Department of State, Office of the Geographer, National Claims to Maritime Jurisdiction 7 (Limits in the Seas, No. 36, 5th rev., 1985). As of 1987, the United States, however, continued to claim only a territorial sea of three nautical miles. See "United States Ocean Policy," The White House, Office of the Press Secretary, Fact Sheet, March 10, 1983, 22 Int'l Leg. Mat. 461, 462 (1983); Feldman and Colson, "The Maritime Boundaries of the United States," 75 Am.J. Int'l L. 729, 730 (1981).

5. *Bays.* One of the earliest rules of maritime international law authorized the coastal state to extend its jurisdiction to areas of the sea surrounded to a large extent by its land territory, *intra fauces terrae.* In order to limit the area thus included in the internal waters of a state, modern international law has imposed various limitations. An indentation of the coast is a "bay" only if its "penetration is in such proportion to the width of its mouth as to contain landlocked waters." The area encompassed in the indentation must be larger than a semicircle whose diameter is a line drawn across the mouth of the indentation or, in the case of islands at the entrance to the bay, a line as long as the sum total of the lines drawn across the different mouths. No bay-closing line may be longer than 24 nautical miles. 1958 Convention on the Territorial Sea and the Contiguous Zone, Art. 7; LOS Convention, Art. 10. Several issues relating to the application of the provisions of the 1958 Convention were resolved in United States v. Louisiana, Reporters' Note 2. In United States v. Maine, *et al.* (Rhode Island and New York Boundary Case), 469 U.S. 504, 105 S.Ct. 992, 83 L.Ed.2d 998 (1985), Long Island and Block Island Sounds were held to be a juridical bay under Article 7 of the 1958 Convention on the Territorial Sea and the Contiguous Zone.

The Chesapeake and Delaware Bays have long been recognized by other states as historic bays of the United States; under contemporary international law, both meet criteria for bays. The Soviet Union's recent claim that the Peter the Great Bay is a historic bay has not been recognized by the United States and several other states. 4 Whiteman, Digest of International Law 235, 250–51 (1965). As to the Libyan claim that the Gulf of Sidra (Sirte) is a historic bay and United States denial of that claim, see [1973] Digest of U.S. Practice in Int'l L. 302–03; 1974 *id.* 293–94; U.N. Docs. S/14632 (1981), and S/14636 (1981), reproduced in 36 U.N. SCOR, Supp. for July-Sept. 1981, at 41, 44; Ratner, "The Gulf of Sidra Incident of 1981," 10 Yale J. Int'l L. 59, 64 (1984). For the rules applicable to "historic bays," see United States v. California, 381 U.S. 139, 85 S.Ct. 1401, 14 L.Ed.2d 296 (1965); United States v. Alaska, Reporters' Note 3. See also United Nations Secretariat, "Juridical Regime of Historic Waters, Including Historic Bays," U.N. Doc. A/CN.4/143, [1962] 2 Y.B. Int'l L. Comm'n 1.

6. *Archipelagic states.* An archipelago is "a group of islands, including parts of islands, interconnecting waters and other natural features which are so closely interrelated that such islands, waters and other natural features form an intrinsic geographical, economic and political entity, or which historically have been regarded as such." LOS Convention, Art. 46(b). An archipelagic state is one constituted wholly by one or more archipelagoes and may include other islands but not continental land territory. See *id.* Art. 46(a). The principal archipelagic states are Indonesia and the Philippines in Asia and the Bahamas in the Western Hemisphere; they succeeded in obtaining recognition of their special status by the Third United Nations Conference on the Law of the Sea. For drawing the baseline of the territorial sea and for tracing the boundaries of the archipelagic states, the LOS Convention takes into account atolls and fringing reefs. Arts. 6 and 47(7).

7. *Exclusive economic zone.* In the decades following the Second World War, several Latin American states, and later a few African states, purported to extend their territorial sea to 200 nautical miles, principally to obtain the exclusive right to fish and to regulate fishing in that area. For some time, major maritime powers, including the United States, resisted that expansion. See § 514. However, in 1976, the United States itself adopted the Fishery Conservation and Management Act, 16 U.S.C. § 1811, which established an exclusive 200-mile fishery zone, and was followed promptly by Canada, Mexico, and several other countries. This development was encouraged by the compromise on the subject developed at the Third United Nations Conference on the Law of the Sea, which gave to the coastal states jurisdiction over certain activities in a 200-mile zone, including "sovereign rights" for the purpose of exploring and exploiting, conserving and managing both the living and nonliving natural resources of that zone, but preserved for maritime states most high seas freedoms.

In 1983, President Reagan, by Proclamation No. 5030, established an exclusive economic zone of the United States and asserted rights over natural resources thereof, both living and nonliving, as well as over economic activities in the zone. 48 F.R. 10601 (1983); 3 C.F.R. 2 (1983 Compilation); 16 U.S.C.A. § 1453

Note; 83 Dep't State Bull., No. 2075, at 71 (1983). The proclamation also asserted United States jurisdiction with regard to all artificial islands, as well as installations and structures in the zone having economic purposes, and in respect of the protection and preservation of the marine environment. See § 514(1)(b) and Comment *c.* The proclamation declared that the United States would exercise its rights to the exclusive economic zone "in accordance with the rules of international law," and that other states will enjoy in that zone "the high seas freedoms of navigation, overflight, the laying of submarine cables and pipelines, and other internationally lawful uses of the sea."

The Soviet Union objected to this proclamation, arguing that it constituted a unilateral attempt to break up "the package" agreed upon at the Law of the Sea Conference. U.N. Doc. A/38/175 (1983); the Group of 77 (representing the developing countries) made similar objections. U.N. Doc. LOS/PCN/5 (1983). Many states that signed the Convention, presumably with intent to ratify it, also proclaimed exclusive economic zones before they ratified the Convention and without waiting for the LOS Convention to come into force. For the 1984 decree as to the exclusive economic zone of the U.S.S.R., see 4 LOS Bull. 31 (1985); see also United Nations, Law of the Sea: National Legislation on the Exclusive Economic Zone, the Economic Zone and the Exclusive Fishery Zone, U.N. Pub. E.85.V.10 (1986), containing the legislation of 78 states with respect to such zones.

8. *Definition of continental shelf.* The Truman Proclamation, § 515, Reporters' Note 1, regarded the continental shelf as "an extension of the land-mass of the coastal nation and thus naturally appurtenant to it." The International Court of Justice also emphasized the character of the shelf as the natural prolongation of the land territory of the coastal state. North Sea Continental Shelf Cases (Federal Republic of Germany/Denmark and the Netherlands), [1969] I.C.J. Rep. 3, 31. It was generally accepted by the Third United Nations Conference on the Law of the Sea, and is now accepted as customary law, that the continental shelf of a coastal state comprises "the sea-bed and subsoil of the submarine areas that extend beyond its territorial sea throughout the natural prolongation of its land territory to the outer edge of the continental margin," and that the continental margin consists of the sea-bed and subsoil of "the shelf, the slope and the rise." LOS Convention, Art. 76(1) and (3). To balance this broad extension of jurisdiction of some coastal states, it has been generally accepted that all coastal states, without regard to geological factors, are entitled to exercise sovereign rights over the resources of the sea-bed and subsoil of the submarine areas extending to a distance of 200 nautical miles from the baseline of the territorial sea "where the outer edge of the continental margin does not extend up to that distance." *Id.* Art. 76(1). As the International Court of Justice pointed out in Case Concerning the Continental Shelf (Libyan Arab Jamahiriya/Malta), the concepts of natural prolongation and distance from shore are complementary, and "where the continental shelf does

not extend as far as 200 miles from the shore, natural prolongation, which in spite of its physical origins has throughout its history become more and more a complex and juridical concept, is in part defined by distance from the shore, irrespective of the physical nature of the intervening sea-bed and subsoil." [1985] I.C.J. Rep. 13, 33.

Where the shelf, as defined, extends beyond 200 nautical miles, international law imposes some limits. In principle, the coastal state may fix the outer edge by using either a line drawn by reference to the thickness of sedimentary rocks and their distance from the nearest point at the foot of the continental slope, or by reference to points no more than 60 nautical miles from the foot of the slope. However, the outer limit of the shelf shall not exceed 350 nautical miles from the baseline of the territorial sea or 100 nautical miles from the 2500-meter isobath (a line connecting points where the waters are 2500 meters deep). To avoid the extension of the authority of a few coastal states to the whole Mid-Atlantic Ridge and similar ridges in other oceans, it was agreed, however, that with respect to submarine ridges the coastal state must observe the 350-mile maximum and cannot benefit from the 2500-meter isobath plus the 100-mile alternative. In view of a special situation north of Alaska and Siberia, the United States and the Soviet Union were able to obtain an exception from these limitations with respect to "submarine elevations that are natural components of the continental margin, such as its plateaux, rises, caps, banks and spurs." LOS Convention, Art. 76(5) and (6). For a diagram explaining these provisions, see Oxman, "The Third United Nations Conference on the Law of the Sea: The Ninth Session (1980)," 75 Am.J.Int'l L. 211, 229 (1981). See also McKelvey, "Interpretation of the UNCLOS III Definition of the Continental Shelf," in D.M. Johnston and Letalik, eds., The Law of the Sea and Ocean Industry: New Opportunities and Restraints 465 (1982).

In view of the complexity of these provisions, the LOS Convention provides for the establishment of a special Commission on the Limits of the Continental Shelf that would determine the limits in cooperation with the coastal state, through a multi-step procedure. LOS Convention, Art. 76(8) and Annex II. This procedure applies only to states parties to the Convention. See Introductory Note to this Part.

§ 512. Coastal State Sovereignty over Territorial Sea

Subject to § 513, the coastal state has the same sovereignty over its territorial sea, and over the air space, sea-bed, and subsoil thereof, as it has in respect of its land territory.

Source Note:

This section follows Articles 1 and 2 of the 1958 Convention on the Territorial Sea and the Contiguous Zone, and Article 2 of the LOS Convention.

Comment:

a. Coastal state sovereignty over territorial sea. The rights of a coastal state in its territorial sea have gradually increased during the past centuries. Today, international law treats the territorial sea like land territory, subject only to the right of passage for foreign vessels. The rights and duties of a state (§ 206) and its jurisdiction (Part IV) are the same in the territorial sea as in its land territory. Any exploration or exploitation of the area's resources, whether living or nonliving, whether natural or man-made (*e.g.*, sunken treasure), whether in the waters, sea-bed, or subsoil, is subject to the consent of the coastal state. No foreign aircraft may fly over the territorial sea without the permission of the coastal state, granted either *ad hoc* or by a general or bilateral international agreement. See § 513, Comment *i.* Aviation agreements regulating overflight of land territory generally apply also to the territorial sea. See § 513, Reporters' Note 6.

The authority of the coastal state in the territorial sea is subject, however, to the right of innocent passage, to the right of transit passage through and over certain straits, and to the right of archipelagic sea lanes passage. See § 513.

b. United States territorial sea and rights of States. The federal Government, rather than the States, has "paramount rights in and power over" the territorial sea, "an incident to which is full dominion over the resources of the soil under that water area, including oil." United States v. California, 332 U.S. 19, 38–39, 67 S.Ct. 1658, 1668, 91 L.Ed. 1889 (1947). In 1953, in the Submerged Lands Act, Congress relinquished to the coastal States the title to and ownership of submerged lands within a three-mile belt, and up to nine miles for some States. 43 U.S.C. § 1301–15. Congress also "approved and confirmed" the "seaward boundary" of each coastal State at three miles from its coastal line, subject to the right of some States to claim a larger historic title. 43 U.S.C. § 1312.

c. Internal waters and ports. In general, maritime ports are open to foreign ships on condition of reciprocity, see Reporters' Note 3, but the coastal state may temporarily suspend access in exceptional cases for imperative reasons, such as the security of the state or public health. It may condition entry of a foreign ship into its internal waters or ports on compliance with its laws and regulations. The coastal state may also exercise jurisdiction to enforce international standards with respect to some activities that occurred prior to entry into its ports or internal waters (for example, illegal discharge of pollutants). LOS Convention, Article 218, see, *e.g.*, Lauritzen v. Larsen, 345 U.S. 571, 577, 73 S.Ct. 921, 925, 97 L.Ed. 1254 (1953). In principle, the coastal state may exercise jurisdiction with respect to a ship in port and over activities on board such ship, but in practice coastal states usually have little interest in exercising jurisdiction over such activities, except when the peace of the port is disturbed. See Reporters' Note 5. With respect to warships, see § 513, Comment *h*.

REPORTERS' NOTES

1. *Coastal state sovereignty over territorial sea.* Early in the 20th century, the status of the territorial sea was still debated, some seeing it as part of the high seas with only a few specific rights conceded to the coastal states. The sovereignty of the coastal state in the territorial sea was later accepted as customary international law and confirmed in the 1958 Convention on the Territorial Sea and the Contiguous Zone, Arts. 1 and 2. See also LOS Convention, Art. 2.

2. *United States territorial sea and rights of States.* In 1947, the Supreme Court held that the three-mile belt of the territorial sea was "in the domain of the Nation" and that, in consequence, the United States was "possessed of paramount rights in, and full dominion and power over, the lands, minerals and other things" underlying the sea to the extent of three nautical miles measured from the low-water mark on the coast or from the outer limit of inland waters; and that the coastal States had "no title thereto or property interest therein." United States v. California, 332 U.S. 19, 67 S.Ct. 1658, 91 L.Ed. 1889 (1947); see also United States v. Louisiana, 339 U.S. 699, 70 S.Ct. 914, 94 L.Ed. 1216 (1950); United States v. Texas, 339 U.S. 707, 70 S.Ct. 918, 94 L.Ed. 1221. The Submerged Lands Act of 1953 ceded to the coastal States all the property rights of the United States in submerged lands within

the three-mile belt (and up to nine miles in the Gulf of Mexico to States able to establish a historic title to such broader area). The Act vested in the States "the right and power to manage, administer, lease, develop and use" the submerged land and natural resources of the ceded area, "all in accordance with applicable State law." The United States retained, however, "powers of regulation and control of said lands and navigable waters for the constitutional purposes of commerce, navigation, national defense, and international affairs." 43 U.S.C. § 1301–15. For disputes between the United States and several coastal States with respect to the boundary between the inland waters and the territorial sea, see § 511, Reporters' Note 3.

The States have long applied their laws to activities in the territorial sea, and State courts have adjudicated disputes arising from activities there. The decision in United States v. California did not purport to modify the State's authority in those respects; the Submerged Lands Act in fact affirmed and approved the area as being within "the seaward boundary of each original coastal State." But an assertion of a wider territorial sea by the United States (as would be permissible under § 511(a) and Article 3 of the LOS Convention; but see § 511, Comment *d*) would not itself give rights in the additional zone to the adjacent States. Unless Congress determined otherwise, the zone between three and twelve miles would be under the exclusive authority of the Federal Government.

3. *Access to ports.* It has been said that, as no civilized state has "the right to isolate itself wholly from the outside world," there is "a corresponding obligation imposed upon each maritime power not to deprive foreign vessels of commerce of access to all of its ports." 1 Hyde, International Law Chiefly as Interpreted and Applied by the United States 581 (2d ed. 1945). The LOS Convention does not mention a right of access of ships to foreign ports, but the customary law on the subject, as reflected in a number of international agreements, has been confirmed by at least one international decision. Thus, the Statute on the International Regime of Maritime Ports of 1923, confirmed the freedom of access to maritime ports by foreign vessels on condition of reciprocity; but it allows the coastal state "in exceptional cases, and for as short a period as possible," to deviate from this provision by measures which that state "is obliged to take in case of an emergency affecting the safety of the state or the vital interest of the country." 58 L.N.T.S. 285, 301, 305; 2 Hudson, International Legislation 1162 (1931). Although this Statute has been ratified by less than 30 states and the United States is not a party to it, the Statute has been accepted as reflecting a customary rule of international law. An arbitral tribunal, relying on this Statute, stated that "[a]ccording to a great principle of international law, ports of every State must be open to foreign

merchant vessels and can only be closed when the vital interests of a State so require." Saudi Arabia v. Arabian American Oil Company (ARAMCO), Award of August 23, 1958, 27 Int'l L.Rep. 117, 212 (1963).

The Institute of International Law has considered this issue in 1898, 1928, and 1957, and each time, after a heated discussion, it affirmed the right of access to ports, subject to various conditions. In 1898, the Institute agreed that, as a general rule, access to ports "is presumed to be free to foreign ships," except when a state, "for reasons of which it is sole judge," declares its ports, or some of them, closed "when the safety of the State or the interest of the public health justifies the order," or when it refuses entrance to ships of a particular nation "as an act of just reprisal." Resolutions of the Institute of International Law 144 (J. Scott ed. 1916). In 1928, the Institute stated that, as a general rule, access to ports "is open to foreign vessels," but, as an exception and for a term as limited as possible, "a state may suspend this access by particular or general measures which it is obliged to take in case of serious events touching the safety of the state or the public health"; it also confirmed the exception in case of reprisals. Institut de Droit International, Tableau Général des Résolutions, 1873–1956, at 102 (Wehberg ed. 1957); 22 Am.J.Int'l L. 844, 847 (1928). In 1957, the Institute distinguished between internal waters and ports, and pointed out that a coastal state may deny access to internal waters, "[s]ubject to the rights of passage sanctioned either by usage or by treaty," but should abstain from denying such access to foreign commercial vessels "save where in exceptional cases this denial of access is imposed by imperative reasons." On the other hand, the Institute declared that "it is consistent with general practice of States to permit free access to ports and harbors by such vessels." [1957] 2 Annuaire de l'Institut de Droit International 485–86. For discussion, see *id.* 171, 180, 194–98, 202–09, 212–22, 253–67; for the text of the 1957 resolution, see also 52 Am.J.Int'l L. 103 (1958).

It seems, therefore, that it is now generally accepted that "in time of peace, commercial ports must be left open to international traffic," and that the "liberty of access to ports granted to foreign vessels implies their right to load and unload their cargoes; embark and disembark their passengers." Colombos, The International Law of the Sea 176 (6th ed. 1967). But see Khedivial Line, S.A.E. v. Seafarers' International Union, 278 F.2d 49, 52 (2d Cir.1960) (plaintiff presented no precedents showing that "the law of nations accords an unrestricted right of access to harbors by vessels of all nations"); Lowe, "The Right of Entry into Maritime Ports in International Law," 14 San Diego L.Rev. 597, 622 (1977) ("the ports of a State which are designated for international trade are, in the absence of express provisions to the contrary made by a port State, presumed to be open to the merchant ships of all States," and they "should not be closed to foreign merchant ships except when the peace, good order, or security of the coastal State necessitates closure").

The general principle of open ports is confirmed by many bilateral agreements. For instance, the Treaty of Friendship, Establishment and Navigation between the United States and Belgium, Brussels, 1961, provides that "[v]essels of either Contracting Party shall have liberty, on equal terms with vessels of the other Party and on equal terms with vessels of any third country, to come with their cargoes to all ports, places and waters of such other Party open to foreign commerce and navigation. Such vessels and cargoes shall in the ports, places and waters of such other Party be accorded in all respects national treatment and most-favored-nation treatment." Art. 13, 14 U.S.T. 1284, T.I.A.S. No. 5432, 480 U.N. T.S. 149. See also [1957] 2 Annuaire de l'Institut de Droit International 209, 216 (according to Paul de La Pradelle, "the many conventions on commerce and navigation which provide for [access to ports] have established a rule of customary law," but others contended that all these treaty provisions would have been superfluous if this right of access were based on customary law).

The parties to the Convention on the Facilitation of International Maritime Traffic, London, April 9, 1965, agreed to adopt "all appropriate measures to facilitate and expedite international maritime traffic and to prevent unnecessary delays to ships [in port] and to persons and property on board." Art. 1, and Annex, para. 2.12, 18 U.S.T. 411, T.I.A.S. No. 6251, 591 U.N.T.S. 265. See also § 501, Reporters' Note 3.

States may impose, however, special restrictions on certain categories of ships. For instance, the Convention on the Liability of Operators of Nuclear-Powered Ships, Brussels, 1962, provides that nothing in that Convention "shall affect any right which a Contracting State may have under international law to deny access to its waters and harbours to nuclear ships licensed by another Contracting State, even when it has formally complied with all the provisions" of that Convention. Art. XVII, 57 Am.J.Int'l L. 268 (1963). See also Reporters' Note 1. In 1985, New Zealand denied to United States nuclear ships access to its ports. See 21 Weekly Comp.Pres. Docs. 147 (1985). A directive of the Council of the European Economic Community regulates the entry into Community ports of oil, gas, and chemical tankers, Dec. 21, 1978, 22 O.J. Eur.Comm. (No. L. 33) 33 (1979); amended Dec. 11, 1979, id. (No. L. 315) 16 (1979). Access to ports by other categories of vessels (e.g., fishing vessels) may also be subject to various restrictions.

A coastal state can condition the entry of foreign ships into its ports on compliance with specified laws and regulations. This jurisdiction to prescribe may extend even to some matters relating to the internal affairs of the ship. See Patterson v. Bark Eudora, 190 U.S. 169, 178, 23 S.Ct. 821, 824, 47 L.Ed. 1002 (1903) (prohibiting prepayment of seamen's wages by certain foreign vessels). See § 513, Comment c. More recently, coastal state jurisdiction has been expanded to allow the state to take steps in the territorial sea necessary to prevent any breach of the conditions imposed by the state on ships proceeding to its internal waters or to a port facility outside these waters. See 1958 Convention on the Territorial Sea and the Contiguous Zone, Art. 16(2); LOS Convention, Art. 25.

The principles governing international aviation differ from those governing shipping; landing rights as well as overflight rights have to be specifically conferred. See § 513, Comment i.

4. *Access to United States coastal waters and ports.* The marine pollution provisions of the Clean Water Act of 1977 were enacted in part as a result of navigation accidents, such as that of the tanker Argo Merchant, which caused considerable damage to the marine environment. The Act prohibited discharge of oil or hazardous substances into or upon the waters of the contiguous zone established by the United States pursuant to Article 24 of the 1958 Convention on the Territorial Sea and the Contiguous Zone, or in other waters where activities "may affect natural resources belonging to, appertaining to, or under the exclusive management authority of the United States (including resources under the Magnuson Fishery Conservation and Management Act)" (16 U.S.C. §§ 1801 *et seq.*), *i.e.*, within 200 nautical miles from the baseline of the territorial sea. 33 U.S.C. § 1321(a)(9) and (b)(1) and (3). Enforcement authority under this Act was limited, however, to the waters of the 12-mile contiguous zone. *Id.* § 1321(m).

Jurisdiction within the 200-mile zone was reasserted by the Port and Tanker Safety Act of 1978, 33 U.S.C. § 1221, which defined the marine environment subject to the Act as including not only the navigable waters of the United States but also "the waters and fishery resources of any area over which the United States asserts exclusive fishery management authority," as well as "the seabed and subsoil of the Outer Continental Shelf of the United States, the resources thereof and the waters superjacent thereto." This Act prohibited operation in the navigable waters of the United States by any "unsafe" vessel (as defined in the Act); imposed civil and criminal penalties on any violator; and authorized the President to conclude agreements with foreign countries to implement this Act. 33 U.S.C. §§ 1222, 1228, 1230, and 1232. See also the 1980 Comprehensive Environmental Response, Compensation, and Liability Act, codified at 42 U.S.C. §§ 9601 *et seq.*, especially § 9601(8). To implement these acts, the United States Department of Transportation issued the Navigational Safety Regulations, which govern navigation procedures, testing, and equipment requirements. These regulations were made applicable only to large vessels operating "in the navigable waters of the United States," including the territorial sea, harbors, and inland waters; such vessels were required, *e.g.*, to test certain equipment 12 hours before entering these navigable waters. 42 Fed. Reg. 5956 (1977), 33 C.F.R. § 164.01. These regulations were later amended to make clear that they do not apply to foreign vessels that are not destined for, or departing from, a United States port, and are in:

(i) innocent passage through the territorial sea of the United States; or

(ii) transit through navigable waters of the United States which form a part of an international strait. 44 Fed. Reg. 66530 (1979), 33 C.F.R. § 164.02.

For an analysis of this legislation and its implementation, see Meese, "When Jurisdictional Interests Collide: International, Domestic and State Efforts to Prevent Source Oil Pollution," 12 Ocean Dev. & Int'l L. 71 (1982).

The Coast Guard can bar the entry of a foreign flag vessel into a United States port under the Special Interest Vessel (SIV) Program, pursuant to classified, unpublished regulations issued by the Secretary of the Treasury under the 1976 Magnuson Act, 50 U.S.C. § 191. (That Act authorized the President in case "the security of the United States is endangered . . . by subversive activities" to issue regulations governing the anchorage and movement of foreign flag vessels.) The Secretary of the Treasury relied on President Truman's Executive Order 10173, 3 C.F.R. § 356 (1949–53 Comp.), which stated that "the security of the United States is endangered by reason of subversive activity." A vessel owned by Swiss nationals, chartered to a Canadian company, and flying the flag of Singapore was excluded under these regulations from Norfolk harbor on the ground that it had a Polish master and Polish officers. It was permitted to enter that harbor only after the Polish officers were disembarked in Baltimore and replaced by non-Communist-bloc officers. When the Canadian company sued the United States for damages caused by this detour, the court found that the regulations, though not published, were valid, but remanded the case for further proceedings on the issue whether the program was administered by the Coast Guard in an arbitrary manner. Canadian Transport Co. v. United States, 663 F.2d 1081, 1087, 1091 (D.C. Cir.1980).

5. *Jurisdiction over foreign vessels in port.* Once a commercial

ship voluntarily enters a port, it becomes subject to the jurisdiction of the coastal state. Cunard S.S. Co. v. Mellon, 262 U.S. 100, 124, 43 S.Ct. 504, 507, 67 L.Ed. 894 (1923); Benz v. Compania Naviera Hidalgo, S.A., 353 U.S. 138, 142, 77 S.Ct. 699, 1 L.Ed.2d 709 (1957). See § 502, Comment *d.*

The coastal state "may out of considerations of public policy choose to forego the exertion of its jurisdiction or to exert the same in only a limited way, but this is a matter resting solely within its discretion." Cunard S.S. Co. v. Mellon, *supra*, at 124, 43 S.Ct. at 507. As was pointed out in Wildenhus's Case, from experience it was found long ago that "it would be beneficial to commerce if the local government would abstain from interfering with the internal discipline of the ship, and the general regulation of the rights and duties of the officers and crew toward the vessel or among themselves." Therefore, it became generally understood that "all matters of discipline and all things done on board which affected only the vessel or those belonging to her, and did not involve the peace or dignity of the country, or the tranquillity of the port, should be left by the local government to be dealt with by the authorities of the nation to which the vessel belonged." 120 U.S. 1, 12, 7 S.Ct. 385, 387, 30 L.Ed. 565 (1887), reiterated in Lauritzen v. Larsen, 345 U.S. 571, 585–86, 73 S.Ct. 921, 930, 97 L.Ed. 1254 (1953). On the other hand, "if crimes are committed on board of a character to disturb the peace and tranquillity of the country to which the vessel has been brought, the offenders have never by comity or usage been entitled to any exemption from the operation of the local laws for their punishment, if the local tribunals see fit to assert their authority." Wildenhus's Case, *supra*, at 12, 7 S.Ct. at 387 (United States law was applied to murder committed on board a foreign ship in a United States port).

Jurisdiction over foreign vessels in port is frequently limited by bilateral agreement. See, *e.g.*, United States-United Kingdom Consular Convention, 1951, Art. 22, 3 U.S.T. 3426, T.I.A.S. No. 2494, 165 U.N. T.S. 121.

The authority of the coastal state generally applies to ships "voluntarily in port," not to ships driven to take refuge in a port by *force majeure* or other necessity. See Kate A. Hoff Claim (United States v. Mexico, 1929), 4 R.Int'l Arb. Awards 444 (1951); but see Cushin and Lewis v. The King, [1935] Can. Exch. 103, [1933–34] Ann. Dig. 207 ("putting into port under constraint does not carry any legal right to exemption from local law or local jurisdiction"). See also statement by Secretary Webster, August 1, 1842, 2 Moore, Digest of International Law 353, 354 (1906).

For a study of the treatment by different states of foreign merchant vessels in port, see reports by the UNCTAD Secretariat, U.N.Docs. TD/B/C.4/136 (1975) and TD/B/C.4/158 (1977).

6. *Warships and other government ships operated for noncommercial purposes.* A warship (§ 501, Reporters' Note 1) in a foreign port must comply with the laws and regulations of the coastal state relating to navigation and safety. See LOS Convention, Art. 21(1) and (4); see also Harvard Research in International Law, The Law of Territorial Waters, 23 Am.J.

Int'l L. Spec. Supp. 328 (1929). For an example of such legislation, see the Spanish order of March 23, 1958, Art. 6, U.N. Legislative Series, National Legislation and Treaties Relating to the Law of the Sea 145, 148 (U.N. Pub. ST/LEG/SER.B/19) (1980). If any such ship does not comply with port regulations, the flag state is internationally responsible for any damage caused, and the ship may be required to leave the port. See LOS Convention, Arts. 30–31.

The coastal state has no jurisdiction over offenses committed on board foreign warships or other government ships operated for non-commercial purposes. See Bustamante Code of Private International Law, Havana, 1928, Art. 300, 86 L.N.T.S. 111, 4 Hudson, International Legislation 2279, 2323 (1931). (The United States is not a party to this instrument.) Under international law, government-owned vessels not used for commercial purposes enjoy immunity from arrest, attachment, or execution. See § 457, Reporters' Note 7. But there is no immunity for a foreign public vessel from a maritime lien based upon a commercial activity of the foreign state. See § 455(4) and Reporters' Note 3 thereto.

7. *Additional jurisdiction to adjudicate by port state.* Traditionally, except for cases within general admiralty jurisdiction, a port state's jurisdiction to adjudicate claims against foreign ships was ordinarily limited to activities by or on board a ship navigating or at anchor in a port. In the 1970s, several international agreements relating to marine pollution broadened the jurisdiction of the port state to allow that state to deal with viola-

tions of international environmental regulations that occurred on the high seas or in the waters of another state. This allows a state to inspect any ship stopping at one of its ports to determine whether it has committed an environmental violation anywhere in the world, and to report the results of the inspection to the flag state. Thus, port jurisdiction has been enlarged from a limited jurisdiction to a general jurisdiction for all port states. See §§ 603–604; see also M'Gonigle and Zacher, Pollution, Politics and International Law 231–34, 249–51 (1979).

Maritime states objected to a coastal state's stopping a ship passing through coastal waters, because the cost of stopping a large tanker was considered very high, but they were willing to accept investigative and judicial proceedings conducted while the ship was loading or unloading in a port. It was also agreed that the ship itself must be permitted to proceed upon posting a bond or other appropriate security, and that only monetary penalties may be imposed, except in the case of a willful and serious act of pollution in the territorial sea. The compromise has been codified in Arts. 218, 228, and 230 of the LOS Convention. See also § 514, Comment *i*.

A European agreement of 1982 established common standards for port state control. See § 603, Reporters' Note 2. The UNCTAD Secretariat concluded that there did not appear to be any evidence that such control was being used to discriminate against ships of any particular flag state. UNCTAD Secretariat, International Maritime Legislation: Treatment of Merchant Vessels in Ports at Regional Level, U.N. Doc. TD/B/C.4/275, at 11 (1984).

§ 513. Passage Through Territorial Sea, Straits, and Archipelagic Waters

(1) (a) Ships of all states have the right of innocent passage through the territorial sea of any coastal state.

(b) Passage is innocent so long as it is not prejudicial to the peace, good order, or security of the coastal state.

(2) (a) Coastal states may not hamper the innocent passage of foreign ships through the territorial sea, nor suspend such passage, except temporarily in specified areas when essential for the protection of national security, and provided that there is no discrimination among ships of different states.

(b) The coastal state may adopt laws and regulations relating to innocent passage through the territorial sea only with regard to safety of navigation, protection of cables and pipelines, fishing, the prevention of pollution, scientific research, and the enforcement of customs, fiscal, immigration, and sanitary regulations.

(3) In straits used for international navigation between one area of the high seas or an exclusive economic zone and another area of the high seas or an exclusive economic zone, all ships and aircraft enjoy the right of transit passage, which the coastal state may neither suspend nor impede.

(4) In archipelagic waters, (a) all ships have the right of innocent passage; and (b) all ships and aircraft enjoy the right of archipelagic sea lanes passage.

Source Note:

This section condenses provisions contained in Articles 14–17 of the 1958 Convention on the Territorial Sea and the Contiguous Zone, and in Articles 17–26, 37–44, and 53 of the LOS Convention.

Comment:

a. Passage. In this section, passage means navigation through the territorial sea, international straits, or archipelagic waters for the purpose of either traversing them without entering internal waters, or proceeding to or from internal waters. Passage must be continuous and expeditious, but a ship may stop and anchor when doing so is incidental to ordinary navigation (*e.g.*, to pick up a pilot), is rendered necessary by *force majeure* or distress, or is required for the purpose of rendering assistance to persons, ships, or aircraft in danger or distress. 1958 Convention on the Territorial Sea and the Contiguous Zone, Article 14(3); LOS Convention, Article 18(2). This section distinguishes between innocent passage (Comments *b–i*) and transit passage through international straits and archipelagic sea lanes passage (Comments *j–k*).

b. *Innocent passage.* Passage through the territorial sea of another state is not innocent if it is prejudicial to the peace, good order, or security of the coastal state, Subsection (1)(b); passage of a foreign ship is considered prejudicial under that subsection if the ship engages in any of the following activities:

(i) Any threat or use of force against the sovereignty, territorial integrity, or political independence of the coastal state, or in any other manner in violation of the principles of international law embodied in the Charter of the United Nations;

(ii) Any exercise or practice with weapons of any kind;

(iii) Any act aimed at collecting information to the prejudice of the defense or security of the coastal state;

(iv) Any act of propaganda aimed at affecting the defense or security of the coastal state;

(v) The launching, landing, or taking on board of any aircraft;

(vi) The launching, landing, or taking on board of any military device;

(vii) The loading or unloading of any commodity or currency or the embarking or disembarking of any person contrary to the customs, fiscal, immigration, or sanitary regulations of the coastal state;

(viii) Any act of willful and serious pollution contrary to international law;

(ix) Any fishing activities;

(x) The carrying out of research or survey activities;

(xi) Any act aimed at interfering with any systems of communication or any other facilities or installations of the coastal state;

(xii) Any other activity not having a direct bearing on passage.

See LOS Convention, Article 19. The coastal state may authorize or consent to such activities, *e.g.*, to fishing or research.

Salvage activities are not included within the right of passage, and therefore cannot be performed in the territorial sea without authorization of the coastal state.

The coastal state may take necessary steps in the territorial sea to protect itself against passage that is not innocent. As to passage of warships and submarines, see Comment *h*.

c. Coastal state jurisdiction to regulate vessels in innocent passage. Subsection (2)(b) follows Article 21(1) of the LOS Convention, which limits the coastal state's jurisdiction to prescribe with respect to ships in innocent passage to the following subjects only:

(i) The safety of navigation and the regulation of maritime traffic;

(ii) The protection of navigational aids and facilities or installations;

(iii) The protection of cables and pipelines;

(iv) The conservation of the living resources of the sea;

(v) The prevention of infringement of the fisheries regulations of the coastal state;

(vi) The preservation of the environment of the coastal state and the prevention, reduction, and control of pollution thereof;

(vii) The conduct of marine scientific research and hydrographic surveys;

(viii) The prevention of infringement of the customs, fiscal, immigration, or sanitary regulations of the coastal state.

A coastal state's laws and regulations may not apply to the design, construction, manning, or equipment of foreign ships in innocent passage through its territorial sea, unless these laws and regulations are in implementation of generally accepted international rules and standards. LOS Convention, Article 21(2).

The basic duty of the coastal state toward foreign ships is not to hamper their innocent passage through the territorial sea or to impose requirements that have that effect. The coastal state may not discriminate against the ships of any state or against ships carrying cargoes to, from, or on behalf of any state. 1958 Convention on the Territorial Sea and the Contiguous Zone, Article 15; LOS Convention, Article 24.

The coastal state may suspend all passage temporarily in specified areas if such suspension is essential for the protection of the state's security, *e.g.*, during weapons exercises; but in such a case there should be no discrimination among ships of different states. Convention on the Territorial Sea and the Contiguous Zone, Article 16(3); LOS Convention, Article 25(3).

Foreign ships exercising the right of innocent passage through the territorial sea are required to comply with laws and regulations of the coastal state adopted in accordance with Subsection (2) and with generally accepted international regulations relating to the prevention of collisions at sea. As to the duty of the flag state to assure compliance by its ships, see § 502(1)(b)(ii). As to coastal state regulation of ships in innocent passage on the way to a port, see § 512, Comment *a* and Reporters' Note 3.

d. Sea lanes and traffic separation schemes. The coastal state may establish sea lanes and traffic separation schemes for ships in innocent passage through its territorial sea where they are necessary to ensure the safety of navigation. The coastal state is required to take into account the recommendations of the competent international organization (principally the International Maritime Organization (IMO), formerly the Inter-Governmental Maritime Consultative Organization (IMCO)); the coastal state is to take account also of channels customarily used for international navigation, the special characteristics of particular ships and channels, and the density of traffic. The coastal state may require all ships to use the sea lanes, or it may impose this requirement only on some ships such as tankers, nuclear-powered ships, and ships carrying nuclear or other inherently dangerous or noxious substances or materials. LOS Convention, Article 22. In addition, since nuclear-powered ships and ships carrying nuclear materials or other hazardous substances present a special danger to the marine environment, they may be required to observe special precautionary measures established by international agreement. *Id.* Article 23. For regulations as to the routing of ships approved by IMCO in 1973, see IMCO Doc. A VIII/Res. 284, 4 Churchill and Nordquist, New Directions in the Law of the Sea 235–43 (1975). For sea lanes and traffic separation schemes in straits and archipelagic waters, see Comments *j* and *k*.

e. Coastal state jurisdiction over foreign ships in territorial sea. The criminal jurisdiction of the coastal state "should not be exercised on board a foreign ship passing through the territorial sea" for the purpose of arresting a person on board the ship or conducting any investigation in connection with any crime committed on board the ship during its passage. A coastal state may, however, take such steps if:

> (i) the consequences of the crime extend to the coastal state;

> (ii) the crime is of a kind to disturb the peace of the coastal state or the good order of the territorial sea;

> (iii) the assistance of the local authorities has been requested by the captain of the ship or by a diplomatic agent or consular officer of the flag state; or

> (iv) such measures are necessary for the suppression of illicit traffic in narcotic drugs or psychotropic substances.

In considering the manner in which such an arrest should be made, the coastal state must pay due regard to the interests of navigation. In no case may the coastal state make an arrest or conduct an investigation aboard a ship in innocent passage in connection with a crime committed before the ship entered the territorial sea if the ship, proceeding from a foreign port, is only passing through the territorial sea without entering internal waters. On the other hand, if the foreign ship is passing through the territorial sea after leaving internal waters of the coastal state, that state has the right to take any steps authorized by its laws for the purpose of an arrest or investigation on board the ship in connection with a crime committed during the ship's sojourn in the state's internal waters. 1958 Convention on the Territorial Sea and the Contiguous Zone, Article 19; LOS Convention, Article 27. The limitations on arrest or investigation applicable to a ship in innocent passage do not apply to a ship in port, but in fact similar restraints are observed there. See, *e.g.*, Wildenhus's Case, 120 U.S. 1, 7 S.Ct. 385, 30 L.Ed. 565 (1887); § 512, Reporters' Note 5. As to enforcement of criminal law beyond a state's territory generally, see § 432.

Similar restrictions apply to the exercise of civil jurisdiction by the coastal state. The coastal state "should not stop or divert a foreign ship passing through the territorial sea for the purpose of exercising civil jurisdiction in relation to a person on board the ship." It "may not levy execution against or arrest the ship for the purpose of any civil proceedings, save only in respect of obligations or liabilities assumed or incurred by the ship itself in the course of or for the purpose of its voyage through the waters of the coastal State." These provisions do not apply, however, to "a foreign ship lying in the territorial sea, or passing through the territorial sea after leaving internal waters." LOS Convention, Article 28; see also 1958 Convention on the Territorial Sea and the Contiguous Zone, Article 20.

f. Contiguous zone. International law permits a coastal state to establish a "contiguous zone," § 511, Comment *k*, in order to protect itself against infringements of its customs, fiscal, immigration, or sanitary regulations committed within its territory or territorial sea. The coastal state can stop a foreign ship in the contiguous zone for the purpose of investigation or arrest in connection with any infringement of the above-mentioned regulations, and may impose punishment for any infringement. 1958 Convention on the Territorial Sea and the Contiguous Zone, Article 24; LOS Convention, Articles 33 and 303. See also § 521, Reporters' Note 6 (control of traffic in archaeological objects). As to searches and arrests beyond the contiguous zone, see § 433, Comment *d* and Reporters' Note 4.

g. Hot pursuit. International law permits a coastal state to engage in hot pursuit of a foreign ship beyond the state's territorial sea if the state has good reason to believe that the ship had violated the state's laws or regulations within its internal waters or its territorial sea. Hot pursuit may begin in the contiguous zone for violation of those regulations for which that zone was designed; it may begin in the exclusive economic zone or over the continental shelf for violations of economic rights of the coastal state committed in that zone or on that shelf. Hot pursuit may be exercised only by a warship, a military aircraft, or a duly authorized ship or aircraft clearly identifiable as being on government service. The right of hot pursuit may be continued only if it has not been interrupted, and ceases as soon as the ship pursued enters the territorial sea of its own state or of a third state. 1958 Convention on the High Seas, Article 23; LOS Convention, Article 111.

h. Warships and other government ships operated for noncommercial purposes. Warships (§ 501, Reporters' Note 1) enjoy the right of innocent passage, but if a warship does not comply with the laws and regulations of the coastal state concerning passage through the territorial sea and disregards any request for compliance, the coastal state may require it to leave the territorial sea immediately. The ship itself is immune from arrest, but the flag state bears international responsibility for any damage resulting from noncompliance with these laws and regulations by a warship, or by any other government ship operated for noncommercial purposes and entitled to immunity under international law. 1958 Convention on the Territorial Sea and the Contiguous Zone, Articles 22–23; LOS Convention, Articles 30–32. As to immunity of government vessels, see § 457, Reporters' Note 7.

International law requires that submarines and other underwater vehicles exercising the right of innocent passage in the territorial sea navigate on the surface and show their flag. 1958 Convention on the Territorial Sea and the Contiguous Zone, Article 14(6); LOS Convention, Article 20. As to submarine passage through straits or archipelagic sea lanes, see Comments *j* and *k*.

i. No right to innocent passage in airspace above territorial sea. The sovereignty of the coastal state in the airspace above its territorial sea is not subject to any right of innocent passage except as provided by international agreement. See Chicago Convention on International Civil Aviation of December 7, 1944, Articles 1–2, 61 Stat. 1180, T.I.A.S. No. 1591, 15 U.N.T.S. 295. See also § 512, Comment *a*. As to aircraft passage over straits or archipelagic sea lanes, see Comments *j* and *k*.

j. Transit passage. Recent practice of states, supported by the broad consensus achieved at the Third United Nations Conference on the Law of the Sea, has effectively established as customary international law the concept and the basic rules of transit passage through international straits and sea-lanes passage through archipelagic waters. Subsections (3) and (4) recognize, therefore, that these two kinds of passage are free from many of the restrictions implied in innocent passage. As compared with the list of activities forbidden to vessels in the territorial sea, Comment *b*, ships in transit passage are obligated only to refrain from "any activities other than those incident to their normal modes of continuous and expeditious transit unless rendered necessary by *force majeure* or by distress." LOS Convention, Article 39(1)(c). The laws and regulations that a coastal state may adopt with respect to transit passage are more limited than those relating to innocent passage, Comment *c*, and include only those that relate to safety of navigation, pollution, fishing, and customs, fiscal, immigration, or sanitary regulations. LOS Convention, Articles 37–44. In the territorial sea, a coastal state may establish sea lanes and traffic separation schemes after "taking into account" the recommendations of the competent international organization, Comment *d*; in international straits the designation of such lanes or schemes requires concurrent action by the strait state (or states) and the competent international organization. The coastal state may temporarily suspend innocent passage through the territorial sea, Comment *c*; it may not suspend transit passage through a strait, but, with the approval of the competent international organization, it may substitute one sea lane for another. The regime of innocent passage requires submarines to surface; transit passage permits them to pass submerged. Airplanes have no right of overflight in innocent passage over territorial sea; they may overfly international straits.

k. Archipelagic sea lanes passage. Under Subsection (4), foreign ships (and aircraft) enjoy the right of passage through designated archipelagic sea lanes (and air routes), which must include all normal passage routes used for international navigation or overflight. Where there are two routes of similar convenience between the same entry and exit points, only one needs to be designated. The sea lanes and air routes are to be designated by agreement between the archipelagic state and the competent international organization (principally IMO). LOS Convention, Article 53. Such passage is generally subject to the same standards as transit passage through straits, Article 54, but the Convention explicitly provides that archipelagic sea lanes passage is allowed in "the normal mode"; for instance, submarines may travel under water. *Compare* Articles 38(2) and 39(1)(c) *with* 53(3). If the archipelagic state has not designated archipelagic sea lanes or routes, "the right of archipelagic sea lanes passage may be exercised through the routes normally used for international navigation." *Id.* Article 53(12). In archipelagic waters other than the designated sea lanes, ships of all states enjoy the right of innocent passage similar to the one they possess in the territorial sea, except in inland waters delimited by straight lines drawn across mouths of rivers, bays, and entrances to ports. See *id.* Articles 50 and 52(1).

REPORTERS' NOTES

1. *Innocent passage.* Customary international law has long recognized the right of innocent passage of foreign ships through territorial waters. The right has been maintained even after international law accepted that in other respects the coastal state enjoys full sovereignty over its territorial sea. What constitutes innocent passage, however, was long a subject of disagreement, and maritime states resisted attempts by coastal states to define certain activities or modalities of passage as not innocent. At the Law of the Sea Conference, it was decided to enumerate the activities that are allowed during the passage and those that are not innocent under international law, as well as the kinds of regulations which the coastal state is entitled to promulgate. See Comments *b* and *c*.

The coastal state may impose limitations on proceeding to a port of a coastal state or departing from it.

No foreign vessel may engage in salvaging operations in territorial waters of the United States, except when authorized by treaty. 46 U.S.C. § 316(d). Treaties conferring a reciprocal right with respect to salvage were concluded with Canada in 1908, 12 Bevans 314, and Mexico in 1935, 9 *id.* 1015. A French decree regulates maritime salvage of French ships sunk on the high seas or in French territorial sea and of foreign vessels sunk in French territorial sea. Decree of Dec. 26, 1961, Arts. 1(3), 14, [1962] Jour. Off. 374. For 1978 revision, which applies also to airplanes, see [1978] *id.* 3063. See also § 521, Reporters' Note 6.

2. *Passage of warships through territorial sea.* Several proposals for requiring prior notification or authorization for the passage of a warship through the territorial sea were discussed at the First Conference on the Law of the Sea, but none was adopted. A number of states entered reservations to the 1958 Convention on the Territorial Sea and the Contiguous Zone, asserting the right to require such prior notification or authorization. See Slonim, "The Right of Innocent Passage and the 1958 Geneva Conference on the Law of the Sea," 5 Colum.J. Transnat'l L. 96, 118–19 (1966). When the 1982 Law of the Sea Convention was adopted, the President of the Conference announced that an amendment to Article 21, which would have allowed the coastal state to adopt laws and regulations for the prevention of infringement of its security, was withdrawn "without prejudice to the rights of coastal states to adopt measures to safeguard their security interests, in accordance with articles 19 and 25" of the Convention. 16 Third U.N. Conf. on LOS, Off. Rec. 136 (1982). Differing interpretations were later given to that statement, some interpreting it as permitting adoption of regulations requiring prior notification or authorization for the passage of warships, and others read it as prohibiting such regulations. For instance, the United States representative pointed out that Articles 19 and 25 do not permit "the imposition of no-

tification or authorization requirements on foreign ships exercising the right of innocent passage." U.N.Doc. A/CONF. 62/WS/37, at 9 (1983). See also Froman, "Uncharted Waters: Non-Innocent Passage of Warships in the Territorial Sea," 21 San Diego L.Rev. 625, 639–44 (1984); Sadurska, "Soviet Submarines in Swedish Waters," 10 Yale J. Int'l L. 34 (1984).

In a case involving drug traffic, a United States court concluded that, as between parties to the 1958 Convention on the Territorial Sea and the Contiguous Zone that accepted it without a reservation on the subject, "a warship of one nation may enter the territorial waters of the other without first giving notification and receiving authorization." United States v. Conroy, 589 F.2d 1258, 1267 (5th Cir.1979), *certiorari denied*, 444 U.S. 831, 100 S.Ct. 60, 62 L.Ed.2d 40 (1979). See also § 433, Reporters' Note 4.

3. *Transit passage through straits.* During the law of the sea negotiations, the major maritime states were unwilling to accept the extension of the breadth of the territorial sea to 12 nautical miles without a guarantee of unimpeded passage through the more than 100 straits that would be affected by that extension. Accordingly, a right of transit passage through straits, equivalent to the freedom of navigation and overflight on the high seas, was agreed to by the coastal states. The states bordering straits agreed not to impede such transit passage and not to suspend it; to designate sea lanes and traffic separation schemes only in accordance with generally accepted international regulations and subject to approval by the competent

international organization; and to adopt laws and regulations relating to transit passage only with respect to certain specified subjects. The maritime states agreed that their ships and aircraft, while exercising the right of transit passage, would refrain from specified activities dangerous to the bordering state and would comply with generally accepted international regulations for safety at sea, and for the prevention, reduction, and control of pollution from ships; that their ships would comply with specified laws and regulations of the bordering states; and that their civil aircraft would observe the Rules of the Air established by ICAO. See LOS Convention, Arts. 39–42.

The right of transit passage is limited to straits used for international navigation between two areas of the high seas or, as will be more common under the new law of the sea regime, between two exclusive economic zones. This right does not apply where the strait is broad enough to allow navigation through a high seas route, or a route through an exclusive economic zone, of similar convenience with respect to navigational and hydrographic characteristics; where the strait is between the mainland and an island belonging to the same state and there is an equally convenient route seaward of the island; or where the strait is between an area of the high seas or an exclusive economic zone and the territorial sea of a foreign state (such as the Strait of Tiran). In the first of these situations, the general provisions relating to high seas freedoms of navigation and overflight apply; in the last two situations the passage is subject to the regime of innocent passage, but such passage cannot be suspended.

LOS Convention, Arts. 36 and 45; compare § 513(2)(a). With respect to the Strait of Tiran, see the Treaty of Peace between Egypt and Israel, 1979, Art. 5(2), 18 Int'l Leg. Mat. 362, 365, 392 (agreed interpretation); Egypt's 1983 declaration on ratification of the Law of the Sea Convention, United Nations, The Law of the Sea: Status of the United Nations Convention on the Law of the Sea 35 (U.N. Pub. E.85.V.5; 1985); and Israel's response, id. at 46; see also the 1982 statements by Israel and the United States, 17 U.N. Conference on the Law of the Sea, Off. Rec. 84 (1984).

The provision as to alternative routes was designed to take account of the Corfu Channel Case (United Kingdom/Albania), where the International Court of Justice held that the Corfu Channel between the mainland and the island of Corfu, though not a "necessary" route between two parts of the high seas, was a "useful route for international maritime traffic" and belonged to "the class of international highways through which passage cannot be prohibited by a coastal state in time of peace." [1949] I.C.J. Rep. 4, 28–29.

The new rules do not affect the legal regime of straits in which passage is regulated by special international conventions of long standing, such as the 1936 Montreux Convention concerning the regime of the straits leading to the Black Sea, 173 L.N.T.S. 213.

4. *Archipelagic sea lanes passage.* Acceptance by the major maritime states of the concept of archipelagic state was conditional on acceptance of the right of archipelagic sea lanes passage. Such sea lanes are defined in detail

in Article 53 of the LOS Convention. The main rules relating to international straits apply, with such modifications as may be necessary, to archipelagic sea lanes passage. See LOS Convention, Arts. 46–54.

5. *Enforcement of United States law beyond territorial sea.* The United States has exercised jurisdiction to prevent smuggling since its early days. By Act of March 2, 1799, 1 Stat. 627, 668, the Congress provided that foreign vessels bound for the United States might, within four marine leagues (12 miles), be boarded by and compelled to show its manifest to United States authorities. The Supreme Court early acknowledged that a state may exercise jurisdiction "beyond the limits of its territory" in order "to secure itself from injury" by means "reasonable and necessary" to prevent violations of its laws. Church v. Hubbart, 6 U.S. (2 Cranch) 187, 234, 2 L.Ed. 249, 264 (1804). The Tariff Act of 1922, 42 Stat. 858, 979, provided for boarding of vessels within 12 miles of the coast whether or not they were bound for United States ports, but, upon protest, the United States released vessels seized beyond the three-mile limit that had not been bound for the United States, unless a hovering vessel had been in contact with the shore. See Cook v. United States, 288 U.S. 102, 114, 53 S.Ct. 305, 309, 77 L.Ed. 641 (1933); The Grace and Ruby, 283 F. 475 (D. Mass. 1922); The Henry L. Marshall, 286 F. 260 (S.D.N.Y.1922), *certiorari denied*, 263 U.S. 712, 44 S.Ct. 38, 68 L.Ed. 519 (1923). See also United States v. Postal, 589 F.2d 862, 880, n. 29 (5th Cir.), *certiorari denied*, 444 U.S. 832, 100 S.Ct. 61, 62 L.Ed.2d 40 (1979) (discussion of other cases dealing with this is-

sue). Conflicts with other states were resolved by a series of treaties. See 1 Hackworth, Digest of International Law 674–79 (1940).

The Anti-Smuggling Act of 1935, 19 U.S.C. § 1701, provided that the President, upon finding that vessels hovering beyond the 12-mile limit of "customs waters" were assisting or threatening to assist "the unlawful introduction or removal into or from the United States of any merchandise or person," might declare a "customs-enforcement area" extending not more than 100 nautical miles from the vicinity of the offending vessels and not more than 50 nautical miles from the outward limit of United States customs waters (*i.e.*, not more than 62 nautical miles from the United States coastline). See The Reidun, 14 F.Supp. 771 and 15 F.Supp. 112 (E.D.N.Y. 1936); People v. Nissen, 97 Misc.2d 1000, 412 N.Y.S.2d 999, 1004 (1979); Jessup, "The Anti-Smuggling Act of 1935," 31 Am.J.Int'l L. 101 (1937). See also Lowe, "The Development of the Concept of the Contiguous Zone," 52 Brit. Y.B. Int'l L. 109 (1981).

The Anti-Smuggling Act also broadened the concept of United States "customs waters" to include, "in the case of a foreign vessel subject to a treaty or other arrangement between a foreign government and the United States enabling or permitting the authorities of the United States to board, examine, search, seize, or otherwise to enforce upon such vessel upon the high seas the laws of the United States, the waters within such distance of the coast of the United States as the said authorities are or may be so enabled or permitted by such treaty or arrangement and, in the case of every other vessel, the waters within four leagues of the coast of the United States." 19 U.S.C. § 1401(j); see also 21 U.S.C. § 955b(a) (applying this provision to the enforcement by the Coast Guard of laws relating to the importation of controlled substances). This provision has been interpreted as allowing the Coast Guard to board and seize a foreign vessel hundreds of miles from the United States coast, if a foreign official has made an "arrangement" by radiotelephone authorizing it; the area where the ship is located is treated as if it were part of United States customs waters. See, *e.g.*, United States v. Romero-Galue, 757 F.2d 1147 (11th Cir.1985); United States v. Bent-Santana, 774 F.2d 1545 (11th Cir.1985); United States v. Gonzalez, 776 F.2d 931, 933–35 (11th Cir. 1985); United States v. Vouloup, 625 F.Supp. 1266 (D. Puerto Rico 1985). For a more elaborate procedure, containing some safeguards for the seized ship and its crew, see 1981 United States-United Kingdom Agreement to Facilitate the Interdiction of Vessels Suspected of Trafficking in Drugs, 1981, § 522, Reporters' Note 8.

In 1981, the United States initiated a program of "high seas interdiction of illegal aliens" under which the Coast Guard was authorized to stop and board defined vessels. The order applied to United States vessels; vessels without nationality; foreign vessels that are owned in whole or in part by the United States or its nationals and that had not been granted foreign nationality in accordance with Article 5 of the 1958 Convention on the High Seas; and vessels of foreign states that have agreed to the United States program. Executive Order 12324,

September 29, 1981, 46 Fed.Reg. 48109, reprinted in 3 C.F.R. 180–82 (Comp. 1982), and in 8 U.S.C.A. § 1182, note. The program was held valid under United States law in Haitian Refugee Center v. Gracey, 600 F.Supp. 1396 (D.D.C. 1985), *dismissed for lack of standing*, 809 F.2d 794 (1987). See also Gutekunst, "Interdiction of Haitian Migrants on the High Seas: A Legal and Policy Analysis," 10 Yale J. Int'l L. 151 (1984). See also § 433, Reporters' Note 4; § 522, Reporters' Note 8.

6. *Right to overfly the territorial sea.* Most coastal states have granted rights to overfly their territorial sea as part of an agreement to overfly their territory generally. See Chicago International Air Services Transit Agreement of December 7, 1944, 59 Stat. 1693, E.A.S. 487, 3 Bevans 916, 84 U.N.T.S. 389. For a comment by the International Civil Aviation Organization, see 1 UNCLOS I, Off. Rec. 336 (1958). See generally Lowenfeld, Aviation Law: Cases and Materials, Chapt. 2 (2d ed. 1981). Military and other state aircraft are not covered by these agreements and enjoy overflight or landing rights only by special agreement.

After a Korean passenger plane was shot down by a Soviet plane near Sakhalin Island in September 1983, the ICAO Assembly adopted in May 1984 an amendment to the 1944 Convention on International Civil Aviation obligating every state to "refrain from resorting to the use of weapons against civil aircraft in flight," and recognizing that "the lives of persons on board and the safety of aircraft must not be endangered." 39 ICAO Bull., No. 6, at 10–11 (1984).

§ **514.   Exclusive Economic Zone**

In the exclusive economic zone (§ 511(d)):

(1) The coastal state has

(a) sovereign rights for the purpose of exploring, exploiting, conserving, and managing the natural resources of the sea-bed and subsoil and of the superjacent waters, and engaging in other activities for the economic exploration and exploitation of the zone, and

(b) authority, subject to limitations, to regulate (i) the establishment and use of artificial islands, and of installations and structures for economic purposes; (ii) marine scientific research; and (iii) the protection of the marine environment.

(2) All states enjoy, as on the high seas, the freedoms of navigation and overflight, freedom to lay submarine cables and pipelines, and the right to engage in other internationally lawful uses of the sea related to these freedoms, such as those associated with the operation of ships or aircraft.

Source Note:

This section is based on Articles 56 and 58 of the LOS Convention, but "authority" is used here instead of "jurisdiction" to avoid confusion with the uses of the term "jurisdiction" in Part IV of this Restatement.

Comment:

a.   Exclusive economic zone as customary law.   Recent practice of states, supported by the broad consensus achieved at the Third United Nations Conference on the Law of the Sea, has effectively established as customary law the concept of the exclusive economic zone, the width of the zone (up to 200 nautical miles), and the basic rules governing it. These are binding, therefore, on states generally even before the LOS Convention comes into effect and thereafter even as to states not party to the Convention. In those respects the Convention is an authoritative statement of customary law. See Introductory Note to this Part and § 511, Reporters' Note 7. Some of the detailed provisions in the Convention, however, do not reflect customary law (as of 1987) and will be binding only when the Convention comes into effect and only on states parties to the Convention. See Comment *j*.

As to the overlap between the exclusive economic zone and the continental shelf, see § 511, Comment *c;* § 515, Comment *a.*

b. *Relation of exclusive economic zone to high seas.* The LOS Convention does not explicitly designate the exclusive economic zone as part of the high seas. See § 521, Comment *a.* According to the United States and other maritime states, however, the Convention reflects the general understanding that, as a matter of customary law as well as under the Convention, the rights and freedoms of other states in the zone, set forth in Subsection (2), are the same as on the high seas. See Comment *e.* As to matters not expressly covered by this section, any conflict that might arise between the interests of a coastal state and those of any other state concerning their respective rights and duties in the exclusive economic zone should be resolved "on the basis of equity and in the light of all the relevant circumstances, taking into account the respective importance of the interests involved to the parties as well as to the international community." LOS Convention, Article 59. Special procedures for settling such disputes are provided in the Convention, but will not apply to states not parties. *Id.* Article 297(1).

c. *Rights of coastal state in exclusive economic zone.* The coastal state does not have sovereignty over the exclusive economic zone but only "sovereign rights" for a specific purpose—the management of natural resources and other economic activities. See § 511, Comment *b.* The coastal state's authority (called "jurisdiction" in the LOS Convention) is even more limited with respect to artificial islands in the exclusive economic zone and such installations and structures as may be required for economic purposes, and with respect to marine scientific research and the protection of the marine environment. See Comments *g–i.* These grants of power are further circumscribed by rules contained in Parts V, XII, and XIII of the Convention, which in large part have already become law by custom and tacit agreement. Among these are rules requiring coastal states to ensure that their laws and regulations for the prevention, reduction, and control of pollution from vessels conform and give effect to generally accepted international rules and standards, to adjust their enforcement measures to the gravity of the violation, and to impose only monetary penalties.

While there is no provision in the Law of the Sea Convention with respect to salvage activities in the exclusive economic zone, the implication in Article 303 of that Convention seems to be that the coastal state may regulate such activities only in the 24-mile contiguous zone. See § 521, Reporters' Note 6.

d.   Rights of other states in exclusive economic zone. In the exclusive economic zone of any state, all other states may exercise most high seas freedoms, such as those of navigation, overflight, and laying of submarine cables and pipelines (§ 521), but their right to participate in fishing is subject to the special rights of the coastal state under Subsection (1). The rights of other states with respect to operation of ships, aircraft, and submarine cables and pipelines are both qualitatively and quantitatively the same as the rights recognized by international law for all states on the high seas. See Subsection 2.

e.   Due regard to rights and duties of other states. The Convention explicitly applies to the exclusive economic zone the principle of customary international law that in exercising its rights a state must do so with due regard to the rights of other states. The coastal state must exercise its rights and perform its duties under Subsection (1) with due regard to the rights and duties of other states under Subsection (2). LOS Convention, Article 56(2). Other states must exercise their rights and perform their duties under Subsection (2) with due regard to the rights of the coastal state under Subsection (1). *Id.* Article 58(3).

f.   Conservation and sharing of living resources. The coastal state is obligated to ensure, through proper conservation and management measures, that living resources in the exclusive economic zone are not endangered by over-exploitation. LOS Convention, Article 61(2). This is an obligation *erga omnes* (to all states) under customary law, codified by the Convention.

In executing this obligation, the coastal state is required to determine: (a) the allowable catch of the living resources in its exclusive economic zone; (b) its own capacity to harvest these resources; and (c) to the extent that it does not have capacity to harvest the entire allowable catch, the conditions (including allocation of quotas) under which other states are given access to the surplus. In making these determinations, the coastal state has substantial discretion. In particular, the objective of management measures is "optimum" utilization of the living resources, not "maximum" exploitation, so that the coastal state may take into account not only the currently harvestable catch but also its future needs. *Id.* Article 62(1). In addition, in determining the allowable catch the coastal state may deviate from maximum sustainable yield in order to take into account the economic needs of coastal fishing communities, other relevant economic and environmental factors (*e.g.*, fishing patterns and interdependence of stocks), and generally recommended international minimum standards, whether subregional, regional, or global. *Id.* Article 61(3). Special rules provide for cooperative management of fishing activities relating to specific stocks (*e.g.*, salmon, tuna, and whales). For additional rights and obligations, which are not established by customary law and apply only to parties to the Convention, see Comment *j*.

g. Artificial islands, installations, and structures. All states are free to build and use islands, installations, and structures on the high seas. LOS Convention, Article 87(1)(d). In an exclusive economic zone, however, the coastal state has the exclusive right to construct and use artificial islands, for any purpose, and to authorize the construction and use of artificial islands by others. Such islands are commonly built to support airfields or nuclear power plants, offshore terminals (superports) for transferring oil from tankers and other bulk cargo, and installations or structures for the exploitation of the oil resources of the continental shelf. The coastal state also has the exclusive right to construct and use, and to authorize others to construct and use, installations and structures in the exclusive economic zone for economic purposes, such as production of energy from the oceans by utilizing currents, tides, winds, and temperature differential, or precipitation of metals from sea water.

The coastal state has exclusive authority over artificial islands and over installations and structures, including jurisdiction to prescribe and enforce customs, fiscal, health, safety, and immigration rules. For the protection of these islands, installations, and structures, the coastal state may establish special safety zones. *Id.* Article 60; § 511, Reporters' Note 2. As of 1986, the United States had not extended the Outer Continental Shelf Lands Act (see § 515, Comment *f*) to the exclusive economic zone and the artificial islands in the zone; however, it adopted special legislation for deepwater ports in the zone. See Reporters' Note 7.

h. Marine scientific research. A coastal state has the right to conduct and regulate marine scientific research in its exclusive economic zone, and no such research may be conducted without its consent. In "normal circumstances," the coastal state is required to grant consent for research to be carried out by another state or its nationals, provided such research is conducted "exclusively for peaceful purposes and in order to increase scientific knowledge for the benefit of all mankind." According to the Convention, "normal circumstances" may exist even in the absence of diplomatic relations between the coastal state and another state that seeks (or whose nationals seek) to conduct research. The coastal state is required to establish rules and procedures ensuring that such consent is not unreasonably delayed or denied. A coastal state may, however, withhold its consent if a project is of direct significance for the exploration and exploitation of natural resources; involves drilling into the continental shelf, or the use of explosives in or the introduction of harmful substances into the marine environment; or involves the construction, operation, or use of artificial islands, installations, or structures. LOS Convention, Article 246. With respect to archaelogical and historical research, see § 521, Reporters' Note 6.

Other states and international organizations engaged in marine scientific research in the exclusive economic zone of a state have the duty to enable that state and its scientists to participate in the project without charge and to provide that state with appropriate reports, data, and samples. There is a general obligation to make the results of research internationally available, but the coastal state may restrict the dissemination of results that are of direct significance for the exploration and exploitation of natural resources. LOS Convention, Article 249.

    i. Protection and preservation of marine environment. With respect to its exclusive economic zone, a coastal state has jurisdiction to adopt laws and regulations for the enforcement of "generally acceptable international rules and standards established through the competent international organization or general diplomatic conference" for the prevention, reduction, and control of pollution from ships of other states. A coastal state can also enforce its own laws and regulations adopted in accordance with applicable international rules and standards, with respect to a violation occurring within its territorial sea or exclusive economic zone. LOS Convention, Articles 211(5) and 220(1). Ordinarily, such enforcement takes place when the ship accused of the violation is voluntarily within a port or at an offshore terminal of the state concerned.

If the coastal state has clear grounds for believing that a foreign ship has violated applicable international rules, or the supplementary laws or regulations of the coastal state, in the exclusive economic zone, and the ship is not in port but is navigating in the exclusive economic zone or territorial sea of the coastal state, that state may require the ship to give information regarding its identity and its port of registry, its last and next port of call, and other relevant information required to establish whether a violation has occurred. If a violation has resulted in a substantial discharge causing significant pollution of the marine environment, and the ship has refused to give information or the information supplied is manifestly at variance with the evident factual situation, the coastal state may undertake physical inspection of the ship for matters relating to the violation. If the discharge causes or threatens to cause major damage to the coastline or related interests of the coastal state, or to any resources of its territorial sea or exclusive economic zone, the coastal state may, if the evidence warrants it, institute proceedings including detention of the ship in accordance with its laws. But the ship must be allowed to proceed on its journey as soon as it has furnished appropriate bond or other financial security. *Id.* Article 220(2)–(7).

Alternatively, in case of a discharge from a ship in violation of generally applicable international rules and standards, the flag state, the coastal state in whose coastal waters the discharge occurred, or the state damaged or threatened by the discharge, may request another state, in whose port or offshore terminal the ship has voluntarily stopped, to undertake investigations and, where warranted by the evidence, to impose penalties on the violators. If the aggrieved state requests it, the port state must transfer the records of the investigation to the coastal state and terminate its proceedings. In addition, any port state proceedings to impose penalties must be suspended if the flag state decides to institute proceedings against the ship in its own courts; but the coastal or port state that has instituted the original proceedings need not suspend them if they relate to an event involving major damage to the coastal state or if the flag state in question "has repeatedly disregarded its obligations to enforce effectively the applicable international rules and standards in respect of violations committed by its vessels." *Id.* Articles 218 and 228. See also § 512, Reporters' Note 7; § 604, Comments *d* and *e*.

j. Additional rights and obligations of parties to LOS Convention. When the Convention enters into force, parties to the Convention will have rights and obligations with respect to the exclusive economic zone in addition to those applicable to all states under this section.

Disputes between parties to the Convention with respect to violations of provisions that relate to "the freedoms and rights of navigation, overflight or the laying of submarine cables and pipelines" in the exclusive economic zone, or to "other internationally lawful uses of the sea related to those freedoms," whether committed by the coastal state or the state exercising those freedoms, would be subject to the jurisdiction of the courts and arbitral tribunals provided for by Article 287 of the Convention. See LOS Convention, Article 297(1). Disputes that relate to the fulfillment by a coastal state of certain obligations with respect to the conservation of and access to living resources of the zone, or with respect to scientific research in the zone, can be submitted to a conciliation commission by any party to the dispute. *Id.*, Article 297(2) and (3).

REPORTERS' NOTES

1. *Exclusive economic zone as customary law.* Prior to the Third United Nations Conference on the Law of the Sea, the United States and several other maritime powers resisted claims by some coastal states to a fishing zone, a "patrimonial sea," or even a territorial sea, extending to 200 (or more) nautical miles from the shore. In the course of the Conference, however, the United States and other maritime states abandoned their opposition and accepted the principle of the exclusive economic zone of 200 miles. The United States itself enacted a 200-mile fishery conservation zone in 1976 (Fishery Conservation and Management Act of 1976, codified at 16 U.S.C. § 1811), and other states quickly followed, enacting either a fishing zone or an exclusive economic zone. By 1981, 90 states had established 200-mile fishing limits, some of them claiming this zone as patrimonial or territorial sea. U.S. Department of State, Office of the Geographer, National Claims to Maritime Jurisdictions 12 (Limits in the Seas, No. 36, 4th rev., 1981). The exclusive economic zone was incorporated into the 1982 LOS Convention without significant dissent as to its fundamentals.

In proclaiming an "Exclusive Economic Zone of the United States" in 1983 (§ 511, Reporters' Note 7), President Reagan stated that the LOS Convention provisions "with respect to traditional uses of the oceans" such as navigation or fishing "generally confirm existing international law and practice and fairly balance the interests of all states," and that "the United States will recognize the rights of other states in the waters off their coasts, as reflected in the Convention, so long as the rights and freedoms of the United States and others under international law are recognized by such coastal states." The fact that 63 other states have taken similar steps confirms that the provisions of the LOS Convention concerning the exclusive economic zone and interrelated navigational provisions have become a part of customary international law, independently of the coming into force of the Convention. For a list of the 64 states with 200-mile economic zones, as of 1985, see U.S. Department of State, Office of the Geographer, National Claims to Maritime Jurisdictions 10 (Limits in the Seas, No. 36, 5th rev., 1985). Additional states proclaimed a 200-mile exclusive economic zone in 1986. See United Nations, Law of the Sea: National Legislation on the Exclusive Economic Zone, the Economic Zone and the Exclusive Fishery Zone, U.N. Pub. E.85.V.10 (1986).

2. *Exclusive economic zone and high seas.* At the Third United Nations Conference on the Law of the Sea, maritime states pressed for having the waters of the exclusive economic zone designated as "high seas" subject to special rights for coastal states in the resources of the area. Coastal states generally insisted that the exclusive economic zone be designated not as high seas but as a special zone of the coastal state subject to rights of navigation and overflight for other states. In the end, the maritime states did not insist on expressly designating the zone as high seas, but the history of the negotiations indicates that they

consider that the zone remains high seas, although it will be subject to exceptional rights in favor of the adjacent coastal state. Conflicts may arise over assertions of rights in the zone, under the principle of freedom of the sea, with respect to matters not explicitly covered in the LOS Convention. As to procedures for settling such conflict, see Comment *b.*

3. *Due regard to rights and duties of other states.* In the Fisheries Jurisdiction Case (United Kingdom v. Iceland), the International Court of Justice observed that the 1958 Convention on the High Seas was "generally declaratory of established principles of international law," and that the Convention declared in Article 2 that the freedoms of the high seas "shall be exercised by all States with reasonable regard to the interests of other States in their exercise of the freedoms of the high seas." The Court held that Iceland's disregard of the rights of the United Kingdom constituted an infringement of this principle. [1974] I.C.J. Rep. 3, 22, 29. Articles 56(2) and 58(3) of the LOS Convention embody the same principle but changed "reasonable regard" to "due regard."

4. *Conservation and sharing of living resources.* After taking the necessary steps to conserve the living resources of the exclusive economic zone and to determine both the allowable catch and the capacity of its fishermen to harvest that catch, the coastal state may find that there is some surplus left. The principle of "optimum utilization" of the living resources of the zone requires that the coastal state arrange for harvesting that surplus. LOS Convention, Art. 62(1) and (2).

In making such arrangements, the coastal state is required to consider various factors but has substantial discretion in balancing them. Among these factors are: the significance of the living resources of the zone to the coastal state's economy and other national interests (*e.g.,* reciprocal fishing arrangements with certain states, or obtaining other benefits from another state in exchange for fishing quotas) (*id.* Art. 62(3)); limited obligation to provide access to these resources, on an equitable basis, to neighboring land-locked and geographically disadvantaged states (*id.* Arts. 69–70); and limited obligation to provide access also to the developing states of the subregion or region and, when needed to minimize economic dislocation, to any state whose nationals have habitually fished in the zone or a state that has made substantial efforts in research or identification of fishing stocks (*id.* Art. 62(3)). In establishing the terms of exploitation by any other state, a coastal state may require payment of fees, or assistance to its own fishing industry in the form of financing, equipment, or training of personnel, or transfer of fisheries technology. *Id.* Art. 62(4) (a) and (j). The participation of other states in the available surplus is also subject to appropriate bilateral, subregional, or regional agreements that may be concluded, and to their obligation to observe the laws and regulations of the coastal state that are consistent with the Convention. *Id.* Arts. 62(2) and (4), 69(2), 70(3). The coastal state may enforce such laws through various means, including boarding, inspection, arrest, and judicial proceedings. However, arrested vessels must be promptly released upon posting of reasonable bond or other security, and members of the crews may not be subjected to imprisonment or corporal punishment. *Id.* Art. 73.

Under the Convention, special rules apply to anadromous stocks, which originate in rivers and spend the greater part of their life cycle in the ocean, and which are primarily regulated by the state of their origin (*id.* Art. 66); to catadromous species, which originate in the ocean and spend the greater part of their life cycle in rivers, and which are primarily regulated by the state in whose rivers they live (*id.* Art. 67); to sedentary species, which at the harvestable stage either are immobile on or under the sea-bed or are unable to move except in constant physical contact with the sea-bed or the subsoil, and which remain subject to the continental shelf regime (*id.* Arts. 68 and 77); to highly migratory species (*e.g.*, tuna), which are to be regulated internationally both within and beyond the exclusive economic zone (*id.* Art. 64); and to marine mammals (*e.g.*, whales), for which special conservation measures designed to increase their populations may be taken by coastal states and the appropriate international organizations (*id.* Art. 65). Whether or not all of these provisions are customary law is in dispute.

5. *United States law concerning fishing.* Even before the United States accepted a 200-mile exclusive economic zone (Reporters' Note 1), it established a 200-mile fishery zone. Fishery Conservation and Management Act of 1976, as amended, 16 U.S.C. § 1811. See Reporters' Note 1. That Act had two purposes: to protect the fisheries in the 200-mile zone from over-

exploitation by foreign fishing fleets, and to reserve a larger share of the resources for United States fishermen. Conservation and management plans for each fish species are developed and constantly revised by eight regional fishery management councils. Each council is composed of representatives of States of the United States bordering on the particular fishing region and fishery experts appointed by the United States Secretary of Commerce from a list of persons nominated by Governors of these States. 16 U.S.C. § 1852. The plans must promote an "optimum" yield from each fishery which would provide "the greatest overall benefit to the Nation, with particular reference to food production and recreational opportunities," and would be based on "the maximum sustainable yield from such fishery, as modified by any relevant economic, social or ecological factor." *Id.* § 1802(18). Access is given to foreign vessels only to the portion of the "optimum yield" not harvested by the United States fishermen, and such access depends on the conclusion of a fishery agreement with the foreign state concerned. *Id.* §§ 1821–1822. For a list of such agreements, see 16 U.S.C. § 1823, note.

The 1983 Proclamation of the exclusive economic zone (§ 511, Reporters' Note 7) announced that there was no change in existing United States policies concerning "marine mammals and fisheries, including highly migratory species of tuna which are not subject to United States jurisdiction and require international agreements for effective management." The accompanying United States Oceans Policy Statement (Introductory Note to this Part) made clear that the proclamation was intended to reinforce the policy of promoting the United States fishing industry.

6. *United States policy concerning scientific research.* In the oceans policy statement accompanying the 1983 proclamation on the exclusive economic zone (Reporters' Note 5 and § 511, Reporters' Note 7), President Reagan announced that the United States elected not to assert the right, recognized by international law, of "jurisdiction over marine scientific research within such a zone," in view of "the United States interest in encouraging marine scientific research and avoiding any unnecessary burdens." Nevertheless, the United States will recognize the right of other coastal states over marine scientific research within their exclusive economic zones "if that jurisdiction is exercised reasonably in a manner consistent with international law." See, Introductory Note to this Part.

7. *Deepwater ports in United States exclusive economic zone.* The Deepwater Port Act of 1974 (33 U.S.C. §§ 1501 *et seq.*) established the legal framework for licensing the construction and operation of port facilities in waters beyond the territorial limits of the United States, in order to facilitate the transport of petroleum supplies obtained from foreign sources. The first applications for licenses to build such ports off the coast of the United States were approved in 1976 by the Secretary of Transportation. The licenses contained provisions to ensure nondiscriminatory access to all carriers and to protect the marine environment. [1976] Digest of U.S. Practice in Int'l L. 374–76.

8. *Previous Restatement.* Section 23 of the previous Restatement dealt with the resources of the continental shelf as originally defined in the 1958 Convention on the Continental Shelf. Conservation of fish beyond the territorial sea was considered in § 36, on the basis of the 1958 Convention on Fishing and Conservation of the Living Resources of the High Seas. See Introductory Note to this Part. This Restatement reflects the intervening development of the law of the exclusive economic zone.

§ 515. Continental Shelf

(1) **The coastal state has sovereign rights over its continental shelf for the purpose of exploring it and exploiting its natural resources.**

(2) **The rights of the coastal state over its continental shelf do not affect the legal status of the superjacent waters or the air space above those waters, and the exercise of these rights must not result in any unjustifiable interference with navigation and other rights and freedoms of other states.**

Source Note:

This section is based on Articles 2–5 of the 1958 Convention on the Continental Shelf, and Articles 77–78 of the LOS Convention.

Comment:

a. Overlap of continental shelf and exclusive economic zone. The continental shelf of a coastal state and its exclusive economic zone largely overlap geographically; the state's rights under the two regimes in respect of natural resources are also largely duplicative. Compare § 511, Comment *b.* As defined by the LOS Convention, and now accepted as customary international law, the continental shelf extends to the outer edge of the continental margin, or to a distance of 200 nautical miles from the baseline of the territorial sea if the margin does not extend that far (or if a state has no continental margin). See § 511, Comment *j.* In many instances, therefore, the continental shelf will be co-extensive with the 200-mile exclusive economic zone. See § 511(c). But some states, *e.g.,* Argentina, Australia, Canada, New Zealand, the Soviet Union, the United Kingdom, and the United States, have extensive areas of continental shelf beyond 200 nautical miles from the coast. Since the coastal state's jurisdiction in its exclusive economic zone includes rights to the resources of the sea-bed, the doctrine of the continental shelf will give a coastal state important additional rights only in areas of the continental shelf beyond 200 nautical miles. Even within 200 nautical miles, however, the coastal state's rights in the sea-bed are somewhat larger under the doctrine of the continental shelf as regards the living resources of the sea-bed, since there is no obligation to manage or to share those resources. See Comment *b.*

Special provisions apply to the area of the continental shelf beyond 200 nautical miles. For instance, in that area the coastal state may not withhold its consent to scientific research on the ground that the project is of direct significance for the exploration and exploitation of natural resources, except where exploitation or detailed exploration have actually started in a specific area or are to occur within a reasonable time. LOS Convention, Article 246(6). In the continental shelf, as distinguished from the exclusive economic zone, the coastal state may not exercise exclusive economic exploration or exploitation rights with respect to such activities as, for example, precipitation of metals in suspension in the water column, see § 514, Comment *g*; such activities above the continental shelf are subject to the regime of the high seas (§ 521).

The coastal states that become parties to the LOS Convention and exploit nonliving resources of the continental shelf beyond 200 nautical miles—with the exception of any developing state that is a net importer of mineral resources produced from its continental shelf—will have to make payments or contributions in kind to the International Sea-Bed Authority, see § 523, Reporters' Note 3. The

Authority is to distribute these funds among other states parties to the Convention, taking into account the interests and needs of developing countries, particularly the least developed and the land-locked among them. LOS Convention, Article 82.

   b. Exclusive rights of coastal states.   As in its exclusive economic zone, the special rights of the coastal state in its continental shelf are exclusive. The coastal state's consent is required for exploring its continental shelf or exploiting its resources. The rights of the coastal state over the continental shelf belong to it automatically; they do not depend on occupation or express proclamation. LOS Convention, Article 77(2) and (3). A coastal state's rights in respect of the natural resources of its continental shelf differ somewhat from the state's rights in respect of the resources of its exclusive economic zone. § 514, Comment *e*. For instance, the coastal state is not obligated to establish conservation measures with respect to the living resources of the continental shelf, or to assure "optimum yield," or to allow any other state, even a developing and geographically disadvantaged state, to participate in the exploitation of either the living or the mineral resources of the continental shelf. LOS Convention, Articles 68 and 77; see Comment *c*. As to the sea-bed within 200 miles from its shore, where a state's continental shelf is also part of its exclusive economic zone, a coastal state may claim the benefits of the regime that is more advantageous to it; thus, it may assert exclusive rights to the resources of that sea-bed without the limitations applicable to the resources of the water above the sea-bed under the regime of the exclusive economic zone. In respect of the exploitation of mineral resources from the shelf beyond 200 nautical miles, however, the LOS Convention would require the coastal states, with the exception of some developing countries, to make some payments to be distributed among other parties to the Convention. See Comment *a*. The United States would be subject to this obligation only if it became party to the Convention.

   c. Resources of continental shelf.   Under this section, the coastal state has exclusive jurisdiction over the resources of the continental shelf. See LOS Convention, Article 77(2). These resources consist of the mineral and other nonliving resources of the sea-bed and subsoil, as well as living organisms belonging to sedentary species, *i.e.*, those that at the harvestable stage are either immobile on or under the sea-bed, or are unable to move except in constant physical contact with the sea-bed or the subsoil. *Id.* Article 77(4). There have been some disagreements as to which species are sedentary. (For a United States list of such species, see 16 U.S.C. § 1802(4).)

d. Scientific research on continental shelf. The restrictions on marine scientific research by other states that are applicable in the exclusive economic zone apply also to research on the continental shelf up to 200 nautical miles from the baseline from which the breadth of the territorial sea is measured. See § 514, Comment *h;* LOS Convention, Articles 246–49; compare 1958 Convention on the Continental Shelf, Article 5(1) and (8); see Reporters' Note 2. The powers of the coastal state are, however, more limited with respect to research on the continental shelf beyond 200 nautical miles. See Comment *a.* The coastal state has the exclusive right to authorize and regulate drilling anywhere on the continental shelf for all purposes, including scientific research. LOS Convention, Article 81.

e. Submarine cables and pipelines. All states are entitled to lay submarine cables and pipelines on the continental shelf, without interference by the coastal state. The consent of the coastal state is required, however, for the delineation of the pipeline's course, and the coastal state may establish conditions for cables or pipelines entering its territory or territorial sea. The coastal state may also take "reasonable measures" for the prevention, reduction, and control of pollution from pipelines. See the 1958 Convention on the High Seas, Article 26; the 1958 Convention on the Continental Shelf, Article 4; and the more elaborate provisions in the LOS Convention, Article 79.

f. Artificial islands, installations, and structures. The principles governing islands, installations, and structures in the exclusive economic zone (§ 514, Comment *g*) apply, *mutatis mutandis*, to the continental shelf. LOS Convention, Article 80.

In the United States, Congress has by law extended to artificial islands and fixed structures erected on the sea-bed of the outer continental shelf "the Constitution and law and civil and political jurisdiction of the United States," including several laws mentioned explicitly, for example the National Labor Relations Act. Outer Continental Shelf Lands Act, 43 U.S.C. §§ 1333, 1356.

REPORTERS' NOTES

1. *Development of concept of continental shelf.* Although the Truman Proclamation, September 28, 1945, 59 Stat. 884, 10 Fed.Reg. 12303, was not the first instrument relating to the continental shelf, it possesses "a special status" and may be regarded as "the starting point of the positive law on the subject." North Sea Continental Shelf Cases (Federal Republic of Germany/Denmark & the Netherlands), [1969] I.C.J. Rep. 3, 32–33. Within a short time the principles laid down in that proclamation secured a general following (*id.* at 53). By 1958

they were embodied in the Convention on the Continental Shelf adopted by the First United Nations Conference on the Law of the Sea, as well as in many national laws and regulations, and accepted as customary law. See United Nations, Laws and Regulations on the Regime of the High Seas, 1 U.N. Legislative Series 3–38; 4 Whiteman, Digest of International Law 789–814 (1965).

Since then, customary law has extended the area of the continental shelf subject to coastal states' jurisdiction, and the LOS Convention imposes some duties on the coastal state in favor of other states and the international community. See Comment a. Some states consider that they have acquired broad areas of the continental shelf beyond 200 miles on the basis of the 1958 Convention on the Continental Shelf. Some developing countries have asserted that their acceptance of the definition of the continental shelf in the 1982 Convention was contingent on agreement that states engaged in production of minerals from the area beyond 200 miles should make payments to an international fund. That position raises the question whether as a matter of customary law a state can claim the resources of that area, or can do so only if it makes the payments provided for in the Convention. See Art. 82.

2. *Scientific research on continental shelf.* The 1958 Convention on the Continental Shelf contained two provisions on scientific research concerning the continental shelf. On the one hand, the coastal state's exploration of its natural resources must not result "in any interference with fundamental oceanographic or other scientific research carried out

with the intention of open publication." Art. 5(1). On the other hand, the "consent of the coastal State shall be obtained in respect of any research concerning the continental shelf and undertaken there", though such consent should not "normally" be withheld if the request is submitted by a qualified institution with a view to "purely scientific research into the physical or biological characteristics of the continental shelf." Art. 5(8). In practice some states have consistently refused to grant consent, alleging that the proposed research was not "purely scientific" but related to the natural resources of the continental shelf. See [1974] Digest of U.S. Practice in Int'l L. 370–74.

In the United States, the Bartlett Act of 1964, 78 Stat. 194, prohibited the taking of any continental shelf fishery resources except for purposes of fishery research by a vessel owned and operated by an international organization of which the United States is a member. That provision seemed to imply that other continental shelf fishery research was prohibited. (The Bartlett Act was repealed by the Fishery Conservation and Management Act of 1976, Sec. 402(b), 90 Stat. 331; see § 514, Reporters' Note 5.)

The LOS Convention deals with scientific research in much greater detail, providing a special regime for research in the exclusive economic zone and on the continental shelf. It requires the coastal state's consent but tries to ensure that it will not be unreasonably denied. See § 514, Comment h, and § 515, Comment d. While coastal states refused to accept international control over their exercise of discretion with respect to marine scientific research, they accepted the jurisdiction of a conciliation commission with respect to certain disputes relating thereto. LOS Convention, Art. 297(2). This conciliation procedure does not apply, however, to states not parties to the Convention.

3. *United States legislation concerning continental shelf.* The Submerged Lands Act of 1953, 43 U.S.C. §§ 1301–15, settled a major controversy between the Federal Government and the States over the ownership of the continental shelf resources, but disputes concerning bays and the baseline of the territorial sea continue. See § 511, Reporters' Note 3. The Submerged Lands Act was accompanied by the Outer Continental Shelf Lands Act of 1953, which regulates the exploration and exploitation of submerged lands lying seaward from the lands granted to States by the Submerged Lands Act (*i.e.* beyond three, or in special cases nine, miles from the baseline of the territorial sea). 43 U.S.C. §§ 1331–43. For regulations relating to mineral leases, the oil, gas, and sulphur operations in the outer continental shelf and the control of pollution, see 30 C.F.R., Part 250. For British objections and United States response to the applicability of United States regulations relating to the operation of foreign mobile offshore drilling units (MODUs) on the outer continental shelf, see [1979] Digest of U.S. Practice in Int'l L. 1323–26.

§ 516. Delimitation of Territorial Sea

Where the coasts of two states are opposite or adjacent to each other, neither of the two states is entitled to extend its territorial sea beyond the median line between them, except (a) by agreement, or (b) where historic title or other special circumstances require a different delimitation.

Source Note:

This provision follows Article 12(1) of the 1958 Convention on the Territorial Sea and the Contiguous Zone, and Article 15 of the LOS Convention.

Comment:

a. *Median line as limit.* The median line is usually defined as a line that is equidistant from the nearest points on the baseline from which the breadth of the territorial sea of the two states is measured. 1958 Convention on the Territorial Sea and the Contiguous Zone, Article 12(1); LOS Convention, Article 15. This section does not establish the median line as a boundary, but forbids neighboring states to extend their limit beyond the median line in the absence of agreement between them.

This section applies only to the territorial sea; for the delimitation of the continental shelf and the exclusive economic zone, see § 517.

b. Special circumstances. The existence of a "historic title" may be established by appropriate evidence. It is uncertain what other "special circumstances" would justify a state in extending its territorial sea beyond the median line. In practice, delimitation has taken into account special geographic factors such as islands so located that they distort the effects of a median-line delimitation. See also § 517, Comment *c*.

REPORTERS' NOTES

1. *Delimitation of territorial sea not controversial.* Unlike the principles governing delimitation of the exclusive economic zone and the continental shelf (§ 517), the principle embodied in this section, as formulated by the First United Nations Conference on the Law of the Sea, was accepted without difficulty by the Third Conference. For various delimitation issues faced by the United States, and agreements on the subject among adjacent states, see 4 Whiteman, Digest of International Law 309–11, 326–27, 333–35 (1965).

2. *Previous Restatement.* Article 12 of the 1958 Convention on the Continental Shelf, substantially identical with this section, was set forth in § 15, Reporters' Note 3, of the previous Restatement without comment.

§ 517. Delimitation of Exclusive Economic Zone and Continental Shelf

(1) The delimitation of the exclusive economic zone or the continental shelf between states with opposite or adjacent coasts is to be effected by agreement.

(2) In the absence of agreement, such boundary is the line resulting from the application of equitable principles that produces an equitable result, taking into account the circumstances of the area concerned.

Source Note:

This section departs to some extent from the language but not the spirit of Articles 74 and 83 of the LOS Convention, adopting the interpretation of these articles by the Chamber of the International Court of Justice in the Case Concerning Delimitation of the Maritime Boundary in the Gulf of Maine Area (Canada/United States), [1984] I.C.J. Rep. 246, 299–300.

Comment:

a. Delimitation of exclusive economic zone and continental shelf. This section applies to the delimitation of both the exclusive economic zone and the continental shelf. The line may be the same for both purposes or it may be different. See Gulf of Maine Case, cited in Source Note, at 301–302, 326–27.

b. Delimitation by agreement. As the International Court of Justice pointed out in the Norwegian Fisheries Case, the "delimitation of sea areas has always an international aspect; it cannot be dependent merely upon the will of the coastal State as expressed in its municipal law," and the validity of any unilateral act of delimitation depends upon its consonance with international law. [1951] I.C.J. Rep. 116, 132. Because of their political sensitivity, sea boundary delimitations involving vast areas of the sea and potentially rich resources are not subject to general rules and require agreement between the states concerned. International law has been able only to provide guidelines for such agreement. According to the International Court of Justice, the parties to a delimitation dispute "are under an obligation to enter into negotiations with a view to arriving at an agreement, and not merely to go through a formal process of negotiation as a sort of prior condition for the automatic application" of some other delimitation principles or methods. In particular, the parties "are under an obligation so to conduct themselves that the negotiations are meaningful, which will not be the case when either of them insists upon its own position without contemplating any modification of it." North Sea Continental Shelf Cases (Federal Republic of Germany/Denmark and the Netherlands), [1969] I.C.J. Rep. 3, 47.

c. Equitable delimitation of boundaries. The International Court of Justice has stated that "the international law of continental shelf delimitation does not involve any imperative rule and permits resort to various principles or methods, as may be appropriate, or a combination of them, provided that, by the application of equitable principles, a reasonable result is arrived at." North Sea Continental Shelf Cases, Comment *b*, at 49. The Court added that "there is no legal limit to the considerations which States may take account of for the purpose of making sure that they apply equitable procedures, and more often than not it is the balancing-up of all such considerations that will produce this result rather than reliance on one to the exclusion of all others." *Id.* at 50. See also Case Concerning the Continental Shelf (Tunisia/Libyan Arab Jamahiriya), [1982] I.C.J. Rep. 18, 59–60; Case Concerning the Continental Shelf (Libyan Arab Jamahiriya/Malta), [1985] I.C.J. Rep. 13, 38–39; Gulf of Maine Case, cited in Source Note, at 321.

Unless the parties agree otherwise, a delimitation of an equitable boundary should "aim at an equal division of areas where the maritime projections of the coasts of the States between which delimitation is to be effected converge and overlap" (Gulf of Maine Case, cited in Source Note, at 327), except when there are "special circumstances in the case which would make that criterion inequitable" (*id.* at 301). The delimitation should, in particular, take into account the physical and political geography of the delimitation area, including such auxiliary factors as the difference within the delimitation area between the lengths of the respective coastlines of the countries concerned, the need to ensure that the delimitation does not cut off one coastline from the maritime area to be divided, and the presence of an island or group of small islands lying off a coast. *Id.* at 328. But such delimitation should not normally consider political and economic factors affecting the parties (Case Concerning the Continental Shelf (Tunisia/Libyan Arab Jamahiriya), *supra*, at 77), unless the overall result is "radically inequitable," *i.e.*, likely to entail catastrophic repercussions for the livelihood and economic well-being of the population of the countries concerned (Gulf of Maine Case, Source Note, at 342).

d. Provisional arrangements. Articles 74 and 83 of the LOS Convention provide that, pending an agreement on delimitation, "the States concerned, in a spirit of understanding and co-operation, shall make every effort to enter into provisional arrangements of a practical nature and, during this transitional period, not to jeopardize or hamper the reaching of the final agreement." Such "arrangements shall be without prejudice to the final delimitation." These provisions reflect general principles of customary law.

e. Procedure for settlement of boundary disputes. No state can be forced to submit a dispute to binding settlement by a third party, but states have often agreed to submit boundary disputes to arbitration or judicial settlement. The LOS Convention provides for a third-party settlement of all disputes arising thereunder and makes special provisions for boundary disputes, Article 298(1)(a), but these provisions apply only to states parties. For the procedure for the delimitation of the outer boundary of the continental shelf, see § 511, Reporters' Note 8.

REPORTERS' NOTES

1. *Development of international guidelines.* The 1958 Convention on the Continental Shelf dealt separately with delimitation of the continental shelf between states with opposite coasts as distinguished from states with adjacent coasts. In both cases the boundary was to be determined by agreement between the states concerned, but

in the absence of agreement, the Convention prescribed somewhat different principles for the two cases. In the case of states with opposite coasts, "the boundary is the median line, every point of which is equidistant from the nearest points of the baselines from which the breadth of the territorial sea of each State is measured." Art. 6(1). In the case of states with adjacent coasts, "the boundary shall be determined by application of the principle of equidistance from the nearest points of the baselines from which the breadth of the territorial sea of each State is measured." Art. 6(2). Both provisions are modified by the addition of the phrase "unless another boundary line is justified by special circumstances." The Convention gives no indication as to the kinds of "special circumstances" that might be invoked.

In the North Sea Continental Shelf Cases, Denmark and the Netherlands contended that the delimitation provision in the 1958 Convention on the Continental Shelf merely codified customary law, and urged before the International Court of Justice that the continental shelf boundaries between them and the Federal Republic of Germany should be based on the equidistance principle. The Court held, however, that the equidistance principle, in particular because of the "special circumstances" exception, was not a principle of international law but merely an application in appropriate situations of a more general rule that "delimitation is to be effected by agreement in accordance with equitable principles, and taking account of all the relevant circumstances." North Sea Continental Shelf Cases (Federal Republic of Germany/Denmark and the Nether-

lands) [1969] I.C.J. Rep. 3, 53. The Court considered as relevant circumstances such factors as:

(a) the general configuration of the coasts of the parties, as well as the presence of any special features;

(b) so far as known or readily ascertainable, the physical and geological structure, and the natural resources, of the continental shelf areas involved;

(c) the element of a reasonable degree of proportionality, which a delimitation carried out in accordance with equitable principles ought to bring about between the extent of the continental shelf appertaining to the coastal State and the length of its coast measured in the general direction of the coastline, account being taken for this purpose of the effects, actual or prospective, of any other continental shelf delimitations between adjacent States in the same region.

Id. at 54. See also Comment c. Similar principles were applied by the Court in Case Concerning the Continental Shelf (Tunisia/Libyan Arab Jamahiriya), [1982] I.C.J. Rep. 18, 92–94.

As a result of the Court's 1969 decision, at the Third United Nations Conference on the Law of the Sea, an early draft of the delimitation provision departed from the 1958 formula and proposed that the "delimitation of the exclusive economic zone [continental shelf] between adjacent or opposite States shall be effected by agreement in accordance with equitable principles, employing, where appropriate, the median or equidistance line, and taking account of all the relevant circumstances." U.N. Doc. A/ CONF.62/WP.10/Rev.1, 51, 57 (1979). This draft was strongly opposed by the defenders of the "principle of equidistance," who emphasized that the practice of states, as reflected in many bilateral agreements, has applied that principle, adjusting the delimitation where necessary to take special circumstances into account.

In 1981, a compromise was reached between the two groups of especially interested states on the following formula, which was inserted in the final text of the LOS Convention:

> The delimitation of the exclusive economic zone [continental shelf] between States with opposite or adjacent coasts shall be effected by agreement on the basis of international law, as referred to in Article 38 of the Statute of the International Court of Justice, in order to achieve an equitable solution.

LOS Convention, Arts. 74 and 83. This section is consistent with these articles, as interpreted by the Court's Chamber in the Gulf of Maine Case.

2. *Gulf of Maine judgment.* The Chamber of the International Court of Justice to which the Gulf of Maine delimitation dispute was submitted noted that the 1982 formula is "singularly concise," but "serves to open the door to continuation of the development effected in this field by international case law." Gulf of Maine Case, cited in Source Note, at 294. Having noted that a "body of detailed rules is not to be looked for in customary international law," and that it would be unrewarding "to look to the general international law to provide a ready-

made set of rules that can be used for solving any delimitation problems that arise," the Chamber decided to seek instead "a better formulation of the fundamental norm . . . whose existence in the legal convictions not only of the Parties to the present dispute, but of all States, is apparent from an examination of the realities of international legal relations." *Id.* at 299. According to the Chamber, this norm is as follows:

> (1) No maritime delimitation between States with opposite or adjacent coasts may be effected unilaterally by one of those States. Such delimitation must be sought and effected by means of an agreement, following negotiations conducted in good faith and with the genuine intention of achieving a positive result. Where, however, such agreement cannot be achieved, delimitation should be effected by recourse to a third party possessing the necessary competence.

> (2) In either case, delimitation is to be effected by the application of equitable criteria and by the use of practical methods capable of ensuring, with regard to the geographic configuration of the area and other relevant circumstances, an equitable result.

Id. at 299–300.

In applying these basic principles, the Chamber refused to apply the equidistance method of the 1958 Convention on the Continental Shelf, since it was requested to draw a single delimitation line for both the continental shelf and the superjacent fishery zones. *Id.* at 301. See Comment *a*. After considering a variety of equitable criteria, *id.* at 312–13, the Chamber decided to aim at "an equal division of areas where the maritime projections" of the two coasts overlap, taking into consideration also such special circumstances as the "by no means negligible difference within the delimitation area between the lengths of the respective coastlines of the countries concerned," the need to correct partially any "cutting off one coastline, or part of it, from its appropriate projection across the maritime expanses to be divided," and "the necessity of granting some effect, however limited, to the presence of a geographical feature such as an island or group of small islands lying off a coast." *Id.* at 327–28, 339. The Chamber considered that political or economic circumstances "are ineligible for consideration" as relevant circumstances or equitable criteria, but it took into account "human and economic geography" in its "assessment of the equitable character of a delimitation first established on the basis of criteria borrowed from physical and political geography." It regarded as "a legitimate scruple" that the overall result should not be "radically inequitable." *Id.* at 278, 340, 342. As the Chamber found "no reason to fear that any such danger will arise," and was "unable to discern any inevitable source of insurmountable disputes" (*id.* at 343), it let the geographically determined line stand as having produced "an equitable overall result" (*id.* at 344). The final line drawn by the Chamber (*id.* at 346) differed considerably from the lines claimed by the two parties, departing from a mid-channel line, but leaving only a small area of Georges Bank on the Canadian side.

3. *Resolution of delimitation disputes.* Several sea boundary disputes have been referred to an international tribunal for adjudication. See, *e.g.*, North Sea Continental Shelf Cases, Reporters' Note 1; 1977 France/United Kingdom Arbitration on the Delimitation of the Continental Shelf, 18 R.Int'l Arb. Awards 3; Case Concerning the Continental Shelf (Tunisia/Libyan Arab Jamahiriya), Reporters' Note 1; Case Concerning Delimitation of the Maritime Boundary in the Gulf of Maine Area, Source Note; Case Concerning the Continental Shelf (Libyan Arab Jamahiriya/Malta), [1985] I.C.J. Rep. 13. In the case concerning the continental shelf between Libya and Tunisia, Reporters' Note 1, at 21, the parties requested the Court to decide it according to "equitable principles, and the relevant circumstances which characterize the area."

The LOS Convention provides for third-party settlement of all disputes arising thereunder, but sea boundary disputes receive special treatment. A state party to the Convention may make a declaration that all such disputes that arose prior to the entry into force of the Convention will not be subject to the obligation to submit them to any third-party decision. But any dispute relating to the maritime boundaries of the declarant that arises subsequent to the coming into force of the Convention can be submitted by either party to the dispute to a conciliation commission (the report of which is not binding). LOS Convention, Art. 298(1)(a) and Annex V, Section 2. These provisions of the Convention do not reflect customary international law; they will apply only after the Convention comes into force, and even then they will apply only to parties to the Convention. See Introductory Note to this

Part. States nonparties may, of course, agree to submit a sea boundary dispute to any tribunal of their choice (for example, the International Court of Justice).

4. *Previous Restatement.* This section reflects the important differ-

ences between the LOS Convention and the 1958 Convention on the Continental Shelf, Article 6 of which was reproduced in the previous Restatement in § 23, Reporters' Note 2.

Chapter Three

HIGH SEAS

---

§ 521. Freedom of High Seas

(1) **The high seas are open and free to all states, whether coastal or land-locked.**

(2) **Freedom of the high seas comprises,** *inter alia*:

(a) **freedom of navigation;**

(b) **freedom of overflight;**

(c) **freedom of fishing;**

(d) **freedom to lay submarine cables and pipelines;**

(e) **freedom to construct artificial islands, installations, and structures; and**

(f) **freedom of scientific research.**

(3) **These freedoms must be exercised by all states with reasonable regard to the interests of other states in their exercise of the freedom of the high seas.**

Source Note:

This section is based on Article 2 of the 1958 Convention on the High Seas, and Articles 87 and 89 of the LOS Convention.

Comment:

a. Area in which high seas freedoms can be exercised. This section applies to all parts of the sea that are not included in the internal waters, the territorial sea, or the exclusive economic zone of any state, or in the archipelagic waters of an archipelagic state. Certain of these freedoms may be exercised also in the exclusive economic zone of other states, as specified in § 514. See LOS Convention, Article 86; compare 1958 Convention on the High Seas, Article 1.

No state may appropriate any part of the high seas or otherwise subject the high seas to its sovereignty. See LOS Convention,

Article 89. For the law governing the exploration and exploitation of the mineral resources of the deep sea-bed, see § 523.

b. Reservation of high seas for peaceful purposes. Article 88 of the LOS Convention specifies that the "high seas shall be reserved for peaceful purposes." That provision does not preclude the use of the high seas by naval forces. Their use for aggressive purposes, which would be in violation of Article 2(4) of the Charter of the United Nations (§ 905, Comment *g*), is forbidden as well by Article 88. See also LOS Convention, Article 301, requiring parties, in exercising their rights and preforming their duties under the Convention, to refrain from any threat or use of force in violation of the Charter.

c. High seas navigation subject to regulation. Due consideration for interests of others requires that ships on the high seas observe rules relating to the safety of navigation, the protection of life at sea, and the prevention, reduction, and control of pollution of the marine environment. For a list of important international agreements on those subjects, see Introductory Note to this Part, note 7. With respect to control of pollution, see §§ 603–604.

d. Overflight. Freedom of overflight, Subsection 2(b), means that all states have the right for their airplanes, both civilian and military, to overfly the high seas. Civil aircraft are obliged to observe the Rules of the Air enacted by the International Civil Aviation Organization (ICAO) pursuant to Article 12 of the 1944 Chicago Convention. 3 Bevans 944, 947, T.I.A.S. No. 1591, 15 U.N. T.S. 295. State aircraft, while not formally subject to ICAO rules, must operate at all times with due regard for the safety of navigation; states normally require their aircraft to comply with the ICAO rules. See LOS Convention, Article 39(3), which relates to straits but embodies a principle applicable to the high seas generally.

e. Fishing. Under international law, all states have "the right for their nationals to engage in fishing on the high seas" (LOS Convention, Article 116), and the obligation to take separately or jointly with other states such measures as may be necessary for the conservation of the living resources of the high seas. These conservation measures may not discriminate in form or in fact against the fishermen of any state. See 1958 Convention on Fishing and Conservation of the Living Resources of the High Seas, Articles 1–4, 7(2)(c); LOS Convention, Articles 87(1)(e), 116–19.

f. Submarine cables and pipelines. The freedom to lay submarine cables and pipelines on the high seas is subject to special rules relating to cables and pipelines on the continental shelf. See

§ 515, Comment *e.* The Convention for the Protection of Submarine Cables of 1884, the provisions of which have been generally accepted as customary international law, obligates a flag state to provide for punishment of those on a ship responsible for willful or negligent breaking of or injury to submarine cables. See 1 Bevans 89; also *id.* at 112–14. See also 1958 Convention on the High Seas, Articles 26–29; LOS Convention, Articles 112–15.

g. Artificial islands, installations, and structures. The freedom to construct artificial islands, installations, and structures is also subject to special rules relating to constructions on the continental shelf and in the exclusive economic zone. See § 514, Comment *g.* As to installations connected with activities relating to the exploration and exploitation of the deep sea-bed, see § 523, Comment *d;* LOS Convention, Article 147.

h. Scientific research. All states, including land-locked states, as well as international organizations, may conduct scientific research on the high seas, Subsection 2(f). LOS Convention, Article 257. The LOS Convention imposes some restrictions on scientific research on the sea-bed and in the subsoil of the continental shelf of another state where the continental shelf extends beyond that state's exclusive economic zone. Article 206(6); see § 515, Comments *b* and *d.*

Marine scientific research on the high seas is governed by the following principles:

> (1) it is to be conducted exclusively for peaceful purposes;

> (2) it may not unjustifiably interfere with other legitimate uses of the sea and in turn is to be duly respected by other users;

> (3) it may not constitute the legal basis for any claim to any part of the marine environment or its resources;

> (4) states and their nationals engaged in such research may deploy and use any type of scientific research installations or equipment, subject to specified conditions.

See LOS Convention, Articles 240–41, 258.

For discussion of research relating to archaeological and historical objects, see Reporters' Note 6.

i. Deep sea-bed mining. With respect to deep sea-bed mining as a freedom of the high seas, see § 523, Comment *b.*

REPORTERS' NOTES

1. *Interference with navigation on high seas.* The use of the high seas by ships is normally subject to regulation and control only by the

flag state; for centuries, the freedom of ships from control or interference by ships of other states has been jealously safeguarded. Small deviations from that rule have been made in order to protect all states against common enemies such as pirates, slave traders, and, more recently, "pirate" broadcasters. See § 404 and Reporters' Note 1 thereto. The increasing concern over illicit traffic in narcotic drugs may lead to a recognition of the right to stop and search foreign vessels suspected of such traffic, and even to confiscate the drugs or arrest the ship and its crew.

The movement of ships in certain areas of the high seas is frequently hampered by naval exercises and the testing of conventional weapons, missiles, and nuclear weapons. As to various attempts to restrict such testing, see 4 Whiteman, Digest of International Law 710–26 (1965). See also McDougal and Schlei, "The Hydrogen Bomb Tests in Perspective: Lawful Measures for Security," 64 Yale L.J. 648 (1955); Margolis, "The Hydrogen Bomb Experiments and International Law," 64 Yale L.J. 629 (1955); Taubenfeld, "Nuclear Testing and International Law," 16 Sw.L.J. 365 (1962). See also Nuclear Tests Cases (Australia and New Zealand v. France), [1974] I.C.J.Rep. 253, 457.

2. *Overflight and air defense.* The United States has established air defense areas, air defense identification zones (ADIZ), and, for Alaska, a distant early warning identification zone (DEWIZ). Some of these zones extend several hundred miles into the sea. Pilots entering these zones are obliged to report promptly and to provide specified data to United States authorities; a foreign aircraft not complying with this requirement is not permitted to enter the air space of the United States. See 14 C.F.R. § 99.23. Similar zones have been established by other states. These zones have been generally accepted. It is uncertain, however, whether a coastal state can apply such regulations to aircraft passing through its declared air defense zone but not planning to enter its airspace. See Note, "Air Defense Identification Zones: Creeping Jurisdiction in the Airspace," 18 Va.J.Int'l L. 485 (1978); 4 Whiteman, Digest of International Law 496–97 (1965). See also § 511, Comment *k*.

3. *Fishing.* Both the 1958 Convention on Fishing and Conservation of the Living Resources of the High Seas and the LOS Convention recognize the freedom of fishing on the high seas; both impose the obligation on states to regulate such fishing in order to conserve the living resources of the oceans. See Comment *e*. In particular, where the nationals of several states are engaged in exploiting identical living resources, or different living resources in the same area of the high seas, states are obligated to cooperate, and to take the necessary joint or parallel measures, either directly or through a regional or subregional fisheries organization with a view to protecting the resources against over-exploitation. 1958 Convention on Fishing and Conservation of the Living Resources of the High Seas, Art. 3; LOS Convention, Art. 118. As the International Court of Justice noted in the Fisheries Jurisdiction Case (United Kingdom v. Iceland), one of the advances in maritime international law is that "the former *laissez-faire* treatment

of the living resources of the sea in the high seas has been replaced by a recognition of a duty to have due regard to the rights of other States and the needs of conservation for the benefit of all." [1974] I.C.J. Rep. 3, at 31.

Special problems have arisen with respect to "straddling stocks," where the same fish stock is to be found within both an exclusive economic zone of a state and a neighboring high seas area. The complex provisions on the subject in the 1958 Convention have not been applied in practice, and the LOS Convention has only a general provision about seeking an agreement on the subject. 1958 Convention on Fishing, *supra*, Arts. 6–12; LOS Convention, Arts. 63, 116(b). For the conservation of highly migratory species and marine mammals, see *id.* Arts. 64–65, 116(b), 120; § 514, Comment *f.*

4. *Freedom to lay submarine cables and pipelines.* As of 1986, the Convention for the Protection of Submarine Cables, Comment *f*, was in force for 40 states including the United States. For a United States-Soviet Union incident in 1959 relating to the application of the 1884 Convention, see 4 Whiteman, Digest of International Law 728–33 (1965).

5. *Freedom of scientific research.* Freedom of scientific research on the high seas (Subsection (2)(f)), LOS Convention, Art. 87(1)(f), was restricted for the first time by Article 5(8) of the 1958 Convention on the Continental Shelf. Further restrictions were introduced by Part XIII of the LOS Convention (especially Article 246). With the emergence of the exclusive economic zone and the extension of the scope of the continental shelf, the areas

subject to restrictions have been enlarged. See § 514, Comment *h*; § 515, Comments *b* and *d*; § 521, Comment *h*.

6. *Archaeological and historical objects.* Under the traditional admiralty rules, shipwrecks and other objects found at sea become the property of the finder, unless his national law or the law of the flag state of the ship engaged in salvage provides otherwise. Hener v. United States, 525 F.Supp. 350, 354–58 (S.D.N.Y.1981); see also Treasure Salvors v. Unidentified Wrecked and Abandoned Sailing Vessel, 569 F.2d 330, 337 (5th Cir.1978), 640 F.2d 560, 567 (5th Cir.1981), and 556 F.Supp. 1319, 1334 (S.D.Fla.1983) (treasure under high seas); Cobb Coin Co. v. Unidentified Wrecked and Abandoned Sailing Vessel, 549 F.Supp. 540, 556 (S.D.Fla.1982) (treasure under territorial sea); Metropolitan Dade County v. One Bronze Cannon, 537 F.Supp. 923 (S.D.Fla.1982) (treasure salvage off the coast of Haiti under an agreement with the Haitian Government). For a comment on these cases, see Shallcross and Giesecke, "Recent Developments in Litigation Concerning the Recovery of Historic Shipwrecks," 10 Syracuse J.Int'l L. & Com. 371 (1983). For discussion of the recovery of warships, see Collins, "The Salvage of Sunken Military Vessels: Project Jennifer: A Dangerous Precedent?" 10 Int'l Law. 681 (1976); 8 J.Mar.L. & Com. 433 (1977). Within the contiguous zone, the coastal state may "control traffic" in archaeological and historical objects, and may "presume" that their removal from the sea-bed without its approval would result in an infringement of its customs and fiscal regulations. LOS Convention, Art. 303. Any such objects

found on the sea-bed beyond the limits of national jurisdiction are to be "preserved or disposed of for the benefit of mankind as a whole, particular regard to be paid for the preferential rights of the State or country of origin, or the State of cultural origin, or the State of historical and archaeological origin." *Id.* Art. 149. It is not clear which

of these states should be given priority in case of a conflict.

7. *Previous Restatement.* The principal reference to high seas in the previous Restatement was contained in § 21, Comment *b*. That Comment is consistent with Subsection (1) of this section and Comment *a*.

§ 522. Enforcement Jurisdiction over Foreign Ships on High Seas

(1) A warship, or other ship owned or operated by a state and used only on government noncommercial service, enjoys complete immunity on the high seas from interference by any other state.

(2) Ships other than those specified in Subsection (1) are not subject to interference on the high seas, but a warship or clearly-marked law enforcement ship of any state may board such a ship if authorized by the flag state, or if there is reason to suspect that the ship

(a) is engaged in piracy, slave trade, or unauthorized broadcasting;

(b) is without nationality; or

(c) though flying a foreign flag or refusing to show its flag, is in fact of the same nationality as the warship or law enforcement ship.

Source Note:

This section follows with minor modifications Articles 8, 9 and 22 of the 1958 Convention on the High Seas, and Articles 95, 96 and 110 of the LOS Convention.

Comment:

a. Immunity of warships and other government ships. A warship (§ 501, Reporters' Note 1) is completely immune from interference by foreign warships. A ship used on government noncommercial service has immunity even if it is not owned by the government so long as it is operated by the government. See LOS Convention, Article 96. With respect to maritime liens, see § 455(4) and Reporters' Note 3.

b. Enforcement procedure. In cases under Subsection (2), the warship or law enforcement ship may proceed to verify a foreign ship's right to fly its flag by examining its documents and, if necessary, by an examination on board the ship. However, if the suspicions prove to be unfounded, and the boarded ship has committed no act justifying those suspicions, the inspecting state is obligated to pay compensation for any loss or damage. 1958 Convention on the High Seas, Article 22; LOS Convention, Article 110.

In specified circumstances warships and law enforcement ships are entitled to engage in hot pursuit. See § 513, Comment *g*.

c. Piracy. Any state may seize a ship or aircraft on the high seas on reasonable suspicion of piracy, arrest the suspected pirates, seize the property on board, try the suspected pirates, and impose penalties on them if convicted. Where the seizure of a ship or aircraft on suspicion of piracy was effected without adequate grounds and the ship was found not to be a pirate ship, the state that made the seizure is liable to the flag state of the seized ship or aircraft for any loss or damage caused by the seizure. 1958 Convention on the High Seas, Articles 19–20; LOS Convention, Articles 105–106.

Not every act of violence committed on the high seas is piracy under international law. Only the following acts are considered piratical:

(i) Any illegal acts of violence, detention, or depredation committed for private ends by the crew or the passengers of a private ship or a private aircraft, and directed against another ship or aircraft on the high seas, or against persons or property on board such other ship or aircraft; or against a ship, aircraft, persons, or property in a place outside the jurisdiction of any state;

(ii) any act of voluntary participation in the operation of a ship or of an aircraft with knowledge of facts making it a pirate ship or aircraft;

(iii) any act of inciting or of intentionally facilitating an act described in subparagraphs (1) or (2).

In addition, acts committed by a mutinous crew of a warship or other government ship or aircraft against another ship or aircraft, may also constitute piracy. 1958 Convention on the High Seas, Articles 15–16; LOS Convention, Articles 101–102.

d. Slave and drug traffic. Because of the general condemnation of slave trade, international law allows the boarding and inspection of vessels suspected of such trade; it does not permit seizure of the vessel or arrest of the crew unless the flag state has consented. Since slave trade is an offense subject to universal jurisdiction (see § 404), the state that boarded the vessel could try members of the crew for violations of its laws, if the flag state consented, and any state could try them later if it obtained jurisdiction over them.

There is movement to extend these rules to illicit traffic in narcotic drugs and psychotropic substances. However, even states, such as the United States, that strongly condemn such traffic do not take steps on the high seas against suspected smugglers except when the ship is without nationality (or is assimilated to such a ship because it uses two or more flags, § 501, Comment *c*), or when permission has been obtained from the flag state (often granted by telegraph or radio) to board, search, and seize the vessel.

  e. Consent of flag state under United States law. Under Subsection (2), interference with a ship that would otherwise be unlawful under international law is permissible if the flag state has consented. However, some actions by the United States in relation to a foreign vessel may violate the United States Constitution even if the flag state consented, and may invalidate an arrest, search, or seizure. See § 433, Comment *d* and Reporters' Note 4.

REPORTERS' NOTES

1. *Warships and other government ships.* A United States Coast Guard ship is considered a warship. United States v. Conroy, 589 F.2d 1258, 1267 (5th Cir.1979), *certiorari denied*, 444 U.S. 831, 100 S.Ct. 60, 62 L.Ed.2d 40 (1979). Some convention provisions grant immunity to "government ships operated for non-commercial purpose" (*e.g.*, 1958 Convention on the Territorial Sea and the Contiguous Zone, Art. 22; LOS Convention, Arts. 31–32); others provide immunity to "ships owned or operated by a State and used only on government non-commercial service" (*e.g.*, 1958 Convention on the High Seas, Art. 9; LOS Convention, Art. 96). It is not clear that any difference was intended. As long as a ship is operated for noncommercial purposes, it is entitled to immunity if it is either owned or operated by the government, for instance, a government-owned ship operated by an oceanographic institute, and engaged on a government-sponsored hydrographic survey, or a private-owned ship chartered by the government for a meteorological service.

2. *Piracy and hijacking.* Acts indicated in Comment *c* are piracy only if they are by private ships and for private ends. Seizure of a ship for political purposes is not considered piracy. See the *Santa Maria* incident in 1961, 4 Whiteman, Digest of International Law 665 (1965). Crew members forced to assist the pirates are not, under the above definition, considered pirates. Wrongful acts by governmental ships are not included in the definition of piracy, but are addressed by general principles of international law governing state responsibility for violations of international obligations. See §§ 207 and 901.

The definition of piracy, Comment c, includes acts by a private ship or aircraft against "another ship or aircraft on the high seas" (para. (1)(a)). That clause was designed to cover acts against a ship or a sea plane floating on the sea; acts committed in the air by one aircraft against another were not included in the definition of piracy but left for regulation outside the framework of the law of the sea. The definition includes also acts committed in "a place outside the jurisdiction of any state" (para. (1)(b)). That reference is to "acts committed by a ship or aircraft on an island constituting *terra nullius* or on the shores of an unoccupied territory," so as to ensure that such acts would not escape all penal jurisdiction. Report of the International Law Commission, [1956] 2 Y.B. Int'l L. Comm'n 282, 11 U.N. GAOR Supp. No. 9 at 28.

As to piracy, see also 1958 Convention on the High Seas, Arts. 14–21; LOS Convention, Arts. 100–107; 18 U.S.C. § 1651 *et seq.*, and 33 U.S.C. § 381 *et seq.*; United States-Thailand Agreement for the Protection of Refugees Against Pirates, 1980, T.I.A.S. No. 9886; In re Piracy Jure Gentium, [1934] A.C. 586 (P.C.); Johnson, "Piracy in Modern International Law," 43 Trans. Grotius Soc'y 63 (1957). For special international agreements relating to the unlawful seizure of aircraft, see § 404, Reporters' Note 1; § 475, Reporters' Note 5; Lowenfeld, Aviation Law: Cases and Materials, ch. 8 (2d ed. 1981).

3. *Slave trade.* A number of 19th century treaties authorized naval and law enforcement vessels of a state to visit, inspect, and seize vessels of another state engaged in slave trade and to bring the traders for trial before special mixed courts of justice. See, *e.g.*, Treaty for the Suppression of African Slave Trade between Great Britain and the United States, 1862, 12 Bevans 136. Most of these treaties are no longer in force; *e.g.*, the treaty with Great Britain was terminated in 1923, pursuant to a notice of termination by the United Kingdom. See [1922] 2 U.S. Foreign Relations 407–408. For United Nations efforts to abolish slave trade, see United Nations Action in the Field of Human Rights 133–40 (U.N. Pub. E.83.XIV.2 (1983).

Unless authorized by special agreement, a ship suspected of slave trade may be visited and inspected by foreign law enforcement ships on the high seas for the purpose of verifying the ship's right to fly its flag, but the ship cannot be seized, unless authorized by the flag state. It is the flag state that has the duty to take effective measures to prevent and punish the transport of slaves in ships authorized to fly its flag and to prevent the unlawful use of its flag for this purpose. See 1958 Convention on the High Seas, Arts. 13 and 22(1)(b); LOS Convention, Arts. 99 and 110(1)(b); §§ 404, 443, 702.

4. *Illicit traffic in narcotic drugs or psychotropic substances.* A ship suspected of traffic in illicit drugs may be visited and inspected by a foreign law enforcement ship with the consent of the ship's master. Absent such consent, it may be visited and searched only pursuant to formal or informal agreement with the flag state, and such agreement is always required for the seizure of the ship. See Reporters' Note 8. No such agreement is nec-

essary, however, when the suspected ship is without nationality or is assimilated to one without nationality. § 501, Comment c; LOS Convention, Arts. 92(2), 110. A state may request the cooperation of other states in suppressing such illicit traffic by ships flying its flag, sometimes even authorizing other states to seize its vessels on the high seas. See LOS Convention, Art. 108; § 433, Reporters' Note 4. In 1983, the United Nations Economic and Social Council noted "the alarming number of private vessels transporting illicit drugs on the high seas," and recommended the "strengthening of international cooperation in combating illicit maritime drug trafficking" and requested that governments "respond promptly to enquiries made for law enforcement purposes by other states regarding the registry of vessels" and take prompt action "to curtail employment of their flag vessels in the illicit drug trade and to impose significant sanctions on persons convicted of such activity." U.N. Doc. E/1983/INF.6, at 4–5 (1983), 1 LOS Bull. 115 (1983). A draft convention prepared for submission to an international conference in Vienna in 1987 was designed to improve international cooperation in combating illicit traffic in narcotic drugs and psychotropic substances; one of its provisions would proclaim trafficking in narcotic drugs and psychotropic substances "a grave crime against humanity." The draft Convention contained no provision on drug smuggling by ship. G.A. Res. 141 (1984), Annex, Article 2, 39 U.N. GAOR, Supp. No. 51, 229, 230; G.A. Res. 122 (1985), para. 4, 40 U.N. GAOR, Supp. No. 53, 237, 238.

5. *Unauthorized broadcasting from high seas.* International law has accepted that any person or ship engaged in unauthorized broadcasting from the high seas may be arrested, and the broadcasting apparatus seized, by a law enforcement ship of any of the following states: the flag state of the broadcasting ship; the state of registry of the installation (as some of the broadcasts are made from abandoned platforms built on the continental shelf); the state of which the person is a national; a state where the transmission can be received; and a state where authorized radio communication is suffering interference. See LOS Convention, Art. 109. As to the European Agreement for the Prevention of Broadcasts Transmitted from Stations Outside National Territories, January 22, 1965, 634 U.N.T.S. 239, see Hunnings, "Pirate Broadcasting in European Waters," 14 Int'l & Comp. L.Q. 410 (1965).

6. *Other situations justifying inspection or seizure.* It may be suggested that the right to inspect and to seize foreign ships be extended to ships carrying stolen nuclear materials or escaping terrorists, but the present international law on the subject is unclear.

7. *Stateless ships.* A stateless vessel is not entitled to the protection of this section against boarding and search. United States v. Cortes, 588 F.2d 106, 109–10 (5th Cir. 1979) (applying the 1958 Convention on the High Seas). See also Molvan v. Attorney General for Palestine, [1948] A.C. 351, 369 (P.C.). A ship displaying two flags, or displaying a flag other than that of the state of registry, may be assimilated to a stateless ship. See 1958 Convention

on the High Seas, Art. 6(2); LOS Convention, Arts. 92(2), 110(1)(d); Legal Opinion of the Chief Counsel of the U.S. Coast Guard, September 1976, [1976] Digest of U.S. Practice in Int'l L. 304; United States v. Martinez, 700 F.2d 1358 (11th Cir. 1983). A ship attempting to change a flag while on the high seas is also assimilated to a stateless ship. United States v. Dominguez, 604 F.2d 304, 307–09 (4th Cir.1979), *certiorari denied*, 444 U.S. 1014, 100 S.Ct. 664, 62 L.Ed.2d 644 (1980).

8. *Consent of flag state to seizure of ships.* Except in cases of privacy, slave trade, or unauthorized broadcasting, Subsection (2), a state may interfere with the ships of another state on the high seas only when expressly authorized by international agreement. 1958 Convention on the High Seas, Art. 22; LOS Convention, Art. 110. States have been reluctant to accord such authority, but a few states have done so in special circumstances.

For instance, by agreement in 1981, the United Kingdom gave permission to United States authorities to board, search, and seize ships under the British flag in an area comprising the Gulf of Mexico, the Caribbean Sea, and a portion of the Atlantic Ocean, in any case in which United States authorities reasonably believe that a ship "has on board a cargo of drugs for importation into the United States in violation of the laws of the United States"; but the United States agreed to release the ship or any United Kingdom national found on board the ship, if the United Kingdom should, within a specified period, "object to the continued exercise of United States jurisdiction" over the ship or person. 1981 Agreement to Facilitate the Interdiction by the United States of Vessels of the United Kingdom Suspected of Trafficking in Drugs, T.I.A.S. No. 10296. This agreement was applied in United States v. Layne, 599 F.Supp. 689 (S.D. Fla.1984); United States v. Reeh, 780 F.2d 1541 (11th Cir.1986); and United States v. Quemener, 789 F.2d 145 (2d Cir. 1986), *certiorari denied*, ___ U.S. ___, 107 S.Ct. 110, 93 L.Ed.2d 58 (1986). In several other instances involving illicit maritime traffic in narcotic drugs, the Coast Guard has relied on informal arrangements with flag state officials providing for consent by radiotelephone. A challenge to this practice was rejected in United States v. Romero-Galue, 757 F.2d 1147 (11th Cir. 1985), and United States v. Gonzalez, 776 F.2d 931 (11th Cir.1985). See also [1976] Digest of U.S. Practice in Int'l L. 302–304; United States v. Hensel, 699 F.2d 18 (1st Cir.1983), *certiorari denied*, 461 U.S. 958, 103 S.Ct. 2431, 77 L.Ed.2d 1317 (1983); United States v. Loalza-Vasquez, 735 F.2d 153 (5th Cir.1984). Congress confirmed the practice in the Maritime Drug Law Enforcement Act, embodied in § 3202 of the Anti-Drug Abuse Act of 1986, Pub. L. 99–570. That statute defines a "vessel of the United States" as including any "vessel registered in a foreign nation where the flag nation has consented or waived objection to the enforcement of United States law by the United States," and provides that such consent "may be obtained by radio, telephone, or similar oral or electronic means, and may be proved by certification of the Secretary of State or the Secretary's designee." *Id.* § 3(b).

In 1981, Haiti authorized United States authorities to board Haitian flag vessels on the high seas for the purpose of ascertaining whether there were any Haitians on board intending to commit an offense against United States immigration laws. The agreement authorized United States authorities to detain any vessel with such migrants aboard, and to return the vessel and persons aboard the vessel to a Haitian port or to release them on the high seas to a representative of Haiti. T.I.A.S. No. 10241. See § 433, Reporters' Note 4; § 513, Reporters' Note 5.

9. *United States jurisdiction over gambling ships.* The Gambling Act of 1948 applies to "any citizen or resident of the United States or any other person who is on an American vessel or is otherwise under or within the jurisdiction of the United States," who commits certain acts on a gambling ship, "if such gambling ship is on the high seas, or is an American vessel or otherwise under or within the jurisdiction of the United States, and is not within the jurisdiction of any State." The Act defines an "Ameri-

can vessel" as either "any vessel documented or numbered under the laws of the United States" or "any vessel which is neither documented or numbered under the laws of the United States nor documented under the laws of any foreign country, if such vessel is owned by, chartered to, or otherwise controlled by one or more citizens or residents of the United States or corporations organized under the laws of the United States or of any State." 18 U.S.C. §§ 1081–1083. This law was applied to defendants engaged in a gambling activity on the high seas on a Greek Line ship on a weekend voyage "to nowhere" from New York harbor, on the grounds that they were United States citizens and residents and that "citizenship alone, apart from locus, suffices to confer upon the United States jurisdiction over extraterritorial acts." United States v. Black, 291 F.Supp. 262, 265–66 (S.D.N.Y.1968). See also § 403, Reporters' Note 9.

Previous Restatement. Enforcement of laws against piracy was dealt with in the previous Restatement in § 34.

§ 523. Exploitation of Mineral Resources of Deep Sea-Bed

(1) **Under international law,**

(a) **no state may claim or exercise sovereignty or sovereign or exclusive rights over any part of the sea-bed and subsoil beyond the limits of national jurisdiction, or over its mineral resources, and no state or person may appropriate any part of that area;**

(b) **unless prohibited by international agreement, a state may engage, or authorize any person to engage, in activities of exploration for and exploitation of the mineral resources of that area, provided that such activities are conducted**

      (i) **without claiming or exercising sovereignty or sovereign or exclusive rights in any part of that area, and**

      (ii) **with reasonable regard for the right of other states or persons to engage in similar activities and to exercise the freedoms of the high seas;**

    (c) **minerals extracted in accordance with paragraph (b) become the property of the mining state or person.**

(2) Under the law of the United States, a citizen of the United States may engage in activities of exploration for, or exploitation of, the mineral resources of the area of the sea-bed and subsoil beyond the limits of national jurisdiction only in accordance with a license issued by the Federal Government pursuant to law or international agreement.

Source Note:

Paragraph (a) of Subsection (1) corresponds to Section 2 (Principles Governing the Area) of Part XI of the LOS Convention, especially Articles 136, 137, 140, and 141. Subsection (2) is based on the United States Deep Seabed Hard Mineral Resources Act of June 28, 1980, 30 U.S.C. § 1401 *et seq.*

Comment:

    a. Sea-bed beyond national jurisdiction. This section applies only to the area "beyond the limits of national jurisdiction," namely the area beyond the territorial sea, exclusive economic zone, and continental shelf of any state. See § 511. The law governing the deep sea-bed differs from the law applicable to the sea-bed of the territorial sea, where the coastal state has sovereignty (§ 512), and from that applicable to the exclusive economic zone and the continental shelf, where the coastal state has some sovereign rights and some exclusive jurisdiction for certain economic purposes (§§ 514 and 515). Unlike the law of the continental shelf, which applies to both mineral and living resources on the sea-bed or in the subsoil (§ 515, Comment *c*), this section applies only to mineral resources. The living resources of the sea-bed and subsoil beyond the limits of national jurisdiction are subject to the same rules as fishing in the waters of the high seas. See § 521(2)(c) and Comment *e* thereto.

    b. Sea-bed mining under customary international law. Subsection (1) restates principles of customary international law.

The principle in Subsection (1)(a) is not in controversy and has been expressly accepted for the United States in the Deep Seabed Hard Mineral Resources Act of 1980, which states that the United States does not "assert sovereignty or sovereign or exclusive rights or jurisdiction over, or the ownership of, any areas or resources in the deep seabed." 30 U.S.C. § 1402(a)(2). Subsection (1) distinguishes between appropriation of the deep sea-bed area or assertion of sovereign or exclusive rights there, which is prohibited by paragraph (a), and exploration or exploitation of mineral resources on a nonexclusive basis, which is permitted by paragraph (b).

Subsection (1) also incorporates the traditional rule that in exercising a freedom of the high seas a state and any person acting under its authority must do so with reasonable regard for the rights of other states or persons engaging in similar activities. See 1958 Convention on the High Seas, Article 2; LOS Convention, Article 87(2). Consequently, miners are obligated not to interfere with activities of other users of the sea, and other users are obligated not to interfere with mining as long as a particular area is actually used for mining operations.

In paragraph (b) of Subsection (1), this Restatement adopts the view of the United States, Reporters' Note 2, that in principle deep sea-bed mining is one of the high seas freedoms. § 521(2). Like high seas fishing, it is permissible under international law and other states may not interfere with it. Although there are important differences between mining and fishing operations, under customary international law the resources of the sea-bed, like the fish in the waters above, may be taken by anyone, provided no claim is made to sovereign or exclusive rights over any area of the sea or sea-bed. See Subsection (1)(a). No state may assert or grant an exclusive right to exploit any area of the deep sea-bed, and no sea-bed mining enterprise may prevent another from mining an area not yet being exploited by it, just as a fishing vessel may not stop another vessel from spreading its nets or traps in an unoccupied area. However, as a fishing vessel may not interfere with nets or traps already put in place by an earlier occupant, a would-be miner may not interfere with a mining activity already begun by another state's enterprise. A claim by a state or a person that it has begun a mining activity and can, therefore, exclude others, must be limited in scope, area and duration to the extent strictly necessary.

c. Mining by persons. Under customary international law, any person, natural or juridical, engaged in activities on the high seas is normally subject to the jurisdiction of the flag state of the ship used for such activity or of the state of which such person is a national. See, *e.g.,* LOS Convention, Article 97 (jurisdiction in collisions on the high seas). A private person may engage in the activities indicated in Subsection (1)(b) only when properly licensed by a state. A state issuing such licenses is obligated to assure that the person licensed respects the rules set forth in this section, and the state is responsible for any violation by such person.

d. Reasonable regard for other activities and marine environment. Under Subsection (1)(b), a state or person engaged in mining activities must conduct them with reasonable regard for the rights of other states or persons to engage in similar activities, and must take special precautions to ensure that installations and activities connected with sea-bed mining do not interfere with international navigation or fishing. See LOS Convention, Article 147(2). Mining states or persons are also required to take the measures necessary to ensure effective protection of the marine environment from harmful consequences of mining activities. See § 603, Comment *c*.

e. Sea-bed regime of LOS Convention. The LOS Convention establishes a comprehensive regime for the deep sea-bed and forbids exploration or exploitation except in accordance with that regime. See Reporters' Note 3. When the LOS Convention comes into effect, it will bind the parties to that Convention; if it is accepted by nations of the world generally, without dissent by an important group of states, the sea-bed mining regime of the Convention may become effective also as customary international law for nonparties. See § 102, Comment *f.* The sea-bed regime of the LOS Convention, however, would not apply to a state, such as the United States, that had rejected it and had insisted on its right to mine the deep sea-bed under present rules of customary international law as stated in Subsection (1)(b). See § 102, Comment *d.*

Under customary law, states are free to establish among themselves a system for granting licenses to exploit areas of the deep sea-bed in a limited area for a limited period, and to require their nationals to respect the licenses of other participating states. See Comment *f.* However, they cannot exclude activities by states not parties to such arrangement nor, subject to § 414, by their licensees. See Comment *f* and Reporters' Note 5.

f. Sea-bed mining under United States law. Subsection (2) reflects the Deep Seabed Hard Mineral Resources Act, 30 U.S.C. § 1401 *et seq.*, which established an interim program to regulate and license deep sea-bed mining by any United States "citizen," defined as any United States national, any United States corporation, or any foreign corporation controlled by a United States national or corporation. The Act provides for arrangements with other states for reciprocity and mutual recognition of licenses. A reciprocating agreement with other potential mining states was concluded on August 3, 1984. See Reporters' Note 5.

REPORTERS' NOTES

1. *Deep sea-bed not subject to state sovereignty or appropriation.* The codification of principles of customary international law, which is contained in Section 2 of Part XI of the LOS Convention, makes clear that no state is entitled to "claim or exercise sovereignty or sovereign rights over any part of the Area [*i.e.*, the sea-bed and ocean floor and subsoil thereof beyond the limits of national jurisdiction, as defined in Article 1(1)(a) of the Convention] or its resources"; that no state or natural or juridical person is entitled to appropriate any part thereof; and that "no such claim or exercise of sovereign rights nor such appropriation shall be recognized." Art. 137(1). These provisions are customary law and are reflected in Subsection (1). But the Convention provides also that all "rights in the resources of the Area are vested in mankind as a whole, on whose behalf the [International Sea-Bed] Authority shall act"; and that no state or natural or juridical person "shall claim, acquire or exercise rights with respect to the minerals recovered from the Area except in accordance" with Part XI and the rules, regulations, and procedures of the Authority. Art. 137(2) and (3). These provisions are not customary international law, and would bind only parties to the Convention; if they should eventually become accepted as customary international law, they would not bind the United States, which has rejected these principles and the power of the Authority to issue rules, regulations, and procedures

binding on states not parties to the Convention. Comment *e*.

2. *Sea-bed mining under customary international law.* Even before the development of the doctrine of the continental shelf and of the concept of the exclusive economic zone (§§ 514–15), there was disagreement, then largely theoretical, as to who owns the sea-bed beyond a state's territorial sea, whether any state could acquire sovereignty or title therein, and whether a state or private person could lawfully exploit the resources of that sea-bed or subsoil and appropriate them to its own use. Discovery in the 1960s of vast mineral resources ("manganese nodules," containing also nickel, copper and cobalt) on the floor of the deep ocean beyond the continental shelves, and the development of technology for obtaining access to these resources, led to three different views as to the applicable law. It was generally agreed that these minerals are the common heritage of mankind (Declaration of Principles Governing the Sea-Bed and the Ocean Floor, and the Subsoil Thereof, Beyond the Limits of National Jurisdiction, adopted by G.A.Res. 2749 (XXV) 25 U.N. GAOR Supp. No. 28, at 24, paras. 1–4, 9 (1970)), but there was disagreement on the application of this concept. Some considered that these minerals could be exploited only by or on behalf of mankind, not by any state or person for its own account; under this view, exploitation would be lawful only pursuant to a generally accepted international agreement. Others argued that, unless a state has

agreed otherwise, it may exploit the resources of the sea-bed freely, and the first claimant in any area is entitled to exclude all others from mining there. See, *e.g.*, Ely, "The Law Governing the Development of Undersea Mineral Resources," 1 Offshore Technology Conference Proc. 19–42 (1969). A third view, which has been accepted by this Restatement, is that like the fish of the high seas the minerals of the deep sea-bed are open to anyone to take. Consequently, any state is entitled to extract and keep them. But no state may conduct or authorize mining operations on an exclusive basis or in such a way as effectively to appropriate large areas of the sea-bed in violation of Subsection (1)(a). See Subsection 1(b)(i). It would therefore not be permissible for any mining enterprise to reserve for itself an area of some 25,000 square miles (equal to the area of Belgium and the Netherlands combined) or more, as some enterprises have suggested.

An analogy may be made also to the law of finds as applied to shipwrecks, the finder having the exclusive right to bring up the find, and others being obliged to stay a reasonable distance away. See, *e.g.*, Hener v. United States, 525 F. Supp. 350, 354 (S.D.N.Y. 1981).

Throughout the long negotiations on the law of the sea, the official view of the United States had been that as long as it did not become party to an international agreement establishing a new international regime, it was free to mine the deep sea-bed. Accordingly, the United States rejected firmly the "moratorium resolution" in which the General Assembly declared that, pending the establishment of an international regime for the deep sea-bed area, "States and persons, physical or juridical, are bound to refrain from all activities of exploitation of the resources of the area" (G.A. Res. 2574D, 24 U.N. GAOR Supp. No. 30, at 11 (1969)). In 1980, when the United States adopted the Deep Seabed Hard Mineral Resources Act, providing for such mining pending an agreed international regime (Reporters' Note 5), it made clear that it was "the legal opinion of the United States that exploration for and commercial recovery of hard mineral resources of the deep seabed are freedoms of the high seas subject to a duty of reasonable regard to the interests of other states in their exercise of those and other freedoms recognized by general principles of international law." 30 U.S.C. § 1401(a)(12).

Disputes between states parties to the Convention are to be resolved in accordance with the provisions of the Convention (Arts. 187(a) and 188(1), and Resolution II, para. 5(c)); those between parties to a reciprocal agreement (Reporters' Note 5) are to be resolved in accordance with that agreement. Should conflicting permits be issued by both the United States and the International Sea-Bed Authority, it is not clear how the conflict would be resolved. It has been suggested that the General Assembly might be asked to submit this question to the International Court of Justice for an advisory opinion.

3. *Sea-bed regime of LOS Convention.* Under the LOS Convention, any deep sea-bed mining would have to be conducted in accordance with rules, regulations, and procedures to be drafted by a Preparato-

ry Commission, and to be adopted and from time to time revised by the International Sea-Bed Authority that will start functioning as soon as 60 states ratify the Convention. (As of January 1, 1987, 159 states have signed the Convention and 32 have ratified it.) The Authority would function through: (a) an Assembly, in which all the members might participate and which would act as the "supreme organ" of the Authority with power to establish "general policies"; (b) a Council of 36 members, seats on which are guaranteed for some states, including "the largest consumer" of minerals derived from the area (the United States, as of 1986) and three Eastern European states, with power to establish "specific policies" and to approve "plans of work" for each mining project; and (c) an "Enterprise," with a separate legal personality, which will carry out mining activities in the area, either directly or through joint ventures with national or private companies. During an interim 25-year period and within defined, strict limits, the Authority would be entitled to establish a production ceiling in order to protect the economies and export earnings of developing countries engaged in the production of certain minerals against the adverse economic effects of sea-bed production.

To facilitate the work of the Enterprise, each applicant for a mining contract would have to present to the Authority two mining sites of equal estimated mining value; the Authority would designate one of them as reserved for the Enterprise, which would be allowed to relinquish it to a developing country. The applicant would also have to arrange for the transfer to the Enterprise (or to a developing coun-

try exploiting a reserved area) on fair and reasonable terms and conditions, to be determined in case of disagreement by commercial arbitration, the technology that the contractor would be using in its sea-bed mining activities. A contractor would have a choice between two methods of payment to the Authority: a production charge which after 12 years of production would reach 12 percent of the market value of the processed metals; or a combination of a smaller production charge (up to 4 percent) with a share of proceeds, on a graduated scale from 35 to 70 percent, payable after the contractor has recovered the development costs.

Since the activities in the deep sea-bed area are to be carried out "for the benefit of mankind as a whole," taking into particular consideration the interests and needs of developing states and of peoples who have not yet attained full independence or self-government, the Authority would have the task of ensuring that such states will share equitably in the financial and other economic benefits derived from these activities. As the Enterprise is not likely to have sufficient funds at the beginning to exploit a reserved site, it was agreed (in Annex IV to the Convention, Art. 11 (3)) that states parties to the Convention would make available to it the necessary funds for one site, in accordance with the scale of assessments for the United Nations general budget. Such funds (estimated at more than one and a half billion dollars in 1986) would be provided half in the form of long-term interest-free loans, and half by guarantee of debts incurred by the Enterprise in raising the remainder.

Amendments to the LOS Convention relating exclusively to activities in the deep sea-bed area can be adopted by a Review Conference by a three-fourths majority of the states parties, and will enter into force for all states parties when ratified by three-fourths of those states.

4. *United States objections to Convention regime.* When the Third United Nations Conference on the Law of the Sea approved the Convention, the United States cast a negative vote (Introductory Note to this Part). In explaining that vote, a spokesman for the United States said that the text was unacceptable as it would deter future development of deep sea-bed mineral resources, because of lack of certainty with regard to the granting of mining contracts, the artificial limitations on sea-bed mineral production, and the imposition of burdensome financial requirements; would not give the United States an adequate role in the decision-making process; would allow amendments to the Convention to enter into force for the United States without its approval; would provide for mandatory transfer of private technology related to sea-bed mining; and would allow the transfer of a portion of funds received from the miners by the International Sea-Bed Authority to national liberation movements. Statements by President Reagan and Ambassador Malone on July 9 and August 12, 1982, respectively, 18 Weekly Comp. of Pres. Docs. 887 (1982), U.S. Dep't of State, Current Policy No. 416 (1982). In a later statement the White House characterized the deep sea-bed mining regime of the Convention as "hopelessly flawed," and announced that the United States would not participate in the work of the Preparatory Commission established by the Conference to draft regulations for sea-bed mining. The Law of the Sea Convention, White House Office of Policy Information, Issue Update No. 10 (April 15, 1983), at 8.

5. *United States Deep Seabed Hard Mineral Resources Act.* In 1980, Congress adopted a statute establishing an interim program to regulate the exploration for and commercial recovery of hard mineral resources of the deep sea-bed by United States citizens, pending the entry into force with respect to the United States of a treaty on the subject. 30 U.S.C. § 1401 *et seq.* Some provisions of the Act parallel the LOS Convention; see *e.g.*, §§ 1401(b)(1), 1402(a)(2) and (b), 1411(c), 1413(a)(2)(D)(ii), 1419 and 1421. The Act authorized issuance of exploration licenses after July 1, 1981, but delayed issuance of permits for commercial recovery of minerals until January 1, 1988. 30 U.S.C. § 1412(c)(1)(D). The Act required the Administrator of the Act, the Administrator of the National Oceanic and Atmospheric Administration (NOAA), before issuing a license or permit, to find in writing that the proposed activity will not unreasonably interfere with the exercise of the freedoms of the high seas by other states; will not create a situation that may reasonably be expected to lead to a breach of international peace and security involving an armed conflict; and cannot reasonably be expected to result in a significant adverse effect on the quality of the environment. § 1415(a). Ten-year licenses for exploration and 20-year permits for exploitation would be issued in order of submission of applications,

and a later licensee or permitee may not interfere with any activity conducted by an earlier one. Licenses and permits issued by any reciprocating state (see below) must be similarly honored. § 1411(b)(3) and (c), § 1417. Only ships documented under the laws of the United States may be used for the commercial recovery or for the processing at sea of the minerals, and at least one so-documented vessel shall be used for the transportation of minerals from the mining site. § 1412(c)(2) and (3). The area covered by a permit must be large enough to satisfy the permittee's reasonable production requirements for an initial 20-year term. § 1413(a)(2)(E)(ii). The Administrator shall require the use of the best available technologies for the protection of safety, health, and the marine environment. § 1419(b).

To prevent conflict between licenses and permits issued by the United States and those issued by other states, the 1980 Act developed the concept of "reciprocating states," *i.e.* states that would regulate the issuance of sea-bed mining licenses and permits in a manner compatible with the United States Act and would establish similar procedures for recognizing licenses and permits issued by the United States and other reciprocating states. § 1428. Several other states have enacted deep sea-bed mining legislation; see, for instance, the laws of France, 21 Int'l Leg.Mat. 808 (1982); Federal Republic of Germany, 20 *id.* 393 (1981) (for amendment, see 21 *id.* 832 (1982); Japan, 22 *id.* 102 (1983); Soviet Union, 21 *id.* 551 (1982); and the United Kingdom, 20 *id.* 1217 (1981).

A preliminary agreement was concluded on September 2, 1982, among the United States, the United Kingdom, the Federal Republic of Germany, and France, establishing interim arrangements for resolving overlapping claims with respect to mining areas for polymetallic nodules of the deep sea-bed. See T.I.A.S. No. 10562; 21 Int'l Leg.Mat. 950 (1982). For negotiations on that subject among other states, initiated by Canada, see U.N. Doc. LOS/PCN/15 (1983). The 1982 agreement was superseded by the Provisional Understanding Regarding Deep Seabed Mining, signed on August 3, 1984, by Belgium, France, the Federal Republic of Germany, Italy, Japan, the Netherlands, the United Kingdom, and the United States. 23 Int'l Leg.Mat. 1354 (1984).

In 1984, four licenses for deep sea-bed exploration were granted by the United States, 49 Fed. Reg. 35973–74, 44661, 44938, 47091, 48205 (1984), 50 *id.* 994 (1985). For a notification by the United States to the United Nations, see 7 U.N. LOS Bull. 74–86 (1986). See also U.S. Department of Commerce, Deep Seabed Mining: Report to Congress 9–19 (Dec. 1985). For objections to the issuance of licenses by the United States, United Kingdom, and the Federal Republic of Germany, see U.N. Doc. LOS/PCN/ 64, 71–74, 76, 78 (1985–86).

In 1986, the Preparatory Commission for the International Sea-Bed Authority made arrangements for assigning an undisputed area in the Indian Ocean to India. It also reached an "understanding" resolving conflicts arising from overlapping claims of other "pioneer investors" in a disputed area in the northeast Pacific Ocean. It did so by accepting the applications of

France, Japan, and the Soviet Union for a portion of their claims, and arranging for those states to relinquish other parts of the contested area for the benefit of other potential pioneer investors (four consortia composed of companies incorporated in the United States, the United Kingdom, Belgium, Canada, the Federal Republic of Germany, Italy, Japan, and the Netherlands), provided they submit their applications before the entry into force of the LOS Convention. U.N. Doc. LOS/PCN/ L.41/Rev.1, at 9–13 (1986); U.N. Press Release SEA/777 (1986).

Part VI

THE LAW OF THE ENVIRONMENT

Introductory Note

Section

Introductory Note:

Since the Second World War, the growth of population, the spread of industrialization, and the increase in automobile, air, and maritime traffic have led to a great increase in pollution of land, air, and water. It soon became obvious that unilateral action by states to control pollution was not sufficient, and that international cooperation and regulation to protect the environment were necessary. Strong impetus to the development of international environmental law was given by the Conference on the Human Environment, held in Stockholm in 1972. That Conference adopted the Stockholm Declaration on the Human Environment and an Action Plan. It also made proposals that led the General Assembly of the United Nations to establish a United Nations Environment Program. See § 601, Reporters' Note 1 and § 602, Reporters' Note 1.

This Part addresses primarily transfrontier and marine pollution. Transfrontier pollution occurs when activities in one state cause significant injury in another (usually neighboring) state, by deleterious effect on that state's ecosystem, its air, land, or water, on the health of its inhabitants, or on its living resources. Marine pollution is the introduction into the marine environment of substances that have or are likely to have deleterious effect on the coasts and coastal waters of states or on marine areas beyond the jurisdiction of any state. International environmental law addresses also pollution of the "global commons," *i.e.*, areas over which no state has jurisdiction or control but which are of common interest to all states—outer space, Antarctica, ice floes, and unoccupied islands.

Environmental harm may be caused by activities other than pollution: a dam may cause erosion, or irrigation may increase the salinity of a river. Other environmental problems of international concern include the need to improve habitat and human settlements; to protect archaeologic treasures, cultural monuments, nature sanctuaries, endangered fauna and flora, and migratory birds; to lessen the consequences of deforestation, overfishing, and weather modification. Where activities in one state cause environmental injuries in another state, the principles of this Part generally apply.

Sources of environmental law. The principles discussed in this Part are rooted in customary international law. They originated in rules relating to the responsibility of a state for injuries caused to another state or to its property, or to persons within another state's territory or their property. The International Court of Justice has noted that one of the "general and well-recognized principles" of international law is "every State's obligation not to allow knowingly its territory to be used for acts contrary to the rights of other States." [1] The United Nations Survey of International Law concluded that "[t]here has been general recognition of the rule that a State must not permit the use of its territory for purposes injurious to the interests of other States in a manner contrary to international law." [2]

Judge Lauterpacht has said that "[a] State is bound to prevent such use of its territory as, having regard to the circumstances, is unduly injurious to the inhabitants of the neighboring State." [3] He added that the maxim *sic utere tuo ut alienum non laedas* (use your own property so as not to injure the property of another) is applicable to relations of states not less than those of individuals; it is one of those general principles of law applicable under Article 38(1)(c) of the Statute of the International Court of Justice. [4]

This general principle has been applied, in particular, to international rivers. As early as 1911, the Institute of International Law expressed the opinion that where a river forms the boundary of two states, neither state may, "on its own territory, utilize or allow the utilization of the water in such a way as seriously to interfere with its utilization by the other State or by individuals, corporations, etc., thereof." [5] The United States stated similarly that "no State might claim to use the waters of an international

---

[1] Corfu Channel Case (Merits) (United Kingdom/Albania), [1949] I.C.J. Rep. 4, 22.

[2] U.N. Doc.A/CN.4/1/Rev.1 (U.N. Pub. 1948. V.1(1)), at 34 (1949).

[3] 1 Oppenheim, International Law 291 (8th ed. by H. Lauterpacht, 1955).

[4] *Id.*, at 346–47.

[5] J.B. Scott, Resolutions of the Institute of International Law Dealing with the Law of Nations 169 (1916). Judge Lauterpacht also pointed out that a state is forbidden to make such use of a river that causes danger to a neighboring state or prevents it from making proper use of the flow of the river. *Supra*, n. 3, at 475.

river in such a way as to cause material injury to the interests of other States."[6]

In a decision applying the general principle to transfrontier air pollution, which has been frequently quoted by other courts and tribunals, a United States-Canadian tribunal, in the *Trail Smelter Arbitration*, concluded that, "under the principles of international law, as well as of the law of the United States, no State has the right to use or permit the use of its territory in such a manner as to cause injury by fumes in or to the territory of another or the properties or persons therein, when the case is of serious consequence and the injury is established by clear and convincing evidence."[7]

In recent years many international agreements have dealt with regional transfrontier pollution. Important guidelines on several aspects of such problems have been adopted, by consensus, by the Organization for Economic Co-operation and Development (OECD).[8]

Marine pollution, International law has established a special regime for marine pollution because of the interdependent character of ocean waters (and air) and the cumulative effect of acts of pollution. Any significant pollution of the marine environment, therefore, is of concern to all states. Any state may complain to the offending state or to an appropriate international agency against violation of generally accepted international rules and standards for the protection of the marine environment by another state or its nationals or ships. Remedies are available to a particular state when the pollution of the marine environment has caused injury to that state or to its nationals. See §§ 604 and 902.

---

[6] 17 U.N. GAOR C. 6 (764th mtg.) at 158 (1962). See also United States notes to Canada and Mexico, [1978] Digest of U.S. Practice in Int'l L. 1116–17, 1121–22.

[7] Trail Smelter Case, 1941, 3 R. Int'l Arb. Awards 1905, 1965 (1949); 35 Am.J. Int'l L. 684, 716 (1941). See also § 601, Reporters' Note 1.

[8] See, *e.g.*, OECD, Non-Discrimination in Relation to Transfrontier Pollution: Leading OECD Documents 8, 32, 49 (1978). See also the Canada-United States joint statement on transboundary air quality. [1979] Digest of U.S. Practice in Int'l L. 1612–15; the Canada-United States Memorandum of Intent Concerning Transboundary Air Pollution, 1980, 32 U.S.T. 2521, T.I.A.S. No. 9856 (expressing "common determination to combat transboundary air pollution in keeping with their existing international rights, obligations, commitments and co-operative practices, including those set forth in the 1909 Boundary Waters Treaty, the 1972 Stockholm Declaration on Human Environment," and in other agreements); and the Mexico-United States Agreement to Co-operate in the Solution of Environmental Problems in the Border Area, 1983, 22 Int'l Leg.Mat. 1025 (1983) (undertaking, "to the fullest extent practical, to adopt the appropriate measures to prevent, reduce and eliminate sources of pollution in their respective territory which affect the border area of the other," the border area being defined for this purpose as "the area situated 100 kilometers on either side of the inland and maritime boundaries" between the parties).

With the rapid growth of maritime traffic after the Second World War, pollution from ships and harm to the marine environment from maritime accidents, particularly those involving large oil tankers, reached alarming proportions. Waste dumped into the sea by ever-growing coastal cities, release of toxic substances including radioactive materials, and spills from oil wells on the continental shelf added greatly to marine pollution.

The 1958 Convention on the High Seas requires states to "draw up regulations to prevent pollution of the seas by the discharge of oil from ships or pipelines or resulting from the exploitation and exploration of the seabed and its subsoil" (Article 24). Every state was also obligated to "take measures to prevent pollution of the seas by the dumping of radioactive waste," and to co-operate with the competent international organizations in preventing pollution of the seas and air space above by "any activities with radioactive materials or other harmful agents" (Article 25).[9]

The 1982 Convention on the Law of the Sea (discussed in Part V) includes provisions for the protection of the marine environment against pollution not only by ships or other activities in the sea, but also from land-based sources or from or through the atmosphere. LOS Convention, Part XII, Articles 192–237. Disputes relating to these provisions are made subject to a compulsory dispute settlement procedure. See, in particular, Article 297(1)(c). The Convention also increases the powers of coastal states, particularly port states, to enforce pollution rules and standards against vessels of foreign states. See § 604. Most of the provisions of the Convention concerning the protection of the marine environment reflect customary international law. See Introductory Note to Part V. The dispute settlement provisions, however, are not customary law and will not bind the United States nor will the United States be able to invoke them unless it becomes a party to the Convention.

In addition to the provisions in the Law of the Sea Convention, there are numerous international conventions on the protection of the marine environment, both global and regional (see § 603, Reporters' Notes 2–5, and § 604, Reporters' Note 1), and several bilateral agreements (see § 604, Reporters' Note 1).

United States law. International aspects of environmental problems, especially of marine pollution, have been the subject of United States legislation. See, *e.g.*, the Acts relating, respectively, to National Environmental Policy, Clean Air, Federal Water Pollution Control, Toxic Substances Control, Oil Pollution, Ocean Dumping, Deepwater Ports, Rivers and Harbors, Coastal Zone Manage-

---

[9] 13 U.S.T. 2312, T.I.A.S. No. 5200, 450 U.N.T.S. 82. (As of 1987, this convention was in force for 57 states, including the United States.)

ment, Outer Continental Shelf Lands, Submerged Lands, Fishery Conservation and Management, Deep Seabed Hard Mineral Resources, Resources Conservation and Recovery, Marine Mammals, Endangered Species, and Marine Sanctuaries. See § 601, Reporters' Note 8, and § 603, Reporters' Note 7.

REPORTERS' NOTES

1. *Bibliography.*

K. Hakapää, Marine Pollution in International Law (1981).

B. Johnson, International Environmental Law (1976).

D. M. Johnson, ed., The Environmental Law of the Sea (1981).

J. Schneider, World Public Order and the Environment (1979).

2. *Previous Restatement.* The previous Restatement dealt incidentally with transfrontier pollution in sections relating to liability of a state for injuries caused in the territory of another state (§ 18, Reporters' Note 3), and to marine pollution resulting from the exploration and exploitation of the seabed (§ 23, Reporters' Note 3).

§ 601. State Obligations with Respect to Environment of Other States and the Common Environment

(1) A state is obligated to take such measures as may be necessary, to the extent practicable under the circumstances, to ensure that activities within its jurisdiction or control

    (a) conform to generally accepted international rules and standards for the prevention, reduction, and control of injury to the environment of another state or of areas beyond the limits of national jurisdiction; and

    (b) are conducted so as not to cause significant injury to the environment of another state or of areas beyond the limits of national jurisdiction.

(2) A state is responsible to all other states

    (a) for any violation of its obligations under Subsection (1)(a), and

    (b) for any significant injury, resulting from such violation, to the environment of areas beyond the limits of national jurisdiction.

(3) A state is responsible for any significant injury, resulting from a violation of its obligations under Subsection (1), to the environment of another state or to its property, or to persons or property within that state's territory or under its jurisdiction or control.

Comment:

a. Application of general principles of state responsibility.
This Part applies to environmental questions the general principles
of international law relating to the responsibility of states for
injury to another state or its property or to persons within its
territory or their property, or for injury to interests common to all
states. A state is responsible under Subsections (2) and (3) for
breach of any of its obligations under Subsection (1). It is responsible under Subsection (2) to all states, and any state may request
that it abate a threat of pollution and make arrangements to
prevent future violations. Under Subsection (3), it is responsible to
an injured state for any significant injury and is required to make
reparation for the injury. The conditions of responsibility and the
remedies available may differ with the circumstances and with the
interests affected. See Comment *d* and § 602; see also the general
principles in § 711 and §§ 901–902.

b. "Generally accepted international rules and standards."
This phrase is adopted from the law of the sea; see § 502, Comment *c*. The obligation under Subsection (1)(a) refers to both
general rules of customary international law (see, *e.g.*, the *Trail
Smelter* case, Reporters' Note 1) and those derived from international conventions, and from standards adopted by international
organizations pursuant to such conventions, that deal with a specific subject, such as oil pollution or radioactive wastes. See Reporters' Notes 3–7 and § 603, Reporters' Notes 4 and 5; see also § 102,
Comments *f* and *g*, and § 103, Comment *c*. A state is also obligated
to comply with an environmental rule or standard that has been
accepted by both it and an injured state, even if that rule or
standard has not been generally accepted.

Where an international rule or standard has been violated, any
state can object to the violation; where a state has been injured in
consequence of such violation, it is entitled to damages or other
appropriate relief from the responsible state; where there is a
threat of injury, the threatened state, or any state acting on behalf
of threatened common interests, is entitled to have the dangerous
activity terminated. See § 602.

*c. "Activities within its jurisdiction" and "significant inju-
ry."* An activity is considered to be within a state's jurisdiction
under this section if the state may exercise jurisdiction to prescribe
law with respect to that activity under §§ 402–403. The phrase
"activities within its jurisdiction or control" includes activities in a
state's territory, on the coastal waters that are under its jurisdiction, Part V, as well as activities on ships flying its flag or on
installations on the high seas operating under its authority. See

§ 502(1)(b) and Comment *c* thereto, § 514, Comment *i* and § 521, Comment *c*. International law does not address internal pollution, but a state is responsible under this section if pollution within its jurisdiction causes significant injuries beyond its borders. "Significant injury" is not defined but references to "significant" impact on the environment are common in both international law and United States law. The word "significant" excludes minor incidents causing minimal damage. In special circumstances, the significance of injury to another state is balanced against the importance of the activity to the state causing the injury. See Reporters' Note 3.

d. Conditions of responsibility. A state is responsible under Subsections (2) and (3) for both its own activities and those of individuals or private or public corporations under its jurisdiction. The state may be responsible, for instance, for not enacting necessary legislation, for not enforcing its laws against persons acting in its territory or against its vessels, or for not preventing or terminating an illegal activity, or for not punishing the person responsible for it. In the case of ships flying its flags, a state is responsible for injury due to the state's own defaults under Subsection (1) but is not responsible for injury due to fault of the operators of the ship. In both cases, a state is responsible only if it has not taken "such measures as may be necessary" to comply with applicable international standards and to avoid causing injury outside its territory, as required by Subsection (1). In general, the applicable international rules and standards do not hold a state responsible when it has taken the necessary and practicable measures; some international agreements provide also for responsibility regardless of fault in case of a discharge of highly dangerous (radioactive, toxic, etc.) substances, or an abnormally dangerous activity (*e.g.*, launching of space satellites). See also the principles applicable to weather modification, Comment *f.* In all cases, however, some defenses may be available to the state; *e.g.*, that it had acted pursuant to a binding decision of the Security Council of the United Nations, or that injury was due to the failure of the injured state to exercise reasonable care to avoid the threatened harm. Compare Restatement, Second, Torts §§ 519, 520, and 524. A state is not responsible for injury due to a natural disaster such as an eruption of a volcano, unless such disaster was triggered or aggravated by a human act, such as nuclear explosion in a volcano's vicinity. But a state is responsible if after a natural disaster has occurred it does not take necessary and practicable steps to prevent or reduce injury to other states.

Under Subsections (2)(b) and (3), responsibility of a state for a significant injury entails payment of appropriate damages if the complaining state proves the existence of a causal link between an activity within the jurisdiction of the responsible state and the injury to the complaining state. Determination of responsibility raises special difficulties in cases of long-range pollution where the link between multiple activities in some distant states and the pollution in the injured state might be difficult to prove. Where more than one state contributes to the pollution causing significant injury, the liability will be apportioned among the states, taking into account, where appropriate, the contribution to the injury of the injured state itself.

A state is responsible under this section for environmental harm proximately caused by activity under its own jurisdiction, not for activity by another state. For instance, a state is not responsible under this section merely because it encourages activities in another state, such as plant eradication programs, that inflict environmental injury in that state or in a third state. Similarly, if a group of states imposes economic sanctions on state A depriving it of oil supplies and requiring state A to use coal, which results in an increase in air pollution in state B, the boycotting states are not responsible under principles of international environmental law for injury resulting to state B.

Although there has been no authoritative consideration of the issue, international environmental law has apparently not extended responsibility beyond the state directly responsible for the activities causing injury, under principles analogous to "product liability" which apply in some national legal systems. Thus, under this section, state A is responsible for a radioactive emission from a nuclear reactor operated in its territory that causes injury to state B, but there is no recognized responsibility to B by state C in which the defective reactor was manufactured or from which it was sold to state A. There may, however, be such responsibility pursuant to an international agreement between state A and state C, and in special circumstances under general principles of state responsibility. See, *e.g.*, §§ 207, 711, and 901. Also, there may be liability by the manufacturer or seller of the defective reactor, whether it is a state or a private person, under principles of national law applicable to the transaction. Compare, for example, Restatement, Second, Torts §§ 388–408.

Under this section, a state is obligated to take all necessary precautionary measures where an activity is contemplated that poses a substantial risk of a significant transfrontier environmental injury; if the activity has already taken place, the state is obligated to take all necessary measures to prevent or reduce pollution beyond its borders. Similarly, where a violation of international environmental rules and standards has already occurred, the violating state is obligated to take promptly all necessary preventive or remedial measures, even if no injury has yet taken place.

For the remedies for breach of obligations under this section, see § 602.

e. Obligation to notify and consult. Under Subsection 1(a), a state has an obligation to warn another state promptly of any situation that may cause significant pollution damage in that state. A state has also an obligation to consult with another state if a proposed activity within its jurisdiction or control poses a substantial risk of significant injury to the environment of the other state, but it need not permit such consultations to delay the proposed activity unduly.

f. Weather modification. Weather modification programs are normally used either to prevent injuries to the environment (*e.g.*, by a storm) or to obtain some benefit (*e.g.*, by causing rain during a drought). A state's weather modification programs have sometimes caused injury to another state, *e.g.*, by bringing it excessive rain or by depriving it of rain, or, by changing the direction of a storm, causing injury to that state's ships at sea, to its shore, or to the marine environment. Under international law, a state engaged in weather modification activities is responsible for any significant injuries if causation can be proved, even if the injury was neither intended nor due to negligence, and even if the state took all necessary measures to prevent or reduce injury. Compare the rule as to abnormally dangerous activities, Comment *d.*

REPORTERS' NOTES

1. *General principles of state responsibility for environmental injury.* Principle 21 of the 1972 Stockholm Declaration on the Human Environment provides that "States have, in accordance with the Charter of the United Nations and the principles of international law, the sovereign right to exploit their own resources pursuant to their own environmental policies and the responsibility to ensure that activities within their jurisdiction or control do not cause damage to the environment of other States or of areas beyond the limits of national jurisdiction." Report of the United Nations Conference on the Human Environment, U.N.Doc. A/CONF. 48/14/Rev.1 (U.N.Pub.E.73.II.A.14), at 3, 5 (1973). According to Principle 22 of the Stockholm Declaration, "States shall co-operate to develop further the international law regarding liability and compensation for the victims of pollution and other environmental damage caused by activities within the jurisdiction or control of such States to areas beyond their jurisdiction." *Id.* In 1973, the Council of the European Communities issued a statement of principles and objectives of Community environmental policy including

the following: "In accordance with the Declaration of the United Nations Conference on Human Environment adopted in Stockholm, care should be taken to ensure that activities carried out in one state do not cause any degradation of the environment in another state." Johnson, The Pollution Control Policy of the European Communities 4 (para. vi) (1979).

In Article 19(3)(d) of the Draft Articles on State Responsibility, adopted provisionally in 1976, the International Law Commission listed among international crimes "a serious breach of an international obligation of essential importance for the safeguarding and preservation of the human environment, such as those prohibiting massive pollution of the atmosphere or of the seas." Report of the International Law Commission, [1976] 2(2) Y.B.Int'l L.Comm. 96, 31 U.N. GAOR, Supp. No. 10, at 226 (1976).

The 1963 Treaty banning certain nuclear weapon tests, Reporters' Note 6, prohibits underground explosions that cause "radioactive debris to be present outside the territorial limits of the State under whose jurisdiction or control such explosion is conducted." The Soviet Union complained when nuclear explosions in Nevada vented and resulted in radioactive debris over Canada, Mexico, and the Eastern Pacific. Similarly, the United States complained when explosions in the Soviet Union resulted in radioactive debris in the air over Japan and the Western Pacific. See U.S. Department of State, "Soviet Noncompliance with Arms Control Agreements," Special Report No. 136, at 8 (1985); Voas, "The Arms-Control Compliance Debate," 28 Survival 8, 13 (1986).

The Convention on Long-Range Transboundary Air Pollution was adopted in Geneva on November 13, 1979, by which more than 30 European states, as well as Canada and the United States, agreed to "endeavour to limit and, as far as possible, gradually reduce and prevent air pollution including long-range transboundary air pollution." Such pollution was defined as air pollution that originates "within the area under the national jurisdiction of one State and which has adverse effects in the area under the jurisdiction of another State at such a distance that it is not generally possible to distinguish the contribution of individual emission sources or groups of sources." The main emphasis of the Convention is on research and exchange of information. T.I.A.S. No. 10541; 18 Int'l Leg.Mat. 1442 (1979). As of 1987, this convention was in force for 31 states including the United States. For a 1984 protocol to the Convention, providing more adequate financing for the program, see 24 Int'l Leg.Mat. 484 (1985). As to the implementation by the United States of the Convention, see Benedick, "Transboundary Air Pollution," U.S. Dep't of State, Current Policy No. 723 (1985). Another 1984 protocol to the 1979 Convention, obligating the parties to reduce annual sulphur emission by at least 30 percent by 1993, was not in force as of 1986 and had not been signed by the United States. U.N. Press Release L/T/3808 (1986).

Two cases involving the United States and Canada illustrate the difficulties that have arisen in dealing with transfrontier injuries to the environment and the development of international law rules on this subject: the *Trail Smelter* case and the *Gut Dam* case.

The *Trail Smelter* case resulted from injuries caused in the State of Washington by large amounts of sulphur dioxide emitted since 1925 by a smelter plant at Trail, British Columbia. Claims for the injury could not be brought in the courts of British Columbia under a doctrine of nuisance since under the law of that province such claims were "local" and could be brought only in the jurisdiction where the injured property was located. See § 602, Reporters' Note 3. The State of Washington, on the other hand, had no jurisdiction over the polluter, a Canadian company, as it was not engaged in any business in that State. (At that time long-arm jurisdiction was not yet available; see § 421(2)(j).) In 1928, the matter was referred to the International Joint Commission established under the Boundary Waters Treaty of 1909, 36 Stat. 2448, T.S. No. 548, 12 Bevans 319, but the Commission's report was rejected by the United States. Further negotiations led to a Convention in 1935 submitting to arbitration two questions: reparation for past injuries and arrangements for the future. 49 Stat. 3245, T.S. No. 893, 6 Bevans 60.

In its final decision, of March 11, 1941, the tribunal recognized a general principle of international law that "[a] State owes at all times a duty to protect other States against injurious acts by individuals from within its jurisdiction." Not finding any international precedents, the tribunal relied on decisions of the Supreme Court of the United States in controversies between States of the United States. From cases such as Missouri v. Illinois, 200 U.S. 496, 520, 526, 26 S.Ct. 268, 269, 272, 50 L.Ed. 572, 578, 581 (1906), New York v. New Jersey, 256 U.S. 296, 309, 41 S.Ct. 492, 496, 65 L.Ed. 937, 943 (1921), and Georgia v. Tennessee Copper Co., 206 U.S. 230, 237–39, 27 S.Ct. 618, 619–620, 51 L.Ed. 1038, 1044–45 (1907), the tribunal deduced the following as a principle not only of United States law but also of international law:

> [N]o state has the right to use or permit the use of its territory in such a manner as to cause injury by fumes in or to the territory of another or the properties or persons therein, when the case is of serious consequence and the injury is established by clear and convincing evidence.

The tribunal held that Canada was responsible in international law for the conduct of the Trail Smelter, and that its Government had "the duty . . . to see to it that this conduct should be in conformity with the obligation of the Dominion under international law." In particular, "the Trail Smelter shall be required to refrain from causing any damage through fumes in the State of Washington"; should any injuries occur, an indemnity should be fixed by agreement of the two Governments, injury being defined for this purpose as any injury which "would be recoverable under the decisions of the courts of the United States in suits between private individuals." 3 R.Int'l Arb.Awards 1911, 1963–66. See Rubin, "Pollution by Analogy: The Trail Smelter Arbitration," 50 Ore.L.Rev. 259, 266–74 (1971).

To prevent future injuries as far as possible, the tribunal established a regime of control over the emission of sulphur dioxide fumes from the smelter, at a capital cost of 20 million dollars (at 1941 prices). See Read, "The Trail Smelter Dispute," 1 Can.Y.B.Int'l L. 213, 221 (1963). However, in case the regime should prove insufficient to abate the nuisance, provision was made for amendment or suspension of the regime through binding decisions by an *ad hoc* commission of three scientists. 3 R.Int'l Arb.Awards 1911, 1978. As the system has apparently functioned well, no need for appointing a commission has arisen.

In 1972, Canada invoked the *Trail Smelter* principle against the United States when an oil spill at Cherry Point, Washington, resulted in a contamination of beaches in British Columbia, 11 Can.Y.B. Int'l L. 333–34 (1973). For a recent application of the *Trail Smelter* principle by a Dutch court, see Lammers, Pollution of International Watercourses 198 (1984).

The Gut Dam, which was built by Canada across the international boundary on the St. Lawrence River with the consent of the United States (Act of June 18, 1902; 32 Stat. 392), raised the water levels of Lake Ontario between 1947 and 1952 and caused injury by erosion and inundation to property owners on the United States shore of the lake. Their attempts to sue Canada in United States courts, and to sue the United States Government, proved unsuccessful. See 3 Whiteman, Digest of International Law 768–71, 860–64 (1964). A United States statute authorized the investigation of the Gut Dam claims by the Foreign Claims Settlement Commission (76 Stat. 387 (1962)), but,

before any decisions were rendered, the United States and Canada agreed to establish an international arbitral tribunal to dispose finally of the claims of United States citizens. 17 U.S.T. 1566, T.I.A.S. No. 6114. See Re, " 'The Foreign Claims Settlement Commission and the Lake Ontario Claims Program," 4 Int'l Leg.Mat. 473 (1965), and the supplementary materials, *id.* at 468–72.

After the tribunal rendered several preliminary decisions in favor of the United States, Canada agreed to pay to the United States $350,000 in full settlement of all claims. The tribunal recorded the settlement and terminated the proceedings. See 8 Int'l Leg.Mat. 118, 133–42 (1969); 7 Can.Y.B.Int'l L. 316–18 (1969).

2. *"Environment" and "pollution" defined.* In the United States, the Council on Environmental Quality has interpreted "human environment" comprehensively as including "the natural and physical environment and the relationship of people with that environment." At the same time, as regards the requirement of an environmental impact statement, Reporters' Note 3, the Council stated that "economic or social effects are not intended by themselves to require preparation" of such a statement, but they must be taken into account in an environmental impact statement when "economic or social and natural or physical environmental effects are interrelated." 40 C.F.R. § 1508.14. See also the Council's Second Annual Report 189–207 (1971), quoted with approval in Crosby v. Young, 512 F.Supp. 1363, 1388 (E.D.Mich. 1981) (such factors as inadequate housing, high crime rates, unsani-

tary conditions, or inadequate education may not be environmental when looked at individually, but when their net effect is to lower the quality of life their combined environmental impact must be considered); Hanly v. Mitchell, 460 F.2d 640 (2d Cir.), *certiorari denied,* 409 U.S. 990, 93 S.Ct. 313, 34 L.Ed.2d 256 (1972) (environmental impact statements must take into consideration not only water and air pollution, but also such factors as noise, overburdened mass transportation systems, crime, and congestion). The Council's regulations define adverse "effects" to be avoided or minimized as including not only ecological ones, but also "aesthetic, historic, cultural, economic, social or health, whether direct, indirect or cumulative." 40 C.F.R. § 1500.2(f) and § 1508.8. (Whether this broad definition of environmental effect applies in international transboundary cases has not been decided.) The Executive Order on Environmental Effects Abroad of Major Federal Actions applies to "the natural and physical environment," excluding "social, economic and other environments." U.S. Exec. Order No. 12114, Jan. 4, 1979, Section 3–4, 44 Fed.Reg. 1957 (1979). See also National Environmental Policy Act of 1969, Section 101, 42 U.S.C. § 4331.

Pollution has been defined as "any introduction by man, directly or indirectly, of substance or energy into the environment resulting in deleterious effects of such a nature as to endanger human health, harm living resources and ecosystems, impair amenities or interfere with other legitimate uses of the environment." See Organization for Economic Co-operation and Development (OECD), Recommendation of the Council for the Implementation of a Regime of Equal Right of Access and Non-Discrimination in Relation to Transfrontier Pollution, May 17, 1977, OECD Doc. C (77) 28 (Final), Annex, Introduction, subpara. (a) (1977); OECD, OECD and the Environment 115, 116 (1979); 16 Int'l Leg.Mat. 977–78 (1977). The International Bank for Reconstruction and Development (World Bank) and its related institutions have made environmental concerns a major part of their economic assistance programs. They interpret those concerns broadly, "as those pertaining to the natural and social conditions surrounding all organisms, particularly mankind, and including future generations." According to the Bank, actions affecting the environment include not only pollution of air, water, and land, but also waste of resources and "despoiling of mankind's aesthetic and cultural heritage." World Bank, Environmental Policies and Procedures 1–2 (1984). For a definition of pollution in the context of the law of the sea, see § 603, Reporters' Note 1.

3. *"Significant" impact or injury.* Both international law and United States law stress "significant" impact or injury, as a requirement for remedial action (see § 602), or for other purposes, such as an impact statement. For instance, according to the 1969 National Environmental Policy Act, an environmental impact statement is required for any major Federal actions "significantly affecting the quality of the human environment." Section 102(2)(C); 42 U.S.C. § 4332(C). In determining the significance of an impact, both its "context" (*e.g.,* the affected region, locality and interests) and "intensity" (*e.g.,* severity of impact, controversial character,

111

danger of unique or unknown risks) are to be considered. See the 1978 regulations of the Council on Environmental Quality (CEQ), 40 C.F.R. § 1508.27. For an interpretation of the statutory provisions, see Hanly v. Kleindienst, 471 F.2d 823, 830–31 (2d Cir. 1972), *certiorari denied,* 412 U.S. 908, 93 S.Ct. 2290, 36 L.Ed. 2d 974 (1973). The Clean Air Act requires the Administrator, in cases of international air pollution, to take steps leading to a revision of the pollutant State's plan for implementing the national "ambient air quality standards," but only when the Administrator "has reason to believe that any air pollutant or pollutants emitted in the United States cause or contribute to air pollution which may reasonably be anticipated to endanger public health or welfare in a foreign country" (42 U.S.C. § 7415(a)); in inter-State cases the Act requires that a State prohibit any stationary source within the State from emitting any air pollutant in amounts that will prevent any other State from attaining or maintaining a national "ambient air quality standard" (42 U.S.C. § 4710(a)(2)(E)(i)(I)). It has been held that this standard is less demanding than one requiring prohibition of emissions having "substantial impact on pollution" in the affected State, though other sections of the Act impose that higher standard for other purposes. State of Conn. v. E.P.A., 696 F.2d 147, 156 (2d Cir.1982). The Executive Order on Environmental Effect Abroad of Major Federal Actions, Reporter's Note 2, states that "an action significantly affects the environment if it does significant harm to the environment even though on balance the agency believes the action to be beneficial to the environment." Section 3–4.

The requirement that injury be "significant", "substantial" or "serious" appears also in several international instruments and arbitral awards. See, *e.g.,* 1980 Memorandum of Intent Concerning Transboundary Air Pollution between United States and Canada, Reporters' Note 4; 1983 Mexico-United States Agreement to Cooperate in the Solution of Environmental Problems in the Border Area, Art. 7, 22 Int'l Leg.Mat. 1025 (1983). G.A. Res. 2995 (XXVII) concerning cooperation between states in the field of the environment, §§ 1 and 2, 27 U.N. GAOR, Supp. No. 30, at 42 (1973); Recommendation of the Council of the Organization for Economic Co-operation and Development on Principles Concerning Transfrontier Pollution, 1974, § 6, OECD, Non-Discrimination in Relations to Transfrontier Pollution: Leading OECD Documents 30, 35 (1978); the draft convention on industrial and agricultural use of international rivers and lakes, prepared by the Inter-American Juridical Committee in 1965, Art. 5, Organization of American States, Rios y Lagos Internacionales 132 (4th ed., 1971); the Helsinki Rules on the Uses of the Waters of International Rivers, Art. 10, International Law Association, Report of the 52d Conference (Helsinki, 1966), 484, 496 (1967); draft on the law of the non-navigational uses of international watercourses, presented to the International Law Commission in 1981, Art. 8(2), U.N. Doc. A/CN.4/348, at 105 (1981). The *Trail Smelter* tribunal imposed liability only in cases "of serious consequence." 3 R.Int'l Arb.Awards 1911, 1965. In the *Lake Lanoux*

Case, the arbitral tribunal noted that the principle prohibiting the upstream state to alter the flow of water applies only where the downstream state has been seriously ("gravement") injured. Award of Nov. 16, 1957, 12 R.Int'l Arb. Awards 281, 308.

In a few cases, the significance of an impact on the environment is balanced against the economic importance of the activity causing the impact. For instance, the 1971 Agreement Concerning Frontier Rivers between Finland and Sweden contains the following provision in Chapter 3, Art. 3(2) (825 U.N.T.S. 191, 282):

> Where the construction would result in a substantial deterioration in the living conditions of the population or cause a permanent change in natural conditions such as might entail substantially diminished comfort for people living in the vicinity or a significant nature conservancy loss or where significant public interests would be otherwise prejudiced, the construction shall be permitted only if it is of particular importance for the economy or for the locality or from some other public standpoint.

There is no need to prove a significant impact or injury when pollution is caused by substances which are highly dangerous to human life and health. Several international agreements contain "black lists" of such substances. See, *e.g.*, 1972 Convention on the Prevention of Marine Pollution by Dumping of Wastes and Other Matter, Annex I, 26 U.S.T. 2403, T.I.A.S. No. 8165. (As of 1987, this convention was in force for 64 states, including the United States.) See also 1978 Agreement between the United States and Canada on Great Lakes Water Quality, Annex, 30 U.S.T. 1383, T.I.A.S. No. 9257. The launching of space objects is considered an abnormally dangerous activity and the launching state is "absolutely liable to pay compensation for damage caused by its space object on the surface of the earth or to aircraft in flight." 1972 Convention on International Liability for Damage Caused by Space Objects, Art. 2, 24 U.S.T. 2389, T.I.A.S. No. 7762, 961 U.N.T.S. 187. (As of 1987, this convention was in force for 80 states, including the United States, as well as for the European Space Agency.) See also the resolution of the International Law Institute on the pollution of rivers and lakes, Art. III(2) (requiring the taking of strict measures in the case of abnormally dangerous activities), 58(2) Institut de Droit International, Annuaire 196 (1979). As to liability for nuclear accidents, see the conventions cited in § 602, Reporters' Note 2.

When two or more states contribute to pollution causing significant injury, liability is apportioned among the responsible states. If the injured state itself contributed to the pollution, that state, too, is included as one of the responsible states in apportioning liability. Compare the principles recognized in respect of damage caused by space objects, 1972 Convention on International Liability for Damage Caused by Space Objects, Arts. 4(2), 5, and 6, *supra*. Compare also, as to the responsibility of private vessels, 1969 International Convention on Civil Liability for Oil Pollution Damage, Art. 3(3), 973 U.N.T.S. 3, 9 Int'l Leg. Mat. 45 (1970). *Cf.* Restatement, Second, Torts §§ 433A,

433B, 875, 881; Michie v. Great Lakes Steel Division, 495 F.2d 213 (6th Cir.), *certiorari denied*, 419 U.S. 997, 95 S.Ct. 310, 42 L.Ed.2d 270 (1974).

Under Subsections (1)(a) and (2)(a), any state that might be affected by a violation of an applicable pollution control standard is entitled to request compliance with that standard even if no significant injury has been caused or is imminent. Pollution control standards usually allow a margin of safety, but a state that might be affected by their violation need not await the erosion of that margin before requesting compliance.

4. *Obligation to notify and consult.* Under some international agreements, there is an obligation to consult or to provide another state with relevant information in case of activities which are likely to cause significant injuries in that state.

The 1974 Recommendation of the Council of the OECD on Principles Concerning Transfrontier Pollution, which has been accepted by almost all members of the organization including the United States and Canada, contains the following principles:

. . . Prior to the initiation in a country of works or undertakings which might create a significant risk of transfrontier pollution, this country should provide early information to other countries which are or may be affected. It should provide these countries with relevant information and data, the transmission of which is not prohibited by legislative provisions or prescriptions or applicable international conven-

tions, and should invite their comments.

. . . Countries should enter into consultation on an existing or foreseeable transfrontier pollution problem at the request of a country which is or may be directly affected and should diligently pursue such consultations on this particular problem over a reasonable period of time.

. . . Countries should refrain from carrying out projects or activities which might create a significant risk of transfrontier pollution without first informing the countries which are or may be affected and, except in cases of extreme urgency, providing a reasonable amount of time in the light of circumstances for diligent consultations. Such consultations held in the best spirit of co-operation and good neighbourliness should not enable a country to unreasonably delay or to impede the activities or projects on which consultations are taking place.

OECD, Non-Discrimination in Relation to Transfrontier Pollution: Leading OECD Documents 35 (1978); 14 Int'l Leg.Mat. 242, 246 (1975). See United Nations Convention on Long-Range Transboundary Air Pollution, Geneva, 1979, Arts. 5 and 8(b), T.I.A.S. No. 10541; 18 Int'l Leg.Mat. 1442 (1979). (As of 1987, this convention was in force for 31 states, including the United States.) See also Scandinavian Convention on the Protection of the Environment, 1974, Art. 11, 13 Int'l Leg. Mat. 591, 595 (1974).

While the Stockholm Conference on the Human Environment was unable to achieve consensus on the scope of the obligation to notify and consult, such an obligation is generally accepted, as long as it does not cause inordinate delays in development projects. See G.A. Res. 2995, 27 U.N. GAOR, Supp. No. 30, at 42; National Environmental Policy Act, § 102, Reporters' Note 2. See also Sohn, "The Stockholm Declaration on the Human Environment," 14 Harv.Int'l L.J. 423, 496, 502 (1973).

In the 1980 Memorandum of Intent Concerning Transboundary Air Pollution, 32 U.S.T. 2521, T.I.A.S. No. 9856, Canada and the United States agreed to continue and expand

> their long-standing practice of advance notification and consultation on proposed actions involving a significant risk or potential risk of causing or increasing transboundary air pollution, including:

> (a) proposed major industrial development or other actions which may cause significant increases in transboundary air pollution: and

> (b) proposed changes of policy, regulations or practices which may significantly affect transboundary air pollution.

As noted in Comment e (and in § 603, Comment e), when a state becomes aware that an activity or incident within its territory may cause significant pollution injury in another state, it has a duty to notify that state of the danger. See Report of J. Barboza to the International Law Commission, U.N.Doc. A/CN.4/402, para. 14 (1986); United Nations, Survey of State Practice Relevant to International Liability for Injurious Consequences Arising Out of Acts not Prohibited by International Law 180–82, U.N.Doc. A/CN.4/384 (1984); Magraw, "Transboundary Harm: The International

Law Commission's Study of 'International Liability,' " 80 Am.J.Int'l L. 305, 312, 327–29 (1986).

In 1986, when an accident at the nuclear reactor in Chernobyl, in the Soviet Union, resulted in radioactive clouds spreading to several European countries, these countries protested that the Soviet Union had not immediately notified them of the impending danger. As a result of this incident, the International Atomic Energy Agency prepared two conventions: one, the Convention on Early Notification of a Nuclear Accident, would strengthen the obligation of a state to provide its neighbors with early notification and information about a nuclear accident that may have a transboundary effect; the other convention, the Convention on Assistance in the Case of a Nuclear Accident or Radiological Emergency, would commit states parties to provide assistance in case of nuclear accident. IAEA Doc. GC/SPL.I/2 (1986); 25 Int'l Leg.Mat. 1370, 1377 (1986). By October 1986, the conventions were signed by 57 states, including the United States. The Notification Convention entered into force on October 27, 1986, but the United States had not yet ratified it. 1 IAEA Newsbriefs, No. 1, at 1 (1986); 2 id. at 2. Many states announced their willingness to apply the two conventions even before they became bound by them. In October 1986 the Soviet Union immediately notified the IAEA of an accident involving a nuclear submarine. See 25 Int'l Leg.Mat. 1369, 1394 (1986).

A 1978 agreement between France and the Soviet Union on the prevention of accidental or unauthorized use of nuclear weapons requires each party immediately to notify the other party "of any accidental occurrence or any other unexplained incident that could lead to the explosion of one of their nuclear weapons which may have harmful effect on the other party." 1036 U.N.T.S. 299.

5. *Antarctica.* Concerning the prohibition of disposal of radioactive waste in Antarctica, see Antarctic Treaty, 1959, Art. 5, 12 U.S.T. 794, T.I.A.S. No. 4780, 402 U.N.T.S. 71. (As of 1987, this treaty was in force for 33 states, including the United States.) The parties to the Antarctic Treaty have adopted various measures for the preservation and conservation of the living resources of the Antarctic and the protection of the Antarctic environment. See, *e.g.,* the recommendations in 13 U.S.T. 1349, T.I.A.S. No. 5094 (1961); 14 U.S.T. 99, T.I.A.S. No. 5274 (1962); 17 U.S.T. 991, T.I.A.S. No. 6058 (1964); 20 U.S.T. 614, T.I.A.S. No. 6668 (1966); 24 U.S.T. 1793, T.I.A.S. No. 7692 (1968); 25 U.S.T. 266, T.I.A.S. No. 7796 (1970); 28 U.S.T. 1138, T.I.A.S. No. 8500 (1972). See also Convention for the Conservation of Antarctic Seals, London, 1972, 29 U.S.T. 441, T.I.A.S. No. 8826 (as of 1987, this convention was in force for 11 states, including the United States); and Convention on the Conservation of Antarctic Marine Living Resources, Canberra, 1980, T.I.A.S. No. 10240 (as of 1987, this convention was in force for 20 states, including the United States, and for the European Economic Community).

6. *Outer Space.* In conducting exploration of outer space, including the moon and other celestial bodies, states parties to the 1967 Treaty on Outer Space have agreed "to avoid their harmful contamination" and to prevent the introduction into the earth's environment of extraterrestrial matter which may cause adverse changes in that environment. Art. 9, 18 U.S.T. 2410, T.I.A.S. No. 6347. (As of 1987, this treaty was in force for 96 states, including the United States.) This treaty also makes a state launching an object into outer space liable for injuries caused by such object to another state or to natural or juridical persons, whether on earth, in the air, or in outer space. Art. 7. This provision has been supplemented by the 1972 Convention on the International Liability for Damage Caused by Space Objects. 24 U.S.T. 2389, T.I.A.S. No. 7762. (As of 1987, this convention was in force for 80 states, including the United States, and for the European Space Agency.) Concerning the payment of compensation for injuries caused by Soviet satellite Cosmos 954, which contained a nuclear reactor and which caused injuries in Canada in 1978, see 18 Int'l Leg.Mat. 899 (1979); Cohen, "Cosmos 954 and the International Law of Satellite Accidents," 10 Yale J. Int'l L. 78 (1984).

A 1963 treaty banned nuclear weapon tests in the atmosphere, in outer space and under water, including both territorial waters and high seas. Testing underground was also prohibited if it caused nuclear emissions outside the testing state's territory. 14 U.S.T. 1313, T.I.A.S. No. 5433, 480 U.N.T.S. 43. As of 1987, this treaty was in force for 114 states, including the United States. But some nonparty states continued to conduct nuclear tests in the atmosphere despite protests by other states. *Cf.* the Nuclear Test Cases (Australia and New Zealand v. France), [1974] I.C.J. Rep. 253, 457.

See Goldie, "Concepts of Strict and Absolute Liability in Terms of Relative Exposure to Risk," 16 Netherlands Y.B. Int'l L. 175, 219–31 (1985).

7. *Weather modification.* The principles of international law relating to weather modification are based on general principles of law common to major legal systems of the world (§ 102(1)(c)), which have evolved in recent years out of a number of domestic cases. While these legal principles are widely accepted, scientists have found it difficult to agree whether an incident was caused by a weather modification activity, and it may be difficult to prove causation in a particular case.

The 1977 Convention on the Prohibition of Military or Any Other Hostile Use of Environmental Modification Techniques prohibited the "military or any other hostile use of environmental modification techniques having widespread, long-lasting or severe effects" as a means of inflicting an injury on another state. Such techniques were defined as "any technique for changing—through the deliberate manipulation of natural processes—the dynamics, composition or structure of the Earth, including its biota, lithosphere, hydrosphere and atmosphere, or of outer space." Arts. 1–2, 31 U.S.T. 333, T.I.A.S. No. 9614. As of 1987, this convention was in force for 57 states, including the United States.

See also the Draft Principles prepared by the World Meteorological Organization's and United Nations Environmental Program's (WMO/UNEP) Informal Meeting on Legal Aspects of Weather Modification, April 1978, [1978] Digest of U.S. Practice in Int'l L. 1204–1205 (including, *inter alia*, the principle that "[s]tates shall take all reasonable steps to ensure that weather modification activities under their jurisdiction or control do not cause adverse environmental effects in areas outside their national jurisdiction"); and the 1975 United States-Canada Agreement relating to the Exchange of Information on Weather Modification Activities, 26 U.S.T. 540, T.I.A.S. No. 8056; Weiss, "International Liability for Weather Modification," 1 Climatic Change 267 (1978).

International law has not yet developed rules relating to large-scale climate modification, such as the depletion of the stratospheric ozone layer protecting earth from solar radiation, or the melting of Arctic ice causing inundation of coastal areas all over the world. See, *e.g.*, Staff Report of Senate Comm. on Aeronautical and Space Sciences, 94th Cong., 1st sess., The International Legal and Institutional Aspects of the Stratosphere Ozone Problem 61–78 (Comm. Print 1975); Ozone Layer: Hearings Before the Subcomm. on Toxic Substances and Environmental Oversight of the Senate Comm. on Environment and Public Works, 97th Cong., 1st sess. (1981). See also Agreement Regarding Monitoring of the Stratosphere, Paris, 1976, 27 U.S.T. 1437, T.I.A.S. No. 8255 (establishing strengthened global stratospheric ozone monitoring capability) (in force for France, United Kingdom, and United States); and Convention for the Protection of the Ozone Layer, Vienna, 1985 (cooperation in monitoring, research, and exchange of information, accompanied by recommendation to control chlorofluorocarbon emissions "to the maximum extent practicable"). See

U.S. Dep't of State, "International Cooperation to Protect the Ozone Layer," Current Policy No. 808 (1986); 8 Envt'l L.Rep. 126 (1985).

8. *United States legislation relating to transfrontier pollution.* The two principal United States acts concerned with the prevention and control of pollution are the Clean Water Act and the Clean Air Act, both of which have international implications. The Clean Water Act started as the Federal Water Pollution Control Act of 1948, was amended several times, especially in 1972 and 1977, and is codified at 33 U.S.C. §§ 1251–1376. The Clean Air Act of 1955 was also frequently amended, especially in 1970 and 1977, and was recodified in 1977 at 42 U.S.C. §§ 7401–7642.

The Clean Water Act, designed to control pollution of navigable waters, applies to transfrontier pollution on condition of reciprocity. When the Administrator of the Environmental Protection Agency has reason to believe that pollution is occurring that endangers the health or welfare of persons in a foreign state, and the Secretary of State requests him to abate such pollution, he is obligated to hold a hearing promptly, provided two conditions are fulfilled: that such pollution is occurring in sufficient quantity to warrant such action; and that the foreign country in question has given the United States essentially the same rights with respect to the prevention and control of pollution occurring in that country as are given to that country by this Act. The foreign country that may be adversely affected by the pollution is to be invited to attend and participate in the hearing. 33 U.S.C. § 1320(a). The Adminis-

trator is required to implement promptly the recommendations of the hearing board for abating the pollution. § 1320(c). Civil enforcement actions under the Act can be brought by "citizens," defined as "a person or persons having an interest which is or may be adversely affected." § 1365(a) and (g). It has not been determined whether an alien meeting the definition can sue. In a parallel situation, access to United States courts was allowed to noncitizens under the National Environmental Policy Act (Reporters' Note 3). See People of Enewetak v. Laird, 353 F.Supp. 811, 820, n. 14 (D.Hawaii 1973); Wilderness Society v. Morton, 463 F.2d 1261, 1262 (D.C.Cir.1972). (The Act contains also provisions relating to marine pollution. See § 603, Reporters' Note 7.)

For the complex relationship between the Federal Water Pollution Control Act, as amended, and remedies available under State laws, see the various actions against the cities of Milwaukee and Hammond decided jointly, after two Supreme Court decisions, in People of the State of Illinois v. Milwaukee, 731 F.2d 403, 409–14 (7th Cir.1984), *certiorari denied*, 469 U.S. 1196, 105 S.Ct. 980, 83 L.Ed.2d 981 (1985) (federal act precludes application of one State's common or statutory law to determine liability and afford a remedy for discharge within another State). A similar problem has arisen in Canada. See Interprovincial Co-operatives Ltd. v. The Queen in Right of Manitoba, 53 D.L.R.3d 321 (1975).

The Clean Air Act has similar provisions for allowing foreign state participation in hearings designed to revise a State implementation plan in order to prevent or eliminate danger to public health or welfare in the foreign state; such hearings and foreign participation are also conditioned on reciprocity. 42 U.S.C. § 7415(c). In implementation of this Act, Congress in 1978 expressed its sense that "the President should make every effort to negotiate a cooperative agreement with the Government of Canada aimed at preserving the mutual airshed of the United States and Canada so as to protect and enhance air resources and insure the attainment and maintenance of air quality protective of public health and welfare." Congress also expressed its sense that the President "should take whatever diplomatic actions appear necessary to reduce or eliminate any undesirable impact upon the United States and Canada resulting from air pollution from any source." 92 Stat. 962, at 990; 42 U.S.C. § 7415, note. This resolution led in turn to the 1980 Memorandum of Intent of the Two Governments Concerning Transboundary Air Pollution, which established a United States/Canada Coordinating Committee charged with negotiating a cooperative agreement on transboundary air pollution. 32 U.S.T. 2521, T.I.A.S. No. 9856. The Committee established a Legal, Institutional and Drafting Working Group charged, *inter alia*, with developing "the legal elements of an agreement[,] such as notification and consultation, equal access, nondiscrimination, liability and compensation." Dep't of State, Press Release No. 209A (August 6, 1980), at 14. In 1980, Canada revised its Clean Air Act of 1971, in order to provide the reciprocity required by 42 U.S.C. § 7415(c). Can. Stat., ch. 45, § 21.1(1) (1980–81).

The Acid Precipitation Act of 1980 sets out guidelines for a 10-year study of the impact of acid rain, and seeks to promote international cooperation in acid precipitation research. 42 U.S.C. §§ 8901–05, 8011–12. See also the New York-Quebec Agreement on Acid Precipitation, July 26, 1982. 21 Int'l Leg.Mat. 721 (1982) (to conduct joint studies and exchange information).

Special problems relating to injuries to the environment caused by hazardous wastes have led to the Comprehensive Environmental Response, Compensation, and Liability Act of 1980 (CERCLA, also known as the Superfund Act), 42 U.S.C. § 9601. A foreign claimant may assert a claim under this Act to the same extent as a United States claimant if there is a treaty or executive agreement with the foreign country involved, or if the Secretary of State certifies that such country provides a comparable remedy for United States claimants. *Id.* § 9611(l). See also Senate Committee on Environment and Public Works, Injuries and Damages from Hazardous Wastes—Analysis and Improvement of Legal Remedies: A Report . . . by the "Superfund Section 301(e) Study Group", Doc. No. 97–12, 97th Cong., 2d sess. (1982).

9. *Impact abroad or upon the "global commons."* In the United States, the National Environmental Policy Act (NEPA) of 1969 provides for the preparation by federal agencies of environmental impact statements for all major federal actions significantly affecting the quality of the human environment. See Reporters' Note 3. While that act is principally directed toward assuring

a healthful environment for the people of the United States, it recognizes "the worldwide and long-range character of environmental problems" and supports the initiation of "programs designed to maximize international cooperation in anticipating and preventing a decline in the quality of mankind's world environment." 42 U.S.C. §§ 4321, 4332(2)(F). Whether this policy declaration indicates that the legal obligation to prepare an environmental impact statement extends to impacts outside the United States is not clear. *Compare* Sierra Club v. Coleman, 405 F.Supp. 53, 421 F.Supp. 63 (D.D.C.1975, 1976) (building highway through Panama and Colombia, requirement of inclusion of environmental impact in foreign country assumed), *vacated*, 578 F.2d 389, 391–92 n. 14 (D.C.Cir. 1978) (finding it unnecessary to decide issue in view of impact in the United States), and National Organization for the Reform of Marijuana Laws (NORML) v. United States Department of State, 452 F.Supp. 1226 (D.C.C.1978) (applicability of NEPA to spraying in Mexico to destroy marijuana plants assumed without being decided), *with* Natural Resources Defense Council, Inc. v. Nuclear Regulatory Commission (NRC), 647 F.2d 1345 (D.C.Cir.1981)

(impact statement not required with respect to issuance of nuclear export license for shipment to the Philippines). The Executive Order on Environmental Effects Abroad of Major Federal Actions (Reporters' Note 2) requires federal agencies to take into consideration environmental impact statements and relevant international environmental studies when approving "major Federal actions significantly affecting the environment of the global commons outside the jurisdiction of any nation (*e.g.*, the oceans or Antarctica)." Section 2–3(a). See also Pincus, "The 'NEPA-Abroad' Controversy: Unresolved by an Executive Order," 30 Buffalo L.Rev. 611 (1981). The Nuclear Regulatory Commission, in connection with investigating the environmental impact of exports of nuclear reactors, has decided to evaluate the effect of a foreign nuclear power project on the "global commons," which it defined as including "areas such as the high seas, Antarctica, and the portions of the atmosphere that are not within the territorial jurisdiction of a single nation state." Cited in Natural Resource Defense Council, Inc. v. Nuclear Regulatory Commission, *supra*, at 1348, n. 8, 1377, n. 68 (1981).

§ 602. Remedies for Violation of Environmental Obligations

(1) A state responsible to another state for violation of § 601 is subject to general interstate remedies (§ 902) to prevent, reduce, or terminate the activity threatening or causing the violation, and to pay reparation for injury caused.

(2) Where pollution originating in a state has caused significant injury to persons outside that state, or has created a significant risk of such injury, the state of origin is obligated to accord to the person injured or

exposed to such risk access to the same judicial or administrative remedies as are available in similar circumstances to persons within the state.

Comment:

a. International law remedies. The remedies referred to in Subsection (1) usually begin with a protest against the violation, accompanied by a demand that the offending state terminate the violation, desist from further violations, and make reparation for past violations. If the matter is not resolved by diplomatic negotiations, the aggrieved state may resort to agreed third-party procedures, such as conciliation, mediation, arbitration, or adjudication. Some neighboring states have established international joint commissions to deal with transboundary problems, including pollution, but usually such commissions can only make recommendations. Strictly limited and reasonable measures of "self help" may be permitted in special circumstances. See § 905. Remedies under international law are to the injured state; whether that state is obligated to pay any reparation received over to any injured person in its territory is a matter of its domestic law. See § 902, Comments *i* and *l*.

Remedies under this section are available for injury to a state's environmental interests within its territory as well as to interests beyond its territory, such as injury to its fishing interests on the high seas; it may pursue remedies, not only for injury to state interests but also to those of its political subdivisions or of its inhabitants or nationals. A state may also pursue appropriate remedies for injury to the common interest in the global commons, such as the high seas.

Even where reparations for past injuries are not appropriate or feasible, a state may demand that violations be discontinued.

b. Local remedies. A state responsible for transfrontier pollution can fulfill its obligation to inhabitants of other states who suffered injuries by giving them access to its tribunals for adjudication of their claims. If such local remedies are available, the person who suffered injuries must exhaust these remedies before the state of which he is a national can bring an international claim on his behalf under Subsection (1). See § 703, Comment *d*; § 713, Comments *b* and *f*; § 902, Comment *k*. The two states, however, may agree at any time to settle the claim or include it in a lump-sum settlement. See § 902, Comment *i*.

Subsection (2) applies the principle of non-discrimination against foreign nationals (§ 711, Comment *f*). This principle requires that a state in which pollution originates avoid discrimination in the enforcement of applicable international rules and standards, as well as give to foreign victims the benefit of its own rules and standards for the protection of the environment, even if they are stricter than the international rules or standards. Subsection (2) applies the principle of nondiscrimination also to remedies. A state must provide the same procedures, and apply the same substantive law and the same measures of compensation, to persons outside its territory as are available to persons injured within its territory. Thus, a state applying the "polluter-pays" principle should apply it to all pollution originating within the state, whether it causes injury at home or abroad. If a state applies the principle of strict liability, a victim of transfrontier pollution will be entitled to the benefit of that principle. On the other hand, if the state makes liability conditional on fault or negligence, the foreign victim can be required to meet that condition even if in the place of injury fault or negligence is not a necessary element for liability. Similarly, if a state's law imposes an obligation to reduce pollution to the lowest level that is attainable by the application of the most advanced technology that is economically feasible, this requirement applies equally to pollution at home and abroad.

When environmental injury in one state results from private activity in another state, a remedy may sometimes be available in the courts of the victim state, or even of a third state, and if the victim has received satisfaction by such a remedy the interstate remedy would abate.

c. *Availability of private remedies under state law.* Under the law of many states, pollution damage is considered a local tort; suit for damages lies only in the state where the injury occurred, not in the state where the pollution originated. If personal jurisdiction over the person responsible for the pollution can be obtained in the state where the injury occurred, a suit for compensation or for an injunction would lie, but such suit might not be possible if the alleged polluter has no business or property in that state. Even if a suit there is brought under a long-arm statute and results in a default judgment, the judgment might not be enforceable in the polluter's home state. See § 421(2)(j) and § 481, Reporters' Note 4.

REPORTERS' NOTES

1. *International law remedies.* A state can present a claim for injury to its environment independently of any claim for injury to its nationals or their property. As was noted by the United States Supreme Court in an analogous context, a State of the United States, as quasi-sovereign, "has an interest independent of and behind the titles of its citizens, in all the earth and air within its domain." It was "a fair and

reasonable demand on the part of a sovereign that the air over its territory should not be polluted on a great scale by sulphurous acid gas, that the forests on its mountains, . . . whatever domestic destruction they have suffered, should not be further destroyed or threatened by the acts of persons beyond its control." The Court said that an injunction would issue should the fumes continue. Georgia v. Tennessee Copper Co., 206 U.S. 230, 237–38, 27 S.Ct. 618, 619, 51 L.Ed. 1038, 1045 (1907). In a later decree against one of the defendants, the Supreme Court set limits on the amount of sulphur which Tennessee may permit to escape and appointed an inspector to supervise compliance. 237 U.S. 474, 35 S.Ct. 631, 59 L.Ed. 1054 (1915).

In this case the Supreme Court applied principles of "federal common law" that resemble and sometimes draw on principles of international law. In respect of water pollution, however, the Supreme Court has held that the growth of comprehensive federal control legislation preempted the "federal common law" of nuisance previously applicable. City of Milwaukee v. Illinois and Michigan, 451 U.S. 304, 101 S.Ct. 1784, 68 L.Ed.2d 114 (1981), on remand, 731 F.2d 403 (7th Cir.1984), *certiorari denied*, 469 U.S. 1196, 105 S.Ct. 979, 83 L.Ed.2d 981 (1985); Middlesex County Sewerage Authority v. National Sea Clammers Ass'n, 453 U.S. 1, 101 S.Ct. 2615, 69 L.Ed.2d 435 (1981).

A few international agreements provide expressly for liability for pollution injuries. See, *e.g.*, the 1960 General Treaty for the Settlement of Frontier Questions between the Netherlands and the Federal Republic of Germany, 508 U.N.T.S. 14, 194, which provides that the party causing pollution injuries within the territory of the other party in violation of obligations under the Treaty "shall be liable for damages." A state is liable under the treaty, however, only if the injured state had objected to the polluting activity, and only for injuries sustained after the objection. Art. 63.

The Boundary Waters Treaty between Canada and the United States, 1909, T.S. No. 548, 36 Stat. 2448, 12 Bevans 319, provides in Article 4 that "boundary waters and waters flowing across the boundary shall not be polluted on either side to the injury of health or property on the other." For pollution situations considered by the International Joint Commission established by the Treaty, see *e.g.*, 3 Whiteman Digest of International Law 828, 853, 869 (1964). More than 20 international bipartite and regional commissions have been established to monitor transfrontier pollution and to propose preventive or remedial measures. See OECD, Transfrontier Pollution and the Role of States, 133, 138 (1981).

Upon recommendation of the 1972 Stockholm Conference on the Human Environment (Introductory Note to this Part), the General Assembly of the United Nations adopted several institutional and financial arrangements for international environmental cooperation. In particular, the General Assembly established (a) the United Nations Environment Program (UNEP), under the direction of an intergovernmental Governing Council, which was mandated to "keep under review the world environmental situation in order to ensure that emerging environmental problems of wide international significance receive appropriate and adequate consideration by Governments"; and (b) an Environment Fund, to be financed by voluntary contributions and to be used to finance programs of general interest, such as "regional and global monitoring, assessment and data-collecting systems," and "the improvement of environmental quality management." G.A. Res. 2994–97, 27 U.N. GAOR Supp. No. 30, at 42–45. In fulfillment of this mandate, various global and regional programs were instituted by the UNEP, and several environmental conventions were concluded. For an assessment of the first 10 years of UNEP's work, see the special report of the Governing Council, 37 U.N. GAOR Supp. No. 25, part I (1982); for UNEP's program for the development and periodic review of environmental law, see U.N. Doc. UNEP/GC.10/5/Add.2 and Corrs. 1 and 2 (1982).

2. *Pollution from multiple sources.* Difficulties have arisen in determining liability for pollution originating in several states, sometimes including the state where damage occurred. Some domestic and regional systems oblige each polluting enterprise to pay a tax, or a compensation, which is proportioned to its share of the total pollution, and often specify maximum liability, but there is as yet no general international agreement on such a system. There are, however, agreements with respect to particular sources of pollution, such as nuclear accidents. See, *e.g.,* Convention on Third Party Liability in the Field of Nuclear Energy, July 29, 1960, Arts. 5(b) and 7, 55 Am.J.Int'l L. 1082 (1961) (as of 1986, this conven-

tion was in force for 14 states, but not for the United States); Convention on Civil Liability for Nuclear Damage, 1963, Arts. 2(3), 4 and 5, 2 Int'l Leg.Mat. 727 (1963) (as of 1986, this convention was in force for 10 states, but not for the United States). For the 1982 Protocols which increased the compensation amounts, see OECD, Nuclear Energy Agency (NEA), 14th Report: Activities in 1985, at 31–32 (1986). See also Subcommittee on Legislation of the Joint Committee on Atomic Energy, Selected Materials on Atomic Energy Indemnity Legislation, 89th Cong., 1st sess. 50, 63, 256, 312 (1965); International Atomic Energy Agency, International Conventions on Civil Liability for Nuclear Damage 7, 22, 43 (Legal Series No. 4, rev. ed. 1976).

3. *Availability of private remedies under state law.* The right to sue for compensation and other relief in transfrontier pollution cases is governed by the law of the state where the suit is brought. Special rules govern environmental injuries to immovable property. Some states permit suits for such injuries only where the property is located; in particular, suits based on trespass theory are considered local. Some states allow suits relating to transboundary pollution in either the place where the pollution originated or the place where the injury occurred. Other states achieve the same result by narrowing the definition of trespass, or by changing the rule and considering suits for compensation (or even requests for an injunction) in environmental cases transitory, *i.e.,* they can be brought outside the jurisdiction in which the property is located.

In British South Africa Company v. Companhia de Moçcambique, the House of Lords decided that only the courts of a jurisdiction where immovable property is situated can adjudicate its title; it held that an English court has no jurisdiction with respect to a claim for compensation relating to a trespass to land situated abroad. [1893] A.C. 602 (H.L.). Various Commonwealth courts have extended this rule to bar suits in the state where pollution originated for injury to property in another state. See, *e.g.,* Albert v. Fraser Companies Ltd., [1937] 1 D.L.R. 39, 45, 11 Mar.Prov. 209, 216 (N.B.C.A.); and see 15 Can. B.Rev. 112–15 (1937). When drilling for oil started in the Beaufort Sea on the Canadian side of the United States-Canadian boundary, the United States expressed concern about the possibility of a spill and inquired as to the availability to United States claimants of remedies provided for in the Canadian Arctic Waters Pollution Act. In view of legal doubts on the subject because of the "local action rule," special arrangements were made requiring the Canadian corporation involved in this oil exploration to post a $20,000,000 bond to secure compensation to potential United States pollution victims, and committing the Canadian Government to accept subsidiary liability in the event this bonding arrangement should prove inadequate. See 16 Can.Y.B. Int'l L. 392–94 (1978) (statements in the Canadian House of Commons); Handl, "State Liability for Accidental Transnational Environmental Damage by Private Persons," 74 Am.J.Int'l L. 525, 547–48 (1980); Bankes, "Canada and the Natural Resources of the Polar Regions," Queen's L.J., International Law: Critical Choices for Canada: 1985–2000, at 292, 306–307 (1986).

The common law rule applies also in the United States in States that still follow the "local action rule" established in Livingston v. Jefferson, 15 F. Cas. 660 (No. 8411) (C.C.D.Va.1811). See, *e.g.,* Ellenwood v. Marietta Chair Co., 158 U.S. 105, 107, 15 S.Ct. 771, 39 L.Ed. 913 (1895). See also Taylor v. Sommers Bros. Match Co., 35 Idaho 30, 204 P. 472 (1922); People of the State of Illinois v. Milwaukee, 731 F.2d 403, 411 n. 3 (7th Cir.1984), *certiorari denied,* 469 U.S. 1196, 105 S.Ct. 980, 83 L.Ed.2d 981 (1985) (actions for damages to real property are local and therefore maintainable only in the State wherein the damaged land is).

In the United States, two exceptions to this principle have developed. In some States, an action *in personam,* for example an action for damages, is transitory even if real property in another State is involved. Huntington v. Attrill, 146 U.S. 657, 669, 13 S.Ct. 224, 228, 36 L.Ed. 1123, 1128 (1892). See also Stone v. United States, 167 U.S. 178, 17 S.Ct. 778, 42 L.Ed. 127 (1897); French v. Clinchfield Coal Co., 407 F.Supp. 13 (D.Del. 1976); Mueller v. Brunn, 105 Wis.2d 171, 313 N.W.2d 790 (1982). See also Michie v. Great Lakes Steel Division, National Steel Corp., 495 F.2d 213 (6th Cir.1974), *certiorari denied,* 419 U.S. 997, 95 S.Ct. 310, 42 L.Ed.2d 270 (1974) (Canadian residents sued three United States corporations for damages; no issue of jurisdiction raised); Ramirez de Arellano v. Weinberger, 745 F.2d 1500, 1529, 1563 (D.C.Cir. 1984) (en banc) (according to a majority of six, where "the court adjudicating the controversy has personal jurisdiction over the defendants, the extraterritorial nature of the property involved in the litigation is no bar to equitable relief," but three judges dissented on the ground, *inter alia*, that "even those few courts which have abandoned the local action rule vis-à-vis other states still recognize its validity where land *in a foreign country* is concerned" (emphasis in the original)). This judgment was vacated by the Supreme Court and the case was remanded because of new developments. 471 U.S. 1113, 105 S.Ct. 2353, 86 L.Ed.2d 255 (1985), on remand, 788 F.2d 762 (D.C.Cir.1986).

If the injury in one State was caused by an act in another State, the wrongful act is considered to have been committed in both States and either of them has jurisdiction. Smith v. Southern Railway Co., 136 Ky. 162, 165, 123 S.W. 678, 678 (1909). See, generally, the annotations in 42 A.L.R. 196 (1926) and 30 A.L.R.2d 1219 (1953); Note, "Local Actions in the Federal Courts," 70 Harv.L.Rev. 708 (1957). See also McCaffrey, "Transboundary Pollution Injuries: Jurisdictional Considerations in Private Litigation between Canada and the United States," 3 Cal.W.Int'l L.J. 191 (1973).

In a few States, even actions for trespass to land situated in another State are considered transitory. Little v. Chicago, St.P.M. & O. Ry. Co., 65 Minn. 48, 67 N.W. 846 (1896); Ingram v. Great Lakes Pipe Line Co., 153 S.W.2d 547 (Mo.App. 1941); N.Y. Real Property Law, § 536, McKinney's Real Property Actions and Proceedings Law, § 121. However, a State might distinguish between actions relating to land in another State and those re-

lating to land in a foreign country. One court expressed the view that in international controversies the local-action rule should continue to apply, "especially if the other jurisdiction would provide no redress if the situation were reversed." Reasor-Hill Corp. v. Harrison, 220 Ark. 521, 525, 249 S.W.2d 994 (1952). Relying on this case, the Restatement, Second, of Conflict of Laws § 87 provides more broadly that "[a] State may entertain an action that seeks to recover compensation for a trespass upon or harm done to land in another State." This principle would seem to apply to both inter-State and international cases, although in the latter cases reciprocity—which is implied in domestic cases—might be required.

The Boundary Waters Treaty between the United States and Canada, Reporters' Note 1, provides in Article 2 that "any interference with or diversion from their natural channel of [waters flowing across the boundary or into boundary waters] on either side of the boundary, resulting in any injury on the other side of the boundary, shall give rise to the same rights and entitle the injured parties to the same legal remedies as if such injury took place in the country where such diversion or interference occurs." 36 Stat. 2448, T.S. No. 548, 12 Bevans 319. Article 4(2) relating to pollution contains no similar provision. As of 1986, the United States had no other such agreement on remedies for pollution.

4. *Equal access to remedies.* In 1977, the Council of the Organization for Economic Co-operation and Development (OECD) adopted unanimously a recommendation for the implementation of a regime of equal

right of access and nondiscrimination in relation to transfrontier pollution. See § 601, Reporters' Note 2. The Council recommended, in particular (in para. 4), that:

(a) Countries of origin should ensure that any person who has suffered transfrontier pollution damage or is exposed to a significant risk of transfrontier pollution, shall at least receive equivalent treatment to that afforded in the Country of origin in cases of domestic pollution and in comparable circumstances, to persons of equivalent condition or status.

(b) From a procedural standpoint, this treatment includes the right to take part in, or have resort to, all administrative and judicial procedures existing within the Country of origin, in order to prevent domestic pollution, to have it abated and/or to obtain compensation for the damage caused.

This recommendation has been generally accepted. It led, *inter alia*, to a proposal by the American and Canadian Bar Associations for a bilateral convention on the subject. See American Bar Association and Canadian Bar Association, Settlement of International Disputes Between Canada and the United States, pp. xiii, 40–56 (1979). This proposal in turn led to the preparation by a Joint Working Group of the Uniform Law Conference of Canada and of the United States National Conference of Commissioners on Uniform State Laws of a Draft Transfrontier Pollution Reciprocal Access Act, which was approved by the two organizations in August 1982. (As of 1987, the Act was adopted by Colorado (Colo.Rev.Stat. § 13–1.5.101) (1984), Montana (Mont.Code Ann. § 75–16–101) (1987), New Jersey (N.J.Stat.Ann. 2A:58A–1) (West 1984), Wisconsin (Wis.Stat.Ann. § 144.995) (West Supp.1987), Manitoba (Man.Stat. 1985, ch. 11), and Ontario (Ont. Stat. 35 Eliz. II, c. 10) (1986).)

Several European agreements recognize the right of equal access in transfrontier pollution cases. See, *e.g.*, the 1974 Scandinavian Convention on the Environment, Art. 3 (§ 601, Reporters' Note 4). In 1976, the European Court of Justice held that within the European Community the victim of transfrontier pollution may sue either before a tribunal of the victim's country or before the tribunal of the polluter's country, and that a decision by either tribunal can be executed in any Community country. Bier v. Mines de Potasse d'Alsace, 1976 Eur.Comm.Ct.J.Rep. 1735. For other recent European decisions dealing with jurisdiction in transfrontier pollution, see OECD, Transfrontier Pollution, 1975–1978, at 26 (1979).

Whether, in the United States, the right of equal access includes a right for nonresident foreign persons, claiming environmental injury resulting from activities by persons in the United States, to bring a class action, in circumstances where such an action would lie for domestic plaintiffs, has not been authoritatively determined. Compare Bersch v. Drexel Firestone, Inc., 519 F.2d 974 (2d Cir.1975), *certiorari denied*, 423 U.S. 1018, 96 S.Ct. 453, 46 L.Ed.2d 389 (1975) (excluding foreign purchasers of defendant's securities from class action for fraud), discussed in § 416, Reporters' Note 2.

§ **603.** State Responsibility for Marine Pollution

    (1) A state is obligated

    (a) to adopt laws and regulations to prevent, reduce, and control any significant pollution of the marine environment that are no less effective than generally accepted international rules and standards; and

    (b) to ensure compliance with the laws and regulations adopted pursuant to clause (a) by ships flying its flag, and, in case of a violation, to impose adequate penalties on the owner or captain of the ship.

    (2) A state is obligated to take, individually and jointly with other states, such measures as may be necessary, to the extent practicable under the circumstances, to prevent, reduce, and control pollution causing or threatening to cause significant injury to the marine environment.

Source Note:

This section is based on Articles 194, 207–12, 217, and 220 of the 1982 Convention on the Law of the Sea.

Comment:

    a. State responsibility for marine pollution. This section applies the principles of § 601 to marine pollution. In fulfilling their obligations under this section, states must use "the best practicable means at their disposal and in accordance with their capabilities," and must "endeavour to harmonize their policies in this connection." LOS Convention, Article 194(1). In taking measures to prevent, reduce, or control pollution, states are obligated to implement any pertinent international rules and standards, and to refrain from unjustifiable interference with activities carried out by other states in exercise of their rights and in pursuance of their duties in conformity with international law. Articles 194(4) and 213–22.

    The measures to be taken must "minimize to the fullest possible extent" the release of toxic, harmful, or noxious substances from land-based sources (such as rivers, estuaries, pipelines, and sewers), from or through the atmosphere, or by dumping of waste. Articles 194(3), 207, 210, and 212. In order to limit pollution from ships, all states must take measures for preventing accidents and dealing with emergencies, ensuring the safety of operations at sea, and preventing harmful discharges, whether intentional or unintentional. Navigational routing systems should also be designed to minimize the danger of accidents. Articles 194(3)(b) and 211(1). For the obligations of flag states, see Comment *b*; for the obligations of states engaged in sea-bed mining, see Comment *c*.

Under the principles of § 601(2) and (3), a state is responsible for injuries caused by pollution resulting from a violation of its obligations under this section to a coast or coastal waters of another state or to the marine areas beyond the limits of national jurisdiction, *i.e.*, areas of the sea not included in internal waters, the territorial sea, or the exclusive economic zone of a state, or in the archipelagic waters of an archipelagic state. See Article 86. State responsibility extends to injuries such as those caused by pollution, *e.g.*, by: toxic or noxious substances flowing down-river into the sea and moving into the coastal waters of a neighboring state; sewage drifting from the coastal waters of one state to the coast of another state; toxic or noxious substances dumped, or garbage or fuel discharged, by ships flying the flag of one state and landing on the coast of another state; or oil spills, mineral tailings, or other discharges from installations for exploration and exploitation of oil or polymetallic nodules that contaminate the high seas or are moved by currents to the waters or coast of another state.

b. Obligations of flag state. The flag state has the primary obligation to ensure that its ships respect generally accepted international anti-pollution rules and standards established through the competent international organization or general diplomatic conference, and that they comply with the state's laws and regulations implementing such rules and standards. A flag state is obligated to prohibit its ships from sailing unless they have complied with such international rules and standards, and have also met standards set by the state's own laws, especially those relating to design, construction, equipment, and manning of ships; to require its ships to carry on board certificates of compliance with the international rules; and to inspect its ships periodically to verify that their condition conforms to the certificates they carry. Other states must accept the certificates issued by the flag state as evidence of the condition of the ship, unless there are clear grounds for believing that the condition of the ship does not correspond substantially to the certificates. Article 217(1)–(3).

The flag state is obligated to provide for penalties for pollution by its vessels adequate in severity to discourage violations. Article 217(8). For further enforcement obligations of the flag state, see § 604, Comment *c*.

c. *Obligations of sea-bed mining states.* States are obligated to adopt laws, regulations, and other measures for preventing, reducing, and controlling pollution of the marine environment arising from or in connection with their exploration and exploitation of the sea-bed and subsoil, or from artificial islands, installations, and structures under their jurisdiction that are operating in the marine environment. Such laws, regulations, and measures must be no less effective than international rules, standards, and recommended practices and procedures. Articles 194(3)(c) and (d) and 208.

d. *Protection of fragile ecosystems.* States are obligated to take measures necessary to protect and preserve rare or fragile ecosystems, and the habitat of depleted, threatened, or endangered species and other forms of marine life. Where the area to be protected forms part of a state's exclusive economic zone, the competent international organization may authorize that state to implement special international rules and standards applicable to such zones. Articles 194(5) and 211(6).

A coastal state also has the right to adopt and enforce non-discriminatory laws and regulations for the prevention, reduction, and control of marine pollution from vessels in ice-covered areas within the limits of its exclusive economic zone, where particularly severe climatic conditions and the presence of ice for most of the year create obstructions or exceptional hazards to navigation, and where pollution of the marine environment could cause major harm to, or irreversible disturbance of, the ecological balance. The coastal state is obligated to base such laws and regulations on the best available scientific evidence and to have due regard to navigation. Article 234.

e. *Obligation to notify.* When a state becomes aware that the marine environment has been injured or is in imminent danger of being injured, it is obligated immediately to notify other states likely to be affected by such injuries as well as the competent global or regional international organization. Article 198.

f. *Joint action in emergencies.* States in an area affected by a maritime pollution disaster are obligated to cooperate in eliminating the effects of pollution and in preventing or minimizing injury. To be able to deal better with such emergencies, neighboring states are obligated to develop and be ready to put into operation contingency plans for responding to pollution incidents affecting the marine environment in their vicinity. Article 199.

g. *Pollution by aircraft.* States are responsible under this section for pollution of the marine environment by aircraft of their registry, *e.g.*, by noxious emissions. States are obligated to adopt laws and regulations to prevent, reduce, and control such pollution, taking into account internationally agreed rules, standards, and recommended practices and procedures adopted by the International Civil Aviation Organization, but must not prejudice thereby the safety of air navigation.   Article 212.

REPORTERS' NOTES

1. *Obligations of polluting state.* Article 194(2) of the Convention on the Law of the Sea provides: "States shall take all measures necessary to ensure that activities under their jurisdiction or control are so conducted as not to cause damage by pollution to other States and their environment, and that pollution arising from incidents or activities under their jurisdiction or control does not spread beyond the areas where they exercise sovereign rights in accordance with this Convention." Such measures should be directed at all sources of pollution of the marine environment. The Convention contains specific provisions for the implementation of internationally agreed rules, standards, and recommended practices and procedures, relating to pollution from land-based sources, sea-bed activities, dumping of waste (from vessels, aircraft, platforms, or other structures at sea), other pollution from vessels, and from or through atmosphere. Arts. 1(1)(5) and 207–12.

The term "pollution of the marine environment" means the introduction by man, directly or indirectly, of substances or energy into the marine environment that results or is likely to result in such deleterious effects as harm to living resources and marine life, hazards to human health, or hindrance to marine activities, including fishing and other legitimate uses of the sea, impair-ment of quality for use of sea water and reduction of amenities such as scenic beauty, or other tourist attractions. See Art. 1(1)(4). A similar definition is included in the 1986 Convention for the Protection and Development of the Natural Resources and Environment of the South Pacific Region, Art. 2(f). 26 Int'l. Leg.Mat. 41, 43 (1987).

2. *Safety at sea and environmental law.* Modern international law of the sea has long been concerned with the prevention of collisions at sea. While in earlier days the emphasis was on avoiding loss of life, increasingly there has been concern also to prevent collisions involving large tankers, which might result in significant injuries to the marine environment. The inadequacy of international rules relating to safety of life at sea led to revisions of the international conventions on that subject in 1960 and 1974. International Convention for the Safety of Life at Sea (SOLAS), London, 1960, 16 U.S.T. 185, T.I.A.S. No. 5780, 536 U.N.T.S. 27. (As of 1987, this convention was in force for 101 states, including the United States.) See also the London Convention, 1974, 32 U.S.T. 47, T.I.A.S. No. 9700, which replaced the 1960 Convention as between the parties to the new one. (As of 1987, 96 states, including the United States, were parties to the 1974 Convention.) A 1978 Protocol to the SOLAS Convention was in force, as of 1987, for

61 states, including the United States. 32 U.S.T. 5577, T.I.A.S. No. 10009. For the 1981 and 1983 amendments to the SOLAS Conventions, see [1986] IMO News, No. 2, at 1–4; they were adopted by the "tacit acceptance" procedure, not requiring ratification, and entered into force in 1984 and 1986 respectively. See also the Merchant Shipping (Minimum Standards) Convention, adopted by the International Labor Conference in 1976 as ILO Convention 147. (As of 1986, this convention was in force for 17 states, but not for the United States.) I.L.O. International Labour Conventions and Recommendations, 1919–81 at 923 (1982), 15 Int'l Leg.Mat. 1288 (1976). Various international regulations for preventing collisions at sea were revised and codified by the London Convention of 1972, 28 U.S.T. 3459, T.I.A.S. No. 8587. (As of 1987, this convention was in force for 97 states, including the United States.) A new International Convention on Load Lines was adopted in London on April 5, 1966, 18 U.S.T. 1857, T.I.A.S. No. 6331, 640 U.N.T.S. 133. (As of 1987, this convention was in force for 108 states, including the United States.)

To provide more effective implementation of these conventions and other conventions for the protection of marine environment, 14 European countries approved, on January 26, 1982, a Memorandum of Understanding on Port State Control to ensure that foreign merchant ships visiting their ports comply with the standards laid down in these instruments. 21 Int'l Leg.Mat. 1 (1982). For the implementation of this memorandum, see [1985] IMO News, No. 1, at 16. See also § 512,

Reporters' Note 7; and § 604, Reporters' Note 2.

3. *Maritime casualties.* A state has the right to take and enforce measures beyond its territorial sea, proportionate to the actual or threatened injury, and to protect its coastline or related interests, including fishing, from pollution or threat of pollution following upon a maritime casualty or acts relating to such a casualty, which may reasonably be expected to result in major harmful consequences. The term "maritime casualty" includes collision of vessels, stranding or other incidents of navigation, or other occurrence on board a vessel or external to it resulting in material injury or imminent threat of such injury to a vessel or its cargo, LOS Convention, Art. 221.

As a result of the Torrey Canyon disaster, in which the United Kingdom destroyed the tanker without the permission of the flag state, a Convention Relating to Intervention on the High Seas in Cases of Oil Pollution Casualties was adopted at Brussels on November 29, 1969. It allows states to take "such measures on the high seas as may be necessary to prevent, mitigate or eliminate grave and imminent danger to their coastline or related interests from pollution or threat of pollution of the sea by oil, following upon a maritime casualty . . . , which may reasonably be expected to result in major harmful consequences." Art. 1, 26 U.S.T. 765, T.I.A.S. No. 8068. (As of 1987, this convention was in force for 50 states, including the United States.) By a 1973 Protocol, the Convention was broadened to include certain substances other than oil, the list of which was to be prepared and revised in accordance with a special procedure by the Marine Environment Committee of IMCO, T.I.A.S. No. 10561; 13 Int'l Leg.Mat. 605 (1974). (As of 1987, this protocol was in force for 21 states, including the United States.)

4. *International agreements on oil pollution.* While states became concerned about oil pollution of their shores and waters as early as the 1920's (see *e.g.*, United States Oil Pollution Act of 1924, as amended, 33 U.S.C. § 131), an international agreement on the subject was not reached until 1954. International Convention for the Prevention of Pollution of the Sea by Oil, London, 1954, Art. 3 and Annex A, 12 U.S.T. 2989, T.I.A.S. No. 4900, 327 U.N.T.S. 3. (As of 1987, this convention was in force for 73 states, including the United States.) The 1954 Convention was amended in 1962 and 1969 in response to several marine disasters involving oil tankers. 17 U.S.T. 1523, T.I.A.S. No. 6109, 600 U.N.T.S. 332; 28 U.S.T. 1205, T.I.A.S. No. 8505. See also Oil Pollution Act of 1961, 33 U.S.C. §§ 1001–16, which implements the Convention: it was replaced, effective October 1983, by 33 U.S.C. §§ 1221–32 and 1901–11, when the 1978 Protocol to the International Convention for the Prevention of Pollution from Ships became effective for the United States. See Reporters' Note 5.

For a review of recent marine oil pollution literature, see the annotated bibliography by R.L. Brown. 13 J.Mar.L. & Com. 373 (1982).

5. *Discharge of waste.* The 1958 Convention on the High Seas deals not only with oil pollution but also with the dumping of radioactive waste and of "other harmful

agents" (Art. 25), 13 U.S.T. 2312, T.I.A.S. No. 5200, 450 U.N.T.S. 82. (As of 1987, this convention was in force for 57 states, including the United States.) The London Convention on the Prevention of Marine Pollution by Dumping of Wastes and Other Matter, 1972, prohibits the dumping at sea, *i.e.*, the deliberate disposal at sea, from ships, aircraft, or platforms, of high level radioactive waste, and makes dumping of other radioactive waste subject to special permits by national authorities. Art. 4(1), Annex 1(6) and Annex 11(D), 26 U.S.T. 2403, T.I.A.S. No. 8165. (As of 1987, this convention was in force for 64 states, including the United States.) See also Finn, "Ocean Disposal of Radioactive Wastes: The Obligation of International Cooperation to Protect the Marine Environment," 21 Va.J.Int'l L. 621 (1981). The 1972 Convention deals also with other harmful wastes, dividing them into three categories: some are completely prohibited, some require a prior special permit, and some require only a prior general permit. See Duncan, "The 1972 Convention on the Prevention of Marine Pollution by Dumping of Wastes at Sea," 5 J.Mar.L. & Com. 299 (1973–74). See also Kiss, "Un cas de pollution internationale: L'affaire des boues rouges," 102 Journal du droit international 207 (1975) (dumping of toxic waste off Corsica by Italian company).

Discharges other than dumping are covered by the International Convention for the Prevention of Pollution from Ships (MARPOL), adopted at London on November 2, 1973, which attempts "to achieve the complete elimination of international pollution of the marine environment by oil and other harmful substances and the minimization of accidental discharge of such substances." Such discharges do not include "dumping," which is dealt with in other conventions. In some designated areas, such as the Mediterranean and Baltic Seas, no discharges are permitted; in other areas a tanker may not discharge within 50 miles from the nearest land, and other ships of more than 400 tons may not do so within 12 miles (Annex 1, Regulations 9 and 10). 12 Int'l Leg.Mat. 1319 (1973). (This convention did not enter into force, but a 1978 protocol incorporating and modifying it (17 id. 546 (1978) was, as of 1987, in force for 43 states, including the United States.) The Act to Prevent Pollution from Ships, of October 21, 1980, designed to implement the Protocol, became effective upon coming into force of the Protocol in October 1983. 33 U.S.C. §§ 1901–11; 33 U.S.C.A. § 1901, note (Supp. 1985).

In addition, there are many regional and special conventions applicable to such areas as the Mediterranean and Baltic Seas, the Persian Gulf (Kuwait Convention), the coastal area off West and Central Africa, South Pacific, and the Caribbean-Gulf of Mexico area. For a historical and analytical summary of these and other agreements discussed in this Reporters' Note, see Hakapää, Marine Pollution in International Law 75–116 (1981). See also Timagenis, International Control of Marine Pollution (1980). A register of international conventions relating to the environment is maintained by the United Nations Environment Program (UNEP). See U.N.Doc. UNEP/GC/INFORMATION/5 (1977), and annual sup-

plements thereto; see also U.N.Doc. A/32/156 (1977), and similar annual reports of the Executive Director of UNEP.

6. *Protection of fragile ecosystems.* The principle in Comment *d* reflects the consensus developed at the Third United Nations Law of the Sea Conference. Previously, controversy was caused by the enactment in 1970 of the Canadian Arctic Waters Pollution Prevention Act, the purpose of which was to preserve "the peculiar ecological balance that now exists in the water, ice and land areas" of the Canadian Arctic. That legislation established, and applied to foreign ships, safety control zones extending 100 nautical miles from the nearest Canadian land, north of the sixtieth parallel of latitude and including both liquid and frozen waters within that area. Ships not complying with far-reaching Canadian regulations were banned from these zones. 18–19 Eliz. II, c. 47 (1969–70), R.S.C., 1970, c. 2 (1st Supp.); 9 Int'l Leg.Mat. 543 (1970). For the United States objections to the Canadian measures and the Canadian response, see 9 Int'l Leg. Mat. 605–15 (1970). New issues arose in 1985, when Canada proclaimed all waters within its Arctic archipelago to be internal waters subject to Canada's full sovereignty and drew straight baselines around the perimeter of that archipelago. Statement in the House of Commons by the Secretary of State for External Affairs, Sept. 10, 1985, 128 Can.H.C.Deb. 6463 (1985). See also Territorial Sea Geographical Coordinates (Area 7) Order in Council, Sept. 10, 1985, implementing this statement, 119 Can.Gaz., Part II, at 3996.

7. *United States legislation on marine pollution.* United States law has been concerned with marine pollution since 1888 when a system of permits for dumping was instituted. See 25 Stat. 209 (1888), 33 U.S.C. §§ 441, 443–44. Rules on the subject are contained in the Clean Water Act (see § 601, Reporters' Note 8), especially in the 1977 amendments thereto. 33 U.S.C. §§ 1251–1376. The Act prohibits "discharges of oil or hazardous substances into or upon the navigable waters of the United States, adjoining shorelines, or into or upon the waters of the contiguous zone." The Act also extends jurisdiction to include ships causing pollution in the 200-mile wide United States fisheries conservation zone established in 1976 (see § 511, Reporters' Note 7), even if the ship is of foreign registry, provided that the owner, operator, or person in charge of the ship is a United States citizen. 33 U.S.C. § 1321(a)(17), (b)(5)(B) and (b)(6)(A).

Other United States statutes dealing with marine pollution are: the Outer Continental Shelf Lands Act of 1953, as amended in 1978, 43 U.S.C. §§ 1331–56; the Marine Protection, Research and Sanctuaries Act of 1972, codified at 33 U.S.C. §§ 1401–43 (ocean dumping) and 16 U.S.C. §§ 1431–34 (marine sanctuaries); Deepwater Port Act of 1974, 33 U.S.C. §§ 1501–24, especially § 1518(c) and § 1521; the National Ocean Pollution Research and Development and Monitoring Planning Act of 1978, 33 U.S.C. §§ 1701–09; the Deep Seabed Hard Mineral Resources Act of 1980, §§ 1401–73 (especially § 1419); and the Comprehensive Environmental Response,

Compensation, and Liability Act of 1980, 42 U.S.C. §§ 9601–57 (the Superfund Act dealing with compensation for hazardous waste injuries on land and at sea). There are also several acts designed to implement international conventions. See, *e.g.*, the 1961 Act to Prevent Pollution from Ships (see Reporters' Note 4); the Intervention on the High Seas Act, 33 U.S.C. §§ 1471–87 (for the relevant Convention, see Reporters' Note 3); and the Act to Prevent Pollution from Ships (1980) (see Reporters' Note 5). For an analysis of several of these statutes, see Mendelsohn and Fidell, "Liability for Oil Pollution: United States Law," 10 J.Mar.L. & Com. 475 (1979). See also Brown, "Marine Oil Pollution Literature: An Annotated Bibliography," 13 J.Mar.L. & Com. 373 (1982).

The 1983 United States Ocean Policy statement declared that "the United States will continue to work through the International Maritime Organization and other appropriate international organizations to develop uniform international measures for the protection of the marine environment while imposing no unreasonable burdens on commercial shipping." See Introductory Note to Part V.

8. *Noise pollution by aircraft.* For international aspects of noise pollution by aircraft, see International Civil Aviation Organization (ICAO), International Standards and Recommended Practices (SARP), Aircraft Noise, Annex 16 to the Convention on International Civil Aviation (1971; 3d ed. 1978); Lowenfeld, Aviation Law, ch. 6, § 6 (2d ed. 1981).

§ 604.   Remedies for Marine Pollution

(1) A state responsible to another state for a violation of the principles of § 603 is subject to general interstate remedies (§ 902) to prevent, reduce, or terminate the activity threatening or causing pollution, and to pay reparation for injury caused.

(2) A state is obligated to ensure that a remedy is available, in accordance with its legal system, to provide prompt and adequate compensation or other relief for an injury to private interests caused by pollution of the marine environment resulting from a violation of § 603.

(3) In addition to remedies that may be available to it under Subsection (1):

(a) a coastal state may detain, and institute proceedings against, a foreign ship:

(i) navigating in its territorial sea, for a violation therein of antipollution laws that the coastal state adopted in accordance with applicable international rules and standards; or

(ii) navigating in its territorial sea or its exclusive economic zone, for a violation in that zone of applicable international antipollution rules and standards that resulted in a discharge causing or threatening a major injury to the coastal state;

(b) a port state may institute proceedings against a foreign ship that has voluntarily come into that state's port,

(i) for a violation of the port state's antipollution laws adopted in accordance with applicable international rules and standards, if the violation had occurred in the port state's territorial sea or exclusive economic zone; or

(ii) for a discharge in violation of applicable international antipollution rules and standards that had occurred beyond the limits of national jurisdiction of any state; and

(c) a port state is obligated to investigate, as far as practicable, whether a foreign ship that has voluntarily come into that state's port was responsible for a discharge in violation of applicable international antipollution rules and standards,

(i) at the request of another state, where the discharge was alleged to have occurred in waters subject to that state's jurisdiction, or to have caused or threatened damage to that state; or

(ii) at the request of the flag state, irrespective of where the violation was alleged to have occurred.

Source Note:

This section is based on Articles 211, 217–18, 220, and 228 of the 1982 Convention on the Law of the Sea.

Comment:

a. Ordinary remedies between states. Subsection (1) states that ordinary international remedies are available for violations of obligations under § 603 as for violation of other obligations under international environmental law (§ 602), or of international obligations generally (§ 902). A state is responsible for a violation of international antipollution rules and standards, resulting from an act or omission by state officials or public vessels, or by ships, aircraft, platforms, or other structures at sea, or by natural or juridical persons, that are under the state's jurisdiction.

Interstate remedies may include claims for reparation for injury to the state or its political subdivisions, or injury to its nationals or inhabitants when they are not afforded reparation by domestic remedy in the offending state. See Subsection (2) and Comment *b.* The obligations of states in respect of the common environment are *erga omnes* and any state may pursue remedies for violations that inflict significant injury on that environment (for instance, to obtain termination of the wrongful conduct). See also Comment *c.*

b. Remedies for private injury. Under Subsection (2), when a natural or juridical person for whose acts a state is responsible under § 601 has caused injury to interests of a private person who is not the state's own national or resident, the state must provide to the injured person access to domestic remedies so that prompt and adequate compensation or preventive or injunctive relief may be obtained. See LOS Convention, Article 235. Where the injury results from a violation by a private ship or installation, the owner is presumably liable under domestic law, and the responsibility of the state is invoked only where adequate reparation is not obtained from the person responsible by domestic remedies. If complex patterns of ownership and agency make it difficult to determine who was legally liable under domestic law for the violation causing the injury, the state is responsible for ensuring that the injured person is compensated.

c. Enforcement by flag states. In addition to the remedies set forth in Comments *a* and *b*, if a ship has committed a violation of applicable international rules and standards, the flag state is obligated to investigate immediately and to institute appropriate proceedings, irrespective of the place of the violation or injury. See LOS Convention, Article 217. The state that is the victim of a violation by a ship (or, in case of pollution of the common environment, any state) may complain to the flag state and request that the guilty persons be punished and be enjoined from further pollution (see Articles 217(6) and 235); if dissatisfied with action taken by the flag state, it may invoke against the flag state the remedies available under international law. Subsection (1) and Comment *a*. In addition, if the flag state has repeatedly disregarded its obligations to enforce effectively the applicable international rules and standards in respect of violations committed by its ships, a port state where proceedings against a ship have been instituted under Subsection (3)(b) or (c) may continue such proceedings and impose penalties, regardless of a request of the flag state that the proceedings be transferred to it. See Comment *e*; LOS Convention, Article 228(1).

d. Enforcement by coastal states. The authority of the coastal state to bring proceedings against an offending foreign vessel (Subsection 3(a)) varies according to where the vessel is located and where the violation occurred. The coastal state has jurisdiction to prescribe, adjudicate, and enforce with respect to acts of pollution committed in its ports. The coastal state can also institute proceedings against a ship voluntarily in port, or against its crew, for a violation of its laws that occurred within its territorial sea or exclusive economic zone, provided that its laws were adopted in accordance with applicable international rules and standards. An offshore terminal is assimilated to a port for these purposes. LOS Convention, Article 220(1).

Where there are clear grounds for believing that a foreign ship, while passing through the territorial sea of the coastal state, violated laws and regulations of that state adopted in accordance with applicable international rules and standards, the coastal state may, subject to certain procedural safeguards (see Article 226), undertake physical inspection of the vessel in the territorial sea in order to ascertain the facts relating to the violation. Where evidence so warrants, the coastal state may institute proceedings against the ship, in accordance with its laws, and may detain the ship pending such proceedings. Article 220(2); see also Articles 19(2)(h), 21(1)(f), and 27.

When a violation of applicable international antipollution rules and standards is committed in the exclusive economic zone of the coastal state, and the ship is still in the zone or in the territorial sea of the coastal state, that state can take various steps, depending on the gravity of the violation. Where there are clear grounds for believing that a violation has occurred, the coastal state may require the ship to identify itself and its port of registry, indicate its last and its next port of call, and provide other relevant information needed to establish whether a violation has occurred. When there are clear grounds for believing that the violation resulted in "a substantial discharge causing or threatening significant pollution of the marine environment," and the ship either refuses to give information or the information supplied is manifestly at variance with the facts, the coastal state is entitled to proceed with a physical inspection. Only if there is "clear objective evidence" that the ship committed the violation and that the discharge is causing or threatens to cause "major damage to the coastline or related interests of the coastal state, or to any resources of its territorial sea or exclusive economic zone," is that state entitled to institute proceedings in accordance with its laws, and to detain the ship. Article 220(3)–(6).

To ensure that a ship is not unduly detained, appropriate procedures must be established, either through the competent international organization or by special agreement, for bonding or other appropriate financial security. If the ship makes the necessary arrangements, the coastal state is obligated to allow the vessel to proceed. Only monetary penalties may be imposed, unless the violation was committed in the territorial sea and the act of pollution was willful and serious, in which case the vessel may be confiscated and the person responsible may be tried and punished. Articles 220(7) and 230.

The principle of sovereign immunity protects warships, warplanes, and other government ships and aircraft on noncommercial service against coastal state proceedings, but the flag state is obligated to ensure that such ships or aircraft act in a manner consistent, as far as is reasonable and practicable, with applicable international rules and standards. Article 236.

e. Enforcement by port states. The jurisdiction of the port state with respect to a foreign ship voluntarily in its port or offshore terminal includes authority for the state to investigate and, where the evidence warrants, to institute proceedings with respect to any discharge from that ship that occurred on the high seas. The port state may also institute proceedings if an unlawful discharge outside its coastal waters caused or is likely to cause pollution within those waters.   If the discharge occurred in the coastal waters of another state, the port state is obligated to institute proceedings, as far as practicable, when requested by that state.   In addition, under Subsection (3)(c), the port state is obligated to conduct an investigation, as far as practicable, when so requested by the flag state, or by a state damaged or threatened by the discharge.   LOS Convention, Article 218(1)–(4).

The records of the investigation carried out by a port state must be transmitted to the state that asked for the investigation if it so requests.   The state in whose coastal waters the violation took place, but not the state where the injury occurred, is entitled to have the proceedings transferred to it.   Once the records, the evidence, and the bonds (or other financial security) are transmitted to the requesting state, the proceedings in the port state must be suspended.   Article 218(4).

The flag state is entitled to have penal proceedings against its ship in a foreign state suspended as soon as the flag state has itself instituted proceedings against the ship.   However, the state that has instituted the proceedings need not suspend them (1) if the violation was committed in its territorial sea; (2) if the coastal state suffered major damage; or (3) if the flag state "has repeatedly disregarded its obligations to enforce effectively the applicable international rules and standards in respect of violations committed by its vessels."   A proceeding that is suspended is to be terminated upon completion of proceedings in the flag state.   Article 228(1).   If the coastal state is dissatisfied with the action taken by the flag state after the case has been transferred, it may protest both to the flag state and to the competent international organization; and if the lack of enforcement recurs, the coastal state may refuse to suspend proceedings on a future occasion.

 f. Liability for wrongful enforcement measures.   If a state has taken measures against a foreign ship that were unlawful or exceeded those reasonably required in the light of available information, it is obligated to pay the flag state for any injury or loss attributable to such measures.   It must provide for recourse in its courts for private actions in respect of such injury or loss.   LOS Convention, Article 232.

REPORTERS' NOTES

1. *Civil liability for marine pollution.*   Several international   conventions deal with liability of persons responsible for the violation

of international antipollution rules. The 1962 Brussels Convention on the Liability of Operators of Nuclear Ships provided that the operator of a nuclear ship "shall be absolutely liable for any nuclear damage upon proof that such damage has been caused by a nuclear incident involving the nuclear fuel of, or radioactive products or waste produced in, such ship." The liability of the operator is limited to 1.5 billion gold francs in respect of any one nuclear incident. The state that authorized the operation of a nuclear ship under its flag is required to ensure the payment of compensation for nuclear injury if the operator's insurance or other financial security proves to be inadequate. Claims may be brought, at the option of the claimant, either before the courts of the licensing state or of the state in whose territory nuclear injury occurred. With respect to obligations arising under this Convention, any immunity from legal process pursuant to national or international law is to be waived. For the text of the Convention, see 57 Am.J.Int'l L. 268 (1963). See also Könz, "The 1962 Brussels Convention on the Liability of Operators of Nuclear Ships," id. at 100. As the United States is not a party to this Convention, there was resistance to admission of the nuclear ship Savannah into foreign ports; the United States Congress, therefore, established a contingency liability fund for this purpose, 42 U.S.C. § 2210(1), and the United States concluded a series of indemnification agreements with a number of foreign governments to cover nuclear incidents. See 9 Whiteman, Digest of International Law 303–304 (1968). Similar agreements were concluded by the Federal Republic of Germany with Liberia and other countries. See U.N. Legislative Series, National Legislation and Treaties Relating to the Law of the Sea, U.N. Doc. ST/LEG/SER.B/18, at 408 (1976).

The International Convention on Civil Liability for Oil Pollution Damage, signed at Brussels on November 29, 1969, applies exclusively to injuries caused by oil pollution on the territory, including the territorial sea, of a state party, and provides for compensation for the cost of measures taken to prevent or minimize such injuries. The liability of the owner of the ship that causes oil pollution injuries is limited to 210 million gold francs, except when the incident occurred as a result of actual fault of, or of someone in privity with, the owner (Art. 5(2)). Compensation claims can be brought only in the courts of a state where the injury occurred, but the judgment is enforceable in any state party to the Convention. Articles 9(1) and 10(1), 9 Int'l Leg.Mat. 45 (1970); U.N. Legislative Series, supra, ST/LEG/SER.B/16, at 447 (1974) (As of 1986, this convention was in force for 56 states, not including the United States.) For a comment on this Convention, see Abecassis, The Law and Practice Relating to Oil Pollution from Ships 172–219 (1978). A 1976 Protocol modified the limit of liability to "14 million units of account" based on Special Drawing Rights of the International Monetary Fund (§ 821, Reporters' Note 1(iii)). See 16 Int'l Leg.Mat. 617 (1977). Another protocol, adopted in 1984, introduced several important changes in the Convention (e.g., extending its territorial scope to the exclusive economic zone). 13 Envt'l Pol'y & L. 66

(1984). See 1984 IMO News, No. 3, at 4.

A United States court held that the limitation of liability under the 1969 Convention applies only to the registered owners of the ship that caused the oil pollution and that the victims are entitled to bring actions in tort outside the Convention against other persons alleged to be responsible for the accident, without limitation as to liability. In re Amoco Cadiz, 20 Env.Rep.Cas. 2041, 2076–77 (N.D.Ill. 1984).

A supplementary compensation and indemnification system was established by the 1971 Brussels Convention on the Establishment of an International Fund for Compensation for Oil Pollution Damage. Contributions to the fund are to be made by persons receiving shipments of oil by sea, in proportion to the tonnage received, and any state receiving oil is obligated to ensure that the contributions are paid. See 11 Int'l Leg.Mat. 284 (1972); U.N. Legislative Series, *supra*, ST/LEG/ SER.B/18, at 387 (1976). (As of 1986, this convention was in force for 30 states, but not for the United States.) For a 1976 Protocol revising the financial arrangements provided for by this convention, see 16 Int'l Leg.Mat. 621 (1977). Further changes were introduced by a 1984 Protocol. 13 Envt'l Pol'y & L. 61 (1984).

Several nongovernmental agreements provide for sharing liability for injuries caused by oil pollution, such as the 1969 Tanker Owners Voluntary Agreement Concerning Liability for Oil Pollution ("TOVALOP"), and the 1971 oil companies Contract Regarding an Interim Supplement in Tanker Liability for Oil Pollution ("CRIS-

TAL"). 8 Int'l Leg.Mat. 497 (1969); 10 *id.* 137 (1971). See Becker, "A Short Cruise on the Good Ships TOVALOP and CRISTAL," 5 J.Mar. L. & Com. 609 (1974). A 1974 Offshore Pollution Liability Agreement ("OPOL") deals with liability for pollution connected with offshore drilling. 13 Int'l Leg.Mat. 1409 (1974).

2. *Joint enforcement by port states.* In 1982, 14 Western European states agreed on a harmonized system of state port control to prevent operation of substandard ships, and to avoid distorting competition between ports and discrimination as to flag. They agreed to enforce standards laid down in seven specified international agreements even with respect to states that are not parties to these agreements. Memorandum of Understanding on Port State Control, Paris, Jan. 26, 1982, 21 *id.* 1 (1982). See also § 512, Reporters' Note 7, and § 603, Reporters' Note 2.

3. *Liability for wrongful enforcement measures.* Liability for wrongful enforcement measures was provided in the 1958 Convention on the High Seas, though environmental measures are not mentioned there. See Arts. 20 (piracy), 22(3) (stopping certain suspected ships on the high seas), and 23(7) (hot pursuit), 13 U.S.T. 2312, T.I. A.S. No. 5200, 450 U.N.T.S. 82. (As of 1987, this convention was in force for 57 states, including the United States.) See also LOS Convention, Arts. 106 (piracy), 110(3) (stopping certain suspected ships on the high seas), 111(8) (hot pursuit), 263(2) (damage to scientific research), 304 (reserving liability under international law). See also Comment *f.* The 1969 International Convention

Relating to Intervention on the High Seas in Cases of Oil Pollution Casualties provides that any Contracting Party violating the convention "shall be obliged to pay compensation to the extent of the damage caused by measures which exceed those reasonably necessary" to prevent, mitigate, or eliminate grave and imminent danger. Art. 6, 26 U.S.T. 765, T.I.A.S. No. 8068. (As of 1987, this convention was in force for 50 states, including the United States.) Under the 1973 International Convention for the Prevention of Pollution from Ships (MARPOL) (see § 603, Reporters' Note 5), a ship that is unduly detained or delayed by measures taken under that convention "shall be entitled to compensation for any loss or damage suffered." Art. 7(2).

Part VII

PROTECTION OF PERSONS
(NATURAL AND JURIDICAL)

Introductory Note:

International law governs primarily relations between states, see § 101, and traditional international jurisprudence insisted that the individual was not a "subject" of international law, see Part II, Introductory Note, but customary international law and numerous international agreements have created obligations for states in relation to persons, both natural and juridical. International law has long held states responsible for "denials of justice" and certain other injuries to nationals of other states. Increasingly, international human rights agreements have created obligations and responsibilities for states in respect of all individuals subject to their jurisdiction, including their own nationals, and a customary international law of human rights has developed and has continued to grow.

The traditional law of responsibility for injury to aliens and the contemporary law of human rights have had separate growth and, originally, different jurisprudential underpinnings. Injury by a state to the nationals of another state implicates relations between those states, and responsibility for such injury was established early as a norm of customary international law. The injury to the person has been seen as an offense to the state of his nationality. The offense being to the state, the remedy for the violation also runs to the state, although the injured person may have to exhaust domestic remedies before the state of nationality can formally seek reparation for the offense. See § 713, Comments *b, c;* § 902(2) and Comment *i* to that section. Under this principle, the state is responsible as well for injury to juridical persons of foreign nationality. (As to the nationality of companies, see §§ 213, 414.)

The contemporary international law of human rights has developed largely since the Second World War. It is concerned with natural persons only, and it applies to all human beings, not to aliens alone. It reflects general acceptance that every individual should have rights in his or her society which the state should recognize, respect, and ensure. See § 701, Comment *a.* It reflects general acceptance, too, that how a state treats individual human beings, including its own citizens, in respect of their human rights, is not the state's own business alone and therefore exclusively within its "domestic jurisdiction," but is a matter of international concern and a proper subject for regulation by international law. One of the purposes for which the United Nations was created was "to achieve international co-operation . . . in promoting and encouraging respect for human rights and fundamental freedoms for all without distinctions as to race, sex, language, or religion." [1] The Universal Declaration of Human Rights, adopted by the United Nations General Assembly in 1948,[2] proclaimed a series of political, civil, economic, social, and cultural rights as a universal standard, and the Declaration has been incorporated or reflected in national constitutions and has contributed to an international law of human rights. The Declaration was also the basis of two international agreements, the International Covenant on Civil and Political Rights and the International Covenant on Economic, Social and Cultural Rights.[3] (The internationally recognized human rights included in the Declaration and the Covenants are summarized in § 701, Reporters' Note 6.) Numerous other international human rights agreements dealing with particular rights have been concluded and have been adhered to by many states. These agreements, and international concern for human rights reflected in other international instruments and in the practice of states, have led also to the development of some customary law of human rights. See § 702.

The difference in history and in jurisprudential origins between the older law of responsibility for injury to aliens and the newer law of human rights should not conceal their essential affinity and their increasing convergence. The law of responsibility to aliens posited

---

[1] U.N. Charter, Article 1(3). See also Articles 55–56, below. Compare the Charter of the Organization of American States, Articles 5(j), 13, 26–29, 2 U.S.T. 2394, T.I.A.S. No. 2361, 119 U.N.T.S. 3, and the Protocol of Buenos Aires, revising that charter, Articles 3(j), 29–50, 21 U.S.T. 607, T.I.A.S. No. 6847 (1967).

[2] G.A. Res. 217, 3 GAOR UN Doc A/810 at 71, Dec. 10, 1948. The Declaration was adopted without dissent, but with eight states abstaining. Since then virtually all states have given at least some indication of support for the Declaration. Compare the American Declaration on the Rights and Duties of Man, Pan American Union, Final Act of the Ninth Conference of American States 38 (1948), reprinted in Sohn and Buergenthal, Basic Documents on International Protection of Human Rights 187 (1973).

An earlier Statement of Essential Human Rights was prepared by a committee appointed by the American Law Institute during World War II. See 243 Annals of the American Academy of Political and Social Sciences 18–26 (1946).

[3] 999 U.N.T.S. 171 and 993 U.N.T.S. 3. See also the Optional Protocol to the International Covenant on Civil and Political Rights, by which states agree that the Human Rights Committee established by the Covenant may consider complaints by individuals, *id.* at 59. 999 U.N.T.S. 171.

For a history of the development of the Covenants, see Pechota, "The Development of the Covenant on Civil and Political Rights," in Henkin, ed., The International Bill of Rights: The Covenant on Civil and Political Rights 32 (1981); Sohn, Supplementary Paper, in The United Nations and Human Rights, Eighteenth Report of the Commission to Study the Organization of the Peace 39, 101 (1968).

and invoked an international standard of justice for individuals, even if dogmas of the international system limited the application of that standard to foreign nationals. That standard of justice, like contemporary human rights law, derived from historic conceptions of natural law, as reflected in the conscience of contemporary mankind and the major cultures and legal systems of the world. As the law of human rights developed, the law of responsibility for injury to aliens, as applied to natural persons, began to refer to violation of their "fundamental human rights," and states began to invoke contemporary human rights norms as the basis for claims for injury to their nationals. See § 711, Comment *c* and Reporters' Note 3.

The traditional law of responsibility for injury to aliens, however, retains independent vitality. It provides an additional foundation for protecting the human rights of foreign nationals, and affords protection also for injuries not seen as violations of human rights. The traditional law of responsibility for injury to aliens also continues to protect juridical persons, which do not have "human" rights.

The international law of the rights of aliens. The traditional law of state responsibility for denials of justice to aliens has been a subject of international controversy in recent decades, see § 712, Reporters' Note 1, but the principles governing responsibility, including those requiring compensation for economic injury to aliens, have not been undermined by that controversy or by the growth of the law of human rights. A state whose national suffers economic injury or other denial of justice by another state may make a claim against the offending state for that violation, whether or not the state might have claimed under the international law of human rights. The state of nationality may hold an offending state responsible also for injury to a juridical person, whether or not that injury might have constituted denial of human rights if the injured person had been a natural person. See Chapter 2.

The international law of human rights. Virtually all states are members of the United Nations and parties to its Charter, a legally binding international agreement. In Articles 55 and 56 of the Charter, all members "pledge themselves to take joint and separate action in cooperation with the [United Nations] Organization for the achievement of," *inter alia,* "universal respect for, and observance of, human rights and fundamental freedoms for all without distinction as to race, sex, language, or religion." The language imports legal obligation, but there has been no agreement or authoritative determination as to the character and extent of the obligation. Compare § 701, Comment *d* and Reporters' Note 4.

Increasingly, the Charter provisions have been linked to the Universal Declaration of Human Rights, the legal character of which has also been debated. See § 701, Reporters' Notes 4 and 5. Few states would agree that any action by a state contrary to any provision of the Declaration is, for that reason alone, a violation of the Charter or of customary international law. On the other hand, almost all states would agree that some infringements of human rights enumerated in the Declaration are violations of the Charter or of customary international law. See § 702.

The international law of human rights includes also a number of international human rights agreements, some of which have been adhered to by many states. (As of 1987, the United States has adhered to very few. See chart below and § 701, Comment *e*.) The principal agreements are the International Covenant on Civil and Political Rights and the International Covenant on Economic, Social, and Cultural Rights.[4] There are also numerous conventions dealing with particular rights. See chart on following pages.[5]

---

[4] As of June 30, 1987, the Covenant on Civil and Political Rights had been accepted by 86 states; the Covenant on Economic, Social, and Cultural Rights by 90 states; the Optional Protocol by 38 states. A convenient collection of human rights documents as of 1983 is Human Rights, A Compilation of International Instruments (U.N. Doc. ST/HR/1/Rev. 2).

Comprehensive regional human rights agreements are the European Convention for the Protection of Human Rights and Fundamental Freedoms, 213 U.N.T.S. 211, E.T.S. 5; the American Convention on Human Rights, O.A.S. Official Records OEA/Ser. K/XVI/Doc. 65, Rev. 1, Corr. 1, Jan. 7, 1970, 9 Int'l Leg.Mat. 101 (1970); the African Charter on Human and Peoples' Rights, June 27, 1981, 21 Int'l Leg.Mat. 59 (1982).

As of 1987, the United States was not a party to any of these agreements.

[5] The International Labour Organization has also sponsored more than 150 conventions, many of which have been accepted by many states. See International Labour Organization, Chart of Ratifications, International Labour Conventions, January 1, 1987.

147

Title of Agreement	Date of Entry into Force	Citation	U.S. Party	No. of Parties 1–1–87
Slavery Convention of 1926	3–9–27	60 L.N.T.S. 253[a]	Yes	93
Convention on the Prevention and Punishment of the Crime of Genocide	1–12–51	78 U.N.T.S. 277	No[b]	96
Convention for the Suppression of the Traffic in Persons and of the Exploitation of the Prostitution of Others	7–25–51	96 U.N.T.S. 271	No	59
Convention Relating to the Status of Refugees	4–22–54	189 U.N.T.S. 137	No	98
Convention on the Political Rights of Women	7–7–54	193 U.N.T.S. 135[c]	Yes	92
Supplementary Convention on the Abolition of Slavery, the Slave Trade, and Institutions and Practices Similar to Slavery	4–30–57	266 U.N.T.S. 3[d]	Yes	102
Convention on the Nationality of Married Women	8–11–58	309 U.N.T.S. 65	No	55
Abolition of Forced Labor Convention	1–17–59	320 U.N.T.S. 291	No	108
Convention Relating to the Status of Stateless Persons	6–6–60	360 U.N.T.S. 117	No	34
Convention Against Discrimination in Education	5–22–62	429 U.N.T.S. 95	No	77
Convention on the International Right of Correction	8–24–62	435 U.N.T.S. 191	No	11
Protocol Relating to the Status of Refugees	10–4–67	606 U.N.T.S. 267[e]	Yes	98
International Convention on the Elimination of All Forms of Racial Discrimination	1–4–69	660 U.N.T.S. 195	No	124
Convention on the Non-Applicability of Statutory Limitations to War Crimes against Humanity	11–11–70	754 U.N.T.S. 73	No	29
Convention on the Reduction of Statelessness	12–13–75	989 U.N.T.S. 175	No	14
International Convention on the Suppression and Punishment of *Apartheid*	7–18–76	1015 U.N.T.S. 244	No	86
Convention on the Elimination of All Forms of Discrimination Against Women	9–3–81	A/Res./34/180	No	91

[a] 46 Stat. 2183, 2 Bevans 607, T.S. 778 (1929). The United States is also party to the 1953 Protocol amending the Convention, 7 U.S.T. 479, T.I.A.S. No. 3532, 182 U.N.T.S. 51 (adhered to by 50 states), but not to other amendments that went into force in 1955, 212 U.N.T.S. 17 (33 parties).

[b] United States ratification was expected in 1988. See this Introductory Note, n. 7.

[c] 27 U.S.T. 1909, T.I.A.S. No. 8289.

[d] 18 U.S.T. 3201, T.I.A.S. No. 6418.

[e] 19 U.S.T. 6223, T.I.A.S. No. 6577.

Title of Agreement	Date of Entry into Force	Citation	U.S. Party	No. of Parties 1-1-87
Convention Against Torture and other Cruel, Inhuman or Degrading Punishment	6–26–87	U.N.Doc.A/39/708, at 6	No	20[f]

International human rights law and agreements have the same status and the same binding character as other international law and agreements. However, international law generally is largely observed because violations directly affect the interests of states, which are alert to deter, prevent, or respond to violations. See Introductory Note to Part I, Chapter 1. Violations of the international law of human rights, on the other hand, generally injure the inhabitants of the violating state; ordinarily, other states are not directly affected by such violations and their concern for human rights in other states has been uneven. Moreover, states are generally reluctant to submit their actions in respect to human rights to scrutiny by other states. Special international "machinery" has been created to monitor compliance with international human rights law, but the effectiveness of those bodies and procedures in helping induce compliance has been variable. (The European Convention regime has had conspicuous success.) The condition of human rights varies widely even among states that have adhered to international human rights agreements.

Human rights in United States foreign relations law. The United Nations Charter and the Charter of the Organization of American States, both of which include human rights provisions, are treaties of the United States. The human rights conventions to which the United States is a party (see § 701, Comment *e*, and chart above) are also treaties of the United States. Obligations assumed by the United States in these agreements are law of the land, either directly if the provisions are self-executing or upon implementation by Congress. See § 111. The customary international law of human rights, § 702, is also law of the United States. § 111(1). Federal statutes refer to "internationally recognized human rights" and have legislated national policy toward governments guilty of "consistent patterns of gross violations" of such rights. See § 702, Reporters' Note 10. The United States has

---

[f] The Convention came into force on June 26, 1987 with the deposit of the 20th instrument of ratification. As of that date the United States had not ratified the Convention.

frequently reiterated its acceptance of the Universal Declaration, and whatever legal character it has applies to the United States.[6]

Several major human rights agreements have been signed by the United States but as of 1987 not yet ratified.[7] In 1978, President Carter transmitted to the Senate the International Covenant on Civil and Political Rights, the International Covenant on Economic, Social and Cultural Rights, the Convention on the Elimination of All Forms of Racial Discrimination, and the American Convention on Human Rights.[8] In 1980, President Carter submitted to the Senate the Covenant on the Elimination of All Forms of Discrimination against Women.[9] If the Senate consents and the President proceeds with ratification of these treaties, they will become law of the United States. Even in the absence of ratification by the United States, some provisions of these covenants and conventions reflect principles of customary international law and thus are a part of the law of the United States. See § 702. The acts forbidden by the covenants and conventions usually are acts that are prohibited by the United States Constitution or by federal or State law; the obligations imposed on the United States by those instruments are in fact generally honored pursuant to federal or State law. See § 701, Reporters' Note 8.[10]

The principal safeguards for individual rights in the United States are those provided by the Constitution and laws of the United States and of the States. Much of that law is properly part of the foreign relations law of the United States, since it "has

---

[6] See note 2 above. United States is also party to the Final Act of the Conference on Security and Cooperation in Europe, Helsinki 1975, 14 Int'l Leg.Mat. 1292 (1975). The Helsinki Accord was not intended to be a legally binding agreement and is therefore not law of the United States. See § 111, Comment *b*; § 301, Comment *e* and Reporters' Note 2. It may, however, constitute an element in the process contributing to the development of customary international law. See § 102, Comments *b, f,* and *i*. In the Final Act, a Declaration of Principles Guiding Relations between Participating States includes principle VII, "Respect for human rights and fundamental freedoms . . . ." *Inter alia,* that principle provides: "In the field of human rights and fundamental freedoms, the participating States will act in conformity with the purposes and principles of the Charter of the United Nations and with the Universal Declaration of Human Rights." The Act also includes "Basket 3" providing for cooperation in fields relating to human rights such as removal of restrictions to family reunification, to marriage between citizens of different states, to travel, and to circulation of, access to, and exchange of information.

[7] The Genocide Convention was signed by President Truman in 1949 and was before the Senate until 1986 when the Senate finally gave consent to its ratification. Ratification by the United States was expected in 1988.

[8] The Executive Branch recommended some reservations. See Four Treaties pertaining to Human Rights, Executives C, D, E, and F, 95th Cong., 2d sess. (1978).

[9] See Ex.Doc. 96–R, Nov. 12, 1980.

[10] See also Henkin, "Rights: American and Human," 79 Colum.L.Rev. 405, 415–20 (1979).

substantial significance for the foreign relations of the United States or has other substantial international consequences." See § 1. At best, however, it is feasible to restate here only so much of that law as may directly implicate United States foreign relations, *e.g.*, the constitutional rights of individuals in foreign relations contexts, the rights of citizens abroad, the rights of aliens. See Chapter 3 of this Part.

Chapter 1 of this Part deals with the obligations of a state to respect the human rights of all persons subject to its jurisdiction, its own nationals as well as others. Those obligations derive largely from international agreements, but customary law obligates states to respect several important rights. Chapter 2 deals with the obligations of a state in respect of nationals of other states as a matter of customary law. It includes both respect for the human rights and other interests of individuals of foreign nationality, and respect for property interests of persons of foreign nationality, juridical as well as natural. Chapter 3 restates selected principles of United States constitutional law that protect individual rights in respects particularly relevant to United States foreign relations.

REPORTERS' NOTES

1. *Bibliography:*

L. Henkin, The Rights of Man Today (1978).

M. McDougal, H. Lasswell & L. Chen, Human Rights and World Public Order (1980).

T. Meron, ed., Human Rights in International Law (1984).

A. H. Robertson, Human Rights in the World (2d ed. 1982).

L. Sohn & T. Buergenthal, The International Protection of Human Rights (1973).

R. Lillich, ed., International Law of State Responsibility for Injuries to Aliens (1983).

2. *Previous Restatement.* Chapter 1 of this Part incorporates concepts of the international law of human rights that have matured since the previous Restatement; Chapter 2 rearranges and condenses materials on state responsibility to aliens treated at length in the previous Restatement, but without departing from them in substance in any major respect. The concept of state responsibility, remedies for failure of responsibility, and the relation of the state to its nationals were dealt with by the previous Restatement largely in the context of injury to aliens. Previous Restatement, Part IV. These matters are generalized in this Restatement. See §§ 207, 211–13, 902, 906–907. The substantive law of state responsibility for injustice or other personal injury to foreign individuals, previous Restatement Part IV, Chapter 2, is here linked to the international law of human rights, see § 711. As to the law on injury to alien property interests, this Restatement, § 712–13, is generally consistent with the previous Restatement, Part IV, Chapter 3.

Chapter One

INTERNATIONAL LAW OF HUMAN RIGHTS

§ 701. Obligation to Respect Human Rights

A state is obligated to respect the human rights of persons subject to its jurisdiction

(a) **that it has undertaken to respect by international agreement;**

(b) **that states generally are bound to respect as a matter of customary international law (§ 702); and**

(c) **that it is required to respect under general principles of law common to the major legal systems of the world.**

Comment:

a. Human rights defined. "Human rights" refers to freedoms, immunities, and benefits which, according to widely accepted contemporary values, every human being should enjoy in the society in which he or she lives. By international law and agreement states have recognized many specific human rights and assumed the obligation to respect them. The rights protected by customary international law are set forth in § 702. Rights protected by the principal international agreements are summarized in Reporters' Note 6.

b. Human rights and sources of international law. The international law of human rights has strong antecedents in natural law, in contemporary moral values, and in the constitutional law of states. Human rights principles come into international law by the same means and from the same sources as other international law, *viz.*, as customary law, by international agreement, or from general principles of law common to the major legal systems of the world. See § 102. This chapter specifies human rights obligations deriving from customary law or international agreement; some obligations

152

deriving from those sources may also be regarded as having been absorbed into international law as general principles common to the major legal systems. As of 1986, it has not been authoritatively determined whether any obligations to observe human rights, in addition to those included in clauses (a) and (b), have been absorbed into international law as general principles common to the major legal systems. See § 102, Comment *b* and Reporters' Note 7.

c. Human rights law as obligations between states. Like international agreements generally, international human rights agreements create legal obligations between the states parties, although the agreements are for the benefit of individuals, including nationals, residents, and others subject to the jurisdiction of the promisor state. Human rights obligations in customary international law generally are obligations to all other states. See § 702. Remedies for violations of human rights obligations are generally state to state (see § 703 and § 902(2)), but some international agreements also provide remedies to individuals whose human rights have been violated, or to individuals or nongovernmental bodies acting on their behalf. See § 703(3) and Comment *c;* § 906, Comment *a* and Reporters' Note 1.

d. Human rights obligations under United Nations Charter. Almost all states are parties to the United Nations Charter, which contains human rights obligations. There has been no authoritative determination of the full content of those obligations, but it is increasingly accepted that states parties to the Charter are legally obligated to respect some of the rights recognized in the Universal Declaration. See Introductory Note to this Part. A violation of the rights protected by customary law, § 702, also may be seen as a violation of the Charter. See Reporters' Note 4.

e. International human rights obligations of the United States. The United States is bound by the international customary law of human rights. See § 702. It is a party to the United Nations Charter and the Charter of the Organization of American States, both of which include general human rights undertakings. The United States has also adhered to the Slavery Convention of 1926 and the Supplementary Convention on the Abolition of Slavery and the Slave Trade, the Convention on the Political Rights of Women, and the Protocol Relating to the Status of Refugees. See Introductory Note to this Part.

REPORTERS' NOTES

1. *Human rights law and sources of international law.* Ordinarily, international law does not assume restrictions on state autonomy. But the universal acceptance of human rights in principle, and

active international concern with human rights, has led to some readiness to conclude that states have assumed human rights obligations. There is a disposition to find legal obligation in indeterminate language about human rights in international agreements, *e.g.*, the United Nations Charter (see Introductory Note to this Part). There is some willingness to find that the practice of states, perhaps under constitutional, political, or moral impetus, is practice with a sense of international legal obligation creating a customary international law of human rights, even though many states sometimes violate these rights, see § 102(2). Absorption into international law of principles common to national legal systems generally is only a secondary source of international law (§ 102(4)), but there is a willingness to conclude that prohibitions common to the constitutions or laws of many states are general principles that have been absorbed into international law.

2. *Practice creating customary human rights law.* International human rights law governs relations between a state and its own inhabitants. Other states are only occasionally involved in monitoring such law through ordinary diplomatic practice. Therefore, the practice of states that is accepted as building customary international law of human rights includes some forms of conduct different from those that build customary international law generally. See § 102, Comment *b*. Practice accepted as building customary human rights law includes: virtually universal adherence to the United Nations Charter and its human rights provisions, and virtually universal and frequently reiterated acceptance of the Universal Declaration of Human Rights even if only in principle; virtually universal participation of states in the preparation and adoption of international agreements recognizing human rights principles generally, or particular rights; the adoption of human rights principles by states in regional organizations in Europe, Latin America, and Africa (see Introductory Note to this Part); general support by states for United Nations resolutions declaring, recognizing, invoking, and applying international human rights principles as international law; action by states to conform their national law or practice to standards or principles declared by international bodies, and the incorporation of human rights provisions, directly or by reference, in national constitutions and laws; invocation of human rights principles in national policy, in diplomatic practice, in international organization activities and actions; and other diplomatic communications or action by states reflecting the view that certain practices violate international human rights law, including condemnation and other adverse state reactions to violations by other states. The International Court of Justice and the International Law Commission have recognized the existence of customary human rights law. See Case Concerning the Barcelona Traction, Light & Power Co., Ltd. (Belgium v. Spain), [1970] I.C.J. Rep. 32, quoted in § 703, Reporters' Note 3; § 702, Reporters' Notes 3, 4. See, generally McDougal, Lasswell and Chen, Human Rights and World Public Order 266 *et seq.*, 313 *et seq.* (1980). Some of these practices may also support the conclusion that particular human rights have been ab-

sorbed into international law as general principles common to the major state legal systems. See § 702, Reporters' Note 1.

3. *Human rights law as obligations among states.* Like multilateral agreements generally, an international human rights agreement creates rights and obligations between each party and every other party. Most multilateral agreements, however, are essentially networks of bilateral agreements, creating obligations between each pair of parties as regards their particular interests *inter se, e.g.,* as to trade or communication between them. In such cases, remedies also are essentially bilateral, by the state victim of a violation against the violating state. Human rights agreements, however, are more genuinely multilateral. The obligations run to all parties equally and do not ordinarily engage the interests of one state more than another; unless otherwise provided, all states parties have the same remedies for violations. See § 703.

Ordinarily, customary law, too, creates obligations between particular states; for example, a violation of the immunity of a diplomat (§ 464) is effectively an offense to the diplomat's state, not to states generally, and states other than the one directly offended do not ordinarily invoke remedies for such a violation. See § 902, Comment *a.* The customary international law of human rights, however, creates obligations by each state to all other states (*erga omnes*), so that a violation by a state of the rights of persons subject to its jurisdiction is a breach of obligation to all other states. In practice, states may not see fit to vindicate such norms except on behalf of persons with whom they identify in some way, *e.g.,* their nationals, or minorities with which they have ethnic, cultural, or other links. In principle, however, every state can pursue remedies against any other state that commits a violation of the rights under customary law of persons subject to its jurisdiction. See § 703(2) and Reporters' Note 2 to that section.

4. *Human rights obligations under United Nations Charter.* It has been argued that the general pledge of members in the Charter, Introductory Note to this Part, has been made definite by the Universal Declaration, and that failure by any member to respect the rights recognized in the Declaration is a violation of the Charter. Alternatively, it has been urged, the Charter, the Universal Declaration, other international resolutions and declarations, and other practice of states have combined to create a customary international law of human rights requiring every state to respect the rights set forth in the Declaration. There are indeed numerous United Nations resolutions and statements referring, for example, to "the duty of states to fully and faithfully observe the provisions of the Universal Declaration." Art. 11, G.A. Res. 1904, 18 U.N. GAOR Supp. No. 15, at 35. See, generally, United Nations Action in the Field of Human Rights, U.N. Doc. ST/HR/2/Rev. 1, 8–15 (1983); McDougal, Lasswell and Chen, Reporters' Note 2, 325 *et seq.*

5. *Human rights provisions of United Nations Charter in United States law.* In Sei Fujii v. California, 38 Cal.2d 718, 722–25, 242 P.2d 617, 621–22 (1952), a lower court

held that the human rights articles of the United Nations Charter had become supreme law of the land in the United States and invalidated State law precluding the ownership of land by certain aliens on account of their race. The Supreme Court of California upheld the judgment on the ground that the State law violated the Equal Protection Clause of the Fourteenth Amendment, but expressly rejected the lower court's reliance on the United Nations Charter provision. The court observed that the Charter provisions "lack the mandatory quality and definiteness which would indicate an intent to create justiciable rights in private persons immediately upon ratification. Instead, they are framed as a promise of future action by the member nation." See also Hitai v. Immigration and Naturalization Service, 343 F.2d 466, 468 (2d Cir.) *certiorari denied,* 382 U.S. 816, 86 S.Ct. 36, 15 L.Ed.2d 63 (1965) (Charter provision not self-executing and does not invalidate provision of immigration law); also Vlissidis v. Anadell, 262 F.2d 398, 400 (7th Cir.1959) (United Nations Charter does not supersede quota system of United States immigration law); Spiess v. C. Itoh & Co. (America), Inc., 643 F.2d 353, 363 (5th Cir.1981) *vacated,* 457 U.S. 1128, 102 S.Ct. 2951, 73 L.Ed.2d 1344 (1982) (Title VII of Civil Rights Act not intended to override treaty provisions permitting New York subsidiary of Japanese corporation to hire only Japanese citizens for managerial and technical positions; United Nations Charter not self-executing and Title VII not designed to implement Charter and does not partake of Charter's character as superior law).

6. *Internationally recognized human rights.* The binding character of the Universal Declaration of Human Rights continues to be debated, Introductory Note to this Part, and Reporters' Notes 4 and 5, but the Declaration has become the accepted general articulation of recognized rights. With some variations, the same rights are recognized by the two principal covenants, the Covenant on Civil and Political Rights and the Covenant on Economic, Social and Cultural Rights. The particular conventions (Introductory Note to this Part) also protect rights that are recognized in the Universal Declaration.

The rights recognized in the Universal Declaration include: the right to life, liberty, and security of the person; freedom from slavery or servitude; freedom from torture or cruel, inhuman or degrading treatment or punishment; the right to recognition as a person before the law; equality before the law and equal protection of the law; the right to a remedy for violations of fundamental rights, granted by law; freedom from arbitrary arrest, detention or exile; a fair and public trial for persons charged with crime, with guarantees necessary for one's defense; the presumption of innocence; the right to be convicted only according to law and to freedom from the application of *ex post facto* law; freedom from arbitrary interference with privacy, family, home or correspondence, and legal protection against such interference; freedom of movement and residence within a country; the right to leave any country and the right to seek asylum; the right to a nationality and not to be arbitrarily deprived of one's nationality, and the right to change one's nationality; the right to marry and found a family, and equality of men and women in marriage and its dissolution; the right to own property and not to be arbitrarily deprived of it; freedom of thought, conscience, and religion, freedom of opinion and expression, assembly and association. The Universal Declaration includes some political rights, for example, the right to take part in government and have equal access to the public service, which are accepted as being human rights for every person but only in relation to "his country." Art. 21(1), (2). (Compare the right of everyone to return "to his country." Art. 13(2).) The Declaration also includes certain "economic and social rights," for example, the right to social security; the right to work, to free choice of employment and protection against unemployment, to just remuneration and equal pay for equal work, and the right to join a trade union; the right to rest and leisure; to a standard of living adequate for oneself and one's family; to education, which at elementary levels must be free and compulsory. The rights set forth in the Declaration are not subject to "distinctions of any kind, such as race, colour, sex, language, religion, political or other opinion, national or social origin, property, birth or other status." Art. 2. Article 29(2) provides: "In the exercise of his rights and freedoms, everyone shall be subject only to such limitations as are determined by law solely for the purpose of securing due recognition and respect for the rights and freedoms of others and of meeting the just requirements of morality, public order and the general welfare in a democratic society."

The rights set forth in the Declaration are restated, generally, in greater detail and with legal precision in the Covenant on Civil and Political Rights and the Covenant on Economic, Social and Cultural Rights. In the former, each state party "undertakes to respect and to ensure to all individuals within its territory and subject to its jurisdiction the rights recognized in the present Covenant." Art. 2(1). In the Covenant on Economic, Social and Cultural Rights, each state party "undertakes to take steps . . . to the maximum of its available resources, with a view to achieving progressively the full realization of the rights recognized in the present Covenant." Art. 2(1). The Covenants include some rights not mentioned in the Universal Declaration. Both Covenants recognize a right of all peoples to self-determination, and all peoples may "freely dispose of their natural wealth and resources without prejudice to any obligations arising out of international economic co-operation, based upon the principle of mutual benefit, and international law." (Art. 1 of each of the Covenants.) The Covenant on Civil and Political Rights forbids imprisonment for inability to fulfill a contractual obligation, a right not mentioned in the Declaration. On the other hand, the right to own property and not to be arbitrarily deprived of it (Universal Declaration, Art. 17) is not expressly mentioned in either Covenant, but that omission has not been construed to be a rejection of the right. See § 711, Comment *d*; also § 702, Comment *k*. A number of the civil-political rights are expressly made subject to limitations; *e.g.*, the freedom of movement and residence within a country, and the right to leave a country, "shall not be subject to any restrictions except those which are provided by law, are necessary to protect national security, public order *(ordre public)*, public health or morals or the rights and freedoms of others." Art. 12(3). The rights in the Covenant on Economic, Social and Cultural Rights are subject "only to such limitations as are determined by law only in so far as this may be compatible with the nature of these rights and solely for the purpose of promoting the general welfare in a democratic society." Art. 4. Most civil-political rights are subject to derogation during public emergency. For a guide to the interpretation of the Covenant on Civil and Political Rights, see Henkin, ed., The International Bill of Rights: The Covenant on Civil and Political Rights (1981).

International human rights principles generally, the Universal Declaration, and, notably, the International Covenant on Civil and Political Rights address the rights of natural persons only. The Covenant on Economic, Social, and Cultural Rights, however, recognizes some rights for trade unions. Art. 8(1). Compare the European Convention on Human Rights, some of whose provisions would apply to juridical persons also; Article 25 of that Convention expressly accords a right of petition to "any person, nongovernmental organization or group of individuals claiming to be a victim of a violation." See Buergenthal, "To Respect and to Ensure: State Obligations and Permissible Derogations" in Henkin, ed., The International Bill of Rights, *supra*, 72, 73.

7. *International human rights standards as source of United States law.* Courts in the United States have increasingly looked to international human rights standards as law in the United States or as a guide to United States law. See cases cited in § 702, Reporters' Notes 5 and 6; compare Reporters' Note 5 to this section. There are numerous references to the Universal Declaration, *e.g.*, Zemel v. Rusk, 381 U.S. 1, 14, n. 13, 85 S.Ct. 1271, 1279, n. 13, 14 L.Ed.2d 179 (1963); Kennedy v. Mendoza-Martinez, 372 U.S. 144, 161, n. 16, 83 S.Ct. 554, 564, n. 16, 9 L.Ed.2d 644 (1965). Several cases have cited the United Nations Standard Minimum Rules for the Treatment of Prisoners (10 GAOR, U.N. Doc. A/Conf. 6/C.1/L.1, 1955), to help determine rights under the due process and the cruel and unusual punishment clauses of the United States Constitution. See Estelle v. Gamble, 429 U.S. 97, 103–104 and n. 8, 97 S.Ct. 285, 290–291 and n. 8, 50 L.Ed.2d 251 (1976); Detainees of Brooklyn House of Detention for Men v. Malcolm, 520 F.2d 392, 396 (2d Cir.1975); Morgan v. Lavallee, 526 F.2d 221 (2d Cir. 1975); Lareau v. Manson, 507 F.Supp. 1177, 1187 and n. 9 (D.Conn.1980), *affirmed in part,* 651 F.2d 96 (2d Cir.1981); see also United States *ex rel.* Wolfish v. Levi, 439 F.Supp. 114, n. 20 (S.D.N.Y. 1977), *affirmed in part* and *reversed in part,* 573 F.2d 118 (2d Cir. 1978), *reversed,* Bell v. Wolfish, 441 U.S. 520, 99 S.Ct. 1861, 60 L.Ed.2d 447 (1979). In Sterling v. Cupp, 290 Or. 611, 625 P.2d 123 (1981), the Supreme Court of Oregon enjoined prison officials from assigning female guards to certain duties in relation to male prisoners, citing the United Nations standards and other international human rights instruments to support its conclusion that "needlessly harsh, degrading, or de-

humanizing treatment of prisoners" violated the Oregon Constitution. 625 P.2d at 131, n. 21.

8. *Effect of future United States ratification of principal international covenants.* Adherence by the United States to the principal international covenants would not effect any major change in the rights enjoyed by inhabitants of the United States under the United States and State constitutions and laws. The International Covenant on Civil and Political Rights requires states parties to the Covenant to respect and ensure rights generally similar to those protected by the United States Constitution. Some provisions in the Covenant parallel express constitutional provisions, for example, the freedoms protected by the First Amendment, and the prohibition on double jeopardy. Other provisions in the Covenant parallel rights that the Supreme Court has found to be constitutionally protected, *e.g.*, the right to vote, Harper v. Virginia Bd. of Elections, 383 U.S. 663, 86 S.Ct. 1079, 16 L.Ed.2d 169 (1966); Wesberry v. Sanders, 376 U.S. 1, 84 S.Ct. 526, 11 L.Ed.2d 481 (1964); Reynolds v. Sims, 377 U.S. 533, 84 S.Ct. 1362, 12 L.Ed.2d 506 (1964); the presumption of innocence, In re Winship, 397 U.S. 358, 90 S.Ct. 1068, 25 L.Ed.2d 368 (1970); the right to travel, Edwards v. California, 314 U.S. 160, 62 S.Ct. 164, 86 L.Ed. 119 (1941); Shapiro v. Thompson, 394 U.S. 618, 629–31, 89 S.Ct. 1322, 1328–30, 22 L.Ed.2d 600 (1969); Oregon v. Mitchell, 400 U.S. 112, 91 S.Ct. 260, 27 L.Ed.2d 272 (1970); Kent v. Dulles, 357 U.S. 116, 78 S.Ct. 1113, 2 L.Ed.2d 1204 (1958); but *cf.* Haig v. Agee, 453 U.S. 280, 101 S.Ct. 2766, 69 L.Ed.2d 640 (1981), cited in § 721, Reporters'

Note 12; the right to marry and have a family, Loving v. Virginia, 388 U.S. 1, 87 S.Ct. 1817, 18 L.Ed.2d 1010 (1967); Zablocki v. Redhail, 434 U.S. 374, 98 S.Ct. 673, 54 L.Ed. 2d 618 (1978); the right of parents to control the moral and religious education of their children, Pierce v. Society of Sisters, 268 U.S. 510, 45 S.Ct. 571, 69 L.Ed. 1070 (1925); Meyer v. Nebraska, 262 U.S. 390, 43 S.Ct. 625, 67 L.Ed. 1042 (1923); cultural and linguistic rights for minority groups, Wisconsin v. Yoder, 406 U.S. 205, 92 S.Ct. 1526, 32 L.Ed.2d 15 (1972). Protection under the Covenant, however, may not be congruent in all respects with that provided by the Constitution. In some respects, United States adherence to the Covenant without material reservations might add somewhat to the rights enjoyed by individuals under the Constitution. *E.g.*, Article 6 of the Covenant outlaws capital punishment for pregnant women and for crimes committed by persons under 18 years of age, which has not been held to be a violation of the United States Constitution. Article 7 would forbid not only cruel and unusual punishment for crime, but all torture, and any cruel, inhuman, or degrading treatment in any circumstances. Compare Ingraham v. Wright, 430 U.S. 651, 97 S.Ct. 1401, 51 L.Ed.2d 711 (1977) (corporal punishment in schools not "punishment" within Eighth Amendment). Under Article 14(7) of the Covenant, individuals accused of crime would apparently be protected against trial by both State and federal authorities for offenses arising out of the same act. Compare Abbate v. United States, 359 U.S. 187, 79 S.Ct. 666, 3 L.Ed.2d 729 (1959); Bartkus v. Illinois, 359 U.S. 121, 79 S.Ct. 676, 3 L.Ed.2d 684

(1959). Some of the rights recognized by the Covenant are given effect in the United States by federal or State law, notably the civil rights laws. For example, honor and reputation, protected by Article 17 of the Covenant, held not "liberty" or "property" within the protection of the due process clause of the Constitution, Paul v. Davis, 424 U.S. 693, 96 S.Ct. 1155, 47 L.Ed.2d 405 (1976), are accorded substantial protection by State libel laws. The right of every child "to such measures of protection as are required by his status as a minor, on the part of his family, society and the State," Art. 24, is also largely given effect by State law. On the other hand, compensation for persons who have suffered punishment as a result of miscarriage of justice, Art. 14(6), is generally given effect in the United States only *ad hoc* as a matter of legislative grace.

Article 20 of the Covenant on Civil and Political Right requires states to prohibit "propaganda for war," and "advocacy of national, racial or religious hatred that constitutes incitement to discrimination, hostility or violence." The United States would have to enter a reservation to or understanding of this article, since, under the Constitution, the United States (or a State) cannot prohibit "propaganda," and can prohibit incitement to unlawful action but not mere advocacy of it. See Yates v. United States, 354 U.S. 298, 77 S.Ct. 1064, 1 L.Ed.2d 1356 (1957), *overruled on other grounds*, Burks v. United States, 437 U.S. 1, 98 S.Ct. 2141, 57 L.Ed.2d 1 (1978); *cf.* Scales v. United States, 367 U.S. 203, 81 S.Ct. 1469, 6 L.Ed.2d 782 (1961); Brandenburg v. Ohio, 395 U.S. 444, 89 S.Ct. 1827, 23 L.Ed.2d 430 (1969).

Adherence to the Covenant on Economic, Social and Cultural Rights would obligate the United States to "take steps . . . to the maximum of its available resources with a view to achieving progressively the full realization of the rights recognized" in that Covenant. Art. 2. Most of the rights set forth in the Covenant are not recognized as rights under the United States Constitution. Compare the cases that held alleged rights not to be constitutionally rooted or otherwise "fundamental" so that distinctions or classifications in respect of the enjoyment of such benefits do not require "strict scrutiny" and a "compelling State interest" under the Equal Protection Clause. Dandridge v. Williams, 397 U.S. 471, 90 S.Ct. 1153, 25 L.Ed.2d 491 (1970), and Lavine v. Milne, 424 U.S. 577, 584 n. 9, 96 S.Ct. 1010, 1015 n. 9, 47 L.Ed.2d 249 (1976) (welfare payments); San Antonio Independent School District v. Rodriguez, 411 U.S. 1, 93 S.Ct. 1278, 36 L.Ed.2d 16 (1973) (education); Massachusetts Bd. of Retirement v. Murgia, 427 U.S. 307, 312–13, 96 S.Ct. 2562, 2566, 49 L.Ed.2d 520 (1976) (right to work); Lindsey v. Normet, 405 U.S. 56, 74, 92 S.Ct. 862, 874, 31 L.Ed.2d 36 (1972) (housing). But, without support in the United States Constitution, economic and social rights, including free education, social security, and other welfare benefits are generally provided pursuant to United States or State law. And the Equal Protection Clause requires that if such benefits are provided they must be provided without discrimination on grounds of race, gender, or other invidious basis. See Plyler v. Doe, 457 U.S. 202, 102 S.Ct. 2382, 72 L.Ed.2d 786 (1982) (children of undocumented aliens may not be denied education provided for other children). See also Serrano v. Priest, 5 Cal.3d 584, 96 Cal.Rptr. 601, 487 P.2d 1241 (1971), *appeal after remand*, 18 Cal.3d 728, 135 Cal.Rptr. 345, 557 P.2d 929 (1976), *certiorari denied*, 432 U.S. 907, 97 S.Ct. 2951, 53 L.Ed. 2d 1079 (1977) (education is fundamental right under California Constitution). Except for those few rights that require no affirmative governmental action, but only abstention from interference, *e.g.*, the right to join a trade union, Art. 8(1) (a), the provisions of this Covenant are inherently non-self-executing. See § 111(3), (4). By adhering to this Covenant, the United States would be obligated to take legislative, executive, and other measures, federal or State, generally of the kind that are already common in the United States, "to the maximum of its available resources," "with a view to achieving progressively the

full realization" of those rights. Since there is no definition or standard in the Covenant, the United States would largely determine for itself the meaning of "full realization" and the speed of realization, and whether it is using "the maximum of its available resources" for this purpose. The United States would, however, be required to submit reports for consideration by the United Nations Economic and Social Council "on the measures which they have adopted and the progress made in achieving the observance of the rights recognized" in the Covenant, Art. 16.

9. *Previous Restatement.* The previous Restatement referred to human rights in relation to the international standard of justice protecting aliens. See § 165, Comment *b.* Section 118, Reporters' Note, refers to the propriety of dealing with human rights by treaty.

§ 702. Customary International Law of Human Rights

A state violates international law if, as a matter of state policy, it practices, encourages, or condones

    (a) genocide,

    (b) slavery or slave trade,

    (c) the murder or causing the disappearance of individuals,

    (d) torture or other cruel, inhuman, or degrading treatment or punishment,

    (e) prolonged arbitrary detention,

    (f) systematic racial discrimination, or

    (g) a consistent pattern of gross violations of internationally recognized human rights.

Comment:

    a. Scope of customary law of human rights. This section includes as customary law only those human rights whose status as customary law is generally accepted (as of 1987) and whose scope and content are generally agreed. See § 701, Reporters' Note 6. The list is not necessarily complete, and is not closed: human rights not listed in this section may have achieved the status of customary law, and some rights might achieve that status in the future. See Comments *j, k,* and *l.*

b. *State policy as violation of customary law.* In general, a state is responsible for acts of officials or official bodies, national or local, even if the acts were not authorized by or known to the responsible national authorities, indeed even if expressly forbidden by law, decree or instruction. § 207, Comment *d.* The violations of human rights cited in this section, however, are violations of customary international law only if practiced, encouraged, or condoned by the government of a state as official policy. A state is not responsible under this section for a violation of human rights by an official that was not authorized, encouraged, or condoned by the responsible governmental authorities of the state. (Compare the different rule as to state responsibility for official injuries to nationals of another state, § 711, Comment *a* and § 207, Comment *d.*)

A government may be presumed to have encouraged or condoned acts prohibited by this section if such acts, especially by its officials, have been repeated or notorious and no steps have been taken to prevent them or to punish the perpetrators. That state law prohibits the violation and provides generally effective remedies is strong evidence that the violation is not state policy. A state is not ordinarily responsible under this section for violations of human rights by individuals, such as individual acts of torture or of racial discrimination. A state would be responsible if, as a matter of state policy, it required, encouraged, or condoned such private violations, but mere failure to enact laws prohibiting private violations of human rights would not ordinarily constitute encouragement or condonation. International law requires a state to outlaw genocide, slavery, and the slave trade, and the state would be responsible under this section if it failed to prohibit them or to enforce the prohibition.

Even when a state is not responsible under this section because a violation is not state policy, the state may be responsible under some international agreement that requires the state to prevent the violation. For example, under the Covenant on Civil and Political Rights, a state party is guilty of a violation if any of the acts listed in this section is perpetrated by officials, persons acting under color of law, or other persons for whose acts the state is responsible under § 207, even when their acts are contrary to state law or policy. See also § 207, Comment *a*. And see Reporters' Note 2 to this section.

c. Customary law of human rights as United States law. The customary law of human rights is part of the law of the United States to be applied as such by State as well as federal courts. See § 111(1).

d. Genocide. Genocide is defined in Article II of the Convention on the Prevention and Punishment of the Crime of Genocide as

> any of the following acts committed with intent to destroy, in whole or in part, a national, ethnical, racial or religious group, as such:
>
> > (a) Killing members of the group;
> >
> > (b) Causing serious bodily or mental harm to members of the group;
> >
> > (c) Deliberately inflicting on the group conditions of life calculated to bring about its physical destruction in whole or in part;
> >
> > (d) Imposing measures intended to prevent births within the group;
> >
> > (e) Forcibly transferring children of the group to another group.

That definition is generally accepted for purposes of customary law under this section.

A state violates customary law if it practices or encourages genocide, fails to make genocide a crime or to punish persons guilty of it, or otherwise condones genocide. Parties to the Genocide Convention are bound also by the provisions requiring states to punish persons guilty of conspiracy, direct and public incitement, or attempt to commit genocide, or complicity in genocide, and to extradite persons accused of genocide. The United States Senate gave consent to ratification of the Convention in 1986 and ratification was expected in 1988. See Introductory Note to this Part, n. 7.

e. Slavery and slave trade. Many states, including the United States, are parties to conventions outlawing slavery and slave trade (see Introductory Note to this Part), but states not parties to any such conventions are bound by essentially the same obligations as a matter of customary law. Slavery is outlawed by the Constitution and laws of the United States and by the law of states generally.

f. Murder as state policy and capital punishment. Under this section, it is a violation of international law for a state to kill an individual other than as lawful punishment pursuant to conviction in accordance with due process of law, or as necessary under exigent circumstances, for example by police officials in line of duty in defense of themselves or of other innocent persons, or to prevent serious crime.

Capital punishment, imposed pursuant to conviction in accordance with due process of law, has not been recognized as a violation of the customary law of human rights. It may, however, constitute cruel or inhuman punishment under clause (d) if grossly disproportionate to the crime. Compare Article 6 of the Covenant on Civil and Political Rights, which provides that capital punishment may be imposed "only for the most serious crimes in accordance with law in force at the time of the commission of the crime." See also Coker v. Georgia, 433 U.S. 584, 97 S.Ct. 2861, 53 L.Ed.2d 982 (1977), where the plurality opinion barred capital punishment for rape of an adult, and would permit such punishment only for unjustified taking of human life.

  g. Torture and other cruel, inhuman, or degrading treatment or punishment. Torture has been defined as "any act by which severe pain or suffering, whether physical or mental, is intentionally inflicted by or at the instigation of a public official on a person for such purposes as obtaining from him or a third person information or confession, punishing him for an act he has committed or is suspected of having committed, or intimidating him or other persons. It does not include pain or suffering arising only from, inherent in, or incidental to, lawful sanctions to the extent consistent with the Standard Minimum Rules for the Treatment of Prisoners." Declaration on the Protection of All Persons from Being Subjected to Torture and Other Cruel, Inhuman or Degrading Treatment or Punishment, Article 1(1), G.A. Res. 3452, 30 U.N. GAOR Supp. No. 34, at 91. Article 1(2) of the Declaration provides: "Torture constitutes an aggravated and deliberate form of cruel, inhuman or degrading treatment or punishment." See also the Convention Against Torture and other Cruel, Inhuman or Degrading Punishment, approved by the General Assembly by consensus on December 10, 1984, U.N.Doc. A/39/708, at 6, noted in the Introductory Note to this Part.

  h. Prolonged arbitrary detention. Detention is arbitrary if it is not pursuant to law; it may be arbitrary also if "it is incompatible with the principles of justice or with the dignity of the human person." Statement of U.S. Delegation, 13 GAOR, U.N.Doc. A/C.3/SR.863 at 137 (1958). Detention is arbitrary if it is supported only by a general warrant, or is not accompanied by notice of charges; if the person detained is not given early opportunity to communicate with family or to consult counsel; or is not brought to trial within a reasonable time. Customary international law probably does not require a state to provide for release on bail pending trial so long as trial is not unreasonably delayed. However, Article 9(3) of the Covenant on Civil and Political Rights provides: "It shall not be the general rule that persons awaiting trial shall be detained in custody, but release may be subject to guarantees to appear for trial, at any other stage of the judicial proceedings, and should occasion arise, for execution of the judgment." A single, brief, arbitrary detention by an official of a state party to one of the principal international agreements might violate that agreement; arbitrary detention violates customary law if it is prolonged and practiced as state policy.

i. Systematic racial discrimination. Discrimination on account of race is prohibited by all the comprehensive international human rights instruments, and is the subject of the Convention on the Elimination of All Forms of Racial Discrimination and of the Convention on the Suppression and Punishment of the Crime of *Apartheid.* See Introductory Note to this Part. It is forbidden also by the constitutions or laws of many states. Racial discrimination is a violation of customary law when it is practiced systematically as a matter of state policy, *e.g., apartheid* in the Republic of South Africa. Occasional official practices of racial discrimination would not violate this section but such acts of discrimination would violate numerous provisions in international covenants or conventions if practiced by officials of states parties.

As to systematic discrimination on account of religion, see Comment *j;* on account of gender, see Comment *l.*

j. Systematic religious discrimination. The United Nations Charter (Articles 1, 13, 55) links religious discrimination with racial discrimination and treats them alike; to the extent that racial discrimination violates the Charter religious discrimination does also. Religious discrimination is also treated identically with racial discrimination in the principal covenants and in the constitutions and laws of many states. There is as yet no convention on the elimination of religious discrimination, and there has been no concerted attack on such discrimination comparable to that on *apartheid,* but there is a strong case that systematic discrimination on grounds of religion as a matter of state policy is also a violation of customary law. See Reporters' Note 8.

k. Right to property. The Universal Declaration of Human Rights includes the right to own and not to be arbitrarily deprived of property. See § 701, Reporters' Note 6, and § 711, Comment *d.* There is, however, wide disagreement among states as to the scope and content of that right, which weighs against the conclusion that a human right to property generally has become a principle of customary law. All states have accepted a limited core of rights to private property, and violation of such rights, as state policy, may already be a violation of customary law. Invasions of rights in private property that have not achieved the status of customary law may nonetheless violate a particular international agreement or, where the victim is a foreign national, the principles of customary law governing state responsibility to foreign nationals. See §§ 711–713.

l. Gender discrimination. The United Nations Charter (Article 1(3)) and the Universal Declaration of Human Rights (Article 2) prohibit discrimination in respect of human rights on various grounds, including sex. Discrimination on the basis of sex in respect of recognized rights is prohibited by a number of international agreements, including the Covenant on Civil and Political Rights, the Covenant on Economic, Social and Cultural Rights, and more generally by the Convention on the Elimination of All Forms of Discrimination Against Women, which, as of 1987, had been ratified by 91 states and signed by a number of others. The United States had signed the Convention but had not yet ratified it. See Introductory Note to this Part. The domestic laws of a number of states, including those of the United States, mandate equality for, or prohibit discrimination against, women generally or in various respects. Gender-based discrimination is still practiced in many states in varying degrees, but freedom from gender discrimination as state policy, in many matters, may already be a principle of customary international law. Discrimination by a state that does not constitute a violation of customary law may violate a particular international agreement if practiced by a state party.

m. Consistent pattern of gross violations of human rights. The acts enumerated in clauses (a) to (f) are violations of customary law even if the practice is not consistent, or not part of a "pattern," and those acts are inherently "gross" violations of human rights. Clause (g) includes other infringements of recognized human rights that are not violations of customary law when committed singly or sporadically (although they may be forbidden to states parties to the International Covenants or other particular agreements); they become violations of customary law if the state is guilty of a "consistent pattern of gross violations" as state policy. A violation is gross if it is particularly shocking because of the importance of the right or the gravity of the violation. All the rights proclaimed in the Universal Declaration and protected by the principal International Covenants (see § 701, Reporters' Note 6) are internationally recognized human rights, but some rights are fundamental and intrinsic to human dignity. Consistent patterns of violation of such rights as state policy may be deemed "gross" *ipso facto.* These include, for example, systematic harassment, invasions of the privacy of the home, arbitrary arrest and detention (even if not prolonged); denial of fair trial in criminal cases; grossly disproportionate punishment; denial of freedom to leave a country; denial of the right to return to one's country; mass uprooting of a country's population; denial of freedom of conscience and religion; denial of personality before the law; denial of basic privacy such as the right to marry and raise a family; and invidious racial or religious discrimination. A state party to the Covenant on Civil and Political Rights is responsible even for a single, isolated violation of any of these rights; any state is liable under customary law for a consistent pattern of violations of any such right as state policy.

n. Customary law of human rights and jus cogens. Not all human rights norms are peremptory norms (*jus cogens*), but those in clauses (a) to (f) of this section are, and an international agreement that violates them is void. See § 331(2).

o. Responsibility to all states (erga omnes). Violations of the rules stated in this section are violations of obligations to all other states and any state may invoke the ordinary remedies available to a state when its rights under customary law are violated. See § 703(2) and Comment *b* to that section, and § 902(2) and Comment *a* to that section.

REPORTERS' NOTES

1. *Customary law of human rights.* This section adopts the view that customary international law prohibits the particular human rights violations indicated, if the violations are state policy. This view is accepted by virtually all states; with the exception of the Republic of South Africa in respect of *apartheid,* no state claims the right to commit the practices set forth in this section as state policy, and few, if any, would deny that they are violations of international law. Other rights may already have become customary law and international law may develop to include additional rights. It has been argued that customary international law is already more comprehensive than here indicated and forbids violation of any of the rights set forth in the Universal Declaration. See § 701, Reporters' Note 4; McDougal, Lasswell, and Chen, Human Rights and World Public Order 273–74, 325–27 (1980); Waldock, "Human Rights in Contemporary International Law and the Significance of the European Convention," in The European Convention on Human Rights 15 (1963) (British Inst. Int'l & Comp. L., Int'l L. Ser. No. 11).

The practice of states has established the principles of this section in customary law, as indicated in the following notes. Clauses (a) through (e) (and perhaps (f)) also reflect general principles common to the major legal systems that may have been absorbed into international law. See § 102(4). The violations listed in this section are also cited as examples in United States legislation denying benefits to states guilty of "consistent patterns of gross violation of internationally recognized human rights." See Reporters' Note 10. See also address of Secretary of State Vance, 76 Dep't State Bull. 505 (1977).

That customary international law protects some human rights was suggested in the Nuremberg Charter, under which the Nazi defendants were charged, *inter alia*, with:

CRIMES AGAINST HUMANITY: namely, murder, extermination, enslavement, deportation, and other inhumane acts committed against any civilian population, before or during the war; or persecutions on political, racial or religious grounds in execution of or in connection with any crime within the jurisdiction of the Tribunal, whether or not in violation of the domestic law of the country where perpetrated.

See Charter of the International Military Tribunal, August 8, 1945, 59 Stat. 1546, 1547, 82 U.N.T.S. 279; Jackson, The Nürnberg Case (1947); see generally Taylor, Nuremberg Trials, War Crimes and International Law, International Conciliation No. 450 (1949). The principles of international law recognized in the Nuremberg Charter and Judgment were unanimously affirmed by the United Nations General Assembly in a resolution proposed by the United States. G.A. Res. 95, 1 GAOR UN Doc. A/64/Add.1, at 188 (1946).

2. *State responsibility for private violations of rights.* Under customary law, the state is responsible for the acts enumerated in this section when committed by its officials as state policy, or, when committed by private persons, if they were encouraged or condoned as state policy. By contrast, under the Covenant on Civil and Political Rights, a state is required not only to respect but also to "ensure" the rights recognized by the Covenant, suggesting an obligation to act to prevent their violation whether by officials or by private persons. See Art. 2. Article 20 expressly requires parties to the Covenant to prohibit by law war propaganda and advocacy of national, racial, or religious hatred. See § 701, Reporters' Note 8.

A violation of rights covered by this section is committed as a matter of state policy when it is required or encouraged by law, clear custom, or usage, or by some official act or statement of a responsible high official. Evidence of condonation might be found in failure to take steps to punish acts of officials that are common or notorious. See Comment *b*.

Under this section, a state is responsible for the acts of individual officials that violate the indicated human rights only if the acts were in furtherance of state policy. A different formulation asserts that a state is responsible for the acts of its officials in such human rights cases as in other cases even if the action was not state policy (see Comment *b*), but there is no violation, and therefore no responsibility, where the state provides an effective domestic remedy. The formulation adopted in this Restatement may produce a different result where the state remedy fails or is not effective for reasons of general domestic jurisprudence, rather than as the result of a state policy to cover up the human rights violation.

3. *Genocide.* The term was not coined until later, but genocide was in fact considered a "crime against humanity" in the indictments brought under the Nuremberg Charter, the principles of which were affirmed by the United Nations General Assembly in a resolution proposed by the United States. See Reporters' Note 1. In another resolution adopted at the same time, the General Assembly declared genocide an international crime. G.A. Res. 96, 1 GAOR UN Doc. A/64/ Add. 1, at 188. The Convention on the Prevention and Punishment of the Crime of Genocide was the first human rights agreement concluded under United Nations auspices. See G.A. Res. 260, 3 U.N. GAOR 810, at 174.

Draft articles on state responsibility provisionally adopted by the International Law Commission would (in Article 19) declare "a serious breach on a widespread scale of an international obligation of essential importance for safeguarding the human being, such as . . . genocide," to be an international crime. See [1980] 2 Y.B. Int'l L. Comm'n 32. Genocide is also one of the offenses subject to universal jurisdiction to prescribe and adjudicate. See §§ 404, 423.

Section 5(b) of the Act to amend the Bretton Woods Agreement Act, 92 Stat. 1052 (1978), declared "the sense of the Congress that the Government of the United States should take steps to dissociate itself from any foreign government which en-

gages in the international crime of genocide." See 22 U.S.C. § 2151 note.

4. *Slavery and slave trade.* Slavery and slave trade are forbidden by international law, both as a matter of customary law and as general principles common to major legal systems. Slavery is outlawed by the constitutions or laws of virtually all states. Building on efforts in the nineteenth century, a convention to outlaw slavery was concluded under the auspices of the League of Nations in 1926, and one on forced labor under the auspices of the International Labour Office (now the International Labour Organization) in 1930. See Introductory Note to this Part. The Universal Declaration of Human Rights declares that slavery and the slave trade shall be prohibited in all their forms. Art. 4. Slavery has been condemned and declared illegal by unanimous resolutions of the United Nations and other international bodies. As of January 1, 1987, 93 states, including the United States, were parties to the 1926 Convention, and 102 states, including the United States, were parties to the Supplementary Convention on Slavery outlawing slavery and the slave trade, which came into force in 1957. See Introductory Note to this Part. The report of the International Law Commission, Reporters' Note 3, cites slavery as example of an international crime. Slavery and slave trade are also offenses subject to universal jurisdiction to prescribe and adjudicate. See §§ 404, 423.

5. *Torture or other cruel, inhuman or degrading treatment or punishment.* Torture as well as other cruel, inhuman, or degrading treatment or punishment, when

practiced as state policy, are violations of customary international law. The prohibition on torture, at least, may also have been absorbed into international law as a general principle common to major legal systems. The prohibition is included in all comprehensive international instruments. "No one shall be subject to torture or to cruel, inhuman or degrading treatment or punishment." Universal Declaration of Human Rights, Art. 5. A similar provision is included in the International Covenant on Civil and Political Rights, Art. 7; the European Convention on Human Rights, Art. 3; the American Convention on Human Rights, Art. 5; the African Charter of Human and Peoples' Rights, Art. 5. The International Covenant adds: "In particular, no one shall be subjected without his free consent to medical or scientific experimentation." Art. 7. The Declaration on the Protection of All Persons from Being Subjected to Torture and Other Cruel, Inhuman, or Degrading Treatment or Punishment, Comment *g*, was adopted unanimously by the General Assembly. Official torture is also barred by the constitutions or laws of states generally. In the United States, torture as punishment is barred by the Eighth Amendment to the Constitution, and confessions of crime obtained by torture are excluded pursuant to the Fifth Amendment; both amendments are incorporated in and made applicable to the States by the Fourteenth Amendment. The Civil Rights Acts provide remedies for torture by State officials, and the courts might provide a remedy also against federal officials. See 18 U.S.C. §§ 242–45; 42 U.S.C. §§ 1981–83, 1985; Screws v. United States, 325 U.S.

91, 65 S.Ct. 1031, 89 L.Ed. 1495 (1945) (State official's beating of prisoner a violation of United States criminal statute); compare Carlson v. Green, 446 U.S. 14, 100 S.Ct. 1468, 64 L.Ed.2d 15 (1980) (Constitution implies civil remedy for violation of Eighth Amendment prohibition of cruel and unusual punishment).

The difference between torture and cruel, inhuman, or degrading treatment or punishment "derives principally from a difference in the intensity of the suffering inflicted." Ireland v. United Kingdom, 25 Pub. Eur.Ct.Hum.Rts., ser. A. para. 167 (1978). See also Tyrer case, 26 *id.* para. 30 (1978).

In a suit brought by an alien residing in the United States against a former official of Paraguay visiting in the United States, alleging torture of the plaintiff's brother leading to his death, the court of appeals ruled that deliberate torture perpetrated under color of official authority was a violation of customary law supporting the jurisdiction of the district courts "of a civil action by an alien for a tort only, committed in violation of the law of nations." 28 U.S.C. § 1350. Filartiga v. Pena-Irala, 630 F.2d 876 (2d Cir.1980), on remand, 577 F.Supp. 860 (D.N.Y.1984); see § 703, Reporters' Note 7. The court said: "Indeed, for purposes of civil liability, the torturer has become like the pirate and the slave trader before him *hostis humanis generis*, an enemy of all mankind." *Id.* at 890. The court found the torture to be a violation of international law even though it could not be attributed to the state. In the case of torture by an official of intermediate rank, it may sometimes be difficult to determine whether the act was state policy, but failure to prevent, punish, or disown the action would constitute condonation of the act as state policy under this section. Whether torture has become a crime subject to universal jurisdiction is uncertain. See § 404, Comment *a* and Reporters' Note 1.

Unlike the Eighth Amendment to the United States Constitution, international law might include corporal punishment of school children within the prohibition, if the particular punishment, imposed as state policy, were "cruel, inhuman or degrading"; see § 701, Reporters' Note 8. A similar standard in the European Convention was held not violated on the facts of the particular case in Campbell and Cosans v. United Kingdom, 15 Eur.Hum.Rts. Rep. 293 (1982).

6. *Prolonged arbitrary detention.* Arbitrary detention is cited as a violation of international law in all comprehensive international human rights instruments, *e.g.*, the Universal Declaration, Art. 9; the International Covenant on Civil and Political Rights; Art. 9, the European Convention, Art. 5; the American Convention, Art. 7; the African Convention, Art. 6. It is included also in United States legislation and national policy statements citing violations of fundamental human rights. See Reporters' Note 10. In Rodriguez-Fernandez v. Wilkinson, 505 F.Supp. 787 (D.Kan.1980), *affirmed*, 654 F.2d 1382 (10th Cir. 1981), the district court held that the United States may not detain indefinitely an alien excluded as ineligible for entry to the United States even if he cannot be deported because no country will receive him. The court said: "Our review of the

sources from which customary international law is derived clearly demonstrates that arbitrary detention is prohibited by customary international law. Therefore, even though the indeterminate detention of an excluded alien cannot be said to violate the United States Constitution or our statutory laws, it is judicially remediable as a violation of international law." *Id.* at 798. The court of appeals affirmed on the ground that, taking account of principles of international and Constitutional law, the relevant statute should be interpreted as not authorizing such detention in the circumstances. Compare Soroa-Gonzales v. Civiletti, 515 F.Supp. 1049, 1061 n. 18 (N.D.Ga.1981), *reversed*, 734 F.2d 576 (11th Cir.1984) (writ of habeas corpus issued to excludable alien detained indefinitely in maximum security prison on basis of United States law, but court added: "were the Court forced to decide . . . the Court would conclude that petitioner's further detention was arbitrary" within the meaning of the Universal Declaration, the Covenant on Civil and Political Rights and the American Convention on Human Rights). Compare Fernandez-Roque v. Smith, 622 F.Supp. 887 (N.D.Ga.1985), *affirmed sub nom.* Garcia-Mir v. Meese, 788 F.2d 1446 (11th Cir. 1986), *certiorari denied*, ___ U.S. ___, 107 S.Ct. 289 (1986) (prolonged detention of Cuban aliens assumed to violate international law, but courts will not enjoin violation committed under authority of Attorney General). Compare also cases that, without addressing claims under international law, upheld the indefinite detention of persons who had not been admitted for entry into the United States and were excludable under United States immigration law. See § 722, Reporters' Note 15.

Detention is arbitrary if it is unlawful or unjust. "In a democratic society subscribing to the rule of law . . . no detention that is arbitrary can ever be regarded as lawful." Winterwerp Case, 33 Pub. Eur.Ct.Hum.R., ser. A. para. 39 (1979). See Dinstein, "The Right to Life, Physical Integrity, and Liberty" in Henkin, ed., The International Bill of Rights 114, 130–35 (1981).

7. *Systematic racial discrimination.* Numerous United Nations resolutions have declared *apartheid* to be a violation of international law. The General Assembly has adopted the International Convention on the Suppression and Punishment of the Crime of *Apartheid* and, as of 1987, 86 states had adhered to it; the United States was not a party. See Introductory Note to this Part: The International Court of Justice has declared *apartheid* to be "a flagrant violation of the purposes and principles of the Charter." See the advisory opinion, Legal Consequences for States of the Continued Presence of South Africa in Namibia, [1971] I.C.J. Rep. 3, 57. *Apartheid* is listed as an example of an international crime in the draft articles provisionally approved by the International Law Commission. See Reporters' Note 3.

The International Convention on the Suppression and Punishment of the Crime of *Apartheid*, Art. II, defines *apartheid* as including "the following inhuman acts committed for the purpose of establishing and maintaining domination by one racial group of persons over any other racial group of persons and systematically oppressing them:

(a) Denial to a member or members of a racial group or groups of the right to life and liberty of the person . . . (b) Deliberate imposition on a racial group or groups of living conditions calculated to cause its or their physical destruction in whole or in part; (c) Any legislative measures and other measures calculated to prevent a racial group or groups from participation in the political, social, economic and cultural life of the country . . . (d) Any measures, including legislative measures, designed to divide the population along racial lines . . . (e) Exploitation of the labour of the members of a racial group or groups, in particular by submitting them to forced labour; (f) Persecution of organizations and persons, by depriving them of fundamental rights and freedoms, because they oppose *apartheid*.

Presumably the same definition would obtain for purposes of the prohibition of *apartheid* under this section, clause (f), and Comment *i.* The Convention also creates obligations beyond those imposed by customary international law. It attaches personal criminal responsibility to all individuals who commit, participate in, incite, abet, encourage or co-operate in the crime. Art. III. The Convention also requires states to suppress, prevent any encouragement of, and punish *apartheid.* Among parties to the Convention, *apartheid* is also effectively made a subject of universal jurisdiction. Art. IV. See § 404, Reporters' Note 1.

The United States Export-Import Bank Act of 1945, as amended, provides that the Bank shall not extend credit in support of "any export which would contribute to enabling the Government of the Republic of South Africa to maintain or enforce apartheid." Sec. 2(b)(8), 12 U.S.C. § 635(b)(9); see also other clauses in that section of the Act.

In 1986, Congress enacted the Comprehensive Anti-Apartheid Act. See § 414, Reporters' Note 10.

8. *Systematic religious discrimination.* Religion is included with race among forbidden grounds of discrimination in the principal international instruments, *e.g.,* United Nations Charter, Arts. 1(3), 13(1)(b), 55(c); the Universal Declaration, Art. 2; International Covenant on Civil and Political Rights, Arts. 2, 26; International Covenant on Economic, Social and Cultural Rights, Art. 2(2); European Convention, Art. 14; American Convention, Art. 1; African Convention, Art. 2. Fear of persecution on account of religion (as well as race) is included in the definition of a "refugee" under the Convention Relating to the Status of Refugees. See Introductory Note to this Part. In 1981, the General Assembly adopted the Declaration on the Elimination of All Forms of Intolerance and of Discrimination Based on Religion or Belief. G.A. Res. 55, 36 U.N. GAOR Supp. No. 51, at 171.

9. *Right to property.* For the view that an expropriation by a state of property of its own nationals does not violate international law, see Jafari v. Islamic Republic of Iran, 539 F.Supp. 209, 214–15 (N.D.Ill.1982). See also the *Lithgow Case* in the European Court of Human Rights, 102 Pub. Eur.Ct.Hum.Rts., ser. A (1986). In December 1986, the United Nations General Assembly adopted a resolution on "Respect for the right of everyone to own property alone as well as in association with others and its contribution to the economic and social development of Member States." U.N. Doc. A/Res./41/132 (1986).

10. *"Consistent pattern of gross violations."* This phrase derives from Res. 1503 of the United Nations Economic and Social Council, which authorized the Subcommission on Prevention of Discrimination and Protection of Minorities of the Commission on Human Rights to appoint a "working group" to consider communications "which appear to reveal a consistent pattern of gross and reliably attested violations of human rights and fundamental freedoms," even by states not parties to any relevant international agreement. Res. 1503, 48 U.N. ESCOR Supp. No. 1A at 8–9. The Subcommission has been implementing that resolution annually since that time. See the annual reports of the United Nations Commission on Human Rights to the Economic and Social Council. See also, for example, the action taken in respect of Chile, Report of the United Nations Commission on Human Rights on its 32d session, 60 U.N. ESCOR Supp. No. 3 (1976); the report dealing with Malawi, Report of the United Nations Commission on Human Rights on its 36th session, U.N. ESCOR Supp. No. 3 (1980). United Nations bodies have recommended measures against particular "consistent patterns of gross violation," notably *apartheid.* See § 703, Reporters' Note 10.

Section 116(a) of the United States Foreign Assistance Act of 1961, as amended, provides that no assistance may be provided "to the government of any country which engages in a consistent pattern of gross violations of internationally recognized human rights, including torture or cruel, inhuman, or degrading treatment or punishment, prolonged detention without charges, or other flagrant denial of the right to life, liberty, and the security of person. . . . " 22 U.S.C. § 2151n(a). The phrase, similarly defined, appears also in Section 502(B) of the Act, 22 U.S.C. § 2304 (no security assistance to such government). See also Agricultural Trade Development and Assistance Act of 1954, as amended, § 112(a), 7 U.S.C. § 1712 (precluding agreement to finance sale of agricultural commodities to such government); International Financial Institutions Act of 1977, § 703, 22 U.S.C. §§ 262d and 262(1) (United States policy to oppose assistance to such governments by international financial institutions except where the program serves "the basic human needs" of the citizens of such country). See also the restrictions on trade with Uganda, 22 U.S.C. § 2151 note (1979), and 50 U.S.C.App. § 2403m, repealed, 93 Stat. 415 (1979); and the restrictions on aid to Chile, 22 U.S.C. § 2370 note. Compare the "Jackson-Vanik Amendment" to the Trade Act of 1974, barring "most favored nation treatment" and participation in United States credit or investment guarantee programs to communist countries that deny their citizens the right to emigrate. 19 U.S.C. § 2432. The President has been given authority to waive that restriction and has done so in some cases. 19 U.S.C. § 2432 note.

"Consistent pattern of gross violations" generally refers to violations of those rights that are universally accepted and that no government would admit to violating as state policy. They are generally civil and political rights such as those enumerated in Comment *m* or in the United States legislation quoted in this note. It would be difficult to claim a gross violation of a right whose definition and application are disputed. States differ, for example, as to whether a single party state provides "genuine elections" (Universal Declaration, Art. 21(3)) and affords every citizen the right "to vote and to be elected at genuine periodic elections which shall be by universal and equal suffrage and shall be held by secret ballot, guaranteeing the free expression of the will of the electors." (International Covenant on Civil and Political Rights, Art. 25(b)). Since the Covenant on Economic, Social and Cultural Rights requires states "to take steps," "to the maximum of available resources," with a view to achieving the full realization of the enumerated rights "progressively," it would be difficult to find a consistent pattern of gross violations of those rights. But there might be such a violation if a state, as a matter of policy, purposefully starved or denied other basic human needs to some or all of its people.

11. *Human rights law and* jus cogens. Not all human rights norms are *jus cogens*, but those in clauses (a) to (f) have that quality. It has been suggested that a human rights norm cannot be deemed *jus cogens* if it is subject to derogation in time of public emergency; see, for example, Art. 4 of the Covenant on Civil and Political Rights, § 701, Reporters' Note 6. Nonderogability in emergency and *jus cogens* are different principles, responding to different concerns, and they are not necessarily congruent. In any

event, the rights recognized in clauses (a) to (f) of this section are not subject to derogation in emergency under the Covenant. Article 4 of the Covenant explicitly excludes from derogation the right to life and freedom from slavery and from torture, as well as from racial discrimination. Freedom from arbitrary detention is not included among the nonderogable provisions, but since derogation is permitted only "in time of public emergency which threatens the life of the nation," and only "to the extent strictly required by the exigencies of the situation," detentions that meet those standards presumably would not be arbitrary. See, generally, McDougal, Lasswell and Chen, Human Rights and World Public Order 338–50 (1980).

12. *State responsibility and individual responsibility.* Though it has not yet been authoritatively determined, violation by a state of customary law of human rights, at least of the violations specified in clauses (a) to (f), may permit prosecution of individual officials responsible for such acts under the laws of any state, as an exercise of universal jurisdiction. See § 404 and Reporters' Note 1.

13. *Previous Restatement.* The customary law of human rights has developed largely since the previous Restatement. However, that Restatement set forth as customary law an international standard of justice that a state must respect in its treatment of foreign nationals. See §§ 164–67, 178–80, 184–85, 197.

§ 703. Remedies for Violation of Human Rights Obligations

(1) A state party to an international human rights agreement has, as against any other state party violating the agreement, the remedies generally available for violation of an international agreement, as well as any special remedies provided by the agreement.

(2) Any state may pursue international remedies against any other state for a violation of the customary international law of human rights (§ 702).

(3) An individual victim of a violation of a human rights agreement may pursue any remedy provided by that agreement or by other applicable international agreements.

Comment:

a. *Remedies for violation of international human rights obligations.* Under international law, a breach of an international obligation, whether deriving from customary law or from international agreement, gives rise to international remedies against the violating state. These remedies include the right to make an international claim; to resort to the International Court of Justice or other international tribunal to whose jurisdiction the complaining and responding states have submitted; and in some circumstances to some measures of self-help. See §§ 901–905. For this purpose, human rights agreements are no different from other international agreements. Unless the human rights agreement provides or clearly implies otherwise, the ordinary remedies are available to any state party against a state party violating the agreement, even if the violation did not affect nationals of the claimant state or any other particular interest of that state. Whether a state may intercede to provide diplomatic protection to an individual who is not its national, see Comment *b* and Reporters' Notes 2 and 4.

Some international human rights agreements provide for special "implementing machinery," for example complaint before an international human rights committee. See Reporters' Note 2. Unless the agreement provides or clearly implies the contrary, such special remedies generally supplement rather than replace the traditional remedies between states.

b. Remedies for violation of customary law of human rights. Since the obligations of the customary law of human rights are *erga omnes* (obligations to all states), § 702, Comment *o*, any state may pursue remedies for their violation, even if the individual victims were not nationals of the complaining state and the violation did not affect any other particular interest of that state. For the remedies available to individual victims against the state or state officials, see Comment *c*.

For remedies against individuals charged with commission of universal crimes, including some that would constitute violations under this section if the state were responsible for them, see § 404.

c. Remedies of individual victims. In general, individuals do not have direct international remedies against a state violating their human rights except where such remedies are provided by international agreement. See § 906. Whether they have a remedy under the law of a state depends on that state's law. See Reporters' Note 7. International human rights agreements generally require a state party to provide such remedies. See, *e.g.*, International Covenant on Civil and Political Rights, Article 2(3). Failure to provide such remedies would constitute an additional violation of the agreement. Lack of an effective remedy under state law for violation of the customary law of human rights might itself be evidence that a violation of rights is state policy, "systematic," or part of a "consistent pattern of gross violations" for purposes of § 702.

d. Exhaustion of domestic remedies. A state may pursue formal, bilateral remedies under Subsections (1) and (2) only after the individual claiming to be a victim of a human rights violation has exhausted available remedies under the domestic law of the accused state. Compare § 713, Comment *b*, as regards remedies for injury to a state's nationals by another state; see § 902, Comment *i*. International agreements providing remedies to individuals, Subsection (3) and Comment *c*, also generally require that the individual first exhaust domestic remedies. That requirement is met if it is shown that none is available or that it would be futile to pursue them. The individual's failure to exhaust remedies is not an obstacle to informal intercession by a state on behalf of an individual, to unilateral "sanctions" by a state against another for human rights violations, or to multilateral measures against violators by United Nations bodies or international financial institutions. See Comments *f* and *g* and Reporters' Note 10, and § 702, Reporters' Note 10.

e. Humanitarian intervention to rescue victims or suppress human rights violations. It is increasingly accepted that a state may take steps to rescue victims or potential victims in an action strictly limited to that purpose and not likely to involve disproportionate destruction of life or property in the state where the rescue takes place. Whether a state may intervene with military force in the territory of another state without its consent, not to rescue the victims but to prevent or terminate human rights violations, is not agreed or authoritatively determined. Such intervention might be acceptable if taken pursuant to resolution of a United Nations body or of a regional organization such as the Organization of American States. See § 905.

f. State sanctions for human rights violations by another state. A state may criticize another state for failure to abide by recognized international human rights standards, and may shape its trade, aid or other national policies so as to dissociate itself from the violating state or to influence that state to discontinue the violations.

g. Consideration by United Nations bodies. Remedies for violation of human rights include possible consideration by international bodies acting within their jurisdiction, notably the United Nations General Assembly, the Economic and Social Council, the Commission on Human Rights, and even the Security Council when "the continuance of . . . the situation is likely to endanger the maintenance of international peace and security." See United Nations Charter, Articles 34, 36. A charge that a state had violated human rights may be brought to such bodies by any member of the United Nations in accordance with the rules and procedures of the Organization.

REPORTERS' NOTES

1. *Rights of parties under international agreements.* In the South West Africa cases, [1966] I.C.J. Rep. 4, Ethiopia and Liberia, two states that had been members of the League of Nations, brought suit in the International Court of Justice against the Republic of South Africa, the mandatory power under the League's mandate for South West Africa, alleging violation of certain rights of the inhabitants of the mandated territory. The Court dismissed the suit, the majority of the Court holding that the mandate did not intend to create enforceable obligations to other members of the League. It was implied, however, that if such an agreement had intended to create rights in another state, the latter would have a remedy for a violation, including suit in the International Court of Justice if both states had accepted the Court's jurisdiction. The dissenting judges took the view that the complaining states, as members of the League, were parties to the mandate and could bring a proceeding in the International Court for infringement of the mandate by violations of the rights of the inhabitants.

2. *Special interstate remedies for human rights violations.* The right of one state party to call another to account before a special body is provided by the Convention on the Elimination of All Forms of Racial Discrimination, Art. 11. In the International Covenant on Civil and Political Rights, Art. 41, and the American Convention, Art. 45, submitting to such a remedy is optional, applying only to states that declare their willingness to submit to such complaints, on a reciprocal basis. The only "enforcement machinery" to which all parties are subject under the International Covenant requires parties to report on their compliance to the Human Rights Committee, Art. 40.

Whether the remedies expressly provided in an agreement supplement or replace general remedies is a matter of interpretation. The presumption should be that unless otherwise indicated the usual remedies remain available. *Compare* Henkin, "International Human Rights and 'Domestic Jurisdiction,'" *with* Frowein, "The Interrelationship between the Helsinki Final Act, the International Covenants on Human Rights, and the European Convention on Human Rights," in Buergenthal, ed., Human Rights, International Law and the Helsinki Accord 21, 71 (1977). Article 62 of the European Convention on Human Rights, Introductory Note to this Part, declares that the remedies there provided are exclusive of other arrangements for dispute settlement between the parties.

In the Case Concerning the Barcelona Traction, Light and Power Company (Belgium v. Spain), the International Court of Justice said that "on the universal level, the instruments which embody human rights do not confer on States the capacity to protect the victims of infringements of such rights irrespective of their nationality." [1970] I.C.J. Rep. 4, 47. See also Reporters' Note 3. Apparently, the Court meant that, as a matter of interpretation, general human rights agreements ordinarily do not contemplate diplomatic protection by one state party on behalf of an individual victim of a violation by another state party, at least where the victim was not a national of the protecting state. However, unless otherwise provided or clearly implied, there appears to be no reason why a party may not make an interstate claim for a violation of such an agreement as for any other multilateral agreement. See § 902. Special "machinery" provided in these agreements ordinarily should be interpreted as affording supplementary "remedies."

A state's claim under Subsection (1) or (2) for violation of an individual's human rights is subject to the rules governing interstate claims generally, see § 902, and § 713, but claims under Subsection (2), being *erga omnes*, cannot be waived or settled by any one state, and in principle a claim for a violation of the human rights of an individual cannot be waived or settled by a state without the consent of the individual. But compare the practice of lump-sum settlement agreements to resolve the claims of nationals. See § 902, Comment *i* and Reporters' Note 8. The Rules of the European Court on Human Rights provide for consultation with the individual applicant before accepting a discontinuance or a friendly settlement of a human rights complaint. See Rules of the European Court of Human Rights, Rule 48, [1982] Y.B.Eur. Conv.Hum.Rts., ch. III, at 5, 20–21.

3. *Remedies for violation of customary law of human rights.* Ordinarily, violations of customary law entail remedies for the state that is the victim of the violation. The customary law of human rights, however, protects individuals subject to each state's jurisdiction,

and the international obligation runs equally to all other states, with no state a victim of the violation more than any other. Any state, therefore, may make a claim against the violating state. Where the complaining and the accused states have agreed to means for settling disputes between them generally—for example, by accepting the jurisdiction of the International Court of Justice or submitting to arbitration—such means are available for alleged violations of this section.

In the *Barcelona Traction* case, Reporters' Note 2, at 32, the International Court of Justice said:

In particular, an essential distinction should be drawn between the obligations of a State towards the international community as a whole, and those arising vis-à-vis another State in the field of diplomatic protection. By their very nature the former are the concern of all States. In view of the importance of the rights involved, all States can be held to have a legal interest in their protection; they are obligations *erga omnes*.

Such obligations derive, for example, in contemporary international law, from the outlawing of acts of aggression, and of genocide, as also from the principles and rules concerning the basic rights of the human person, including protection from slavery and racial discrimination. Some of the corresponding rights of protection have entered into the body of general international law . . . ; others are conferred by international instruments of a universal or quasi-universal character.

Obligations the performance of which is the subject of diplomatic protection are not of the same category. It cannot be held, when one such obligation in particular is in question, in a specific case, that all States have a legal interest in its observance.

The Court seemed to distinguish diplomatic protection in general, including protection for ordinary violations of human rights, which is available only for nationals of the complaining state (see Reporters' Note 2), from protection against violations of the "basic rights of the human person" set forth in this section, as to which "all States can be held to have a legal interest in their protection."

4. *Remedies regardless of nationality of individual victim.* Remedies available to states parties under international human rights agreements (Subsection (1)), and remedies available to all states for violation by any state of the customary law of human rights (Subsection (2)), do not depend on the nationality of the individual victim. But see Reporters' Note 2, distinguishing between interstate claims and diplomatic protection under international human rights agreements. In practice, states are more likely to intercede on behalf of individuals who are their own nationals or with whom they have other links. But see the South West Africa cases, Reporters' Note 1.

5. *Remedies of individual victims.* The principal international human rights agreements have optional provisions for individual complaints. Under the Optional Protocol to the International Covenant on Civil and Political Rights, the Human Rights Committee may re-ceive and consider private "communications" alleging violation of rights under the Covenant. See also Art. 14 of the Convention on the Elimination of All Forms of Racial Discrimination; European Convention, Art. 25. In the American Convention, the provision for private complaints is not optional; under Article 44, any person, group of persons, or nongovernmental entity may lodge complaints with the Inter-American Commission on Human Rights alleging violation by any state party. The African Convention also provides for communications "other than those of States" which the African Commission may decide to consider. Arts. 55–59. See also the procedure for considering individual complaints of a "consistent pattern of gross violations" by a working group of the Subcommission on Prevention of Discrimination and Protection of Minorities of the United Nations Commission on Human Rights, pursuant to Res. 1503 of the U.N. Economic and Social Council, § 702, Reporters' Note 10.

For discussion of the legal character of the rights of the individual under international human rights law, see Henkin, "International Human Rights as 'Rights,'" 1 Cardozo L.Rev. 425, 438 (1979).

6. *Exhaustion of domestic remedies.* Exhaustion of remedies is expressly made a precondition for consideration of an interstate complaint under the International Covenant on Civil and Political Rights, Art. 41(c), and the Convention on the Elimination of All Forms of Racial Discrimination, Art. 11. It is a precondition for consideration of private complaints under the Optional Protocol to the Covenant (Art.

5) and Art. 14(7) of the Racial Discrimination Convention. See also the American Convention, Art. 46(a); the European Convention, Art. 26; the African Convention, Arts. 50, 56(b). *Cf.* Parratt v. Taylor, 451 U.S. 527, 101 S.Ct. 1908, 68 L.Ed.2d 420 (1981) (no civil rights action for deprivation of property by State officials where complainant did not avail himself of State remedy). See § 713, Comment *f* and Reporters' Note 5.

7. *Individual remedies under United States law.* Since 1790, the United States district courts have had jurisdiction "of a civil action by an alien for a tort only, committed in violation of the law of nations." 28 U.S.C. § 1350. In Filartiga v. Pena-Irala, 630 F.2d 876 (2d Cir. 1980), the court of appeals held that under that statute the district court had jurisdiction of a suit in tort by an alien against a Paraguayan official alleged to have tortured the plaintiff's brother to death, since such torture was a violation of the law of nations. See § 702, Reporters' Note 5. On remand, the district court awarded punitive as well as actual damages, 577 F.Supp. 860 (E.D.N.Y.1984). But *cf.* Tel-Oren v. Libyan Arab Republic, 517 F.Supp. 542 (D.D.C.1981), *affirmed,* 726 F.2d 774 (D.C.Cir.1984), *certiorari denied,* 470 U.S. 1003, 105 S.Ct. 1354, 84 L.Ed.2d 377 (1985), dismissing a suit by victims of a terrorist attack on an Israeli bus, the district court ruling, *inter alia,* that § 1350 does not support jurisdiction unless international law or a treaty of the United States clearly contemplated an individual remedy for the violation. See also Rodriguez-Fernandez v. Wilkinson, 505 F.Supp. 787 (D.Kan.1980), *affirmed,* 654 F.2d 1382 (10th Cir.1981), § 702, Re-

porters' Note 6, which held that prolonged and arbitrary detention was "judicially remediable as a violation of international law," and a detained alien could seek a writ of habeas corpus for his release. (The court of appeals affirmed on the ground that detention in the circumstances was not authorized by Congress.) And see Fernandez-Roque v. Smith, § 702, Reporters' Note 6, which assumed the right of an individual to object to detention as a violation of international law but refused to enjoin a violation of international law committed under the authority of the Attorney General. See generally Henkin, "The Constitution and United States Sovereignty: A Century of *Chinese Exclusion* and Its Progeny," 100 Harv.L. Rev. 853, 883–85 (1987). Violations of international law were also asserted in cases involving detention of Cubans or Haitians not lawfully admitted to the United States, but the cases were decided under United States domestic law. See, *e.g.,* Jean v. Nelson, 727 F.2d 957 (11th Cir.1984) (en banc), *affirmed on other grounds,* 472 U.S. 846, 105 S.Ct. 2992, 86 L.Ed.2d 664 (1985); Soroa-Gonzales v. Civiletti, 515 F.Supp. 1049, 1054 n. 2 (N.D.Ga. 1981), *reversed,* 734 F.2d 576 (11th Cir.1984).

8. *Humanitarian intervention.* Since 1945, the law as to humanitarian intervention has turned largely on the interpretation of Article 2(4) of the United Nations Charter and its effect on prior customary law. Article 2(4) obligates member states "to refrain in their international relations from the threat or use of force against the territorial integrity or political independence of any state, or in any other manner inconsistent with the Purposes of the

United Nations." Missions strictly for rescue, such as that by Belgium and the United States in Stanleyville, the Congo, in 1965, or by Israel at Entebbe, Uganda, in 1976, were commonly thought not to violate Article 2(4), either because they did not involve the "use of force," or were not against "the territorial integrity or political independence" of the target state, within the meaning of Article 2(4). It is far more difficult to justify an implied exception to Article 2(4) that would permit a use of force otherwise contrary to that Article on the ground that the purpose is to suppress or prevent violations of human rights. See Brownlie, International Law and the Use of Force by States 301 (1963); Lillich, ed., Humanitarian Intervention and the United Nations (1973); Lillich, "Humanitarian Intervention: A Reply to Dr. Brownlie and a Plea for Constructive Alternatives," in Moore, ed., Law and Civil War in the Modern World 229 (1974). Of course, if the violation of human rights were itself accomplished or accompanied by a use of armed force in violation of Article 2(4), the Charter would permit the use of force in individual or collective self defense under Article 51, or pursuant to appropriate United Nations authorization. See § 905(2) and Comment *g* to that section.

9. *State criticism and sanctions for violations by other states.* Although states occasionally reject charges that they are violating human rights as interference in their internal affairs, such charges are not unlawful intervention or other improper interference under international law. Virtually every state has criticized some other state for its human rights practices, both directly and by statement or vote in international bodies. See, *e.g.*, the numerous resolutions condemning *apartheid* in South Africa, approved by virtually all the members of the United Nations, *e.g.*, G.A. Res. 1761, 17 U.N. GAOR Supp. No. 17, at 9; see also Henkin, "International Human Rights and 'Domestic Jurisdiction,'" Reporters' Note 2.

United States legislation requires the Department of State to publish annual reports on the condition of human rights in all countries, and provides for denial of assistance, loans, or trade benefits to countries guilty of a "consistent pattern of gross violations" of human rights. See § 702, Reporters' Note 10.

10. *Consideration by United Nations bodies.* Increasingly, the United Nations Commission on Human Rights has been considering complaints of human rights violations by particular states. The reports of the Commission are considered, and sometimes acted on, by its parent body, the Economic and Social Council. Occasionally, violations of human rights have been considered by the United Nations General Assembly, *e.g.*, the refusal of the U.S.S.R. to permit Russian wives of foreign nationals to leave the country (G.A. Res. 285, 3 GAOR, U.N.Doc. A/900, at 34; see also 3 U.N. GAOR, U.N.Doc. A/560 (1948). Violations of human rights by the Republic of South Africa, whether in Namibia (South West Africa) or in the territory of the Republic, have been on the agenda of the General Assembly at almost every session. The Security Council declared that South African violations disturbed international peace and security and called for an arms embargo against that country. See

S.C.Res. 181, 18 U.N. SCOR Resolutions and Decisions (S/INF/18/Rev. 1) at 7 (1963); S.C.Res. 282, 25 *id.* (S/INF/25) at 12 (1970); S.C.Res. 418, 32 *id.* (S/INF/33) at 5 (1977) (first Security Council action under Chapter VII of the United Nations Charter, upon finding that South African policies were "fraught with danger to international peace and security"). The United States voted for the 1963 and 1977 resolutions and abstained in 1970. The General Assembly has repeatedly called on the Security Council to impose mandatory economic sanctions against South Africa, see, *e.g.,* G.A. Res. 183, 33 U.N. GAOR Supp. No. 45, at 27–34; as of 1987, the Security Council has not done so.

Chapter Two

INJURY TO NATIONALS OF OTHER STATES

§ 711. State Responsibility for Injury to Nationals of Other States

A state is responsible under international law for injury to a national of another state caused by an official act or omission that violates

(a) a human right that, under § 701, a state is obligated to respect for all persons subject to its authority;

(b) a personal right that, under international law, a state is obligated to respect for individuals of foreign nationality; or

(c) a right to property or another economic interest that, under international law, a state is obligated to respect for persons, natural or juridical, of foreign nationality, as provided in § 712.

Comment:

a. Human rights, "denial of justice," and injury. This chapter deals with a state's responsibility for injury to nationals of other states. See Introductory Note to this Part. Any injury to an alien for which a state is responsible under this chapter has sometimes been characterized as a "denial of justice." More commonly the phrase "denial of justice" is used narrowly, to refer only to injury consisting of, or resulting from, denial of access to courts, or denial of procedural fairness and due process in relation to judicial proceedings, whether criminal or civil. As regards natural persons, most injuries that in the past would have been characterized as "denials of justice" are now subsumed as human rights violations under clause (a). Clauses (b) and (c) include injuries that are not commonly recognized as violations of human rights but for which a state is nonetheless responsible under international law when the victim is a foreign national. See Comment *e* and § 712.

As used in this chapter, "injury" means any loss, detriment, or damage to liberty, property, or other interest, of the kind that is generally protected by law under the major legal systems of the world. It includes loss, detriment, or damage resulting from violation of customary law or of an international agreement protecting rights or interests of the individual.

This chapter does not address claims based on the fact that a state exceeded its jurisdiction to prescribe, adjudicate, or enforce in relation to nationals of another state. See Part IV. However, under this section, a state may claim that a particular excess of jurisdiction caused injury to its national, for example, by violating the principle against foreign government compulsion (§ 441), by seizing a national's vessel on the high seas (§ 522), or by denying him elements of fair procedure in enforcement (§§ 431–32).

A state's responsibility under this section is for official acts or omissions, ordinarily not for those of private individuals. The principles governing state responsibility for the acts of its officials and others are set forth in § 207. Remedies for a state's failure to meet its responsibilities generally are considered in § 902. For the requirement of proximate causation, see § 207, Comment *e* and Reporters' Note 6. As to state responsibility for human rights violations, see § 702, Comment *b* and Reporters' Note 1.

This chapter sets forth general principles of international law governing state responsibility of one state to another, not rights or obligations a state may have under particular international agreements. For rights and remedies that a foreign national may have under an international agreement between states, or under the domestic law of one or more states, see § 712, Comments *a* and *h*, § 713, and § 906.

  b. International human rights as minimum standard. Under international law, a state is responsible for injury to foreign nationals resulting from violations of their internationally recognized human rights, as well as for injury resulting from violation of other interests for which international law provides special protections to foreign nationals. Under clause (a), the state is responsible for injury due to violation of those rights which the state is obligated to respect for all persons subject to its authority, whether pursuant to international human rights agreements to which it is party or under the customary law of human rights (§ 702); aliens enjoy these rights equally with the state's own nationals. Clause (b) declares that, in respect of foreign nationals, a state is responsi-

185

ble also for injury due to violation of those internationally recognized human rights that may not fall under § 702 and would not be protected by international law as regards the state's own nationals in the absence of international agreement. Under clause (c), a state is responsible for injury to property and other economic interests of foreign nationals that may not be recognized as human rights, and that are protected for foreign juridical persons as well as for foreign individuals. See § 712. A foreign national may also enjoy other rights under special treaties, such as those of the European Economic Community; under the Convention or the Protocol relating to the Status of Refugees (see Reporters' Note 7); under a treaty of friendship, commerce, and navigation between the state of his nationality and the state in which he resides or is present; or under the domestic law of the state of his residence or of another state.

  c. *Obligation to respect human rights of foreign nationals as customary law.* A state's responsibility to individuals of foreign nationality under customary law includes the obligation to respect the civil and political rights articulated in the principal international human rights instruments—the Universal Declaration and the International Covenant on Civil and Political Rights—as rights of human beings generally (see Introductory Note to this Part), but not political rights that are recognized as human rights only in relation to a person's country of citizenship, such as the right to vote and hold office, or the right to return to one's country (Universal Declaration, Articles 13(2), 21; Covenant on Civil and Political Rights, Articles 12(4), 25)). See § 701, Reporters' Note 6. Thus, a state party to the Covenant on Civil and Political Rights is responsible for any violation of any of its provisions in relation to any human being subject to its jurisdiction, regardless of the individual's nationality; but every state, whether or not a party to the Covenant, is responsible for denying to nationals of another state any right specified in the Covenant that is guaranteed by rules of customary law relating to the protection of foreign nationals. Customary law also holds a state responsible for a "consistent pattern of gross violations" of human rights of any persons subject to its jurisdiction. § 702(g). As regards foreign nationals, however, a state is responsible even for a single violation of many of the civil and political rights proclaimed in the Universal Declaration (other than those applicable only to citizens), even if it is not "gross." See § 702, Comment *m.*

  The Universal Declaration proclaims also certain economic, social, and cultural rights, later developed in the Covenant on Economic, Social and Cultural Rights. See Introductory Note to this Part, and § 701, Reporters' Note 6. The traditional responsibility of states under customary law does not include the obligation to extend such rights to foreign nationals. See Reporters' Note 2. Customary law, however, requires that foreign nationals be accorded the equal protection of the laws and forbids unreasonable distinctions between aliens and nationals. Distinctions between aliens and nationals in regard to some economic, social or cultural rights may not be unreasonable. See Comments *f* and *g* and Reporters' Note 3.

This chapter generally deals with the rights of aliens admitted for residence. International law also recognizes many rights for aliens admitted temporarily or for special purposes, *e.g.*, migrant or guest workers, and some rights even for aliens unlawfully in the country. See Comment *i* and Reporters' Note 3.

d. Right to property as human right. Article 17 of the Universal Declaration of Human Rights declares:

> 1. Everyone has the right to own property alone as well as in association with others.

> 2. No one shall be arbitrarily deprived of his property.

There is lack of agreement on the scope of this right and permissible limitations on it, but the right of an individual to own some property and not to be deprived of it arbitrarily is recognized as a human right. See § 702, Comment *k*. Under this section, clause (a), therefore, a state is responsible for violation of that right with respect to an individual who is a national of a foreign state. Customary international law accords additional protection to the property and other economic interests of foreign nationals, as provided in clause (c) and in § 712. For limitations on the right of aliens to acquire property or bring it into the state, see § 712, Comment *i*, and § 722, Comment *g*.

e. Other injury to individuals of foreign nationality. A state is responsible under clause (b) for injury to some interests of individuals of foreign nationality that have not been recognized as human rights under the Universal Declaration of Human Rights or the principal covenants and conventions, or whose recognition as human rights is uncertain. For instance, a state is responsible for injury resulting to a foreign national or his property from the state's failure to provide reasonable police protection. A state does not guarantee the safety of an alien or of alien property, but it is responsible for injury when police protection falls below a minimum standard of reasonableness. What constitutes reasonable police protection depends on all the circumstances, including the state's available resources; ordinarily, the standard of police protection for foreign nationals is unreasonable if it is less than is provided generally for the state's nationals. The state is responsible *a fortiori* for injuries resulting from private violence encouraged by government officials. A state is not responsible if a foreign national was warned not to court special danger in circumstances in which the authorities could not assure the person's safety and he assumed the risk.

A state is also responsible if it fails to provide to an alien remedies for injury to person or property, whether inflicted by the state or by private persons in circumstances in which a remedy would be provided by the major legal systems of the world. That such remedy might not be available because under domestic law the state or an official is immune from suit does not diminish the state's responsibility under international law.

Clause (b) refers to individuals but the interests of a juridical person of foreign nationality also enjoy some protection, for instance, against denials of procedural justice; for a juridical person, such violations would normally result in economic injury and fall within clause (c) and § 712.

f. Discrimination between nationals and aliens. Internationally recognized human rights generally apply to aliens as to nationals. Comment *b.* Discrimination against aliens in matters that are not themselves human rights may nonetheless constitute a denial to the individual of the equal protection of the laws. Equal protection does not, however, preclude reasonable classifications and distinctions, and some distinctions between nationals and aliens are permissible. See § 712, Comment *i*; compare § 722. Whether and to what extent a state may treat nationals better than aliens in respect of economic and social rights is uncertain. See Comment *b.* Compare § 722, Reporters' Note 6.

g. Discrimination among aliens of different nationalities. The human rights of foreign nationals which a state is obligated to respect, clause (a), includes a right to the equal protection of the laws. Therefore, a state may not discriminate among aliens even in matters not related to their human rights when the distinction has no reasonable basis. Comment *f.* This section does not preclude a state from conferring special advantages on aliens of a particular nationality pursuant to treaty or domestic legislation, usually on conditions of reciprocity. See Comment *b.* Even where international law permits retaliation for violation by a state of its international obligations, see § 905, Comment *f,* a state may not retaliate against another state by violating the human rights of the latter's nationals, or by injuring them in other respects forbidden under clauses (b) and (c) of this section. See also § 712, Comment *f.*

Aliens admitted for limited times and special purposes—for example, migrant labor or guest workers—may be subjected to special regimes but may not be denied basic human rights. See Reporters' Note 3; compare § 722, Comment *j*.

h. Enemy aliens during war or other emergency. Under international law prior to 1945, enemy aliens in time of war could be expelled, interned, or otherwise restricted, and their property frozen or confiscated. The provisions of the United Nations Charter prohibiting the use of force (see § 905, Comment *g*) were apparently intended also to outlaw "war," thereby creating uncertainty as to whether there can now be a legal state of war under international law, and consequently raising questions as to the concept and status of "enemy alien." Compare § 336, Comment *d*, as to the effect of hostilities on international agreements.

Under contemporary international law, even a state engaged in lawful hostilities in self-defense pursuant to Article 51 of the United Nations Charter may not abridge certain rights of nationals of other states, even those of the aggressor state. The Covenant on Civil and Political Rights (Article 4) permits a state to take measures derogating from its obligations under the Covenant "in time of public emergency which threatens the life of the nation," but "only to the extent strictly required by the exigencies of the situation." Such measures must not be inconsistent with the state's other obligations under international law, and must not involve "discrimination solely on the ground of race, colour, sex, language, religion or social origin." No derogation is permitted from the articles protecting the right to life, freedom from torture and mistreatment, from slavery, and from the application of *ex post facto* law, or the provisions safeguarding the right to recognition as a person before the law, or freedom of conscience and religion. "To the extent strictly required by the exigencies of the situation," however, a state could lawfully seize or regulate property and detain or regulate the activities of persons, whether nationals or aliens. The derogations permissible in emergency under the Covenant are presumably permissible also under this section in relation to nationals of other states as a matter of customary law.

i. Different categories of aliens. The responsibility of a state under this section applies fully to foreign nationals admitted for residence in its territory. Persons admitted for temporary sojourn and limited purposes, *e.g.*, tourists, are also entitled to the protections of this section generally, but do not enjoy those rights commonly linked to residence, for example, the freedom to choose one's place of residence in a country or the right to work. Aliens admitted under special regimes, such as migrant or guest workers, generally may not claim rights to residence or work beyond the terms of that admission. Some additional distinctions between resident aliens and others may also not be unreasonable and therefore not a denial of the equal protection of the laws. See Comments *c* and *g*. All aliens, even those unlawfully in the country, are entitled to the basic civil rights such as the right to life, freedom from slavery and from torture or arbitrary prolonged detention, and the right to fair trial. A person unlawfully in a country, however, is subject to the penalties provided by law for illegal entry or sojourn. See Reporters' Note 3. Compare the rights of such aliens under United States law, § 722, and Comment *k* thereto.

REPORTERS' NOTES

1. *Injury to aliens and human rights standards.* In the early decades of the 20th century, there was substantial agreement among the countries of Europe and North America on basic rules as to the protection to be afforded to foreign nationals. The countries of Latin America, most of which were recipients of foreign persons and capital, rejected these rules. See § 712, Reporters' Note 1. After the Second World War, with the emergence of many new importing states, and with the development of the law of human rights, opposition to special protection for aliens increased. It is generally accepted that states may invoke recognized international human rights standards on behalf of their nationals; attempts to invoke protections going beyond international human rights standards, as in clauses (b) and (c) of this section, might be resisted by some states.

2. *Rights of foreign nationals recognized under customary law.* Before the development of the contemporary law of human rights, states were held responsible for injury to aliens consisting of, or resulting from, various acts or omissions deemed to violate an international standard of justice or other standards accepted in customary international law. See generally Roth, The Minimum Standard of International Law Applied to Aliens (1949); Freeman, The International Responsibility of States for Denial of Justice (1938) (cited here as "Freeman"). The law of responsibility for such injuries was largely developed by claims practice, by negotiation and agreement concerning liability and compensation, and by decisions of arbitral tribunals and claims commissions established pursuant to international agreement, notably, for the United States, the General Claims Convention of 1923 between the United States and Mexico, 43 Stat. 1730, 9 Bevans 935. (The opinions of the Commissioners under that Convention are cited here as "G.C.C."). See, *e.g.*, Sohn and Buergenthal, International Protection of Human Rights, Chapters 1 and 2 (1973). Claims that have been made by or against the United States since the 19th century are summarized in 6 Moore, Digest of International Law 651–883 (1906) (cited here as "Moore, Digest") and in Moore, History and Digest of International Arbitrations (1898) (cited here as "Moore, Arbitrations"); 5 Hackworth, Digest of International

Law 526–657 (1943) (cited here as "Hackworth"); 2 Hyde, International Law Chiefly as Interpreted and Applied by the United States 909–52 (2d ed. 1945); 8 Whiteman, Digest of International Law 697–906 (1967) (cited here as "Whiteman, Digest"); and in corresponding sections of the annual Digest of U.S. Practice in International Law. See also Whiteman, Damages in International Law (1937–43).

This body of state practice and decision may be summarized as follows:

A. States have been held responsible for injury due to various actions that have since been accepted as violations of human rights in the Universal Declaration on Human Rights or the Covenant on Civil and Political Rights:

—*Denials of due process in criminal proceedings:*

—arbitrary arrest (*Levin*, Nielsen, Opinions and Reports 688) (1937)

—unlawful or prolonged detention or interrogation (*Roberts*, G.C.C. 100) (1927); (*Dyches*, G.C.C. 193) (1929)

—prolonged arbitrary imprisonment (*Turner*, G.C.C. 416) (1927)

—excessive bail (*Jones*, 4 Moore, Arbitrations 3253) (1880)

—delayed trial (*Chattin*, G.C.C. 422) (1927)

—unfair trial (*Cotesworth and Powell*, 2 Moore, Arbitrations 2050) (1875)

—being tried twice for the same offense (*Coles and Croswell*, 78 Brit. & For. State Papers 1301) (1885)

—failure to render a decision (*Fabiani* (France v. Venezuela), 5 Moore, Arbitrations 4877) (1896)

—tribunal manipulated by the executive (*Idler v. Venezuela*, 4 Moore, Arbitrations 3491) (1886)

—denial of right to defend oneself and confront witnesses (*Havana Packet* (1881), in LaFontaine, Pasicrisie Internationale, 1794–1900 (Histoire Documentaire des Arbitrages Internationaux) 240) (1902) (cited here as "La Fontaine")

—conviction without diligent and competent counsel (*White*, LaFontaine, 46) (1863); (*Parrish*, G.C.C. 473) (1927)

—denial of an interpreter (*Bell and Sterling*, 66 Brit. & For. State Papers 315) (1874)

—denial to accused of communication with representatives of his government (*Farrell*, G.C.C. 157) (1931)

—*Arbitrary use of force by officials:*

—arbitrary or excessive use of force by state officials (*Trumbull*, 4 Moore, Arbitrations 3255) (1892)

—inhuman treatment (*Gahagan*, 4 Moore, Arbitrations 3240) (1842) (wrongfully arrested, loaded with irons, and thrown into dungeon without food)

—arbitrary molestation of the person; torture to elicit "confession" (compare *Chevreau v. United Kingdom* (1931), 27 Am.J.Int'l L. 153 (1933))

—*Other violations of recognized rights*: Claims were also made on behalf of aliens for other actions violating rights later recognized in the Universal Declaration, such as freedom of speech, freedom of religion, freedom to travel within a country, and the right to marry. See, *e.g.*, 8 Whiteman, Digest 402; L. of N. Doc C.26.M.21. 1929, II, 32; Freeman 511. There is some authority in international law to support such claims, but these freedoms might be restricted to resident aliens, and might be denied in time of national emergency.

There were also claims for injury due to denial to foreign nationals of benefits enjoyed by nationals, such as social security or aid to indigents or incompetents, or due to other discrimination between aliens and nationals or against aliens of particular nationality. See 3 Hackworth 650–52; 8 Whiteman, Digest 387. International law forbids some such discriminations, but others are permitted. See § 712, Comments *f* and *i.* Compare the corresponding jurisprudence under the "equal protection" clause of the Fourteenth Amendment to the United States Constitution, § 722.

There appears to be no record, however, of a state objecting to imprisonment of its nationals for debt, although that is prohibited by Article 11 of the Covenant on Civil and Political Rights. Some states may question whether they must accord alien men and women equal rights as to marriage, during marriage, and at its dissolution (Universal Declaration, Art. 16) when, for religious or traditional reasons, they do not grant such equality to their citizens.

B. State practice and arbitral decisions have supported state responsibility for several kinds of injury to aliens that have not been recognized as violations of human rights,

clause (b) of this section. They include:

—*Failure to protect foreign nationals.* The rule that developed out of the arbitral awards before World War II was that a state was responsible for injuries inflicted upon aliens by private individuals only if the state failed, by intention or neglect, to provide adequate police protection for those aliens. Comment e. See, *e.g., Noyes* (United States v. Panama), Hunt's Report 155 (1933). A state incurs no liability for injury to aliens by acts of revolutionary forces if the state is unable to protect the aliens from such injury. If the revolutionary forces succeed, the state may become liable for their actions during the struggle for power. See § 207, Comment *b.* A state has greater and more specific duties under customary law and under some international agreements to protect certain classes of aliens, such as diplomatic or consular personnel. The seizure of the United States Embassy and the taking of United States hostages in Iran in 1979–80 may have been initially the act of a mob which the authorities could not prevent, but was soon ratified and became state policy for which Iran was responsible. See Case Concerning United States Diplomatic and Consular Staff in Tehran (United States v. Iran), [1980] I.C.J. Rep. 3; § 207, Reporters' Note 4; § 464, Reporters' Note 6.

—*Failure to punish offenses against aliens.* There is support for a rule obligating a state to act vigorously and diligently to punish crimes against aliens. See, *e.g.,* the decisions of the Mexican-American Claims Commission, *e.g., Kennedy,* G.C.C. 289 [1927] (imposition of inadequate penalty); *Mallen, id.* at 254 (1927) (failure to enforce penalty); *West, id.* at 404 (1927) (amnesty and pardon unduly granted); *Putnam, id.* at 222 (1927) (allowing prisoner to escape). It is argued that failure to punish shows contempt for the alien's state and increases the possibility of harm befalling other nationals of that state. For an argument against liability in such circumstances, see Art. 13 of the draft Convention on the International Responsibility of States for Injuries to Aliens, prepared by Professors Sohn and Baxter, reprinted in 55 Am.J.Int'l L. 545 (1961), and in the volume by Garcia-Amador, Sohn, and Baxter cited in Reporters' Note 8.

—*Failure to provide aliens a legal remedy.* It is a wrong under international law for a state to deny a foreign national access to domestic courts. *Van Bokkelen,* 2 Moore, Arbitrations 1842 (1888). That is the central meaning of "denial of justice." See Comment *a.* Treaties of friendship, commerce, and navigation generally provide that each party shall give to nationals of the other party access to its courts on the same basis as to its own nationals. See treaties collected in Freeman, 123 n. 2. However, states reserve the right to deny access to their courts to corporations that have not registered or qualified to do business in the state, although they in fact do business within the jurisdiction.

United States law generally affords aliens access to courts even in the absence of international agreement, although in respect of some claims against the United States, the right is conditioned on reciprocity by the alien's country of nationality. See Nippon Hodo Co. v. United States, 152 Ct.Cl. 190, 285 F.2d 766 (1961) (giving effect to reciprocity provisions in 28 U.S.C. § 2052 as regards contract claims against the United States); 46 U.S.C. § 785 (reciprocity required in suits in admiralty against United States). Access to courts is extended even to illegal aliens. See, *e.g.,* Janusis v. Long, 284 Mass. 403, 188 N.E. 228 (1933). See also the cases recognizing constitutional rights for illegal aliens, § 722, Reporters' Note 14.

C. States have been deemed not responsible under international law for

—*Certain alleged procedural insufficiencies:*

—witness did not take oath (*Chattin, supra*)

—reasonable security for costs was required (Freeman 224, n. 5)

—court incorrectly but in good faith applied or interpreted the law (*Barron, Forbes, & Co.* 3 Moore, Arbitrations 2525) (1872)

—case dismissed for lack of jurisdiction (when another forum was available) (Freeman 227)

—"technical objections" or "minor irregularities" (Ralston, Venezuelan Arbitrations of 1903, 67–68)

—*Such restrictions on aliens as:*

—exclusion from public employment

—limiting access to certain professions and occupations

—denying access to public facilities or resources

—denying right to own or inherit certain property or interests in property

—requiring aliens to register or be otherwise identified

—deporting or expelling aliens pursuant to law

—requiring aliens to serve on juries or testify as witnesses or experts (Freeman 510).

3. *Human rights of various categories of aliens.* The language of the Universal Declaration, as of the principal international covenants, applies to all individuals; clauses intended to be limited to nationals so indicate. See Comment *b.* However, a study prepared by Baroness Elles, Special Rapporteur of the Sub-Commission on Prevention of Discrimination and Protection of Minorities, concludes that "the wording of international instruments as they relate to aliens is unclear and imprecise, 'nationality' not being included in the non-discrimination clauses." See International Provisions Protecting the Human Rights of Non-Citizens (U.N. Doc. E/CN.4/Sub. 2/392/Rev. 1) at 49. That argument is not persuasive as regards alien residents generally, but may be relevant to aliens admitted for special purposes, such as migrant or guest workers, who appear to have been the principal concern of the Report.

As regards economic and social rights in particular, the Elles Report, *supra*, states: "A realistic approach is however necessary. With the present wide disparities in economic and social development there is no reason to suppose that the progressive achievement of those standards implies equal and simultaneous progress for all individuals within the jurisdiction of the member State, including aliens." *Id.* at 7. On the other hand, when the International Covenant on Econom-

ic, Social and Cultural Rights wished to reserve a right to discriminate against aliens, it did so expressly. See Art. 2(3). ("Developing countries, with due regard to human rights and their national economy, may determine to what extent they would guarantee the economic rights recognized in the present Covenant to non-nationals.")

The Elles Report, *supra*, at 53, appended a "Draft Declaration on the Human Rights of Individuals who are not Citizens of the Country in which they Live." That declaration appears designed to clarify the status and rights of migrant or guest workers in particular. Article 4 of the draft declaration states that noncitizens shall enjoy "at least" specified rights, listing most, but not all, of the rights in the Universal Declaration. Other rights are mentioned in the Preamble and some in later articles of the draft. Not mentioned, in addition to rights of political participation, are the right to seek asylum and the right to a nationality. There is no specific mention of the right not to be held in slavery or servitude, but Article 8 of the Draft Declaration provides that the non-citizen shall enjoy "the right to just and favorable conditions of work, to equal pay for equal work, and to just and fair remuneration," as well as other economic and social benefits. See also U.N. Doc. A/C.3/38/ 11 (1983).

4. *Discrimination among aliens of different nationality.* The principles of state responsibility for injury to aliens, including nondiscrimination, developed contemporaneously with a growing network of treaties of friendship, commerce,

and navigation which provided rights and benefits for nationals of the parties, including most favored nation treatment or even treatment equal to that of nationals. See Reporters' Note 6.

The United States objected to alleged discrimination against United States nationals by Cuba. See § 712, Reporters' Note 5. For United States measures against Iranian nationals in response to seizure of the United States embassy and personnel in 1979, see § 722, Reporters' Note 6.

5. *Enemy aliens and other "designated" aliens.* Since the adoption of the United Nations Charter, there has been little recorded treatment of foreign nationals as enemy aliens, or other discrimination against designated aliens. But see Reporters' Note 4. For the treatment of enemy aliens during the Second World War, see generally Domke, Trading with the Enemy in World War II (1943); also, Domke, The Control of Alien Property (1947). For the law of the United States, see § 722, Comment *h.*

6. *Special treaty rights of aliens of particular nationality.* The European Economic Community gives workers who are nationals of member states freedom of movement and protection against discrimination in employment, and gives to nationals of member states the right to establish themselves and conduct business in the states of the Community. Treaty of Rome Establishing the European Economic Community, 1957, Arts. 48–51, 298 U.N.T.S. 3, 11. Many states have networks of treaties of friendship, commerce, and navigation which give to nationals of the other state, generally on a reciprocal basis, such rights as freedom of travel, security of the person and of property, access to courts and equality before the law, access to ports for vessels, most favored nation treatment for imports, and the right to engage in trade and employment. See generally Walker, "Modern Treaties of Friendship, Commerce and Navigation," 42 Minn.L. Rev. 805 (1958); Wilson, United States Commercial Treaties and International Law (1960); also American Bar Ass'n, Commercial Treaty Index (1976). See also, *e.g.,* Asakura v. Seattle, 265 U.S. 332, 44 S.Ct. 515, 68 L.Ed. 1041 (1924), and other cases cited in § 111, Reporters' Note 5; Sumitomo Shoji America, Inc. v. Avagliano, 457 U.S. 176, 102 S.Ct. 2374, 72 L.Ed.2d 765 (1982).

7. *Refugees.* The Convention Relating to the Status of Refugees (1951) and the Protocol Relating to the Status of Refugees (1976) (see Introductory Note to this Part), give to refugees from political or religious persecution defined civil, economic, and social rights. States parties also undertake to accord to such refugees treatment no less favorable than that accorded to aliens generally, in some respects the most favorable treatment accorded to nationals of any foreign country, in other respects the treatment accorded to nationals. A refugee may not be expelled to territory where his life or freedom would be threatened (*"non-refoulement"*) and refugees are accorded some protection against expulsion generally. The United States is a party to the Protocol, 19 U.S.T. 6223, T.I. A.S. No. 6577, 606 U.N.T.S. 267, which has been implemented by the Refugee Act of 1980, 8 U.S.C. § 1101. In Yiu Sing Chun v. Sava, 708 F.2d 869, 877 (2d Cir.1983), the court said:

a refugee who has a "well-founded fear of persecution" in his homeland has a protectable interest recognized by both treaty and statute, and his interest in not being returned may well enjoy some due process protection not available to an alien claiming only admission.

In 1981, President Reagan ordered the interdiction on the high seas of vessels suspected of bringing illegal aliens to the United States. See Proclamation 4865, Executive Order 12324, Sept. 29, 1981, 46 Fed.Reg. 48109 (1981). Whether the instructions and the proposed procedures would satisfy the obligations of the United States of *"non-refoulement,"* under the Protocol, if any persons on board the vessels should qualify as refugees, has not been adjudicated. Compare Haitian Refugee Center, Inc. v. Gracey, 600 F.Supp. 1396 (D.D.C.1985), *affirmed on other grounds*, 809 F.2d 794 (D.C. Cir. 1987).

The rights of refugees under these instruments are given special "diplomatic protection" by the United Nations Office of the High Commissioner for Refugees. See, G.A. Res. 428(V), 5 U.N. GAOR Supp. No. 20, at 46, and the statute of the Office annexed thereto. For a collection of the resolutions relating to the Office,

see U.N. Doc. HCR/INF/48/Rev. 2 and Add. I–5 (1975–80).

For a discussion of possible human rights limitations on extradition, see Errera, "L'extradition et la protection des droits individuels," Rev. fr. Droit adm. 158 (mars-avr. 1985). See also § 476, Comment *h*.

A selective bibliography is provided in Jacobs, "Political Asylum, Refuge and Sanctuary," [1987] Rec. A.B. City N.Y. 561–72.

8. *Studies of state responsibility.* A study of state responsibility for injury to aliens, with draft articles, was prepared for the International Law Commission by its Special Rapporteur, F.V. Garcia-Amador, and considered by the Commission between 1956–1960. Beginning in 1962 the International Law Commission, with a new Special Rapporteur, Roberto Ago, dealt with state responsibility generally, not with its application in particular contexts. See [1980] 2 Y.B.Int'l L. Comm'n 26. Garcia-Amador's study, together with a draft convention prepared by Sohn and Baxter (essentially completed in 1961), are published as Garcia-Amador, Sohn and Baxter, Recent Codification of the Law of State Responsibility for Injuries to Aliens (1974).

§ 712.   State Responsibility for Economic Injury to Nationals of Other States

A state is responsible under international law for injury resulting from:

(1) a taking by the state of the property of a national of another state that

(a) is not for a public purpose, or

(b) is discriminatory, or

(c) is not accompanied by provision for just compensation;

For compensation to be just under this Subsection, it must, in the absence of exceptional circumstances, be in an amount equivalent to the value of the property taken and be paid at the time of taking, or within a reasonable time thereafter with interest from the date of taking, and in a form economically usable by the foreign national;

(2) a repudiation or breach by the state of a contract with a national of another state

(a) where the repudiation or breach is (i) discriminatory; or (ii) motivated by noncommercial considerations, and compensatory damages are not paid; or

(b) where the foreign national is not given an adequate forum to determine his claim of repudiation or breach, or is not compensated for any repudiation or breach determined to have occurred; or

(3) other arbitrary or discriminatory acts or omissions by the state that impair property or other economic interests of a national of another state.

Comment:

a. *Responsibility under general principles of international law.* This section sets forth the responsibility of a state under customary international law for certain economic injury to foreign nationals. A state may have additional obligations under international agreements to which it is party. The remedies available to a state whose national suffered injury, or to the injured person, are dealt with in § 713; see also § 906. As to remedies available to the injured person in the courts of the United States, see also § 907, §§ 451–60 (sovereign immunity) and §§ 443–44 (act of state).

This section deals with state responsibility under international law. For the obligations of the United States and of the States with respect to aliens and their property under the United States Constitution, see §§ 721 and 722.

A state is responsible under this section for injury to property and other economic interests of private persons who are foreign nationals. Injury by a state to property or economic interests of another state or state instrumentality is covered by general principles of state responsibility, § 206, Comment e and Reporters' Note 1. See also the principles of state responsibility to other states in regard to particular matters, such as economic interests in the sea (Part V) or pollution of the environment (Part VI).

b. Expropriation of alien property under international law. Subsection (1) states the traditional rules of international law on expropriation of alien properties and takes essentially the same substantive positions as the previous Restatement, §§ 187–90. These rules have been challenged in recent years, but this Restatement reaffirms that they continue to be valid and effective principles of international law. In particular, international law requires that when foreign properties are expropriated there must be compensation and such compensation must be just. See Comments *c* and *d*.

c. Requirement and standard of compensation. International law requires that a taking of the property of a foreign national, whether a natural or juridical person, be compensated. There are authoritative declarations that under international law the compensation to be paid must be "appropriate." This Restatement maintains the view that compensation must also be "just." Compare the Fifth Amendment to the United States Constitution: "nor shall private property be taken for public use, without just compensation." See Comment *d*.

The United States Government has consistently taken the position in diplomatic exchanges and in international fora that under international law compensation must be "prompt, adequate and effective," and those terms have been included in United States legislation. See Reporters' Note 2. That formulation has met strong resistance from developing states and has not made its way into multilateral agreements or declarations or been universally utilized by international tribunals, but it has been incorporated into a substantial number of bilateral agreements negotiated by the United States as well as by other capital-exporting states both among themselves and with developing states.

d. Just compensation. The elements constituting just compensation are not fixed or precise, but, in the absence of exceptional circumstances, compensation to be just must be equivalent to the value of the property taken and must be paid at the time of taking or with interest from that date and in an economically useful form.

—There must be payment for the full value of the property, usually "fair market value" where that can be determined. Such value should take into account "going concern value," if any, and other generally recognized principles of valuation.

—Provision for compensation must be based on value at the time of taking; as in United States domestic law, if compensation is not paid at or before the time of taking but is delayed pending administrative, legislative, or judicial processes for fixing compensation, interest must be paid from the time of the taking.

—Compensation should be in convertible currency without restriction on repatriation, but payment in bonds may satisfy the requirement of just compensation if they bear interest at an economically reasonable rate and if there is a market for them through which their equivalent in convertible currency can be realized.

Various forms of payment have been provided in negotiated settlements which would not be held to satisfy the requirements of just compensation, *e.g.*, payment in nonconvertible currency that can be used for investment in productive assets in the taking state, or even payment in kind, as in the case of expropriation of investment in natural resources.

In exceptional circumstances, some deviation from the standard of compensation set forth in Subsection (1) might satisfy the requirement of just compensation. Whether circumstances are so exceptional as to warrant such deviation, and whether in the circumstances the particular deviation satisfies the requirement of just compensation, are questions of international law. An instance of exceptional circumstances that has been specifically suggested and extensively debated, but never authoritatively passed upon by an international tribunal, involves national programs of agricultural land reform. See Reporters' Note 3. A departure from the general rule on the ground of such exceptional circumstances is unwarranted if (i) the property taken had been used in a business enterprise that was specifically authorized or encouraged by the state; (ii) the property was an enterprise taken for operation as a going concern by the state; (iii) the taking program did not apply equally to nationals of the taking state; or (iv) the taking itself was otherwise wrongful under Subsection (1)(a) or (b).

Exceptional circumstances that would permit deviation from the standard of compensation set forth in Subsection (1) might include takings of alien property during war or similar exigency. As to alien enemies in time of war, see § 711, Comment *h*.

When, by an international agreement, a state has undertaken not to expropriate the properties of nationals of another state, or has agreed that in the event of such expropriation it will provide compensation in accordance with a particular standard, any claim of a right to terminate, suspend, or modify that obligation on grounds of special circumstances is governed by the law of international agreements, including the principle of *rebus sic stantibus*. See § 336.

e. Taking for public purpose. The requirement that a taking be for a public purpose is reiterated in most formulations of the rules of international law on expropriation of foreign property. That limitation, however, has not figured prominently in international claims practice, perhaps because the concept of public purpose is broad and not subject to effective reexamination by other states. Presumably, a seizure by a dictator or oligarchy for private use could be challenged under this rule.

f. Discriminatory takings. Formulations of the rules on expropriation generally include a prohibition of discrimination, implying that a program of taking that singles out aliens generally, or aliens of a particular nationality, or particular aliens, would violate international law. Where discrimination is charged, or where the public purpose is challenged, Comment *e,* there is often also a failure to pay just compensation, and a program of takings that did not meet the requirements of equal treatment and public purpose but did provide just compensation under Subsection (1) might not in fact be successfully challenged.

Discrimination implies unreasonable distinction. Takings that invidiously single out property of persons of a particular nationality would be unreasonable; classifications, even if based on nationality, that are rationally related to the state's security or economic policies might not be unreasonable. Discrimination may be difficult to determine where there is no comparable enterprise owned by local nationals or by nationals of other countries, or where nationals of the taking state are treated equally with aliens but by discrete actions separated in time.

Whether a state can take the property of private persons in response to a violation of international law by their state of nationality, even in retaliation for unlawful takings of private property by that state, is doubtful. See previous Restatement § 200. For other forms of response to a violation of international law, see § 905, Comments *b* and *f* and Reporters' Note 2. As to the taking of the property of enemy aliens during war, see § 711, Comment *h.*

g. Expropriation or regulation. Subsection (1) applies not only to avowed expropriations in which the government formally takes title to property, but also to other actions of the government that have the effect of "taking" the property, in whole or in large part, outright or in stages ("creeping expropriation"). A state is responsible as for an expropriation of property under Subsection (1) when it subjects alien property to taxation, regulation, or other action that is confiscatory, or that prevents, unreasonably interferes with, or unduly delays, effective enjoyment of an alien's property or its removal from the state's territory. Depriving an alien of control of his property, as by an order freezing his assets, might become a taking if it is long extended. A state is not responsible for loss of property or for other economic disadvantage resulting from bona fide general taxation, regulation, forfeiture for crime, or other action of the kind that is commonly accepted as within the police power of states, if it is not discriminatory, Comment *f*, and is not designed to cause the alien to abandon the property to the state or sell it at a distress price. As under United States constitutional law, the line between "taking" and regulation is sometimes uncertain. See Reporters' Note 6.

h. Repudiation or breach of contract by state. A state party to a contract with a foreign national is liable for a repudiation or breach of that contract under applicable national law, but not every repudiation or breach by a state of a contract with a foreign national constitutes a violation of international law. Under Subsection (2), a state is responsible for such a repudiation or breach only if it is discriminatory, Comment *f*, or if it is akin to an expropriation in that the contract is repudiated or breached for governmental rather than commercial reasons and the state is not prepared to pay damages. A state's repudiation or failure to perform is not a violation of international law under this section if it is based on a bona fide dispute about the obligation or its performance, if it is due to the state's inability to perform, or if nonperformance is motivated by commercial considerations and the state is prepared to pay damages or to submit to adjudication or arbitration and to abide by the judgment or award.

With respect to any repudiation or breach of a contract with a foreign national, a state may be responsible for a denial of justice under international law if it denies to the alien an effective domestic forum to resolve the dispute and has not agreed to any other forum; or if, having committed itself to a special forum for dispute settlement, such as arbitration, it fails to honor such commitment; or if it fails to carry out a judgment or award rendered by such domestic or special forum. See Comment *j*.

A breach of contract by a state may sometimes constitute "creeping expropriation," Comment *g*, for example, if the breach makes impossible the continued operation of the project that is the subject of the contract.

i. Other economic injury. Under Subsection (1), a state is responsible for expropriation of alien property without just compensation even if property of nationals is treated similarly, but economic injuries that fall within Subsection (3) are generally unlawful because they involve discrimination or are otherwise arbitrary. An alien enterprise that has been lawfully established is protected by international law against changes in the rules governing its operations that are discriminatory, Comment *f*, or are so completely without basis as to be arbitrary in the international sense, *i.e.*, unfair. In general, in the absence of international agreement to the contrary, a state may deny to foreign nationals the right to acquire property or to invest within the state. See § 711, Comment *d*. Compare § 722, Comments *f* and *g*.

Under bilateral treaties of friendship, commerce, and navigation, nationals of both states are usually accorded rights to establish businesses, to invest, and to engage in trade or a profession, often on a most-favored-nation basis, sometimes equally with nationals. Such treaties generally permit each state to exclude the other's nationals from sensitive industries. Some foreign nationals enjoy extensive rights under multilateral arrangements, such as those of the European Economic Community. Such favorable treatment is not unlawful discrimination against aliens who do not have comparable treaty rights.

j. Economic injury and denial of justice. Economic injury to foreign nationals is often intertwined with a denial of domestic remedies. If no effective administrative or judicial remedy is available to the alien to review the legality under international law of an action causing economic injury, the state may be liable for a denial of justice, as well as for the violation of economic rights. See § 711, Comment *a*. In the case of a taking of property, Subsection (1), an impartial determination is required by international law, particularly as to whether the compensation provided is just. In the case of repudiation or breach of a contract with an alien, Subsection (2)(b), an impartial determination is required to review the adequacy of the asserted justification for the repudiation or breach and to assess damages if appropriate. Such a determination might be made by an independent domestic tribunal, an *ad hoc* or previously agreed arbitration, or an international tribunal. In the case of other acts that impair the economic interests of aliens, Subsection (3), the denial of an adequate remedy may confirm the arbitrary or discriminatory character of the act.

REPORTERS' NOTES

1. *Status of international law on expropriation.* Subsection (1) restates the traditional principles of international law on expropriation. Early in this century these principles were settled law. See, *e.g.*, The Factory at Chorzow, P.C.I.J. ser. A, No. 17 (1928). See also Case Concerning German Interests in Polish Upper Silesia, P.C.I.J. ser. A, No. 7, at 32 (1926). Compare Schachter, "Compensation for Expropriation," 78 Am.J.Int'l L. 121, 122–24 (1984).

The first major challenge to these principles was posed by the U.S.S.R., which rejected the traditional rule, claiming that an alien enters the territory of another state or acquires property there subject wholly to local law. The principles were challenged also by Latin American governments. In 1938, in a famous exchange between Secretary of State Hull and the Minister of Foreign Relations of Mexico, the United States insisted that property of aliens was protected by an international standard under which expropriation was subject to limitations, notably that there must be "prompt, adequate and effective compensation." In contrast, the Government of Mexico insisted that international law required only that foreign nationals be treated no less favorably than were nationals, at least in the case of "expropriations of a general and impersonal character like those which Mexico has carried out for the purpose of redistribution of land." 3 Hackworth, Digest of International Law 655–61 (1942).

After the Second World War, with the coming of many new states and the rise of the "Third World" to influence, opposition to the traditional view received widespread support. For the new majority of states, a people's right to dispose of its national resources became "economic self-determination," and was designated a "human right" and placed at the head of both the International Covenant on Civil and Political Rights and the International Covenant on Economic, Social and Cultural Rights. See § 701, Reporters' Note 6. In 1962, however, the United Nations General Assembly declared that in cases of expropriation of natural resources "the own-er shall be paid appropriate compensation . . . in accordance with international law." G.A. Res. 1803, Permanent Sovereignty over Natural Resources, 17 U.N. GAOR, Supp. 17, at 15; the United States voted in favor of that resolution. See Reporters' Note 2. See Schwebel, "The Story of the UN's Declaration on Permanent Sovereignty over Natural Resources," 49 A.B. A.J. 463 (1963).

Divisions became sharper in 1974 when the United Nations General Assembly adopted the Charter of Economic Rights and Duties of States, which dealt with the subject without making any reference to international law. The Charter declared that every state has the right

to nationalize, expropriate or transfer ownership of foreign property, in which case appropriate compensation should be paid by the State adopting such measures, taking into account its relevant laws and regulations and all circumstances that the State considers pertinent. In any case where the question of compensation gives rise to a controversy, it shall be settled under the domestic law of the nationalizing State and by its tribunals . . . [unless otherwise agreed].

The Charter was adopted by 120 in favor, 6 against, and 10 abstentions, the vote reflecting the views of the majority as developing states, with the United States among the dissenters and the other developed Western states either dissenting or abstaining. *Compare* Brower and Tepe, "The Charter of Economic Rights and Duties of States: A Reflection or Rejection of International Law?," 9 Int'l Law. 295 (1975), *with* Weston, "The Charter of Economic Rights and Duties of States and the Deprivation of Foreign Owned Wealth," 75 Am.J.Int'l. L. 437 (1981).

The United States and other capital exporting states have rejected the challenge by developing states, have refused to agree to any change in the traditional principles, and have denied that these have been replaced or modified in customary law by state practice. See, e.g., Clagett, "The Expropriation Issue Before the Iran-United States Claims Tribunal: Is 'Just Compensation' Required by International Law or Not?" 16 L. & Pol'y in Int'l Bus. 813, 818 (1984). Those states have taken the position that the traditional requirements are solidly based on both the moral rights of property owners and on the needs of an effective international system of private investment. Moreover, they argued, whatever objections might be made to the traditional rules as applied to investments established during the colonial era, the traditional rules should clearly apply to arrangements made between investors and independent governments negotiated on a commercial basis. That view was supported by the arbitrator in Texas Overseas Petroleum Co. v. Libyan Arab Republic (1977), 17 Int'l Leg. Mat. 1, 27–30 (1978), who concluded that the traditional rule prevailed, if only because the capital exporting states had not assented to its undoing or modification. Other arbitrations under agreements between states and foreign investors, as well as judgments of an Iran-United States Claims Tribunal, Reporters' Note 2, have also supported the traditional rule.

Both before and after the adoption of the Charter of Economic Rights and Duties of States, many states, including many developing states that supported the Charter (though not generally states in Latin America), concluded bilateral agreements that included provisions for compensation in the case of expropriation. Some of those provisions are contained in treaties of friendship, commerce, and navigation, as part of broader accommodations for foreign trade and investment. See, e.g., Art. IV(3) of the Convention of Establishment between the United States and France, 1959, 11 U.S.T. 2398, T.I. A.S. No. 4625. Others appear in agreements aimed particularly at the security of foreign investment, e.g., Agreement between Egypt and the United Kingdom, 1975, 14 Int'l Leg.Mat. 1470, and Agreement between Singapore and the United Kingdom, 1975, 15 Int'l Leg.Mat. 591. For a comprehensive listing of such agreements, numbering about 200 (as of 1986), see International Chamber of Commerce, Bilateral Treaties for International Investment (1977), updated. The United States began a program of negotiating such bilateral agreements in 1980 and as of 1986 had signed, but not ratified, agreements with some 10 countries, including Egypt, Panama, and Turkey. See Gann, "The U.S. Bilateral Investment Treaties Program," 21 Stan. J. Int'l L. 373 (1986). Some provisions for compensation appear in arrangements whereby a state guarantees the investments of its nationals against loss due to expropriation, after agreement with the state host to the investment. See, e.g., Agreement between the United States and Indonesia, 1967, 18 U.S.T. 1850, T.I.

A.S. No. 6330. It has been argued that the growing network of such agreements constitutes state practice that provides further support for the rule of compensation set forth in this section. See Dolzer, "New Foundations of the Law of Expropriation of Alien Property," 75 Am.J.Int'l L. 553, 565–66 (1981). An effort under the aegis of the OECD to conclude a multilateral agreement, which provided for just compensation, defined as "the genuine value of the property affected", failed to achieve consensus. See Schwarzenberger, Foreign Investments in International Law, 153–59 (1969).

There have been numerous settlements by aliens or their governments with expropriating states, but these do not provide persuasive evidence as to what the parties to the settlement believed the relevant law to be. Such settlements are often made for political or larger economic reasons, and it is uncertain whether the expropriating state is paying with a sense of international legal obligation to compensate, or what view as to the required measure of compensation is reflected in the amount of the settlement. See the discussion of the settlement in 1974 by the Government of Chile with the Kennecott Copper Co. in Steiner and Vagts, Transnational Legal Problems 522–24 (3d ed.1986); the agreement between the United States and Peru resolving the Marcona Mining Company Expropriation, 1976, 27 U.S.T. 3993, T.I.A.S. No. 8417; Gantz, "The Marcona Settlement," 71 Am. J.Int'l L. 474 (1977). (In the *Marcona* settlement, however, the United States Department of State declared that the settlement satisfied the requirement of just compensa-

tion. See Contemporary Practice, 71 Am.J.Int'l L. 139 (1977).) Lump-sum settlement agreements are also ambiguous. It has been argued that, while they may be some evidence of a sense of legal obligation to compensate, they suggest that only modest compensation need be paid. However, the International Court of Justice, in the Case concerning Barcelona Traction Light and Power Co. (Belgium v. Spain), [1970] I.C.J. Rep. 4, 40, stated that such settlements "are *sui generis* and provide no guide" as to general international practice. See also Banco Nacional de Cuba v. Chase Manhattan Bank, 505 F.Supp. 412, 433 (S.D.N.Y.1980), *modified*, 658 F.2d 875 (2d Cir.1981) ("Such settlements are all influenced and distorted by the relative political and economic power of the parties, and their desire to regularize disrupted relationships, factors which are not relevant in attempting to set forth neutral principles of international law.") Domestic national practice, which might be relevant as "general principles common to the major legal systems" (§ 102(4) and Comment *l* to that section), also varies widely. See Lowenfeld, ed., Expropriation in the Americas (1971).

In 1964, the Supreme Court of the United States stated: "there are few if any issues in international law today on which opinion seems to be so divided as the limitations of a state's power to expropriate the property of aliens." Banco Nacional de Cuba v. Sabbatino, 376 U.S. 398, 428, 84 S.Ct. 923, 940, 11 L.Ed. 2d 804 (1964). See also Banco Nacional de Cuba v. Chase Manhattan Bank, *supra*, at 658 F.2d 888. Since 1974, the controversy as to the state of customary law has been dormant, and investing states have come to rely on bilateral agreements, though Latin American states generally have not concluded such agreements. International arbitral tribunals have consistently applied the traditional rule as set forth in Subsection (1) but they have differed in their formulation of the standard of compensation to be applied. See Reporters' Note 2.

Even those who have challenged the traditional rule as to compensation for nationalization programs generally accept it as to "a discrete expropriation of particular items of property." See Sedco, Inc. v. National Iranian Oil Co., __ Iran-U.S. C.T.R. __ (1986), 25 Int'l Leg.Mat. 636 (1986).

2. *Standard of compensation.* The 1962 Resolution of the United Nations General Assembly, Reporters' Note 1, affirming that a taking of property of foreign nationals required compensation, declared that compensation had to be "appropriate." The United States had proposed the phrase "prompt, adequate and effective" compensation, the formula asserted by Secretary of State Hull in 1938, see Reporters' Note 1, but it accepted and voted for the 1962 resolution; it declared that in its view the word "appropriate" was the equivalent of "prompt, adequate and effective." UN Doc. A/C.2/S.R. 850 at 327 (1962). On the other hand, Mexico asserted that "appropriate compensation" was satisfied by the standard it had applied in 1938, *i.e.,* if aliens were compensated to the same extent as nationals. See UN Doc. A/PV. 1194, at 1136. A Soviet amendment which would have had the Resolution refer to the inalienable right to "unobstructed . . . expropriation" was defeated. U.N. Doc. A/PV.

1193 at 1131. The Charter of Economic Rights and Duties of States also adopted "appropriate" compensation as the standard, but only as required by the law of the expropriating state, rejecting by implication any obligation of compensation under international law.

International tribunals have differed in their formulation of the standard of compensation to be applied, although their phraseology may be intended to have equivalent meaning. In Libyan American Oil Co. v. Libyan Arab Republic, (1977) 20 Int'l Leg.Mat. 1, 86 (1982), the arbitrator adopted "equitable compensation" with "the classical formula of 'prompt, adequate and effective compensation' remaining as a maximum and a practical guide." In Kuwait v. American Independent Oil Co. (1982), 21 Int'l Leg.Mat. 976, 1033 (1982), the arbitrators used "appropriate" compensation, "determined by means of an enquiry into all the circumstances." The Iran-United States Claims Tribunal in American Int'l Group v. Islamic Rep. of Iran, 4 Iran-U.S. C.T.R. 96, 105, 109 (1983), held as "a general principle of public international law" that foreign nationals are entitled to "the value of the property taken," and referred to the need to determine "the going concern or fair market value" of the property. Subsequently, in Tippetts, Abbett, McCarthy, Stratton v. TAMS–AFFA, 6 Iran-U.S. C.T.R. 219, 225 (1984), the Tribunal stated the Standard of Compensation to be "the full value" of the property of which the claimant was deprived. See also, Sedco, Inc. v. National Iranian Oil Co., __ Iran-U.S. C.T.R. __, 25 Int'l Leg.Mat. 629, 635 (1986) and *id.* at 636, 647 (separate opinion of Judge Brower). The Tribunal has also applied the 1957 Treaty of Amity between Iran and the United States, 8 U.S.T. 900, T.I. A.S. No. 3853, calling for the payment of "just compensation" defined in part as "the full equivalent of the property taken". Phelps Dodge Corp. v. Islamic Rep. of Iran, 25 Int'l Leg. Mat. 619, 626–27 (1986). The network of bilateral agreements, Reporters' Note 1, uses different formulae, with a substantial number of them providing for all or some of the terms "prompt, adequate and effective" compensation. See generally Schachter, Reporters' Note 1.

The Executive Branch and the Congress of the United States have held resolutely to the view that international law requires compensation that is "prompt, adequate and effective." In the First Hickenlooper Amendment, Congress referred to the obligation of states taking property of United States citizens as including "speedy compensation in convertible foreign exchange equivalent to the full value thereof, as required by international law." 22 U.S.C. § 2370(e)(1). That standard is presumably incorporated by reference in the Second Hickenlooper Amendment, 22 U.S.C. § 2370(e)(2). See § 444, Comment c. United States representatives to international financial institutions are directed to oppose loans to countries that have expropriated property of United States citizens without prompt, adequate, and effective compensation, in the absence of certain exceptional circumstances. See e.g., 22 U.S.C. §§ 283r, 285o, 290g–8. The benefits of the generalized system of tariff preferences for less-developed countries may be denied to countries that fail to compensate in accordance with that standard. 19 U.S.C. § 2462(b)(4). The President and the State Department frequently reiterate the traditional formula in general policy statements. See, e.g., 66 Dept.State Bull. 152–54 (1972); [1975] Digest of U.S. Practice in Int'l L. 488; [1978] id. 1226–27; 19 Weekly Comp.Pres.Docs. No. 36 (Sept. 12, 1983), at 1217.

3. *Just compensation.* No formula defining just compensation can suit all circumstances. In interpreting the requirement of just compensation in the United States Constitution, the Supreme Court said:

> The Court in its construction of the constitutional provision has been careful not to reduce the concept of "just compensation" to a formula. The political ethics reflected in the Fifth Amendment reject confiscation as a measure of justice. But the Amendment does not contain any definite standards of fairness by which the measure of "just compensation" is to be determined.

United States v. Cors. 337 U.S. 325, 332, 69 S.Ct. 1086, 1090, 93 L.Ed. 1392 (1949). Compare United States v. Commodities Trading Corp., 339 U.S. 121, 123, 70 S.Ct. 547, 549, 94 L.Ed. 707 (1950):

> This Court has never attempted to prescribe a rigid rule for determining just compensation under all circumstances and in all cases. Fair market value has normally been accepted as a just standard. But when market value has been too difficult to find, or when its application would result in manifest injustice to owner or public, courts have fashioned or applied other standards.

—*Valuation.* In the absence of exceptional circumstances, just compensation requires payment of full value, usually "fair market value." Comment *d.* Compare Olson v. United States, 292 U.S. 246, 255, 54 S.Ct. 704, 708, 78 L.Ed. 1236 (1934) (for purposes of the Fifth Amendment, just compensation is normally to be measured by "the market value of the property at the time of the taking contemporaneously paid in money"), reaffirmed in United States v. 50 Acres of Land, 469 U.S. 24, 105 S.Ct. 451, 83 L.Ed.2d 376 (1984). Such market value would include the "going concern" value of the enterprise, since a willing buyer would be receiving that value. Where the foreign national's property is unique—a mine or large manufacturing entity—it may be hard to find comparable assets or a willing buyer, and hence difficult to find a market value. Another method of valuation that would capture going concern value is to calculate the present value of the future earnings of the enterprise. When a taking arises out of a revolutionary situation that might affect the prospects of the enterprise in the eyes of a hypothetical purchaser, the situation should be taken into account in evaluating the property for purposes of compensation. See Banco Nacional de Cuba v. Chase Manhattan Bank, 658 F.2d 875 (2d Cir. 1981); American Int'l Group v. Islamic Republic of Iran, Reporters' Note 2.

—*Time.* The First Hickenlooper Amendment, Reporters' Note 2, requires the expropriating state to take appropriate steps to fix compensation within a reasonable time (six months). The payment is generally regarded as having been timely if compensation is tendered at the time of the taking or if compensation plus interest from that time is paid at a later date. Compare Kirby Forest Indus. v. United States, 467 U.S. 1, 104 S.Ct. 2187, 81 L.Ed.2d 1 (1984), on remand 635 F.Supp. 705 (E.D.Tex.1986), holding that just compensation requires only that interest be paid from the date the government acquired title to land, not from the date on which condemnation proceedings were commenced.

—*Usable form.* Payment meets the requirement of just compensation if it is in a form that is usable by the alien. This includes deferred payments, as by bonds, provided that they bear interest realistically related to market rates. Compare the decision of the Constitutional Council of France that the provision in the Declaration of the Rights of Man and of the Citizen of 1789, incorporated into the French Constitution, which provides that property can be taken only "on condition of a just and prior indemnification," was satisfied by compensation otherwise just but payable in negotiable interest bearing bonds to be paid on the average in 7½ years, Jour. Off. 17 Jan. 1982, at 299.

—*Exceptional circumstances.* Subsection (1) sets forth the elements constituting just compensation in the absence of exceptional circumstances. Compare United States v. Commodities Trading Corp., quoted above; also suggestion in that case, 339 U.S. at 126, that "exceptional circumstances" might warrant different standard for compensation under the Fifth Amendment; United States v. Virginia Electric & Power Co., 365 U.S. 624, 633, 81 S.Ct. 784, 790, 5 L.Ed. 2d 838 (1961) ("fair market value" not "an absolute standard"). The limitations on the exception for "exceptional circumstances" set forth in Comment *d* derive from the previous Restatement § 188.

One exception that has been frequently asserted involves expropriation as part of a national program of agricultural land reform. Such land reform programs, unlike, for example, nationalizations of investments in natural resources, would often not be possible if full compensation had to be paid. From the time of the exchange of notes between Mexico and the United States in 1938, see Reporters' Note 1, Latin American countries in particular have insisted that full compensation was not payable in such cases if the state could not afford full payment so long as aliens were treated equally with nationals. It may be with a view to such programs that Latin American countries generally have refrained from concluding bilateral investment agreements promising full compensation. See Reporters' Note 1. The United States has consistently rejected the exception, from the exchange of notes with Mexico in 1938, Reporters' Note 1, through exchanges with Guatemala (1953) and Cuba (1959). See 8 Whiteman, Digest of International Law 1156–63, 1167–70 (1967). United States military government authorities in Japan insisted upon the exclusion of property of allied nationals from a land reform program, the constitutionality of which, as applied to Japanese landowners, was sustained by the Supreme Court of Japan even though it provided less than full compensation. *Id.* at 1152–55.

The land reform exception was accepted by some scholars in developed states, see 1 Oppenheim, International Law 352 (8th ed. Lauterpacht 1955), but rejected by others. See the varying views expressed in 43(1) Annuaire de l'Institut de Droit International 42 (1950). The land reform exception has been supported on the ground that takings of agricultural land, unlike takings of mineral resources or of a going business concern, typically do not generate funds from which the government could make compensation. If a requirement of compensation fully in accord with the standard set forth in Subsection (1) would prevent the program, the obligation to compensate might be satisfied by a lower standard. Latin American states that have framed this exception have not denied that aliens had to be treated no less favorably than nationals as to compensation. As of 1987, no international tribunal had passed upon this exception.

As to exceptional circumstances generally, see dicta in separate opinions in cases before the Iran-U.S. Claims Tribunal by Judges Lagergren and Holtzmann in INA Corp. v. Islamic Republic of Iran (Sept. 15, 1985) and by Judge Brower in Sedco, Inc. v. National Iranian Oil Co., ___ Iran-U.S. C.T.R. ___, 25 Int'l Leg.Mat. 636, 647, n. 31 (1986).

4. *Expropriation for public purpose.* In the controversy as to the current state of the international law on expropriation of alien property, Reporters' Note 1, there has been little specific challenge to the traditional requirement that expropriation be for a public purpose. The public purpose requirement is included in the typical United States treaty of friendship, commerce, and navigation and was declared in the 1962 United Nations General As-

209

sembly Resolution on Permanent Sovereignty over Natural Resources, Reporters' Note 1. However, case law applying or interpreting the rule has been scarce and the few cases have also involved a denial of compensation by the taking state. Walter Fletcher Smith, 1929, 2 R. Int'l Arb.Awards 913; Finlay Claim, 39 Br. & For. State Papers 410 (1849); Banco Nacional de Cuba v. Sabbatino, 193 F.Supp. 375, 381 (S.D.N.Y.1961), *affirmed,* 307 F.2d 845 (2d Cir.1962), *reversed on other grounds,* 376 U.S. 398, 84 S.Ct. 923, 11 L.Ed.2d 804 (1964). As the general understanding of "public purpose" broadens, the likelihood of a successful challenge on that basis grows smaller. Compare the requirement in the Fifth Amendment to the United States Constitution that takings be for a "public use." There appears to be no case in which a taking by the United States Government was successfully challenged as not being for a public use. Compare Berman v. Parker, 348 U.S. 26, 32, 75 S.Ct. 98, 102, 99 L.Ed. 27 (1954) (taking for aesthetic purposes); United States *ex rel.* TVA v. Welch, 327 U.S. 546, 551–52, 66 S.Ct. 715, 717, 90 L.Ed. 843 (1946) (deference to judgment of Congress and federal agency). A broad interpretation of public purpose has been accepted also in respect of takings by States of the United States, to which a similar standard applies through the due process clause of the Fourteenth Amendment. Hawaii Housing Authority v. Midkiff, 467 U.S. 229, 104 S.Ct. 2321, 81 L.Ed.2d 184 (1984) (taking of fee simple for purpose of dispersing land ownership). Compare the decision of the Constitutional Council of France, Reporters' Note 3, that the legislative judgment as to the public necessity for nationalization cannot be reviewed in the absence of manifest error.

5. *Discriminatory expropriation.* Discrimination has not been a prominent objection if the expropriating state paid compensation, but the expropriation of United States properties by Cuba was held to be in violation of international law because, *inter alia,* its purpose was to retaliate against United States nationals for acts of their Government, and was directed against United States nationals exclusively. Banco Nacional de Cuba v. Farr, 243 F.Supp. 957 (S.D.N.Y.1965), *affirmed,* 383 F.2d 166 (2d Cir.1967), *certiorari denied,* 390 U.S. 956, 88 S.Ct. 1038, 19 L.Ed.2d 1151 (1968). See also the arbitration in Texas Overseas Petroleum Co. v. Libyan Arab Republic (1977), 17 Int'l Leg. Mat. 1 (1978), in which investors referred to the Libyan statement that expropriation had been undertaken as a "cold slap in the insolent face" of the investors' government; and BP Exploration Co. v. Libyan Arab Republic (1974), 53 Int'l L. Rep. 297 (1979), in which the investor cited the Libyan statement that expropriation had been undertaken as retaliation for political action of the investor's government directed at a third state. For a finding that nationalizing one company but not another did not violate international law when there was no discrimination on the basis of the nationality of the two companies and there were "adequate reasons" for distinguishing between them, see the decision of the tribunal in the arbitration between Kuwait and the American Independent Oil Co. (1982), 21 Int'l Leg.Mat. 976, 1019–1020 (1982).

Expropriation programs that discriminate in favor of aliens do not violate this section. Compare the decision of the French Constitutional Council, Reporters' Note 3, that the constitutional principle of equality is not violated when largely domestic banks are nationalized while largely foreign banks are not.

6. *Taking or regulation.* It is often necessary to determine, in the light of all the circumstances, whether an action by a state constitutes a taking and requires compensation under international law, or is a police power regulation or tax that does not give rise to an obligation to compensate even though a foreign national suffers loss as a consequence. In general, the line in international law is similar to that drawn in United States jurisprudence for purposes of the Fifth and Fourteenth Amendments to the Constitution in determining whether there has been a taking requiring compensation. *Compare* Pennsylvania Coal Co. v. Mahon, 260 U.S. 393, 43 S.Ct. 158, 67 L.Ed. 322 (1927); United States v. Pewee Coal Co., 341 U.S. 114, 71 S.Ct. 670, 95 L.Ed. 809 (1951); and Kaiser Aetna v. United States, 444 U.S. 164, 100 S.Ct. 383, 62 L.Ed.2d 332 (1979) (finding government actions constituted takings), *with* Goldblatt v. City of Hempstead, 369 U.S. 590, 82 S.Ct. 987, 8 L.Ed.2d 130 (1962); and Penn-Central Transp. Co. v. New York City, 438 U.S. 104, 98 S.Ct. 2646, 57 L.Ed.2d 631 (1978) (finding government actions constituted regulations, not takings). See also Ruckelshaus v. Monsanto Co., 467 U.S. 986, 104 S.Ct. 2862, 81 L.Ed.2d 815 (1984). See generally Greenawalt, "United States of America," in Lowenfeld, ed., Expropriation in the Americas: A Comparative Law Study 307 (1971).

International cases addressing the problem of distinguishing expropriation from regulation include Harza Engineering Co. v. Islamic Rep. of Iran, 1 Iran-U.S. C.T.R. 499 (1982), in which a panel of the tribunal dismissed a claim that the Iranian state bank had in effect expropriated claimant's bank accounts by dishonoring claimant's check and frustrating its attempts to authenticate its officer's signature; Sedco, Inc. v. National Iranian Oil Co., ____ Iran-U.S. C.T.R. ____, 25 Int'l Leg.Mat. 636 (1985), holding that the appointment by Iran of "temporary directors" *prima facie* fixed the date of expropriation; Parsons (Great Britain v. United States), 1925, 6 R.Int'l Arb.Awards 165, in which an arbitrator rejected a British claim for compensation for the destruction of a British national's stock of liquor during a rebellion in the Philippines; and Kügele v. Polish State, [1931–32] Ann.Dig.Int'l L. 69, in which the Upper Silesian Arbitral Tribunal dismissed a claim that a series of license fees imposed by Poland had forced the claimant to close his brewery, and Poland had therefore taken that property. See Christie, "What Constitutes a Taking of Property Under International Law," [1962] Brit.Y.B.Int'l L. 307. Compare the majority and concurring opinions in Starrett Housing Corp. v. Islamic Rep. of Iran, 4 Iran-U.S. C.T.R. 122, 23 Int'l Leg.Mat. 1090 (1984).

One test suggested for determining whether regulation and taxation programs are intended to achieve expropriation is whether they are applied only to alien enterprises. In many instances, however, particularly in developing countries, there may be no comparable locally-owned enterprise. Another test, emphasized in connection with OPIC insurance, § 713, Reporters' Note 7, is the degree to which the government action deprives the investor of effective control over the enterprise. In other cases, however, though the government does not assume control it makes it impossible for the firm to operate at a profit, and the alien (or his government) claims that the purpose is to effect expropriation. A challenged regulation might be compared with the practice of major legal systems; the fact that a given regulation is supported by guidelines adopted by an international agency to guide the behavior of multinationals may be seen as evidence of its legitimacy. See § 213, Reporters' Note 7.

A temporary deprivation of control, as by a freezing of assets under the International Emergency Economic Powers Act (IEEPA), 50 U.S.C. § 1701, is probably not a taking but may become one if deprivation is for an extended or indefinite period. See Comment g. See Sardino v. Federal Res. Bank, 361 F.2d 106, 111 (2d Cir.), *certiorari denied*, 385 U.S. 898, 87 S.Ct. 203, 17 L.Ed.2d 130 (1966). Thus, government appointment of an "interventor" or "receiver" to manage the enterprise might constitute a taking. A temporary deprivation of an alien's control over his property may in some cases cause significant injury and give rise to a claim for damages. Compare First English Evangelical Lutheran Church v. County of Los Angeles, ___ U.S. ___, 107 S.Ct. 2378 (1987) (requiring pay-

ment for temporary takings of property.) As to the freezing of the private assets of a foreign national in response to a violation of international law or agreement by the state of the alien's nationality, see § 905, Comment b and Reporters' Note 2.

7. *"Creeping expropriation."* Formal expropriation involves a taking by the state and transfer of title to the state, but a state may seek to achieve the same result by taxation and regulatory measures designed to make continued operation of a project uneconomical so that it is abandoned. In some cases the owner, faced with the prospect of continuing losses, sells to the government, accepting a modest price, but later asserts that the transaction was, in fact, not a sale but a taking. See Weston, "Constructive Takings under International Law," 16 Va.J.Int'l L. 103 (1975); Vagts, "Coercion and Foreign Investment Rearrangements," 72 Am.J.Int'l L. 17 (1978).

8. *Repudiation or breach of state contract with foreign national.* The term "repudiate" has been interpreted as meaning an outright disclaimer by the state of any liability under the contract. Matter of Revere Copper & Brass Co. and Overseas Private Investment Corp., 14 Int'l Leg.Mat. 1321, 1345 (1978) (interpreting OPIC insurance policy); [1979] Digest of U.S. Practice in Int'l L. 1217 (interpreting Second Hickenlooper Amendment). The prevailing view is that, in principle, international law is not implicated if a state repudiates or breaches a commercial contract with a foreign national for commercial reasons as a private contractor might, *e.g.*, due

to inability of the state to pay or otherwise perform, or because performance has become uneconomical; or because of controversy about the contractor's performance. In such circumstances, the state is liable for damages under applicable law and remedies are usually available in some forum. It is a violation of international law if, in repudiating or breaching the contract, the state is acting essentially from governmental motives (akin to those that operate in cases of expropriation) rather than for commercial reasons, and fails to pay compensation or to accept an agreed dispute settlement procedure.

The protection provided in Subsection (2) is sometimes stated as a rule that a state is responsible for "arbitrary" repudiation of a contract. It is not clear whether any breach or repudiation would be deemed "arbitrary" unless it violated the principles of Subsection (2), or constituted expropriation or creeping expropriation, Comment *g.* In any case, failure of a state to afford an adequate remedy to determine an asserted breach of contract is a denial of justice in violation of international law. Comment *j.*

Some commentators consider "arbitrary" any unreasonable departure from principles recognized by the principal legal systems of the world in their law of government contracts. See Sohn and Baxter, Draft Convention on the International Responsibility of States for Injuries to Aliens, Art. 12(a), 55 Am. J.Int'l L. 545 (1961). However, the propriety of governmental action affecting rights under state contracts has been uncertain under national law, too. See, for example, the cases applying the clause in the

United States Constitution forbidding States to impair the obligation of contracts (Article I, Section 10). *Compare* El Paso v. Simmons, 379 U.S. 497, 85 S.Ct. 577, 13 L.Ed.2d 446 (1965), *with* United States Trust Co. v. New Jersey, 431 U.S. 1, 97 S.Ct. 1505, 52 L.Ed.2d 92 (1977).

A state is generally responsible in international law for wrongs done by local subdivisions, see § 207(b), but there is authority that such responsibility does not extend to breach by local subdivisions of contracts with foreign contractors. See Sohn and Baxter, *supra*, Art. 12(1), and previous Restatement § 193, Comment *l.*

9. *"Internationalization" of concession or development agreements.* Repudiations by governments have resulted in controversy particularly in respect of concession or development agreements involving the exploitation of natural resources, since such contracts have sometimes become symbols of interference with the state's sovereignty over its natural resources. On the other hand, recovery of the alien's large capital investment requires a long period of contractual security. The 1962 Resolution of the General Assembly on Permanent Sovereignty over Natural Resources, Reporters' Note 1, recognized in Article 8 that "[f]oreign investment agreements freely entered into by or between sovereign states shall be observed in good faith."

The rights of the alien may depend on the form of the concession or development contract. The rights of the investor may be greater if the contract includes a provision that it shall be governed by "general principles of the law of nations" or "principles of the law of [the state party] not inconsistent with international law." Even if the contract provides that it shall be governed by local law, the contract is subject to the principles of Subsection (2).

The significance of such a clause has been disputed. Private parties to agreements containing such clauses have sometimes claimed that the clause converts the agreement into an international agreement, and breach of the contract into a violation of international law; that by such a clause, it is argued, a state submits its actions to international law and should be held to its bargain. On the other hand, some developing states have viewed such a clause as without effect because it derogates from the state's inalienable sovereignty, particularly its sovereign rights over its natural resources. Under an intermediate view, followed in this Restatement, such a clause authorizes courts or arbitrators to develop a body of rules for the resolution of disputes under such contracts, either modeled after the rules governing international agreements (Part III of this Restatement), or distilled from relevant general principles of various national legal systems. Such a clause does not, however, render the contract an international agreement subject to the rules of Part III, or to international remedies under Part IX.

Breaches of development or concession contracts are similar to, and often allied with, expropriations, Subsection (1), and international law tends to treat the two similarly. The law of the United States does so, too. The First Hickenlooper Amendment, Reporters' Note 2, made both such breaches and expro-

priations cause for the termination of aid. See § 444, Comment c. Legislation authorizing investment guarantees by the Overseas Private Investment Corporation (see § 713, Reporters' Note 7) defines "expropriation" to include "any abrogation, repudiation, or impairment by a foreign government of its own contract with an investor . . . where such abrogation, repudiation, or impairment is not caused by the investor's own fault or misconduct, and materially adversely affects the continued operation of the project." 22 U.S.C. § 2198(b).

10. *State contracts other than development agreements.* The principles of international law restated in Subsection (2) are relevant for international contract practice to different extents in respect of different types of contract disputes. For example:

(a) A state having entered into a contract to deliver goods of a certain quality, the foreign buyer claims that the product delivered was inferior. Such disputes are typically resolved by arbitration according to commercial rules, or in the ordinary or administrative courts of the contracting state or of the state of the private party's nationality. No issue of international law arises unless the contracting state interferes with the normal course of remedies.

(b) A state, having borrowed money abroad, fails to meet an installment of interest when it falls due. Such cases are typically adjusted by direct negotiation between the state and the lenders, with an international institution such as the International Monetary Fund acting as intermediary. The bond or loan agreement frequently contains a waiver of the state's immunity to suit in the courts of other states. See § 467, Reporters' Notes 3 and 4. In such cases, issues of state responsibility under international law or of international remedy rarely arise in modern practice. See Case of Certain Norwegian Loans (France v. Norway), [1957] I.C.J. Rep. 9, where the issue was raised but the Court decided it had no jurisdiction.

(c) A state, having entered into a long-term development (concession) agreement for a mining project, cancels the agreement in order to operate the project through a state agency. The state's action disrupts an established economic activity and is equivalent to a taking of property. Such action is sometimes intertwined in fact with a formal taking of property. The rules as to taking (Subsection (1)) generally apply. For cases in which arbitrators considered repudiations of concession agreements as takings, see Libyan American Oil Co. v. Libyan Arab Republic, (1977), 20 Int'l Leg.Mat. 1 (1981); Kuwait v. American Independent Oil Co. (1982), 21 Int'l Leg. Mat. 976 (1982); Texaco Overseas Petroleum Co. v. Libyan Arab Republic (1977), 17 Int'l Leg.Mat. 1 (1978).

(d) A state, having entered into a long term contract with a foreign national, then changes its tax or regulatory laws, bringing about a sharp reduction of the expected economic value of the contract to the foreign party. If the contract is one of many, the principle of international law forbidding discriminatory treatment requires similar treatment for all and will tend to discourage radical measures. Where the foreign contractor is virtually the only party affected, however, discrimination may not be the issue, and an international rule against discrimination may not provide the remedy. The private party may obtain a provision in the contract that "internationalizes" the contract, Reporters' Note 9, or a provision that expressly or by implication purports to "stabilize" the arrangement by barring the state from passing certain types of legislation during the term of the contract. If coupled with an arbitration clause, such a stabilization clause will be given effect by the arbitrator. For discussion of stabilization clauses, see the majority and concurring opinions in Kuwait v. American Independent Oil Co., (1982), 21 Int'l Leg.Mat. 976 (1982). Inclusion of such clauses may be resisted by some states, however, on the ground that they constitute a derogation from the state's sovereignty. Under Subsection (2), a state violating its obligation under a contract would be responsible, even in the absence of such a clause, if the repudiation or breach violated Subsection (2)(a) or if no remedy were provided, Subsection (2)(b).

In each of these types of disputes a state would incur responsibility under international law if it failed to provide access to an adequate forum for dispute resolution or failed to carry out a determination by a forum thus provided. Subsection (2)(b); see § 713.

11. *"Arbitrary" economic injury.* "Arbitrary" in Subsection (3) is used in a sense analogous to its use in connection with repudiation of contracts, Reporters' Note 8. It re-

fers to an act that is unfair and unreasonable, and inflicts serious injury to established rights of foreign nationals, though falling short of an act that would constitute an expropriation under Comment *g*.

12. *Economic injury and rights under international agreements.* Particularly among the developed countries, there is a network of bilateral international agreements that provide for extensive rights for the nationals of one state party within the territory of the other. These include the right to establish oneself in business or to invest in enterprises controlled by others, subject to the right of the host state to exclude aliens from certain "sensitive" businesses such as communications, air transport, banking, and natural resources. Once such enterprises are established, they are generally entitled to the same treatment as nationals of the host state, subject to narrow exceptions. Within the European Economic Community, extensive rights of establishment have been conferred upon nationals of the member states, and the Commission was authorized to develop a timetable for the removal of remaining restrictions on entry. In 1976, the member states of the Organization for Economic Cooperation and Development signed a Declaration on International Investment and Multinational Enterprises, 75 Dep't

State Bull. 83, which stated that each member state should afford enterprises owned or controlled by nationals of other member states treatment "no less favourable than that accorded in like situations to domestic enterprises." Whether a treaty gives private persons rights and remedies under the national law of the parties depends on interpretation of the treaty and on the domestic law of the state where the right or remedy is sought to be asserted. See § 111, Reporters' Note 4; § 713(2) and Comment *h* to that section; § 906.

13. *Previous Restatement.* The previous Restatement dealt with economic injuries to aliens in §§ 184–96. The subject is treated here in fewer sections, and is sometimes distributed differently among black letter, Comment, and Reporters' Notes, but without major change in substance. Thus, the standard of "just compensation" for a taking of property of a foreign national, §§ 187–90 in the previous Restatement, is dealt with here in Subsection (1), Comment *d*, and Reporters' Notes 2 and 3. Breach by a state of a contract with a foreign national, § 193 in the previous Restatement, is treated here in Subsection (2), Comment *h* and Reporters' Notes 8–10. Remedies for economic injury to foreign nationals are made more explicit in this Restatement, in § 713; see also § 906.

§ 713. Remedies for Injury to Nationals of Other States

(1) A state whose national has suffered injury under § 711 or § 712 has, as against the state responsible for the injury, the remedies generally available between states for violation of customary law, § 902, as well as any special remedies provided by any international agreement applicable between the two states.

(2) A person of foreign nationality injured by a violation of § 711 or § 712 may pursue any remedy provided by

> (a) international agreement between the person's state of nationality and the state responsible for the injury;
>
> (b) the law of the state responsible for the injury,
>
> (c) the law of another state, or
>
> (d) agreement between the person injured and the state responsible for the injury.

Comments:

a. Remedies under international law. A state whose national has suffered injury under § 711 or § 712 may resort to any of the remedies usually available to a state that has been the victim of a breach of international law, including international claims procedures and other diplomatic measures or permissible international responses. See § 902. The offended state may also invoke any special measures applicable by agreement between the two states, including arbitration or adjudication. Treaties of friendship, commerce, and navigation and other bilateral agreements commonly provide for resort to the International Court of Justice or to arbitration to resolve a claim that rights protected under the agreement have been violated. See §§ 903–904. In the case of economic rights guaranteed to nationals of member states of the European Communities, the special remedies provided by the treaties creating the Communities are available. The European Communities agreements provide for special remedies for violation by one member state of the rights of nationals of other Community members. See Comment *h.*

In principle, the responsibility of a state under §§ 711 and 712 is to the state of the alien's nationality and gives that state a claim against the offending state. The claim derives from injury to an individual, but once espoused it is the state's claim, and can be waived by the state. However, the derivative character of the claim has practical consequences: for example, damages are often measured by the damage to the individual, not by the loss to the state or the affront to its honor. The derivative character of the claim is reflected also in the traditional rule that the accused state can reject an international claim if the individual victim has not exhausted domestic remedies, Comment *f,* or if the individual has reached a voluntary settlement with the respondent state, Comment *g.* See also § 902.

b. Diplomatic protection. A state has the right to afford its nationals diplomatic protection against violation by another state of obligations under §§ 711 and 712. A state is entitled to communicate with a national arrested or charged with crime, to provide him assistance, and to have a representative present at his trial. A state may also intercede to assure other human rights of its nationals, their personal safety, or their property or other interests protected by §§ 711 and 712. Formal diplomatic espousal usually awaits exhaustion of local remedies (Comment *f*), but governments often intercede informally without regard to the person's domestic remedies.

For the special international protection available to refugees, see § 711, Reporters' Note 7.

c. Protection of persons of multiple nationality. Except as otherwise agreed by the parties, a state may refuse a claim or intercession by another state on behalf of an individual who is that state's national if the victim is (a) also a national of the responding state, or (b) also a national of a third state, and the responding state treats the person as a national of that state for the matter in question. However, the responding state may not refuse the claim or intercession if the nationality of the claimant state is "dominant", *i.e.*, if the individual has stronger links to that state, such as extended residence or sojourn or ties of family or property in that state. See § 211, Comment *f* and Reporters' Note 1; § 212, Reporters' Note 3.

For protection of subsidiaries of multinational companies, see Comment *e*.

d. Stateless persons. Since responsibility under §§ 711 and 712 is to the state of nationality, the principles stated in these sections provide no protection for persons who have no nationality; and the responsibility of the offending state to the state of nationality ceases if the alien has voluntarily given up that nationality or has lost or been deprived of it under the law of that state. However, the human rights of an alien who has no nationality are protected under general human rights law (Chapter 1 of this Part), which applies to all persons subject to a state's jurisdiction, regardless of nationality. Stateless persons may also have status, rights, and protections under the Convention relating to the Status of Stateless Persons (see Introductory Note to this Part), or as refugees, § 711, Reporters' Note 7.

e. Protection of corporations. Section 711(c) and § 712 apply to all persons of foreign nationality, natural as well as juridical, but since most foreign investment is in corporate form, the protections of those provisions are invoked largely by corporations. Under the rule stated in § 213, a corporation has the nationality of the state of its incorporation and that state is entitled to provide the company diplomatic protection. If the state of a corporation's nationality is not effectively representing the corporation, or if the injury was aimed at and incurred by shareholders of a particular nationality, the state of the shareholders' nationality has sometimes proceeded on their behalf. See § 213, Comment *d* and Reporters' Notes 2 and 3.

Much foreign investment is carried on through subsidiaries of multinational enterprises, the subsidiary being incorporated in the state where it is active. The United States and other capital exporting states, as the states of nationality of the parent corporation, have protested and made international claims when the property of a local subsidiary is expropriated or when the subsidiary sustains other economic injury in violation of § 712. The legal justification asserted for protection by the state of nationality of the parent varies. In some cases it is asserted that as a result of the expropriation or other injury the subsidiary has in fact ceased to exist so that the loss is that of the parent company. In other cases the argument is made that the expropriation or other act was aimed at the parent company or at the state of the parent's nationality. For issues arising out of regulation of multinational enterprises, see § 414, Comment *a*.

f. Exhaustion of remedies. Under international law, ordinarily a state is not required to consider a claim by another state for an injury to its national until that person has exhausted domestic remedies, unless such remedies are clearly sham or inadequate, or their application is unreasonably prolonged. There is no need to exhaust local remedies when the claim is for injury for which the respondent state firmly denies responsibility, for example a claim for injury due to the shooting down of a foreign commercial aircraft where the respondent state contends that the act was justified under international law. When a person has obtained a favorable decision in a domestic court, but that decision has not been complied with, no further remedies need be exhausted. For exhaustion of remedies for violations of human rights, see § 703, Comment *d*.

g. Waiver and "Calvo" clauses. A state's claim against another state for injury to its nationals fails if, after the injury, the person waives the claim or otherwise reaches a settlement with the respondent state.

Some states have attempted to immunize themselves against responsibility for an injury to an alien under §§ 711 and 712 by a "Calvo law," providing that an alien who acquires or invests in property waives the protection of his state of nationality, or by a "Calvo clause" in a contract with the state whereby the alien expressly waives such protection. The United States regards companies that sign such clauses or submit to such laws as waiving rights that are not theirs to waive, since, in principle, the injury is to the state, Comment a. In the view of the United States, such "waiver" by the private party does not preclude a claim by the state for denial of justice (§ 711), unjust enrichment, or on any other basis not depending on contract. See Reporters' Note 6.

h. *Remedies provided to injured persons by international agreement.* Under treaties of friendship, commerce, and navigation, nationals of one state party are generally assured access to the courts of the other state party on the same terms as nationals. In the European Economic Community, a national of a member state aggrieved by a violation of the agreement creating the community, may in appropriate cases obtain a resolution of the dispute by the European Court of Justice.

i. *Remedies for injured persons under state law.* The law of many states provides foreign nationals some remedy for many of the injuries resulting from violations of §§ 711 and 712. Often, these remedies are provided by the ordinary civil courts or a regular administrative tribunal; in some cases an exceptional body is established. As regards state contracts with foreign nationals, remedies before established tribunals are generally adequate to satisfy the requirements of § 712(2)(b). A special body may also be satisfactory unless it lacks the independence necessary to assure that the remedy is adequate. Inadequacy of remedy may also constitute a separate wrong of denial of justice. See § 711, Comment a; also § 712(2)(b).

Remedies are sometimes available in the injured person's home state. Thus, courts in the United States may exercise jurisdiction over claims against a foreign state arising out of certain commercial activities (§ 453(2)); over many claims in tort, if the injury occurred in the United States (§ 454, Comment e); and over some claims to property taken in violation of international law (§ 455(3)). Such remedies, however, may be subject to limitations such as the act of state doctrine. See §§ 443, 444. Many other countries also provide such remedies in principle, although in practice a state's courts frequently grant relief to investors of the state's nationality, less frequently to nationals of other countries.

j. *Remedies for foreign investors by special arrangement.* Various devices have been used, by agreement with the host state, to provide additional security to foreign investors and contractors. In contracts between a state and nationals of other states, it is sometimes provided that the contract shall be governed by the law of another state. Often there is provision for arbitration under procedures developed for international trade in general, *e.g.*, those of the International Chamber of Commerce, and such arbitral awards are enforceable in state courts under the 1958 Convention on the Enforcement of Foreign Arbitral Awards, Reporters' Note 4. Development (concession) agreements often provide for special arbitral procedures designed to immunize the contract from unilateral state action. The United States (through the Overseas Private Investment Corporation (OPIC)) and other capital exporting countries afford their nationals opportunity to buy insurance against expropriation of their investments in certain countries. In 1985, the governors of the World Bank launched a proposal for a Multilateral Investment Guarantee Agency (MIGA), but it was not yet in effect in 1987. See Reporters' Note 7. Special remedies are provided by the International Centre for the Settlement of Investment Disputes (ICSID): a state that is party to the agreement creating ICSID may include in its contracts with foreign nationals a clause referring disputes to ICSID, and an award by an ICSID arbitration will be enforced in the courts of member states. See Reporters' Note 4.

k. Compensation as remedy for unlawful expropriation or for repudiation of contract. The reparation for any taking in violation of § 712(1) is generally monetary compensation. An expropriation unlawful because of lack of just compensation gives rise to a claim for damages. A taking that is unlawful only because it was discriminatory or not for a public purpose, but was accompanied by just compensation, might bring only nominal damages. See § 712, Comment *f*. Restoration of ownership to the original owner is virtually unknown in expropriation cases. See Reporters' Note 7. In the United States, the Second Hickenlooper Amendment, 22 U.S.C. § 2370(e)(2), apparently contemplated that if property taken without compensation is brought into the United States, a court might allow the former owner to recover the property. See § 444.

For unlawful repudiation of contract, generally the remedy is monetary compensation. An arbitrator's award declaring that there has been an unlawful repudiation will generally be accompanied by an award of money damages (or followed by a money settlement).

REPORTERS' NOTES

1. *Remedies under international law.* The remedies for violations of §§ 711–12 include the diplomatic measures and international claims procedures available generally to a state claiming any breach of the international obligation by another state, § 902. See Comment *b*.

For a survey of United States actions to obtain reparation for economic injury to its nationals, see Kearney, "Diplomatic Protection of United States Foreign Investments," in International Project Finance, [1975] Fordham Corp. Law Inst. 243. Claims under §§ 711–12 may also go to arbitration or adjudication if the states involved have agreed, or agree *ad hoc*, to such resolution. In several cases, resort to the International Court of Justice to vindicate claims of economic injury to nationals failed on jurisdictional grounds. See Anglo-Iranian Oil Co. Case (United Kingdom v. Iran), [1952] I.C.J. Rep. 89; Nottebohm Case (Liechtenstein v. Guatemala), [1955] I.C.J. Rep. 4; Interhandel Case (Switzerland v. United States), [1959] I.C.J. Rep. 4; Barcelona Traction Case (Belgium v. Spain), [1970] I.C.J. Rep. 4.

Some treaties of friendship, commerce, and navigation provide that if a dispute over alleged denial to a person of a treaty right has not been resolved in the national courts or by diplomatic negotiation, it may be submitted to arbitration or to the International Court of Justice. In the European Communities, a member state may vindicate the rights of its nationals by resort to the European Court of Justice or to one of the other branches of the Communities system. By international agreement, states have also created special tribunals to resolve claims of alleged injury by one state to the nationals of the other. See Reporters' Note 9 and § 902, Reporters' Note 8.

2. *Protection of persons of multiple nationality.* In United States *ex rel.* Mergé v. Italian Republic, 1955, 14 R.Int'l Arb.Awards 236, the Italian–United States Conciliation Commission decided that the United States could not claim on behalf of the relator, a United States citizen by birth, since she also held Italian nationality, had resided in Italy with her husband, traveled on an Italian passport, and lived with him in Japan where he was an official of the Italian Embassy, and was therefore not "dominantly" a United States national within the meaning of the Treaty of Peace with Italy. See also Canevaro Case (Italy-Peru), Permanent Court of Arbitration, 1912, 1 Scott, Hague Court Reports 284 (1916). In Esphahanian v. Bank Tejarat, 2 Iran-U.S. C.T.R. 157 (1983), a Chamber of the Iran-United States Claims Tribunal permitted the United States to claim on behalf of a person possessing dual nationality, finding his United States nationality to be "dominant and effective." The Tribunal as a whole affirmed on the same ground. 78 Am.J.Int'l L. 914 (1984).

3. *Remedies for injured persons.* Treaties of friendship, commerce, and navigation generally provide that nationals of a state party have access to the courts of the other state on the same terms as nationals of that state. See, *e.g.*, Asakura v. Seattle, 265 U.S. 332, 44 S.Ct. 515, 68 L.Ed. 1041 (1924), and other cases cited in § 111, Reporters' Note 5; § 906, Reporters' Note 2. Even when there is no applicable treaty, the laws of many states provide foreign individuals local remedies for injuries covered by §§ 711–12. States that launch major expropriation programs sometimes establish special bodies to consider claims arising out of such programs, but in some cases, for example the Chilean Copper Program of 1971 (10 Int'l

Leg.Mat. 1067 (1971); 12 *id.* 983 (1973)), the independence of the tribunal and therefore the adequacy of the remedy are open to question. Comment *i.* In general, the availability of a domestic remedy does not relieve the state of responsibility for the injury under international law, although in principle the domestic remedy must be exhausted before international remedies can be pursued. Comment *f.*

In the United States, highly developed remedies for breach of contract or for a taking by the government are generally available to foreign nationals, and satisfy the requirements of both international and constitutional law. See § 721, Reporters' Note 7, and § 722, Reporters' Note 3. The United States Government takes private property for public use either by depositing the estimated amount of the property's value in court, or by taking the property and remitting the former owner to a suit under the Tucker Act. United States v. Cobb, 328 F.2d 115 (9th Cir.1964). Under either procedure, interest must be paid from the time of taking. Occasionally, in a massive taking, special remedies are provided for valuation after the taking. See Regional Rail Reorganization Act Cases, 419 U.S. 102, 156, 95 S.Ct. 335, 365, 42 L.Ed. 2d 320 (1974). Contract claims against the United States may be vindicated by suit in the courts, chiefly the Court of Claims, or through administrative procedures, chiefly the Boards of Contract Appeals of the various executive departments. Subject to domestic jurisdictional limitations, both United States and State courts are open to foreign nationals claiming injury by taking or other acts of States of the

United States. See § 722, Comments *a, c.*

Civil law systems tend to distinguish between commercial and administrative contracts, remitting disputes about the latter to administrative tribunals. As to the *contrat administratif,* see Friedmann, The Changing Structure of International Law 200–206 (1964).

A national of state X may have a remedy for a taking or for a breach of contract by state Y in the courts of state X or even of state Z. Thus, pursuant to the Foreign Sovereign Immunities Act and the Second Hickenlooper Amendment, United States courts are open to suits against a foreign state for compensation for expropriation of property if the property or its proceeds are present in the United States; or to suits in damages for breach of contract resulting from commercial activities of the foreign state. See §§ 453 and 455. Verlinden B.V. v. Central Bank of Nigeria, 461 U.S. 480, 103 S.Ct. 1962, 76 L.Ed.2d 81 (1983), upheld the provision in the Foreign Sovereign Immunities Act permitting a foreign national to sue a third state in the United States on a contract claim. See § 457, Reporters' Note 5.

The courts of other states have sometimes granted relief to their own nationals in expropriation cases, but have been less free in assisting nationals of third states. For cases arising from the Iranian oil nationalization of 1953, see Brower, "The Future of Foreign Investment—Recent Developments in the International Law of Expropriation and Compensation," in Private Investors Abroad—Problems and Solutions in International Business in 1975, at 93, 165, 173 (1976). For cases arising from the Chilean copper nationalization of 1971, see Mac-Crate, "International Arbitration in a New Climate of Foreign Nationalization," *id.* at 1, 24–25. See also Hunt v. Coastal States Gas Producing Co., Reporters' Note 8; Occidental of Umm al Qaywayn, Inc. v. A Certain Cargo, 577 F.2d 1196 (5th Cir.1978), *certiorari denied*, 442 U.S. 928, 99 S.Ct. 2857, 61 L.Ed.2d 296 (1979).

4. *Remedies pursuant to special contractual arrangements.* It is common for traders and investors dealing with foreign governments to seek clauses in their contracts providing for the resolution of disputes outside of national legal systems. See MacCrate, Reporters' Note 3. For example, a private party may seek to have disputes resolved through one of the channels commonly used in international trade, such as the Court of Arbitration of the International Chamber of Commerce. Such agreements are generally regarded as effectively waiving sovereign immunity and are enforceable in the courts of other states under the Convention on the Recognition and Enforcement of Arbitral Awards, 21 U.S.T. 2517, T.I.A.S. No. 6997, 330 U.N.T.S. 3. See § 456, Reporters' Note 3 and § 487; see generally Delaume, "State Contracts and Transnational Arbitration," 75 Am.J.Int'l L. 784 (1981).

In development contracts, reference might be to ICSID, *infra*, or to a special *ad hoc* tribunal. Such arrangements have resulted in a number of important arbitral awards, *e.g.*, Petroleum Development Ltd. v. Sheikh of Abu Dhabi (1951), 18 Int'l L.Rep. 144 (1953); Sapphire Int'l Petroleum Ltd. v. National Iranian Oil Co. (1963), 35 Int'l L.Rep. 136 (1967); Saudi Arabia v. Arabian American Oil Co. (1958), 27 Int'l L.Rep. 117 (1963). Three arbitrations arose from the cancellation of oil concession agreements by Libya: Texas Overseas Petroleum Co. v. Libyan Arab Republic (1977), 17 Int'l Leg.Mat. 1 (1978); BP Exploration Co. v. Libyan Arab Republic (1974), 53 Int'l L.Rep. 297 (1979); Libyan American Oil Co. v. Libyan Arab Republic (1977), 20 Int'l Leg. Mat. 1 (1981). See, generally, von Mehren and Kourides, "International Arbitration Between States and Foreign Private Parties: The Libyan Nationalization Cases," 75 Am.J. Int'l L. 476 (1981). For difficulties encountered in Switzerland and the United States in enforcing the Libyan-American award, see *id.* at 548, and Delaume, *supra*, at 788.

As regards investment disputes, as of 1987, 89 states were parties to the Convention on the Settlement of Investment Disputes between States and Nationals of Other States, 17 U.S.T. 1270, T.I.A.S. No. 6090, 575 U.N.T.S. 159 (1965), sponsored by the World Bank. A state party to that Convention may include in its legislation or in a contract with a foreign investor a clause referring disagreements to the International Centre for the Settlement of Investment Disputes (ICSID). As of 1986, 22 disputes had been referred to panels of arbitrators drawn from ICSID's roster; five had been disposed of by opinions of arbitrators; several had been settled by the parties; and two had been referred to conciliation proceedings. See ICSID Annual Reports. The Convention obligates states parties to enforce awards of ICSID tribunals. That obligation is implemented in the United States by

22 U.S.C. §§ 1650, 1650a. The states parties to the Convention have agreed not to espouse diplomatically claims by their nationals in respect of disputes within the jurisdiction of the Centre.

5. *Exhaustion of domestic remedies.* In the Interhandel Case (Switzerland v. United States), [1959] I.C.J. Rep. 6, 26–27, the International Court of Justice noted that "[t]he rule that local remedies must be exhausted before international proceedings may be instituted is a well-established rule of customary international law"; and that this rule "has been generally observed in cases in which a State has adopted the cause of its national whose rights are claimed to have been disregarded in another State in violation of international law." The Court added that "[b]efore resort may be had to an international court in such a situation, it has been considered necessary that the State where the violation occurred should have an opportunity to redress it by its own means, within the framework of its own domestic legal system."

In that case, the United States had vested the assets of Interhandel during the Second World War, claiming that Interhandel, though incorporated in Switzerland, was controlled by a German company and therefore could properly be considered an enemy alien. Interhandel brought suit in the United States district court in 1946 to recover its assets; a judgment dismissing Interhandel's suit was affirmed in the court of appeals. While a petition for certiorari by Interhandel was pending before the United States Supreme Court in 1959, Switzerland brought a proceeding against the United States in the International Court of Justice.

The Supreme Court of the United States granted Interhandel's petition for certiorari and reversed and remanded the case to the district court. Société Internationale pour Participations Industrielles et Commerciales, S.A. v. Rogers, 357 U.S. 197, 78 S.Ct. 1087, 2 L.Ed.2d 1255 (1958), § 442, Reporters' Note 6. The International Court of Justice dismissed the proceeding before it. The Court said that the exhaustion of local remedies rule must be observed *a fortiori* when the domestic proceedings are still pending, especially when both the domestic and the international actions are designed to obtain the same result, *i.e.,* the restitution of Interhandel's assets.

As was stated in the Ambatielos Case (Greece v. United Kingdom), 1951, 12 R.Int'l Arb.Awards 91, 120, 122, the phrase "local remedies" should be interpreted broadly, including "the whole system of legal protection, as provided by municipal law," not only the courts and tribunals but also "the use of procedural facilities which municipal law makes available to litigants." There, the claimant lost the case in the lower court because he failed to call a crucial witness, and the Court of Appeals refused "to give leave to adduce [this] evidence." The tribunal held that the claimant had failed to exhaust local remedies, as it was due to his own action that the appeal became futile.

It is generally accepted that the claimant must utilize all available procedural means, presenting all pertinent evidence, raising all substantive arguments, both issues of law and fact, and exhausting all appeals. See Finnish Ships Case (Finland v. United Kingdom), 1934, 3 R.Int'l Arb.Awards 1484, 1498–1505. If, however, a higher tribunal is not competent to deal with a particular contention, for instance if appeals are limited to issues of law and the claim is based primarily on a matter of fact, an appeal is not required and remedies are considered exhausted. *Id.* at 1535–43. "There can be no need to resort to the municipal courts if those courts have no jurisdiction to afford relief; nor is it necessary again to resort to those courts if the result must be a repetition of a decision already given." Panevezys-Saldutiskis Railway Case (Estonia v. Lithuania), P.C.I.J., ser. A/B, No. 76 at 18 (1939). See also Finnish Ships Case, *supra,* at 1495, 1504.

An arbitration clause in a contract between a state and a national of another state, or another forum selection clause, is not subject to the requirement of exhaustion of domestic remedies in the contracting state unless otherwise agreed. The 1965 Convention on the Settlement of Investment Disputes Between States and Nationals of Other States, Reporters' Note 4, provides in Article 26 that consent to arbitration under that Convention is deemed to exclude any other remedy, unless the contracting state requires "the exhaustion of local administrative or judicial remedies as a condition of its consent to arbitration under this Convention." 17 U.S.T. 1270, T.I.A.S. No. 6090, 575 U.N.T.S. 159.

6. *Waiver of rights by injured person.* Some Latin American states have long advocated a Calvo Doctrine (named after an Argentine diplomat and writer) to the effect

that states owed aliens no duty beyond treatment equal to that accorded to nationals. See § 712, Reporters' Note 1. The United States and other states denied the validity of the Doctrine and the effectiveness of a Calvo law or clause, Comment *g,* reflecting that doctrine. See [1976] Digest of U.S. Practice in Int'l Law 435. Arbitrations during the 1920's left the effectiveness of such a provision in doubt; in particular, they indicated, the clause was not effective in cases of denial of justice or in cases where the claim did not arise under the contract. See Shea, The Calvo Clause (1955). There has been no significant arbitral ruling since that time. See Note, "The Calvo Clause," 6 Texas Int'l.L.Forum 289 (1971).

Settlement by the injured person, after the alleged wrong but before espousal of the claim by the state of nationality, is generally regarded as effective if the settlement was voluntary. However, the United States has taken the position that it will not be bound if its national accepts less than adequate compensation. [1975] Digest of U.S. Practice in Int'l Law 488–89.

7. *Expropriation insurance.* The United States has offered insurance against expropriation since shortly after World War II; the program is currently administered by the Overseas Private Investment Corporation (OPIC), a government corporation established under 22 U.S.C. §§ 2191–2200a. OPIC charges premiums and acts like a commercial insurance firm in some respects, but it is backed by the full faith and credit of the United States and it pursues various policies of the United States in selecting projects to insure. OPIC insures an

investment only if the host state agrees. Upon entering into a guaranty agreement, the investor is insured against loss through expropriation of the funds it has invested, usually less a deductible amount. (War risk and inconvertibility coverage are also available.) If an expropriation occurs, the investor presents a claim to OPIC; if an amicable settlement cannot be reached with the investor, the investor may resort to arbitration. 22 U.S.C. § 2197(i). If OPIC pays a claim, it is subrogated to the investor's rights; it may pursue the matter with the expropriating state, and may resort to international remedies, including arbitration, if necessary. Other capital exporting states administer similar programs. See Meron, Investment Insurance in International Law (1976).

In 1985, the World Bank prepared a Convention Establishing the Multilateral Investment Guarantee Agency (MIGA), 24 Int'l Leg.Mat. 1598 (1985), but the Convention was not yet in effect as of 1987.

8. *Compensation as remedy for unlawful expropriation or repudiation of contract.* In Factory at Chorzów, P.C.I.J. ser. A, No. 17, at 46–48 (1928), the Permanent Court of International Justice seemed to distinguish between takings in violation of a treaty, the remedy for which was restitution, and takings that were otherwise unlawful, which effectively passed title but gave rise to an obligation to compensate. Where restitution was the appropriate remedy but was not practicable, the claimant was entitled to compensation, including the higher measure if the property had appreciated in value between the time of the taking and the judgment

date. Contemporary cases generally involve disputes about just compensation rather than restitution. Governments generally accept and arbitrators generally award monetary compensation. Compare the law of the United States as to taking of Indian property, where Congress made compensation the exclusive remedy even when the taking was alleged to be unconstitutional because not for a public use. Oglala Sioux Tribe of Pine Ridge Indian Reservation v. United States, 650 F.2d 140 (8th Cir.1981), *certiorari denied*, 455 U.S. 907, 102 S.Ct. 1252, 71 L.Ed.2d 445 (1982).

The Second Hickenlooper Amendment (§ 444) directs the courts not to apply the Act of State doctrine and "to give effect to the principles of international law in a case in which a claim of title or other right to property" is asserted based upon an unlawful expropriation. See § 444, Comment *a*. The statute does not indicate what remedies the court may give, but the possibility of restitution seems contemplated. Cases holding the amendment inapplicable to breach of contract include Hunt v. Coastal States Gas Producing Co., 583 S.W.2d 322 (Tex. 1979), *certiorari denied*, 444 U.S. 992, 100 S.Ct. 523, 62 L.Ed.2d 421 (1979); French v. Banco Nacional de Cuba, 23 N.Y.2d 46, 242 N.E.2d 704, 295 N.Y.S.2d 434 (1968).

In other contexts, illegality under international law has been claimed to vitiate title. For example, the United Nations has sought to render minerals extracted in Namibia under the authority of the South African government unmarketable, by decreeing that such authority is invalid and that the title to such products remains in Namibia as represented by the United Nations Council on Namibia. See Schermers, "The Namibia Decree in National Courts," 26 Int'l & Comp. L.Q. 81 (1977).

Whether and in what circumstances specific performance may be ordered for a repudiation of a contract in violation of § 712(2) is not settled. See, e.g., Award in Dispute Between British Petroleum and Libya (1973), 53 Int'l L.Rep. 297, and Award in Dispute Between Libyan American Oil Co. and Libyan Arab Republic (1977), 20 Int'l Leg. Mat. 1, 61–64 (1981), denying specific performance but awarding compensation. In Texas Overseas Petroleum Co. and Libyan Arab Republic (1977), 17 Int'l Leg.Mat. 1, 32–37 (1978), the arbitrator, after extended discussion of restitution, declared that Libya was "legally bound to perform its contract"; the dispute was settled on a monetary basis (paid in oil).

9. *Diplomatic protection and claims settlement by the United States.* Throughout its history, the United States has provided active diplomatic protection for United States nationals and has pressed numerous claims for violations of their rights and interests in accordance with the principles of § 711.

United States practice in respect of claims for injury to United States nationals reflects the character of international remedies and United States claims practice generally. See § 902 and Reporters' Note 8 thereto. In 1853, when the United States was contemplating settling several claims against Chile, the Secretary of State first stated that "having originally taken up the subject at the instance of the claimants, and for their benefit, it would be altogether inexpedient to pursue it, without the attempt at least to obtain their consent beforehand to the measures adopted." He added that a contrary course would be imprudent as it "might lay the foundations for an onerous demand upon Congress." Later it was explained that this statement did not imply that it was "indispensable to obtain the consent of the claimants in order to make a convention." 6 Moore, Digest of International Law 1015 (1906).

The Supreme Court has referred to Congressional authorization of payment to claimants as a result of an international claims settlement as "payments of grace." See cases cited in § 721, Reporters' Note 8. For a parallel Swiss case, see Gschwind v. Swiss Confederation, [1931–32] Annual Dig. 242.

As to whether the settlement of a claim of a United States national may constitute "taking" of private property, see § 721, Reporters' Note 8.

After the Second World War, several bloc settlement agreements led to the creation in 1949 of the International Claims Commission (renamed "Foreign Claims Settlement Commission" in 1954 and "Foreign Claims Settlement Commission of the United States" in 1982, when the Commission was transferred from the Department of State to the Department of Justice "as a separate agency"). Its function is to distribute funds received from foreign governments among the various claimants, after considering each claim separately and deciding on its validity and the amount due to each claimant on the basis of "applicable principles of international law, justice, and equity." 22 U.S.C. §§ 1621–1645o, as amended. In some instances, groups of claims have been referred to the Commission even prior to a settlement agreement for a preliminary assessment (*e.g.*, with respect to Vietnam in 1980, see 22 U.S.C. § 1645). There is a standing appropriation for the distribution of funds received by the United States from a foreign government and deposited in the Miscellaneous Receipts account of the Treasury. 22 U.S.C. § 2668a. For a summary report on United States settlements of claims for compensation for nationalization of property of United States nationals, see United States brief as *amicus curiae* at 30–32, Banco Nacional De Cuba v. Sabbatino, 376 U.S. 398, 84 S.Ct. 923, 11 L.Ed.2d 804 (1964), reprinted in 2 Int'l Leg.Mat. 1009, 1019 (1963).

A number of United States settlement agreements provided for the establishment of claims commissions to adjudicate private claims. Notable among such bodies were the claims commission established by the General Claims Convention of 1923 between the United States and Mexico, § 711, Reporters' Note 2, and the Iran-United States Claims Tribunal created under the Algiers Declaration, § 487, Reporters' Note 6.

10. *Previous Restatement.* In the previous Restatement, the rules governing remedies for injury to foreign nationals were not set forth in one section. The requirement that local remedies be exhausted was treated in §§ 206–10, the effectiveness of waiver by the claimant in §§ 202–205, the practice of the United States in regard to claims in §§ 211–14. Questions about the nationality of the claimant for claims purposes were treated in §§ 171–73.

Chapter Three

INDIVIDUAL RIGHTS IN FOREIGN
RELATIONS: LAW OF THE
UNITED STATES

Section
721. Applicability of Constitutional Safeguards
722. Rights of Aliens

§ 721. Applicability of Constitutional Safeguards

The provisions of the United States Constitution safeguarding individual rights generally control the United States government in the conduct of its foreign relations as well as in domestic matters, and generally limit governmental authority whether it is exercised in the United States or abroad, and whether such authority is exercised unilaterally or by international agreement.

Comment:

a. United States foreign relations subject to constitutional restraints. Any exercise of authority by the United States in the conduct of foreign relations is subject to the Bill of Rights and other constitutional restraints protecting individual rights. That principle applies equally to authority exercised pursuant to powers expressed in the Constitution, for example the power of Congress to regulate commerce with foreign nations (Article I, Section 8), as to foreign affairs powers not enumerated in the Constitution but inherent in the United States "as necessary concomitants of nationality." United States v. Curtiss-Wright Export Corp., 299 U.S. 304, 318, 57 S.Ct. 216, 220, 81 L.Ed. 255 (1936); see § 1, Reporters' Note 1. Treaties and other international agreements are also subject to such constitutional restraints. See Reporters' Note 1.

b. Applicability of Constitution outside United States territory. The Constitution governs the exercise of authority by the United States government over United States citizens outside United States territory, for example on the high seas, and even on foreign soil. Although the matter has not been definitely adjudicated, the Constitution probably governs also at least some exercises of authority by the United States in respect of some aliens abroad. See § 722, Reporters' Note 16.

c. Incorporated and unincorporated territories. The Constitution limits the exercise of governmental authority in territories that Congress has formally incorporated into the United States as within States of the United States. Early in this century, the Supreme Court decided that in territories acquired by the United States that Congress has not incorporated, only "fundamental" constitutional rights apply. See Reporters' Note 3.

d. First Amendment freedoms. The freedoms of speech, press, religion, and assembly, and the right not to be subject to an establishment of religion, are protected against infringement in the exercise of foreign relations power as in domestic affairs. There is a heavy presumption against the validity of "prior restraints of expression," such as judicial injunctions against publication of classified materials relating to foreign affairs. However, insofar as restraints (for example, on time, place, or manner of communication) are judged by balancing the private right against the public need, national foreign affairs interests weigh heavily in the balance. For example, Congress may prohibit picketing near foreign embassies.

e. Unreasonable searches and seizures. It is not unreasonable search and seizure, even in the absence of a warrant, for United States customs officials to inspect baggage entering or leaving the country, or for immigration officers to stop and inspect automobiles at check points in border areas. As regards Coast Guard arrest and search of vessels, see § 433, Comment *d* and Reporters' Note 4.

f. Due process of law and equal protection of the laws. The due process clause requires fair procedure in matters relating to foreign relations, in civil as in criminal matters, for aliens as for citizens. See § 722. What process is due, however, differs with the circumstances. Presidential decisions generally, even when they affect private interests, are not judicial in character and do not require judicial kinds of procedures. Thus, for example, a hearing is not required as of constitutional right before the President exercises his constitutional authority, or authority delegated to him by Congress, to suggest immunity from suit (see Introductory Note to Part IV, Chapter 5, Subchapter A), to impose a tariff, to invoke the act of state doctrine (§ 444 and Comment *f* thereto), to extradite an individual for trial by a foreign country (§ 478), or to settle an international claim (§ 713, Comment *a*, and this section, Comment *g*).

The due process clause also gives some substantive protection to life, liberty, or property affected, for example, by a regulation of foreign commerce or of the right to travel. Comment *i*. To date, the due process clause has not been held to prevent deportation of an alien, even one long resident in the United States, for whatever reason Congress chooses, so long as notice, hearing, and fair procedures are provided. See § 722, Comment *i* and Reporters' Note 12.

The due process clause of the Fifth Amendment also incorporates the requirement that the federal government afford the equal protection of the laws. For equal protection of the laws as applied to aliens, see § 722, Comments *c* and *d*.

g. Taking of private property. In matters affecting foreign relations as in domestic matters, it is not always easy to distinguish a regulation that is within the police power of the United States from a taking of private property requiring just compensation under the Fifth Amendment. See § 712, Comment *g* and Reporters' Note 6. In foreign relations, the distinction must take account of the conceptions and traditions of international law. For example, under international law and practice, claims between a national or resident of the United States and a foreign state, its national or resident, are seen as claims between the United States and the other state which they can settle by international agreement. See § 713, Comment *a* and Reporters' Note 9, and § 902, Comment *i* and Reporters' Note 8. Usually, the Executive Branch consults with representatives of claimants, and Congress has generally made monies received in settlement available for distribution to the private claimants. In general, a settlement by treaty or executive agreement of foreign claims of United States nationals or residents neither deprives them of their property without due process of law (see Comment *f*) nor constitutes a taking of their property requiring compensation. In special circumstances, however, a sacrifice of private claims for a national purpose may constitute a taking requiring compensation. See Reporters' Note 8.

h. Safeguards in criminal procedure. Criminal trials implicating foreign affairs are subject to the usual constitutional safeguards for the accused. Except as regards members of the armed forces and others subject to military law during war, a trial held under the authority of the United States must conform to the requirements of the Fifth and Sixth Amendments, including right to counsel and to jury trial and respect for the privilege against self-incrimination, whether the trial is held in the United States or abroad. A United States court has held that these safeguards, including a jury trial, are required in a trial of an alien under United States authority in Berlin. See Reporters' Note 9, and § 722, Reporters' Note 16. Whether a jury trial is required where the court has mixed character, serving both as a court of the United States and as a local court, may depend on the circumstances, including the gravity of the offense. See Reporters' Note 3 and § 722, Reporters' Note 16. As to United States law on extradition, see §§ 475–478.

i. Right to travel. "The right to travel abroad is part of the 'liberty' of which the citizen cannot be deprived without due process of law . . . . Freedom of movement is basic in our scheme of values." Kent v. Dulles, 357 U.S. 116, 125–26, 78 S.Ct. 1113, 1122, 2 L.Ed.2d 1204 (1958). As a fundamental right, it may not be curtailed lightly and the Executive may limit such travel only if clearly authorized by Congress. The right to travel may not be denied or limited on grounds that would infringe First Amendment rights, *e.g.*, because of a person's political opinions. But in Haig v. Agee, 453 U.S. 280, 306–307, 101 S.Ct. 2766, 2781, 69 L.Ed.2d 640 (1981), the Court distinguished "the *freedom* to travel outside the United States" from "the *right* to travel within the United States," the former being "no more than an aspect of the 'liberty' protected by the Due Process Clause of the Fifth Amendment." The Secretary of State may revoke a passport when he determines that the individual's activities abroad are causing or are likely to cause serious damage to the national security or foreign policy of the United States. The Secretary may also forbid the use of the passport for travel to designated countries and, upon appropriate findings of fact, may confiscate the passport if it is abused; under 22 U.S.C. § 211a, enacted in 1978, the Secretary can impose such restrictions in respect of a country with which the United States is at war, where armed hostilities are in progress, or where there is imminent danger to the health or safety of United States travelers.

j. Acquisition and loss of citizenship. United States law on acquisition and loss of citizenship is set forth in § 212.

k. Rights protected against infringement by States of the United States. Although foreign affairs are within the exclusive authority of the federal government, the actions of States also often impinge on the foreign relations of the United States. See § 1, Reporters' Note 5. Rights of persons are protected by provisions in Article I, Section 10, that may have foreign affairs applications, *e.g.*, the provisions forbidding States to pass "any bill of attainder, *ex post facto* law, or law impairing the obligation of contracts," or to lay any duties on imports or exports without the consent of Congress. The Thirteenth Amendment supports the international obligations of the United States to outlaw slavery and slave trade. See § 702, Reporters' Note 4. The Fourteenth Amendment establishes national citizenship, and forbids States to abridge the privileges or immunities of citizens of the United States, including, for example, "free access to its seaports, through which all operations of foreign commerce are conducted," and the right "to demand the care and protection of the federal government over his life, liberty, and property when on the high seas or within the jurisdiction of a foreign government." Slaughter-House Cases, 83 U.S. (16 Wall.) 36, 79, 21 L.Ed. 394 (1873). States may not deprive persons of life, liberty, or property without due process of law, or deny them the equal protection of the laws. A person may invoke the due process clause to challenge excessive exercises of jurisdiction by a State. The due process clause of the Fourteenth Amendment provides the same protections against the States as the due process clause of the Fifth Amendment provides against the Federal Government. See Comment *f*. It also requires States that take property for public use to provide just compensation. Compare Comment *g*. The Fourteenth Amendment also incorporates and applies to the States most of the provisions of the Bill of Rights.

For the rights of aliens protected against State violation, see § 722.

l. Rights of foreign governments and officials under the United States Constitution and laws. Subject to international agreements and to immunities and other principles of international law (Part IV, Chapter 5), a foreign state or international organization, engaged in activities or party to any suit in the United States, is generally treated as a person for purposes of United States law. A foreign state or an international organization is not a "person" enjoying rights under the United States Constitution generally, but foreign states are accorded procedural due process and may claim also the minimum due process requirements for the exercise of *in personam* jurisdiction by courts in the United States. See § 453, Reporters' Note 3. Their status under international law apart, accredited diplomatic representatives and officials of foreign governments or of international organizations have status and rights under the Constitution similar to those of other aliens admitted to the United States temporarily for special purposes (see § 722, Comment *j*), but are subject to different procedures in respect of entry to and departure from the United States.

REPORTERS' NOTES

1. *United States foreign relations subject to constitutional restraints.* "The restrictions confining Congress in the exercise of any of the powers expressly delegated to it in the Constitution apply with equal vigor when that body seeks to regulate our relations with other nations." Perez v. Brownell, 356 U.S. 44, 58, 78 S.Ct. 568, 576, 2 L.Ed.2d 603 (1955). The powers of the United States inherent in sovereignty,

although not explicit in the Constitution, are subject to constitutional limitations. United States v. Curtiss-Wright Export Corp., 299 U.S. 304, 320, 57 S.Ct. 216, 221, 81 L.Ed. 255 (1936). Treaties and executive agreements are similarly limited. "The prohibitions of the Constitution were designed to apply to all branches of the National Government and they cannot be nullified by the Executive or by the Executive and Senate combined." Reid v. Covert, 354 U.S. 1, 17, 77 S.Ct. 1222, 1230, 1 L.Ed.2d 1148 (1957) (plurality opinion of Black, J.). See § 302(2) and Reporters' Note 1. Constitutional prohibitions apply to acts of the United States abroad as well as at home, for wherever the United States acts "it can only act in accordance with the limitations imposed by the Constitution." Reid v. Covert, 354 U.S. at 6, 77 S.Ct. at 1225. But "[m]atters intimately related to foreign policy and national security are rarely proper subjects for judicial intervention." Haig v. Agee, 453 U.S. 280, 292, 101 S.Ct. 2766, 2774, 69 L.Ed.2d 640 (1981). Sometimes issues raised by such matters are deemed "political questions" and not justiciable. See § 1, Reporters' Note 4.

The courts have occasionally invalidated actions related to foreign affairs, in various contexts, *e.g.*, Afroyim v. Rusk, 387 U.S. 253, 87 S.Ct. 1660, 18 L.Ed.2d 757 (1967) (invalidating act of Congress depriving person of United States citizenship for voting in foreign election); Reid v. Covert, *supra* (dependent of United States serviceman cannot be tried abroad by court-martial without a jury); Faruki v. Rogers, 349 F.Supp. 723 (D.D.C.1972) (invalidating act requiring naturalized citizen to have been citizen for ten years to

be eligible for United States Foreign Service). As of 1987, no provision in an international agreement of the United States has been declared unconstitutional by the Supreme Court.

2. *Applicability of Constitution outside United States territory.* In In re Ross, 140 U.S. 453, 464, 11 S.Ct. 897, 900, 35 L.Ed. 581 (1890), the Supreme Court said: "The Constitution can have no operation in another country." That case and its doctrine have been dismissed as "a relic from a different era." Reid v. Covert, Reporters' Note 1, 354 U.S. at 12, 77 S.Ct. at 1228 (plurality opinion of Black, J.). The Constitution has been given effect outside territory of the United States in Reid v. Covert, and in Kinsella v. United States *ex rel.* Singleton, 361 U.S. 234, 80 S.Ct. 297, 4 L.Ed.2d 268 (1960) (dependent of United States serviceman or civilian defense employee cannot be tried abroad for crime by court-martial without a jury); also Seery v. United States, 130 Ct. Cl. 481, 127 F.Supp. 601 (1955) (requiring compensation for taking by United States military authorities of property of United States citizen in Austria). In Berlin Democratic Club v. Rumsfeld, 410 F.Supp. 144 (D.D.C. 1976), the district court held justiciable the claims of United States citizens abroad against United States army officials for violations of civil rights and other harassment and intimidation. The Constitution governs actions by United States authorities on the high seas. See § 433, Comment *d*. For the applicability of the Constitution to aliens abroad, see § 722, Comment *m*.

3. *Incorporated and unincorporated territories.* The distinc-

tion between incorporated and unincorporated territories was established in The Insular Cases, Downes v. Bidwell, 182 U.S. 244, 21 S.Ct. 770, 45 L.Ed. 1088 (1901) (Puerto Rico then not part of United States for purposes of revenue clauses of Constitution); Hawaii v. Mankichi, 190 U.S. 197, 23 S.Ct. 787, 47 L.Ed. 1016 (1903) (upholding conviction under Hawaiian law by less-than-unanimous jury verdict, since Hawaii then unincorporated territory); Dorr v. United States, 195 U.S. 138, 24 S.Ct. 808, 49 L.Ed. 128 (1904) (same); Balzac v. Porto Rico, 258 U.S. 298, 42 S.Ct. 343, 66 L.Ed. 627 (1922) (Sixth Amendment jury trial requirement not applicable in unincorporated territory). The continued validity of the distinction between incorporated and unincorporated territories was questioned in Justice Black's opinion in Reid v. Covert, Reporters' Note 1, 354 U.S. at 14, 77 S.Ct. at 1228, but has survived. See, *e.g.*, Torres v. Puerto Rico, 442 U.S. 465, 468–70, 99 S.Ct. 2425, 2428–29, 61 L.Ed.2d 1 (1979). In that case, the Court held that the prohibition on search and seizure and the exclusionary rule applied in Puerto Rico, but the Court divided on the basis for that conclusion; the majority treated Puerto Rico as unincorporated territory within the doctrine of the *Insular Cases, supra,* but found the constitutional provision applicable. The status of Puerto Rico is *sui generis*; the relationship of Puerto Rico to the United States "has no parallel in our history." Examining Board v. Flores de Otero, 426 U.S. 572, 596, 96 S.Ct. 2264, 2278, 49 L.Ed.2d 65 (1976). Although individuals enjoy constitutional rights there, Congress may distinguish between Puerto Rico and the States for many purposes. Compare Harris v. Rosario, 446 U.S. 651, 100 S.Ct. 1929, 64 L.Ed.2d 587 (1980) (Congress may provide Puerto Rico less assistance than to the States in meeting needs of dependent children).

Other cases have upheld claims to constitutional protections in United States territories. *E.g.*, Ralpho v. Bell, 569 F.2d 607 (D.C.Cir.1977) (national of United States trust territory entitled to judicial review of claim that Micronesian Claims Commission created by Congress denied him due process of law). See also King v. Morton, 520 F.2d 1140, 1147 (D.C.Cir.1975), holding that a jury trial should be provided an accused in American Samoa unless it would be "impractical and anomalous," and, on remand, King v. Andrus, 452 F.Supp. 11 (D.D.C.1977), deciding that the jury system would not be impractical or anomalous in that territory in serious cases. Compare 48 U.S.C. § 1421b extending certain provisions of the United States Constitution to Guam; § 1561 (Virgin Islands); and § 1681 note (Section 501(a) of the Covenant of the Northern Mariana Islands); see also § 1004(a) of the Covenant of the Northern Mariana Islands, *ibid.*, authorizing the President of the United States to suspend the application there of any provision of the United States Constitution "which would otherwise apply" until termination of the Trusteeship Agreement, if he finds that such provision would be inconsistent with the Trusteeship Agreement.

4. *First Amendment freedoms.* The "Pentagon Papers" case, New

York Times v. United States, 403 U.S. 713, 91 S.Ct. 2140, 29 L.Ed.2d 822 (1971), denied the Executive Branch an injunction against the publication of classified documents, the publication of which, it was alleged, would damage the military and foreign policy interests of the United States. The Supreme Court held that the Government had failed to overcome a heavy presumption against "prior restraints of expression."

A District of Columbia law forbidding picketing within 500 feet of an embassy was upheld in Frend v. United States, 100 F.2d 691 (D.C. Cir.1938), *certiorari denied,* 306 U.S. 640, 59 S.Ct. 488, 83 L.Ed. 1040 (1939); and again in Finzer v. Barry, 798 F.2d 1450 (D.C.Cir.1986); compare United States v. Grace, 461 U.S. 171 (1983), holding a statute unconstitutional as applied to forbid distributing leaflets on sidewalk in front of the United States Supreme Court.

A United States statute authorizing the Post Office Department to retain all mail from abroad determined to be "Communist political propaganda," and to forward it to the addressee only upon his request, was held invalid as inhibiting the exercise of the First Amendment right to receive information. Lamont v. Postmaster General, 381 U.S. 301, 85 S.Ct. 1493, 14 L.Ed.2d 398 (1965). But the First Amendment rights of persons in the United States were deemed not violated by the denial of a visa to an alien scholar whom they had invited to lecture in the United States, Kleindienst v. Mandel, 408 U.S. 753, 92 S.Ct. 2576, 33 L.Ed.2d 683 (1972), relying in part on the fact that applicant had violated a condition on a prior visa.

There has been no definitive adjudication, but issues under the First Amendment would arise if the United States entered into arrangements with a foreign country that involved foreign assistance or other expenditures of United States funds for religious purposes, or other official involvement in religion (*e.g.,* through the Peace Corps); or agreements or other arrangements with a foreign country that entailed discrimination against United States citizens because of their religion. But *cf.* American Jewish Congress v. Vance, 575 F.2d 939 (D.C.Cir. 1978) (challenge to United States arrangements with Saudi Arabia as involving discrimination against United States citizens who were Jewish dismissed as raising political question).

5. *Unreasonable searches and seizures.* The constitutional guarantee against unreasonable searches and seizures is applied with some modifications to border searches. An automobile may not be searched without a warrant or probable cause to believe that the occupants are engaged in a violation of law. Almeida-Sanchez v. United States, 413 U.S. 266, 93 S.Ct. 2535, 37 L.Ed. 2d 596 (1973) (search by roving patrol in border area); United States v. Ortiz, 422 U.S. 891, 95 S.Ct. 2585, 45 L.Ed.2d 623 (1975) (search at permanent check point); compare Delaware v. Prouse, 440 U.S. 648, 663, 99 S.Ct. 1391, 1402, 59 L.Ed.2d 660 (1979) (random stopping of automobiles to check driver's license or vehicle registration without "articulable and reasonable suspicion" of violation of law contravenes Fourth Amendment). A roving patrol may not stop a vehicle near the Mexican border and question occupants about their citizenship merely be-

cause they appear to be of Mexican ancestry. United States v. Brignoni-Ponce, 422 U.S. 873, 95 S.Ct. 2574, 45 L.Ed.2d 607 (1975). However, United States officials may question occupants at permanent check points near the national borders, without a warrant or any probable cause to suspect smuggling by the particular vehicle or other illegal activity by the occupants. United States v. Martinez-Fuerte, 428 U.S. 543, 96 S.Ct. 3074, 49 L.Ed.2d 1116 (1976).

Evidence obtained abroad by foreign officials, by means which would have been invalid as unreasonable search and seizure if used by United States officials, is admissible in courts in the United States unless United States officials were in fact implicated in the search and seizure. See § 433(3).

In 1886, the United States Supreme Court held that a person arrested by United States officials in a foreign country in violation of international law could nonetheless be tried in the United States. Ker v. Illinois, 119 U.S. 436, 7 S.Ct. 225, 30 L.Ed. 421 (1886). See § 433, Comment b.

6. *Due process of law and equal protection.* The due process clause provides procedural safeguards as well as substantive limitations on governmental regulation of life, liberty, and property; both safeguards and limitations apply to foreign as well as to domestic matters. See Comments f, g, and k. The due process clause safeguards also against excessive exercises of jurisdiction. See Pennoyer v. Neff, 95 U.S. (5 Otto) 714, 733, 24 L.Ed. 565 (1878); International Shoe Co. v. Washington, 326 U.S. 310, 316, 66 S.Ct. 154, 158, 90 L.Ed. 95 (1945);

Guaranty Trust Co. v. Virginia, 305 U.S. 19, 23, 59 S.Ct. 1, 3, 83 L.Ed. 16 (1938); also Helicopteros Nacionales de Colombia v. Hall, 466 U.S. 408, 104 S.Ct. 1868, 80 L.Ed.2d 404 (1984). See also Asahi Metal Industry Co., Ltd. v. Superior Court, ___ U.S. ___, 107 S.Ct. 1026, 94 L.Ed. 92 (1987), on remand, ___ Cal. ___, 236 Cal.Rptr. 153, 734 P.2d 989 (1987).

The meaning and scope of due process have developed largely in the application of the clause of the Fourteenth Amendment governing action by the States, but it is established that due process has essentially the same meaning and scope in the Fifth Amendment as applied to the Federal Government. The due process clause of the Fourteenth Amendment includes the implication that a State may take private property only for a public use and upon payment of just compensation. Fallbrook Irrigation Dist. v. Bradley, 164 U.S. 112, 158–59, 17 S.Ct. 56, 63, 41 L.Ed. 369 (1896) (public use); Chicago, B. & Q. R.R. v. Chicago, 166 U.S. 226, 233, 235–37, 17 S.Ct. 581, 583, 584–85, 41 L.Ed. 979 (1897) (just compensation). That implication has not been found in the due process clause of the Fifth Amendment, since that Amendment contains an additional provision expressly requiring just compensation for a taking of property for public use. See Comment g. Also, the due process clause of the Fourteenth Amendment (or perhaps the Amendment as a whole) has been held to "incorporate" most of the provisions of the Bill of Rights and render them applicable to the States (see Comment k); of course, no such incorporating effect is found in the due process clause of the Fifth Amendment.

In one important respect the due process clause of the Fifth Amendment has been given content beyond that of the same clause in the Fourteenth Amendment. Since the Fourteenth Amendment expressly forbids States to deny to any person the equal protection of the laws, equal protection has not been deemed to be implied in the due process clause of that Amendment. There being no equal protection clause in the Bill of Rights, the due process clause of the Fifth Amendment has been held to incorporate the principle of equal protection of the laws. Contemporary constitutional jurisprudence has given to equal protection as implied in the Fifth Amendment the same scope and content as those of the express provision in the Fourteenth Amendment applicable to the States. Bolling v. Sharpe, 347 U.S. 497, 499, 74 S.Ct. 693, 694, 98 L.Ed. 884 (1954) (outlawing segregated schools in the District of Columbia). "Equal protection analysis in the Fifth Amendment area is the same as that under the Fourteenth Amendment." Buckley v. Valeo, 424 U.S. 1, 93, 96 S.Ct. 612, 670, 46 L.Ed.2d 659 (1976). See Weinberger v. Wiesenfeld, 420 U.S. 636, 638, n. 2, 95 S.Ct. 1225, 1228, n. 2, 43 L.Ed.2d 514 (1975); Hampton v. Moo Sun Wong, 426 U.S. 88, 100, 96 S.Ct. 1895, 1903, 48 L.Ed.2d 495 (1976); compare Rostker v. Goldberg, 453 U.S. 57, 101 S.Ct. 2646, 69 L.Ed.2d 478 (1981) (applying general equal protection principles in upholding registration of men for military service without registration of women). See also Schneider v. Rusk, 377 U.S. 163, 84 S.Ct. 1187, 12 L.Ed.2d 218 (1964) (invalidating law that penalized foreign residence by natural-ized citizens but not by natural-born citizens).

7. *Taking of private property.* The Fifth Amendment provision that property shall not be taken for public use without just compensation applies also to property of United States citizens abroad, see Reporters' Note 2, and to the property of aliens (other than alien enemies) in the United States, and probably also abroad. § 722, Reporters' Note 3. And see Reporters' Note 8.

8. *Settlement of claims of United States nationals as "taking" of private property.* The United States has concluded numerous treaties and other international agreements settling claims of its nationals against foreign governments or foreign nationals, usually in exchange for a lump sum payment to the United States. The United States has made such settlements sometimes with the consent of, and after consultation with, the private claimants, but sometimes without such consent or consultation, and taking into account national interests in a settlement, not the interests of the claimants alone. Usually, Congress has provided for distribution of the proceeds among the claimants. In 1949, Congress established a Foreign Claims Settlement Commission to adjudicate individual claims and determine their validity or amount. International Claims Settlement Act of 1949, as amended by Foreign Claims Settlement Commission Act, 22 U.S.C. § 1621. But there is no appeal from the Commission to a court, 22 U.S.C. § 1623h. The Supreme Court has referred to payments authorized by Congress following an international settlement as "payments as of grace, and not of

right." Blagge v. Balch, 162 U.S. 439, 457, 16 S.Ct. 853, 856, 40 L.Ed. 1032, 1036 (1896); see also La Abra Silver Mining Co. v. United States, 175 U.S. 423, 20 S.Ct. 168, 44 L.Ed. 223 (1899); United States *ex rel.* Boynton v. Blaine, 139 U.S. 306, 11 S.Ct. 607, 35 L.Ed. 183 (1891); Frelinghuysen v. United States *ex rel.* Key, 110 U.S. 63, 3 S.Ct. 462, 28 L.Ed. 71 (1884); *cf.* Z. & F. Assets Realization Corp. v. Hull, 311 U.S. 470, 61 S.Ct. 351, 85 L.Ed. 288 (1941). Courts have refused to consider a challenge to an international settlement by a claimant, or a claim for compensation for loss as a result of a settlement. See, *e.g.*, Shanghai Power Co. v. United States, 4 Ct. Cl. 237 (1983), *affirmed*, 765 F.2d 159 (Fed. Cir.), *certiorari denied*, 106 S.Ct. 279 (1985); Aris Gloves, Inc. v. United States, 190 Ct. Cl. 367, 420 F.2d 1386 (1970). Perhaps the courts refuse to see such settlements as a "taking," since usually the claimant has no assured right against a foreign national, even less against a foreign government. Perhaps the courts have been reluctant to scrutinize the political judgment that the settlement was usually in the best interests of the claimants as well as of the United States.

In the famous "French Spoliation" case, however, the United States agreed to dispose of claims of United States nationals against France by setting them off against claims by France against the United States. The Court of Claims, in what was in effect an advisory opinion to Congress, concluded that "the citizen whose property is thus sacrificed for the safety and welfare of his country . . . has a right to compensation." See Gray v. United States, 21 Ct.Cl. 340, 392–93 (1886);

See Henkin, Foreign Affairs and the Constitution, 259–66, 496–99 (1972). In Dames & Moore v. Regan, 453 U.S. 654, 101 S.Ct. 2972, 69 L.Ed.2d 918 (1981), the Iranian Hostage Settlement case, the Supreme Court found that the claim that the United States had "taken" private claims against Iran for the public use of obtaining the release of the hostages was not ripe for consideration. Compare In re Aircrash in Bali, 684 F.2d 1301 (9th Cir.1982) (plaintiffs have right to compensation if their claims have been unreasonably impaired by limitation on liability in Warsaw Convention).

9. *Safeguards in criminal procedure.* Reid v. Covert and Kinsella v. United States *ex rel.* Singleton, Reporters' Note 2, held that the constitutional safeguards in criminal procedure apply also to trials for civilians under United States authority outside the United States in time of peace. See also § 722, Reporters' Note 16.

Periodically, there have been proposals to establish an international criminal court to try persons guilty of certain acts declared to be international crimes. For a provision that anticipated the possible creation of such an international court to try persons guilty of genocide, see Art. VI, Convention on the Prevention and Punishment of the Crime of Genocide, 1948, 78 U.N. T.S. 277. No such international tribunal has been created by states, and constitutional issues that might arise if the United States adhered to such a tribunal are hypothetical. For a study of such hypothetical issues, see Henkin, Arms Control and Inspection in American Law ch. 8 (1958); also Henkin, Foreign Affairs and the Constitution 198–201 (1972).

10. *Rights of members of United States armed forces.* Members of the armed forces charged with crime enjoy the same rights as civilians if they are tried in civil courts. When tried by court martial, they are entitled to "due process" and other rights conferred in the Uniform Code of Military Justice, 10 U.S.C. §§ 801–940.

The constitutional rights of members of the United States armed forces are in principle the same when they serve abroad as when they are stationed in the United States. A United States serviceman can be tried by court-martial even for a non-service-connected crime committed in the United States in time of peace. Solorio v. United States, ___ U.S. ___, 107 S.Ct. 2924, 97 L.Ed.2d 364 (1987), *overruling* O'Callahan v. Parker, 395 U.S. 258, 89 S.Ct. 1683, 23 L.Ed.2d 291 (1969). It is not a violation of the constitutional rights of a member of the armed forces that he is assigned abroad, effectively subjected to the jurisdiction of a foreign state, and, if charged with crime, that he does not have all the safeguards he would enjoy in United States courts or even in a United States court-martial. The United States may enter into a status of forces agreement pursuant to which United States forces stationed in the territory of another state are subject to the criminal jurisdiction of that state for all or some offenses; and, pursuant to such agreement, the United States may deliver a member of the United States armed forces to the authorities of the host state for criminal trial in accordance with local law and procedure. Wil-

son v. Girard, 354 U.S. 524, 77 S.Ct. 1409, 1 L.Ed.2d 1544 (1957). The NATO Status of Forces Agreement, and other status of forces agreements, however, include a "bill of rights" which the host state undertakes to provide to members of visiting armed forces tried for crime. The Agreement guarantees the accused a right to a prompt and speedy trial; to be informed in advance of charges against him; to be confronted with witnesses against him and to have compulsory process for obtaining witnesses in his favor; a right to counsel of his own choice or free legal representation made available to him; to an interpreter, if necessary; and the right to communicate with a representative of his government, and ordinarily to have such representative present at the trial. See North Atlantic Treaty Status of Forces Agreement, 1951, Art. VII, 4 U.S.T. 1792, T.I.A.S. No. 2846, 199 U.N.T.S. 67; also the Panama Canal Treaty, Annex D, 16 Int'l Leg.Mat. 1022 (1977).

11. *United States cooperation in foreign criminal enforcement.* Pursuant to treaty and implementing legislation, the United States offers assistance to foreign consuls, and to friendly foreign forces in the United States, in arresting, interrogating, and imprisoning persons subject to their jurisdictions. See, *e.g.,* Consular Convention between the United States of America and Ireland, 1950, Arts. 21–27, 5 U.S.T. 949, T.I.A.S. No. 2984; 22 U.S.C. §§ 256–258a; NATO Status of Forces Agreement, Reporters' Note 10, Art. VII, § 7b; Service Courts of Friendly Foreign Forces Act, 22 U.S.C. §§ 701–706. The United States has concluded treaties pursuant to which nationals of one state party serving in prisons of the other

state may, at their request, be transferred to complete their sentence in the prison of their home state, but they must waive any right to challenge their conviction. *E.g.*, United States-Mexico Treaty on the Execution of Penal Sentences, 1976, 28 U.S.T. 7399, T.I. A.S. No. 8718; United States-Canada Treaty on the Execution of Penal Sentences, 1977, 30 U.S.T. 6263, T.I. A.S. No. 9552; United States-Bolivia Treaty, 1978, 30 U.S.T. 796, T.I.A.S. No. 9219. The validity of these treaties as applied to United States nationals convicted in Mexico and transferred to complete their sentences in the United States was upheld in Rosado v. Civiletti, 621 F.2d 1179 (2d Cir.1980), *certiorari denied*, 449 U.S. 856, 101 S.Ct. 153, 66 L.Ed.2d 70 (1980); Pfeifer v. United States Bureau of Prisons, 468 F.Supp. 920 (S.D.Cal.1979), *affirmed*, 615 F.2d 873 (9th Cir.1980), *certiorari denied*, 447 U.S. 908, 100 S.Ct. 2993, 64 L.Ed.2d 858 (1980); Kanasola v. Civiletti, 630 F.2d 472 (6th Cir.1980), *certiorari denied*, 450 U.S. 930, 101 S.Ct. 1390, 67 L.Ed.2d 363 (1981).

As to extradition, see §§ 475–78.

12. *Right to travel.* The right to travel was declared to be a liberty protected by the due process clause in Kent v. Dulles, 357 U.S. 116, 78 S.Ct. 1113, 2 L.Ed.2d 1204 (1958). In Aptheker v. Secretary of State, 378 U.S. 500, 84 S.Ct. 1659, 12 L.Ed.2d 992 (1964), the Supreme Court struck down a statutory provision that made it unlawful for any member of the Communist Party to apply for or use a passport. But while the constitutional right of travel within the United States is "virtually unqualified," the right of international travel "is subordinate

to national security and foreign policy considerations" and "can be regulated within the bounds of due process." Califano v. Aznavorian, 439 U.S. 170, 176, 99 S.Ct. 471, 475, 58 L.Ed.2d 435 (1978). The authority of the Secretary of State to refuse to issue passports valid for travel to designated countries was upheld in Zemel v. Rusk, 381 U.S. 1, 85 S.Ct. 1271, 14 L.Ed.2d 179 (1965). The authority of the Secretary to refuse to renew a passport for one who had violated such restrictions and refused to undertake not to do so in future was upheld in Worthy v. Herter, 270 F.2d 905 (D.C.Cir.1959), *certiorari denied*, 361 U.S. 918, 80 S.Ct. 255, 4 L.Ed.2d 186 (1959). But the Court of Appeals later held that the Secretary could not deny a passport to one who refused to undertake not to travel to a restricted area. Lynd v. Rusk, 389 F.2d 940 (D.C.Cir.1967). And Congress has not made travel in violation of an "area restriction" in a passport a crime. United States v. Laub, 385 U.S. 475, 87 S.Ct. 574, 17 L.Ed.2d 526 (1967). In Haig v. Agee, 453 U.S. 280, 101 S.Ct. 2766, 69 L.Ed.2d 640 (1981), the Court upheld revocation by the Secretary of State of the passport of a person engaged in a campaign to expose United States intelligence officers and agents abroad, pursuant to a regulation, held authorized by Congress, permitting revocation where the "Secretary determines that the national's activities abroad are causing or are likely to cause serious damage to the national security or the foreign policy of the United States." In Regan v. Wald, 468 U.S. 222, 104 S.Ct. 3026, 82 L.Ed.2d 171 (1984), the Court upheld Treasury Regulations forbidding citizens to expend money for travel to Cuba and for living expenses there; the Regulations were held to be within authority delegated by Congress and not to violate the due process clause of the Fifth Amendment.

13. *Remedies for violation of individual rights.* The United States Civil Rights Acts may have some application in cases with significance for United States foreign relations. 18 U.S.C. §§ 242–43, and 42 U.S.C. §§ 1981 *et seq.*, which provide criminal and civil remedies for violations by State officials or persons conspiring with them, apply to violations of rights of "persons," therefore including aliens. 18 U.S.C. § 242 has also been held to apply to federal officials acting under color of federal law who deprive aliens of federal rights. United States v. Otherson, 637 F.2d 1276 (9th Cir.1980), *certiorari denied,* 454 U.S. 840, 102 S.Ct. 149, 70 L.Ed. 2d 123 (1981) (upholding conviction of United States border patrol agents for assaulting illegal aliens). See Screws v. United States, 325 U.S. 91, 108, 65 S.Ct. 1031, 1038, 89 L.Ed. 1495 (1945), and cases in 325 U.S. at 97, n. 2. There are some judicially created remedies against federal officials for violations of constitutional rights which might be applied or extended to circumstances significant for United States foreign relations. See Bivens v. Six Unknown Named Agents, 403 U.S. 388, 91 S.Ct. 1999, 29 L.Ed. 2d 619 (1971) (remedy for unlawful search and seizure); Carlson v. Green, 446 U.S. 14, 100 S.Ct. 1468, 64 L.Ed.2d 15 (1980) (remedy for violation of Eighth Amendment).

Some United States civil rights legislation protects United States nationals outside the United States. See, *e.g.,* Bryant v. International Schools Services, Inc., 502 F.Supp. 472 (D.N.J.1980) (Title VII of United States Civil Rights Act forbidding discrimination in employment on basis of gender applies to employment of United States citizens in school operated by United States nationals in Iran), *reversed on other grounds,* 675 F.2d 562 (3d Cir.1982) (findings of fact failed to substantiate discrimination charge).

14. *Previous Restatement.* The previous Restatement did not specifically deal with the subject of this section. Constitutional safeguards for individual rights were mentioned in connection with the NATO Status of Forces Agreement, § 62, Reporters' Note 2, and in respect of aliens, § 167, Comment *b.*

§ 722. Rights of Aliens

(1) An alien in the United States is entitled to the guarantees of the United States Constitution other than those expressly reserved for citizens.

(2) Under Subsection (1), an alien in the United States may not be denied the equal protection of the laws, but equal protection does not preclude reasonable distinctions between aliens and citizens, or between different categories of aliens.

Comment:

a. Constitutional rights of aliens. The Bill of Rights of the United States Constitution (Amendments I–X) declares the rights of persons, not of citizens only. Aliens in the United States therefore enjoy, notably, the freedoms of speech, press, religion, and assembly (Amendment I), the rights of privacy and freedom from unreasonable arrest and search or seizure (Amendment IV), the safeguards for fair trial in criminal process (Amendments V, VI, and VIII), the due process protections for life, liberty, and property (Amendment V), the right to jury trial in civil cases (Amendment VII). Aliens are also protected from slavery (Amendment XIII). Unlike citizens, however, aliens may be subject to deportation, and aliens admitted other than for permanent residence are subject to the conditions of their entry. See Comments *i* and *j*.

The principal provisions of the Fourteenth Amendment safeguarding individual rights against violation by the States also prescribe rights of persons, not only of citizens: "nor shall any State deprive any person of life, liberty, or property, without due process of the law; nor deny to any person within its jurisdiction the equal protection of the laws." Since the Fourteenth Amendment has been held to make most provisions of the Bill of Rights applicable to the States, aliens enjoy those protections against the States as well. Aliens are protected also against State impairment of the obligation of contracts, bills of attainder, and *ex post facto* laws. Article I, Section 10; see § 721, Comment *k*. Aliens need not, however, be accorded those rights implied in the citizenship clause of the Fourteenth Amendment, the privileges and immunities of citizens of the United States (Amendment XIV, Section 1), or the privileges and immunities of citizens of the several States (Article IV, Section 2). The Constitution reserves for citizens the office of President and Vice President (Article I, Sections 2, 3) and membership in the House of Representatives and the Senate (Article II, Section 2; Amendment XII). The Constitution does not limit voting to citizens, but leaves qualifications for voting to be determined by the States, subject to regulation by Congress. See Comment *c* and Reporters' Note 3. Apparently, however, the Constitution assumes that only citizens would be allowed to vote: several Amendments bar denial of the right of "citizens of the United States" to vote, on account of race, sex, nonpayment of a tax, or age (for persons 18 or older). Amendments XV, XIX, XXIV, XXVI.

In general, this section applies to all aliens in the United States, including those admitted for limited purposes and those present in the United States unlawfully. See Comments *j* and *k*. As regards aliens subject to United States authority outside the United States, see Comment *m*.

This section addresses the rights of aliens under United States constitutional law. For the rights of aliens under international law, see §§ 711–13.

b. Federal supremacy in regulation of aliens. Aliens are generally subject to the laws of the United States and of the States equally with citizens. Congress also has power under the Constitution to prescribe special law with respect to aliens, and the status, interests, and rights of foreign nationals have been frequently regulated by treaty or other international agreements.

States cannot regulate aliens in ways inconsistent with laws of Congress or with international agreements of the United States. States cannot regulate where regulation is preempted by Congress (*e.g.*, the registration of aliens) or by international agreement. That aliens were admitted to permanent residence in the United States implies a Congressional policy that they are to be free to engage in gainful employment, and States may not deny aliens ordinary employment. See Reporters' Note 2; also Comment *c*. States may not regulate aliens in ways which "intrude" on the foreign relations of the United States. Zschernig v. Miller, 389 U.S. 429, 88 S.Ct. 664, 19 L.Ed.2d 683 (1968); see Reporters' Note 2, and § 1, Reporters' Note 5.

c. Equal protection for resident aliens by States of the United States. The equal protection of the laws does not forbid all classifications or distinctions, only those that are unreasonable. Discriminations against resident aliens by the States, however, are generally suspect and will be subject to strict scrutiny and upheld only if they serve a compelling State interest. (Considerations of cost and "fiscal integrity" are not compelling interests.) Therefore, States cannot deny resident aliens the right to practice a profession, to be employed in the classified civil service, or to have access to welfare programs. However, strict scrutiny will not be applied and a compelling state interest not required where the State deals "with matters firmly within a state's constitutional prerogative" and seeks "to preserve the basic conception of a political community." Foley v. Connelie, 435 U.S. 291, 295–96, 98 S.Ct. 1067, 1070, 55 L.Ed.2d 287 (1978). States may, therefore, deny aliens the right to vote and to hold public office, Comment *a*, and apparently all States do. Since "the right to govern belongs to citizens," a State may also deny aliens access to public employment that "fulfills a most fundamental obligation of government to its constituency" (*id.*, 435 U.S. at 297, 98 S.Ct. at 1071), including employment as teachers in the public schools or as members of the police force. A State may probably deny to aliens what it may deny to citizens of other States, *e.g.*, access to its public parks and lands, publicly owned game, and other natural resources. For State distinctions between resident and nonresident aliens, see Comment *j*.

d. Discrimination against or among aliens by United States Government. The authority of Congress to regulate aliens is subject to constitutional restraints, Subsection (1), including the requirement of equal protection held to be incorporated in the due process clause of the Fifth Amendment. See § 721, Comment *f* and Reporters' Note 6. Unreasonable distinctions between citizens and aliens, or among aliens, then, are in principle invalid. But the regulation of aliens has been seen as related to war and peace, national security, and foreign policy, and judgments of the political branches in such matters have been accorded great deference. Congress has imposed special burdens on aliens, *e.g.* registration. At various times it has denied them the right to own property in territories of the United States, has excluded them from some forms of investment and enterprise, has authorized their exclusion from the Civil Service, and denied them access to benefits provided with public funds. Congress has also given aliens rights conditioned on reciprocity for United States citizens by the state of their nationality. Unlike discriminations by the States, Comment *c*, the courts have not declared that discriminations by Congress are suspect, requiring strict scrutiny and a compelling national interest to sustain them. Apparently, no distinction between citizens and aliens by Congress has been held invalid as a denial of equal protection.

e. Alien companies in the United States. Congress has the power under the Constitution to exclude or regulate alien companies, both under its power to regulate commerce with foreign nations (Article I, Section 8) and under the power to regulate aliens inherent in the nationhood of the United States. See § 1, Reporters' Note 1. Alien companies may be regulated also by treaty or other international agreement. Subject to federal regulation or preemption, a State may also regulate and tax alien companies and their activities in the State. By implication, however, the Commerce Clause forbids a State to exclude or discriminate against foreign commerce, or burden such commerce unduly. A State may not insist that an alien company incorporate in the State as a condition of doing interstate or international business, but it may require that the company obtain a license to do local business. A State may subject the company to its laws and to the jurisdiction of its courts, for example, by reasonable "long-arm" statutes.

f. Alien investment in the United States. The powers of Congress and of the States to exclude or regulate foreign investment in the United States are essentially the same as their powers with regard to alien companies. Comment *e.* Both the United States and the States have restricted investment by foreign interests in United States companies in some industries. Investment by resident aliens, however, is protected by the equal protection and due process clauses and only reasonable discriminations are permitted. See Comments *a, c, d,* and *h.*

g. Alien ownership of land in the United States. In principle, the authority of the United States and of the States to regulate ownership of land by aliens is the same as for other alien activities. Comments *e* and *f.* In practice, however, Congress has not purported to regulate alien ownership of land (other than in territories belonging to the United States), while virtually all States have regulated such ownership at some time. For current regulations, see Reporters' Note 9. Alien rights in land have also been the subject of treaties of friendship, commerce, and navigation, and their provisions supersede any inconsistent provisions in State law.

h. Enemy and other designated aliens during war or emergency. Under the United States Constitution and laws, the United States government may, in time of war, arrest and intern enemy aliens and seize their assets, and may even deport them summarily. See Reporters' Note 11. An enemy alien is not entitled to a hearing as a matter of constitutional right. Under international law since the adoption of the United Nations Charter, the status of "war" and of "enemy alien" is unclear (see § 711, Comment *h*); United States legislation dealing with enemy aliens would presumably be drafted or interpreted in the light of the international obligations of the United States, but the constitutional authority of Congress is not affected. See §§ 114, 115.

Under Article I, Section 9, Congress can suspend the privilege of the writ of habeas corpus "when in Cases of Rebellion or Invasion the Public Safety may require it." That provision permits the suspension of that particular remedy, not of any rights or other remedies. See *Ex parte* Milligan, 71 U.S. (4 Wall.) 2, 120–21, 18 L.Ed. 281 (1866). There is no authority as to whether in emergency Congress could suspend the privilege of the writ on a basis that discriminates among friendly aliens.

Distinctions between designated aliens and others, in respects that do not impinge on their constitutional rights, raise issues of equal protection, but are valid if reasonable. See Comment *d.*

i. Deportation of resident aliens. Although persons admitted for permanent residence have very largely the same status and rights as citizens, in the past the Supreme Court ruled that the United States had authority to deport an alien even if the person had been admitted for permanent residence and had peacefully resided in the United States for many years. The alien could be deported even for activities which Congress could not define and punish as crime, for example, political activities that Congress could not prohibit because of the limitations of the First Amendment. However, the alien could be deported only pursuant to law and was entitled to procedural due process of law, including a fair hearing and judicial review. The power of Congress to deport aliens has not been recently reexamined. See Reporters' Note 12.

j. Aliens admitted temporarily for limited purposes. Aliens may be admitted temporarily for limited purposes, for example, tourism, study, or trade. It has been assumed that Congress may also admit aliens for a fixed period for residence or for particular activity, for example, as "guest workers." Aliens who violate the terms of their admission may be punished for violation of the immigration laws, or deported, or both. Punishment must be by ordinary criminal process in full conformity with due process of law. Deportation of such aliens also requires due process of law, but the procedures prescribed by Congress will satisfy due process if they are fair and reasonable.

Some distinctions between aliens admitted temporarily and resident aliens may be reasonable and consistent with equal protection, but such a distinction made by a State may be subject to strict judicial scrutiny and require an important, if not compelling, State interest to sustain it. Such distinctions by a State may also be precluded by federal supremacy or preemption in fixing the consequences of different immigration status. See Reporters' Notes 2 and 13.

k. Illegal or "undocumented" aliens. Persons not lawfully admitted to the United States, or who violate the terms of their admission, may be deported. They may be temporarily detained pending their deportation. They may also be punished for violation of the immigration laws. See Comment *j*. While they remain in the United States or subject to United States jurisdiction, they generally enjoy the constitutional protections enjoyed by lawful aliens under this section. Some distinctions between undocumented and lawfully admitted aliens may be reasonable, but such a distinction if made by a State is subject to judicial scrutiny and may require an important, if not a compelling, State interest to sustain it.

l. Exclusion of aliens. It was long assumed that there are no constitutional limitations on the power of Congress to determine whom it will admit to or exclude from the United States. It is now open to question, however, whether Congress could exclude an alien on certain grounds, for example, solely on account of race or religion.

m. Aliens outside the United States. Although the matter has not been authoritatively adjudicated, at least some actions by the United States in respect of foreign nationals outside the country are also subject to constitutional limitations. Thus, trial of an alien under United States authority has been held subject to constitutional safeguards. See Reporters' Note 16. Similarly, the taking by United States authorities abroad for public use of property of a foreign national may give the former owner a right to just compensation under the Fifth Amendment. Some remedies, including judicial remedies, available to persons in the United States for such violations, may not be available to aliens abroad.

REPORTERS' NOTES

1. *Federal regulation of aliens.* The power to regulate aliens is inherent in the nationhood and sovereignty of the United States. See § 721, Comment *a.* The Supreme Court has also found authority for "specialized regulation of the conduct of an alien before naturalization" in the power of Congress (Art. I, Sec. 8) to "establish an Uniform Rule of Naturalization." See Hines v. Davidowitz, 312 U.S. 52, 66, 61 S.Ct. 399, 403, 85 L.Ed. 581 (1941). Congress has enacted laws regulating aliens since the early history of the United States, for example, the Alien Enemies Act of 1798, 1 Stat. 577 (1798). The power of Congress to regulate aliens has never been seriously doubted and was upheld in numerous cases in the nineteenth century, *e.g.,* The Chinese Exclusion Case, 130 U.S. 581, 9 S.Ct. 623, 32 L.Ed. 1068 (1889). In Mathews v. Diaz, 426 U.S. 67, 81, 96 S.Ct. 1883, 1892, 48 L.Ed.2d 478 (1976), the Court said:

For reasons long recognized as valid, the responsibility for regulating the relationship between the United States and our alien visitors has been committed to the political branches of the Federal Government. Since decisions in these matters may implicate our relations with foreign powers, and since a wide variety of classifications must be defined in the light of changing political and economic circumstances, such decisions are frequently of a character more appropriate to either the Legislature or the Executive than to the Judiciary . . . . The reasons that preclude judicial review of political questions also dictate a narrow standard of review of decisions made by the Congress or the President in the area of immigration and naturalization.

As of 1987, no regulation of aliens has been held to be beyond the power of Congress.

Congress has enacted special legislation for aliens, *e.g.*, the requirement of registration. 8 U.S.C. §§ 1301–1306. It has also prohibited certain activities to aliens, limited certain benefits to citizens, and provided differently for citizens and aliens. See Comment *d* and Reporters' Note 6. Congress has also given benefits to aliens on a condition of reciprocity, *i.e.*, that the state of an alien's nationality accord similar benefits to United States nationals, *e.g.*, 28 U.S.C. § 2502 (access to Court of Claims). For other examples, see Henkin, "The Treaty Makers and the Law Makers," 107 U.Pa. L.Rev. 903, 921, n. 41 (1959). United States bilateral treaties, especially treaties of friendship, commerce, and navigation, often give to nationals of one party rights to carry on certain activities in the territory of the other, or "most favored nation" or "national" treatment in respects indicated. See § 711, Reporters' Note 6; § 801, Comments *a* and *b*.

2. *Federal supremacy in regulation of aliens.* State laws generally apply to aliens as to citizens. The Constitution does not prevent the application of State law to aliens except where it would constitute "an intrusion by the State into the field of foreign affairs which the Constitution entrusts to the President and the Congress." Zschernig v. Miller, 389 U.S. 429, 432, 88 S.Ct. 664, 666, 19 L.Ed.2d 683 (1968). In that case, the Court invalidated an Oregon statute under which the State court had denied an inheritance to a resident of East Germany because he could not satisfy the court that his country allowed United States citizens to inherit estates in that country, and that he would receive payments from the Oregon estate without confiscation. There

has been no other case in which the Supreme Court invalidated State law under this doctrine.

State regulations of aliens that are inconsistent with federal law are invalid under the Supremacy Clause, Article VI, clause 2. The Supreme Court has held that State laws denying ordinary employment to a resident alien are inconsistent with "the right to work for a living in the common occupations of the community" implied in the decision of Congress to admit the alien to the country for residence. Takahashi v. Fish & Game Comm'n, 334 U.S. 410, 68 S.Ct. 1138, 92 L.Ed. 1478 (1947). See also Toll v. Moreno, Reporters' Note 13.

In Hines v. Davidowitz, Reporters' Note 1, the Supreme Court held that a federal alien registration system enacted by Congress "occupied the field" and precluded similar registration of aliens by the States. The Court said:

. . . Consequently the regulation of aliens is so intimately blended and intertwined with responsibilities of the national government that where it acts, and the state also acts on the same subject, "the act of Congress, or the treaty, is supreme; and the law of the State, though enacted in the exercise of powers not controverted, must yield to it." And where the federal government, in the exercise of its superior authority in this field, has enacted a complete scheme of regulation and has therein provided a standard for the registration of aliens, states cannot, inconsistently with the purpose of Congress, conflict or interfere with, curtail or complement, the federal law, or enforce additional or auxiliary regulations.

312 U.S. at 66–67, 61 S.Ct. at 403–404. See also Takahashi v. Fish & Game Comm'n, *supra.*

State legislation prohibiting the employment of undocumented aliens was held not to be precluded by the exclusive constitutional powers of Congress over immigration or preempted by the immigration laws. DeCanas v. Bica, 424 U.S. 351, 96 S.Ct. 933, 47 L.Ed.2d 43 (1976).

3. *Constitutional rights of aliens.* Cases upholding constitutional rights of aliens include Yick Wo v. Hopkins, 118 U.S. 356, 6 S.Ct. 1064, 30 L.Ed. 220 (1886) (equal protection), quoted in Reporters' Note 4; Wong Wing v. United States, 163 U.S. 228, 16 S.Ct. 977, 41 L.Ed. 140 (1896) (due process of law); Truax v. Raich, 239 U.S. 33, 36 S.Ct. 7, 60 L.Ed. 131 (1915) (right to work protected by due process), quoted in Reporters' Note 5; Russian Volunteer Fleet v. United States, 282 U.S. 481, 51 S.Ct. 229, 75 L.Ed. 473 (1931) (right to just compensation for taking of property). See also cases cited in Reporters' Notes 5 and 6. See, generally, "The Alien and the Constitution," 20 U.Chi.L. Rev. 547 (1953); Mutharika, The Alien under American Law (1980).

4. *Protection of aliens under Fourteenth Amendment.* "The Fourteenth Amendment to the Constitution is not confined to the protection of citizens." Yick Wo v. Hopkins, Reporters' Note 3, 118 U.S. at 369, 6 S.Ct. at 1070.

In Barbier v. Connolly, 113 U.S. 27, 31, 5 S.Ct. 357, 359, 28 L.Ed. 923 (1885), the Supreme Court said:

The Fourteenth Amendment, in declaring that no State "shall deprive any person of life, liberty, or property without due process of law, nor deny to any person within its jurisdiction the equal protection of the laws," undoubtedly intended not only that there should be no arbitrary deprivation of life or liberty, or arbitrary spoliation of property, but that equal protection and security should be given to all under like circumstances in the enjoyment of their personal and civil rights; that all persons should be equally entitled to pursue their happiness and acquire and enjoy property; that they should have like access to the courts of the country for the protection of their persons and property, the prevention and redress of wrongs, and the enforcement of contracts; that no impediment should be interposed to the pursuits of any one except as applied to the same pursuits by others under like circumstances; that no greater burdens should be laid upon one than are laid upon others in the same calling and condition, and that in the administration of criminal justice no different or higher punishment should be imposed upon one than such as is prescribed to all for like offences.

The statement is quoted with approval and applied to aliens in Yick Wo v. Hopkins, Reporters' Note 3, 118 U.S. at 367–68, invalidating the conviction of an alien for violation of a municipal ordinance that was administered so as to discriminate against persons of Chinese descent.

5. *State discrimination against aliens.* The principal case confirming the constitutional rights of

aliens established their right to the equal protection of the laws. Yick Wo v. Hopkins, Reporters' Note 3. In 1915, the Supreme Court held that a state provision requiring that 80% of the employees of certain businesses be citizens infringed the alien's "right to work for a living in the common occupations of the community." Truax v. Raich, Reporters' Note 3, 239 U.S. at 41, 36 S.Ct. at 10. For some time, the Court upheld some State discriminations against aliens, *e.g.*, Ohio *ex rel.* Clarke v. Deckebach, 274 U.S. 392, 47 S.Ct. 630, 71 L.Ed. 1115 (1927); Terrace v. Thompson, 263 U.S. 197, 44 S.Ct. 15, 68 L.Ed. 255 (1923); Heim v. McCall, 239 U.S. 175, 36 S.Ct. 78, 60 L.Ed. 206 (1915). But aliens benefited from the flourishing of rights generally after the Second World War. See, *e.g.*, Takahashi v. Fish & Game Comm'n, Reporters' Note 2. In 1971, the Supreme Court declared that distinctions in State law between aliens and citizens are suspect and will be sharply scrutinized, and such distinctions can be sustained only for a compelling state interest. Graham v. Richardson, 403 U.S. 365, 372, 91 S.Ct. 1818, 1852, 29 L.Ed.2d 534 (1971). In that case, the Court found that concern for the State's fiscal integrity was not a compelling interest and invalidated the denial by a State of welfare assistance to aliens. Later cases scrutinized and invalidated the exclusion of aliens from the practice of law and other licensed professions; In re Griffiths, 413 U.S. 717, 93 S.Ct. 2851, 37 L.Ed.2d 910 (1973) (law practice); Examining Bd. v. Flores de Otero, 426 U.S. 572, 96 S.Ct. 2264, 49 L.Ed. 2d 65 (1976) (right to practice civil engineering in Puerto Rico); Bernal v. Fainter, 467 U.S. 216, 104 S.Ct.

2312, 81 L.Ed.2d 175 (1984) (notaries public); from public employment generally, Sugarman v. Dougall, 413 U.S. 634, 93 S.Ct. 2842, 37 L.Ed. 2d 853 (1973) (permanent positions in competitive civil service); from educational benefits, Nyquist v. Mauclet, 432 U.S. 1, 97 S.Ct. 2120, 53 L.Ed.2d 63 (1977) (state scholarships). The Court has held, however, that restrictions on aliens are not suspect, and will not require a higher level of scrutiny and a compelling State interest to sustain them, where the State deals "with matters firmly within a State's constitutional prerogatives," for example, "a state's historical power to exclude aliens from participation in its democratic political institutions," and "to preserve the basic conception of a political community." Foley v. Connelie, 435 U.S. 291, 295–96, 98 S.Ct. 1067, 1070, 55 L.Ed.2d 287 (1978), quoting from Sugarman v. Dougall, *supra*, 413 U.S. at 647–48, 93 S.Ct. at 2850. In *Foley*, the Court upheld the exclusion of aliens from the State police force. The Court followed *Foley* in upholding state exclusion of aliens from teaching in the public schools, Ambach v. Norwick, 441 U.S. 68, 99 S.Ct. 1589, 60 L.Ed.2d 49 (1979), and from serving as "peace officers," including deputy probation officers, Cabell v. Chavez-Salido, 454 U.S. 432, 102 S.Ct. 735, 70 L.Ed.2d 677 (1982). See also Perkins v. Smith, 370 F.Supp. 134 (D.Md.1974), *affirmed*, 426 U.S. 913, 96 S.Ct. 2616, 49 L.Ed. 2d 368 (1976) (upholding exclusion of aliens from State and federal juries).

A State can probably deny to aliens what it can constitutionally deny to citizens of other States, *e.g.*, access to its public parks and lands, publicly owned game, and other natural resources. *Compare* Baldwin v. Montana Fish and Game Comm'n, 436 U.S. 371, 98 S.Ct. 1852, 56 L.Ed. 2d 354 (1978) (Montana may impose higher hunting-license fees on residents of other States), *with* Toomer v. Witsell, 334 U.S. 385, 68 S.Ct. 1156, 92 L.Ed. 1460 (1948) (invalidating State restrictions on commercial fishing by nonresidents); but see Hicklin v. Orbeck, 437 U.S. 518, 98 S.Ct. 2482, 57 L.Ed.2d 397 (1978) (invalidating preference for State residents in certain jobs).

States may not discriminate among aliens on foreign policy grounds. See Tayyari v. New Mexico State University, 495 F.Supp. 1365 (D.N.M.1980) (denial of admission by State university to nationals of foreign state holding United States citizens hostage held to deny equal protection of the laws and to frustrate federal authority in foreign affairs). See Reporters' Notes 2 and 13. For reliance on federal preemption, in addition to, or instead of, the equal protection clause, to invalidate state restrictions on aliens, see Takahashi v. Fish & Game Comm'n, Reporters' Note 2, and Toll v. Moreno, Reporters' Note 13.

6. *Discrimination against or among aliens by the United States Government.* The Supreme Court has not considered whether and in what circumstances a distinction between aliens and citizens in federal law or treaty might be suspect and require a higher level of scrutiny and a compelling interest to sustain the distinction. Compare Comments *c* and *d.*

In Hampton v. Wong, 426 U.S. 88, 96 S.Ct. 1895, 48 L.Ed.2d 495 (1976), the Court invalidated a regulation of the Civil Service Commission gen-erally barring resident aliens from the Civil Service. The Court said:

When the Federal Government asserts an overriding national interest as justification for a discriminatory rule which would violate the Equal Protection Clause if adopted by a State, due process requires that there be a legitimate basis for presuming that the rule was actually intended to serve that interest. If the agency which promulgates the rule has direct responsibility for fostering or protecting that interest, it may reasonably be presumed that the asserted interest was the actual predicate for the rule . . . . Alternatively, if the rule were expressly mandated by the Congress or the President, we might presume that any interest which might rationally be served by the rule did in fact give rise to its adoption.

. . . We may assume with the [Government] that if the Congress or the President had expressly imposed the citizenship requirement, it would be justified by the national interest in providing an incentive for aliens to become naturalized, or possibly even as providing the President with an expendable token for treaty negotiating purposes; but we are not willing to presume that the Chairman of the Civil Service Commission . . . was deliberately fostering an interest so far removed from his normal responsibilities.

426 U.S. at 103, 105, 96 S.Ct. at 1905, 1906.

After the *Wong* case, the President issued an executive order excluding aliens from the Civil Service. The exclusion was upheld in the lower courts. Vergara v. Hampton, 581 F.2d 1281 (7th Cir. 1978), *certiorari denied*, 441 U.S. 905, 99 S.Ct. 1993, 60 L.Ed.2d 373 (1979); Jalil v. Campbell, 590 F.2d 1120 (D.C.Cir.1978).

In Mathews v. Diaz, 426 U.S. 67, 96 S.Ct. 1883, 48 L.Ed.2d 478 (1976), the Supreme Court upheld a federal statute denying medicare benefits to aliens unless they had been admitted to permanent residence and have resided in the United States for five years. The Court said:

> Since it is obvious that Congress has no constitutional duty to provide *all aliens* with the welfare benefits provided to citizens, the party challenging the constitutionality of the particular line Congress has drawn has the burden of advancing principled reasoning that will at once invalidate that line and yet tolerate a different line separating some aliens from others.

426 U.S. at 82, 96 S.Ct. at 1892.

In Narenji v. Civiletti, 617 F.2d 745 (D.C.Cir.1979), *certiorari denied*, 446 U.S. 957, 100 S.Ct. 2928, 64 L.Ed.2d 815 (1980), the court of appeals upheld Executive regulations requiring all Iranian nationals in the United States holding student visas to report their current status and whereabouts to the Immigration and Naturalization Service, as a discrimination among aliens that had a rational basis in view of the relations between the United States and Iran during the then-pending hostage crisis. But compare State discrimination on such grounds, Reporters' Note 5.

The Fisheries Conservation and Management Act was upheld although it discriminates against non-resident aliens and foreign fishing vessels. United States v. Tsuda Maru, 479 F.Supp. 519 (D.Alaska 1979); United States v. Kaiyo Maru, 503 F.Supp. 1075, 1086 (D.Alaska 1980), *affirmed*, 699 F.2d 989 (9th Cir.1983).

Discriminations against aliens under United States law include: exclusion from service on grand or petit jury (28 U.S.C. § 1861); ineligibility for appointment to commissioned grades in armed services or as officers in merchant marine (10 U.S.C. § 532, 46 U.S.C. § 221); denial of communication licenses (47 U.S.C. § 310); ineligibility to serve as national bank directors (12 U.S.C. § 72); social security payments suspended if alien is outside the United States for more than six consecutive months (42 U.S.C. § 402(t)(1)). See also Comments *c* and *f* and Reporters' Notes 7, 8, 9, and 10; also § 501, Reporters' Note 4 (ownership of vessels).

7. *Protection for aliens under United States civil rights law.* The Civil Rights Act of 1870 granted basic civil rights to "persons," thus to aliens equally with citizens. 42 U.S.C. §§ 1981 *et seq.* See also 18 U.S.C. §§ 241–42 providing criminal penalties for violation of civil rights of "persons." Some provisions apply only to citizens, *e.g.*, 42 U.S.C. § 1982 ("property rights of citizens"). Some provisions protect "any citizen of the United States or other persons within the jurisdiction thereof." 42 U.S.C. § 1983 (civil action for deprivation of rights). Recent civil rights legislation continues and extends protection for all "persons" (including aliens), with protection for citizens only in particular respects, principally the right to vote. See, *e.g.*, Civil Rights Act

of 1964, 42 U.S.C. §§ 2000a *et seq.;* Civil Rights Act of 1976, 18 U.S.C. § 246. The United States has not purported to confer the right to vote on aliens or to interfere with State dispositions in this respect.

8. *Alien companies in the United States.* Federal regulation of alien companies has been sporadic, responding to specific concerns (*e.g.,* excessive competition in particular industries, national security, or the desire to prevent foreign companies from enjoying United States government benefits). At present, United States law restricts or prohibits the activities of alien corporations in the following areas: merchant shipping, air commerce, banking, defense contracting, the sale and lease of federal land and mineral rights (see Reporters' Note 9), radio and television broadcasting, and the use and production of radioactive materials. See Vagts, "The Corporate Alien," 74 Harv.L. Rev. 1489 (1961).

States have not legislated extensively with respect to alien companies. In general, State laws do not distinguish between other-country and other-State corporations, requiring all to obtain a license to do local business. Generally, this involves payment of a fee, submission of data pertaining to the corporation's organization and financial condition, and appointment of an agent for service of process.

For federal and State law in regard to the nationality of corporations, see § 213, Reporters' Note 5.

9. *Alien ownership of land.* Federal law limits the right of aliens who have not declared their intention to become citizens to own land in the territories of the United States. 48 U.S.C. §§ 1501, 1508;

but title held in contravention of the Act is subject to attack only through escheat proceedings brought by the Attorney General of the United States, 48 U.S.C. § 1501. These limitations are not applicable in the District of Columbia. See Larkin v. Washington Loan & Trust Co., 31 F.2d 635 (D.C.Cir.), *certiorari denied,* 279 U.S. 867, 49 S.Ct. 481, 73 L.Ed. 1004 (1929). Aliens may inherit real property in the territories or obtain such property in the collection of debts, but such property must be disposed of within 10 years.

State laws concerning alien ownership of land vary widely. Approximately one third of the States have completely eliminated alien disabilities to own land. Some 15 States restrict the rights of special categories of aliens only (*i.e.,* enemy aliens, aliens not eligible for citizenship). The remaining States limit the rights of nonresident aliens, or of all aliens. Restrictions range from prohibition on the inheritance of land by a nonresident alien whose government does not grant reciprocal rights to United States nationals, to a limitation of six years on the ownership of land by any alien who does not become a citizen. See 1 Powell, The Law of Real Property ¶¶ 101–108 (Rohan rev. 1977).

In 1923, the Supreme Court upheld State law denying aliens the right to own real property (Terrace v. Thompson, Reporters' Note 5), but the continued vitality of that case has been questioned in view of the development of equal protection principles with respect to aliens. *Ibid.*

State laws limiting ownership of land by aliens have sometimes been superseded by United States treaty. See, *e.g.*, Hauenstein v. Lynham, 100 U.S. (10 Otto) 483, 25 L.Ed. 628 (1880) (State limitation on inheritance by alien invalidated). In general, however, treaties of friendship, commerce, and navigation have avoided restricting the States' power to control ownership of land by aliens. 1 Hyde, International Law Chiefly as Interpreted and Applied by the United States § 203 (2d ed. 1945). Growing concern about alien land ownership led to the passage of a federal law requiring reporting of certain land acquisitions by aliens. Foreign Agriculture Investment Disclosure Act of 1978, 7 U.S.C. §§ 3501–3508.

10. *Alien participation in United States companies.* For an example of federal exclusion of aliens, see the Federal Aviation Act § 101(3), (16), and § 401, 49 U.S.C. § 1301(3), (16), and § 1371, limiting the issuance of certificates as "air carrier" to citizens of the United States or to corporations in which the president and two-thirds of the directors are citizens of the United States and at least 75% of the voting interest is owned or controlled by citizens. See generally Vagts, Reporters' Note 8. See also 12 U.S.C. § 619; 47 U.S.C. § 17.

11. *Restrictions on aliens during war.* During the Second World War, the Supreme Court upheld curfew for and relocation of aliens, and even of citizens. Hirabayashi v. United States, 320 U.S. 81, 63 S.Ct. 1375, 87 L.Ed. 1774 (1943) (curfew for persons of Japanese ancestry); Korematsu v. United States, 323 U.S. 214, 65 S.Ct. 193, 89 L.Ed. 194 (1944) (relocation), conviction later set aside on writ of *coram nobis,* 584 F.Supp. 1406 (N.D.Cal.1984).

The Supreme Court upheld detention of alien enemies, see Comment *h,* but invalidated detention of citizens whose loyalty was conceded. *Ex parte* Endo, 323 U.S. 283, 65 S.Ct. 208, 89 L.Ed. 243 (1944). After the war, the United States provided some reimbursement for property loss (50 U.S.C.App. §§ 1981– 87). In 1980, Congress established a Commission on Wartime Relocation and Internment of Civilians, 50 U.S.C.App. § 1981 note. A suit against the United States for damages and declaratory relief was dismissed, but a claim for a taking of property was remanded. Hohri v. United States, 586 F.Supp. 769 (D.D.C.1984), *reversed in part,* 782 F.2d 227 (D.C.Cir.1986).

Enemy aliens in time of war may be arrested and interned and their assets seized. Ludecke v. Watkins, 335 U.S. 160, 68 S.Ct. 1429, 92 L.Ed. 1881 (1948); Johnson v. Eisentrager, 339 U.S. 763, 70 S.Ct. 936, 94 L.Ed. 1255 (1950).

12. *Deportation of resident aliens.* Long ago it was established that the control of Congress over immigration includes the power to deport even lawfully resident aliens on any ground. The plenary authority of Congress was reaffirmed during the years immediately following the Second World War. Carlson v. Landon, 342 U.S. 524, 72 S.Ct. 525, 96 L.Ed. 547 (1952); Shaughnessy v. United States *ex rel.* Mezei, 345 U.S. 206, 73 S.Ct. 625, 97 L.Ed. 956 (1953). The alien is entitled to a hearing satisfying the requirement of procedural due process. Wong Wing v. United States, Reporters' Note 3. Also Landon v. Plasencia, 459 U.S. 21, 32, 103 S.Ct. 321, 329, 74 L.Ed.2d 21 (1982), and Kwong Hai Chew v.

Colding, 344 U.S. 590, 73 S.Ct. 472, 97 L.Ed. 576 (1953) (resident alien denied entry upon returning from visit abroad entitled to due process). The principle that the power of Congress to provide for deportation of aliens is unlimited has not been reexamined by the Supreme Court, but doubts have been raised as to its consistency with the constitutional rights of aliens that have flowered since the principle was established. It may be doubted, for example, whether Congress may deport resident aliens solely on account of their race or religion. Some have argued that deportation except on reasonable grounds would deprive the alien of liberty and other important interests without due process of law, and indeed that the alien should not be deportable except for an important if not a compelling interest. See, *e.g.*, Bullitt, "Deportation as a Denial of Substantive Due Process," 28 Geo. Wash.L.Rev. 205 (1953); Hesse, "The Constitutional Status of the Lawfully Admitted Permanent Resident Alien," 68 Yale L.J. 1578 (1959). In Galvan v. Press, 347 U.S. 522, 530–31, 74 S.Ct. 737, 742–43, 98 L.Ed. 911 (1954), while upholding a deportation, the Court said:

> In light of the expansion of the concept of substantive due process . . . much could be said for the view, were we writing on a clean slate, that the Due Process Clause qualifies the scope of political discretion heretofore recognized as belonging to Congress in regulating the entry and deportation of aliens. And since the intrinsic consequences of deportation are so close to punishment for crime, it might fairly be said also that the *ex post facto* Clause

. . . should be applied to deportation.

In *Mezei, supra,* the Supreme Court upheld the authority of the United States to keep an alien in detention even for an extended period pending deportation. In 1985, a majority of the Supreme Court avoided an opportunity to reexamine *Mezei,* but dissenting Justices challenged its continuing validity. See Jean v. Nelson, Reporters' Note 15; Henkin, "The Constitution as Compact and as Conscience," 27 Wm. and Mary L.Rev. 11 (1985); Henkin, "The Constitution and United States Sovereignty: A Century of *Chinese Exclusion* and Its Progeny," 100 Harv.L.Rev. 853 (1987).

13. *Aliens admitted temporarily for limited purposes.* In the "bracero program," Congress admitted aliens for a fixed period for work and residence. 65 Stat. 119 (1951). Presumably, Congress could admit an alien for residence without other limitations but for a fixed term, since it can deport aliens admitted without limitation. See Reporters' Note 12. Doubts have been raised, however, about the validity of proposed programs that would admit aliens for a fixed period of residence and would also limit their right to travel or to change residence or employment. Some distinctions between resident and nonresident aliens would doubtless be reasonable and consistent with the equal protection of the laws. See Zschernig v. Miller, Reporters' Note 2 (Harlan, J., concurring); Blake v. McClung, 172 U.S. 239, 260–61, 19 S.Ct. 165, 173–74, 43 L.Ed. 432 (1899). States may not impose certain additional burdens, *e.g.*, higher tuition fees, on nonimmigrant aliens. Toll v. Moreno, 458

U.S. 1, 102 S.Ct. 2977, 73 L.Ed.2d 563 (1982) (State provisions preempted by federal statutes).

14. *Illegal or undocumented aliens.* Aliens unlawfully in the United States are also entitled to constitutional protections. Such an alien is protected by the due process clause, Matthews v. Diaz, Reporters' Note 6, 426 U.S. at 77, 96 S.Ct. at 1890; also Shaughnessy v. United States *ex rel.* Mezei, Reporters' Note 12; Leng May Ma v. Barber, 357 U.S. 185, 187, 78 S.Ct. 1072, 1073, 2 L.Ed.2d 1246 (1958); and the equal protection clause, Plyler v. Doe, 457 U.S. 202, 102 S.Ct. 2382, 72 L.Ed.2d 786 (1982) (State may not deny undocumented school-age children free public education provided for citizen or resident alien children, where such discrimination does not further substantial State interest); *cf.* Holley v. Lavine, 529 F.2d 1294 (2d Cir.), *certiorari denied,* 426 U.S. 954, 96 S.Ct. 3181, 49 L.Ed.2d 1193 (1976) (equal protection claims of illegal alien who was denied welfare benefits for minor children cannot be dismissed out of hand). See Bolanos v. Kiley, 509 F.2d 1023, 1025 (2d Cir.1975).

Undocumented aliens were also held to be within the protection of the Civil Rights Act, 18 U.S.C. § 242. United States v. Otherson, 637 F.2d 1276 (9th Cir.1980), *certiorari denied,* 454 U.S. 840, 102 S.Ct. 149, 70 L.Ed.2d 123 (1981) (affirming conviction of United States border patrol agents for assaulting aliens who had entered United States illegally).

For the special protection of refugees, by United States treaty and act of Congress, against deportation to a country where their life or freedom would be threatened, see § 711, Reporters' Note 7.

15. *Exclusion of aliens.* The power of Congress to exclude aliens was held to be plenary and not subject to constitutional limitations. Chinese Exclusion Case, Reporters' Note 1; United States *ex rel.* Knauff v. Shaughnessy, Reporters' Note 12. The procedures prescribed by Congress for determining admission or exclusion are the only process due the alien. Those principles have not been recently reexamined by the Supreme Court. It may be doubted, for example, whether Congress could exclude aliens solely on account of their race or religion.

The fiction that an alien who has not been admitted to the United States is not here, and is not entitled to constitutional protections and remedies, was rejected in Rodriguez-Fernandez v. Wilkinson, 505 F.Supp. 787 (D.Kan.1980), *affirmed,* 654 F.2d 1382 (10th Cir.1981). In that case, the court ordered the Attorney General to release from prolonged detention an alien ineligible for admission to the United States whom the United States was unable to deport because his country of nationality would not accept him. See § 702, Reporters' Note 6. Compare Jean v. Nelson, 727 F.2d 957 (11th Cir.1984) *en banc* (denying Fifth Amendment protections for unadmitted aliens, on the authority of *Mezei,* Reporters' Note 12), *affirmed on other grounds,* 472 U.S. 846, 105 S.Ct. 2992, 86 L.Ed.2d 664 (1985) (court of appeals should not have reached the constitutional issue). Justices Marshall and Brennan dissented in that case, and would have rejected application of *Mezei.* "Only the most perverse reading of the Constitution would deny detained aliens the right to bring constitutional challenges to the most basic conditions of their confinement." 472 U.S. at 873, 105 S.Ct. at 3008. They asserted that due process and equal protection principles are applicable to undocumented aliens physically present in the United States.

See also Augustin v. Sava, 735 F.2d 32, 37, 38 (2d Cir.1984) (alien present in U.S. has procedural right to effective translation in deportation hearing, and the rights may also be required by constitutional due process).

16. *Aliens outside the United States.* In United States v. Belmont, the Court said: "Our Constitution, laws and policies have no extraterritorial operation, unless in respect of our own citizens." 301 U.S. 324, 332 (1939). But later language, in Reid v. Covert, 354 U.S. 1, 6, 77 S.Ct. 1222, 1228, 1 L.Ed.2d 1148 (1957), declaring that any exercise of authority by the United States is subject to constitutional limitations (§ 721, Reporters' Notes 1 and 2) would seem to apply as well to acts in respect of any alien anywhere. In United States v. Caltex, Inc., 344 U.S. 149, 73 S.Ct. 200, 97 L.Ed. 157 (1952), the Court considered claims for compensation under the Fifth Amendment by alien corporations for takings in the Philippines. Apparently, no case since *Reid* has denied the protections of the Constitution to aliens abroad; and the Constitution has been held to apply to searches and seizures on the high seas, in cases involving foreign vessels and non-United States nationals. In United States v. Tiede, 86 F.R.D. 227 (1979), the United States Court for Berlin held that a Polish national tried in Berlin by that court, established under the post-war occupation authority of the United States, had to be given a jury trial as a matter of constitutional right. The court distinguished Madsen v. Kinsella, 343 U.S. 341, 72 S.Ct. 699, 96 L.Ed. 988 (1952), which had upheld the conviction of a United States citizen by a court established under United States occupation authority without a jury, on the ground that the earlier court was established under the authority of the Commander-in-Chief in occupied territory while the United States was still at war. Compare Dostal v. Haig, 652 F.2d 173 (D.C.Cir.1981), accepting arguendo the applicability of the Bill of Rights to United States action in Berlin, but holding that failure by United States authorities to provide a judicial forum, or to forego invoking sovereign immunity, did not deny alien plaintiffs due process since the injury complained of impaired neither liberty nor property interests.

Aliens outside the United States, "by the policy and practice of the courts of this country, are ordinarily permitted to resort to the courts for the redress of wrongs and the protection of their rights." Disconto Gesellschaft v. Umbreit, 208 U.S. 570, 578, 28 S.Ct. 337, 339, 52 L.Ed. 625 (1908); but *cf.* Kukatush Mining Co. v. SEC, 309 F.2d 647 (D.C.Cir. 1962) (denying standing to Canadian corporation, a nonresident alien without assets in United States, to seek injunction to have its name stricken from "restricted list"). In Berlin Democratic Club v. Rumsfeld, 410 F.Supp. 144 (D.D.C.1976), the court denied standing to an alien abroad to sue United States military officials in Germany for harassment and intimidation. The court assumed a general rule that nonresident aliens have no standing to sue in United States courts except: where the alien claims in respect of a *res* within the jurisdiction of the court; where a United States statute authorizes relief to a nonresident alien; or where the nonresident alien is brought from abroad for criminal prosecution. 410 F.Supp. at 152. In wartime, however, nonresident alien enemies imprisoned abroad under military authority could not claim access to the courts of the United States for a writ of habeas corpus. Johnson v. Eisentrager, 339 U.S. 763, 70 S.Ct. 936, 94 L.Ed. 1255 (1950). In re Yamashita, 327 U.S. 1, 66 S.Ct. 340, 90 L.Ed. 499 (1946), was distinguished on the ground that the petitioner was held in the Philippines, then territory subject to United States authority.

17. *Previous Restatement.* The previous Restatement (§ 167, Comment *b*) stated that the requirements of the United States Constitution as to the protection of personal and property rights are applicable to aliens as well as to nationals.

Part VIII

SELECTED LAW OF INTERNATIONAL ECONOMIC RELATIONS

Introductory Note:

The law of international economic relations in its broadest sense includes all the international law and international agreements governing economic transactions that cross state boundaries or that otherwise have implications for more than one state, such as those involving the movement of goods, funds, persons, intangibles, technology, vessels or aircraft. This Restatement, however, deals only with selected aspects of that law. For example, it does not address the international regulation of shipping, air transportation, or telecommunications. It deals with rules that govern the behavior of states rather than of private persons directly.[1] It does not consider rules of commercial law applicable to international transactions by private persons, such as sales of goods, letters of credit or technology licensing.

International economic activity often reflects tension between policies of states that maximize their particular and direct economic interest and other policies that would contribute to general economic welfare. The law of international economic relations is designed, generally, to specify actions that states may take unilaterally without transgressing international norms—for example, the imposition of taxes, environmental controls, or safety regulations—and to impose restraints on other types of actions that might have adverse impact on foreign states or on the international economy as a whole—for example, tariffs, import quotas, or exchange controls.

There has been little customary international law of economic relations, but the interest of states in an efficient global economy has resulted in a variety of international agreements and arrangements. As of 1987, no multilateral agreement of general application had established comprehensive rules governing international investment. The principal multilateral agreements concerning trade in goods and those concerning international monetary affairs,

---

[1] Some rules set forth elsewhere in this Restatement are relevant to international economic relations as well. For example, the movement of individuals to pursue employment or other economic activity abroad implicates state responsibility for the treatment of aliens, dealt with in § 711. The security of foreign investment and related contracts is dealt with in §§ 712 and 713. Questions as to the jurisdiction of states, dealt with in Part IV, apply to economic as to other international activities.

along with related law of the United States, are addressed in this Part.

The previous Restatement did not address the subjects here covered.

Chapter One

LAW OF INTERNATIONAL TRADE

Introductory Note

Introductory Note:

After World War II, there was a general sense that the cycle of intensely protectionist measures and countermeasures of the 1930's, with high tariffs, competitive currency devaluations, and exchange controls, had done severe damage to the international economy and should not be allowed to recur. As to trade in goods, that conviction found expression in the General Agreement on Tariffs and Trade (the GATT). The GATT came into being as part of an attempt to draft an elaborate agreement for a strong International Trade Organization. When it became apparent that such an institution could not win early approval, a partial agreement was concluded. It came into effect when a group of initial members signed the Protocol of Provisional Application of October 30, 1947.[1] That "temporary" agreement remains in effect, and as of 1987, 92 states had become members of the GATT, including all of the major industrial states other than the Soviet Union.

The GATT as originally concluded consisted of three parts. Part I deals largely with tariffs but contains other general principles applicable to all trade restraints. Part II deals largely with restrictions other than tariffs and includes a number of exceptions to the commitments not to restrict trade. Part III contains procedural and administrative provisions as well as ground rules for

---

[1] 61 Stat. A(3), (5), (6); T.I.A.S. No. 1700, 55 U.N.T.S. 308.

tariff negotiations. Part IV, dealing with developing states, was added in 1965. See § 810.

The key provisions as to tariffs are Article I, whereby member states undertake to grant each other most-favored-nation treatment, see § 802, and Article II, containing a commitment by each party to adhere to the tariffs listed in the schedules that it has negotiated pursuant to GATT, see § 803. Those two sections in effect replaced the bilateral negotiation process of the 1930's with a multilateral process designed to enable states to balance all the concessions they make to all parties against all concessions they receive, regardless of which party granted them.

The GATT tariff structure developed through a series of negotiating rounds in which the parties sought to lower tariffs through reciprocal concessions. The so-called Tokyo Round of Multilateral Trade Negotiations (MTN), culminating in 1979, shifted the GATT's major emphasis to non-tariff barriers. It produced a series of specialized codes, not subscribed to by all members, dealing with such topics as subsidies and countervailing duties (§ 806), discrimination against foreign goods in government procurement and quality specifications that operate to hamper foreign imports (§ 805), and the unification of rules as to dumping (§ 807).[2] In 1986, preparations were initiated for a new round of multilateral negotiations, which would address for the first time restraints on trade in services, such as insurance, banking, and transportation, and perhaps also other matters, such as protection for intellectual property and international investment.

The GATT is an international agreement, but its status as international law cannot be stated simply. Like other agreements, it is binding upon states that are parties to it, § 321. Certain provisions of GATT, however, permit states to withdraw from obligations they have undertaken, though at some cost; see § 803, Comment b. In addition, Article XXV of the Agreement provides that the Contracting Parties may, by a two-thirds majority of the votes cast, waive an obligation imposed on a party by the Agree-

---

[2] The nine Tokyo Round agreements are: (1) Agreement on Interpretation and Application of Articles VI, XVI and XXIII of the GATT (Subsidies Code), (2) Agreement on Implementation of Article VI of the GATT (Anti-dumping Code), (3) Agreement on Implementation of Article VII of the GATT (Customs Valuation Code), (4) Agreement on Government Procurement, (5) Agreement on Technical Barriers to Trade, (6) Agreement on Import Licensing Procedures, (7) Agreement on Trade in Civil Aircraft, (8) International Dairy Arrangement, and (9) Agreement Regarding Bovine Meat. These agreements are reprinted in Agreements Reached in the Tokyo Round of the Multilateral Trade Negotiations, H.R.Doc. 96–153, 96th Cong., 1st sess. (1979). Some of the agreements have been published in the United States Treaties series. See 31 U.S.T. 405 (Standards); 513 (Subsidies); 619 (Civil Aircraft); 679 (Dairy Products); 4919 (Anti-Dumping); 32 U.S.T. 293 (Bovine Meat); 1985 (Import Licensing Procedures).

ment either unconditionally or subject to conditions and time limits. Other GATT provisions set forth principles so general that they have not been understood to impose legal obligations, see § 805, Comment *a*; it was the purpose of the Tokyo Round to make those commitments more specific and enforceable, sometimes at the cost of making them narrower. Furthermore, GATT does not possess an institutional apparatus like that of other international organizations. The drafters did not intend that GATT become an organization; they provided that any necessary action be taken by the Contracting Parties acting jointly. Over its history, however, the GATT has evolved procedures and institutional practices, and a web of obligations requiring states to submit their actions in respect of trade to international scrutiny, to negotiate about them, and to consider the reactions of other states. While some GATT obligations have not been meticulously observed at the margin, overall the Agreement constitutes the prevailing norm of international trade among member states.

The United States adhered to GATT through the Protocol of Provisional Application signed by the President under the authority of the Reciprocal Trade Agreements Act. Despite some attempts by Congress to distance itself from the Agreement,[3] its status as a commitment of the United States is not in doubt, and courts in the United States assume its binding character.

The GATT has a status in United States law different from that described in §§ 111–15 of this Restatement for international agreements generally. The Protocol of Provisional Application binds the parties without qualification to apply Parts I and III of the GATT, but the commitment as to Part II (Articles III through XXIII) applies only "to the fullest extent not inconsistent with existing legislation." Comparable provisions appear in protocols of accession to the GATT by other states. Thus, United States trade laws enacted prior to 1947 remained in force (unless repealed by Congress) even when inconsistent with Part II of the GATT, and post-1947 actions taken under those laws did not entitle other member states to compensation. The ancillary codes negotiated in the Tokyo Round did not contain any comparable "grandfather clause," and United States law had to be changed in a number of respects to achieve compliance with the Codes. See, *e.g.*, § 806, Comment *f* and Reporters' Note 3, on the requirement of a finding of injury prior to imposition of countervailing duties against subsidized imports. In several statutes, Congress has directed the President to act in conformity with the GATT, as in § 122(a) of the Trade Act of 1974, 19 U.S.C. § 2132(a) (balance of payments restric-

---

[3] See *e.g.*, § 121(d) of the Trade Act of 1974, 19 U.S.C. § 2131(d).

tions). In § 203(k) of that Act, 19 U.S.C. § 2253(k), dealing with import relief, the President is directed to proceed "after consideration of the relation of such actions to the international obligations of the United States." In approving the series of multilateral codes adopted in the Tokyo Round, Congress provided that in case of conflict United States law rather than the pertinent code shall prevail.[4]

Article XXIV(12) of the GATT binds each party to "take such reasonable measures as may be available to it" to ensure observance of the GATT by regional and local governments. In the United States, prior State legislation inconsistent with GATT has been held to be superseded by GATT despite the grandfather clause. See § 805, Reporters' Note 2.

With rare exceptions, the GATT itself has not provided rights for private parties directly. See § 805, Reporters' Note 2. In § 3(f) of the Trade Agreements Act of 1979, 19 U.S.C. § 2504(d), Congress said that adoption of the Tokyo Round agreements shall not be "construed as creating any private right of action or remedy for which provision is not explicitly made" in the legislation. Many provisions of United States law, however, mirror international obligations contained in GATT or its ancillary codes and confer rights on private parties affected by imports. Exporters from the United States must seek the intervention of the Executive Branch in order to obtain the benefits of the Agreement in respect of import restraints or other measures imposed by foreign states.[5]

United States law concerning international trade. Under the United States Constitution, the Federal Government may impose duties on imports but not on exports. Article I, Sections 8 and 9. The States may not impose duties on exports or imports without the consent of Congress, Article I, Section 10, and no instance of such consent is known.

The last full legislative tariff was the Smoot-Hawley Tariff Act of 1930, 46 Stat. 590, seen by many as a significant cause of the world-wide decline in international trade during the Great Depression of the 1930's. When the Franklin Roosevelt administration came into office, it secured passage by Congress of the Reciprocal Trade Agreement Act of 1934, 48 Stat. 943, which authorized the President, subject to stated conditions, to negotiate reductions of duties with other states on the basis of mutual exchange of benefits, and to proclaim the lower duties on a general most-favored-nation basis. Since 1934, the Reciprocal Trade Agreements Pro-

---

[4] Section 3 of the Trade Agreements Act of 1979, 19 U.S.C. § 2504.

[5] See § 301 of the Trade Act of 1974, 19 U.S.C. § 2411.

gram has been the principal basis of United States foreign trade law.

Until 1945, negotiations of duty reductions took place on a bilateral basis. Following creation of the GATT in 1947, most negotiations in respect of duties have been carried on multilaterally, and reduced duties were extended to goods from virtually all United States trading partners, even those not members of GATT or participants in the negotiations.[6] Until 1945, the President's authority to reduce duties in implementation of trade agreements was based on the 1930 rates. Subsequent acts of Congress granted the President authority to reduce rates from then prevailing levels. For example, the 1949 Act authorized reduction in individual tariffs by up to 50 percent of the rates prevailing in 1945, the 1955 Act authorized reductions by up to 15 percent of the 1955 rates, and the 1958 Act authorized reductions by up to 20 percent of their 1958 level. Each of these authorities carried a time limit, and each set the ground rules for successive GATT negotiations.

A major overhaul of United States trade legislation was adopted in the Trade Expansion Act (TEA) of 1962, 76 Stat. 872, designed in part as a response to the emergence of the European Common Market and the rise of Japan as a major economic power. Under the TEA, the President was authorized not only to negotiate item-by-item, but to make "linear tariff cuts," *i.e.*, across-the-board reductions in duties on classes of goods and to conduct sectoral negotiations. A further major revision was made by the Trade Act of 1974, 88 Stat. 1978, for the first time authorizing and directing negotiations on so-called "non-tariff barriers," including subsidies, dumping, restrictive government procurement, and technical standards with protectionist intent or effect. The Tokyo Round, negotiated over the period 1973–79, reflected many of the goals of this initiative; its results were made part of United States domestic law by the Trade Agreements Act of 1979, 93 Stat. 144.

As of 1986, the basic trade legislation for the United States remained the Trade Act of 1974, but portions of the 1962 and 1979 acts, plus the Trade and Tariff Act of 1984, 98 Stat. 2948, are reflected in this chapter.[7] As of 1986, only limited authority to conduct trade negotiation remained in effect, but it was assumed that if the major trading states agreed to hold a new round of trade negotiations—possibly going beyond goods to services and more closely linked than in the past to international monetary arrange-

---

[6] For exceptions to this statement, see § 802, Reporters' Note 2.

[7] The foreign trade legislation of the United States appears in Title 19 of the U.S. Code. The Trade Act of 1974 begins at 19 U.S.C. § 2101.

ments—Congress would be asked to grant new negotiating authority to the President.

REPORTERS' NOTES

1. Bibliography.

On trade law:

G. Curzon, Multilateral Commercial Diplomacy (1965)

K. Dam, The GATT: Law and International Economic Organization (1970)

R. Hudec, The GATT Legal System and World Trade Diplomacy (1975)

J. Jackson, World Trade and the Law of GATT (1969)

J. Jackson & W. Davey, Legal Problems of International Economic Relations (2d ed. 1986)

A. Lowenfeld, Public Controls on International Trade (2d ed. 1983)

E. Rossides, U.S. Import Trade Regulation (1986)

Most official actions by GATT bodies are reported in Basic Instruments and Selected Documents with periodic supplements (cited "BISD, __ Supp.").

On export controls:

A. Lowenfeld, Trade Controls for Political Ends (2d ed. 1983).

§ 801. Definitions

Under the General Agreement on Tariffs and Trade and other international agreements, an obligation by a state to accord to another state

(1) "most-favored-nation" treatment is an obligation to treat that state, its nationals or goods, no less favorably than any other state, its nationals or goods;

(2) "national treatment" is an obligation to treat the nationals or goods of another state as the state treats its own nationals or goods;

(3) "reciprocity" is an obligation to treat another state, its nationals or goods, as the other state treats the promisor state, its nationals or goods;

(4) a "preference" is an obligation to grant another state, its nationals or goods, a benefit not accorded to all other states, their nationals or goods.

Comment:

a. Most-favored-nation treatment. If a state promises most-favored-nation (MFN) treatment to another state by bilateral treaty, the promisor state thereby undertakes to give to the promisee state the benefit of any concession it has given, or may later give, to any third state. A most-favored-nation clause in a multilateral agreement, as in the GATT (§ 802), is effectively a rule of nondiscrimination among all parties.

A most-favored-nation clause may be limited in subject matter, or may cover all aspects of trade, other international intercourse, or the treatment of foreign nationals. The treatment may apply to a state, to its nationals, or to its goods.

A most-favored-nation clause is said to be "unconditional" if state *A* grants to state *B* the treatment given to state *C*, without requiring state *B* to give state *A* any benefit in return. A clause is said to be "conditional" if, as a consideration for receiving the benefits given by *A* to *C*, *B* must give to *A* a benefit comparable to that given to *A* by *C*.

The treatment afforded to the beneficiary of a most-favored-nation clause is not fixed as of the time the clause goes into effect; it rises or falls as the treatment afforded to the most favored nation changes.

b. Most-favored-nation and national treatment contrasted. A grant of most-favored-nation treatment by state *A* to state *B* is a grant of treatment equivalent to that which *A* grants to *C*, the nation receiving the most favorable treatment; a grant of national treatment by *A* to *B* is a grant of treatment for *B*'s nationals or goods equivalent to that which *A* accords to its own nationals or goods. The same international agreement may contain clauses of both types.

c. Reciprocity. A grant by state *A* to state *B* of a benefit on the basis of reciprocity is a grant by *A* to *B* equivalent to that which *B* grants to *A*. A reciprocity clause in a treaty is usually a means of saying that *A* and *B* (or all states parties to a multilateral treaty) bind themselves to give the same benefit to each other's nationals or goods. A reciprocity clause serves to permit *A* thereafter to diminish the benefit to nationals of *B* to the extent that *B* diminishes benefits to nationals of *A*. A benefit on condition of reciprocity is often granted unilaterally by statute; the state grants benefits to another state if that state grants comparable benefits to the enacting state. In contrast to reciprocity clauses in international agreements, such a clause in national legislation can ordinarily be repealed or modified by the enacting state without violating any international obligation.

d. Preferences. The term "preference" is used to refer to various kinds of benefits granted by a state to nationals or goods of another state but not to the nationals or goods of all other states. Increasingly, the term is used particularly to refer to those differentiations that are permitted as exceptions under the GATT or other international agreements, despite general guarantees of most-favored-nation treatment to all parties. For example, the GATT permits preferences to be granted by developed states to developing states notwithstanding the general GATT requirement of most-favored-nation treatment. Typically, such preferences accord to developing countries benefits not granted to other states, such as duty-free treatment for their goods or exemption from prohibitions against subsidies, and are granted without expectation of reciprocal benefits to the granting state. See § 810.

REPORTERS' NOTES

1. *History of most-favored-nation clauses.* By the middle of the 19th century, unconditional most-favored nation clauses had become common in treaties between European states, although their scope varied. McNair, Law of Treaties ch. XV (1961). The League of Nations, seeking to achieve "equitable treatment for the commerce of all members," conducted studies of the political and legal questions raised by most-favored-nation clauses. In the 1970's, the International Law Commission undertook a general study of most-favored-nation clauses. See, *e.g.,* [1978] 1 Y.B. Int'l L.Comm'n 241. In United States practice, the conditional most-favored-nation clause predominated in trade agreements until the 1920's, but since then MFN clauses have been generally unconditional. See § 802.

2. *Most-favored-nation clauses in non-trade contexts.* Most-favored-nation clauses appear also in contexts other than trade. A clause granting such treatment in connection with the right of foreign nationals to acquire or possess property was given effect in Kolovrat v. Oregon, 366 U.S. 187, 81 S.Ct. 922, 6 L.Ed.2d 218 (1961). It has been used also in relation to rights of navigation, industrial property rights, consular matters, and tonnage or other taxes. See Most-Favored-Nation Clause, Report by Ustor, [1969] 2 Y.B.Int'l L. Comm'n 157.

§ 802.   Most-Favored-Nation Treatment as to Imports

(1) **Under the General Agreement on Tariffs and Trade or a comparable international agreement, a state party is obligated, with specified exceptions, to accord most-favored-nation treatment to products of other states parties.**

(2) **Under the law of the United States, products of all states are entitled to most-favored-nation treatment, except as otherwise provided by law.**

Source Note:

GATT, Article I; § 126, Trade Act of 1974, 19 U.S.C. §§ 2136, 2431.

Comment:

a. Agreements for most-favored-nation treatment as to trade. In addition to the central most-favored-nation obligation in Article I of the GATT, that agreement contains most-favored-nation clauses applicable to particular matters, such as marks of origin (Article IX(1)), quantitative restrictions (Article XIII(1)), and export controls on goods in short supply (Article XX(j)). The GATT also contains exceptions to these obligations, *e.g.*, permitting preferences for developing countries (§ 810), or permitting customs unions and free trade areas under stated conditions (§ 809). Each of these exceptions is a specified and limited departure from the most-favored-nation rule, and no implied departures from most-favored-nation treatment may be read into the General Agreement.

An obligation to accord most-favored-nation treatment as to trade matters also appears commonly in treaties of friendship, commerce, and navigation.

b. Most-favored-nation treatment in United States law. As stated in Subsection (2), United States law extends most-favored-nation treatment to states generally, even those not parties to the GATT, but Congress has restricted the President's authority to grant most-favored-nation treatment to non-market, *i.e.* Communist, states. United States law also authorizes departures from the most-favored-nation principle in several respects, such as the generalized preference rules for developing states (§ 810), which parallel the GATT exceptions. See Comment *a.*

c. Like products. The most-favored-nation principle applies regardless of insignificant differentiations. A state may make reasonable classifications based on distinctions of commercial significance, but may not manipulate distinctions to discriminate among states.

REPORTERS' NOTES

1. *Multilateral trade negotiation codes and most-favored-nation treatment.* New codes negotiated under GATT auspices as supplements to GATT (rather than as amendments thereto) confer specific benefits on signatories to the code on the basis of reciprocity only, thus deviating from the most-favored-nation principle underlying the GATT generally. Signatories to these codes include the United States and all states members of the Organization for Economic Cooperation and Development but, as of 1986, few of the developing

states members of GATT had adhered to them.

Under the Trade Agreements Act of 1979, benefits of the Government Procurement Code, the Technical Barriers Code, and the Subsidies Code were specifically limited to parties to those codes or to states that assumed comparable obligations. Sections 101, 301 of the Trade Agreements Act of 1979, 19 U.S.C. §§ 1671, 2511. For discussion of the United States legislation, see Rubin, "Most-Favored-Nation Treatment and the Multilateral Trade Negotiations", 6 Int'l Trade L.J. 221 (1981); Hufbauer, Erb and Starr, "The GATT Codes and the Unconditional Most-Favored-Nation Principle", 12 L. & Pol'y in Int'l Bus. 59 (1980).

2. *United States statutes on most-favored-nation treatment in trade.* The general principle of nondiscrimination was adopted in the Trade Agreements Act of 1934, and restated in § 126(a) of the Trade Act of 1974 (19 U.S.C. § 2136(a)):

> Except as otherwise provided in this Act or in any other provision of law, any duty . . . proclaimed in carrying out any trade agreement under this subchapter shall apply to products of all foreign countries . . . .

An exception to generalized MFN, applicable to Communist countries, was written into United States trade law in 1951 and has continued in various forms since that time. As of 1986, sections 401–10 of the Trade Act of 1974 (19 U.S.C. §§ 2431–40) denied most-favored-nation treatment to most Communist states unless a commercial agreement is in effect with them, and limit the authority of the President to enter into such commercial agreements. These provisions of the 1974 Act were intended primarily to induce the U.S.S.R. to modify its behavior with respect to granting permission to emigrate, to obtain information as to persons missing in action in South East Asia, and to achieve the resolution of claims against Czechoslovakia. Most-favored-nation treatment has been extended by bilateral agreements pursuant to the 1974 Act to Hungary, Rumania, and the People's Republic of China; Poland and Yugoslavia had become beneficiaries of most-favored-nation treatment before that Act. The President suspended most-favored-nation treatment for Poland in 1982 after martial law was imposed there. 47 Fed.Reg. 49005 (1982).

3. *Like products.* Most-favored-nation treatment as to goods, generally applies only to "like products." The history of tariffs provides some striking examples of attempts to define a concession to state X so narrowly as to deny its benefits to state Y under a most-favored-nation clause. For example, in 1904, Germany, in a treaty with Switzerland, reduced its tariff on cattle reared at least 300 meters above sea level and having at least one month's grazing each year at least 800 meters above sea level, qualifications beyond the capacity of Denmark or the Netherlands. The Contracting Parties to GATT have considered the "like product" concept in several instances but have not succeeded in substantially clarifying it. See, *e.g.*, Treatment by Germany of Imports of Sardines, BISD, 1st Supp. 53–59 (1953); Australian Sulphate Case, BISD, Volume II 188 (1952); Brazilian Cognac Case, *id.* at 181.

Attempts have been made to simplify the vast variety of customs classifications and to make them internationally uniform. Most major trading states use the Brussels Tariff Nomenclature (BTN) as the basis of their tariffs. As of 1986, the United States had not adopted that nomenclature, but it was a party to the convention establishing the Customs Cooperation Council, which administers the BTN, 22 U.S.T. 320, T.I.A.S. No. 7063, 157 U.N.T.S. 129. A revised tariff schedule, based on a "Harmonized Commodity Description and Coding System" developed by the Customs Cooperation Council, was in preparation for submission to Congress. 46 Fed.Reg. 47897 (1981); 51 *id.* 30933 (1986).

§ 803.   Commitment to Tariffs Bound by International Agreement

(1) Under the General Agreement on Tariffs and Trade, a state party, subject to specified exceptions,

(a) is obligated not to increase a tariff to a level above the rate to which it is bound by schedule,

(b) may withdraw a binding on a product if, in negotiation with the principal beneficiaries of the original binding, it offers to give them substantially equivalent concessions.

(2) Under the law of the United States, the President, by authority delegated to him by Congress, may proclaim modification of tariffs in implementation of international agreements.

Source Note:

GATT, Articles II, XXVIII; 19 U.S.C. § 1202 (Tariff Schedules of the United States).

Comment:

a. Binding of tariffs. Together with the most-favored-nation obligation of § 802, the obligation not to increase customs duties above those at which a country has bound them is the cornerstone of the GATT system. A tariff is "bound" when a state has filed with the GATT a commitment either not to increase an existing rate or to lower it; the commitment is indicated by including it in a tariff schedule. A tariff is bound as the outcome of a negotiating process through which the state that is bound obtains, in return for its bindings, concessions from other states that it deems to be of equivalent value. That process is multilateral, as contrasted with the bilateral procedures involved in earlier trade agreements such as those concluded pursuant to the Trade Agreements Act of 1934 and subsequent acts. A state may bind other kinds of restrictions on imports; for example, it may agree not to extend a requirement that a category of goods sold within the state contain a specified proportion of parts of local origin.

   b. Deviation from bound tariffs. Though a tariff is bound, the GATT provides for withdrawal of a binding under certain conditions. Article XXVIII provides that every three years (beginning January 1, 1958) a state may modify or withdraw any concession by agreement with the party with which it was originally negotiated and with any other party found "to have a principal supplying interest." Article XXVIII contemplates that the state withdrawing a concession will afford equivalent concessions on other goods. If no agreement is reached, the state "proposing to modify or withdraw the concession shall, nevertheless, be free to do so," and the other negotiating parties may withdraw "substantially equivalent concessions initially negotiated with the applicant contracting party." A state may reserve in advance the right to renegotiate at off-cycle intervals. Article XXVIII(5). The GATT authorizes renegotiation other than at the three-year intervals in special circumstances. Article XXVIII(4). These qualifications, designed to overcome reluctance to agree to tariff reductions, have not often been used by the important trading states.

   At the creation of a customs union (§ 809), renegotiation of external tariffs of the custom union's individual members is, according to Article XXIV(6), to be conducted through the procedures set forth in Article XXVIII. Apart from renegotiation under that article, a state may take action under Article XIX in response to injury resulting from imports. See § 808.

   c. Delegation of Congressional authority. The United States Constitution grants Congress the power to regulate commerce with foreign nations. It also grants Congress the power to lay duties, Article I, Section 8, and denies such power to the States without the consent of Congress, Article I, Section 10. The tariff rates established by Congress appear in the Tariff Schedules of the United States, 19 U.S.C. § 1202, in Column 2. However, Congress has delegated authority to the President to deviate from the rates it sets. Modified rates proclaimed by the President appear in Column 1. See Reporters' Note 4. Imports on most products are subject to the rates set forth in Column 1, reflecting the results of negotiations under the trade agreements program; those rates are applicable to products from all states entitled to most-favored-nation treatment under the law or treaties of the United States; see § 802, Reporters' Note 2. (Another column captioned "GSP Item" indicates the products designated by the President to be eligible for the general system of preferences; see § 810, Comment *c.*)

REPORTERS' NOTES

1. *The binding process.* The binding process takes place largely at the successive meetings of the Contracting Parties of the GATT, referred to as "rounds". Past "rounds" have taken place as follows: Geneva, 1947; Annecy, 1948; Torquay, 1950; Geneva, 1956; Geneva, 1960–61 ("Dillon"); Geneva, 1964–67 ("Kennedy"); and Geneva, 1973–79 ("Tokyo").

The presence of all the Contracting Parties makes it possible for State X to make a concession that benefits State Y even though it receives no corresponding concession from that state, because it simultaneously receives one from State Z. As a result of the most-favored-nation provisions in GATT, any concession benefits not only the state that negotiated the concession but all other states as well. Negotiating rules are established prior to each round. In the earlier rounds, the rules provided for negotiation item-by-item with the principal supplier; beginning with the Kennedy Round, a "linear technique" was used, under which states were expected to offer to cut all tariffs according to an agreed formula, and to negotiate about exceptions.

2. *"Principal supplier."* The determination of who has a "principal supplying interest" (Comment *b*) affects both negotiations of concessions and renegotiations after withdrawal of concessions. Note 4 to Paragraph 1 ad Article XXVIII provides that a party should be found to have such an interest only if it "had, over a reasonable period of time prior to the negotiations, a larger share in the market of the applicant contracting party than a

contracting party with which the concession was initially negotiated." The note also provides for situations in which discriminatory restrictions prevented a party from achieving such a share. The United States was in such a situation vis-á-vis the Federal Republic of Germany, with respect to poultry following the creation of the European Economic Community. Germany had become bound as a result of negotiations with Denmark. In 1958, the United States had sold only one-third as much poultry to Germany as did Denmark; it had moved to approximate equality with Denmark in 1959, and exceeded it in 1960. Thereafter, import restraints pursuant to the Common Agricultural Policy led to a sharp decline in imports of poultry into the EEC, and the United States filed a formal complaint with the GATT. A GATT panel subsequently ruled on the amount of compensation due to the United States, assuming (without formally deciding) that the United States had standing under Article XXVIII as a principal supplier, although the concession was originally granted to Denmark. See Report of Panel on Poultry. GATT Doc. No. L/2088 (Nov. 21, 1963), repr. 3 Int'l Leg.Mat. 116 (1964); Walker, "Dispute Settlement: The Chicken War," 58 Am.J.Int'l L. 671 (1964); 1 Chayes, Ehrlich and Lowenfeld, International Legal Process 249–305 (1968). The United States withdrew concessions in an amount equal to that found by the GATT panel, selecting products of which the EEC was a principal supplier, but generalizing the increased duties to all suppliers of those products. See

United States v. Star Industries, Inc., 462 F.2d 557 (C.C.P.A.), *certiorari denied*, 409 U.S. 1076, 93 S.Ct. 678, 34 L.Ed.2d 663 (1972); Lowenfeld, "Doing Unto Others, The Chicken War Ten Years After," 4 J.Mar.L. & C. 599 (1973).

3. *Measurement of "substantially equivalent concessions."* The simplest measure of substantial equivalence is the amount of trade in the period before the binding, unbinding, or impairment of a concession, in some instances adjusted to reflect trends. Thus, if state X withdraws a concession covering $25 million of exports from state Y, Y may levy a burden on $25 million of X's exports. A more sophisticated measure would be the change in the rate of the tariff, or the trade effect of such change, but such calculations are regarded as so complex as often to be administratively not feasible. See the decision, of the panel on poultry, Reporters' Note 2.

4. *Tariff-negotiating authority in United States law.* Beginning in the 19th century, Congress delegated increasing authority to the President to negotiate and put into effect lower tariffs, as well as authority to increase tariffs. Though repeatedly challenged in the courts as unreasonable delegations of Congressional power, each of these enactments was sustained. Reporters' Note 5.

The Reciprocal Trade Agreement program authorized in the Trade Agreements Act of 1934 was expanded after 1945 to include multilateral negotiations under GATT. As GATT progressed through round after round, Reporters' Note 1, more specific authority was granted the President,

usually limited both as to duration and as to the amount of tariff reduction permitted.

Most grants to the President of negotiating authority contained in the Trade Act of 1974 expired in 1979, but the Trade and Tariff Act of 1984 renewed some grants and created new ones. The Act continued, with different conditions and limitations, the power to grant preferences to developing states under Title V of the Trade Act of 1974; see this Restatement, § 810. It granted specific new authority with respect to trade in services, trade in high technology items, and trade with Israel. The President continues to have authority to compensate other states for withdrawal of concessions previously granted, for example under the import relief procedures. See § 808.

5. *Presidential authority under United States law.* Presidential claims of independent constitutional authority to alter tariffs have been rejected. Compare United States v. Guy W. Capps, Inc., 204 F.2d 655, 659 (4th Cir. 1953), *affirmed on other grounds*, 348 U.S. 296, 75 S.Ct. 326, 99 L.Ed. 329 (1955). However, Congressional delegation to the President of the authority to amend tariff levels has been uniformly upheld. In Field v. Clark, 143 U.S. 649, 12 S.Ct. 495, 36 L.Ed. 294 (1892), the Supreme Court upheld a grant of authority to the President to increase duties on listed articles to rates specified in the statute, if the President found that the other state was imposing unequal and unreasonable duties on United States trade. In J.W. Hampton, Jr. & Co. v. United States, 276 U.S. 394, 48

S.Ct. 348, 72 L.Ed. 624 (1928), the Supreme Court sustained a grant of power to the President to change duties in order to equalize costs of production between the United States and other states. In Star-Kist Foods, Inc. v. United States, 47 C.C.P.A. 52, 275 F.2d 472 (1959), the Courts of Customs and Patent Appeals upheld the President's action in reducing the duty on tuna pursuant to authority granted in the Trade Agreements Act of 1934. See also United States v. Yoshida International, Inc., 63 C.C.P.A. 15, 526 F.2d 560 (1975), sustaining a Presidential emergency tariff surcharge under the Trading with the Enemy Act. *Cf.* The Brig Aurora v. United States, 11 U.S. (7 Cranch) 382, 3 L.Ed. 378 (1813) (giving effect to a statute authorizing the President to suspend and reinstitute the Non-Intercourse Act).

The exercise by the President of power delegated by Congress must comply with its terms. "[T]he executive cannot, through its communications, manage foreign commerce in a manner lying outside a comprehensive regulatory scheme Congress has enacted pursuant to its Article I, § 8 power." Consumers Union of U.S., Inc. v. Kissinger, 506 F.2d 136, 149 (D.C.Cir.1974), *certiorari denied*, 421 U.S. 1004, 95 S.Ct. 2406, 44 L.Ed.2d 673 (1975) (concurring opinion). See also United States v. Guy W. Capps, Inc., *supra*.

6. *Procedure before reduction of barriers.* Congress commonly requires that certain procedures be followed before tariffs or other import barriers are reduced. The procedures, 19 U.S.C. §§ 2151–55, are designed to ensure that the Presi-

dent has the advice of the United States International Trade Commission, of the Departments of Agriculture, Commerce, Defense, Interior, Labor, State, and Treasury, and of the private sector, to make him aware of competitive conditions in the industries producing the articles in question, and the likely impact on employment, profits, and prices. The Office of the United States Trade Representative and the Advisory Committee for Trade Negotiations assist in the process. As a further safeguard, the Trade Act of 1974 provides that ten members of Congress are to be "official advisers" to United States delegations to international conferences relating to trade agreements. See 19 U.S.C. § 2211.

7. *Challenges to tariff rulings.* There are special procedures for challenging an adverse customs ruling. An importer may import the goods, and if the Customs Service decides to impose a duty at a rate different from that claimed, the importer may file a protest. If the protest is denied, review may be obtained from the United States Court of International Trade (prior to 1980, the Customs Court), and an appeal may be taken to the Court of Appeals for the Federal Circuit (prior to 1982, to the Court of Customs and Patent Appeals). Importers may also request an advance classification ruling. Domestic interested parties, including manufacturers, unions, or trade associations may also challenge Custom Service decisions in these courts. 19 U.S.C. §§ 1514–16. See 1 Feller, U.S. Customs and International Trade Guide, ch. 4 (1980); Rossides, U.S. Import Trade Regulation 531–58 (1986).

§ 804.   Quantitative Restrictions on Imports

(1) Under the General Agreement on Tariffs and Trade, a state party may not impose quantitative restrictions on imports from other states parties, except as necessary for reasons of national security, for balance of payments purposes, as part of an agricultural commodity support, or as a measure of general law enforcement.

(2) Under the law of the United States, quantitative restrictions on imports are authorized in situations of emergency import relief (§ 808) and for particular products as expressly authorized by statute.

Source Note:

GATT, Articles XI–XIV, XIX–XXI; 19 U.S.C. §§ 2135, 2411, 2436, 7 U.S.C. § 624.

Comment:

a. Permissible uses of quantitative restrictions. Article XI of the GATT prohibits quantitative import restrictions, with various exceptions. The most significant exception permits quantitative restrictions in the case of "any agricultural or fisheries product" necessary to the enforcement of programs that attempt to restrict the domestic output of the product in question or of some closely related product. Article XI(2)(c). Such programs may not alter the proportion of imports to domestic production that might otherwise be expected to prevail.

Article XII permits quantitative restrictions for balance of payments purposes. Two articles of the GATT provide for exceptions to all provisions, therefore also to prohibitions on quantitative restrictions. Article XX allows quantitative and other restrictions for various general law enforcement purposes, such as the protection of public morals, national treasures, or human or animal health, and the prevention of deceptive practices. Article XXI allows such restrictions to protect a contracting party's essential security interests.

Quantitative restrictions on imports may also be imposed in connection with escape clause cases under Article XIX (§ 808), but not countervailing duty cases (§ 806) or antidumping cases (§ 807) under Article VI. No quantitative restriction may be applied to imports from one party to GATT unless it is similarly applied to all other GATT countries, and quotas that are permitted must be allocated among supplying states so as to preserve the shares of imports they might have been expected to have in the absence of quantitative restrictions. Article XIII. For similar restrictions imposed by orderly marketing agreements, see § 808, Comment *b*.

REPORTERS' NOTES

1. *Effect of quantitative restrictions.* The GATT limits the use of quantitative restrictions because, unlike tariffs, such quotas cannot be surmounted by a change in price and can have severe effect on prices and competition in the protected market. Moreover, a quota may give rise to problems of allocation among exporting countries, among producers, and often among importers. Allocations also tend to freeze historical patterns of supply. See Comment *a*. The revenue from a tariff inures to the state imposing it; in contrast, a quota results in a higher profit for those exporters who are allocated portions of the quota and for those domestic producers who are able to raise prices without fear of foreign competition.

2. *Quantitative restrictions on agricultural products.* The United States agriculture commodity program has relied heavily upon quantitative restrictions, some dating back to the Agricultural Adjustment Act of 1933, as amended, 7 U.S.C. § 624. In 1952, a GATT resolution found that the United States action on dairy products under this legislation impaired the value of concessions made to the Netherlands under the GATT within the meaning of Article XXIII and infringed Article XI; the resolution authorized the Netherlands to suspend its concessions on United States wheat. See BISD, 1st, 2d, 3d, 8th and 14th Supps. (1952–66). In 1955, GATT granted the United States a "hard-core" waiver for products covered by the Agricultural Adjustment Act. From time to

time special United States legislation has restricted products such as sugar. Other GATT parties, including Japan and the European Economic Community, have also protected domestic agriculture through special programs. The variable levy imposed by the Community under its Common Agricultural Policy has aspects of both tariffs and quotas, as well as of subsidies, and has been the subject of continuing controversy. See § 806, Reporters' Note 2. See also § 809.

3. *Multilateral agreements on trade in textiles.* Beginning in the mid-1950's, the industrial states of the West perceived a threat to their established textile industries from imports from low-wage states in the Far East and the developing countries. Following a series of formal and informal quantitative restraints imposed by developed states on textile imports, the Contracting Parties of the GATT decided in 1960 that a situation of "Market Disruption," § 808, Reporters' Note 1, existed with respect to cotton textiles. BISD, 9th Supp. at 26 (1961). Thereafter, a Short-Term and subsequently a Long-Term Arrangement Regarding International Trade in Cotton Textiles, were concluded. BISD, 10th Supp. at 18 (1962); BISD, 11th Supp. at 25 (1963). The thrust of these arrangements was that, in return for acceptance by importing states of reasonable amounts of cotton textiles, increasing gradually and in parallel, the exporting states accepted restraints on the amount of imports. In general, the restraints were imposed

through bilateral agreements within the framework of the multilateral arrangement, but in some instances they were imposed unilaterally by the importing states. The Long Term Arrangement (LTA) was extended several times until it was replaced in 1973 by the so-called Multifibre Arrangement (MFA), covering not only cotton but wool and man-made fiber textiles as well. BISD, 21st Supp. at 3 (1975), 25 U.S.T. 1001, T.I.A.S. No. 7840, extended several times thereafter, through 1991. For discussion of the origins of the textile agreements and their relation to GATT, see Dam, The GATT; Law and International Economic Organization 296–315 (1970); for a judicial discussion of the MFA and its implementation in the United States, see American Association of Exporters and Importers—Textile and Apparel Group v. United States, 751 F.2d 1239 (Fed.Cir. 1985).

4. *Quantitative restrictions and voluntary restraint agreements.* Numerous controversies over perceived excesses of imports of particular products have been "settled" through imposition of restraints by the exporting rather than the importing country. In some instances the voluntary restraints have been in fact or in form unilateral; in other instances they have been the result of so-called "orderly marketing agreements." See § 808, Reporters' Note 5. From the point of view of the economics of trade, a quantitative limit on exports of a particular product to a particular country has much the same effect as an import quota. However, the practice under the GATT has been to regard such restraints as not violating Article XI, because the injured party—*i.e.,* the

exporting country—has given its consent.

5. *National security restrictions.* The United States Mandatory Oil Import Program of quotas on oil, in effect from 1959 to 1973, was stated to be based upon "national security grounds," as defined in Section 232 of the Trade Expansion Act of 1962, 19 U.S.C. § 1862, and prior statutes. A Presidential change from quotas to a license fee system was sustained in Federal Energy Admin. v. Algonquin SNG, Inc., 426 U.S. 548, 96 S.Ct. 2295, 49 L.Ed.2d 49 (1976). Except with respect to oil, the national security section of the trade legislation has not been resorted to by the United States. GATT has not developed an international test for "national security." See § 812, Comment *a.*

6. *Quantitative restrictions for balance of payments purposes.* The GATT authorizes resort to quantitative restrictions (but not tariff surcharges) for states in balance of payments difficulties. See Art. XII and, in relation to developing states, Art. XVIII, Section B. States resorting to quantitative restrictions must consult at specified intervals with the GATT Contracting Parties, and the IMF is given an authoritative role in those consultations. Art. XV. See § 821, Reporters' Note 4. When Great Britain in (1964) and the United States (in 1971) encountered balance of payments problems, they resorted to tariff surcharges rather than quantitative restrictions. See United States v. Yoshida Int'l, Inc., 63 C.C. P.A. 15, 526 F.2d 560 (1975). For current Presidential authority to impose temporary duty surcharges or import quotas for balance of payments purposes, see Section 122(a) of

the Trade Act of 1974, 19 U.S.C. § 2132(a).

7. *Presidential authority as to quantitative restrictions.* The President may impose a quota in response to actions of other states, 19 U.S.C. §§ 2135, 2411, as part of emergency action to protect domestic producers, § 808, 19 U.S.C. §§ 2252 and 2436, or under the International Emergency Economic Powers Act. "Voluntary restrictions" on the quantity of exports

imposed by the state of the producer have been used by the Executive Branch to settle countervailing duty and antidumping cases, see § 806, Reporters' Note 6, as well as to resolve other trade controversies. See Reporters' Note 4. The Trade Agreements Act of 1979, 19 U.S.C. § 2581, authorizes the President to sell import licenses at auction but instructs him to "insure against inequitable sharing of imports by . . . larger importers."

§ 805.   Indirect Barriers to Imports

(1) **Under the General Agreement on Tariffs and Trade, a state party may not apply internal taxes or other restrictions that unreasonably burden imports from other states parties.**

(2) **Under the law of the United States, the United States may not impose restrictions forbidden by Subsection (1).**

Source Note:

GATT, Articles III, VII, XVII; Standards Code, 31 U.S.T. 405, T.I.A.S. No. 9616; Customs Valuation Code, ___ U.S.T. ___, T.I.A.S. No. 10402; Government Procurement Code, ___ U.S.T. ___, T.I.A.S. No. 10403; 19 U.S.C. §§ 2511–18, 2531–71.

Comment:

a. *GATT and indirect barriers.* In order to make effective the limitations on duties (§ 803) and on quantitative restrictions (§ 804), GATT also proscribes requirements of local law that have the purpose and effect of excluding imports. These are to be distinguished from *bona fide* rules protecting legitimate interests such as health or safety. See § 804, Comment a. Article III(1) of the GATT provides that "internal taxes and other . . . regulations and requirements affecting the internal sale . . . purchase, transportation, distribution or use of products . . . should not be applied . . . so as to afford protection to domestic production." Article III(2) and Article III(4) call for national treatment in respect of such regulations, taxes, or requirements. Article VIII calls upon members to minimize the incidence and complexity of import formalities. The obligations set forth in Subsection (1) are further defined in ancillary codes relating to (a) technical standards; (b)

281

customs procedures and formalities; and (c) government procurement. See Introductory Note to this Part.

Article XVII provides that, as to purchases involving imports or sales involving exports, state trading enterprises shall act "solely in accordance with non-discriminatory commercial considerations." However, imports for use by the government itself—*i.e.*, not for resale or for use in the production of goods for sale—are exempt from the requirement of nondiscrimination, and are subject only to a requirement of "fair and equitable treatment." Article XVII(2). Article III contains a corresponding exemption for noncommercial government purchases.

b. United States law on indirect barriers. Limitations on government procurement in United States law that disadvantaged foreign bidders (see, *e.g.*, 41 U.S.C. §§ 10a–10d, the "Buy American" Act of 1933), and customs procedures thought to be unnecessarily burdensome and restrictive, came within the grandfather clause in the Protocol of Provisional Application of GATT or the exemption of Article III(8), and were allowed to remain in effect. They were, however, later superseded by the 1979 MTN Codes in various respects. See Introductory Note to this Chapter.

The Commerce Clause of the United States Constitution, Article I, section 8, as construed by the Supreme Court, bars the States from imposing undue burdens on foreign as well as domestic commerce. See § 1, Reporters' Note 1(e). Rules adopted by the States, unlike federal rules, were not covered by the grandfather clause and where in conflict with the GATT, or with the ancillary codes referred to in Comment *a*, have been held to be superseded. See Reporters' Note 2.

REPORTERS' NOTES

1. *GATT and United States government procurement.* The United States has become a party to the Agreement on Government Procurement, T.I.A.S. No. 10403, which limits the effect of the Buy American Act. The Agreement, one of the Codes resulting from the Tokyo Round, provides for national and most-favored-nation treatment in the procurement of goods for governmental use, and seeks to eliminate procedures tending to favor national suppliers. However, only agencies listed in Annex I are governed by the Code; the United States listing exempts various major Department of Defense programs as well as small and minority business "set-asides" and school lunch programs.

Acceptance of the Agreement on Government Procurement, and Presidential action thereunder to set aside existing restrictions, were authorized by Section 2 of the Trade Agreements Act of 1979, 19 U.S.C. §§ 2503(c)(2), 2511–2518, and implemented by Executive Order No. 12260, 46 Fed.Reg. 1653 (1980).

2. *GATT and State legislation.* Several decisions have held that State "Buy American" legislation, applied to purchases for governmental purposes, was superseded by GATT or was an unconstitutional intrusion on federal power. See, *e.g.*, Bethlehem Steel Corp. v. Board of Comm'rs, 276 Cal.App.2d 221, 80 Cal.Rptr. 800 (1969); Baldwin-Lima-Hamilton Corp. v. Superior Court, 208 Cal.App.2d 803, 25 Cal.Rptr. 798 (1962). In *Baldwin*, the holding that the GATT obligation was violated involved a finding that the generation of electric power constituted "the production of goods for sale," so that the exemption in GATT Articles III(8) and XVII for purchase for governmental purposes was not available. Compare K.S.B. Technical Sales Corp. v. North Jersey Dist. Water Supply Comm'n, 75 N.J. 272, 381 A.2d 774 (1977), *appeal dismissed*, 435 U.S. 982, 98 S.Ct. 1635, 56 L.Ed.2d 76 (1978). See also Territory of Hawaii v. Ho, 41 Haw. 565 (1957).

3. *United States law and technical standards.* The United States has incorporated into domestic law its understanding of the obligations of the Agreement on Technical Barriers to Trade, sections 401–53 of the Trade Agreements Act of 1979, 19 U.S.C. §§ 2531–73. That legislation forbids any federal agency from engaging in "any standard-related activity that creates unnecessary obstacles" to trade, and provides specifically for nondiscrimination in testing, for the use of international rather than national standards where appropriate, and for the use of performance criteria rather than design criteria. "It is

the sense of the Congress" (*id.* § 2533) that State as well as private standard-related activities should not create unnecessary obstacles to trade. The United States Trade Representative is charged with coordinating these policies and negotiating with foreign countries and with international institutions that set and coordinate technical standards. Complaints about violations of these rules on the part of United States parties are to be handled through the United States Trade Representative. In general, no private right of action is created to enforce these rules or recover damages for their violation (*id.* § 2551).

4. *Customs valuation procedures.* Effective international controls on tariffs depend on at least minimum clarity and uniformity in the valuations to which rates (typically percentages *ad valorem*) are applied. In general, the price agreed between importer and exporter should be determinative but, in transactions between parties not dealing at arm's length, price may not be reliable.

The American Selling Price system, which prevailed as to certain chemical products imported into the United States, valued imports for tariff purposes at prices established by producers within the United States. It was eliminated pursuant to the Tokyo Round and the Agreement on the Implementation of Article VII (the Customs Valuation Code), T.I.A.S. No. 10402 and similar valuation systems would be inconsistent with the Code. See generally Sherman, "Reflections on the New Customs Valuation Code", 12 L. & Pol'y in Int'l Bus. 119 (1980).

5. *Harmonization by other international organizations.* Var-

ious international organizations other than GATT have sought to harmonize divergent national rules that create barriers to trade. The powers and areas of concentration of different organizations vary. The European Economic Community has given its institutions sweeping powers to issue regulations and directives designed, directly or through national implementing legislation, to eliminate national rules about technical standards, value added taxes, customs procedures, etc., that hamper trade within the Community. The European Free Trade Area has generated harmonizing standards. The United Nations Economic Commission for Europe has studied the possibility of simplifying the documentation associated with international trade. See, *e.g.*, Facilitation Measures Related to International Trade Procedures, ECE/Trade/141 (1981). Conventions designed to eliminate unnecessary diversity in private law aspects of international trade have been drafted by the United Nations Commission on International Trade Law. See Symposium, "Unification of International Trade Law: UNCITRAL's First Decade", 27 Am.J. Comp.L. 201 (1979).

§ 806.   Subsidies and Countervailing Duties

(1) **Under the General Agreement on Tariffs and Trade, a state party may not grant a subsidy on the export of any product (other than a primary product) that results in an export price that is lower than the comparable domestic price.**

(2) **Under the Agreement on Subsidies and Countervailing Measures, a state party other than a developing country may not grant any subsidy on the export of a product (other than certain primary products).**

(3) **Under the General Agreement on Tariffs and Trade, a state party may impose a countervailing duty on imports of products that have benefited from a subsidy, whether or not the subsidy was related to exports or resulted in a price lower than the domestic price in the exporting country, provided that the imports cause or threaten material injury to a domestic industry and that the countervailing duty does not exceed the amount of the subsidy.**

(4) **Under the law of the United States,**

(a) **a countervailing duty may be imposed on imports of products that have benefited from a subsidy, whether on manufacture, production, or export;**

(b) **if such imports have originated in a state party to the Agreement on Subsidies and Countervailing Measures or comparable agreement, a** countervailing duty may be imposed only if the imports are determined to cause or threaten material injury to a domestic industry.

Source Note:

GATT, Articles VI, XVI; Subsidies Code, 31 U.S.T. 513, T.I.A.S. No. 9619; 19 U.S.C. §§ 1671–1671f, 1675, 1677.

Comment:

a. Subsidies and dumping distinguished. A subsidy is a benefit given by a state to producers or exporters; dumping is a practice by an exporter itself to sell a product abroad for lower prices than are charged in the domestic market. See § 807. Some products may both benefit from subsidies and be sold at prices that come within the definition of dumping. This is particularly common for state trading countries or industries having close connections with the state (*e.g.,* the steel industries in France and Great Britain). It may be difficult, however, to identify a subsidy in the context of a fully state-controlled economy, and some producers have attempted to counter "unfair trade" from state-controlled enterprises through antidumping proceedings. See, *e.g.,* 19 U.S.C. § 1677b(c). Countervailing and antidumping duties may be imposed in respect of the same product, but not in such a way as to provide a duplicate response to a single effect of a foreign practice. GATT, Article VI(5).

b. Subsidies under GATT and the Subsidies Code. The GATT prohibits export subsidies only when the result is an export price lower than the comparable domestic price; the Subsidies Code, Reporters' Note 1, prohibits export subsidies without regard to a differential effect on prices. Neither the GATT nor the Code prohibits domestic or production subsidies, but the Code recognizes that such subsidies may cause or threaten injury to industries in other states and requires parties to "seek to avoid causing such effects." Under the Code, both export and production subsidies may give rise to consultations and dispute settlement, but under somewhat different schedules and ground rules. *Compare* Subsidies Code, Articles 12(1) and 13(1) *with id.,* Articles 12(3) and 13(2). Since export subsidies are prohibited by the Code, it is not necessary to show injury when challenging such subsidies through the GATT procedures; in contrast, a complaint about production subsidies may be brought only upon a showing of injury to the complaining state's domestic industry or serious prejudice to its export interests. In addition, or instead, an importing state may impose a countervailing duty in conformity with Subsection (3), upon determination by its own authorities that a domestic industry has sustained or is threatened with material injury as a result of the subsidy. A countervailing duty may be imposed notwithstanding the fact that ordinary duties on the product in question are bound (§ 803), and notwithstanding departure from most-favored-nation treatment (§ 802). The prohibition on export subsidies in the Subsidies Code applies to exports to nonmember as well as member states, because such subsidies may impair the export opportunities of member states.

c. Subsidies on primary products. Article XVI of the GATT provides that contracting parties "should seek to avoid the use of subsidies on the export of primary products." If subsidies are granted on such products, they "shall not be applied in a manner which results in [the granting state] having more than an equitable share of world export trade" in the product in question. The Subsidies Code spells out this standard, by comparison to a "previous representative period," normally to the three most recent calendar years in which normal market conditions existed. Article 10.

d. Obligation to notify. Article XVI(1) of the GATT obligates member states that grant or maintain subsidies having the effect of increasing their exports or reducing their imports to notify the other contracting parties and to consult with any party seriously prejudiced by such subsidies about the possibility of limiting the subsidization.

e. Injury under GATT. Article VI(6) of the GATT authorizes countervailing duties on the importation of subsidized products only if the effect of the subsidization "is such as to cause or threaten material injury to," or "to retard materially the establishment of" a domestic industry. The Subsidies Code (in Article 6) spells out the criteria for defining "domestic industry" and for evaluating "injury." A determination of injury requires consideration whether there has been a significant increase in subsidized imports, either in absolute or in relative terms, and whether there has been significant price undercutting or other depressing effect on prices by the subsidized imports. These criteria were incorporated in substance into the United States countervailing duty statute as it was amended by the Trade Agreements Act of 1979, Reporters' Note 1.

f. Countervailing duties under United States law. Under United States law since 1979, a countervailing duty may be imposed with respect to a subsidy on any product, whether or not dutiable. For dutiable products, a determination of injury is required if the product originates in a state party to the Subsidies Code or comparable agreement. For nondutiable products, determination of injury is required if the product originates in a state party to the GATT, whether or not the state is a party to the Subsidies Code, because countervailing duties on nondutiable products are not covered by the grandfather clause of the Protocol of Provisional Application, Introductory Note to this chapter. It has been held that where an imported product has the benefit of subsidy from several countries, the International Trade Commission should consider the cumulative effect of all the imports in determining whether there has been injury to the domestic industry.

g. *Amount of countervailing duty.* United States law provides that the amount of the countervailing duty shall be equal to the amount of the net subsidy. The Subsidies Code, Article 4, provides that no countervailing duty shall exceed the amount of the subsidy, and that it is desirable that the duty be in a lesser amount if that would be adequate to remove the injury.

REPORTERS' NOTES

1. *The GATT Subsidies Code.* Since the GATT itself does not define its concept of subsidy, an important objective in the Tokyo Round was to negotiate a code that would do so. The United States and other states became parties in 1979 to an "Agreement on Interpretation and Application of Articles VI, XVI and XXIII of the General Agreement on Tariffs and Trade" (Subsidies Code), T.I.A.S. No. 9619.

That Code regularizes the procedures in countervailing duty cases and provides notice and opportunity to be heard to foreign parties. The Subsidies Code provides for a Committee of Signatories composed of representatives from each state. Upon request, the Committee establishes a panel to make findings of fact about a matter in controversy, to assist the parties to arrive at a settlement and, if necessary, to report to the Committee. The Committee may make recommendations to the parties and, if they are not heeded, may authorize countermeasures. See Hudec, "GATT Dispute Settlement after the Tokyo Round: An Unfinished Business," 13 Cornell Int'l L.J. 145 (1980).

2. *Subsidies and primary products.* The exclusion of primary products from even the limited prohibition on export subsidies in the GATT reflects the fact that in the 1940's there were many programs, notably in the United States, designed to safeguard the interests of agricultural producers faced with large surpluses. See § 804. The GATT Subsidies Code provides that subsidies on a primary product may aim at achieving no more than an "equitable" share of international trade. As of 1986, a major controversy centered on the operation of the Common Agricultural Policy of the European Economic Community, which used import levies to maintain artificially high prices in the Community and used the proceeds of the levy to reduce the price of surpluses sold abroad. See Boger, "The United States-European Community Agricultural Export

Subsidies Dispute," 16 L. & Pol'y in Int'l Bus. 173 (1984).

3. *Subsidies in United States law.* Prior to 1979, the United States law on subsidies differed from the GATT provision, Comment *b*, chiefly in that no injury to producers had to be shown as a condition of imposing a countervailing duty. As a result, assessment of countervailing duties was usually a one-step process, committed to the Treasury Department, without the participation by the Tariff Commission (later the International Trade Commission). That deviation from GATT was permitted by the grandfather clause of the Protocol of Provisional Application, Introductory Note to this chapter. United States law, 19 U.S.C. § 1671, now requires a finding of injury in cases involving states parties to the Subsidies Code and some other states described in that section, as well as in most cases involving duty-free merchandise. See Comment *f.* Thus, in such cases, imposition of countervailing duties, like imposition of antidumping duties, is now a two-step process, with the existence of a subsidy determined by the Commerce Department, an executive agency, and existence of injury determined by the International Trade Commission, an independent regulatory agency. As to the compatibility of the denial of such treatment to other states with the most-favored-nation principle, see § 802, Reporters' Note 1.

Prior to 1979, United States authorities developed their own definitions of subsidy or bounty. Downs v. United States, 187 U.S. 496, 23 S.Ct. 222, 47 L.Ed. 275 (1903), held that Russia had conferred a bounty on exporters of sugar when it gave them a saleable certificate of freedom from excise taxes. Nicholas & Co. v. United States, 249 U.S. 34, 39 S.Ct. 218, 63 L.Ed. 461 (1919), upheld a countervailing duty upon imports of liquor from Great Britain, which granted an allowance against excise taxes when liquor was exported. More recently, however, in Zenith Radio Corp. v. United States, 437 U.S. 443, 98 S.Ct. 2441, 57 L.Ed. 2d 337 (1978), the Supreme Court sustained a ruling of the Secretary of the Treasury that a remission of the Japanese Commodity Tax on exported consumer electronic goods was not a bounty. It interpreted the *Downs* and *Nicholas* cases, *supra*, as referring only to "excessive" remissions, *i.e.*, those that exceed the amount of tax originally paid, and noted that this construction had been incorporated into GATT. See GATT, Art. VI(4), Note d ad Art. XVI; Subsidies Code, Annex, para. (g).

In Michelin Tire Corp. v. United States, 15 Customs Bull. & Dec. (No. 47) 17 (Ct. Int'l Trade 1981), the court sustained imposition of countervailing duties with respect to subsidies given by Canada to industries established in depressed areas, although the subsidies were not directly linked to exports.

In ASG Industries, Inc. v. United States, 67 C.C.P.A. 11, 610 F.2d 770 (1979), a divided court held that benefits given by the West German government to float glass manufacturers constituted a bounty, although the Secretary of the Treasury had found that they did not, because of the small amount of glass exported and the small value of the benefit. The court held that, once it was found that any benefit had been received, the Secretary could not refuse to impose a countervailing duty except by exercise of the limited waiver authority given by 19 U.S.C. § 1303(d)(2).

In British Steel Corp. v. United States, 605 F.Supp. 286 (Ct. Int'l Trade 1985), appeal after remand, 632 F.Supp. 59 (1986), the court sustained a Department of Commerce finding that equity infusions by the United Kingdom on terms inconsistent with commercial considerations, and funds used to close redundant facilities or purchase idled assets, constituted subsidies and were, subject to countervailing duties. See also British Steel Corp. v. United States, 632 F.Supp. 59 (Ct. Int'l Trade 1986). Neither the GATT nor the Subsidies Code contains any provision about how to measure subsidies other than export subsidies. Nor does the Subsidies Code require an importing state to define subsidies for purposes of its countervailing duty legislation in the same way as GATT defines them for purposes of an exporting state's obligation not to grant subsidies. The United States has taken the position that it is free to apply an expansive definition of the term. Since 1979, United States legislation has included definitions of export subsidies taken from an Annex to the Subsidies Code containing an "Illustrative List of Export Subsidies" as well as illustrative examples of domestic or production subsidies. For example, since 1984 the law included "upstream subsidies." 19 U.S.C. § 1677–1. The Code illustrations of subsidies include only forms of government assistance that treat exports differently from goods destined for domestic consumption since only such subsidies

are forbidden by the Code. However, Article 11 of the Code lists other kinds of benefits that may cause injury to a domestic industry of another state, such as government retraining projects, research and development programs, or aid to disadvantaged regions, and importing states appear to be free to impose countervailing duties against such subsidiaries as well. See Barceló, "Subsidies, Countervailing Duties and Antidumping after the Tokyo Round," 13 Cornell Int'l L.J. 257 (1980).

4. *Countervailing duty procedures in United States law.* Under the 1979 Trade Agreements Act, 19 U.S.C. § 1671a, as amended by the Trade and Tariff Act of 1984, a proceeding, termed an "investigation," may be commenced by the Secretary of Commerce on his own motion, and a proceeding must be commenced if a petition is filed by an "interested party." United States v. Roses, Inc., 706 F.2d 1563 (Fed.Cir.1983). "Interested party" includes the government of a country in which merchandise is produced; a foreign or domestic manufacturer; an importer or wholesaler; or a union or trade association representing an industry. "Industry" is defined to mean the domestic producers whose output contributes a major portion of the total domestic output of a like product. 19 U.S.C. § 1677(4) and (9). The International Trade Commission, after investigation, makes a preliminary determination as to injury where such a determination is required. Reporters' Note 3. The Secretary, after investigation, is to make a preliminary determination whether there had been a subsidy. If both determinations are affirmative, importers must post security in the amount of

the net subsidy preliminarily determined to exist. Following fact-finding and the submission of evidence by the parties, the Secretary makes a final determination as to the existence of a subsidy. If the Secretary's determination is affirmative, the case is submitted to the International Trade Commission for a final determination of injury. If the Commission's determination is also affirmative, a countervailing duty order is issued which imposes a duty in the amount of the net subsidy determined to exist. Deadlines are set for preliminary and final determinations as to both injury and subsidy. Some preliminary and all final decisions may be appealed to the Court of International Trade. See § 807, Reporters' Note 2. For summary guides to these procedures see, Lowenfeld, Public Controls on International Trade 372–74 (2d ed. 1983); Ehrenhaft, "What the Antidumping and Countervailing Duty Provisions of the Trade Agreements Act [Can] [Will] [Should] Mean for U.S. Trade Policy," 11 L. & Pol'y in Int'l Bus. 1361 (1979); Macrory and Suchman, eds., Current Aspects of International Trade Law, App. C (1982); Bello and Holmer, "The Trade and Tariff Act of 1984: Principal Anti-dumping and Countervailing Duty Provisions," 19 Int'l Law. 639 (1985).

5. *Evidence in countervailing duty cases.* Countervailing duty proceedings in the United States are called "investigations," Reporters' Note 4, but they have many of the characteristics of judicial proceedings. They are not controlled by the private party initiating them, but they are adversarial as between the foreign party and the United States government. *See* Ehrenhaft, "The Judicialization of Trade Law,"

56 Notre Dame Law. 595 (1981); Palmer, "Torquemada and the Tariff Act," 20 Bus.Law. 641 (1986). Discovery of the type contemplated by the Federal Rules of Civil Procedure does not apply, but the foreign party to a proceeding is asked to respond to government questionnaires, to produce evidence, and to permit verification by United States government personnel at its home country plants and offices. Failure to comply is subject to sanction through operation of the rule that the administering authority may not rely upon unverified submissions in making determinations under the law but may employ the "best information available to it . . ., which may include . . . the information submitted in support of the petition." 19 U.S.C. § 1677e(a). Unlike other demands for evidence by United States courts and agencies (see § 442, Comment *b*), these investigations have not evoked objections, and disclosure and compliance have been the general practice. Evidence thus provided may be covered by a protective order precluding disclosure to competitors, but it is usually open for examination by retained (as distinguished from corporate) counsel for the various parties. The rules and experience in antidumping proceedings are similar. See § 807.

6. *Termination of countervailing duty proceedings by consent.* Countervailing duty proceedings in the United States often end without determinations. The exporters may agree to cease exports or offer "undertakings" to eliminate the injurious effects of subsidized sale, and 19 U.S.C. §§ 1671c and 1673c permit suspension of investigations if such undertakings meet certain standards. Also, foreign

governments may offer acceptable quantitative restraints on subsidized exports, 19 U.S.C. § 1671c(c)(3), and in some cases, domestic petitioners have withdrawn their petition upon agreement by the foreign government to restrain exports. See the case of Certain Steel Products, 47 Fed. Reg. 49508, 21 Int'l Leg.Mat. 1372 (1982); Lowenfeld, Public Controls on International Trade 420–49 (2d ed. 1983). Under the 1984 Act, the administering authority must find the resolution "in the public interest" before ending the investigation. 19 U.S.C. § 1671c(a)(2)(A), and (d)(1)(a).

7. *The Subsidies Code and taxation.* The Subsidies Code did not resolve issues between the United States and other GATT members as to the permissibility of certain forms of tax relief for exporters. In the case of the United States, the measure under attack was legislation allowing exporters to create Domestic International Sales Corporations (DISCs) in order to defer tax on income derived from export operations. A GATT panel found that the DISC provisions created a subsidy not permitted by GATT; it also found various forms of tax relief by three other states to be impermissible. BISD, 23d Supp. at 98 (1977); See Jackson, "The Jurisprudence of International Trade: The DISC Case in GATT," 72 Am.J.Int'l L. 747 (1978). In 1981, the GATT Council adopted the panel reports, 16 J. World Trade L. 361–62 (1982). The controversy was apparently resolved in 1984 through the repeal of the DISC provisions and the substitution of provisions permitting the creation of Foreign Sales Companies that, unlike DISCs, are not organized under United States law. 26 U.S.C. §§ 921–27.

8. *European Community and OECD rules on investment incentives.* An investment incentive may cause an investor to locate a plant where it would not otherwise be located and cause trade to follow channels not indicated by economic forces. Article 92 of the Treaty of Rome forbids any member state to grant any aid that distorts competition within the Community by favoring certain undertakings, but excepts aid such as disaster relief and aid to disadvantaged areas.

In 1976, the states members of the Organization for Economic Cooperation and Development (OECD) signed a Declaration on International Investment and Multinational Enterprises recognizing the need to give due weight to the interests of other states affected by official incentives to international direct investment. Later, the OECD Council decided that there should be consultation at the request of member states adversely affected by investment incentives with the "purpose of reducing such effects to a minimum." See OECD, International Investment and Multinational Enterprises (Rev. ed. 1979).

§ 807. Dumping and Antidumping Duties

(1) **Under the General Agreement on Tariffs and Trade, a state party may impose an antidumping duty upon an imported product offered for sale at less than**

its normal value in the exporting state if such sale causes or threatens material injury to a domestic industry in the importing state.

(2) Under the law of the United States, an antidumping duty will be imposed if imported goods are sold at a price that is lower than the foreign market value and such sales cause or threaten material injury to a domestic industry.

Source Note:

GATT, Article VI; Anti-Dumping Code, 31 U.S.T. 4919, T.I.A.S. No. 9650; 19 U.S.C. §§ 1673–1677h; 15 U.S.C. § 72.

Comment:

a. Dumping under GATT. Dumping is defined in the GATT (Article VI(1)) as sale in the importing state below "normal value." Normal value means, in the first instance, the price of the same product when destined for consumption in the exporting state. If there is no such price, the basis for comparison is the price charged in exports to third countries, or the cost of production (including a reasonable allowance for cost of sales and for profit), whichever is higher. The GATT permits the antidumping duty to be in the full amount of the margin of dumping, but the Anti-Dumping Code, Reporters' Note 3, states that "it is desirable" that the duty be lower "if a lesser amount would be adequate to remove the injury." Article 8(1). Article VI of the GATT, pertaining to both subsidies and dumping, requires a showing of material injury or threat thereof to justify a duty by the importing state. See § 806, Comment *e.*

b. Dumping in United States law. The 1979 Trade Agreements Act was intended to bring United States law into conformity with the revised GATT Anti-Dumping Code. Under United States law, dumping is defined as sale of a product in the United States at less than fair value, 19 U.S.C. § 1673, which in turn is defined as a sale in which the "United States price" (§ 1677a) is lower than "foreign market value" (§ 1677b). The "United States price" is the purchase price from the foreign producer or the exporter's sale price, *i.e.*, the price at which the exporter offers the goods for sale to the first unrelated purchaser in the United States. Freight is subtracted from the United States sale price and adjustments are made for taxes, duties, commissions, and other expenses. The "foreign market value" is the price at which such or similar merchandise is sold in the home market, or, if such sales are too few to be indicative, the price at which the product is sold or offered for sale in third countries. Sales in the home market or in third countries below cost of production are disregarded in determining foreign market value. See 19 U.S.C. § 1677b. When no foreign market value can be determined after disregarding such sales, the United States price is measured against "a constructed value," including (i) cost of materials and labor, (ii) overhead and general expenses equal to at least ten percent of cost of materials and labor, and (iii) profit, equal to at least eight percent of (i) plus (ii). 19 U.S.C. § 1677b(e).

The Trade Agreements Act of 1979 replaced the antidumping statute of 1921 but not the Act of 1916, 15 U.S.C. § 72. The provisions of the 1916 Act resemble the price discrimination and predatory pricing provisions of the Clayton Antitrust Act. The 1916 Act provides for criminal penalties and private treble damage actions for sales at prices below those in the country of origin or in any third state, made with the intent of destroying or injuring an industry in the United States, but it does not provide for administrative enforcement by the government. The Act has been rarely invoked.

REPORTERS' NOTES

1. *United States antidumping duty procedures.* The procedures for handling dumping cases, 19 U.S.C. §§ 1673–1677(h), are substantially similar (except as to deadlines) to those for subsidies cases described in § 806, Reporters' Notes 4–6. In parallel with subsidies cases, determinations as to "material injury" are assigned to the International Trade Commission, and determinations as to sales at less than half value to the Secretary of Commerce. See 19 C.F.R. Part 353; Macrory and Suchman, eds, Current Aspects of International Trade Law, App. B (1982); 1 Kaye, Plain, and Hertzberg, International Trade Practice, ch. 23–27 (1981). The measure of relief is the margin of dumping, *i.e.,* the amount by which foreign market value, Comment *b*, exceeds the United States price, 19 U.S.C. § 1673.

2. *Judicial review.* Since 1974, both affirmative and negative determinations by the Executive Branch of the existence of dumping (as well as of a countervailable subsidy) have been subject to judicial review; since 1979, affirmative as well as negative determinations of injury by the International Trade Commission are also subject to judicial review. 19 U.S.C. § 1516a, as amended by the Trade Agreements Act of 1979. Review of final determinations (and of some preliminary determinations after final decision) may be sought by the complainant (*e.g.* the domestic producer, union, or trade association), or by the importer. Exclusive jurisdiction under § 1516a to review determinations of the Department of Commerce and the International Trade Commission is vested in the Court of International Trade (formerly the Customs Court), 28 U.S.C. §§ 1581–85,

§§ 2631–46. The decisions of the Court of International Trade may be appealed to the United States Court of Appeals for the Federal Circuit, created in 1982 as successor (among other functions) to the United States Court of Customs and Patent Appeals, 28 U.S.C. § 1295(a)(5).

3. *The GATT Anti-Dumping Code.* Due to the lack of sufficient detail in the GATT, the United States and some 25 other countries adopted an antidumping code in 1967. 19 U.S.T. 4348, T.I.A.S. No. 6431. That code was superseded in 1979 by an "Agreement on the Implementation of Article VI of the General Agreement on Tariffs and Trade" (Anti-Dumping Code), 31 U.S.T. 4919, T.I.A.S. No. 9650, one of the codes adopted in the Tokyo Round of Multinational Trade Negotiations, Introductory Note to this chapter. The revised Anti-Dumping Code, like the Subsidies Code, § 806, Reporters' Note 1, seeks to make national procedures more "transparent" (more fully disclosed) and orderly, and provides for an international committee with functions similar to those of the committee established pursuant to the Subsidies Code. See § 806, Reporters' Note 1.

4. *Antidumping practice in the European Economic Community.* The European Community adopted antidumping regulations for the first time in 1968, and revised them to comply with the revised Anti-Dumping Code of 1979, Reporters' Note 3. EEC procedures are more informal than those of the United States, and more commonly result in undertakings by importers to raise their prices to a negotiated "normal value," rather than in the imposition of definitive antidumping duties. See Davey, "An Analysis of European Communities Legislation Relating to Antidumping and Countervailing Duties," in 1983 Fordham Corp. L. Inst. 39 (Hawk ed. 1984); Norall, "New Trends in Anti-Dumping Practice in Brussels," 9 World Economy 97 (1986).

§ 808. Emergency Action to Protect Domestic Producers

(1) Under the General Agreement on Tariffs and Trade, a state party may suspend its obligation or withdraw or modify a concession with respect to a product if, as a result of unforeseen developments and of the effect of the obligation incurred, including a tariff concession, the product is being imported into its territory in such increased quantities and under such conditions as to cause or threaten serious injury to domestic producers.

(2) Under the law of the United States, upon a finding by the International Trade Commission that increased imports are a substantial cause of serious injury or threat of serious injury to domestic producers, the President may provide relief to affected domestic parties by

(a) **restricting imports through tariffs or quantitative restrictions, or**

(b) **negotiating an orderly marketing agreement.**

Source Note:

GATT, Article XIX; 19 U.S.C. §§ 2251–2394.

Comment:

a. Emergency action under GATT. The escape clause actions indicated in Subsection (1) are to be taken only in case of emergency, and only for as long as necessary to meet the emergency. Under Article XIX(2), a state must give advance notice to the Contracting Parties and to states having a substantial interest as exporters. Except in "critical circumstances," a state proposing to take "escape clause" action is required to consult with the parties primarily affected before taking action. If the matter is not resolved by negotiation, the parties injured by the action may respond by suspending substantially equivalent concessions on imports from the state resorting to the escape clause action.

b. Alternatives to escape clause action. The GATT provides several alternatives to use of the escape clause permitted under this Section. Article XXVIII provides for renegotiation of tariff concessions at specified intervals if suitable compensation is provided. See § 803, Comment *b.* Members of the GATT may respond to an emergency created by unexpected increases in imports through an orderly marketing agreement, permitted under the GATT so long as both exporting and importing members agree and third parties are not adversely affected. Under such an agreement, the exporting state (or states) agrees to restrict its exports, often in exchange for a commitment by the importing state to phase out the restriction by a certain date, or to allow the exports in question to increase over time or in proportion to growth of consumption in the importing state. Whether in emergency or otherwise, developing states may restrict imports temporarily to aid domestic industries, under Article XVIII(4)(a) and (9). See § 810.

c. United States escape clause procedures. As of 1987, United States law as to emergency action provides for an original investigation and findings by the International Trade Commission, without participation by the Department of Commerce or other executive agency. If the Commission determines that there is no need for import relief, the case is closed. If the Commission finds that there is a threat of serious injury substantially caused by increased imports, it must report its findings to the President together with its recommendation for relief. Upon receiving a report from the Commission recommending relief, the President is required, usually within 60 days, to provide import relief for the industry affected, unless he determines that such relief is not in the national economic interest of the United States. To provide import relief, he may choose one or more of the following options: he may impose higher duties, tariff quotas, or quantitative import restrictions; he may negotiate orderly marketing agreements with exporting countries; he may make adjustment assistance available to affected producers, employees, and communities. Import restrictions under the escape clause authority are limited to five years, and tariffs may not be increased by more than 50 per cent *ad valorem*. A quota may not limit imports, in quantity or value, to a level below what they were during the last period found to be normal. If the President declines to grant import relief, or if he takes action different from that recommended by the Commission, Congress may by joint resolution require him to take the action recommended. Section 203 of the Trade Act of 1974, as amended, 19 U.S.C. § 2253(c)(1). Neither an affirmative nor a negative determination by the International Trade Commission in an escape clause action, nor the action of the President upon the Commission's affirmative recommendation, is subject to judicial review, except as to compliance with the procedural requirements of the statute. See Reporters' Note 2. Under Section 406 of the Trade Act of 1974, 19 U.S.C. § 2436, simpler procedures may be used in the case of market disruption "a significant cause" of which is the increase of imports from a Communist country.

REPORTERS' NOTES

1. *Rationale of "escape clause."* The rule in this section recognizes that, even if a state as a whole benefits from the lower cost of imported goods, the burden on some domestic producers, their employees, and the surrounding community of "market disruption" may be severe. The hope is that after a time the injured industry will either regain its ability to compete with imports or its resources will be shifted to a new line of production. In general, it has been assumed that states will be more likely to reduce restrictions on imports and make other trade concessions if they know that they will be permit-ted to take emergency relief action in the event of unforeseen developments.

2. *Escape clause and "unfair trade" actions compared.* Escape clause actions as described in this section, and countervailing duty and antidumping actions discussed in §§ 806 and 807, differ in several respects. Antidumping and countervailing duty actions focus primarily on the behavior of an exporter or foreign state, whereas escape clause actions focus only on the injury to the domestic industry. In the United States, the statutory criteria are similar, but the threshold

of injury attributable to imports necessary to justify import relief appears to be higher in escape clause proceedings, where no unfair conduct can be ascribed to the foreign exporters. Antidumping and countervailing duty actions require a two-step administrative process, one before the Department of Commerce to determine whether there has been dumping or subsidization and if so the amount of the corrective duty to be imposed, a second proceeding before the International Trade Commission to ascertain whether there has been injury; see § 806, Reporters' Notes 6 and 7, § 807, Reporters' Note 1; escape clause actions, in contrast, are brought directly before the International Trade Commission. Also, whereas the determinations of both the Commerce Department and the ITC in antidumping and countervailing duty cases are subject to judicial review, see § 807, Reporters' Note 2, but not to Presidential intervention, a determination of the Commission in escape clause actions is reviewable only as to compliance with the procedural requirements of the statute, see Maple Leaf Fish Co. v. United States, 762 F.2d 86 (Fed. Cir.1985), and the final decision by the President upon an affirmative recommendation of the Commission is subject to review by Congress but not to judicial review.

3. *Attempt at "safeguards code."* When, in the 1970's, attention shifted from tariff reduction to lowering other barriers to trade, an attempt was made by the GATT member states to develop a "safeguards" code that would restrict and regularize escape clause procedures. Suggestions for reform included international scrutiny of safeguard actions, time limits on safeguards, limits on discrimination in safeguards as between imports from different countries, and improved procedures for international notification and mediation. No safeguards code was adopted in the Tokyo Round, in part because of differences over a requirement of nondiscrimination among exporters in the application of safeguards by injured states.

4. *United States law on "injury."* Different formulations have been used for the link between imports and injury to domestic industry, which must be found before restrictive action is taken. The GATT escape clause was modeled upon then current United States legislation, but that law has been amended from time to time. In the 1951 version, increased imports to justify escape clause action had to "cause or threaten serious injury." In 1955, the standard was changed to require that imports "contribute substantially towards causing or threatening serious injury." The Trade Expansion Act of 1962 required, as a condition for import relief, that increases in imports resulting in major part from trade agreement concessions, "cause, or threaten to cause, serious injury," and that they must have been "the major factor in causing" the injury. The Trade Act of 1974 required that the increased import be "a substantial cause of serious injury," and eliminated the requirement that the increase in imports be due to trade agreement concessions. "Substantial cause" was defined to mean "a cause which is important and not less than any other cause." In Certain Motor Vehicles and Certain Chassis and Bodies Therefor, 45 Fed.Reg. 85194 (1980), the International Trade Commission deter-

mined that although imports were an important cause of injury to the car industry they were less significant than the decline in demand for cars; relief was thus not available. The elimination of the requirement that as a condition for import relief, the increase in imports be due to trade agreement concessions may raise questions under GATT, Article XIX. For further refinement of the factors and proof required to establish injury for the purposes of escape clause actions, see 19 U.S.C. 2251(b), as amended by Section 249(b) of the Trade and Tariff Act of 1984, 98 Stat. 2998.

5. *United States law on orderly marketing agreements.* The Trade Expansion Act of 1962, 19 U.S.C. § 1982, authorized the President to negotiate "orderly marketing agreements" with foreign countries, designed to limit exports to the United States, and Section 203 of the Trade Act of 1974, 19 U.S.C. § 2253, made negotiation of such agreements one of the options for import relief, Comment *c.* The legality of two orderly marketing agreements with Taiwan and South Korea as to athletic footwear was sustained against argument, *inter alia,* that they violated the GATT, in Sneaker Circus, Inc. v. Carter, 457 F.Supp. 771 (E.D.N.Y.1978), *affirmed,* 614 F.2d 1290 (2d Cir.1979). However, concluding a voluntary restraint agreement with private foreign producers would not be within the President's authority under the Act and such an agreement might constitute an agreement in restraint of trade in violation of the Sherman Act. *Cf.* Consumers Union of U.S., Inc. v. Kissinger, 506 F.2d 136 (D.C. Cir.1974), *certiorari denied,* 421 U.S. 1004, 95 S.Ct. 2406, 44 L.Ed.2d 673 (1975). Section 607 of the Trade Act of 1974, 19 U.S.C. § 2485, relieved all parties of antitrust liability on account of pre-1975 steel agreements restraining exports of steel to the United States.

6. *Trade adjustment assistance in United States law.* An alternative to restrictions on imports is "adjustment assistance," introduced in the Trade Expansion Act of 1962 and amended several times. Adjustment assistance does not restrain imports but seeks to cushion the impact of imports through grant or loan of federal funds and other assistance to injured firms or workers. In its original version, eligibility for adjustment assistance was determined by the Tariff Commission under the same criteria as applied to requests for import relief. Since the Trade Act of 1974, worker petitions are addressed to the Secretary of Labor, 19 U.S.C. §§ 2271– 2321, and petitions by firms are addressed to the Secretary of Commerce, 19 U.S.C. §§ 2341–51. A group of workers (or a firm) is eligible for adjustment assistance if the Secretary of Labor (or Commerce) determines that a significant number or proportion of the workers in the relevant firm have become or are threatened with becoming totally or partially separated from employment; that sales or production or both of the firm have decreased; and that increased imports of like or directly competitive articles "contributed importantly" to worker separation and to the decline in sales or production. 19 U.S.C. §§ 2272, 2341. A determination of noneligibility for relief is subject to review by the Court of International Trade, with appeal to the Court of Appeals for the Federal Circuit. 19 U.S.C. § 2395.

Workers certified for adjustment assistance may be eligible for unemployment compensation beyond the term of standard unemployment insurance, and for employment service, retraining, job search, and relocation benefits. A firm certified for adjustment assistance may receive both technical assistance and loans or loan guarantees, designed to make the firm competitive either in its original product line or in a new line. In its first quarter century, adjustment assistance has, to a limited extent, eased the plight of firms and workers faced with surges of import competition; it has not fulfilled the promise of facilitating redirection of productive resources in response to changes in comparative advantage. The program has been extended to 1992. See generally, Bratt, "Issues in Worker Certification and Questions of Future Direction in the Trade Adjustment Assistance Program," 14 Law & Pol'y in Int'l Bus. 819 (1982).

§ 809. Customs Unions and Free Trade Areas

Under the General Agreement on Tariffs and Trade, two or more states parties may form a customs union or free trade area, provided that

(a) the resulting tariffs and other restrictions on trade with states not parties to the arrangement are on the whole not higher or more restrictive than the general incidence of duties and other regulations of commerce previously applicable in the territory of the union or area; and

(b) duties and other restrictions on substantially all trade within the territory of the customs union or free trade area are eliminated.

Source Note:

GATT, Article XXIV.

Comment:

a. Customs union and free trade area distinguished. A customs union is a grouping of states in which duties and other restrictions are eliminated with respect to substantially all trade among the members, and substantially the same duties and other regulations are applied by all members of the union to imports from all other states. A free trade area also eliminates barriers on trade among the members, but leaves each member state free to determine barriers to the outside world. The European Economic Community is a customs union, as distinguished from the European Free Trade Association.

b. Customs unions, free trade areas, and GATT. If no special provision had been made, both customs unions and free trade areas involving parties to the GATT would violate Articles I and II of the GATT, since such arrangements deny most-favored-nation treatment to the products of outside states. See § 802. Moreover, the creation of a common external tariff by a customs union typically involves raising some tariffs to levels higher than the prior tariff schedules to which the member states are bound. See § 803.

Article XXIV of the GATT, however, permits a customs union or free trade area if it meets several criteria. First, the purpose of the customs union or free trade area should be to facilitate trade between the participants, not to raise barriers to the trade of other states parties to the GATT. Second, in order to preclude special arrangements with discriminatory effect, the customs union or free trade area is to apply to "substantially all the trade between the constituent territories." Third, the resulting external barriers "shall not on the whole be higher" than those that prevailed before. Fourth, the parties to the arrangement must follow procedures specified in Article XXIV for notification to the GATT, consultation with the Contracting Parties, and negotiation with particularly affected states. See § 803, Comment *b* and Reporters' Note 2. However, the Contracting Parties, by a two-thirds majority, may approve a proposal for a customs union or free trade area that does not fully comply with Article XXIV, provided that such proposal will lead to a customs union or free trade area fully consistent with that Article.

The GATT has been interpreted as permitting a customs union or a free trade area that includes nonmembers of the GATT. The Caribbean Basin Initiative for example, was approved although it includes several states not party to the GATT.

REPORTERS' NOTES

1. *Rationale for customs unions.* *Prima facie,* a customs union may damage trading partners left outside the union, in that products originating in state *X* that is within the union will enjoy an advantage over the same product originating in state *Y* outside the customs union, as to exports into another member of the customs union, state *Z.* Nevertheless, the GATT permits customs unions, in the expectation that such a union meeting the prescribed conditions will be a more efficient and prosperous economic unit and overall, trade with outside states will increase. The expectation has been borne out in the experience of the European Economic Community, at least in respect of industrial products.

2. *Examples of customs unions and free trade areas.* Article I, Paragraph 2 of the GATT excepted from the most-favored-nation requirement various preferences then in force, some of which might have been within the scope of this section. The

300

excepted preferences included arrangements between the United Kingdom and specified Commonwealth territories; among territories of the French Union; within the Benelux customs union; among the United States, its dependent territories, and the Republic of the Philippines; between Chile and its neighbors; and among Lebanon, Syria, Palestine, and Transjordan. Of the arrangements that have come into being since that time, the most prominent are the European Economic Community (EEC), Reporters' Note 4, and the European Free Trade Association consisting, as of 1986, of Norway, Sweden, Switzerland, Austria, and Finland. The United Kingdom, Denmark and Ireland, which were founding members of EFTA, joined the Common Market in 1973 and Portugal joined in 1986. The Latin American Integration Association (1981) (formerly Latin American Free Trade Association (1960)), the Andean Common Market, the Caribbean Common Market (formerly Caribbean Free Trade Area), and the Central American Common Market have at various times, and with various degrees of success, attempted to remove trade barriers among their members and to harmonize their economic policies. In Africa, the Economic Community of West African States, the West African Economic Community (Communauté Economique de l'Afrique de l'Ouest), and the Customs and Economic Union of Central Africa have made similar attempts. In 1985, the United States and Israel created a free trade area. 24 Int'l Leg.Mat. 653 (1985). These customs unions and free trade areas differ widely in the degree of integration they have achieved and in their compliance with GATT Article XXIV.

3. *Canadian-United States Automotive Products Agreement.* In 1965, the United States and Canada entered into an Automotive Products Agreement, 17 U.S.T. 1372, T.I. A.S. No. 6093, which provided (subject to some exceptions for established firms) for free movement of automobiles and parts between the two countries. A GATT working party determined that the United States was in violation of Article I of the GATT because the duty-free treatment given to products of Canada was not extended to products of other states, and the Agreement did not come within the definition of a customs union. However, the Contracting Parties granted a waiver to the United States. BISD 14th Supp. 37, 20 Dec. 1965. Canada, having extended its tariff concessions to all other Contracting Parties, asserted that it had adhered to the most-favored-nation principle. See 1 Chayes, Ehrlich and Lowenfeld, International Legal Process 307–83 (1968). In 1987, the United States and Canada announced a tentative agreement on free trade, but as of November 1, 1987, its details were not published and it was not known whether they conform to Article XXIV of the GATT requiring that such an agreement must cover "substantially all the trade" between the two states.

4. *The European Economic Community.* The European Economic Community was created in 1957 by the Treaty of Rome, 298 U.N.T.S. 11, and enlarged in 1973, 1981, and 1986. A central feature of that treaty is the commitment of the member states to a staged reduction of their internal trade barriers. There has also been a progressive elimination of barriers to the movement of labor and of invest-

ment capital. The process has been supervised by the Community institutions, principally, the Council of Ministers, the Commission and the Court of Justice, institutions which the Economic Community shares with the European Coal and Steel Community and European Atomic Commission [EURATOM]. See, *e.g.*, Stein, Hay and Walbroeck, European Community Law and Institutions in Perspective (1976); Smit and Herzog, eds., The Law of the European Economic Community (1976–and supplements).

In trade relations with non-member states, the Community now generally negotiates on behalf of member states, both within the GATT and bilaterally, except with Communist bloc states.

The European Economic Community is itself a customs union, but the same status does not attach to the arrangements between the Community and other states. Among these arrangements are bilateral arrangements with Turkey, Israel, Tunisia, Algeria, and Morocco (and formerly with Greece), as well as multilateral arrangements with developing countries (chiefly the Yaoundé (1963) and Lomé (1975 and 1979) Conventions to which about 50 states are parties). These arrangements involve preferences said to be justified under the provisions as to developing states set forth in § 810, but in a number of cases the United States has challenged the arrangements as creating unjustified discrimination against United States products.

§ 810. Developing States

(1) Under the General Agreement on Tariffs and Trade, a state party may, notwithstanding other obligations under the Agreement,

    (a) if it is a developing state, restrict imports and take other measures to promote domestic industry;

    (b) if it is a developed state, grant specially favorable treatment to developing states.

(2) Under the law of the United States, the President may, subject to the conditions set forth in legislation, eliminate or reduce duties on the products of developing states.

Source Note:

GATT, Articles XVIII, XXXVI–XXXVIII; 19 U.S.C. §§ 2461–65.

Comment:

    a. Deviations by developing states. Article XVIII of the GATT, as amended in 1955, permits states with "low standards of living" and in "the early stages of development" to deviate from their GATT commitments, by imposing tariffs or quantitative restrictions, by granting subsidies, or by taking other steps to protect domestic industries or the balance of payments that would otherwise entitle states injured by such measures to compensation.

b. Preferences and most-favored-nation principle. Articles XXXVI–XXXVII, adopted in 1965 as Part IV of the GATT, recognize the special needs of developing countries, and urge developed states to open their markets to developing states without requiring reciprocal benefits. In 1971, the Contracting Parties granted a general waiver to permit developed countries to make tariff concessions to developing states that they did not grant other states. That waiver was incorporated during the Tokyo Round in Agreements relating to the Framework for the Conduct of International Trade, "Differential and More Favourable Treatment, Reciprocity and Fuller Participation of Developing Countries." How far developing state parties may depart from normal GATT obligations has not been determined. The United States has taken the position that it is not consistent with GATT for a developing state to grant a preference to a developed state in return for a preference given to it. In principle, the grant by a developed state (or group of states, such as the European Economic Community) of a preference to one developing state (or group of states) but not to others also seems inconsistent with the GATT. However, such discrimination is widely practiced and generally tolerated, not only by developed states (which may lack standing to complain), but also by other developing states.

c. United States law on preferences for developing states. Title V of the Trade Act of 1974 authorizes a Generalized System of Preferences, adopted in response to the GATT waiver of 1971. That legislation, renewed in 1984, authorizes the President to designate states as eligible to introduce eligible goods free of duty or subject to reduced duties. GSP treatment is not available, however, for products of Communist countries not entitled to MFN treatment (§ 802, Reporters' Note 2). Further, products of the following categories of states are ineligible for GSP treatment: members of the Organization of Petroleum Exporting Countries and similar cartel arrangements; states affording trade preferences to developed states other than the United States; states refusing to cooperate with the United States in narcotics control; states refusing to honor awards resulting from arbitrations with United States citizens; states that have expropriated investments or otherwise impaired the rights of United States investors in violation of international law, as defined in the Hickenlooper Amendment (§ 712, Reporters' Note 2), unless the President determines that designation of the state will be in the national economic interest of the United States. Products likely to damage domestic industries, including textile and apparel articles, watches, and import-sensitive steel and electronic articles, are ineligible for GSP benefits. The goods that may be exempt from duty are limited to a fixed amount per year per country for any product category, adjusted for changes in the gross national product of the United States. In addition, if imports of any product from any country reach or exceed 50 percent of all imports of that product, then (subject to stated exceptions) duty-free imports of that product shall cease.

REPORTERS' NOTES

1. *Definition of developing state.* The GATT speaks of "less-developed" states, although "developing" is now preferred. Article XVIII refers to economies "which can only support low standards of living and are in the early stages of development." Interpretative Notes ad Article XVIII specify: (1) that only normal conditions and not such factors as exceptionally favorable conditions for a country's exports should be taken into account in determining its status; and (2) that "early stages of development" should apply even to somewhat advanced economies that are industrializing in order to free themselves from dependence on primary production. A GATT panel concluded that Ceylon (Sri Lanka) qualified, since it had a *per capita* gross national product of $128 (in 1955 terms) and manufacturing provided only 10 percent of its GNP. See Jackson, World Trade and the Law of GATT 651–53 (1969).

In 1971, the United Nations General Assembly approved a list of "hard core least developed countries" reported by the Committee for Development Planning. G.A. Res. 2768, 26 U.N. GAOR Supp. No. 29, at 52.

International organizations employ various criteria in determining which states qualify as developing states entitled to benefits, and which are to carry financial burdens and in what measure. See, *e.g.,* Jackson, "The Legal Framework of United Nations Financing: Peacekeeping and Penury," 51 Calif.L. Rev. 79, 95–98 (1963). For a listing of the other terms used to describe developing states for different purposes, see Meagher, An International Redistribution of Wealth and Power, App. B (1979).

Various provisions of United States law conferring benefits on developing countries authorize the President to designate qualifying states, usually from a list of eligible states. See, *e.g.,* 19 U.S.C. § 2462 (beneficiaries of generalized system of preferences); former Int.Rev. Code 26 U.S.C. § 4916(b), 78 Stat. 827 (less developed states exempt from application of former Interest Equalization Tax); former Int.Rev. Code 26 U.S.C. § 955(c)(3), 76 Stat. 1013, (defining less developed country in connection with income tax benefits); 22 U.S.C. § 2151v (aid to "relatively least developed countries, as determined on the basis of criteria comparable to those used for the United Nations General Assembly list"); 22 U.S.C. § 2191 (OPIC to foster investment in "less developed friendly countries"). For a judicial discussion of the United States system of preferences and the scope of administrative and judicial review, see Florsheim Shoe Co., Div. of Interco, Inc. v. United States, 744 F.2d 787 (Fed.Cir.1984).

2. *GATT and other institutions for development.* In the mid-1960's, the developing states, which had begun to meet for political purposes as "non-aligned" states, turned to institutions outside of GATT for economic purposes. A group of 77 Developing Countries—numbering 122 as of 1986—has served to focus the economic demands of the developing states, par-

ticularly in the United Nations Conference on Trade and Development (UNCTAD). That body first met in 1964 and has since then become a permanent institution affiliated with the United Nations General Assembly. Trade issues may be discussed in either UNCTAD or GATT and the existence of UNCTAD has helped to make GATT more responsive to the needs of developing states, but UNCTAD has not supplanted GATT as a rule-making organization. Efforts by UNCTAD to use commodity agreements, § 811, to achieve transfer of resources to developing states have generally not been accepted by developed commodity-importing states. See § 811, Reporters' Note 3.

§ 811. Commodity Agreements

Under the General Agreement on Tariffs and Trade, states parties may enter into commodity agreements, provided that these

    (a) are open to participation by both exporting and importing states; and

    (b) are designed to assure the availability of supplies adequate to meet demand at stable prices.

Source Note:

GATT, Article XX(h); Note ad Article XX; Article XXIX, incorporating proposed Havana Charter Articles 60 and 63 (1948).

Comment:

a. Definition of commodity agreement. A commodity agreement is an international agreement that regulates international trade in a commodity, usually an agricultural product such as wheat or coffee, or a natural resource such as tin. A commodity agreement, in conformity with Subsection (a), must include states that are consumers and importers as well as states that are producers and exporters, and it must be open to all states. The definition excludes a producer cartel such as the Organization of Petroleum Exporting Countries (OPEC). The Agreement regarding International Trade in Textiles (the Multi-Fibre Agreement), extended several times, is considered an orderly marketing agreement, § 808, Comment *b*, rather than a commodity agreement.

To stabilize prices, commodity agreements use several techniques, separately or together. They may allocate export quotas to the producing states, in some instances policed by importing states; they may establish a buffer stock for which purchases are to be made when prices are low and from which sales are made when prices are high; they may commit the importing states to purchase specified quantities at minimum prices and the exporting states to sell specified quantities at maximum prices.

Decisions under a commodity agreement are typically made by a weighted voting system. In the International Coffee Agreement, for example, the exporting Members and importing Members each hold 1,000 votes. Each Member has five basic votes and the remaining votes are allocated according to a Member's export quotas or historic imports of coffee.

REPORTERS' NOTES

1. *GATT and commodity agreements.* The Charter of the proposed International Trade Organization (Arts. 57–63), Introductory Note to this chapter, set forth principles for the governance of commodity agreements along the lines of this section. However, when the GATT became effective in its stead, commodity agreements were mentioned only in Article XX(h), which made a general exception to GATT obligations for agreements not disapproved by the Contracting Parties. A Note ad Article XX(h) extended this exception to agreements in conformity with principles approved by the United Nations Economic and Social Council Resolution 30 (IV) of 28 March 1947. Part IV, added in 1965 to deal with Trade and Development, includes various references to the primary products of less-developed contracting parties and to the need to obtain stable, equitable and remunerative prices for them. Art. XXXVIII(2)(a).

2. *Status of agreements.* As of 1986, the United States was party to the following commodity agreements: (1) the International Coffee Agreement, 1983, T.I.A.S. No. 10439; (2) the International Natural Rubber Agreement, 1979, T.I.A.S. No. 10379; (3) the International Sugar Agreement, 1985, T.I.A.S. No. 10467; and (4) the International Wheat Agreement, 1971, 22 U.S.T. 821, T.I.A.S. No. 7144, with Protocol of 1979, 32 U.S.T. 2785, T.I.A.S. No. 9878 and Protocol for the Further Extension of the Agreement, 1983. Agreements to which the United States was not a party included the International Olive Oil Agreement, 1979, the International Cocoa Agreement, 1980, and a Sixth International Tin Agreement, 1982. See, generally, Khan, The Law and Organisation of International Commodity Agreements (1982).

3. *Stability in commodity agreements.* Article 57(c) of the draft Charter of the International Trade Organization, Reporters'

Note 1, declared a goal of commodity agreements to be the attainment of a "reasonable degree of stability" in export prices. Subsequent practice has not developed a clear meaning for the phrase. The aim of such agreements is to free the economies of producer states, which frequently are dependent upon export earnings of a single commodity, from the impact of sharp price fluctuations. However, the effect will sometimes be to stabilize prices at a higher level than would prevail absent the agreement. Stabilization of the price may also be undone by fluctuation in the demand for or supply of the product. See Gerhard, "Commodity Trade Stabilization through International Agreements," 28 L. & Contemp.Prob. 276 (1963); Meier, "UNCTAD Proposals for International Economic Reform," 19 Stan.L.Rev. 1173, 1195 (1967). For a description of the collapse of the International Tin Agreement in 1985, see McFadden, "The Collapse of Tin: Restructuring a Failed Commodity Agreement," 80 Am.J.Int'l L. 811 (1986).

4. *Commodity price stabilization through other means.* The pressure from developing countries for relief from price fluctuation problems has been intense. See, *e.g.*, The Charter of Economic Rights and Duties of States, G.A. Res. 3281, 29 U.N. GAOR Supp. No. 31, at 50, Art. 6; Kreinin and Finger, "A Critical Survey of the New International Economic Order," 10 J. World Trade L. 493 (1976). One consequence has been the establishment of a Compensatory Finance Facility under the IMF, on which developing states may draw by showing the impact on their economy of fluctuations in commodity prices, without meeting the usual conditions for drawing on the Fund. See § 821, Comment *e.* See Finger and Derosa, "The Compensatory Finance Facility and Export Instability," 14 J. World Trade L. 14 (1980). The Lomé Conventions between the European Economic Community and various developing countries establish a STABEX fund, also intended to ease the difficulties of developing states attributable to unexpected fall in commodity prices. See Yelpaala, "The Lomé Conventions and the Political Economy of the African-Caribbean-Pacific Countries: a critical analysis of the Trade Provisions," 13 N.Y.U. J. Int'l L. & Pol. 807 (1981).

§ 812.   Export Controls

(1) Under the General Agreement on Tariffs and Trade, a state party may not impose restrictions on exports to achieve economic advantage for its products.

(2) Under the law of the United States, the President may, upon making determinations required by statute, restrict exports to safeguard the national security, to further foreign policy, to comply with international obligations of the United States, or to conserve resources in short supply.

Source Note:

GATT, Articles XI, XIII, XX, XXI; 50 U.S.C.App. §§ 2401 *et seq.*, 22 U.S.C. § 287c.

Comment:

a. *Export controls for non-economic purposes.* Articles I and XI of the GATT in terms apply to restrictions on exports as well as imports, without any express distinction as to the purpose of the restriction. In operation, however, the GATT has regulated devices employed by states to gain economic advantage for their products over the products of other states; it has been thought to be inapplicable to trade practices to achieve non-economic ends such as national security or foreign policy purposes. Thus, export controls not used to promote economic advantage generally do not raise issues under the GATT even if they are discriminatory.

b. *Short supply controls.* The GATT authorizes the imposition of export controls to prevent "critical shortages of foodstuffs or other products essential" to the exporting state (Article XI), and allows measures "essential to the acquisition or distribution of products in general or local short supply" (Article XX(j)). Such measures are to be used to relieve hardships in the exporting state, not to benefit local processors at the expense of foreign competitors. The short supply authorization in United States legislation, Comment *c*, is interpreted similarly.

c. *Export controls in United States law.* Export controls have been authorized in the United States since 1949. The criteria for imposing them have varied from time to time, but they have generally aimed at denying strategic materials and technology to potential adversaries. Export controls have also been used to deter or protest conduct by states deemed hostile to the national interests of the United States, such as states supporting terrorism or engaging in gross violations of human rights. Export controls have been applied to all "persons subject to the jurisdiction of the United States," including foreign affiliates of United States corporations. Such controls have also been applied to the foreign transferees of goods or technology of United States origin. See §§ 402, 403; Comment *b* and Reporters' Notes 3, 4, and 6; § 414, Reporters' Note 4; § 431, Reporters' Note 3.

Presidents have asserted some authority to control exports under their general constitutional power in foreign affairs, though usually together with a claim of statutory authorization; there has been no authoritative judicial determination as to whether the President has such authority in the absence of Congressional authorization and, if so, what is the scope of such authority.

REPORTERS' NOTES

1. *Application of GATT rules on exports.* Only a small number of complaints about export controls have been raised in GATT. See Roessler, "GATT and Access to Supplies," 9 J. World Trade L. 25 (1975). The principal targets of export controls by the United States and by the Western European states have generally not been members of GATT, or under GATT (Art. XXXV) did not have negotiating rights with the states that imposed the controls. Similarly, most of the states involved in the oil embargo imposed by Arab states against the United States and the Netherlands in 1973 were not GATT members.

Interdiction of exports, especially if done collectively, might be subject to challenge on principles of international law other than those in GATT. Thus, the 1973 oil embargo, it was argued, constituted unlawful intervention in the affairs of other states. *Compare* Paust and Blaustein, "The Arab Oil Weapon—A Threat to International Peace," 68 Am.J.Int'l L. 410 (1974), *with* Shihata, "Destination Embargo of Arab Oil: Its Legality Under International Law," *id.* at 591. Collective export restrictions as sanctions under the authority of the United Nations Security Council are lawful. See Diggs v. Shultz, 470 F.2d 461 (D.C.Cir.1972), *certiorari denied,* 411 U.S. 931, 93 S.Ct. 1897, 36 L.Ed. 2d 390 (1973). In some circumstances, the victim of a violation of international law may resort to a boycott as an appropriate remedy. See § 905.

2. *United States export controls.* Exports of commodities and of unpublished technology from the United States have been regulated under the Export Control Act of 1949, the Export Administration Acts of 1969 and 1979, and various amendments and renewals thereof. The constitutionality of export controls was upheld in Moon v. Freeman, 379 F.2d 382 (9th Cir.1967). Action under the Export Administration Act is expressly exempt from judicial review, 50 U.S.C. App. § 2412, and, except for enforcement actions, Reporters' Note 3, from the Administrative Procedure Act, 5 U.S.C. §§ 551 *et seq.*

All commercial exports from the United States, both of goods and of technology, require licenses as a condition for leaving a United States port. Most exports are conducted pursuant to *general license, i.e.,* a published notice that the commodity or technology may be exported to all—or all but specified—countries. For some products, typically those deemed to have potential strategic value and embodying advanced technology, a particular or *validated license* is required for export to most or all countries, and the application for such a license must specify the end-user and often be accompanied by assurance against re-export. A validated license may be issued for an individual transaction or for a series of related transactions.

Authority to impose export controls is vested in the President; he has delegated administrative functions to the Secretary of Commerce. Decisions as to whether export of particular products shall be restrained are subject to inter-agency review, with an important role for the Department of Defense.

Since 1979, the basic authority for export controls has distinguished between national security controls, 50 U.S.C. App. § 2404, and controls for foreign policy reasons, *id.* § 2405. National security controls largely concern "dual use" equipment and technology, such as computers and advanced telecommunications devices, which may have both civilian and military value. Foreign policy controls are designed to implement expressions of disapproval of the policies of particular foreign states, and may include products of no strategic value.

The criteria to be considered by the President before imposing controls, and the requirements for consultation with the Congress and with industry, are significantly different under the two sections, but the operative authority is the same. The list of goods and technology subject to national security controls must be reviewed by the Secretaries of Commerce and Defense, but the controls do not expire automatically. Foreign policy controls may not be maintained longer than one year unless extended by the President. *Id.* § 2405(a)(3). In some instances a President has declared that both national security and foreign policy considerations supported imposition of particular controls, such as the grain embargo imposed against the Soviet Union in 1980 following the invasion of Afghanistan and the embargo on exports connected with the U.S.S.R.-Western Europe natural gas pipeline in 1981–82. See § 414, Reporters' Note 8. The 1985 amendments to the Export Administration Act prohibit imposition of national security controls on agri-

cultural commodities; foreign policy controls on any such commodity may be imposed only for a period of up to 60 days, unless Congress within that time adopts a joint resolution authorizing the President to impose such controls for a period up to one year. In the 1985 amendments, Congress provided that the President may impose export controls for foreign policy purposes only if he determines, *inter alia* that the reaction of other countries to such imposition "is not likely to render the controls ineffective . . . or to be counterproductive to United States foreign policy interests." 50 U.S.C. App. § 2405(b)(1)(c).

3. *Enforcement of United States export controls.* Enforcement of export controls is carried out in the first instance by the Customs Service at the place of export. Export without a license or in violation of its limitations is a crime, 50 U.S.C. App. § 2410(a) and (b); civil penalties are also authorized. *Id.* § 2410(c)(1).

In practice, criminal prosecution has been rare; civil penalties have been used primarily to enforce the provisions of the Act prohibiting cooperation with the Arab boycott against Israel. 50 U.S.C. App. § 2407. The usual sanction is partial or total denial of "export privileges." See § 431, Reporters' Note 3. A party accused of a violation normally receives a charging letter, and is afforded an opportunity for a hearing, and for appeal, within the Department of Commerce. The majority of cases are settled. In some instances, the Department may apply *ex parte* for a "temporary denial order" suspending the accused party's export privileges; it may also suspend or revoke outstanding validated licenses. See 15 C.F.R. Pt. 388.

When a person is subject to a denial order, all other persons subject to the jurisdiction of the United States are prohibited from participating with that person in any transaction covered by the order, whether as exporter, importer, carrier, warehouser, or end-user. Denial orders are published in the Federal Register, as well as in the Export Bulletin of the Department of Commerce.

4. *Other United States authorities for export controls.* Complete embargoes on exports, without differentiation among products or elaborate licensing procedures, have been imposed under the Trading with the Enemy Act, 50 U.S.C. App. § 5(b) (1941–77), and the International Emergency Economic Powers Act, 50 U.S.C. §§ 1701–1706 (1977). These acts have also been invoked to keep export controls in effect in periods between expiration and renewal of export control legislation. See, *e.g.,* Executive Order 12470 of March 30, 1984, 49 Fed.Reg. 13099 (April 3, 1984). The Arms Export Control Act, 22 U.S.C. § 2751–93, and the export control provisions of the Atomic Energy Act of 1954, as amended by the Nuclear Non-Proliferation Act of 1978, 42 U.S.C. §§ 2074 *et seq.,* impose separate controls on munitions and nuclear fuel and equipment.

5. *Multilateral export controls.* Since 1949, the member states of the North Atlantic Treaty Organization (except Iceland), and Japan, have participated in a Coordinating Committee (CoCom) concerned with controls on export of strategic goods and technology to the Soviet Union and its allies. CoCom develops lists of items the export of which member states agree to restrict, and provides a forum for exchange of information on enforcement. In theory, CoCom acts by unanimous decision; however, nothing precludes a member from imposing controls on a wider range of products than those on the CoCom lists, and the United States has done so regularly. CoCom is not an international organization, see § 221, but the Export Administration Act contains detailed instructions to the President on negotiating in CoCom. 50 U.S.C. App. § 2404(i). If the Department of Commerce tentatively approves an application for export license for an item on a CoCom list, it must submit the applcation to CoCom for review. If CoCom does not make a determination within 40 days, the license issues unless the Secretary of Commerce determines that issuance of the license "would prove detrimental to the national security of the United States," for instance because it would undermine United States efforts to restrict exports of another item by another member of CoCom.

The United States has from time to time sought to organize joint action on export controls for other purposes, for instance to punish states that support terrorism or violate human rights. Such efforts have generally failed to achieve consensus but have not been resisted as inconsistent with obligations under the GATT. See, generally, Lowenfeld, Trade Controls for Political Ends (2d ed. 1983); Berman and Garson, "United States Export Controls—Past, Present, and Future," 67 Colum.L.Rev. 791 (1967); Abbott, "Linking Trade to Political Goals: Foreign Policy Export Controls in the 1970's and 1980's," 65 Minn.L. Rev. 739 (1981); Ray, Guide to Export Controls (1985). Moyer and Mabry, "Export Controls as Instruments of Foreign Policy: The History, Legal Issues, and Policy Lessons of Three Recent Cases," 15 L. & Pol'y Int'l Bus. 1 (1983).

Chapter Two

INTERNATIONAL MONETARY LAW

Introductory Note

Introductory Note:

As World War II was ending, the allied nations, led by the United States and Great Britain, met at Bretton Woods, N.H., to lay the groundwork for post-war international cooperation in monetary and financial matters. The Bretton Woods Conference of July 1944 created two international institutions, the International Monetary Fund (IMF) and the International Bank for Reconstruction and Development (The World Bank). The World Bank was designed to mobilize resources for long-term economic development—originally in the war-torn states, and later in the less-developed and newly independent states. The International Monetary Fund, in contrast, was designed to provide short- or medium-term funds for states needing reserves, to develop and administer a code of conduct for states in international financial matters, and to serve as a forum for consideration of international financial issues. Nearly all states other than the Soviet Union and the members of the Soviet bloc are members of the International Monetary Fund—151 as of 1986. Almost all members of the Fund are also members of the World Bank.[1]

The role of the IMF as a forum for discussion of financial issues has continued since its inauguration in 1946. Its role as a

---

[1] The Soviet Union participated in the Bretton Woods Conference, but did not become a member of these organizations. Czechoslovakia, Cuba, and Poland, which were original members, withdrew. Romania and Hungary became members of the IMF in 1972 and 1982, respectively. Poland became a member again in 1986. Under Article II(1) of the Articles of Agreement of the World Bank, membership in the IMF is a prerequisite for membership in the Bank; the Articles of Agreement of the Fund contain no corresponding provision requiring membership in the Bank. Switzerland had not, as of 1986, joined the IMF, but has maintained close relations with the Fund.

source of funds for member states has also continued, but the conditions for use of these funds have become increasingly controversial. See § 821, Comment *e*. The code of conduct developed at Bretton Woods lasted for roughly a quarter century without change, but broke down in significant part in 1971.

Article IV of the original Bretton Woods agreement created a system of fixed par values of member state currencies, which could be altered only with the concurrence of the Fund and only in conditions of "fundamental disequilibrium." Currency values were denominated in terms of gold, and member states undertook, by intervention in exchange markets in their territory or otherwise, to maintain the value of their currencies within one percent of parity. In 1971, faced with an international economy vastly different from that of the early postwar years, the United States announced that it would no longer assure the convertibility of the United States dollar into gold or other reserve assets. After some efforts to preserve the par value system on the basis of realigned exchange rates, the international monetary system early in 1973 moved to a system of floating exchange rates, *i.e.*, a system in which the issuers of major currencies did not undertake to maintain any specific exchange rate with other currencies or with gold, and did not commit themselves to intervene in the exchange market.

In the period 1971–76, a process of adaptation took place that significantly changed the rules governing exchange arrangements, but kept substantially intact the institutional arrangements of the Bretton Woods agreement, as well as much of the code of conduct, including the provisions concerning exchange controls. See § 821(3). A conference in Jamaica in January 1976 resulted in agreement on amended Articles of Agreement of the International Monetary Fund, which entered into force on April 1, 1978. The most important change was a complete recasting of Article IV, which maintains the overriding concept that the value and behavior of currencies of member states are matters of international concern, but recognizes and permits a system of floating currencies.[2]

Section 821 of this Restatement sets forth the principal provisions of the amended Articles of Agreement, concerning exchange arrangements, notification and consultation, and exchange controls. Section 822 addresses the provision that has given rise to most of the litigation involving the Fund's Articles of Agreement, the effect in one member state of exchange controls maintained by another

---

[2] Article IV(4) and Schedule C(1) of the amended Articles provide for eventual return to a general par value system based on "stable but adjustable" par values, without need for further amendment of the Articles of Agreement, but only if the Fund so determines by an 85 percent majority of the total voting power.

member state. Other obligations under the Articles of Agreement not addressed in those sections are mentioned in the Comments and Reporters' Notes.

Section 823 addresses the problem of translating foreign currency obligations for purposes of judgments rendered in the United States. That subject is not dealt with in the IMF Articles of Agreement, but replacement of the par value system under the original Articles by a system of floating (and often widely fluctuating) exchange rates has given increased importance to the problem, and has underscored the need for a governing principle of general application.

REPORTERS' NOTES

1. Bibliography. Official actions by the IMF are collected in Selected Decisions of the International Monetary Fund (11th issue 1985). Commentaries by IMF officials are published in the International Monetary Fund Pamphlet Series.

The former counsel of the IMF, Sir Joseph Gold, has written extensively on legal aspects of the International Monetary Fund, including The Fund Agreement in the Courts, Vol. I (1962), Vol. II (1982), Vol. III (1986); The Stand-By Arrangements of the International Monetary Fund (1970); Voting and Decisions in the International Monetary Fund (1972); Membership and Nonmembership in the International Monetary Fund (1974); Developments in the International Monetary System, the International Monetary Fund and International Monetary Law since 1971 (Hague Academy of Int'l. L., 174 Recueil des Cours 107, 1982); and Legal and Institutional Aspects of the International Monetary System: Selected Essays, Vol. I (1979), Vol. II (1985).

See also K. Dam, The Rules of the Game: Reform and Evolution in the International Monetary System (1982); R. Edwards, International Monetary Collaboration (1985); A Lowenfeld, The International Monetary System (2d ed. 1984); F. Mann, The Legal Aspect of Money (4th ed. 1982).

2. Previous Restatement. The previous Restatement did not cover this topic. Section 144 of the Restatement, Second, of Conflict of Laws deals with the time for conversion of foreign currency obligations, but on the assumption, no longer conclusive, that courts in common law countries may render a money judgment only in the currency of the forum. See § 823, Reporters' Note 1.

§ 821.   Principal Obligations of Member States of the International Monetary Fund

Under the Articles of Agreement of the International Monetary Fund:

(1) A member state is free to adopt any exchange arrangement consistent with orderly economic growth and reasonable price stability, but such arrangement may not

(a) be linked to gold, or

(b) involve multiple currency practices, or discriminate against the currency of any member state, except with the approval of the Fund.

(2) A member state must cooperate with the Fund in its oversight of the international monetary system

(a) by furnishing information to the Fund as required for surveillance of its exchange rate policies, and

(b) by consulting with the Fund with respect to those policies periodically and on request.

(3) A member state may not, without approval of the Fund, maintain or impose restrictions on the making of payments or transfers for current international transactions, unless it has reserved the right to avail itself of transitional arrangements that include such restrictions.

(4) A member state may not manipulate exchange rates in order to prevent effective balance of payments adjustment or to gain unfair competitive advantage over other member states.

Source Note:

Articles of Agreement of the International Monetary Fund, Second Amendment, April 30, 1976, 29 U.S.T. 2203; T.I.A.S. No. 8937.

Comment:

a. Obligations with respect to exchange arrangements. Under the Articles of Agreement, a member state may permit its currency to float freely (*i.e.*, without intervention in the market by governmental authorities); it may tie the value of its currency to a particular currency, such as the United States dollar or the French franc; it may tie the value of its currency to the value of Special Drawing Rights (Reporters' Note 1(iii)) or to any other basket of currencies; or it may link its currency in a cooperative arrangement with currencies of other states, as the members of the European Monetary System have done. While the provisions of the original Articles of Agreement requiring members to maintain a par value for their currencies have been eliminated from the amended Articles (Introductory Note to this Chapter), the principle that exchange rates are a subject of international concern is maintained, and is the basis of the obligations stated in Subsection (2). Under Article IV(2) of the amended Articles, each member state must notify the Fund of the exchange arrangements it intends to apply and of any changes in those arrangements. Notification need not be given in advance of their implementation, but must be given promptly thereafter. Members are expected to respond to questions from the Fund and, on request, to consult with the Fund on these arrangements and on the effect they may have on other member states or on the international economy as a whole.

b. *Consultation and surveillance.* Article IV(3)(b) of the amended Articles of Agreement states that the Fund shall exercise "firm surveillance over the exchange rate policies of members, and shall adopt specific principles for the guidance of all members with respect to those policies." As of 1987, the relevant principles had not been fully elaborated, but a major Decision on Surveillance over Exchange Rate Policies of April 29, 1977, and several subsequent Decisions, had given some content both to the procedures required of member states and to the scope of the surveillance by the Fund:

(i) *Procedure.* Each member state is required to consult regularly with the Fund, in principle annually, in practice at intervals of up to 18 months. Within three months of completion of these consultations, the results are to be reported to the Executive Board by the Managing Director, and the Board is to reach conclusions thereon. The conclusions may include directions to the Managing Director to have further discussions with the member state if there is doubt about its observance of the principles of Article IV. The Managing Director may also initiate discussions with a member state in the interval between the annual consultations, either on his own motion or on motion of another member state.

(ii) *Scope of consultations.* It is clear that the term "exchange rate policies," as to which member states must inform and consult with the Fund under Subsection (2), goes beyond the "exchange arrangements" provided for in Article IV(2) and reflected in Subsection (1) and Comment a. Exchange rate policies include such matters as member state intervention (or non-intervention) in the foreign exchange market, the level of official borrowing or lending for balance of payments purposes, and restrictions on or incentives to current transactions or capital transfers. Whereas the jurisdiction of the Fund under Article IV(3)(b) to conduct surveillance is addressed to exchange rate policies, Article IV(1) refers to "the orderly underlying conditions that are necessary for financial and economic stability," and the 1977 Decision on Surveillance provides that the Fund's appraisal of a member's exchange rate policies "shall be made within the framework of a comprehensive analysis of the . . . economic policy strategy of the member, and shall recognize that domestic as well as external policies can contribute to timely adjustment of the balance of payments." Ex. Bd. Decision No. 5392 (77/63), April 29, 1977, Selected Decisions of the IMF 10, 13 (11th issue 1985). In addition to these obligations under Article IV, member states have other obligations to consult with the Fund, including consultations in connection with drawings, Comment *e*, with exchange restrictions, Comment *d*, and with use of Special Drawing Rights, Reporters' Note 1(iii).

c. Obligations as to exchange rate policies. In addition to elaborating the surveillance of exchange rate policies prescribed in Article IV of the amended Articles of Agreement, the 1977 Decision on Surveillance, Comment *b*, addresses three specific practices. It states that members (i) *shall* avoid manipulating exchange rates in order to prevent effective balance of payments adjustments; (ii) *should* intervene in the exchange market if necessary to counter disorderly conditions in the exchange value of their currency; and (iii) *should take into account* in their intervention policies the interests of other member states. The first rule is clearly mandatory and repeats Article IV(1)(iii), reflected in Subsection (4) of this section; the degree to which points (ii) and (iii) had matured into obligations was not clear as of 1987. Failure to observe any of the principles, however, could form part of the agenda in consultations with the Fund, Comment *b*, as well as in negotiations concerning use of the Fund's resources, Comment *e*.

d. Obligations as to exchange restrictions.

(i) *Current and capital transactions contrasted.* Article VI(3) of the original Articles of Agreement, unchanged in the amended Articles, provides that members may "exercise such controls as are necessary" to regulate international capital movements, but not "in a manner which will restrict payments for current transactions." In contrast, Article VIII, also unchanged in this respect in the amended Articles and reflected in Subsection (3), provides that states accepting its provisions (see below) are not permitted to restrict payments for current transactions without approval of the Fund.

(ii) *Article VIII and Article XIV states contrasted.* Article VIII reflects the principle that exchange restrictions on current transactions are disfavored and states that "no member shall, without the approval of the Fund," impose such restrictions. Not all states were prepared in 1944 to assume the obligations of Article VIII. Hence, Article XIV of the original Articles, retained (with minor changes) in the amended Articles, provides that member states may declare, when they join the Fund, that they intend to maintain restrictions on current transactions for a transitional period, notwithstanding the prohibitions in Article VIII. No limit is stated for the transitional period, which in many instances has lasted for several decades, and the amended Articles continue to speak of "transitional arrangements," without reference to any period. A state that has made a declaration under Article XIV is permitted to maintain restrictions on current payments, and adapt them to changing circumstances, without approval of the Fund, but is obligated to endeavor to withdraw them as soon as conditions permit, and to consult with the Fund annually to that end. Imposition of new restrictions, or reimposition of a restriction previously terminated, requires approval of the Fund. Once a state has declared that it accepts the obligations of Article VIII, it is not permitted to revert to Article XIV status.

For the effect of exchange controls of member states in courts of other states, see § 822.

e. Use of Fund's resources. Subject to the Articles of Agreement and Decisions thereunder, member states may apply to use the resources of the Fund to assist them in solving their balance of payments problems. Article V. The Fund's resources—typically "freely usable" currencies such as dollars, pounds sterling, marks, francs, or yen, but in principle any member's currency—are sold to member states in return for the member's own currency. The sale is subject to an obligation to repurchase in a stated period, as well as to conditions negotiated with the Fund concerning the member's economic policies during that period. The conditions may be negotiated either at the time the member draws on the Fund's resources, or in advance in connection with grant of a stand-by commitment. See Reporters' Note 1(ii). If a member state, without excuse, fails to fulfill its repurchase requirements as required by a drawing, the Executive Board may, by a simple majority, declare it ineligible to use the general resources of the Fund. A decision to this effect was made with respect to Peru in 1986.

The basic condition for use of the Fund's resources is that they must be used in a manner consistent with the Articles of Agreement. Except for drawings within the member's reserve tranche position (*i.e.*, its contribution of reserves to the Fund, Reporters' Note 1(i)) and drawings under certain special facilities, the Fund will examine the economic situation and policies of a member state prior to approval of a drawing or stand-by. The Fund may negotiate arrangements with the state's authorities with respect to economic policies to be pursued by the state during the period the drawing or stand-by is outstanding. Such arrangements are not international agreements in the sense that non-compliance is a breach of an international obligation, see §§ 321, 335. However, an unjustified failure to live up to an arrangement with the Fund in connection with a drawing or stand-by may be a basis for non-renewal of a stand-by or for limitations on future drawings, and failure to achieve performance criteria in a stand-by arrangement may interrupt the right to make further drawings thereunder.

f. Consequences of breach of obligation under Articles of Agreement. Some breaches of the Articles of Agreement carry specific penalties, such as ineligibility to use the resources of the Fund. Articles V(5), VI(1), XXVI(2)(a). More important, the Articles of Agreement and Decisions serve as standards by which the conduct of states is measured, both when they apply to use the Fund's resources, Comment *e*, and in connection with lending and restructuring arrangements with other states and with commercial banks, Reporters' Note 5.

REPORTERS' NOTES

1. *Definitions.*

   (i) Reserve tranche *and credit* tranches. Drawings by members of the IMF on the resources of the Fund, Comment *e*, are generally made in tranches, representing one quarter (or multiples of one quarter) of the member's quota. Since one quarter of the member's quota was contributed in gold (under the original Articles) or in SDR's or other reserve assets (since the Second Amendment), when a member draws funds equal to the first tranche it is in effect drawing against its own assets, formerly called the *gold tranche* and since 1978 the *reserve tranche*. No challenges are made to drawings under the reserve tranche; drawings under the credit tranches are subject to conditions, generally increasingly stringent for successive tranches. Under Article V(3)(b)(iii), drawings are not permitted that would cause the Fund's holdings of a member's currency to exceed 200 percent of its quota, but various waivers and special facilities have reduced the importance of this limit.

   (ii) *Stand-by.* A stand-by arrangement with the IMF assures a member state that it will be able to draw on the resources of the Fund up to a stated amount within a stated period, without further examination of its economic situation or policies, on the strength of intentions stated and understandings reached at the time the stand-by is issued. Since the 1970's, stand-by arrangements have sometimes included performance criteria, Comment *e*.

(iii) *Special Drawing Rights (SDR's)*. SDR's are reserve assets created from time to time by the Fund and allocated to member states participating in the Special Drawing Rights Department in proportion to their quotas. The original purpose of SDR's was to overcome an expected shortage of world reserves, by creating reserves free from the vagaries of the production and use of gold, or of balance of payments deficits of reserve currency states (principally the United States). The expected reserve shortage did not develop, and as of 1986 SDR's constituted only about 4 percent of world reserves excluding gold and 2 percent of total reserves, but they assumed other functions during the 1970's, both as a vehicle for transactions with the IMF and as a relatively stable unit of account. SDR's may now be used to settle official balances among states, and also to meet their general reserve asset subscription obligations, paragraph (i) *supra*.

Originally, one SDR equalled one United States dollar. After the demise of the par value system based on a fixed relationship between dollars and gold, Introductory Note to this Chapter, the SDR was assigned a value not linked to any one currency but measured by a "basket" of specified currencies, so that it would be more stable than any single currency. The method of valuation has been changed from time to time, but the use of the SDR, as valued by the Fund, as a global unit of account has spread, not only in transactions by and with the Fund and in official settlements, but in international agreements, including long-term loans, construction and mining contracts, and limitations on liability by shipowners, airlines, and other carriers. See Gold, "The SDR in Treaty Practice: A Checklist," 22 Int'l Leg.Mat. 209 (1983); Trans World Airlines, Inc. v. Franklin Mint Corp., 466 U.S. 243, 257, 104 S.Ct. 1776, 1785, 80 L.Ed.2d 273 (1984).

(iv) *Quotas in the Fund.* Each member state is assigned a quota, in principle designed to reflect the state's relative position in the international economy. A member state's quota largely determines its voting strength in the Fund, Reporters' Note 2, as well as its required contribution to the Fund. Under the original Articles of Agreement, one quarter of the contribution (with exceptions not here relevant) was to be paid in gold, the rest in the member's own currency. Under the amended Articles, one quarter of the quota is normally to be paid in SDR's or in currencies specified by the Fund, the remainder in the member's own currency. Quotas of member states may be changed from time to time, but only with the member's consent. Overall quotas, which (apart from borrowing by the Fund) determine the resources available to the Fund, are subject to review at intervals of not more than five years. From an initial amount of $8.8 billion in 1946, the total amount of quotas in the Fund had as of 1986 been raised to about SDR 90 billion, equivalent to about U.S. $106 billion.

(v) *Current and capital transactions.* While the distinction between current and capital transactions is sometimes difficult to draw, in general current transactions include payments for goods and services, interest on debt, dividends on shares, royalties and license fees, short-term financing of export-import transactions, insurance premiums and claims, payment of moderate amounts for amortization of loans or depreciation of direct investment, and most unrequited transfers; capital transactions include direct international investment, purchase and sale of shares of stock, long-term loans and repayment of such loans at maturity, and repatriation or redemption of capital.

2. *Governance of IMF.* In contrast to the GATT, Introductory Note to Chapter 1, the Articles of Agreement of the International Monetary Fund contain detailed provisions concerning organization and governance. Under Article XII, all powers of the Fund not otherwise assigned are vested in its Board of Governors, which consists of representatives of each member state—generally the minister of finance or the president of the central bank. The Board of Governors convenes at the Fund's annual meeting (always held in conjunction with the annual meeting of the World Bank) and may take actions between meetings by mail or cable ballot. Most decisions of the Fund are made by the Executive Board, consisting of five Executive Directors appointed by the five states having the largest quotas, and 15 or more Executive Directors elected every two years by other member states under a procedure designed to produce representation for compatible groups of states according to economic and geographic criteria. In some cir-

cumstances, a large creditor of the Fund that does not otherwise appoint an Executive Director—Saudi Arabia in the early 1980's—is entitled to appoint an additional Executive Director. The Executive Board functions in continuous session throughout the year. The Managing Director is head of the staff and chairman of the Executive Board, but without vote except in case of an equal division.

Votes in both the Board of Governors and the Executive Board are weighted according to the size of a member's quota. Each member has 250 "basic votes" reflecting the principle of equality of states, plus one additional vote for each part of its quota equivalent to SDR 100,000. As of 1986, the United States held 19.64 percent of the voting power, Great Britain, the second largest member, 6.63 percent, and all developing member states together close to 40 percent. In practice, votes are rarely cast; under Rule C–10 of the Fund's Rules and Regulations, the Chairman "shall ordinarily ascertain the sense of the meeting in lieu of a formal vote." Decisions of the Executive Board and Board of Governors of general application are published from time to time in *Selected Decisions of the International Monetary Fund.*

Approval by the Fund, when required by the Articles of Agreement or Decisions thereunder, is given by the Executive Board, on recommendation of the Managing Director. Unless otherwise provided, approval of the action of a member state is granted on the basis of a simple majority of the votes cast.

3. *Gold in international monetary system.* Under the amended Articles of Agreement, gold has

been eliminated as the common denominator for exchange rate purposes, and member states may not maintain the value of their currencies in terms of gold. Subsection (1)(a). Also, transactions between member states and the Fund are no longer conducted in gold but in SDR's (or in some instances in specified currencies). However, gold may continue to be counted by a member state among its reserve assets, valued either at (or in proportion to) market price, or at some prior price, as is the United States practice. Member states may also use gold in official transactions among themselves, either to settle balances or, as has been more common, as collateral. A commission created by the United States Congress recommended in 1982 against restoration of a gold standard, but urged both the Fund and the United States to retain their existing stock of gold. Since December 1974, United States citizens may freely buy or sell gold.

4. *IMF and GATT.* Article XV(1) of the GATT calls for cooperation between the GATT and the IMF, particularly in determining whether import quotas otherwise prohibited come within the balance of payments exception of the GATT. See § 804(1) and Reporters' Note 6. Article XV(2) of the GATT states that the GATT Contracting Parties *"shall accept* all findings of statistical and other facts presented by the Fund relating to foreign exchange, monetary reserves and balance of payments, and *shall accept* the determination of the Fund as to whether action by a contracting party is in accordance with the Articles of Agreement of the . . . Fund. . . ." There is no comparable provision in the Fund Articles of Agreement concerning trade implications of exchange arrangements or controls. However, the Fund regularly engages in informal consultations with the staff of GATT, and, at least for states that are members of both organizations, compliance with GATT obligations is an important criterion considered by the Fund in consultations with member states, Comment *b*, and in negotiations concerning use of the Fund's resources, Comment *e*.

5. *IMF and developing country debt.* In part to avoid the conditions associated with drawings from the IMF and in part to gain access to funds deposited by oil-producing states in "money-center" commercial banks, many developing countries turned to private sector banks for substantial loans in the decade following the first massive rise in oil prices achieved by OPEC in 1973. In the period 1982–86, when first Mexico, then Brazil, and thereafter a number of other states were unable to meet their obligations on these loans, the international financial community, both public and private, worked out a series of restructuring arrangements under the supervision of the IMF. Typically, more funds were lent to the debtor states and repayment obligations were stretched out; in return, the debtor states gave specific undertakings concerning controls on inflation, limits on budgetary deficits, restraints on subsidies to state-owned enterprises, and balance of payments targets, usually (though not always) subject to monitoring or "enhanced surveillance" by the IMF. See generally "Symposium, The International Debt Crisis," 17 N.Y.U.J.Int'l L. & Pol. 483 *et seq.*, including bibliography.

6. *United States law and International Monetary Fund.* The United States became a member of the Fund pursuant to the Bretton Woods Agreements Act of 1945, 59 Stat. 512, 22 U.S.C. §§ 286 *et seq.* The Act authorized the President to accept membership for the United States in the Fund (as well as in the World Bank), to appoint, with the advice and consent of the Senate, a Governor of the Fund and Bank, and an Executive Director for the Fund and one for the Bank. The Act also authorized payment by the United States of its quota in the Fund, and authorized the President to furnish information required by the Fund under Article VIII(5) of the Articles of Agreement. Section 5 of the Act prohibited the President from consenting to any change in the United States quota in the Fund, or to any change in the par value of the United States dollar, without authorization by Congress. The requirement of authorization by Congress of any change in the United States quota remains in effect, and each proposal to increase the overall quota of the Fund, Reporters' Note 1(iv), has been submitted to Congress for its approval. The prohibition concerning changes in the par value of the dollar became obsolete when the Second Amendment to the Articles of Agreement of the Fund entered into force. It has been replaced by a provision prohibiting the President from making or consenting to any proposal for a par value for the United States dollar without authorization by Congress. 90 Stat. 2660, § 3, amending 22 U.S.C. § 286c. Since 1980, Congress has attached to quota authorizations various riders containing "directives" concerning positions to be taken on behalf of the United States; see 22 U.S.C. § 286s–gg. For directives concerning violations of human rights, see § 702, Reporters' Note 9. In general, such directives have been followed, but whether they are legally binding is not settled.

§ 822. Exchange Controls and Exchange Contracts in Courts of Member States

Under the Articles of Agreement of the International Monetary Fund, a member state may not enforce exchange contracts involving the currency of another member state if such contracts are contrary to that state's exchange control regulations maintained or imposed consistently with the Articles of Agreement.

Source Note:

Article VIII(2)(b) of the IMF Articles of Agreement.

Comment:

a. Exchange controls, public policy, and choice of law. The traditional (pre-Bretton Woods) view of the courts of most states was that exchange control regulations, like tax and penal laws, were entitled to recognition only in the territory of the state that issued them. This section, following Article VIII(2)(b) of the Articles of Agreement, regards that view, based on the so-called "revenue rule," as obsolete, at least with respect to actions to enforce exchange contracts covered by Article VIII(2)(b). See § 483, Reporters' Note 1. Thus, if a court of one state hearing an action to enforce a contract is presented with a defense founded on the alleged inconsistency of the contract with the exchange control regulations of another state, it will (i) decide whether the regulation is applicable to the transaction in question; (ii) inquire whether the control was imposed or is maintained consistently with the Articles of Agreement, Comment *c;* (iii) determine whether the contract is an "exchange contract" under Article VIII(2)(b) (see Comment *b*); and (iv) determine whether the contract "involves the currency" of the member imposing the regulation. If the answers to all four questions are affirmative, the court must give effect to the foreign exchange control and deny the claim. An alleged violation of an exchange control imposed or maintained consistently with the Fund Agreement may also be the basis of a claim or defense in an action on a contract not qualifying as an "exchange contract," and it may be the basis of a claim or defense in another state, but the Articles of Agreement do not require the courts of member states to recognize or apply foreign exchange controls in such cases. See Reporters' Note 2.

b. Meaning of "exchange contracts." Neither Article VIII 2(b) nor the definitions article (Article XXX) of the IMF Articles of Agreement contains a definition of the term "exchange contract." At least two distinct interpretations of the term have emerged in judicial decisions and scholarly writings. At a minimum, this section applies to transactions that have as their immediate object the exchange of one currency for another, such as the conversion of marks into yen or the purchase of sterling futures with dollars. Under a more expansive interpretation of the term "exchange contract," this section might apply also to other contracts, including contracts for international sale of goods, charter of ships, deposit of funds, and similar transactions that have an effect on the member state's balance of payments or exchange resources. United States courts that have addressed the question have favored the narrow interpretation; British courts have also generally favored the narrow interpretation, but they have applied Article VIII(2)(b) to sales contracts found to be monetary transactions in disguise. Some courts of other states have favored or expressly adopted the wider interpretation. See Reporters' Note 2.

c. Exchange controls maintained or imposed consistently with IMF Articles. In principle, all exchange regulations of member states must be notified to the Fund, whether or not they require the Fund's approval under Article VIII. See § 821(3) and Comment *d.* Ordinarily, the Fund will not approve restrictions on payments for current account imposed by "Article VIII states," but it may do so in some circumstances. Restrictions on current account payments imposed by "Article XIV states" do not require approval if they are continuations or adaptations of restrictions in effect when the state became a member, but do require approval if they are new or different. Restrictions on capital transfers do not require approval by the Fund. See § 821, Comment *d*(i) and Reporters' Note 1(v).

The Fund does not publicly announce whether a given measure of exchange control has been approved, nor does description of a measure in the Fund's Annual Report on Exchange Arrangements and Exchange Restrictions indicate that it has been either approved or disapproved. Since consistency of a particular exchange restriction with the Articles of Agreement often cannot be determined simply by reference to the Articles, it may be necessary for a court to seek advice of the Fund before passing on the question, and the Fund will normally respond to such inquiries. See Reporters' Note 1. A statement by the Fund that a particular control is not maintained or imposed consistently with the Articles of Agreement is conclusive; a statement that the control is maintained or imposed consistently with the Articles of Agreement is entitled to great weight, but the court will make the final decision. If an exchange control regulation is determined not to be maintained or imposed consistently with the Articles of Agreement, a court would normally proceed in accordance with the pre-Bretton Woods approach to exchange controls, Comment *a;* if the restriction is maintained or imposed consistently with the Agreement, a court would still have to rule whether the restriction is applicable to the transaction before it, and whether that transaction is an "exchange contract" within the meaning of Article VIII(2)(b). See Comment *b.*

REPORTERS' NOTES

1. *Exchange controls maintained or imposed consistently with the Fund Agreement.* Article VIII(2)(b) provides that "Exchange contracts which involve the currency of any member and which are contrary to the exchange control regulations of that member maintained or imposed consistently with this Agreement shall be unenforceable in the territories of any member." The International Monetary Fund has not issued a definition of "exchange contract," Comment *b,* and would probably not respond to an inquiry from a court as to whether a given transaction was an exchange contract within the meaning of Article VIII(2)(b). It is prepared, however, to respond to inquiries from a court or from parties to litigation as to whether a given ex-

change regulation is maintained or imposed consistently with the Fund Agreement. Ex.Bd.Decision No. 446–4 of June 10, 1949, Selected Decisions of the International Monetary Fund 251 (11th Issue 1985), reproduced in 14 Fed.Reg. 5208 (August 19, 1949). In explaining Article VIII(2)(b) in this decision, the Executive Board of the Fund stated:

> Parties entering into exchange contracts involving the currency of any member of the Fund and contrary to exchange control regulations of that member which are maintained or imposed consistently with the [IMF Articles of] Agreement will not receive the assistance of the judicial or administrative authorities of other members in obtaining the performance of such contracts.

Thus, for example, courts of member states are not to order performance of such contracts or award damages for their non-performance. In further explanation, the decision states that:

> . . . if a party to an exchange contract of the kind referred to in Article VIII, Section 2(b) seeks to enforce such a contract, the tribunal of the member country before which the proceedings are brought will not, on the ground that they are contrary to the public policy (ordre public) of the forum, refuse recognition of the exchange control regulations of the other member which are maintained or imposed consistently with the Fund Agreement. It also follows that such contracts will be treated as unenforceable notwithstanding that under the private international law of the forum, the law under which the

foreign exchange control regulations are maintained or imposed is not the law which governs the exchange contract or its performance.

Thus, even if an exchange contract is, by its terms or by the choice of law rules of the forum, not subject to the laws of the member state imposing the controls, the court may not disregard that state's controls, nor may it do so on the ground that recognition of foreign exchange controls is contrary to the public policy of the forum. For discussion of the scope and effect of the Fund's advice, see 2 Gold, The Fund Agreement in the Courts, esp. 119, 191, 358–59 (1982); Edwards, International Monetary Collaboration 481–84 (1985). See also Callejo v. Bancomer, S.A., 764 F.2d 1101, 1119–20 (5th Cir.1985).

2. *Exchange controls as defense to contract claim.* Numerous cases have considered claims by suppliers of goods or services against residents of foreign states who fail to make payments called for by a contract, claiming that the payment (or the contract itself) is contrary to the exchange controls of the state where the debtor resides. In general, the defense that payment would be contrary to applicable exchange controls has failed, sometimes on the ground that the contract was not an "exchange contract" and therefore not within the prohibition of Article VIII(2)(b), e.g., Wilson, Smithett & Cope Ltd. v. Terruzzi, [1976] Q.B. 683, 709 (U.K. Ct.App.); sometimes on the ground that the regulation in question did not preclude payment, e.g., Weston Banking Corp. v. Turkiye Garanti Bankasi, A.S., 57 N.Y.2d 315, 456 N.Y.S.2d 684, 442 N.E.2d 1195

(1982); and sometimes on the ground that under the applicable choice of law rules the law of the forum governed the transaction, *e.g.,* J. Zeevi & Sons, Ltd. v. Grindlays Bank (Uganda) Ltd., 37 N.Y.2d 220, 371 N.Y.S.2d 892, 333 N.E.2d 168 (1975), *certiorari denied,* 423 U.S. 866, 96 S.Ct. 126, 46 L.Ed.2d 95 (1975).

European courts have been more willing to accept the defense. See, *e.g.,* A v. B Co., 1962 Aussenwirtschaftsdienst des Betriebs-Beraters 146 (Sup.Ct., Fed.Rep. of Germany, April 9, 1962), discussed in 2 Gold, The Fund Agreement in the Courts, 18–21 (1982); Lessinger v. Mirau, 22 Int'l L.Rep. 725 (1955) (Schleswig-Holstein Court of Appeal 1954); Clearing Dollars Case, 22 Int'l L.Rep. 730 (1955) (Commercial Court of Hamburg 1954); Moojen v. Von Reichert, 89 Journal du Droit International 718 (Cour d'Appel Paris, 1st Chamber 1961); Société Filature et Tissage X. Jourdain v. Époux Heynen-Bintner, 22 Int'l L.Rep. 727 (1955) (Tribunal D'Arrondissement de Luxembourg (Civil) 1956). See generally Gold, *supra* (periodically updated); also Baker, "Enforcement of Contracts Violating Foreign Exchange Control Laws," 3 Int'l Trade L.J. 247, 254–258, 266–67 (1977); Edwards, International Monetary Collaboration 484–89 (1985). When a successful party in a British court sought to enforce its judgment against the defaulting debtor in Italy, the Supreme Court of Italy declined enforcement of the judgment, on the ground that the British judgment was contrary to Italy's public policy *(ordine pubblico).* Wilson Smithett & Cope Ltd. v. Terruzzi, (Corte di Cassazione, July 2, 1981), 18 Riv. di Diritto Internazionale Privato e

Processuale 107 (1982). In United City Merchants (Investments) Ltd. v. Royal Bank of Canada, [1983] 1 A.C. 168 (H.L. (E)), an English seller and a Peruvian buyer agreed on the dollar purchase price of a factory, to be paid through a letter of credit at twice the factory's actual value, with the understanding that the seller would remit the proceeds in excess of the actual value to an account in the United States controlled by the buyer. The object of the transaction was to use a genuine purchase as a device to move funds from Peru to the United States, in contravention of Peruvian exchange controls. When the confirming bank under the letter of credit refused payment, relying (in part) on Article VIII(2)(b), the House of Lords divided the transaction in two, holding the confirming bank liable for so much of the draft drawn against the letter of credit as represented the actual value of the goods sold plus freight, but not liable for the amount that reflected an unenforceable monetary transaction.

3. *Claims based on violation of foreign exchange controls.* In Banco do Brasil v. A.C. Israel Commodity Co., 12 N.Y.2d 371, 239 N.Y.S.2d 872, 190 N.E.2d 235 (1963), *certiorari denied,* 376 U.S. 906, 84 S.Ct. 657, 11 L.Ed.2d 605 (1964), the central bank of Brazil sought to recover in tort from a New York buyer of coffee exported from Brazil, alleging that the buyer had participated in a scheme to use forged export documents to deprive the central bank of the dollar proceeds of the sale due to it under Brazilian exchange control regulations. The court held (by a vote of 4 to 3) that the claim based on Article VIII(2)(b) must fail. Even if the contracts for

the sale of coffee were "exchange contracts," Comment *b*, which the court doubted, Article VIII(2)(b) only required that exchange contracts in violation of a member state's exchange controls maintained or imposed consistently with the Articles of Agreement be unenforceable in the courts of other member states; it did not imply an obligation on other states to impose tort liability on those who have executed such contracts. In Banco Frances e Brasileiro S.A. v. Doe, 36 N.Y.2d 592, 370 N.Y.S.2d 534, 331 N.E.2d 502 (1975), *certiorari denied*, 423 U.S. 867, 96 S.Ct. 129, 46 L.Ed.2d 96 (1975), a private Brazilian bank sought to recover dollar travelers checks allegedly obtained by defendants through fraudulent applications to Brazilian exchange control authorities in the name of persons who either did not exist at all or had no intention of traveling abroad. The New York Court of Appeals reversed dismissal of the action, on the ground that the "revenue rule," if it retained validity at all, see § 483, Reporters' Note 1, should not be applied to actions of private parties. Article VIII(2)(b) did not obligate member states to provide tort recoveries for conspiracies to violate foreign exchange controls, but that Article did not prevent states from doing so, and it made it "impossible to conclude that the currency control laws of other member States [of the IMF] are offensive to this State's public policy. . . ." 36 N.Y.2d at 598, 370 N.Y.S.2d at 539, 331 N.E.2d at 506. See also Kolovrat v. Oregon, 366 U.S. 187, 197–98, 81 S.Ct. 922, 928, 6 L.Ed.2d 218 (1961), involving inheritance of property under State law, in which the United States Supreme Court declared that federal policy as evidenced by the IMF Agreement superseded State policy.

4. *Exchange controls for security purposes.* The principal purpose of most exchange controls, as well as of IMF scrutiny of such controls, is economic regulation. From time to time, however, states impose restrictions on the movement of funds for reasons of national or international security, and the acceptability of such restrictions is governed by other standards. Under Ex.Bd.Decision No. 144–(52/51) of August 14, 1952, Selected Decisions of the IMF 253 (11th Issue 1985), a member state that has imposed or intends to impose controls solely for national security purposes should give notice to the Fund; unless the Fund informs the member state within 30 days that it is not satisfied that such restrictions are imposed solely for security purposes, "the member may assume that the Fund has no objection to the imposition of the restrictions." For example, during the Iranian hostage crisis of 1979 the United States imposed restrictions on transfer of Iranian dollar assets held in the United States or in foreign branches of United States banks; since it gave notice to the Fund pursuant to Decision No. 144, and the Fund did not communicate its disapproval, it was asserted in litigation in France and in the United Kingdom that the United States controls were restrictions maintained consistently with the Articles of Agreement. See Edwards, "Extraterritorial Application of the U.S. Iranian Assets Control Regulations," 75 Am.J.Int'l L. 870 (1981); 2 Gold, The Fund Agreement in the Courts 360–427 (1982). Earlier, Decision No. 144 was invoked in connection with United States controls

under the Trading with the Enemy Act against Cuba, Indian restrictions against Pakistan, and controls by Great Britain and some other states against Rhodesia. See 1 Horsefield, The International Monetary Fund 1945–1965, at 275–76 (1969); Edwards, International Monetary Collaboration 415–20 (1985).

5. *Choice of law rules and exchange controls.* A substantial number of cases have arisen out of claims to funds held by banks or insurance companies doing business in the United States or the United Kingdom, derived from transactions alleged to be contrary to exchange controls of Czechoslovakia, Yugoslavia, Cuba, and other states where political upheavals had induced large-scale emigration. In some cases the exchange controls of a member state maintained consistently with the Articles of Agreement of the IMF have been upheld. Perutz v. Bohemian Discount Bank in Liquidation, 304 N.Y. 533, 110 N.E.2d 6 (1953); Kraus v. Zivnostenska Banka, 187 Misc. 681, 64 N.Y.S.2d 208 (Queens Cty. 1946); Confederation Life Assn. v. Ugalde, 164 So.2d 1 (Fla.1964), *certiorari denied,* 379 U.S. 915, 85 S.Ct. 263, 13 L.Ed.2d 186 (1964); Kahler v. Midland Bank, Ltd., [1950] A.C. 24 (H.L. (E)). In other cases the courts have found the controls inapplicable because payment was to be made (or could be made) outside the state imposing the controls. See, *e.g.,* Pan American Life Insurance Co. v. Blanco, 362 F.2d 167 (5th Cir. 1966); Theye y Ajuria v. Pan American Life Ins. Co., 245 La. 755, 161 So.2d 70 (1964), *certiorari denied,* 377 U.S. 997, 84 S.Ct. 1922, 12 L.Ed. 2d 1046 (1964). See also "The Cuban Insurance Cases" in 2 Gold, The Fund Agreement in the Courts, 43–

94 (1982). When the state imposing the control has withdrawn from the IMF, as Czechoslovakia did in 1955 and Cuba did in 1964, the recognition of its foreign exchange controls is no longer required. See, *e.g.,* Stephen v. Zivnostenska Banka, National Corp., 31 Misc.2d 45, 140 N.Y.S.2d 323 (N.Y.Cty.1955), *affirmed,* 286 App.Div. 999, 145 N.Y.S.2d 310 (1955); Gold, *supra,* at 87–88.

6. *Foreign debt moratoria and private actions on loans.* In several cases related to the difficulties of developing states in the early 1980's in meeting their debt service obligations, § 821, Reporters' Note 5, the issue arose whether a United States court may enforce a loan obligation payable in the United States when the state of the borrower had imposed a debt moratorium or restructuring in connection with an economic recovery program approved by the International Monetary Fund. One district judge in New York held that a loan agreement entered into by several Costa Rican banks to borrow United States dollars, repayable in New York, was not an exchange contract for purposes of Article VIII(2)(b) of the IMF Articles of Agreement, but that even if it were, the defendants relying on a prohibition by the government of Costa Rica against payment of foreign exchange had not shown that the prohibition was "maintained or imposed consistently with the [Fund] Agreement." Libra Bank Ltd. v. Banco Nacional de Costa Rica, 570 F.Supp. 870, 896–902 (S.D.N.Y.1983). Another district judge in New York, in a case arising out of the same Costa Rican decree, held that the act of state doctrine (see § 443, this Restatement) precluded adjudication of a claim on an

overdue loan brought on behalf of a syndicate of 39 banks. Allied Bank International v. Banco Credito Agricola de Cartago, 566 F.Supp. 1440 (S.D.N.Y.1983). While appeal from that decision was pending, the Government of Costa Rica and its central bank signed a financing agreement with all but one of the banks in the syndicate, linked to a state-to-state ("Paris Club") restructuring of Costa Rica's sovereign debt, which in turn was linked to maintenance of a stand-by arrangement with the IMF. See § 821, Reporters' Note 1(ii). On appeal on behalf of the non-concurring creditor bank, the Court of Appeals first affirmed dismissal of the action on the ground that the actions of Costa Rica resulting in the debt moratorium were consistent with the law and policy of the United States, and

were analogous to reorganization of a business pursuant to Chapter XI of the United States bankruptcy code. On rehearing, following submissions on the part of the United States government that the actions of the Costa Rican government had not been consistent with United States policy, the court of appeals withdrew its earlier decision and reversed, holding also that the act of state doctrine was not applicable, because for act of state purposes, see § 443, Reporters' Note 4, the property taken (*i.e.*, the obligation to repay the loan) was not situated in the taking state. Allied Bank International v. Banco Credito Agricola de Cartago, 757 F.2d 516 (2d Cir.), *certiorari dismissed,* 473 U.S. 934, 106 S.Ct. 30, 87 L.Ed.2d 706 (1985).

§ 823. Judgments on Obligations in Foreign Currency: Law of the United States

(1) **Courts in the United States ordinarily give judgment on causes of action arising in another state, or denominated in a foreign currency, in United States dollars, but they are not precluded from giving judgment in the currency in which the obligation is denominated or the loss was incurred.**

(2) **If, in a case arising out of a foreign currency obligation, the court gives judgment in dollars, the conversion from foreign currency to dollars is to be made at such rate as to make the creditor whole and to avoid rewarding a debtor who has delayed in carrying out the obligation.**

Comment:

a. Foreign currency obligations in State and federal courts. When obligations in foreign currency arise in State courts or in federal courts exercising diversity jurisdiction, the rules for conversion have depended on State law; when such obligations have arisen in federal courts in exercise of other bases of federal jurisdiction, including admiralty, the federal courts have fashioned their own rules. This section applies both to State and to federal courts, and in federal courts regardless of the basis on which jurisdiction is exercised.

b. *Judgments in foreign currencies.* The traditional United States rule has been that courts in the United States are required to render money judgments payable in United States dollars only, regardless of the currency of obligation or loss. Those courts that have analyzed the basis for this rule, Reporters' Note 1, have attributed it either to a 1792 statute that seems to have had a different purpose but in any event has been repealed, or to the assertion that it is required by Anglo-American common law, an assertion repudiated by the British House of Lords in 1976, Reporters' Note 6. Given a fundamentally changed system of exchange rates, in which all major currencies, including the United States dollar, fluctuate in value against each other (see Introductory Note to this Chapter), and given the absence of conclusive authority to the contrary, this section, like § 3-107 of the Uniform Commercial Code, and Section 27 of the New York Judiciary Law, Reporters' Note 1, takes the position that there is no impediment to issuance by a court in the United States of a judgment denominated in a foreign currency. However, a judgment in a foreign currency should be issued only when requested by the judgment creditor, and only when it would best accomplish the objective stated in Subsection (2).

A judgment denominated in a foreign currency may be satisfied either in that currency or by payment of an equivalent amount in dollars measured by the rate of exchange in effect on the date of payment.

c. *Making the injured party whole.* The objective of civil money judgments is, in general, to place the judgment creditor (*i.e.,* the injured party) in a position as close as possible to that in which he would have been if the obligation had been carried out by the judgment debtor or if the injury had not occurred. When obligations are incurred in currencies other than the currency of the forum, the same objectives govern. While the preference of the judgment creditor is to be taken into account, the decision is to be made by the court, which should assure that neither party receives a windfall or is penalized as a result of currency conversion. If the court gives judgment in United States dollars, as is the general practice, the date used for conversion should depend on whether the currency of obligation has appreciated or depreciated relative to the dollar. In general, if the foreign currency has depreciated since the injury or breach, judgment should be given at the rate of exchange applicable on the date of injury or breach; if the foreign currency has appreciated since the injury or breach, judgment should be given at the rate of exchange applicable on the date of judgment or the date of payment. See Reporters' Note 4. The court is free, however, to depart from those guidelines when the interests of justice require it, for instance if a judgment creditor refrains from pursuing remedies in the state where the obligation arose in anticipation of a more advantageous result in the United States.

d. Alternative conversion rules. Under Subsection (2), and Comment *c*, a judgment in dollars should be given on the basis of conversion at whichever date would serve the ends of justice in the circumstances.

(i) *Breach date.* When the breach date is applied for conversion of foreign obligations, Comment *c*, an obligation to pay a sum of money is convertible as of the date it was payable; an obligation to deliver goods or perform services is convertible as of the last date on which the obligation could be performed in compliance with the agreement on which it was based, or the date on which default was declared. For an obligation not arising out of contract, such as a tort or ships' collision, the date for conversion is the date of the event giving rise to the claim. When a judgment is based on multiple obligations, conversion should be made separately in respect of each obligation.

(ii) *Judgment date.* When the judgment date rule is applied for conversion of foreign obligations, the obligation is convertible into dollars as of the date on which the judgment is rendered, regardless of the duration of any appeal.

(iii) *Payment date.* When judgment is given in a foreign currency, it may be paid in that currency within the normal time for payment of judgments, or in the dollar equivalent on the date of payment.

If payment was to be made on more than one date, the conversion must be made separately on each date of payment. If execution is levied against the property of a judgment debtor in the case of a judgment expressed in foreign currency, the conversion should be made as of the date of levy.

e. Interest. The date for commencement of interest on an obligation or a judgment is determined by the law of the forum, including its rules on choice of law. When a statutory rate of interest is applicable in the forum, that rate must be applied, even if the judgment is given in foreign currency. If no statutory rate of interest is applicable, the court may, in appropriate cases, order interest to be based on the interest rate applicable at the principal financial center of the state issuing the currency in which the judgment is payable.

f. Set-off. If adverse parties in a single suit prevail in respect of separate claims, each claim is subject to a judgment in accordance with this section. If the judgments so rendered are in different currencies, the judgment for the smaller sum may be converted into the currency of the judgment for the larger sum as of the date of payment and used as set-off.

REPORTERS' NOTES

1. *Dollar judgment rule reexamined.* Courts in the United States have generally assumed that their judgments, when calling for payment of a sum of money, must be denominated in United States dollars. Most courts have made this assumption without any discussion, both in enforcing foreign judgments, see § 481, Reporters' Note 8, and in issuing judgments based on foreign claims. See, *e.g.,* Deutsche Bank Filiale Nurnberg v. Humphrey, 272 U.S. 517, 47 S.Ct. 166, 71 L.Ed. 383 (1926). Some courts have attributed the rule to the common law, probably based on concepts of sovereignty, see, *e.g.,* Guiness v. Miller, 291 F. 769 (S.D. N.Y.1923), *affirmed,* 299 F. 538 (2d Cir.1924), *affirmed,* Hicks v. Guiness, 269 U.S. 71, 46 S.Ct. 46, 70 L.Ed. 168 (1925); Liberty National Bank v. Burr, 270 F. 251 (E.D.Pa. 1921). That rule, however, has not been codified in the United States, and was abandoned in Great Britain in 1976, Reporters' Note 6. Some courts have referred to § 20 of the Coinage Act of 1792, formerly found in 31 U.S.C. § 371, which stated, in pertinent part, "The money of account of the United States shall be expressed in dollars or units, dimes or tenths, cents or hundredths, . . . and all accounts in the public offices and all proceedings in the courts shall be kept and had in conformity to this regulation." See, *e.g.,* Shaw, Savill, Albion & Co. Ltd. v. The Fredericksburg, 189 F.2d 952 (2d Cir.1951); International Silk Guild Inc. v. Rogers, 262 F.2d 219 (D.C.Cir.1958). Other courts questioned whether the Coinage Act in fact prohibited entry of a judgment in foreign currency. See Baumlin & Ernst, Ltd. v. Gemini, Ltd., 637 F.2d 238 (4th Cir.1980). When the law concerning money and finance was revised and codified in 1982, the Coinage Act was reenacted without the passage concerning units of account. 96 Stat. 877 at 980, 31 U.S.C. § 5101. The report of the Judiciary Committee indicates that the passage was "omitted as surplus," suggesting that accounts of United States courts must continue to be kept in United States dollars, but that the statute has no bearing on the question whether courts in the United States may give judgments in foreign currencies. See H.R. Rept. No. 97–651, 97th Cong., 2d sess., at 146–47 (1982).

When § 3–107(2) of the Uniform Commercial Code came before the New York legislature, the last sentence, expressly providing for payment in foreign currency of instruments denominated in a foreign currency, was omitted from the

New York version, apparently because the New York Clearing House Association was concerned that its member banks might be required to maintain large amounts of foreign currencies. See Penney, "New York Revisits the Code: Some Variations in the New York Enactment of the Uniform Commercial Code," 62 Colum.L.Rev. 992, 997–98 (1962). In 1987, a New York statute authorized entry of judgments in foreign currency, if the underlying obligation was in that currency, to be converted into U.S. dollars at the rate of exchange prevailing on the date of entry of the judgment. N.Y. Laws 1987, ch. 326, amending N.Y. Judiciary Law § 27. For a decision enforcing a foreign arbitral award partly in United States dollars and partly in pounds sterling, see Waterside Ocean Navigation Co., Inc. v. International Navigation Ltd., 737 F.2d 150 (2d Cir.1984).

2. *"Breach-Date" and "Judgment Date" rules in State and federal courts.* Prior to Erie R. Co. v. Tompkins, 304 U.S. 64, 58 S.Ct. 817, 82 L.Ed. 1188 (1938), federal courts distinguished between obligations that arose in the United States, in which case the date of breach was used for conversion, Hicks v. Guiness, 269 U.S. 71, 46 S.Ct. 46, 70 L.Ed. 168 (1925), and obligations that arose or were to be performed in a foreign state, in which case the date of conversion was the date of filing of the complaint, Deutsche Bank Filiale Nurnberg v. Humphrey, 272 U.S. 517, 47 S.Ct. 166, 71 L.Ed. 383 (1926). State courts did not treat the issue as one of federal law, and tended to follow the so-called "New York rule," under which the date of breach was used for conversion of foreign currency obligations, regardless of where the cause of action arose. Hoppe v. Russo-Asiatic Bank, 235 N.Y. 37, 138 N.E. 497 (1923); Parker v. Hoppe, 257 N.Y. 333, 178 N.E. 550 (1931), *on rehearing,* 258 N.Y. 365, 179 N.E. 770 (1932). Following the *Erie* decision, federal courts exercising diversity jurisdiction have generally applied State law. Compania Engraw Comercial e Industrial, S.A. v. Schenley Distillers Corporation, 181 F.2d 876 (9th Cir.1950); Meinrath v. Singer Co., 87 F.R.D. 422 (S.D.N.Y.1980); Vishipco Line v. Chase Manhattan Bank, N.A. (I), 660 F.2d 854 (2d Cir. 1981), *certiorari denied,* 459 U.S. 976, 103 S.Ct. 313, 74 L.Ed.2d 291 (1982); Competex, S.A. v. LaBow 783 F.2d 333 (2d Cir.1986). Federal courts exercising federal jurisdiction on other bases, including admiralty, have purported to apply federal law, but no uniform rule has developed. *Compare* Shaw, Savill, Albion & Co. v. The Fredericksburg, 189 F.2d 952 (2d Cir.1951), and Paris v. Central Chiclera, 193 F.2d 960 (5th Cir.1952) (judgment date rule applied to foreign cause of action), *with* Bamberger v. Clark, 390 F.2d 485 (D.C.Cir.1968) (breach date rule applied to foreign cause of action).

3. *Currency in which loss occurred.* The rules in this section are applicable whether the claim is one for liquidated or unliquidated damages, and whether the claim is founded in contract, in tort, or on some other basis. In the case of personal injury or death, the relevant currency would ordinarily be the currency in use at the injured person's domicile or habitual residence, see, *e.g.* Hoffman v. Sofaer, [1982] 1 W.L.R. 1350, 1358 (U.K. Q.B.); in the case of damage to property, the relevant currency of

loss would be the currency expended to make repairs, or (if the property is sold in damaged condition) the currency for which the property was sold. In the case of a contract for sale of goods, damages should ordinarily be assessed in the currency in which the price is expressed, except where the injured party was obliged to incur expenses (including mitigation of damages) in some other currency. See, *e.g.*, The Despina R. [1979] A.C. 685 (H.L. (E.)); Shaw, Savill, Albion & Co. Ltd. v. The Fredericksburg, 189 F.2d 952 (2d Cir.1951).

4. *Making injured party whole.* As the cases in Reporters' Note 2 indicate, neither State nor federal courts in the United States have been consistent in their choice of dates for conversion into dollars of obligations stated in foreign currencies. In general, however, courts have endeavored to select the rule that, in a given case, will prevent the loss due to fluctuation of exchange rates from being borne by the injured or non-breaching party. Thus, for instance, in Jamaica Nutrition Holdings, Ltd. v. United Shipping Co., Ltd., 643 F.2d 376 (5th Cir.1981), a cargo owner was required, because of the ship owner's default, to pay for cleaning the pipes of a ship in Jamaica, using Jamaican currency. Subsequently, the Jamaican dollar was devalued relative to the United States dollar. The court ordered the defendant to pay damages equal to the amount expended by plaintiff in acquiring Jamaican currency at the time of the repairs, *i.e.*, the date of breach. In B.V. Bureau Wijsmuller v. United States, 487 F.Supp. 156 (S.D.N.Y. 1979), *affirmed*, 633 F.2d 202 (2d Cir.1980), a Dutch salvor of a United States Navy vessel was permitted an "uplift" in his claim for services, to make up for a decline in the dollar relative to the guilder in the period between the salvage and the judgment, in effect awarding the salvor the judgment date value of his guilder claim. Similarly, in Librairie Hachette, S.A. v. Paris Book Center, Inc., 62 Misc.2d 873, 309 N.Y.S.2d 701 (N.Y.Cty.1970), a United States purchaser had defaulted in paying for books ordered in French francs from a French publisher. Thereafter, the French franc was devalued. The New York court held that the equities favored application of the breach date rule, and ordered the defaulting buyer to pay at the rate applicable when the obligation was due. Subsection (2) is in accord with this result; if in *Librairie Hachette*, the franc had appreciated, this section would call for judgment either in French francs or in dollars converted as of the judgment date. For other cases in which the conversion date was chosen consistently with the principle reflected in Subsection (2), see, *e.g.*, Shaw, Savill, Albion & Co. v. The Fredericksburg, Reporters' Note 3; The Gylfe v. The Trujillo, 209 F.2d 386 (2d Cir.1954); Competex, S.A. v. LaBow, Reporters' Note 2. In *Competex*, plaintiff brought suit in the United States on an English judgment, and the United States court entered judgment for the dollar equivalent of the English judgment on the day it became due. When the pound sterling depreciated thereafter, the debtor sought to discharge his obligation by paying the original judgment in (now depreciated) sterling, but the district court held that the United States judgment could be satisfied only by payment of the full dollar equivalent of the English judgment

on the day it was issued. Had the pound sterling risen in value between the time of the English and the United States judgments, a court prepared to follow this section might have given judgment in sterling (or the dollar equivalent on date of payment); the opinion of the Court of Appeals criticizes that suggestion. 783 F.2d at 336.

5. *Ascertainment of exchange rate.* Ordinarily, when a court in the United States converts a foreign currency obligation into dollars, it applies the exchange rate prevailing at the forum (or at the principal financial center, *i.e.,* New York). When no market for the currency in question existed at the forum on the relevant date, the court may look to the official rate for dollars existing in the state of issue of the currency in question. If there was no such rate or if it did not reflect actual economic conditions, the court may look to any market rate that reasonably reflects economic reality on the relevant date. See Vishipco Line v. Chase Manhattan Bank, N.A. (II), 754 F.2d 452 (2d Cir.1985).

6. *Practice in other states.* The courts of many states whose currencies were unstable over extended periods of time, including Austria, Germany, Italy, and Brazil, have been prepared to grant judgments in foreign currencies. In other states, for instance France and Belgium, judgments must be expressed in the currency of the forum, but courts have authorized conversion as of the date of payment, which is substantially equivalent to judgment in the foreign currency, Comment *d*(iii). See Mann, The Legal Aspect of Money 340 (4th ed. 1982), and sources there cited. In Great Britain, the rule was that judgments could be given only in pounds sterling, see Manners v. Pearson & Son, [1898] 1 Ch. 581 (C.A.); In re United Railways of Havana and Regla Warehouses Ltd., [1961] A.C. 1007, (H.L. (E.)), giving rise to controversies about the date for conversion similar to those in the United States, Reporters' Notes 2 and 4. See, *e.g.,* The Teh Hu, [1970] P. 106. In a series of decisions in the 1970's, culminating in the decision of the House of Lords in Miliangos v. George Frank (Textiles) Ltd., [1976] A.C. 443 (H.L. (E.)), British courts abandoned the "common law" rule, stating that in an age of floating currencies (see Introductory Note to this Chapter), it had "nothing but precedent to commend it." *Id.* at 464. Thus, in a suit for the purchase price of goods sold for Swiss francs, the seller was permitted to recover francs, which gave him "neither more nor less than he bargained for." *Id.* at 466. Experience with the new British rule, which entitles the claimant, in effect, to elect whether he wants the currency of the obligation or the currency of the forum, see Comment *b*, appears to have been favorable. See The Law Commission, Private International Law: Foreign Money Liabilities (Working Paper No. 80, 1981). For the present British rule, incorporating the *Miliangos* decision, see [1985] The Supreme Court Practice, Vol. II, ¶ 724; Practice Direction (Judgment: Foreign Currency), [1976] 1 W.L.R. 83, as amended [1977] 1 W.L.R. 197.

Part IX

REMEDIES FOR VIOLATIONS OF INTERNATIONAL LAW

Introductory Note

Section
901. Redress for Breach of International Law
902. Interstate Claims and Remedies
903. International Court of Justice
904. Interstate Arbitration
905. Unilateral Remedies
906. Private Remedies for Violation of International Law
907. Private Remedies for Violation of International Law: Law of the United States

Introductory Note:

Remedies in international law are not as developed as remedies in the domestic law of most states, but both the principles and the modes of relief are similar. A state that has violated an international obligation is required to terminate the wrongful conduct and, in appropriate cases, to provide restitution, to restore the *status quo ante*, to render specific performance of an undertaking, or to pay compensation. See § 901. Acknowledgment of the violation and an apology are also a common remedy. For most injuries restoration is the preferred remedy, with compensation as an alternative. In case of a violation of an international agreement (§ 301), the injured party may suspend or terminate the agreement or seek specific performance, money damages, or other redress. See § 335 and Comment *e*. For some treaty obligations special remedies may be provided, *e.g.*, withdrawal of equivalent concessions for violations of GATT obligations. See §§ 806(3) and 807(1). In different circumstances different remedies may be pursued simultaneously or successively. Legal and political remedies may be pursued at the same time.

Most disputes involving a claim of violation of international law are resolved by negotiation. The general expectation of states that legal obligations will be observed tends to promote such resolution. If negotiations do not result in a settlement, there may be resort to a third party for assistance, an advisory opinion, or binding decision. Such reference to a third party may be either *ad hoc* or

338

pursuant to prior agreement. The International Court of Justice provides a permanent forum for resolving international disputes between states, but only if the parties agree to submit a particular dispute to the Court or had previously agreed to accept the Court's jurisdiction over a category of disputes that includes the particular dispute. See § 903. Interstate arbitration is common and resembles international adjudication, except that parties to the dispute are free to choose the arbitrators, the procedure, and the law to be applied. See § 904; compare § 487, Reporters' Notes 1–6, for commercial arbitration. In many instances, states prefer to settle their disputes in a political forum rather than by legal processes and in accordance with legal principles, and the international political system provides a variety of procedures for this purpose. See § 902, Comment *d* and Reporters' Note 5.

In some circumstances the victim state is entitled to take some peaceful measures of self-help—to regain what was unlawfully taken, to reduce or repair losses, to terminate relationships, or to retaliate. See § 905. Self-help often promotes negotiation or third-party resolution. The unilateral use of force, however, once common as a remedy for violations of international law, is now prohibited by the Charter of the United Nations except in special circumstances. See § 905, Comment *g*.

Although the international community has no organized criminal law system, collective action against aggression under the aegis of the United Nations or of a regional organization is a possible remedy for that particular violation of international law, and international law requires states to refrain from recognizing territorial gains resulting from such aggression. See § 202(2) and Comment *e*; § 210, Reporters' Note 7. States sometimes respond collectively to other serious violations of international law.

Generally, only the state that is the victim of a breach of an international obligation has standing to make a formal claim or to resort to third-party settlement procedures. Some international obligations, however, are *erga omnes* (to all states), and as to these any state may pursue a remedy. Many obligations under international law benefit private persons, see Part VII, but the principal remedies for violation of these obligations are interstate only; international private remedies for violations of international law are still rare. See §§ 906, 907. Private persons, and sometimes states, may obtain redress for a violation of an international obligation under state law and in state tribunals. *Ibid.* See also §§ 111(2) and 115. Exhaustion of available domestic remedies is often required before a formal international claim may be made. See § 703, Comment *d;* § 902, Comment *k*.

The general principles of remedies are considered in this Part; remedies for particular violations of international law may be found, *e.g.*, in §§ 602 and 604, dealing with the protection of the environment, and §§ 703 and 713, dealing with injuries to private persons.

REPORTERS' NOTES

1. *Bibliography.*

K. Carlston, The Process of International Arbitration (1946).

F. Jeantet, ed., International Courts (1958).

J. Merrils, International Dispute Settlement (1980).

J. Mosler & R. Bernhardt, eds., Judicial Settlement of International Disputes (1974).

S. Rosenne, The Law and Practice of the International Court (1965).

J. Wetter, The International Arbitral Process, Public and Private (1979).

2. *Previous Restatement.* The previous Restatement contained no separate treatment of remedies but dealt with some aspects of this subject in connection with responsibility of states (§§ 200, 202–14) and the effect of violations of international law (§ 3).

§ 901. Redress for Breach of International Law

Under international law, a state that has violated a legal obligation to another state is required to terminate the violation and, ordinarily, to make reparation, including in appropriate circumstances restitution or compensation for loss or injury.

Comment:

a. International obligation to provide redress. This section states the basic principle of the international law of remedies. A state that has violated an international obligation to another state, or to an international organization, has the further obligation to provide redress for the violation. The obligation to provide redress presupposes that there had been an international obligation, that the obligation was violated, and that the violation was not justified or excused under international law.

A state may not be liable for a violation if its act was due to an irresistible force or other event beyond its control (*force majeure*). Other defenses, comparable to those in domestic legal systems generally, such as duress, impossibility, waiver, acquiescence, and perhaps estoppel, may also be applicable to states and their agents. These defenses usually provide full exoneration for the action taken; extenuating circumstances, such as contributory fault, may reduce the extent of liability. That the violation was compelled or authorized by the state's domestic law is not a defense. See § 115, Comment *e*.

In general, the state seeking redress has the burden of proving the existence of an international obligation and its breach; the responding state has the burden of establishing any justification or excuse. As in some domestic legal systems, the burden of proof may shift to the party that has control over the evidence.

Ordinarily, claims for damages require injury, but other forms of redress may be available even if there is no injury, or to prevent an injury. See Introductory Note to this Part and Comment *c* to this section.

b. State interests subject to international remedies. A state may seek redress under international law for any violation of its legal interests, including those concerning its political subdivisions (States, provinces, cantons, or regions), public corporations, or private persons (principally its nationals, but in special circumstances other persons as well, § 902, Comment *j*).

c. Obligation to discontinue violation. The obligation of a state to terminate a violation of international law may include discontinuance, revocation, or cancellation of the act (whether legislative, administrative, or judicial) that caused the violation; abstention from further violation; or performance of an act that the state was obligated but failed to perform. For instance, there is an obligation to repeal a law illegally annexing a foreign territory, to release from jail an illegally arrested foreign ambassador, to stop releasing toxic fumes into another state's territory, and to clean up an oil spill threatening the shores of a neighboring state. There is also an obligation to carry out a treaty undertaking that has not been performed, *e.g.*, to cede a territory, to pay money, to provide landing rights to another state's airline, or to allow access to the sea to a land-locked state.

d. Forms of reparation. All forms of reparation are designed to provide redress for the breach of the international obligation that gave rise to the claim. Ordinarily, emphasis is on forms of redress that will undo the effect of the violation, such as restoration of the *status quo ante*, restitution, or specific performance of an undertaking. For instance, if a foreign embassy has been occupied by a mob, there is an obligation to remove the mob and to return the embassy to its diplomatic staff; there may also be an obligation to pay compensation for the damage to the building and to its contents, and for the injuries and indignities suffered by the embassy's staff. Compensation is a common remedy for monetary damage, Comment *e*, and in some instances compensation may be required even though no monetary damage had occurred. Acknowledgment of a violation and an apology are common forms of redress, sometimes supplemented by compensation. There is variety also in the remedies that may be ordered by a third party to which a claim has been presented for resolution. Principles of international law concerning remedies are not rigid or formalistic and give an international tribunal wide latitude to develop and shape remedies, but the tribunal is usually restricted to measures proposed by the parties.

e. Principle and measure of compensation. Monetary compensation is the usual remedy in cases of economic injury. Compensation ordinarily is limited to the loss directly sustained, but in appropriate circumstances may include also damages for injuries caused indirectly by the wrongful act or omission. For instance, compensation in case of an oil spill may include the cost of clean-up, replacement of the property destroyed, and damages for lost tourist business; compensation for a wrongful seizure of a ship may include cost of repair, seamen's wages paid during the seizure, and lost revenue; compensation for nonpayment of debt may include payment of the principal and interest. When compensation is awarded for an economic loss, interest is generally payable from the date of the injury to the date of payment. When an intergovernmental claim derives from an injury to a private person, the compensation to the state need not be measured by or limited to the loss suffered by the individual, although that loss usually provides a basis for calculating the compensation due to the state. In some circumstances, the remedy for a violation may reflect such elements as malice or the repetitive character of the violation.

REPORTERS' NOTES

1. *International obligation as basis for international redress.* The obligation of a state to make reparation for a violation of international law ordinarily runs to the state injured by the violation, but it may run to a state otherwise entitled to present a claim based on the violation, either because the obligation is *erga omnes,* for example a claim for an injury to the marine environment, or because the obligation runs to all parties of a multilateral agreement, such as a human rights convention. The International Law Commission, in its draft articles concerning responsibility of states, declared that some violations of international obligations are international crimes rather than merely delicts. The Commission defined an international crime as a violation of an international obligation that is "so essential for the protection of fundamental interests of the international community that its breach is recognized as a crime by the international community as a whole."

[1976] 2(2) Y.B.Int'l L.Comm'n 95, 31 U.N. GAOR Supp. No. 10, at 226 (1976). Although the implications of declaring a violation to be an international crime are not indicated, presumably a crime is an offense against the community of states as a whole and the obligation to remedy also runs to all states and may be the subject of a collective response. For the rules governing international responsibility of states, see § 207.

The International Law Commission has also considered "circumstances precluding wrongfulness" and prepared articles concerning consent, legitimate countermeasures, *force majeure* and fortuitous event, extreme distress, state of necessity, and self-defense. For text and comments on these subjects, see [1979] 2(2) Y.B.Int'l L.Comm'n 106–36, [1980] 2(2) *id.* 34–62; 34 U.N. GAOR Supp. No. 10, at 284–369 (1979); 35 U.N. GAOR Supp. No. 10, at 69–135 (1980); for the text of the Commission's other draft articles on responsibility of states, see [1980] 2(2) Y.B.Int'l L.Comm'n 30–34; 35 U.N. GAOR Supp. No. 10, at 59–69 (1980).

The question of estoppel as a bar to a claim arose in two cases before the International Court of Justice. In a case involving an arbitral award by the King of Spain made in 1906, the Court held that the award was valid and that it was no longer open to Nicaragua to challenge its validity, as Nicaragua by express declaration and by conduct had recognized the award as valid; only a dissenting opinion discussed the question of estoppel. Case Concerning the Arbitral Award Made by the King of Spain (Honduras v. Nicaragua), [1960] I.C.J. Rep. 192,

213, 222, 236. When Thailand claimed that a frontier agreement was not binding because it was based on error, the Court held that Thailand was precluded by its subsequent conduct from challenging the validity of the treaty. Temple of Preah Vihear Case (Cambodia v. Thailand), [1962] I.C.J. Rep. 6, 32.

2. *Obligation to discontinue violation.* The obligation to discontinue a violation has sometimes been implemented by an order of a tribunal. For instance, in the *Hostages* case, the International Court of Justice decided that Iran "must immediately take all steps to redress the situation," and in particular "must immediately terminate the unlawful detention" of the diplomatic and consular staff and other United States nationals held hostage in Iran, and "must immediately place in the hands of the protecting Power the premises, property, archives and documents" of the United States Embassy and Consulates in Iran. Case Concerning United States Diplomatic and Consular Staff in Tehran (United States v. Iran), [1980] I.C.J. Rep. 3, 44–45.

3. *Forms of reparation.* The essential principle of international law is "that reparation must, as far as possible, wipe out all the consequences of the illegal act and reestablish the situation which would, in all probability, have existed if that act had not been committed." Chorzów Factory (Indemnity) Case (Germany v. Poland), P.C.I.J., ser. A, No. 17, at 47 (1928). The Court added that this result can be accomplished in several ways: through restitution in kind; or, if this is not possible, through "payment of a sum corresponding to the value which a restitution in kind would

bear"; and "the award, if need be, of damages for loss sustained which would not be covered by restitution in kind or payment in place of it." *Ibid.* A few years later, however, in Central Rhodope Forests Case (Greece v. Bulgaria), 1933, the arbitrator (Undén, Sweden) rejected a request for restitution on the ground that it was hardly likely that the forests were in the same condition in 1933 as when they were seized by Bulgaria in 1918. 2 Whiteman, Damages in International Law 1460, 1483–84 (1937); 3 R.Int'l Arb.Awards 1405, 1432. In the *Temple of Preah Vihear* case, Reporters' Note 1, [1962] I.C.J. Rep. at 36–37, the International Court of Justice ordered Thailand to "restore to Cambodia any objects . . . removed from the Temple or the Temple area by the Thai authorities."

In an arbitration between a state and a private company, Texas Overseas Petroleum Co. v. Libyan Arab Republic (1977), 53 Int'l L.Rep. 389, 507–09, 511 (1979), the arbitrator (Dupuy, France) held that restitution is, "under the principles of international law, the normal sanction for non-performance of contractual obligations and that it is inapplicable only to the extent that restoration of the *status quo ante* is impossible"; called upon Libya "to perform specifically its own obligations"; decided that Libya "is legally bound to perform these contracts and to give them full effect"; and reserved for further proceedings the question what should be done if the award were not implemented. But in the parallel case of B.P. (British Petroleum) v. Libya, the arbitrator (Lagergren, Sweden) rejected the claim that the company be restored to the full enjoyment of its rights, and awarded damages instead (1973), 53 Int'l L.Rep. 297, 356–57. Accord, Libyan American Oil Co. v. Libya (by Mahmassani, Lebanon, 1977), 20 Int'l Leg.Mat. 1, 122–25 (1981) (restitution is inconsistent with "respect due for the sovereignty of the nationalizing state"). See Fatouros, "International Law and the Internationalized Contract," 74 Am.J.Int'l L. 134 (1980); see also § 713, Reporters' Note 8.

4. *Principle and measure of compensation.* The rules relating to compensation for a violation are unclear in a number of respects, such as the calculation of direct and indirect damages, prospective profits, rate of exchange, interest, incidental expenses, and costs connected with the preparation and presentation of the claim. For many decisions dealing with these topics, see 3 Whiteman, Damages in International Law 1765–2031 (1943); for a table summarizing the amounts claimed and awarded in 101 international arbitrations, and by 36 domestic claims commissions, see *id.* at 2068a. For later cases, see 8 Whiteman, Digest of International Law 1143–1216 (1967).

5. *Punitive or exemplary damages.* If a violation is not merely a delict but an international crime, see Reporters' Note 1, punitive damages may be awarded. In fixing the amount of an award, some international tribunals have taken into consideration the seriousness of the offense and included an element of punishment in the award. Borchard, The Diplomatic Protection of Citizens Abroad 419 (1915); see the case of The I'm Alone, 1935, 3 R.Int'l Arb.Awards 1616, 1618 (1949) ("as a material amend in respect of the wrong, the United States should pay the sum of

$25,000" to Canada). For a contrary view, see Judge Parker's opinion in Lusitania Cases (United States v. Germany), 1923, 7 R.Int'l Arb. Awards 32, 38–44 ("counsel has failed to point us to any money award by an international arbitral tribunal where exemplary, punitive, or vindictive damages have been assessed against one sovereign nation in favor of another presenting a claim in behalf of its nationals"). In the United States, the Foreign Sovereign Immunities Act excludes punitive damages against a foreign state, but allows them against an agency or instrumentality of the foreign state. 28 U.S.C. § 1606.

§ 902. Interstate Claims and Remedies

(1) A state may bring a claim against another state for a violation of an international obligation owed to the claimant state or to states generally, either through diplomatic channels or through any procedure to which the two states have agreed.

(2) Under Subsection (1), a state may bring claims, *inter alia*, for violations of international obligations resulting in injury to its nationals or to other persons on whose behalf it is entitled to make a claim under international law.

Comment:

a. Standing to make claims. Ordinarily, claims for violation of an international obligation may be made only by the state to whom the obligation was owed. See § 901, Comment *b* and Reporters' Note 1. When a state has violated an obligation owed to the international community as a whole, any state may bring a claim in accordance with this section without showing that it suffered any particular injury. Thus, any state may call on the violating state to terminate a significant injury to the general environment, § 602, Comment *a*, or pursue a remedy for a denial of human rights in violation of customary international law, § 703(2). Some multilateral international agreements, such as regional human rights agreements, may also give standing to any state party to raise a claim of violation of the agreement without having to show injury to its particular interest.

For the forms of reparation and the principle and measure of monetary compensation, see § 901, Comments *d* and *e* and Reporters' Notes 3–5.

b. Ripeness. Ordinarily, a state may bring a formal claim against another state or resort to available third-party procedures only after a violation has actually occurred, but it can make an informal protest in advance of a violation that it reasonably believes is impending. A claim may be made for a violation even if an injury has not yet been suffered.

c. Lapse of time. No general rule of international law limits the time within which a claim can be made. However, international tribunals have barred claims because of a delay in presentation to the respondent state if the delay was due to the negligence or laches of the claimant state.

d. Means for settling international disputes. Most international disputes are resolved by direct negotiations between the parties. If the parties to the dispute do not maintain diplomatic relations, negotiations may be facilitated by a third state or a high international official (*e.g.*, the Secretary-General of the United Nations). Parties that are members of an international organization may resort to its procedures for settling a dispute. Parties may also agree, *ad hoc* or in advance, to resort to third parties for help in resolving a dispute. See Comment *e*. Third parties may volunteer their assistance in resolving a dispute, and such an offer may not be considered an unfriendly act. A state to which a claim is presented is required to negotiate in good faith to resolve it and to submit the dispute to a claim settlement procedure where it has agreed to do so.

e. Third-party settlement. Dispute settlement by third parties depends on consent of the parties. Such consent may be given expressly by international agreement, *ad hoc* or in advance, or may be implied from submission of pleadings or arguments to an international tribunal without challenging its jurisdiction. Some international agreements require a specified sequence of proceedings; for instance, many agreements providing for conciliation prohibit submission of a dispute to an international tribunal before the conciliation proceeding is completed, unless the parties agree otherwise.

In accepting third-party jurisdiction, the parties to the dispute may authorize the third party to try to settle the claim through good offices, mediation, inquiry, or conciliation; to render an advisory opinion; or to render a decision binding on the parties. The third party may be a state or a group of states, an individual or a group of individuals, a domestic institution, an international court, or an arbitral tribunal.

f. Negotiation as condition to third-party settlement. An international agreement providing for the settlement of a dispute by specified means, such as conciliation, arbitration, or by decision of an international tribunal, often makes resort to such procedures conditional on previous attempt to resolve the matter by negotiation. A failure of a state to respond in good faith to a request for negotiation may itself constitute a breach of an international obligation. If the respondent rejects the claim or refuses to negotiate, or if negotiations have continued for a substantial time without progress, resort to agreed procedures is appropriate.

g. Withdrawal or settlement of claim. A claim may be terminated by withdrawal of the claim, by settlement, or by judgment or award with which the parties have complied. A settlement reached by the parties after the commencement of third-party proceedings usually terminates such proceedings, but a proceeding before an international court cannot be terminated by the parties without leave of the court. See, *e.g.*, International Court of Justice, Rules of Court, Articles 88–89; European Court of Human Rights, Rules of the Court, Rule 47.

h. Ex gratia *relief.* A state charged with a violation of an international obligation may offer an *ex gratia* (voluntary) payment or other relief, without acknowledgment of liability. If the claimant state accepts the offer without reservation, the dispute is resolved; if the claimant state declines to accept the offer in full settlement, or accepts it only on conditions not acceptable to the state that made the offer, the offer of *ex gratia* relief is not to be taken as an admission of liability.

i. State claims deriving from injury to private persons. Like other claims for violation of an international obligation, a state's claim for a violation that caused injury to rights or interests of private persons is a claim of the state and is under the state's control. The state may determine what international remedies to pursue, may abandon the claim, or settle it. The state may merge the claim with other claims with a view to an *en bloc* settlement. The claimant state may set these claims off against claims against it by the respondent state. Any reparation is, in principle, for the violation of the obligation to the state, and any payment made is to the state.

State claims deriving from private injury differ from other interstate claims in some respects. The injured person may disable the state from making the claim by failing to exhaust local remedies, § 713, Comment *b*. The person may waive or settle the claim. (But see § 713, Comment *f*). The person is often consulted or otherwise involved in the claims process. Money damages paid are generally measured, in fact, by the injury to the individual (rather than by the offense to the state), and the state ordinarily pays over to the person the compensation it receives. Some international agreements to resolve claims may give the private person direct access to an international tribunal, *e.g.*, the United States–Iran Claims Tribunal. See § 487, Reporters' Note 6.

A state that makes a claim for a violation of an obligation *erga omnes* can abandon or settle its own claim, but not those of other states or of the community at large. As regards waiver or settlement of a claim by a state for a violation of the human rights of an individual, see § 703, Reporters' Note 2.

j. Nationals and other private persons represented. For the most part, state claims under Subsection (2) are for injury due to violations of the rights of nationals under §§ 711, 712. See § 713. In some circumstances, a state may present a claim on behalf of persons who are not its nationals, such as permanent residents, aliens injured aboard a ship or an airplane of the claimant state, or a foreign corporation or vessel substantially owned by nationals of the claimant state. Under some international agreements and the customary international law of human rights, a state may bring a claim on behalf of any person whose human rights were violated by another state, including a national of the respondent state. See § 703 and Comment *b* and Reporters' Note 4 thereto.

k. Exhaustion of local remedies. Under international law, before a state can make a formal claim on behalf of a private person, Comment *i*, that person must ordinarily exhaust domestic remedies available in the responding state. See § 703, Comment *d*; § 713, Comments *b* and *f*. Local remedies need not be exhausted for violations of international law not involving private persons; a state is not required to seek a remedy for violations of its rights in the courts of the responsible state, even where the state suffered injury to its own interests as a result of a violation of international law that also caused injury to its nationals.

l. International claims under United States law. In the United States, the presentation of claims against foreign governments, including those on behalf of private persons, is the responsibility of the President and the Executive Branch. The President may refuse to present a claim, settle it by negotiation, abandon it, or join it with other claims for *en bloc* resolution; he may also agree to submit the claim for international dispute settlement, whether or not the United States is obligated to do so by international agreement. While some claims settlements have been made by treaty, a majority of them have been by executive agreement, and the authority of the President to make such agreements has been upheld by the Supreme Court. The money received from a foreign government as a result of an international award, or in settlement, belongs to the United States and is placed in the

Miscellaneous Receipts account of the Treasury, but Congress has usually provided for payment to private claimants, especially to those whose claims are settled in accordance with decisions of a special United States claims commission dividing a lump-sum settlement. See § 713, Reporters' Note 9.

REPORTERS' NOTES

1. *Standing to claim.* In South West Africa Cases (Second Phase) (Ethiopia and Liberia v. South Africa), the International Court of Justice rejected the contention that international law recognizes "the equivalent of an *'actio popularis,'* or right resident in any member of a community to take legal action in vindication of a public interest." [1966] I.C.J. Rep. 6, 47. A few years later, however, the Court declared that

> an essential distinction should be drawn between the obligations of a State towards the international community as a whole, and those arising vis-à-vis another State in the field of diplomatic protection. By their very nature the former are the concern of all States. In view of the importance of the rights involved, all States can be held to have a legal interest in their protection; they are obligations *erga omnes.*

Such obligations derive, for example, in contemporary international law, from the outlawing of acts of aggression, and of genocide, as also from the principles and rules concerning the basic rights of the human person, including protection from slavery and racial discrimination. Some of the corresponding rights of protection have entered into the body of general international law [Reservations to the Convention on the Prevention and Punishment of the Crime of Genocide (Advisory Opinion), [1951] I.C.J. Rep. 15, 23]; others are conferred by international instruments of a universal or quasi-universal character.

Case Concerning the Barcelona Traction, Light and Power Co., Ltd. (Belgium v. Spain), [1970] I.C.J. Rep. 3, 32. Some universal and some regional human rights conventions allow any party to the convention to bring before an international commission or court any breach of the convention by another party, provided both parties have accepted an optional clause on the subject. See, *e.g.,* International Convention on the Elimination of All Forms of Racial Discrimination, Arts. 11, 22, 20 U.N. GAOR Supp. No. 14, at 47 (1965), 660 U.N.T.S. 195; European Convention for the Protection of Human Rights and Fundamental Freedoms (1950), Arts. 24 and 48(c), 213 U.N.T.S. 221, 45 Am.J.Int'l L.Supp. 24 (1951).

2. *Lapse of time.* In the George W. Cook case, 1927, the General Claims Commission between United States and Mexico stated that there is "no rule of international law putting a limitation of time on diplomatic action or upon the presentation of an international claim to an international tribunal." 4 R.Int'l Arb.Awards 213, 214. On the other hand, in the Walter H. Faulkner case (1926) before the same Commission, it was noted that interna-

tional "tribunals have in some instances declared that one government should not call upon another government to respond in damages when such action, after a long lapse of time, clearly puts the respondent government in an unfair position in making its defense, particularly in the matter of collecting evidence." Separate opinion of American Commissioner (Nielsen), *id.* 67, at 74. See also Ralston, The Law and Procedure of International Tribunals 375–83 (1926), and Supp. 185–87 (1936).

In the *Ambatielos* case, 1956, the arbitral tribunal did not accept the British contention that the Greek claim ought to be rejected because of undue delay in its presentation. The tribunal endorsed the principle stated by the Institute of International Law in 1925 that it is "left to the unfettered discretion of the international tribunal" to determine the existence of an "undue delay." 12 R.Int'l Arb.Awards 81, 103–104; see 32 Institut de Droit International, Annuaire 558–60 (1925). In Lighthouses Case (France/Greece), 1956, Greece invoked a delay of more than 40 years as barring the French claims, but the tribunal rejected the defense in the circumstances, especially in view of the troubled conditions caused by successive wars between 1912 and 1923. 12 R.Int'l Arb.Awards 161, 186.

3. *Consent to third-party settlement.* "It is well established in international law that no State can, without its consent, be compelled to submit its disputes with other States either to mediation or to arbitration, or to any other kind of pacific settlement." Eastern Carelia, P.C.I.J., ser. B, No. 5, at 27 (1923)

(Advisory Opinion). International claims "cannot, in the present state of the law as to international jurisdiction, be submitted to a tribunal, except with the consent of the States concerned." Reparation for Injuries, [1949] I.C.J.Rep. 174, 177–78 (Advisory Opinion).

The Permanent Court of International Justice held that "the consent of a State to the submission of a dispute to the Court may not only result from an express declaration, but may also be inferred from acts conclusively establishing it," such as "the submission of arguments on the merits, without making reservations in regard to the question of jurisdiction." Rights of Minorities in Upper Silesia (Minority Schools) Case (Germany v. Poland), P.C.I.J., ser. A, No. 15, at 24 (1928). See also the Haya de la Torre Case (Colombia v. Peru), [1951] I.C.J. Rep. 71, 78.

4. *Forms of third-party settlement.* The most common means for the settlement of international disputes are good offices, mediation, commissions of inquiry, and conciliation commissions. See United Nations Charter, Art. 33. While some international agreements draw clear distinctions among these procedures, in practice they are often combined. International organizations also use these procedures, but their mandates to commissions, committees, or individuals often confuse the various functions, especially good offices and mediation.

If relations between parties are severed or strained, they may ask for, or accept, the *good offices* of a third party. The third party may bring them to the negotiating table, induce them to resort to arbitration, or help them to reach a solution on the merits.

A *mediator* tries to reconcile the views and claims of the parties and in appropriate cases makes confidential suggestions for this purpose. Such suggestions have no binding force.

An offer of good offices or mediation "can never be regarded by either of the parties in dispute as an unfriendly act." Convention on the Pacific Settlement of International Disputes, The Hague, 1907, Art. 3(3), T.S. 536, 1 Bevans 577, 586.

The main function of a *commission of inquiry* is to elucidate the facts by means of an impartial and conscientious investigation, which may involve hearing witnesses or a visit to the area where the breach of international obligation is said to have occurred. Such a commission often includes representatives of both parties and sometimes consists solely of such representatives.

A *conciliation commission* examines the claims of the parties and the evidence submitted by them, and makes proposals to them for an amicable settlement. If an agreement is not reached, the commission prepares a report stating its conclusions on all questions of fact or law relevant to the matter in dispute, together with such recommendations as the commission may deem appropriate for an amicable settlement. Neither its conclusions nor its recommendations are binding upon the parties.

5. *Dispute settlement in or by international organization.* An agreement establishing an international organization may empower the organization to deal with disputes between its members and sometimes also with those involving non-members. The United Nations, its specialized agencies, regional organizations, such as the Organization of American States, the Organization of African Unity, and the Council of Europe, and organizations such as the General Agreement on Tariff and Trade (GATT) and the organizations established by various commodity agreements, frequently deal with international disputes by arranging for good offices, mediation, or commissions of inquiry or conciliation. The European Commission of Human Rights considers disputes between states involving human rights violations within the framework of the European Human Rights Convention, and presents reports on them, which are then considered by the Committee of Ministers of the Council of Europe. For a discussion of an interstate proceeding, see *e.g.*, Becket, "The Greek Case Before the European Human Rights Commission," 1 Human Rights 91 (1970).

Under some agreements, the parties are obligated to refer some categories of disputes to a bilateral commission, such as the joint boundary waters commissions between the United States and Canada and between the United States and Mexico.

The Charter of the United Nations authorizes any member state to bring any dispute (even one to which the member state is not a party), or any situation which is likely to endanger the maintenance of international peace and security, to the attention of the Security Council or of the General Assembly. Even a non-member state may bring to the attention of these organs any dispute to which it is a party. United Nations Charter, Art. 35(1) and

(2). The Security Council may recommend appropriate procedures or methods of adjustment, or may recommend such terms of settlement as it considers appropriate. *Id.*, Arts. 36(1) and 37(2). The General Assembly "may recommend measures for the peaceful adjustment of any situation, regardless of origin which it deems likely to impair the general welfare or friendly relations among nations." *Id.*, Art. 14. Many disputes have been submitted to the Security Council and the General Assembly under these provisions, and a solution acceptable to the parties was found in a number of them. For a comprehensive list of measures taken by the Security Council in the 41 disputes submitted to it between January 1970 and December 1978, see Repertory of Practice of United Nations Organs, Supp. No. 5, Vol. II, at 20–33 (U.N. Pub. Sales No. E.85.V.8) (1986).

Under some regional agreements, there is an obligation to resort to regional bodies or procedures prior to bringing the matter before the United Nations. For instance, the Charter of the Organization of American States provides that "[a]ll international disputes that may arise between American States shall be submitted to the peaceful procedures set forth in the Charter, before being referred to the Security Council of the United Nations." Original 1948 text, Art. 20, 2 U.S.T. 2394, T.I.A.S. No. 2361, 119 U.N.T.S. 3; revised 1967 text, Art. 23, 21 U.S.T. 607, T.I.A.S. No. 6847. (As of 1986, this Charter was in force for 32 states, including the United States.) Members of the United Nations that are parties to regional arrangements are obligated to make every effort to achieve pacific settlement of local disputes through such regional arrangements before referring them to the Security Council, but any dispute likely to endanger the maintenance of peace and security may be referred directly to the United Nations. United Nations Charter, Art. 52(2) and (4).

Some international agreements empower an organization to render binding decisions, *e.g.*, United Nations Charter, Arts. 25, 39, 41, 42 (Security Council decisions may not, however, impose a settlement of a dispute). See also Articles of Agreement of the International Monetary Fund, Second Amendment, 1976, Art. 29, 29 U.S.T. 2203, T.I.A.S. No. 8937, entered into force for the United States in 1978; Articles of Agreement of the International Bank for Reconstruction and Development (World Bank), 1945, Art. 9, T.I.A.S. No. 1502, 3 Bevans 1390, 2 U.N.T.S. 134; Convention on International Civil Aviation, 1944, Art. 84, 3 Bevans 944. Other agreements provide for non-binding reports by special committees or working parties (*e.g.*, the General Agreement on Tariff and Trade, Arts. 22 and 23), or for arbitration (*e.g.*, the Convention of the World Meteorological Organization, 1947, Art. 29, 1 U.S.T. 281, T.I.A.S. No. 2052, 77 U.N.T.S. 143; as of 1987, the United States and 159 other states were parties). See Hudec, "GATT Dispute Settlement After the Tokyo Round: An Unfinished Business," 13 Cornell Int'l L.J. 145 (1980); Sohn, "Settlement of Disputes Relating to the Interpretation and Application of Treaties," Hague Academy, 150 Recueil des Cours 195, at 264–66 (1976).

6. *Negotiation as condition to third-party settlement.* According to the Permanent Court of Interna-

tional Justice, the obligation to negotiate is "not only to enter into negotiations, but also to pursue them as far as possible, with a view to concluding agreements," although it is not necessarily an obligation to reach an agreement. Railway Traffic between Lithuania and Poland, P.C.I.J., ser. A/B, No. 42, at 108, 116 (1931) (Advisory Opinion). The International Court of Justice also pointed out that "the parties are under an obligation to enter into negotiations with a view to arriving at an agreement . . . ; they are under an obligation so to conduct themselves that the negotiations are meaningful, which will not be the case when either of them insists upon its own position without contemplating any modification of it." North Sea Continental Shelf Cases (Fed. Rep. of Germany/Denmark and the Netherlands), [1969] I.C.J. Rep. 3, at 47.

Many international agreements require negotiation or consultation prior to resort to more institutionalized procedures for the settlement of disputes. In particular, many international agreements relating to the pacific settlement of disputes provide that other means of settlement can be resorted to only with respect to disputes "which it has not been possible to settle by diplomacy." See, e.g., the Geneva General Act for the Pacific Settlement of International Disputes, 1928, Art. 1, 93 L.N.T.S. 345, which provides for conciliation, arbitration, and judicial settlement of all disputes (as of 1986, it had been acceded to by 22 states, but some of these had denounced it; the United States was not a party); and the Revised General Act for the Pacific Settlement of International Disputes, 1949, Art. 1, 71 U.N.T.S. 101, which adapted

the 1928 Act to the United Nations system (as of 1986 it had been acceded to by seven states, but the United States was not a party). For a list of other such treaties containing this requirement, see United Nations, Systematic Survey of Treaties for the Pacific Settlement of International Disputes, 1928–1948, at 13–23 (1949); for a list of 20 pre-World War II United States conciliation treaties, resort to which is conditional on failure of "ordinary diplomatic proceedings," see id. at 21–22.

Whether a negotiation has become futile or whether all means have been exhausted is not easy to determine. The Permanent Court of International Justice said that "the question of the importance and chances of diplomatic negotiations is essentially a relative one." Negotiations "do not of necessity always presuppose a more or less lengthy series of notes and despatches; it may suffice that a discussion has been commenced, and . . . a deadlock is reached, or if finally a point is reached at which one of the Parties definitely declares himself unable, or refuses, to give way." Mavrommatis Palestine Concessions Case (Greece v. U.K.), P.C.I.J., ser. A, No. 2, at 13 (1924); quoted with approval in South West Africa Cases (Preliminary Objections) (Ethiopia and Liberia v. South Africa), [1962] I.C.J. Rep. 319, 345.

7. *Dispute as prerequisite to resort to settlement procedures.* Before resorting to some settlement procedures, the claimant state must prove the existence of an "international dispute," but ordinarily such proof is not difficult. The Permanent Court of International Justice defined a dispute broadly as "a disa-

greement on a point of law or fact, a conflict of legal views or of interests between two persons" or states. Mavrommatis Palestine Concessions, Reporters' Note 6, at 11–12. See also German Interests in Polish Upper Silesia (Jurisdiction) (Germany v. Poland), P.C.I.J., ser. A, No. 6, at 14 (1925). See § 903, Reporters' Note 5.

8. *International claims practice of the United States.* The United States has a long tradition of settling international claims by negotiation or international arbitration. Some claims implicated national interests directly, such as boundary disputes; some claims by the United States were for injury to private interests of its nationals. See Comment *i* and § 713. Sometimes a single dispute was settled or arbitrated, sometimes several disputes were combined; sometimes a dispute involved large numbers of claims, usually private claims. Thus, in 1794, the United States and Great Britain referred to a mixed commission more than 500 claims relating to maritime seizures. 1 Moore, History and Digest of International Arbitrations 299–349 (1898). The United States-Mexican Commission established in 1868 disposed of some 2,000 claims. 2 *id.* at 1287–1359. Two United States-Mexico claims commissions were established in 1923 to deal with more than 6,000 claims, mostly by the United States against Mexico, and a few by Mexico against the United States. See Feller, The Mexican Claims Commissions, 1923–34 (1935). Under the Algiers Declaration of 1981, 20 Int'l Leg.Mat. 230 (1981), more than 3,000 claims were submitted to an Iran-United States Claims Tribunal, most of them by United States nationals against Iran, some by Iranians against the United States, and some claims were between the two governments. See § 487, Reporters' Note 6. See generally, Lillich, ed., The Iran-United States Claims Tribunal (1984).

Matters affecting the national interest directly are generally resolved or submitted to international arbitration by treaty made with the consent of the United States Senate; most agreements settling claims of nationals have been made by executive agreement. The validity of such executive agreements was upheld in United States v. Belmont, 301 U.S. 324, 57 S.Ct. 758, 81 L.Ed. 1134 (1937), and United States v. Pink, 315 U.S. 203, 62 S.Ct. 552, 86 L.Ed. 796 (1942). See also Ozanic v. United States, 188 F.2d 228, 231 (2d Cir.1951); Shanghai Power Co. v. United States, 4 Ct.Cl. 237, 244, 247 (1983). Presidential action in the case of Iran was sustained in *Dames and Moore v. Regan,* 453 U.S. 654, 101 S.Ct. 2972, 69 L.Ed.2d 918 (1981), § 721, Reporters' Note 8. As the Supreme Court noted in *Dames and Moore,* Congress has generally acquiesced in this exercise of presidential power. In 1974, however, Congress found a proposed agreement with Czechoslovakia unacceptable and adopted the Gravel Amendment to the Trade Act of 1974 (88 Stat. 1978, § 408), requesting that the agreement be renegotiated and submitted to Congress as part of any agreement entered under that Act; gold belonging to Czechoslovakia was not to be released to that country. For difficulties which arose as a result of that legislation, see [1974] Digest of U.S. Practice in Int'l L. 422–25; [1976] *id.* 439–41; [1977] *id.* 695–98; [1978] *id.* 1220–26.

The Department of State is authorized to pay any small (less than $15,000) "meritorious claim" against the United States presented by a foreign government. 22 U.S.C. § 2669(b). See also 22 U.S.C. § 2669(f), 28 U.S.C. § 2672 and 31 U.S.C. § 3725.

For United States practice in respect of claims for injury to United States nationals, see § 713, Reporters' Note 8.

9. *Previous Restatement.* The previous Restatement dealt with remedies in the special context of responsibility of states for injuries to aliens, §§ 164–214. Compare this Restatement, § 713.

§ 903. International Court of Justice

(1) A state party to a dispute with another state may submit that dispute to the International Court of Justice for adjudication, and the Court has jurisdiction over that dispute, if the parties:

(a) have, by a special agreement (*compromis*) or otherwise, agreed to bring that dispute before the Court; or

(b) are bound by an agreement providing for the submission to the Court of a category of disputes that includes the dispute in question; or

(c) have made declarations under Article 36(2) of the Statute of the Court accepting the jurisdiction of the Court generally or in respect of a category of legal disputes that includes the dispute in question.

(2) The Court may render an advisory opinion at the request of:

(a) the General Assembly or the Security Council on any legal question; or

(b) other organs and specialized agencies of the United Nations, authorized by the General Assembly to request such an opinion, on legal questions arising within the scope of their activities.

(3) The Court has authority to determine whether it has jurisdiction to decide a dispute submitted to it, or whether to issue an advisory opinion requested of it.

Comment:

a. Jurisdiction of International Court of Justice. The Court has two kinds of jurisdiction: to decide contentious cases between parties and to render advisory opinions. Only a state may be a party to a contentious case before the Court, not an international organization or a private person. I.C.J. Statute, Article 34(1). Only a state party to the Court's Statute can be a party to a case before the Court. Article 35(1). All states members of the United Nations are automatically parties to the Statute, as are a few non-members, such as Switzerland, pursuant to Article 93 of the United Nations Charter. The Court is open to a state not party to the Statute under conditions prescribed by the Security Council. I.C.J. Statute, Article 35(2); [1985–86] I.C.J. Y.B. 45–48. See Reporters' Note 2.

The jurisdiction of the Court in contentious cases is based on consent of the parties, either express or implied. Compare § 902, Comment *e* and Reporters' Note 3. Under Article 36(1) of the Statute, consent may be given *ad hoc*, or by prior agreement, for example by provision in an international agreement giving the Court jurisdiction over a dispute between parties to that agreement as to its interpretation or application. Subsections (1)(a) and (b). Contentious cases may be brought also under the compulsory jurisdiction of the Court between states that have made declarations under Article 36(2) of the Statute. Subsection (1)(c), see also Comment *b*. Although the jurisdiction of the Court is based on the consent of the parties, they cannot terminate a proceeding before the Court without its consent.

By accepting the Statute of the Court, states accept also its incidental jurisdiction, *i.e.*, its authority to decide whether the Court has jurisdiction with respect to a particular case, Subsection (3) of this section and Article 36(6) of the Statute; to indicate (*indiquer*) provisional measures to preserve the rights of the parties, Article 41; to construe a judgment in the event of a dispute as to its meaning, Article 60; to revise a judgment upon discovery of a decisive fact, Article 61; and to allow a third party to intervene, Article 62.

For the jurisdiction of the Court to give advisory opinions, Subsection (2), see Comment *h*.

b. Compulsory jurisdiction under Article 36(2). Under the Statute of the Court, a state may declare that it recognizes as compulsory the jurisdiction of the Court with respect to all legal disputes concerning the interpretation of a treaty, any question of international law, the existence of any fact constituting a breach of an international obligation, or the nature or extent of the reparation for such a breach. Such a declaration by a state applies only in relation to another state that has made a similar declaration. A declaration may accept the jurisdiction of the court for all legal disputes, or may exclude certain categories of disputes. A declaration is, however, subject to reciprocity, and a defendant state against which a proceeding is brought may invoke an exclusion or other reservation not stipulated in its own declaration but included in the declaration of the plaintiff state. A declaration may be of indefinite duration, or for a limited time only. A declaration for a given time is binding for the period indicated. A declaration of indefinite duration may be cancelled at any time but is binding in respect of any proceeding brought before cancellation.

c. *The United States and the International Court of Justice.* By becoming a member of the United Nations, the United States became *ipso facto* a party to the Statute of the Court. See Comment *a.* In 1946, the United States accepted the jurisdiction of the Court under Article 36(2) of the Statute of the Court by a special declaration. That declaration reserved the right of cancellation on six months' notice. In October 1985, the United States gave notice of cancellation and the United States declaration was thereby terminated in April 1986. See Reporters' Note 3.

The United States declaration applied only to cases brought under Article 36(2) of the Statute. The United States has accepted the jurisdiction of the Court under Article 36(1) in numerous bilateral and multilateral agreements, in which the United States has agreed that any party may submit a dispute arising under the treaty to the Court. See Comment *a.* The termination of the declaration under Article 36(2) does not affect the jurisdiction of the Court based on such a provision in a bilateral or multilateral agreement.

d. *Legal disputes.* The jurisdiction of the Court, pursuant to the declarations made under Article 36(2) of the Court's Statute (Subsection (1)(c)), is expressly limited to "legal disputes." No such limitation appears in respect of the Court's jurisdiction under Article 36(1). Cases brought pursuant to prior agreement (Subsection (1)(b)) generally involve legal disputes as to the interpretation or application of an international agreement. But the Court may accept a case submitted to it by the parties even though it involves a political rather than a legal dispute. In such a case the Court is in effect asked to decide the case *ex aequo et bono.* See Article 38(2) of the Court's Statute. Under that article, the Court may decide even a legal dispute *ex aequo et bono,* rather than according to international legal principles, if the parties agree. See Reporters' Note 9.

e. *Provisional measures.* If the Court considers that circumstances so require, it may "indicate" any provisional measures for the parties to take in order to preserve their respective rights.

I.C.J. Statute, Article 41. Such measures may be indicated by the Court either at the request of a party or on the Court's own initiative. The Court may indicate measures other than those requested, including measures to be taken by the requesting party. I.C.J. Rules of Court, Articles 73–75. The Court usually asks both parties to avoid any action that may aggravate the tension between them or render the dispute more difficult to resolve. The Court has not ruled whether an order "indicating" provisional measures is mandatory on the parties. It is not clear what effect the failure of a state to comply with provisional measures has on the decision in the principal case.

f. Declaratory judgments. In submitting a case to the Court, the parties may agree that the Court should issue only a declaratory judgment and award no relief. In any contentious case, the Court may also, of its own accord, limit the decision to a declaration that a violation has occurred.

g. Enforcement of judgments. Judgments of the Court are binding between the parties. I.C.J. Statute, Article 59. Under Article 94(1) of the Charter of the United Nations, all members of the United Nations have undertaken to comply with a judgment of the Court in any case to which they are parties. If any party fails to comply with the judgment of the Court, any other party may call on the Security Council to enforce the judgment. The Council may, if it deems it necessary, make recommendations or decide upon measures (such as economic measures provided for in Article 41 of the Charter) to give effect to the judgment. Article 94(2). Members of the United Nations have agreed to accept and carry out any such decision of the Council. Article 25. Whether provisional measures, Comment *e*, are enforceable by the Security Council has not been determined.

h. Advisory jurisdiction. The General Assembly and the Security Council of the United Nations are authorized to request the International Court of Justice to give an advisory opinion on "any legal question." United Nations Charter, Article 96(1). In addition, the General Assembly may authorize any other organ of the United Nations and any specialized agency to request advisory opinions of the Court on "any legal questions arising within the scope of their activities." Article 96(2). Parties to a dispute may agree that an advisory opinion of the Court will be binding on them.

REPORTERS' NOTES

1. *Statute of International Court of Justice.* The Statute of the Court is annexed to the Charter of the United Nations and forms an integral part of it. United Nations Charter, Art. 92. The Statute of

the Court is based on the statute of its predecessor, the Permanent Court of International Justice (*id.*) and differs from it only slightly. The Court has frequently followed the precedents established by its predecessor. (The United States was not a party to the Permanent Court. See Hudson, The World Court, 1921–1938, pp. 237–321 (1938).)

The Court consists of 15 independent judges, no two of whom may be nationals of the same state. I.C.J. Statute, Art. 3(1). Judges are elected, at separate meetings held simultaneously, by the General Assembly and the Security Council of the United Nations by an absolute majority of votes of each body. The voting in the Security Council is not subject to the veto that applies with respect to other substantive issues. *Id.* Arts. 4, 8, and 10. The members of the Court are elected for nine years and may be re-elected. The elections are held in rotation, with five judges elected every three years. *Id.* Art. 13. A member elected to fill a vacancy holds office only for the remainder of his predecessor's term. *Id.* Art. 15.

The Court decides cases either by a full bench or in a chamber of three or more judges established to deal with a particular case or category of cases. There is also a chamber of summary procedure, composed of five judges, designed for speedy dispatch of business. *Id.* Arts. 25–29.

All questions are decided by a majority of the judges present. In case of a tie vote, the President of the Court has a casting vote, *id.* Art. 55. This happened in South West Africa Cases (Second Phase) (Ethiopia and Liberia v. South Africa), [1966] I.C.J. Rep. 6, 51.

2. *Access to and jurisdiction of the International Court.* States members of the United Nations are automatically parties to the Court's Statute. States not members of the United Nations may become parties to the Statute of the Court by accepting both the Statute and the obligations of a member state under Article 94 of the Charter of the United Nations concerning compliance with, and enforcement of, the judgments of the Court. Art. 93(2) of the Statute of the Court, as implemented by G.A. Res. 91(I), U.N. Doc. A/64/Add 1, at 182 (1947). Switzerland, Liechtenstein, and San Marino have deposited such instruments of acceptance. [1985–86] I.C. J. Y.B. 45–46. Without becoming a party to the Statute, a state may by special declaration accept the obligations of the Statute and of Article 94 of the Charter, either in respect of a particular dispute or with respect to all or some future disputes. Art. 35(2) of the Statute of the Court, as implemented by S.C.Res. 9 (1946). Several states did so prior to becoming members of the United Nations, but their declarations expired upon their admission to membership. [1985–86] I.C.J. Y.B. 46–48.

International organizations may not bring a contentious case before the Court, but the Court may ask them to present information to the Court relevant to cases before it, or they may present such information to the Court on their own initiative (an international version of an amicus brief). This may be done, in particular, whenever the construction of the constituent instrument of an international organization, or of an international convention adopted pursuant to that instrument, is in question before the Court. I.C.J. Statute, Art. 34(2) and (3). As to requests, by international organizations for advisory opinions, see Reporters' Note 12.

Article 36(1) of the Statute of the Court confers jurisdiction on the Court with respect to "all cases which the parties refer to it."

The consent of the parties to the jurisdiction of the Court need not be expressed in advance or in any particular form. See Corfu Channel Case (United Kingdom v. Albania), [1948] I.C.J. Rep. 15, 27. When a party to a dispute submits a case to the Court, the other party, though it had not previously accepted the Court's jurisdiction, may accept it for that proceeding, either explicitly or by responding on the merits without raising a jurisdictional objection. Jurisdiction as *forum prorogatum* requires some conduct or statement by the respondent state "which involves an element of consent regarding the jurisdiction of the Court." Anglo-Iranian Oil Co. Case (United Kingdom v. Iran), [1952] I.C.J. Rep. 93, 114. In that case, the Court held that it had no jurisdiction since the government of Iran had consistently denied the Court's jurisdiction. In the Corfu Channel Case, the Albanian Government, while denying the right of the United Kingdom to bring the case to the Court by unilateral application, sent a letter to the Court announcing that, notwithstanding the irregularity of the United Kingdom action, Albania was prepared to appear before the Court, but that "its acceptance of the Court's jurisdiction for this case cannot constitute a precedent for the future." *Supra,* at 18–

19. The Court held that this letter constituted a "a voluntary and indisputable acceptance of the Court's jurisdiction." *Id.* at 27. In another case, the Court held that, as all "the questions submitted to it have been argued by them on the merits, and no objection has been made to a decision on the merits," the parties' conduct was sufficient to confer jurisdiction on the Court. Haya de la Torre Case (Colombia v. Peru), [1951] I.C.J. Rep. 71, 78. For a discussion of the Court's jurisprudence on *forum prorogatum,* see H. Lauterpacht, The Development of International Law by the International Court 103–107 (1958).

Many states have consented to the jurisdiction of the Court by becoming parties (i) to bilateral or multilateral agreements for the peaceful settlement of disputes that provide for the submission to the Court of any legal disputes arising between them, or (ii) to agreements on particular subjects containing a provision for reference to the Court of any dispute between the parties relating to the interpretation of application of the agreement. There are some 250 such agreements. See [1985–86] I.C.J. Y.B. 54–59, 93–109. In addition, many agreements which originally conferred jurisdiction on the Permanent Court of International Justice are still in force, and any dispute arising under them may, pursuant to Article 37 of the Statute of the International Court of Justice, be referred to that Court. While parties sometimes refer cases to the Court by *ad hoc* agreement, most cases are brought before the Court under bilateral and multilateral agreements, either those transferred from the predecessor Court or those concluded since 1945.

As of 1986, 57 states had made declarations under Article 36(2) of the Statute of the Court accepting compulsory jurisdiction of the Court; 11 of these declarations have expired or have been terminated. Forty-six declarations are in force; 44 by members of the United Nations, and two by non-members (Liechtenstein and Switzerland). Declarations in effect are by states of Western Europe, the Americas, Africa, Asia, and the Pacific; there are no declarations by states of Eastern Europe. Several of the declarations antedate the International Court of Justice and originally conferred jurisdiction on the Permanent Court of International Justice, but under Article 36(5) of the Statute of the International Court of Justice such declarations are deemed to be acceptances of the jurisdiction of the successor Court.

Some of the declarations are without limit of time; others are for a specific period (usually five or ten years), in many instances with an automatic renewal clause. Many declarations reserve the right to terminate by a notice of withdrawal effective upon receipt by the Secretary-General of the United Nations. Some declarations specify that they apply only to disputes arising after the declaration was made or concerning situations or facts subsequent to a specified date. Seventeen declarations are without any reservation; the remaining declarations are accompanied by a variety of reservations. Many states have modified their reservations, some of them several times.

The most common reservation excludes disputes committed by the parties to other tribunals or which the parties have agreed to settle by other means of settlement. Another common reservation excludes disputes relating to matters that are "exclusively" or "essentially" within the domestic jurisdiction of the declarant state; some of these reservations provide in addition that the question whether a dispute is essentially within the domestic jurisdiction is to be determined by the declaring state (a so-called "self-judging" clause). Several declarations exclude disputes arising under a multilateral treaty "unless all parties to the treaty affected by the decision are also parties to the case before the Court" or, more broadly, "unless all parties to the treaty are also parties to the case before the Court." Some reservations exclude disputes as to a particular subject, such as territorial or maritime boundaries or other law of the sea issues.

A few declarations, using various formulas, exclude disputes arising out of hostilities to which the declarant state is a party; the most comprehensive of these reservations is that of India which excludes "disputes relating to or connected with facts or situations of hostilities, armed conflicts, individual or collective actions taken in self-defense, resistance to aggression, fulfillment of obligations imposed by international bodies, and other similar or related acts, measures or situations in which India is, has been or may in future be involved." A reservation of the United Kingdom made in 1957 excluded disputes "relating to any question which, in the opinion of the Government of the United Kingdom, affects the national security of the United Kingdom or of any of its dependent territories"; this clause was restricted in the United Kingdom's 1958 declaration to certain past disputes and was omitted in its 1963 declaration.

An increasing number of states have added to their declarations clauses designed to avoid surprise suits by states that accept the Court's jurisdiction and immediately bring a case against another state. For instance, some states have excluded any dispute that was brought before the Court by a party to a dispute less than 12 months after the party had accepted the jurisdiction of the Court with respect to that category of disputes. Many states have reserved the right to modify or terminate a declaration peremptorily by means of a notification to the Secretary-General of the United Nations, with effect from the moment of that notification.

In 27 contentious cases (as of 1986), objections were raised as to the Court's jurisdiction or the admissibility of an application; the Court dismissed almost half of these cases. A few cases were terminated by the Court when it was informed that the defendant had not previously accepted the Court's jurisdiction and was not willing to accept it *ad hoc* for the particular case. Several cases were discontinued by agreement between the parties. See [1985–86] I.C.J. Y.B. 48, 50, 123, 124.

3. *The United States and the International Court of Justice.* In 1946, the United States made a declaration under Article 36(2) of the Statute of the Court, accepting the Court's jurisdiction but excluding:

(a) disputes the solution of which the parties shall entrust to other tribunals by virtue of agreements already in existence or which may be concluded in the future;

(b) disputes with regard to matters which are essentially within the domestic jurisdiction of the United States of America as determined by the United States of America; and

(c) disputes arising under a multilateral treaty, unless (1) all parties to the treaty affected by the decision are also parties to the case before the Court, or (2) the United States of America specially agrees to jurisdiction.

These reservations applied only to the Court's jurisdiction pursuant to Article 36(2). They did not apply to a suit that was within the Court's jurisdiction under Article 36(1) of the Court's Statute and was brought pursuant to an international agreement in which the United States agreed to the jurisdiction of the Court with respect to any dispute relating to the interpretation or application of that agreement (See Coment *c*). According to a report of the Senate Committee on Foreign Relations regarding the 1958 Law of the Sea Convention, 86th Cong., 2d sess., Exec. Rep. No. 5, at 9, the acceptance of such a provision "means that with respect to subjects covered by these conventions the United States would not attempt to reserve to itself the right to determine whether or not a matter lay within the domestic jurisdiction of the United States." Such a provision is common in United States treaties of friendship, commerce, and navigation, and in several constitutions of international organizations of which the United States is a member, as well as in various multilateral treaties accepted by the United States. For instance, by the 1961 Protocol to the Vienna Convention on Diplomatic

Relations, the United States and about 50 other states agreed to the jurisdiction of the Court for all disputes arising out of the interpretation or application of that Convention. 23 U.S.T. 3374, T.I.A.S. No. 7502, 500 U.N.T.S. 241. That Protocol provided jurisdiction for the Court in the case brought by the United States relating to the U.S. Diplomatic and Consular Staff in Tehran (United States v. Iran), [1980] I.C.J. Rep. 3. For a list of multipartite treaties containing such provisions to which the United States is party, see Sen. Comm. on Foreign Relations, International Convention on the Prevention of the Crime of Genocide, S. Exec. Rep. No. 98–50, 98th Cong. 2d sess., at 37–41 (1984); see also 106 Cong. Rec. 11194 (1960). In consenting to the ratification of the Genocide Convention the United States Senate required a reservation to the clause accepting the jurisdiction of the Court for disputes under the Convention. 132 Cong. Rec. S1377 (1986).

—*Domestic jurisdiction reservation.* Paragraph (b) of the United States declaration (including the self-judging clause, the so-called Connally Amendment) did not reflect reluctance to submit to the jurisdiction of the Court generally, but fear that the Court might be persuaded to assert jurisdiction over certain questions that were essentially within the domestic jurisdiction of the United States, such as the issues that might arise under United States immigration or tariff laws or with respect to the Panama Canal. See the statement by Senator Connally, 92 Cong.Rec. 10624 (1946); see also a series of articles in 40 Am.J.Int'l L. 699–736, 778–81 (1946). In a report to the Senate

Foreign Relations Committee in 1959, the Department of State declared that it

> was the understanding of the Senate when the automatic proviso was adopted that this reservation would never be improperly invoked and that the United States would be bound in good faith to accept the Court's jurisdiction in every case involving matters not essentially within the domestic jurisdiction of the United States. Thus, the United States as a matter of policy would expect to invoke the reservation only in those cases in which the Court itself would probably uphold a plea of domestic jurisdiction if interposed by the United States on the basis of the domestic jurisdiction reservation without the automatic proviso.

12 Whiteman, Digest of International Law 1309 (1971).

The United States did not interpret paragraph (b) as reserving an absolute right to refuse to submit to the jurisdiction of the Court. It was the United States policy, therefore, that the determination whether a matter is essentially within its domestic jurisdiction will be made in good faith. For example, a question of treaty interpretation is not a question "essentially within the domestic jurisdiction of the United States." However, the Department of State interpreted paragraph (b) to mean that, while the reservation should be exercised in good faith, any determination by the United States that a matter was essentially within the domestic jurisdiction of the United States was not reviewable by the Court. Since the declaration was subject to reciprocity, that interpretation applied also when the United States brought a claim against another state and the latter invoked the United States reservation.

In Certain Norwegian Loans Case, the Court allowed Norway to invoke, on the basis of reciprocity, a Connally-type reservation in the French declaration; the French claim was dismissed for want of jurisdiction. [1957] I.C.J. Rep. 9, 27. The United States invoked the reservation in the *Interhandel* case brought against it by Switzerland, but the Court dismissed the case on other grounds. [1959] I.C.J. Rep. 6, 25–26. When the United States brought a claim against Bulgaria arising from the shooting down of an Israeli aircraft carrying several United States nationals, Bulgaria invoked the United States reservation by reciprocity. After first contending that the reservation could not be invoked for matters that were clearly international, and that the Bulgarian objection to the Court's jurisdiction should be rejected as not being *bona fide*, the United States changed its position; it agreed that, while to apply the reservation to such matters was an abuse of the reservation, its invocation by a party was final and binding on the Court. Consequently, the United States withdrew the case. Case Concerning the Aerial Incident of 27 July 1955, [1960] I.C.J. Rep. 146; see Gross, "Bulgaria Invokes the Connally Amendment," 56 Am.J. Int'l L. 357 (1962).

Since a declaration under Article 36 is optional, the declaring state can, subject to the Court's Statute, determine the scope and limits of its acceptance of the Court's jurisdiction. After a declaration is deposited, however, its proper interpretation is a question of international law; later interpretations by the declaring state are entitled to some weight but are not conclusive. Anglo-Iranian Oil Co. Case (United Kingdom v. Iran), [1952] I.C.J. Rep. 93, 106–07. Compare § 325. Since the Court has authority to determine whether it has jurisdiction over a dispute submitted to it (Subsection (3)), it would have to decide whether a particular invocation of the declaration to support or defeat the Court's jurisdiction was in accordance with the proper meaning of the declaration. The Court has not had occasion to consider the State Department's interpretation of "the Connally Amendment," paragraph (b) in the United States Declaration. In Case Concerning Military and Paramilitary Activities in and Against Nicaragua (Nicaragua v. United States), the United States informed the Court that it had decided not to invoke the Connally Amendment at this time, but "without prejudice to the rights of the United States under the proviso in relation to any subsequent pleadings, proceedings, or cases before this Court." [1984] I.C.J. Rep. 392, 422. Nevertheless, in later stages of the case, the United States refrained from invoking this reservation.

—*Multilateral treaty reservation.* This reservation was originally suggested by Senator Vandenberg, and was sometimes called the "Vandenberg Amendment." It excluded disputes "arising under a multilateral treaty," and required that "all parties to the treaty affected by the decision" be parties to the case before the Court. In Nicaragua v. United States, *supra*, as Nicaragua relied in its application on the Charter of the United Nations, the Charter of the Organization of American States, and two other inter-American treaties, the United States contended that the Court had no jurisdiction unless all states parties to these treaties that would be affected by a decision were parties before the Court, and that Nicaragua's three neighbors—Honduras, Costa Rica, and El Salvador—would clearly be affected, "in a legal and practical sense," by adjudication of the claims submitted by Nicaragua. [1984] I.C.J. Rep. 392, 422. The Court pointed out that these three states had made declarations accepting the compulsory jurisdiction of the Court, that once Nicaragua was also bound by that jurisdiction, these states were free to institute proceedings against Nicaragua, or to resort to the incidental procedure for intervention under Articles 62 and 63 of the Court's Statute. *Id.* at 425. The Court held that "the question of what States may be 'affected' by the decision on the merits is not in itself a jurisdictional problem," and that, consequently, the United States objection based on the multilateral treaty reservation "does not possess, in the circumstances of the case, an exclusively preliminary character" and does not constitute an obstacle to further proceedings. *Id.* at 425–26. The Court also noted that in any event the multilateral treaty reservation would not warrant the Court in dismissing the claims of Nicaragua under principles of customary international law, such as those relating to non-use of force, non-intervention, or respect for the independence and territorial integrity of states. Although these principles have been enshrined in multilateral conventions, they continue to be binding as part of customary international law,

"even as regards countries that are parties to such conventions." *Id.* at 424. In its decision on the merits, the Court decided that it could not apply the multilateral treaties invoked by Nicaragua, since El Salvador would be "affected" by the decision of the Court on the lawfulness of resort by the United States to collective self-defense under those treaties; but the Court held that the United States reservation does not bar the application of identical rules of customary international law. [1986] I.C.J. Rep. 14, 36, 38, 95.

—Modification of United States declaration. The United States declaration of 1946 provided that it "shall remain in force for a period of five years and thereafter until the expiration of six months after notice may be given to terminate this declaration." In 1984 the United States, having learned that Nicaragua was about to bring a claim against the United States before the International Court of Justice, deposited with the Secretary-General of the United Nations a declaration stating that:

> . . . the aforesaid declaration shall not apply to disputes with any Central American State or arising out of or related to events in Central America, any of which disputes shall be settled in such manner as the parties to them may agree.

> Notwithstanding the terms of the aforesaid declaration, this provision shall take effect immediately and shall remain in force for two years . . . .

[1984–85] I.C.J. Y.B. 100.

The United States argued that since its new declaration did not terminate but only modified its 1946 declaration, it was not subject to the six-month notice clause; and that the new declaration, therefore, was effective immediately and the Court did not have jurisdiction over the case brought by Nicaragua against the United States. The Court rejected the United States distinction between a modification and a termination of a declaration, and held that the United States notification was intended "to secure a partial and temporary termination" of the United States obligation "to subject itself to the Court's jurisdiction with regard to any application concerning disputes with Central American States." [1984] I.C.J. Rep. 392, 417–18. Even if a state perhaps has the right to terminate a declaration of indefinite duration, the principle of good faith requires a reasonable period of notice, and a period of a few days (in this case from April 6 to 9) would not amount to a "reasonable time." *Id.* at 420.

—Termination of United States declaration. The 1984 modification was to expire in April 1986, but on October 7, 1985, the United States delivered to the Secretary General of the United Nations a note terminating the 1946 declaration, effective six months from the date of delivery. 85 Dep't State Bull. 82 (1985). This termination of the United States declaration under Article 36(2) of the Court's Statute did not affect the jurisdiction of the Court under Article 36(1) over cases as to which the United States accepted jurisdiction by an international agreement. See Comment *c* and Reporters' Note 2.

See generally Damrosch, ed., The International Court of Justice at a Crossroads (1987).

4. *Appellate jurisdiction of the Court.* In addition to its original jurisdiction, the Court also has a limited appellate jurisdiction. For instance, the Convention on International Civil Aviation (1944) provides for appeals to the Court from the decisions of the Council of the International Civil Aviation Organization (ICAO). Art. 84, 3 Bevans 944, 15 U.N.T.S. 295. The International Air Services Transit Agreement (1944) utilizes the same procedure for disputes arising thereunder. See Art. 2(2), 3 Bevans 916, 84 U.N.T.S. 389. When India appealed to the Court from a decision of the ICAO Council in favor of Pakistan, Pakistan contended that the Court had no jurisdiction because India's appeal related to the Council's decision concerning its jurisdiction, not to a final decision on the merits. The Court held that a jurisdictional decision was a "substantive" decision and the appeal could be heard. Appeal Relating to the Jurisdiction of the ICAO Council (India v. Pakistan). [1972] I.C.J. Rep. 46, 52–57.

The Court has also reviewed several judgments of administrative tribunals of international organizations in the exercise of its advisory jurisdiction (Reporters' Note 12). See Judgments of the Administrative Tribunal of the International Labour Organization upon Complaints Made Against UNESCO, [1956] I.C.J. Rep. 77 (Advisory Opinion); Application for Review of Judgment No. 158 of the United Nations Administrative Tribunal, [1973] *id.* 166 (Advisory Opinion); Application for Review of Judgment No. 273 of the United Nations Administrative Tribunal, [1982] *id.* 325 (Advisory Opinion); and Application for Review of Judgment No. 333 of the United Nations Administrative

Tribunal, [1987] *id.* 18 (Advisory Opinion). The last three cases were submitted to the Court by the Committee on Applications for Review of Administrative Tribunal Judgments established especially for that purpose by the General Assembly in 1955. G.A. Res. 957, 10 U.N. GAOR Supp. No. 19, at 30–31; the 1982 case was sent to the Court on request of the United States [1982] I.C.J. Rep. 325, 330.

5. *Requirement of legal dispute.* The jurisdiction of the Court is limited to "disputes," Comment *d.* In Nuclear Tests Cases (Australia and New Zealand v. France), the International Court of Justice stated that "the Court can exercise its jurisdiction in contentious proceedings only when a dispute genuinely exists between the parties." [1974] I.C.J. Rep. 253, 271; 457, 476. The term "dispute" is defined loosely. See § 902, Reporters' Note 7. The Permanent Court of International Justice said that "the manifestation of the existence of the dispute in a specific manner, as for instance by diplomatic negotiations, is not required." The Court added, however, that it "would no doubt be desirable that a State should not proceed to take as serious a step as summoning another State to appear before the Court without having previously, within reasonable limits, endeavoured to make it quite clear that a difference of views is in question which has not been capable of being otherwise overcome." Interpretation of Judgments Nos. 7 and 8 (Factory at Chorzów Case (Germany v. Poland)), P.C.I.J., ser. A, No. 13, at 10–11 (1927). In some cases the Court has rejected a claim on the ground that the claimant did not establish the existence of a dispute. See, *e.g.,* Electricity Company of So-

fia and Bulgaria Case (Belgium v. Bulgaria), P.C.I.J., ser. A/B, No. 77, at 64, 83 (1939). While the jurisdiction of the Court over cases brought pursuant to declarations under Article 36(2) of the Courts Statute (Subsection 1(c)) is limited to "legal disputes," the framers of the Statute rejected a proposal to impose that limitation also on cases submitted by the parties *ad hoc* pursuant to Article 36(1). "[W]hen parties agreed to go before the Court, the Court's jurisdiction should not be limited with respect to the nature of the dispute" 14 Docs.U.N.Conf. on Int'l Org. 204–205, 221–29, 288, 318 (1945).

Except where parties agree to submit a political dispute for decision *ex aequo et bono* (see Reporters' Note 9), the Court may hear only disputes that are essentially legal. This is implied in Article 38(1) of the Statute, which specifies that the function of the Court is "to decide in accordance with international law such disputes as are submitted to it." In Northern Cameroons Case, the Court noted:

There are inherent limitations on the exercise of the judicial function which the Court, as a court of justice, can never ignore. There may thus be an incompatibility between the desires of an applicant, or, indeed, of both parties to a case, on the one hand, and on the other the duty of the Court to maintain its judicial character. The Court itself, and not the parties, must be the guardian of the Court's judicial integrity.

Northern Cameroons Case (Cameroon v. United Kingdom), [1963] I.C.J. Rep. 15, 29. In that case the Court refused to consider the plaintiff's claims since its judgment would have no practical effect on the existing situation and an examination of the merits of the claim would serve no purpose. The Court has not rejected any case on the ground that it involved nonlegal issues. Judges Dillard, Jiménez de Aréchaga, Onyeama and Sir Humphrey Waldock, in their dissenting opinion in Nuclear Tests Cases (Australia and New Zealand v. France), stated that "[n]either in contentious cases nor in requests for advisory opinions has the Permanent Court [of International Justice] or [the International Court of Justice] ever at any time admitted the idea that an intrinsically legal issue could lose its legal character by reasons of political considerations surrounding it." [1974] I.C.J. Rep. 312, 366–67.

In Case Concerning United States Diplomatic and Consular Staff in Tehran, Reporters' Note 3, Iran contended that the conflict between the United States and Iran was not one relating to interpretation and application of treaties but arose from a political "situation containing much more fundamental and more complex elements." The Court pointed out that "legal disputes between sovereign States by their very nature are likely to occur in political contexts, and often form only one element in a wider and long standing political dispute." The Court found unacceptable the view that, "because a legal dispute submitted to the Court is only one aspect of a political dispute, the Court should decline to resolve for the parties the legal questions at issue between them"; it refused to impose such "a far reaching and unwarranted restriction upon the role of the Court in the peaceful solution of international disputes." [1980] I.C.J. Rep.

3, 19–20. The Court rejected a similar objection in the Nicaragua v. United States case. [1984] I.C.J. Rep. 392, 439–40.

6. *Provisional measures.* The Court treats a request for provisional measures of interim protection under Article 41 of its Statute as a matter of urgency. I.C.J., Rules of Court, Article 61. Consequently, the Court has not been willing to postpone ordering such measures until it definitely resolved objections to its jurisdiction; it has indicated interim measures as soon as it has ascertained that plaintiff's claims appear *prima facie* to fall within the Court's jurisdiction. See Nuclear Tests Cases (Australia and New Zealand v. France) (Interim Protection), [1973] I.C.J. Rep. 99, 103; 135, 139–40. In Nicaragua v. United States (Reporters' Note 3), when Nicaragua requested provisional measures, the Court held that in order to "indicate" such measures it did not have to satisfy itself finally that it had jurisdiction on the merits of the case, but only that there appeared to be a *prima facie* basis for the Court's jurisdiction. The Court proceeded to indicate provisional measures but reserved the question of its jurisdiction on the merits for future determination. [1984] I.C.J. Rep. 169, 179, 186.

As of 1986, the Court had considered requests for interim measures of protection in 11 cases; the request was granted, *inter alia*, in Nuclear Tests Cases, *supra*; Nicaragua v. United States, Reporters' Note 3; and Frontier Dispute (Burkina Faso/Mali) (Provisional Measures), [1986] I.C.J. Rep. 3; it was denied, *inter alia*, in Interhandel Case (Switzerland v. United States) (Interim Protection), [1957]

I.C.J. Rep. 105. In most cases the respondents refused to comply with an interim order, usually on the ground that the Court had no jurisdiction over the case. See, *e.g.*, Anglo-Iranian Oil Co. Case (United Kingdom v. Iran) (Interim Protection), [1951] I.C.J. Rep. 89. In that case, the United Kingdom asked the Security Council to call upon Iran to act in conformity with the Court's order, but in view of doubts about the authority of the Council to enforce non-final decisions, the Council decided to postpone the matter until the Court had ruled on its own jurisdiction. United Nations, [1946–51] Repertoire of Practice of the Security Council 235–38 (1951).

The Court usually includes in its interim orders a request that the parties avoid any action that may aggravate the tension between the parties or render the dispute more difficult of solution. See, *e.g.*, Case Concerning United States Diplomatic and Consular Staff in Tehran (United States v. Iran) (Provisional Measures), [1979] I.C.J. Rep. 7, 21. In its later judgment in that case, the Court noted that the attempt by the United States to rescue the hostages through an incursion into the territory of Iran while the Court was deliberating on the judgment was "of a kind calculated to undermine respect for the judicial process in international relations." [1980] I.C.J. Rep. 3, 43.

Another purpose of the provisional measures is to prevent irreparable prejudice to the rights that are the subject of dispute. In Nuclear Tests Cases, *supra*, the Court concluded that possible radioactive fallout from the French tests might cause damage to Australia that would be irreparable. [1973] I.C.J. Rep. 99, 105; 135, 141.

In Case Concerning the Frontier Dispute (Burkina Faso/Mali), when grave incidents took place between the armed forces in the border region between the two countries, each party requested the Chamber of the Court (to which the case was submitted by agreement) to indicate differing provisional measures. The Chamber indicated that both Governments "should withdraw their armed forces" to agreed positions and that failing an agreement on the terms of the troop withdrawal "the Chamber will itself indicate them." [1986] I.C.J. Rep. 3, at 11–12. The parties complied with the request. Report of the I.C.J., 41 U.N. GAOR Supp. No. 4, at 18 (1986).

As the Statute of the Court uses the ambiguous word "indicate" rather than "order" or "determine," there has been uncertainty as to whether the Court's orders indicating provisional measures are binding. The General Acts for the Settlement of International Disputes of 1928 and 1949 (see § 904, Reporters' Note 4) expressly provide that the "parties to the dispute shall be bound to accept" the provisional measures adopted in the Court (or by an arbitral tribunal). Art. 33(1). Opinions of scholars are divided on the subject. The binding character of provisional measures is supported by Fitzmaurice, "The Law and Procedure of the International Court of Justice, 1951–4," 34 Brit. Y.B. Int'l L. 1, 122 (1958) (the "whole logic of the jurisdiction to indicate interim measures entails that, when indicated, they are binding"); Hudson, The Permanent Court of International Justice,

1920–1942, at 426 (1943) ("a State is under an obligation to respect the Court's indication of provisional measures"); Stone, Legal Controls of International Conflict 132 (1959) (Article 41 "represents the only respect in which by mere acceptance of the Statute a State renders itself liable to the imposition of obligations by Court action"). See also Elkind, Interim Protection: A Functional Approach 153–66 (1981), supporting this view, and Dumbauld, Interim Measures of Protection in International Controversies 168–69 (1932), supporting an intermediate view that the Court merely declares "what action is required by international law to safeguard legal rights of the parties"; the parties have the duty "to fulfill their obligations under international law," and it is the law, not the order of the Court, that is binding on them. But see Rosenne, Procedure in the International Court 149–57 (1983) ("these indications are of an advisory character, imposing upon the States to which they are directed no more than an obligation to examine them in good faith"); Schwarzenberger and Brown, A Manual of International Law 204 (6th ed. 1976) ("the effect of such interlocutory order is moral rather than legal"); Sztucki, Interim Measures in the Hague Court 283–84 (1983) (citing a number of authors adhering to the view that interim measures are not binding). See also Reichert, "Provisional Measures in International Litigation: A Comprehensive Bibliography," 19 Int'l Law. 1429 (1985).

7. *Intervention.* The Statute of the Court provides for intervention by a state in a case between other states in two circumstances: a state that considers that "it has an interest of a legal nature which may be affected by the decision in the case" may be permitted by the Court to intervene, Art. 62; a state that is a party to a convention the construction of which is before the Court has the right to intervene in the proceedings, Art. 63. In both circumstances the decision of the Court is binding on the intervening party. In the Permanent Court of International Justice, there was only one case of intervention, by the Government of Poland in the Wimbledon Case, which involved the interpretation of the Peace Treaty of Versailles of 1919. P.C.I.J., ser. A, No. 1 at 11–13 (1923). In 1951, the International Court of Justice allowed Cuba to intervene in the Haya de la Torre Case between Colombia and Peru, which involved the interpretation of the 1928 Havana Convention on Asylum, to which Cuba was a party. [1951] I.C.J. Rep. 71, 76–77. In later cases involving permissive interventions under Article 62, the Court took a more restrictive attitude and refused to grant permission to intervene. See Nuclear Tests Cases, Reporters' Note 3, [1974] I.C.J. Rep. 530, 535 (Fiji's application to intervene lapsed when the proceedings were terminated because the main case "no longer has any object"); Case Concerning the Continental Shelf (Tunisia/Libyan Arab Jamahiriya) (Application of Malta for Permission to Intervene), [1981] I.C.J. Rep. 3, 19 (Malta's interests were no greater than those of other Mediterranean states, and her application was so restricted by various reservations that the decision in the case could not affect any of her legal interests); Case Concerning the Continental Shelf (Libyan Arab Jamahiriya/Malta) (Application of

Italy for Permission to Intervene), [1984] I.C.J. Rep. 3, 18–28 (to permit Italy to intervene would introduce a fresh dispute; Article 62 was not intended as an alternative means of bringing an additional dispute as a case before the Court); Case Concerning Military and Paramilitary Activities in and Against Nicaragua (Nicaragua v. United States) (Declaration of Intervention of the Republic of El Salvador), [1984] I.C.J. Rep. 215, 216 (although El Salvador's declaration invoked Article 63, this declaration addressed the substance of the dispute and was inadmissible at the stage of proceedings relating only to the Court's jurisdiction). Later, in a decision concluding that it had jurisdiction of the case, the Court noted that if Costa Rica, El Salvador, and Honduras should find that "they might be affected by the future decision of the Court" in the case, they would be free to institute proceedings against Nicaragua or resort to the incidental procedures for intervention under Articles 62 and 63 of the Statute. [1984] I.C.J. Rep. 392, 425. No further action was taken by Costa Rica or Honduras, but proceedings against them were instituted by Nicaragua in 1986. 25 Int'l Leg.Mat. 1290, 1293 (1986) (applications by Nicaragua); [1986] I.C.J. Rep. 548, 551 (procedural orders); [1987] *id.* 182 (order recording the discontinuance by Nicaragua of the proceedings against Costa Rica).

8. *Sources of law and Court decisions.* The sources of law to be applied by the Court are specified in Article 38 of the Statute (quoted in § 102, Reporters' Note 1). While Article 59 provides that a "decision of the Court has no binding force except between the parties and in respect of that particular case," the Court's decisions are generally considered authoritative statements of international law. See § 103, Comment *b*; see also § 102, Reporters' Note 1. The Court seldom cites decisions of other tribunals, but it frequently relies on its own prior decisions and advisory opinions and on those of its predecessor, the Permanent Court of International Justice.

9. *Equity and* ex aequo et bono. Under Article 38(2) of the Statute of the Court, the parties may authorize the Court to decide a case *ex aequo et bono, i.e.,* according to what is equitable and good, departing if necessary from existing legal principles. This should be distinguished from application by the Court of the basic principles of equity that are part of customary international law. See § 102, Comment *m*; Sohn, "The Role of Equity in the Jurisprudence of the International Court of Justice," in Mélanges Georges Perrin 303 (1984). As of 1987, there had been no case in which the parties authorized the Court to decide *ex aequo et bono.*

The 1982 Convention on the Law of the Sea provides that the delimitation of maritime boundaries in the exclusive economic zone or on the continental shelf shall be by agreement "in order to achieve an equitable solution." Arts. 74 and 83; see § 517(2) and Comment *c.* In two cases relating to maritime boundaries, the Court was authorized by the parties to apply, and did apply, equitable principles. Continental Shelf Case (Tunisia/Libyan Arab Jamahiriya) [1982] I.C.J. Rep. 18, 21, 58–60 (the Court should "take account of equitable principles and the relevant circumstances which characterize the area"); Continental Shelf Case (Libyan Arab

Jamahiriya/Malta) [1985] I.C.J. Rep. 13, 31, 38–40, 57 ("the delimitation is to be effected in accordance with equitable principles and taking account of all relevant circumstances, so as to arrive at an equitable result").

10. *Declaratory judgments.* In the Corfu Channel Case (United Kingdom v. Albania); the International Court of Justice declared that the action of the British Navy had constituted a violation of Albanian sovereignty. It added that this declaration "is in itself appropriate satisfaction." [1949] I.C.J. Rep. 4, 35. In the Eastern Greenland Case, the Permanent Court of International Justice declared that the 1931 proclamation placing Eastern Greenland under Norwegian sovereignty and later steps taken by the Norwegian Government "constitute a violation of the existing legal situation and are accordingly unlawful and invalid." P.C.I.J. ser. A/B No. 53, at 75 (1933). Two days later Norway revoked the 1931 proclamation. 3 Hudson, World Court Reports 148 (1938). In the North Sea Continental Shelf Cases (Fed. Rep. of Germany/Denmark and the Netherlands), the International Court of Justice was asked to decide what "principles and rules of international law are applicable to the delimitation" of the continental shelf areas in the North Sea. The parties had agreed that they would delimit the shelf as between them pursuant to the decision of the Court, and after the Court established the basic principles, the parties delimited their boundary accordingly. [1969] I.C.J. Rep. 3, 6, 53–54; for the 1971 agreements, see 10 Int'l Leg.Mat. 600–12 (1971). A similar procedure was followed in Continental Shelf Case

(Tunisia/Libyan Arab Jamahiriya) [1982] I.C.J. Rep. 18, 21, 92–94.

11. *Compliance with judgments of the Court.* The judgments of the Court have been generally complied with, but there have been exceptions. For instance, Albania did not comply with the Court's judgment in the Corfu Channel Case (Reporters' Note 10) awarding compensation to the United Kingdom for damage to its warships and the loss of life caused thereby; and Iran failed to comply with the Court's judgment in the United States Diplomatic and Consular Staff in Tehran Case (Reporters' Note 5). In 10 cases submitted to the Court by application of a party to a dispute, the other party failed to appear; when judgment was rendered against it, it refused to comply. For a list of these cases, see [1985–86] I.C.J. Y.B. 124, n. 1.

In the Nicaragua v. United States case, after the Court rejected the arguments of the United States and decided that it had jurisdiction, the United States refused to participate further in the proceedings and reserved "its rights in respect of any decision by the Court regarding Nicaragua's claims." [1986] I.C.J. Rep. 14, 23. The Court declared that this reservation has "no effect on the validity" of its judgment. *Id.* at 23–24. In July 1986, the United States vetoed a resolution of the Security Council calling for compliance with the Court's 1986 judgment in this case. U.N. Docs. S/18250 (1986) and S/PV. 2704 (1986), reprinted in 25 Int. Leg.Mat. 1352–65 (1986). The General Assembly adopted a resolution calling for "full and immediate compliance" with the Court's Judgment. U.N. Doc. A/RES/41/31 (1986).

12. *Advisory opinions.* Under the Court's Statute, some international organizations may request advisory opinions; states have no right to request an advisory opinion or to demand that an international organization do so.

Some international agreements between an international organization and a state provide that disputes relating to the interpretation or application of the agreement shall be submitted to the Court for an advisory opinion, which "shall be accepted as decisive by the parties," See, *e.g.*, Convention on the Privileges and Immunities of the United Nations, 1946, sec. 30, 21 U.S.T. 1418, T.I.A.S. No. 6900, 1 U.N.T.S. 16.

In addition to the General Assembly and the Security Council, four other organs of the United Nations have been authorized by the General Assembly to request advisory opinions: the Economic and Social Council, the Trusteeship Council, the Interim Committee of the General Assembly (which stopped functioning in 1952), and the Committee on Applications for Review of Administrative Tribunal Judgments (which has requested three opinions). Fifteen specialized agencies have also been authorized to request advisory opinions, and three of these (UNESCO, WHO, and IMCO) have made one request each. As to the development of the advisory jurisdiction of the Court, see 2 Rosenne, The Law and Practice of the International Court 651–757 (1965). As of 1986, the Court had rendered 18 advisory opinions. For a list, see [1985–86] I.C.J. Y.B. 51, nn. 3–4, and 52, nn. 1–4.

13. *Jurisprudence of the Court and its predecessor.* The International Court of Justice frequently follows the jurisprudence of its predecessor, the Permanent Court of International Justice. See Reporters' Note 1. In the 65 disputes that came before it, the Permanent Court rendered 32 judgments, 27 advisory opinions, and more than 200 orders. It effected settlement of numerous disputes, each of which was important to the parties and some of which were of wider significance. The matters considered by the Court included several disputes between Poland and Germany and between Poland and Danzig; a number of disputes between other Eastern European countries relating to the interpretation and application of treaties for the protection of minorities; a claim of domestic jurisdiction in the Anglo-French dispute concerning nationality decrees in Tunis and Morocco; boundary disputes between Czechoslovakia and Poland, Iraq and Turkey, and France and Switzerland (concerning the Free Zones); sovereignty over Eastern Greenland (Denmark v. Norway); the attempted customs union between Germany and Austria; jurisdiction of states in cases of collisions at sea; competence of the International Labour Organization with respect to regulation of agricultural labor, women in supervisory positions, and incidental work of employers; restoration of railway traffic between Poland and Lithuania; navigation on the Danube and Oder Rivers and through the Kiel Canal; diversion of water from the River Meuse by Belgium (the first Court decision on the basis of equity); validity of the gold clause in international loans; and various claims involving violations of international law with respect to private persons and the

right of states to present claims on their behalf.

The cases that have come before the International Court of Justice are also impressive. Since the first application was submitted to the Court in 1947, 73 cases had been presented to it by 1986, and by that date the Court had rendered 48 judgments, 18 advisory opinions, and 213 orders (mostly procedural). [1985–86] I.C.J. Y.B. 3. It has rendered several decisions relating to the law of the sea—Norway's maritime boundary, transit of warships through the Corfu Channel, the delimitation of the North Sea continental shelf, fisheries jurisdiction of Iceland, the continental shelf boundaries between Tunisia and Libya and between Libya and Malta, the maritime boundary between Canada and the United States in the Gulf of Maine area, the last a decision by a panel of the Court; it dealt with several territorial disputes—between France and the United Kingdom concerning the Minquiers and Ecrehos islands, the boundary between Honduras and Nicaragua, sovereignty over certain Belgian enclaves in the Netherlands, the ownership of the Temple of Preah Vihear on the Cambodia-Thailand boundary; right of asylum (Colombia-Peru); claims on behalf of stockholders in a foreign company (Barcelona Traction Case); and safety of diplomatic and consular personnel (United States-Iran). The Court's advisory opinions dealt with: the right of the United Nations to present claims on behalf of its injured officials; several issues relating to South West Africa (Namibia); the admission of members to the United Nations; decisions of the United Nations Administrative Tribunal; the effect of reservations to general international agreements; the authority of the United Nations to engage in peacekeeping activities and the obligation of member states to pay for those activities; the interpretation of an agreement relating to a regional office of an international organization; and the status of Western Sahara.

14. *Other international courts.* There are several specialized international courts. The Court of Justice of the European Communities has broad jurisdiction and is open not only to states but also to the organs of the Community and to private persons. The European Court of Human Rights and the Inter-American Court of Human Rights have jurisdiction relating to human rights questions. These courts can render binding decisions, and there are special provisions for the execution of their judgments. Treaty Establishing the European Community, Arts. 187, 192 (decisions of the Court of Justice of the European Communities that impose a pecuniary obligation on persons other than states are to be enforced pursuant to rules of civil procedure in force in the state in whose territory the execution takes place); European Convention for the Protection of Human Rights and Fundamental Freedoms, Art. 54 (§ 906, Reporters' Note 1) (the Committee of Ministers of the Council of Europe shall supervise the execution of the judgments of the European Court of Human Rights); American Convention on Human Rights, Art. 68 (a judgment of the Inter-American Court of Human Rights that stipulates compensatory damages may be executed in the country concerned in accordance with domestic procedure governing the execution of judgment against

the state). The Inter-American Court has broad jurisdiction to render advisory opinions. On the scope of that jurisdiction, see Advisory Opinion of Sept. 24, 1982, Inter-Am. Court Hum.Rt., ser. A, No. 1, 22 Int'l Leg.Mat. 51 (1983). The International Tribunal of the Law of the Sea to be established under Annex VI of the Convention on the Law of the Sea (see Part V of this Restatement) will have jurisdiction not only over disputes between states but also over disputes involving international organizations, state enterprises, or natural or juridical persons. LOS Convention, Art. 187, and Annex VI, Art. 20.

15. *Previous Restatement.* There was no comprehensive treatment of the International Court of Justice in the previous Restatement; there were references to its jurisdiction in § 3, Comments *c* and *d*, and § 148, Reporters' Note 1, and to various decisions of the Court where appropriate.

§ 904. Interstate Arbitration

(1) States parties to a dispute may submit it to arbitration by special agreement (*compromis*).

(2) A state party to a dispute with another state may submit the dispute to an arbitral tribunal pursuant to a bilateral or multilateral agreement providing for the submission to arbitration of a category of disputes that includes the claim in question.

(3) An award by an arbitral tribunal is binding on the parties unless they have agreed otherwise.

Comment:

a. Interstate arbitration. This section applies to arbitration of disputes between states under international law. For commercial arbitration between a state and a private person, see § 487, Reporters' Notes 1–6; § 713, Comment *j*.

b. Consent requirement. A state may not be compelled to submit to arbitration without its consent. Consent to arbitration is indicated either by agreement between the parties to arbitrate a particular dispute (Subsection (1)), or by agreement authorizing either party to submit to arbitration any dispute with the other party, or a dispute belonging to a specified category of disputes, *e.g.*, those arising out of a particular agreement or relating to a particular subject (Subsection (2)). Agreement to proceed to arbitration is usually embodied in a special agreement (*compromis*) between states parties to the dispute. Some arbitration agreements, both bilateral and multilateral, provide a method for the preparation of a *compromis* if the parties cannot agree upon it, either by a third party or by the tribunal itself once it is constituted; an agreement may designate an appropriate authority to assist in the selection of the members of the tribunal so that they may prepare the *compromis.*

    c. Jurisdiction of arbitral tribunal. The jurisdiction of the tribunal is usually specified in the *compromis*, as are the questions to be submitted for decision (or advisory opinion). The tribunal ordinarily is judge of its own competence, determined on the basis of its interpretation of the *compromis* and any other relevant instrument.

    d. Provisional measures. Once a case has been submitted to arbitration, the parties generally are obligated to abstain from any action that may aggravate or extend the dispute, or prejudice the execution of the arbitral decision. An arbitral tribunal, or in case of urgency its president, ordinarily is granted or is deemed to have authority to prescribe provisional measures to preserve the rights of the parties or to protect the integrity and effectiveness of the arbitration; sometimes a *compromis* contains specific provisions for an interim regime to govern the matter in dispute pending the conclusion of the arbitration. As to measures of self-help prior to constitution of the tribunal, see § 905, Reporters' Note 4.

    e. Compliance with arbitral awards. In general, an arbitral award is binding upon the parties, but some arbitration agreements provide that the award shall be only advisory. An agreement to arbitrate is presumed to imply an agreement to comply with the award, and noncompliance is a violation of the international agreement to arbitrate and, therefore, of international law. Although arbitration agreements do not generally contain special enforcement provisions, arbitral awards are usually complied with. A few awards have been rejected, usually on the ground that the tribunal has exceeded its jurisdiction, or that there was a fundamental fault in the procedure, fraud in evidence presented to the tribunal, or some manifest error in applying international law.

REPORTERS' NOTES

    1. *Consent requirement.* In Ambatielos Case (Obligation to Arbitrate) (Greece v. United Kingdom), the International Court of Justice identified two issues involved in determining whether the parties had consented to submit a particular claim to an arbitral tribunal. First, whether there has been consent to arbitrate, for a state "may not be compelled to submit its disputes to arbitration without its consent." Second, whether the consent of the parties extends to the claim submitted to the tribunal. [1953] I.C.J. Rep. 10, 19.

    2. Compromis. Most arbitrations are based on a special agreement (*compromis*) concluded after a dispute has arisen. Such an agreement may relate to a single dispute or to a group of disputes; it

may involve a claim or claims by one state against the other, or by each state against the other. The main purpose of the agreement is to define the subject of the dispute, and it often specifies the exact questions to be answered by the tribunal. It usually specifies, in addition, the method of constituting the tribunal; the number of arbitrators; a third party authorized to appoint the arbitrators, if not designated in due time by one or both of the parties; the rules of law to be applied by the tribunal, including sometimes the exact principles to be applied, or an authorization to the tribunal to decide *ex aequo et bono* (§ 903, Reporters' Note 9); the procedure to be followed by the tribunal; the majority vote required for an award; the time within which the award is to be rendered; whether the members of the tribunal may attach dissenting or individual opinions to the award; how the costs of the arbitration are to be apportioned. See International Law Commission, Model Rules of Arbitral Procedure, Reporters' Note 4, Art. 2. For a recent example of a complex *compromis*, see the Declaration Concerning the Settlement of Claims by the Government of the United States of America and the Government of the Islamic Republic of Iran, Algiers, 1981, 20 Int'l Leg.Mat. 230 (1981). See also the *compromis* of arbitration between the United States and Italy relating to the interpretation of an air transport agreement between the two countries, 1964, 15 U.S.T. 1471, T.I.A.S. No. 5624.

3. *Failure to agree on terms of* compromis. Many states, including the United States, are parties to treaties that provide for compulsory arbitration, *i.e.*, arbitration that may be initiated by unilateral application of one party if the two states cannot agree on a *compromis*. Such treaties often specify that if the *compromis* is not concluded within a certain time, usually three to six months, either party may initiate a special procedure for supplying the terms of reference for the arbitration. Some treaties provide for third-party appointment of members of an arbitral tribunal who then draw up the *compromis*; a few treaties provide for the appointment of a special commission for the sole purpose of preparing the *compromis*. For the texts of various provisions, see United Nations, Systematic Survey of Treaties for the Pacific Settlement of International Disputes, 1928–1948 (Sohn, ed.), at 78–107 (1949). The Model Rules on Arbitral Procedure, prepared by the International Law Commission (see Reporters' Note 4), envisage the possibility of the tribunal proceeding to hear and decide the case on the application of either party even without a *compromis*. Art. 8(3).

4. *Arbitration procedure.* Most agreements to arbitrate do not specify the details of the arbitration procedure but refer to some generally accepted treaty on the subject (though the parties to the *compromis* may not be parties to that treaty), or to model rules prepared by an international institution. Such rules were first codified in the 1899 Hague Convention for the Pacific Settlement of International Disputes, T.S. 392, 1 Bevans 230, and considerably revised by the 1907 Hague Convention, T.S. 536, 1 Berans 577. (As of 1986, this convention was in force for the United States and 74 other states.) These conventions established the Perma-

nent Court of Arbitration, which is not a court but a panel of available arbitrators consisting of four persons appointed by each state party for six-year terms.

Many arbitration agreements follow the General Act for the Pacific Settlement of International Disputes, adopted under the auspices of the League of Nations in 1928, 93 L.N.T.S. 343, and revised by the United Nations in 1949, 71 U.N.T.S. 101. Similar provisions, with some variations, are contained in the 1957 European Convention for the Peaceful Settlement of Disputes. 320 U.N.T.S. 243. Different patterns have been followed by the 1948 American Treaty on Pacific Settlement ("Pact of Bogotá"), 30 U.N.T.S. 55; and by the 1964 Protocol to the Charter of the Organization of African Unity, which established the Commission of Mediation, Conciliation and Arbitration, from whose 21 members an arbitral tribunal may be chosen by the parties. 1 Sohn, Basic Documents of African Regional Organizations 69 (1971); 3 Int'l Leg.Mat. 1116 (1964).

The International Law Commission submitted to the General Assembly in 1958 "Model Rules on Arbitral Procedure," which the General Assembly approved for possible use by member states in drawing up treaties of arbitration or compromis. 13 U.N. GAOR Supp. No. 9, at 5–8; G.A. Res. 1262, 13 U.N. GAOR Supp. No. 18, at 53. For the difficulties connected with the approval of this document, see Briggs, The International Law Commission 285–91 (1965). Some international agreements provide for arbitration pursuant to these Model Rules. See, e.g., the Treaty Concerning the Reciprocal Encourage-ment and Protection of Investments between the United States and Egypt, 1982, Art. 8(3)(f), 21 Int'l Leg.Mat. 927, 943 (1982) (as of 1986, this treaty was not in force).

5. *Provisional measures.* An agreement to arbitrate may expressly authorize the arbitral tribunal to adopt provisional measures necessary to safeguard the rights of the parties, but such jurisdiction may also be implied; in some cases it has been exercised without any basis in the agreement. See, *e.g.,* Case Concerning the Air Service Agreement between the United States and France, 1978, 18 R.Int'l Arb.Awards 417, 445–46 (tribunal has power to decide on interim measures of protection, "regardless of whether this power is expressly mentioned or implied in its statute"); United Nations Tribunal in Libya, Case Concerning the Administration of Certain Properties of the State in Libya (Italy v. United Kingdom and Libya) (Request for Interim Measures), 1952, 12 R.Int'l Arb.Awards 359 (rules of procedure adopted by tribunal empowered it to protect jeopardized rights of parties); decisions of the Mixed Arbitral Tribunals cited in Ralston, Supplement to the Law and Procedure of International Tribunals 95 (1936); and Guggenheim, "Les mesures conservatoires dans la procédure arbitrale et judiciaire," Hague Academy, 40 Recueil des Cours 645, 720–43 (a provisional measure issued in accordance with the rules of the tribunal cannot be construed as an infringement of the sovereignty of the state). See also Sztucki, Interim Measures in the Hague Court 4–11 (1983).

6. *Binding force of arbitral awards.* Most arbitral awards are

intended to be binding, but some are intended to be advisory only. A *compromis* may provide expressly that the award will be final and binding. See, *e.g.*, the Declaration Concerning the Settlement of Claims by the United States and Iran, Reporters' Note 2, Art. 4(1), 20 Int'l Leg.Mat. 230, 232 (1981) (providing also that any "award which the Tribunal may render against either government shall be enforceable against such government in the courts of any nation in accordance with its laws," Art. 4(3)). Some international agreements, however, provide that the dispute should be submitted to a tribunal for "an advisory report"; they sometimes provide also that the parties "will use their best efforts under the powers available to them to put into effect the opinion expressed in any such advisory report." See, *e.g.*, Air Transport Services Agreement between the United States and France, as modified in 1951, Art. 10, 2 U.S.T. 1033, T.I.A.S. No. 2257, 139 U.N.T.S. 151. As to self-help in case of non-compliance, see § 905, Reporters' Note 4.

7. *Compliance with arbitral awards.* A study of the execution of some 300 arbitral awards between 1794 and 1936 uncovered only 20 cases of noncompliance. Hambro, L'exécution des sentences internationales 11–29 (1936). A few instances of noncompliance have occurred since 1936, *e.g.*, with respect to an award concerning the dispute over the Beagle Channel islands between Argentina and Chile. See 17 Int'l Leg.Mat. 634, 738–53, 1198–1205 (1978). This dispute was finally settled by mediation in 1985. 24 *id.* 1 (1985). For a detailed list of international arbitrations and

data on their execution, see Stuyt, Survey of International Arbitrations, 1794–1970 (2d ed. 1972).

Article 35 of the Model Rules on Arbitral Procedure, prepared by the International Law Commission (Reporters' Note 4), allows a party to challenge the validity of an arbitral award only on the following grounds:

(a) that the tribunal exceeded its powers;

(b) that there was corruption on the part of a member of the tribunal;

(c) that there was a failure to state the reasons for the award or a serious departure from a fundamental rule of procedure;

(d) that the undertaking to arbitrate or the *compromis* is a nullity.

This Article does not include among the grounds for invalidity either errors of law or erroneous findings of fact. Article 38, however, envisages the possibility of revising an award if a fact is discovered "of such nature as to constitute a decisive factor, provided that when the award was rendered that fact was unknown to the tribunal and to the party requesting revision." For a study of alleged violations of international law by international arbitral tribunals, such as non-observance of minimum procedural standards, lack or excess of jurisdiction, or essential error (as distinguished from mere mistake), and of the finality of arbitral awards and proposals for instituting an appeals procedure, see Carlston, The Process of International Arbitration (1946).

8. *Previous Restatement.* International arbitration is not dealt

with in the previous Restatement but is mentioned as one of the means for the settlement of international disputes (§ 3, Comment c).

§ 905.   Unilateral Remedies

(1) Subject to Subsection (2), a state victim of a violation of an international obligation by another state may resort to countermeasures that might otherwise be unlawful, if such measures

(a) are necessary to terminate the violation or prevent further violation, or to remedy the violation; and

(b) are not out of proportion to the violation and the injury suffered.

(2) The threat or use of force in response to a violation of international law is subject to prohibitions on the threat or use of force in the United Nations Charter, as well as to Subsection (1).

Comment:

a. Permissibility of unilateral remedies under international law. In general, international law encourages the settlement of legal disputes by negotiation or third-party resolution, and discourages self-help unless it becomes necessary. Subsection (1)(a) and Comment *c.* Even when self-help is necessary, the measures taken must not be out of proportion to the violation or the injury. Subsection (1)(b) and Comment *d.* The use of force against another state, even in response to a violation of international obligation, is generally prohibited by the United Nations Charter. Subsection (2) and Comment *g.*

Under this section, a state may take limited measures that would be unlawful were they not in response to a violation, measures such as termination or suspension of treaty obligations, or seizure of the offending state's assets. See Comment *b.* A state may also respond to a violation by measures that, while abnormal and perhaps "unfriendly," do not violate any international obligation and are, therefore, not governed by this section. Thus, a state may express its displeasure over a violation by "cooling" relations with the offending state, taking the violation into account in political decisions, withholding future benefits, refraining from entering into new arrangements, or taking other steps not prohibited by international law or agreement. In general, however, diplomatic relations, communication, and trade are fundamentals of interstate intercourse and in practice are governed by considerations of necessity and proportionality, and hence are not seriously disrupted for any but the grossest violations. When an international agreement provides for a particular response by a party to violation by another party, other responses are generally precluded. See, for example, the General Agreement on Tariffs and Trade (GATT), Introductory Note to Part VIII and §§ 804, 806–808.

The principles governing unilateral countermeasures apply as well when a state responds to a violation of an obligation to all states *(erga omnes)*. See § 703(2) and Comment *a*. This section does not address actions in response to violations that are taken by states pursuant to resolutions of appropriate organs of international organizations, such as the United Nations Security Council (United Nations Charter, Articles 41 and 42), or the Organ of Consultation under Article 8 of the Inter-American Treaty of Reciprocal Assistance (the Rio Treaty), 4 Bevans 559, 21 U.N.T.S. 77.

b. Range of permissible countermeasures. The measures that a state may take under this section (subject to the principles of necessity and proportionality) include: suspension or termination of treaty relations generally or of a particular international agreement or provision; freezing of assets of the offending state; imposition of other economic sanctions. Self-help measures against the offending state may not include measures against the state's nationals that are contrary to the principles governing human rights and the treatment of foreign nationals. See § 711, Comments *f, g,* and *h,* and § 712, Comment *f*; see also § 335, Comment *c.* Under the law of the United States, certain actions in retaliation against nationals of an offending state may be forbidden by the Constitution. See § 722, Comments *d* and *h,* and Reporters' Note 6.

c. Necessity. Under this section, countermeasures in response to a violation of an international obligation are ordinarily justified only when the accused state wholly denies the violation or its responsibility for the violation; rejects or ignores requests to terminate the violation or pay compensation; or rejects or ignores proposals for negotiation or third-party resolution. Countermeasures are to be avoided as long as genuine negotiation or third-party settlement is available and offers some promise of resolving the matter. A showing of necessity is particularly important before any drastic measures of self-help are taken. In a dispute between members of an international organization, there may be a requirement that the dispute be submitted to the dispute settlement procedures of the organization, and countermeasures are precluded before that procedure has been concluded or terminated without success.

d. Proportionality. Countermeasures are ordinarily related to the violation. For instance, if a state has violated an obligation in respect of trade, the response of the other state will generally be limited to a corresponding trade restriction rather than a measure such as denial of airline landing rights. But an unrelated response is not unlawful so long as it is not excessive in relation to the violation. Different steps may be taken at different stages of a dispute. For instance, limited measures may be taken when a state refuses to negotiate (*e.g.*, freezing the offending state's assets); stronger measures may be used when a state refuses to comply with a judgment of an international tribunal (*e.g.*, seizure and appropriation of assets).

e. Response to violation of international agreement. A material breach of a bilateral agreement by one of the parties entitles the other to suspend or terminate the agreement in whole or in part. See § 335(1). Similarly, a party affected by a breach of a multilateral agreement may suspend its operation in whole or in part as between itself and the defaulting state. See § 335(2)(b). Some international agreements specify the responses that may be made to a breach of the agreement; *e.g.*, GATT specifies the compensatory actions that may be taken, see Part VIII, especially §§ 806 and 807. Some of these agreements provide, or may be interpreted as implying, that the specified actions are the only responses permitted. See Comment *a* and Reporters' Note 6. The aggrieved state may also take countermeasures unrelated to the agreement, subject to the limitations of this section.

f. Retaliation. The principle of necessity ordinarily precludes measures designed only as retribution for a violation and not as an incentive to terminate a violation or to remedy it. A state may retaliate, however, by acts of "retorsion" which are not otherwise illegal, such as the "unfriendly" acts indicated in Comment *a*. Retorsion is to be distinguished from "reprisal"; traditionally, reprisal was punitive in character and commonly involved the use of force, such as bombardment or temporary occupation of part of the offending state's territory. To the extent that reprisal involves threat or use of force, its use is now limited by the principles of the United Nations Charter. See Comment *g*.

g. Use of force in response to violation. The use or threat of force in response to a violation of international law is subject both to the requirements of necessity and proportionality (Subsection (1)) and to the prohibitions of the United Nations Charter (Subsection (2)). Virtually all states are parties to the Charter, and its rules in respect of the use of force are also binding as customary law and are *jus cogens*. See § 102, Comment *k*.

Article 2(4) of the Charter forbids the "threat or use of force against the territorial integrity or political independence of any state, or in any other manner inconsistent with the Purposes of the United Nations." However, that provision is subject to "the inherent right of individual or collective self-defense if an armed attack occurs." Article 51.

Article 2(4) prohibits the threat or use of military force; it does not address the threat or use of economic force or pressure. It prohibits the threat or use of force generally, whether or not in response to a violation of international law. Important issues as to the scope of the prohibition in Article 2(4) have never been authoritatively resolved, but it is clear that it was designed, *inter alia*, to outlaw "gunboat diplomacy" even in response to violations of international law. However, an armed attack in violation of the law of the Charter permits the use of force in the exercise of the right of self-defense (Article 51), but important issues as to the scope of that right, too, remain unresolved.

It is generally accepted that Article 2(4) does not forbid limited use of force in the territory of another state incidental to attempts to rescue persons whose lives are endangered there, as in the rescue at Entebbe in 1976. That interpretation of the Charter, however, would not justify the use of force by one state on its own authority to conquer another state or overthrow its government even if that government had been guilty of persecution of minorities or other gross violations of human rights. See § 703, Comment *e* and Reporters' Note 8.

h. Authority to take measures in response to violation: law of the United States. Authority to take countermeasures on behalf of the United States in response to a violation by another state rests generally with the President, but some measures may require Congressional authorization. The President may, on his own authority, terminate or limit diplomatic relations with the offending state, and he may deploy forces under his command for purposes not involving engagement in hostilities. Successive Presidents and Congresses have differed as to the President's authority to use force in hostilities short of war. In time of peace, the President probably may not, without authorization from Congress, expel aliens or freeze assets of foreign states or their nationals. See § 712, Comment *f.* A State of the United States, unless authorized by Congress, may not take measures of self-help against a foreign state that has violated an international obligation to the United States. *Cf.* United States Constitution, Article I, Section 10; also § 1, Reporters' Note 5. See § 722, Reporters' Note 5.

A decision to resort to countermeasures is a political, not a judicial, decision. Courts in the United States will not decide whether and how the United States should respond to a violation by another state. For example, if a provision in a treaty of the United States is violated by another party to that treaty, it is for the President and not for the courts to decide whether to respond by suspending the treaty or ceasing to carry out obligations under it. See § 339, Reporters' Note 1 and § 475, Reporters' Note 4. The courts will generally consider whether Executive acts against foreign nationals or their interests in the United States, in response to a violation of international law by another state, violate the Constitutional rights of the alien (§ 722), or are beyond the President's authority under the Constitution or acts of Congress. Courts will also entertain an objection, in an appropriate case, that the measure taken violates international law under this section because it is not necessary or because it is excessive, except where Congress directed or clearly authorized such measures (§ 115, Comment *a*), and except also, perhaps, when the action is within the President's constitutional authority and he has made an authoritative determination to take the action even though it would constitute a violation of international law by the United States. See § 115, Reporters' Note 3.

REPORTERS' NOTES

1. *Permissibility of unilateral remedies under international law.* There has been continuing uncertainty as to which measures of self-help are permissible under international law in response to violations of international obligations, in which circumstances, and subject to what limitations. There have been few judicial pronouncements on the subject, and the practice of states, though abundant, has not clarified either the circumstances in which unilateral countermeasures can be employed or the limits that need to be observed. See Stone, Legal Control of International Conflicts 285 (1954). This section distills a general principle from few cases and a confusion of precedents.

John Bassett Moore listed non-amicable processes for settling international differences in the order of their coercive nature. He began with "withdrawal of diplomatic rela-

tions, retorsion or retaliation, and the display of force"; then came "reprisals, 'pacific' blockade, embargo and non-intercourse." Those measures, he explained, though described as being "short of war," sometimes involved acts of war, but "if they are not opposed, they may not result in the legal condition of things called a state of war." Quoted in 2 Hyde, International Law Chiefly as Interpreted and Applied by the United States 1654, n. 1 (2d ed. 1945).

The United Nations Charter imposes strict limits on the use of force in self-help (see Comment *g*), but it provides no clear guidance as to what is a use of force within the meaning of the Charter, or what use of force is to be considered to be "against the territorial integrity or political independence" of another state. No international agreement or other authoritative instrument has clarified the scope and limits of self-help by means other than use of force.

In Corfu Channel Case (United Kingdom v. Albania), when two United Kingdom destroyers were damaged by mines in Albanian territorial waters, the United Kingdom resorted to a minesweeping operation in those waters, which it justified by invoking the right of "self-protection or self-help." The International Court of Justice refused to accept this defense. While the Court recognized that the Albanian Government failed to remove the mines after the explosions and was dilatory in answering diplomatic notes, it considered that "to ensure respect for international law, of which it is the organ, the Court must declare that the action of the British Navy constituted a violation of Albanian sovereignty." [1949] I.C.J. Rep. 4, 35.

In Case Concerning Military and Paramilitary Activities in and Against Nicaragua (Nicaragua v. United States), [1986] I.C.J. Rep. 14, 127, the Court held that the acts of which Nicaragua was accused "could only have justified proportionate counter-measures on the part of the State which had been the victim of these acts, namely El Salvador, Honduras or Costa Rica"; they "could not justify counter-measures taken by a third State, the United States, and particularly could not justify intervention involving the use of force."

In its draft on state responsibility, the International Law Commission proposed an article on "countermeasures in respect of an internationally wrongful act" substantially consistent with this section. Art. 30, 34 U.N. GAOR Supp.

No. 10, at 311 (1979). The Commission considered but did not express conclusions on such questions as whether reprisals are legitimate under international law, whether countermeasures require a prior attempt to secure reparation, or whether proportionality between the injury suffered and the particular reaction is required. Id. at 314. See also Zoller, Peacetime Unilateral Remedies: An Analysis of Countermeasures 67–75 (1984).

2. *Range of permissible countermeasures.* State responses to alleged violations of international obligations have varied. States have suspended sales of arms, technology, and even food, or military or economic assistance; limited fishing in their coastal waters by nationals of the offending state; or cancelled landing rights for its airlines or access to ports for its ships. For an early listing of instances in which non-military measures of self-help were used or authorized, see Wild, Sanctions and Treaty Enforcement 160–80 (1934).

States have also responded to violations by withholding benefits. Comment *a*. In the First Hickenlooper Amendment, Congress directed the President to suspend foreign assistance to any state that nationalized properties of United States nationals without providing compensation as required by international law. Foreign Assistance Act of 1961, as amended, 22 U.S.C. § 2370(e). See § 444, Comment *c*. Congress has denied military and economic assistance to states guilty of consistent patterns of gross violations of internationally recognized human rights. See § 702, Reporters' Note 10. Under the Fisherman's Protective Act of 1954, as amended in 1967, the United States reimbursed American fishermen fined for fishing in zones not recognized by the United States as being within the jurisdiction of a foreign state, and the amount was deducted from United States aid funds designated for that state. 22 U.S.C. §§ 1971–80; but see 90 Stat. 331 (1976).

In response to the seizure of United States diplomatic and consular personnel as hostages by Iran in 1979, the United States discontinued purchases from Iran, blocked Iranian government assets, restricted the number of Iranian diplomatic and consular personnel in the United States, and intensified the enforcement of immigration regulations against Iranian students in the United States. See Narenji v. Civiletti, 617 F.2d 745 (D.C.Cir.1979), *certiorari denied*, 446 U.S. 957, 100 S.Ct. 2928, 64 L.Ed.2d 815 (1980) discussed in § 722, Reporters' Note 6; Lowenfeld, Trade Controls for Political Ends, ch. V (2d ed. 1983). Later the United States broke off diplomatic relations with Iran, prohibited exports to that country, cancelled all visas issued to Iranian citizens for future entry, prohibited travel to Iran by United States citizens, and took other economic measures, including the blockage of private assets of Iranian nationals. In United States Diplomatic and Consular Staff in Tehran Case (United States v. Iran), the International Court of Justice cited these countermeasures and appeared to accept them as not unlawful in the circumstances. [1980] I.C.J. Rep. 3, 17. See 80 Dep't State Bull. 56–57, May 1980; but see Reporters' Note 4.

Measures permitted under this section are, usually, measures against the offending state and its instrumentalities. Some question the propriety, generally, of responses directed against the nationals of the offending state. But see Sardino v. Federal Reserve Bank of New York, 361 F.2d 106, 111 (2d Cir.1966), *certiorari denied*, 385 U.S. 898, 87 S.Ct. 203, 17 L.Ed.2d 130 (1966), upholding regulations that prohibited the transfer outside of the United States, without special authorization, of property owned by Cuban nationals. The court said: "It does not follow, however, that in dealing with the property of an alien the United States must be blind to the acts of the country of which he is a national; the Constitution protects the alien from arbitrary action by our government but not from reasonable response to such action by his own." Mass expulsion of nationals of the offending state would presumably be barred by the general prohibition on expulsion of aliens contained in some international agreements. See, *e.g.*, African Charter on Human and Peoples' Rights, Art. 12(5), 21 Int'l Leg.Mat. 59 (1982); American Convention on Human Rights, Art. 22(9), O.A.S.T.S., No. 36; Protocol No. 4 to the European Convention for the Protection of Human Rights and Fundamental Freedoms, Art. 4, Eur. T.S., No. 46. (The United States has signed the American Convention but as of 1987 had not ratified it.) Measures against nationals of the offending state are clearly forbidden if they are contrary to the principles governing human rights and the treatment of foreign nationals. Comment *b;* § 711, Comments *g* and *h;* § 712, Comments *d* and *f.* Measures against selected nationals of the offending state are open to challenge as discriminatory (*ibid.*), but in particular circumstances, measures directed against only some of the offending state's nationals, if not selected on an invidious basis, might be acceptable, whereas measures against all such nationals might be excessive and disproportional under Subsection (1)(b). Compare Narenji v. Civiletti, *supra,* upholding regulations issued during the hostages crisis that required Iranian nationals in student status to report to the Immigration Service.

3. *Necessity.* During an insurrection in Canada in 1837, the rebels were supplied from United States territory by the steamer Caroline. A British force entered United States territory, destroyed the steamer, and in the skirmish killed two United States citizens. The British Government justified this action by emphasizing "the necessity of self-defense and preservation." In his famous communication to the British Government, Secretary of State Webster stressed that the exceptions permitting self-defense should be confined to cases in which the "necessity of self-defence is instant, overwhelming, and leaving no choice of means, and no moment for deliberation". Earlier he had written that the British Government was required to show that the Canadian authorities "did nothing unreasonable or excessive; since the act justified by the necessity of self-defence, must be limited by that necessity, and kept clearly within it." See Jennings, "The Caroline and McLeod Cases," 32 Am.J.Int'l L. 82, 85, 89 (1938). Although the principle of necessity was asserted in that instance to support a use of force in self-defense, it is accepted that the principle applies as well to other means of self-help that would

be unlawful were they not in response to a violation. Necessity may justify self-help, in particular, if all attempts to settle the issue, to achieve a cessation of the violation, or to obtain adequate compensation for the damage caused by the violation have proved fruitless. Tucker, "Reprisals and Self-Defense: The Customary Law," 66 Am.J.Int'l L. 586, 592 (1972) ("the necessity legitimizing reprisals is defined in terms of the injured state's inability to obtain redress by other, and peaceful, means"). Necessity disappears, however, once the case has been submitted to an international tribunal, and the tribunal is in a position to decide on interim measures of protection. Case Concerning Air Service Agreement (U.S.-France), 1978, 18 R.Int'l Arb.Awards 417, 445–46.

The requirements of necessity and proportionality (Reporters' Note 5) are concurrent. Necessity may justify prompt action, but such action may not exceed the bounds of proportionality, and should cease when it is no longer necessary. The practice of states confirms that ordinarily an action justified by necessity is proportional, and is terminated when the violation of international law has stopped. For instance, in 1949, when Hungary refused to allow a United States consul to visit a United States citizen accused of espionage and sabotage, the United States closed two Hungarian consulates in the United States; as soon as the accused person was released and allowed to leave Hungary, the United States permitted the reopening of the consulates. See 8 Whiteman, Digest of International Law 867–73 (1967).

4. *Exhaustion of other remedies as condition for self-help.* An

early study by the Institute of International Law concluded that measures of self-help are prohibited when redress can be obtained through available procedures for peaceful settlement, notably when the matter is within the jurisdiction of a court or tribunal and that court or tribunal can provide interim measures of protection. In addition, measures of self-help are not permitted while the case is pending (except as interim protection where the court or tribunal is unable to provide it), or when the defendant has complied with the decision of the court or tribunal. 38 Institut de Droit International, Annuaire 708–11 (1934); see also *id.* 1–166, 623–94, for an extensive discussion of retaliatory measures, based on a report by Nicolas Politis. In United States Diplomatic and Consular Staff in Tehran Case (Reporters' Note 2), the International Court of Justice criticized the United States for resorting to self-help to free the hostages while the case was before the Court. [1980] I.C.J. Rep. at 43. Compare Case Concerning Air Service Agreement, Reporters' Note 5, where the tribunal accepted measures of self-help implemented when there was yet no tribunal in existence to order measures of protection.

The 1907 Hague Convention Respecting the Limitation of the Employment of Force for the Recovery of Contract Debts made the offer of arbitration by the state seeking payment on behalf of its nationals, and the refusal thereof by the debtor state, a condition precedent to the use of armed force by the claimant state. Art. 1, T.S. No. 537, 1 Bevans 607 (the undertaking not to use force is "not applicable when the debtor state refuses or neglects to reply to an offer of arbitration, or, after accepting the offer, prevents any *compromis* from being agreed on, or, after arbitration, fails to submit to the award"). The Hague Convention has been largely overtaken by the more comprehensive prohibitions on the use of force of the United Nations Charter (Comment *g*), but the Convention is still in effect to the extent that it is not inconsistent with the Charter (Art. 103); as of 1986, the United States and 27 other states were parties to this Convention, some of them having acceded to it recently.

5. *Proportionality.* In considering countermeasures taken by the United States when France had allegedly violated an air services agreement between the two countries, the international arbitral tribunal addressed the requirement of proportionality. It pointed out that a state that is satisfied that another state has violated an international obligation to it is entitled, "within the limits set by the general rules of international law pertaining to the use of armed force, to affirm its rights through 'countermeasures.'" Countermeasures must "have some degree of equivalence with the alleged breach," and their aim should be "to restore equality between the Parties and to encourage them to continue negotiations with mutual desire to reach an acceptable solution," and to avoid escalation that would lead to a worsening of the conflict. The Tribunal upheld the denial by the United States to France of air service rights corresponding to those that France had denied to the United States. Case Concerning Air Service Agreement (U.S.-France), 1978, R.Int'l Arb. Awards 417, 443–45 (1980). For other examples of proportionality,

see 2 Oppenheim, International Law 141 (7th ed. H. Lauterpacht 1952).

Even before the United Nations Charter, when forcible reprisals were not forbidden in principle, it was held by a German-Portuguese arbitral tribunal in the *Naulilaa* case, 1928, that the German action in destroying certain forts and posts and causing death of many persons, in reprisal for the killing of an official and two officers, was disproportionate. "Even if it were admitted that the law of nations does not demand that reprisals be in approximate proportion to the offense, it would nevertheless be necessary to consider as excessive and illegal any reprisals that are out of all proportion to the act motivating them." 2 R.Int'l Arb.Awards 1011, 1028. See also 6 Hackworth, Digest of International Law 154, 155 (1943).

6. *Response to violation of international agreement.* Some international agreements provide for responses to violations other than those specified in the Vienna Convention on the Law of Treaties. See § 335. The General Agreement on Tariffs and Trade (GATT) authorizes certain unilateral compensatory measures in cases of violations of that Agreement, especially when a state has refused to accept a report of a Working Party that has proposed a way to settle a dispute. See § 806, Reporters' Note 1.

In 1982, the states parties to the General Agreement on Tariffs and Trade (GATT) undertook "to abstain from taking restrictive trade measures, for reasons of a non-economic character, not consistent with the General Agreement," GATT, B.I. S.D., Supp. No. 29 (1983), at 9, 11. Relying on that undertaking, *inter alia*, the General Assembly of the

United Nations reaffirmed that "developed countries should refrain from threatening or applying trade restrictions, blockades, embargoes and other economic sanctions, incompatible with the Charter of the United Nations and in violation of undertakings contracted, multilaterally or bilaterally, against developing countries as a form of political and economic coercion which affects their economic, political and social development." G.A. Res. 210, 39 U.N. GAOR Supp. No. 51, at 160. The United States and 18 other states voted against this resolution. For a report of the Secretary-General and comments by various states, see U.N. Doc. A/39/415 (1984).

The parties to the 1980 Convention on the Conservation of Antarctic Marine Living Resources undertook "to exert appropriate efforts, consistent with the Charter of the United Nations, to the end that no one engages in any activity contrary to the objectives" of that convention. T.I.A.S. No. 10240, Art. 22(1). As of 1986, the United States and 15 other states and the European Economic Community were parties to this convention.

7. *United Nations Charter prohibitions on use of force.* A number of issues in the interpretation of Articles 2(4) and 51 of the Charter have not been authoritatively resolved. See generally Henkin, Pugh, Schachter, and Smit, International Law, Cases and Materials 676 *et seq.* (2d ed. 1987); *compare* McDougal, "The Soviet-Cuban Quarantine and Self-Defense," 57 Am.J. Int'l L. 597, 599–601 (1963), *with* Henkin, How Nations Behave 139–45, 290–300 (2d ed. 1979); see also Bowett, Self-Defense in International Law 29–114, 182–99 (1958);

Brownlie, International Law and the Use of Force by States 251–349, 372–73 (1963).

8. *Retaliation, retorsion, and reprisal.* Traditional international law permitted both "retorsion" and "reprisal," but their scope and the distinction between them have been a subject of controversy, and the traditional law as to reprisal has been modified by the law forbidding use of force. Comment *g*. Retorsion generally consisted of acts not involving the use of force in response to any unfriendly act, whether illegal or not. See, *e.g.*, Stone, Legal Control of International Conflict 289–90 (1954); 2 Hyde, International Law Chiefly as Interpreted by the United States 1657–59 (2d ed. 1945); 7 Moore, Digest of International Law 105 (1906). A reprisal often involved some use of force and could be done only in response to a gross violation of international law. In the *Naulilaa* case, Reporters' Note 5, the German-Portuguese arbitral tribunal defined reprisal as follows:

> Reprisals are acts of self-help by the injured State, acts in retaliation for acts contrary to international law on the part of the offending State, which have remained unredressed after a demand for amends. In consequence of such measures, the observance of this or that rule of international law is temporarily suspended, in the relations between the two States. They are limited by considerations of humanity and the rules of good faith, applicable in the relations between States. They are illegal unless they are based upon a previous act contrary to international law. They seek to impose on the

offending State reparation for the offence, the return to legality and the avoidance of new offences.

2 R.Int'l Arb.Awards 1011, 1026; 12 Whiteman, Digest of International Law 149 (1971). Reprisals have also been defined as "such injurious and otherwise internationally illegal acts of one State against another as are exceptionally permitted for the purpose of compelling the latter to consent to settlement of a difference created by its own international delinquency." 2 Oppenheim, International Law 136 (7th ed. H. Lauterpacht 1948).

The provision in the United Nations Charter (Art. 2(4)), Comment *g*, proscribing "the threat or use of force" by one state against another has been generally interpreted as prohibiting reprisals that involve the use of force. See Brownlie, International Law and the Use of Force by States 281–82 (1963), and sources cited at 281 n. 4. In one of its early decisions, the Security Council decided that no party was permitted to violate the truce between Israel and the Arab states on the ground that it was undertaking reprisal or retaliation against the other party. Resolution 56 (1948), 3 S.C.O.R., Resolutions and Decisions of the Security Council 24 (1948). Similarly, in connection with the British retaliatory action against Yemen (the Harib Incident), the Security Council condemned "reprisals as incompatible with the purposes and principles of the United Nations." Resolution 188 (1964), 19 *id.* 9 (1964). See also Resolution 228 (1966), 21 *id.* 11 (1966), censuring Israel ("actions of military reprisal cannot be tolerated"). The Declaration of Principles of International Law Concerning Friendly Relations and Co-operation Among States proclaims that "States have a duty to refrain from acts of reprisal involving the use of force." 25 U.N. GAOR Supp. No. 28, at 122 (1970). In 1974, the Department of State noted that it "has supported and supports" the principle contained in the Declaration, and pointed out that it is "desirable to endeavor to maintain the distinction between acts of lawful self-defense and unlawful reprisal." [1974] Digest of U.S. Practice in Int'l L. 700.

9. *Presidential authority to use self-help: Law of the United States.* The authority of the President to use measures of self-help in response to a violation of international law is an aspect of his general authority to conduct foreign relations and is subject to the general limitations on that authority. The President's authority to respond to violations by suspending or limiting diplomatic relations has been generally accepted. His authority to terminate an international agreement for breach by the other party is also commonly acknowledged. See § 339. Measures affecting individual interests are generally taken pursuant to authorization by Congress. Thus, retaliation for violation of United States rights with respect to foreign trade is authorized and limited by such statutes as the Trade Act of 1974. 19 U.S.C. §§ 2101 *et seq.*, especially § 2112. See § 803, Reporters' Note 5; § 804, Reporters' Note 7. The Internal Revenue Code authorizes the President to double the taxes of nationals of states that subject United States nationals to discriminatory or extraterritorial taxes. 26 U.S.C. § 891. The United States freezes assets in response to a violation of its rights under international law

pursuant to legislation such as the Trading with the Enemy Act (50 U.S.C. App. §§ 5(b)) or the International Emergency Economic Powers Act (50 U.S.C. §§ 1701 *et seq.*). See also Reporters' Note 2.

The President has on many occasions taken measures of self-help involving the use of armed forces abroad, usually to protect American lives and property, sometimes in retaliation for an alleged violation of international law. The authority of the President to use force without Congressional authorization has been a subject of continuing controversy. In a number of instances, the President obtained Congressional authorization. For comprehensive lists of the instances of use of United States armed forces abroad, see House Comm. on Foreign Affairs, Background Information on the Use of United States Armed Forces in Foreign Countries, H.Rep. No. 127, 82d Cong., 1st sess. 55–62 (1951), supplemented by 1970 Revision, 91st Cong., 2d sess. 15 *et seq.*, and Appendices I and II. The 1973 War Powers Resolution, 87 Stat. 555, adopted over the President's veto, included in Section 2(c) the following declaration by Congress:

The constitutional powers of the President as Commander-in-Chief to introduce United States Armed Forces into hostilities, or into situations where imminent involvement in hostilities is clearly indicated by the circumstances, are exercised only pursuant to (1) a declaration of war, (2) specific statutory authorization, or (3) a national emergency created by attack upon the United States, its territories or possessions, or its armed forces.

United States courts have ordinarily refrained from interfering with military action taken by the President, following in this respect the statement by Chief Justice Marshall that retaliation "is a political and not a legal measure," and that it is not for the courts "to interfere with the proceedings of the nation and to thwart its views." The Nereide, 13 U.S. (9 Cranch) 388, 422, 3 L.Ed. 769 (1815). Compare the lower court cases holding that the President's authority to send forces to fight in Vietnam was a political question not subject to judicial review. See § 1, Reporters' Note 4.

10. *Previous Restatement.* Section 200 of the previous Restatement dealt only with the question whether a state is entitled to retaliate against an alien for acts of the state of the alien's nationality.

§ 906. Private Remedies for Violation of International Law

A private person, whether natural or juridical, injured by a violation of an international obligation by a state, may bring a claim against that state or assert that violation as a defense

(a) **in a competent international forum when the state has consented to the jurisdiction of that forum with respect to such private claims;**

(b) **in a court or other tribunal of that state pursuant to its law; or**

(c) **in a court or other tribunal of the injured person's state of nationality or of a third state, pursuant to the law of such state, subject to limitations under international law.**

Comment:

a. International remedies available to private persons. International tribunals and other fora are generally not open to claims by private persons. However, the increasing recognition of the rights of private persons, whether natural or juridical, under international law, has led to a variety of remedies and arrangements to protect these rights. A few international agreements have given private persons access to an international forum where the agreement establishing the forum allows such extension of its jurisdiction. For instance, the International Tribunal for the Law of the Sea, when established, will be open to "entities other than States Parties" in any case submitted pursuant to "an agreement conferring jurisdiction on the Tribunal which is accepted by all the parties to that case." United Nations Convention on the Law of the Sea (see Part V of this Restatement), Annex VI, Article 20. See § 903, Reporters' Note 14. Some human rights agreements grant individuals the right to present petitions to specified international institutions. See § 703, Comment *c*. On the other hand, a state cannot agree to have individuals submit claims against it to the International Court of Justice, since that Court is open only to states. See § 903, Comment *a*.

   b. Domestic remedies for private persons. Private remedies against a state in a domestic forum for violations of international law are subject to the law of the forum and to the limitations imposed by international law. For example, suits against the foreign state or execution on its property may be barred by sovereign immunity, Part IV, Chapter 5. The forum state must have jurisdiction to adjudicate (§§ 421–23), and the substantive law to be applied must be within its jurisdiction to prescribe (§§ 402–403).

   In some circumstances, a state is obligated to provide a domestic forum for certain claims, for example, for some violations of human rights (§ 703) or to foreign nationals claiming denial of justice. See § 713, Comment *h*. Special tribunals are sometimes established for certain claims of foreign nationals. See § 713, Comment *i*. Ordinarily, exhaustion of domestic remedies is required before resorting to an international remedy. See § 713, Comments *b* and *f*. A state may provide a domestic remedy for its own violations of international law even where not obligated to do so.

REPORTERS' NOTES

   1. *International fora.* Some international agreements have given individuals direct access to international tribunals. For instance, private claimants were given access to the Iran-United States Arbitral Tribunal established in 1981. 20 Int'l Leg.Mat. 230–33 (1981). See § 487, Reporters' Note 6, and § 713, Reporters' Note 9. Private persons may bring claims before the Court of Justice of the European Communities against the main organs of the Communities but not against member states. See, *e.g.,* the Treaty Establishing the European Economic Community, March 25, 1957, Arts. 173, 175, 178–79, 181, 298 U.N.T.S. 11.

   The 1950 European Convention for the Protection of Human Rights and Freedoms, 213 U.N.T.S. 222, and the 1969 American Convention on Human Rights, O.A.S.T.S. No. 36, give individuals the right to bring complaints against states to an international commission. European Convention, Art. 25; American Convention, Art. 44. The individual may not institute proceedings before the European Court of Human Rights, but once a case has been brought before the Court by the Commission or one of the states concerned, under the Rules of the Court, as revised in 1982, the individual may "present his own case" to the Court either directly or by an advocate. Rule 30. There is no parallel right for individuals in the Inter-American Court of Human Rights. A right of individual petition to an international forum exists also under the Charter of the United Nations (with respect to inhabitants of trust territories, Art. 87), under the Optional Protocol to the International Covenant on Civil and Political Rights (1966), and under the International Convention on the Elimination of All Forms of Racial Discrimination (1965). See § 703, Reporters' Note 5. As of 1987, the United States was not a party to the Protocol or the Racial Convention.

The European Convention on State Immunity does not permit execution of judgments against states but imposes an obligation on states to give effect to judgments rendered against them. The Additional Protocol to the Convention provides that a private party seeking such enforcement (even one who is not a national of a state party to that Convention) may ask the European Tribunal in Matters of State Immunity to consider whether a contracting state has the obligation to give effect to a judgment rendered against it in proceedings in another state. Additional Protocol to the European Convention on State Immunity, 11 Int'l Leg.Mat. 470, at 485 (1972); Council of Europe, Explanatory Reports on the European Convention on State Immunity and the Additional Protocol 42 (1972). The protocol came into force and the Tribunal was inaugurated on May 28, 1985. Council of Europe, Press Communiqué C(85) 39 (1985).

The 1965 Convention on the Settlement of Investment Disputes between States and Nationals of Other States established a Center for the settlement of such disputes in any case in which parties to the dispute consent in writing to submit to the Center's jurisdiction. See

§ 487, Reporters' Notes 4 and 5, and § 713, Reporters' Note 4.

2. *Domestic fora.* Many bilateral treaties provide that nationals of one state party shall have access to the courts and other tribunals of the other state party on equal terms with nationals of that state. See, *e.g.,* Convention of Establishment between the United States and France, Nov. 25, 1959, Art. 3(1), 11 U.S.T. 2398, T.I.A.S. No. 4625, 401 U.N.T.S. 75. Thus, if a national of France is entitled to present claims for injury resulting from a violation of international law in French courts, whether against France or a third state, nationals of the United States are also entitled to present such claims in French courts, subject only to the same limitations as are applicable to French nationals, such as sovereign immunity. For a similar multilateral provision, see the 1955 European Convention on Establishment, Art. 7, 529 U.N.T.S. 141, 148.

3. *Domestic claims commissions.* Some states give individuals (usually only their nationals) access to a domestic claims commission authorized to adjudicate specified claims against foreign states. In some cases, these commissions divide among the claimants a lump sum obtained in a settlement with a foreign government; in others, there is a preadjudication of claims pending a settlement, which provides the claimant an opportunity to obtain a preliminary determination of the merits and the value of the claim before evidence is lost and witnesses disappear or die. See Lillich, International Claims: Their Adjudication by National Commissions (1962). For United States claims

practice, see § 713, Reporters' Note 9, and § 902, Reporters' Note 8.

4. *Previous Restatement.* This section elaborates on § 3 of the previous Restatement.

§ 907. Private Remedies for Violation of International Law: Law of the United States

(1) A private person having rights against the United States under an international agreement may assert those rights in courts in the United States of appropriate jurisdiction either by way of claim or defense.

(2) A private person having rights against a foreign state under an international agreement of the United States may assert those rights against that state in courts in the United States of appropriate jurisdiction by way of claim or defense, subject to limitations under international law.

Comment:

a. Claims under international agreements of the United States. This section applies only to claims based on an international agreement to which the United States is a party. In principle this section applies not only to United States nationals but also to foreign individuals and foreign corporations even if they are not resident or doing business in the United States, provided they meet other jurisdictional requirements. However, a plaintiff who is a foreign national without any important link to the United States is likely to face the obstacle of *forum non conveniens* in a claim against a foreign state. Hence, it would be possible for him to bring a claim against another state, even under a United States treaty, only in exceptional circumstances, such as those discussed in § 453, Reporters' Note 4.

International agreements, even those directly benefiting private persons, generally do not create private rights or provide for a private cause of action in domestic courts, but there are exceptions with respect to both rights and remedies. Whether an international agreement provides a right or requires that a remedy be made available to a private person is a matter of interpretation of the agreement. Where a remedy was intended, suit against a foreign state (or the United States) might nonetheless be barred by principles of sovereign immunity, unless such immunity is found to have been waived. See Comment *c.*

A claim by a United States citizen under a treaty of another state might also be justiciable in courts in the United States. Although courts in the United States are open to "transitory" suits in some circumstances, a claim by a foreign national against a foreign state for violation of a treaty to which the United States is not a party, even where the defense of sovereign immunity would not apply, would probably fail if only for *forum non conveniens.*

Generally, customary international law does not grant rights to private persons that would serve as a basis for remedies in domestic courts. But see Reporters' Note 4. If a rule of customary international law has become a part of United States law, a domestic remedy may be available for its enforcement. Some principles of customary law are available as a defense, for example, diplomatic immunity, § 464.

  b. Jurisdiction of federal courts over claims for violations of international law. The remedies indicated in this section may be in either State or federal courts. Federal courts have jurisdiction over cases arising under international law and international agreements of the United States. See § 111, Comments *e* and *f;* § 455, Comment *c;* § 713, Comment *i* and Reporters' Note 3; 28 U.S.C. §§ 1330, 1331, 1350 and 1605; The Paquete Habana, 175 U.S. 677, 700, 20 S.Ct. 290, 299, 44 L.Ed. 320 (1900). With respect to remedies in State courts, see Comment *c;* § 713, Reporters' Note 3; § 722, Comments *a* and *c.*

  c. Sovereign immunity as defense. Suits under this section against a foreign state are subject to the defense of sovereign immunity. See §§ 451–60. Suits against the United States are subject to the domestic counterpart of that doctrine, and such suits will not lie unless the United States has consented. Whether such consent may be implied in a treaty, or whether in each case or category of cases statutory authorization is required, is not clear. The United States has consented to suits by foreign nationals in some circumstances, and the Foreign Sovereign Immunities Act explicitly contemplates suits against foreign states for some violations of international law. See § 455(3). Even if a suit against the sovereign is barred, there may be a remedy by suit against a responsible official. For instance, the immunity of the United States does not preclude suit against a United States official on the ground that his action was unconstitutional or contrary to law or treaty, or where such suit is specifically authorized by Congress.

  Private persons have frequently invoked rights under international agreements of the United States to invalidate inconsistent acts of the States or municipalities, sometimes even prior inconsistent federal acts. See § 111, Comment *e* and Reporters' Note 4.

REPORTERS' NOTES

1. *Claims under treaty or other agreement of the United States.* As the Supreme Court stated in Head Money Cases, 112 U.S. 580, 598–99, 5 S.Ct. 247, 254, 28 L.Ed. 798 (1884), a treaty in addition to being "a compact between independent nations" may contain also "provisions which confer certain rights upon the citizens or subjects of one of the nations residing in the territorial limits of the other, which partake of the nature of municipal law, and which are capable of enforcement as between private parties in the courts of the country," *e.g*, rights of property by descent or inheritance. A treaty "is a law of the land as an act of Congress is, whenever its provisions prescribe a rule by which the rights of the private citizen or subject may be determined. And when such rights are of a nature to be enforced in a court of justice, that court resorts to the treaty for a rule of decision for the case before it as it would to a statute." See § 111, Comment *h* and Reporters' Note 5.

2. *Claims against the United States for violations of international law.* Claims against the United States for violations of international law are subject to limitations applicable to claims against the United States generally. The United States cannot be sued in courts in the United States unless Congress by general or special enactment has consented to such suits. See the statement by Chief Justice Marshall in Cohens v. Virginia, 19 U.S. (6 Wheat.) 264, 411–412, 5 L.Ed. 257 (1821); United States v. Lee, 106 U.S. 196, 207, 1 S.Ct. 240, 249–50, 27 L.Ed. 171 (1882); see also Hart and Wechsler, The Federal Courts and the Federal System 1339 *et seq.* (2d ed., Bator *et al.*, 1973). Several statutes have authorized bringing various claims against the United States, including claims for violations of international law.

The Court of Claims, established in 1855 and renamed "United States Claims Court" in 1982, has been given jurisdiction over claims founded upon the United States Constitution or any law of Congress, upon any executive regulation, or upon any express or implied contract with the Federal Government, and over claims for damages, liquidated or unliquidated. Codified in 28 U.S.C. § 1491. (For the concurrent jurisdiction of the district courts over some claims against the United States, see 28 U.S.C. § 1346; concerning maritime claims, see 46 U.S.C. §§ 741 *et seq.*, §§ 781 *et seq.*) The Claims Court does not have jurisdiction over claims against the United States growing out of or dependent upon an international agreement (*id.* § 1502). The Supreme Court has held, however, that the "treaty exception" does not defeat the jurisdiction of the Claims Court with respect to any claim against the United States that is founded upon the Constitution (*e.g.*, whether the suspension of claims under the 1981 agreements with Iran constituted an unconstitutional taking). Dames & Moore v. Regan, 453 U.S. 654, 689–90, 101 S.Ct. 2972, 2992, 69 L.Ed.2d 918 (1981); see also Magraw, "Jurisdiction of Cases Related to Treaties: The Claims Court's Treaty Exception," 26 Va. J. Int'l L. 1 (1985).

Claims by aliens are within the jurisdiction of the Court of Claims only if they are nationals of states that accord reciprocal privileges to United States nationals. 28 U.S.C. § 2502. See 15 Wright, Miller and Cooper, Federal Practice and Procedure: Jurisdiction §§ 3810, 3814 (1976).

When a judgment has been rendered by the Claims Court, its payment depends upon authorization and appropriation of funds by Congress. There have been at least 15 instances in which Congress has failed to appropriate funds to pay a judgment. See Glidden Co. v. Zdanok, 370 U.S. 530, 570, 82 S.Ct. 1459, 1483, 8 L.Ed.2d 671 (1962), citing Note, "The Court of Claims: Judicial Power and Congressional Review," 46 Harv.L.Rev. 677, 685–86, n. 63 (1933). However, in 1982, the Federal Courts Improvement Act authorized the payment of every judgment of the Claims Court against the United States out of a "general appropriation" available therefor. 28 U.S.C. § 2517. The general appropriation is found in 31 U.S.C. § 1304(a)(3)(A).

On various occasions Congress conferred on the Claims Court special jurisdiction over particular claims involving aliens. In some cases this step was taken in response to diplomatic protests by the claimant's government. See, e.g., S.S. Zeelandia (Royal Holland Lloyd v. United States), 73 Ct.Cl. 722 (1931); In re Government of Norway (Hannevig), 145 Ct.Cl. 470, 172 F.Supp. 651 (1959), 14 Whiteman, Digest of International Law 299–300 (1970).

The Federal Tort Claims Act excludes claims against the United States "arising in a foreign coun-try." 28 U.S.C. § 2680(k). Some United States statutes provide, however, for the settlement by the United States of certain small tort claims arising in a foreign country. See, e.g., 22 U.S.C. § 2669(b) and (f), which allow resort to the procedure provided for in 28 U.S.C. § 2672. If the amount of the claim exceeds the maximum allowed in the legislation, the only way in which a claim can be paid is by a special act of Congress, or by a special provision in an appropriation act. 8 Whiteman, Digest of International Law 814 (1967). In paying such claims, the United States takes into consideration their validity under international law. See id. at 812–15.

An official of the United States is not protected by the sovereign immunity of the United States if his action is challenged as unconstitutional, or contrary to law (including international law) or treaty. See Ex parte Young, 209 U.S. 123, 28 S.Ct. 441, 52 L.Ed. 714 (1908); Larson v. Domestic and Foreign Commerce Corp., 337 U.S. 682, 696, 69 S.Ct. 1457, 1464, 93 L.Ed. 1628 (1949). A suit against officials of the United States may also be specifically authorized by Congress: for instance, in actions involving nonresident aliens, courts have held that the Administrative Procedure Act, 5 U.S.C. § 1009(a) and (e), made "a clear waiver of sovereign immunity in actions to which it applies." Estrada v. Ahrens, 296 F.2d 690, 698 (5th Cir. 1961); Constructores Civiles de Centroamerica v. Hannah, 459 F.2d 1183, 1191 (D.C.Cir.1972).

Suits against a State of the United States for violations of international law or an international agreement of the United States are also subject to some constitutional limitations. By the Eleventh Amendment to the United States Constitution, the judicial power of the United States does not "extend to any suit in law or equity, prosecuted against one of the United States . . . by citizens or subjects of any foreign state." A State is immune also from suits by its own citizens or by a foreign state. Hans v. Louisiana, 134 U.S. 1, 11, 10 S.Ct. 504, 506, 33 L.Ed. 842 (1890); Principality of Monaco v. Mississippi, 292 U.S. 313, 54 S.Ct. 745, 78 L.Ed. 1282 (1934). However, a suit against a State official alleging that the State statute under which he acted was unconstitutional, or that his act was beyond his statutory authority, or was in willful and negligent disregard of State laws, is not barred by the Eleventh Amendment. Osborn v. Bank of the United States, 22 U.S. (9 Wheat.) 737, 858–59, 868, 6 L.Ed. 204 (1821); Pennoyer v. McConnaughy, 140 U.S. 1, 11 S.Ct. 699, 35 L.Ed. 363 (1894); Johnson v. Lankford, 245 U.S. 541, 38 S.Ct. 203, 62 L.Ed. 460 (1918). See Block, "Suit against Government Officers and the Sovereign Immunity Doctrine," 59 Harv.L.Rev. 1060 (1946). A foreign national may benefit from all these exceptions to the sovereign immunity doctrine.

3. *Claims against foreign state for violations of international law.* In Verlinden B.V. v. Central Bank of Nigeria, 461 U.S. 480, 103 S.Ct. 1962, 76 L.Ed.2d 81 (1983), a Dutch corporation brought a suit against the Government of Nigeria under the Foreign Sovereign Immunity Act, 28 U.S.C. § 1330, relying on the commercial activities exception in § 1605(a)(2). The Supreme Court recognized that the Act was primarily designed to assure to United States citizens access to the courts but held that the legislative history did not reveal an intent to limit jurisdiction to actions by citizens. See § 457, Comment *h* and Reporters' Note 5. Presumably, such suits could involve claims for violations of international law.

4. *Jurisdiction over tort claims in violation of international law.* For the jurisdiction of United States courts to consider claims by aliens based on torts "in violation of the law of nations," see Filartiga v. Pena-Irala, 630 F.2d 876, 878 (2d Cir.1980); and Tel-Oren v. Libyan Arab Republic, 726 F.2d 774 (D.C. Cir.1984), *certiorari denied*, 470 U.S. 1003, 105 S.Ct. 1354, 84 L.Ed. 2d 377 (1985). These cases are discussed in § 702, Reporters' Note 5, § 703, Reporters' Note 7.

5. *Previous Restatement.* Section 3, Comment *j*, of the previous Restatement dealt with the application of international law in the courts of the United States. Otherwise, the previous Restatement did not consider the questions discussed in this section.

*

TABLES

*

Tables

TABLE OF CASES

1. UNITED STATES AND STATE COURTS

A

Abbate v. United States—§ 483, RN 3; § 701, RN 8.

Aboujdid v. Singapore Airlines, Ltd.—§ 453, RN 4; § 456, RN 4; § 457, RN 4.

Abu Eain v. Adams—§ 476, RN 6; § 478, RN 3.

Ackerman v. Ackerman—§ 482, RN 4.

Adickes v. S. H. Kress & Co.—§ 207, RN 4.

Afroyim v. Rusk—§ 1, RN 1; § 212, RN 4; § 721, RN 1.

Aircrash in Bali, Indonesia, In re—§ 721, RN 8.

Air France v. Saks—§ 325, RN 1; § 325, RN 2.

Aktiebolaget Kreuger & Toll, In re—§ 481, RN 2.

Alaska, United States v.—§ 511, RN 3.

Albano, United States v.—§ 433, RN 4.

Alberti v. Empresa Nicaraguense de la Carne—§ 457, RN 1.

Alcan Aluminium Ltd. v. Dep't of Revenue of Oregon—§ 412, RN 7.

Alco Standard Corp. v. Benalal—§ 472, RN 2.

Alfred Dunhill of London, Inc. v. Republic of Cuba—§ 443, RN 2, 3, 4, 6, 8; § 455, RN 1, 2.

Alifieris v. American Airlines, Inc.—§ 458, RN 1.

Allied Bank Int'l. v. Banco Credito Agricola de Cartago—§ 443, RN 4; § 455, RN 2; § 822, RN 6.

Almeida-Sanchez v. United States—§ 721, RN 5.

Aluminum Co. of America, United States v.—§ 403, RN 2; § 415, RN 2.

Alva S.S. Co., Ltd., Petition of—§ 452, RN 1.

Alvez v. American Export Lines, Inc.—§ 112, RN 2.

Ambach v. Norwick—§ 722, RN 5.

Ambatielos v. Foundation Co.—§ 482, RN 1.

Amerada Hess Shipping Corp. v. Argentine Republic—§ 454, RN 1; § 457, RN 5.

American Ass'n of Exporters and Importers-Textile and Apparel Group v. United States—§ 804, RN 3.

American Banana Co v. United Fruit Co.—§ 415, RN 2; § 441, RN 4.

American Bell Int'l Inc. v. Islamic Republic of Iran—§ 205, RN 1.

American Cetacean Soc. v. Baldrige—§ 115, RN 5.

American Infra-Red Radiant Co. v. Lambert Industries, Inc.—§ 474, RN 10.

American Int'l Group, Inc. v. Islamic Republic of Iran—§ 456, RN 1.

American Jewish Congress v. Vance—§ 721, RN 4.

Ames v. State of Kansas—§ 464, RN 16.

Anderson v. Villela—§ 465, RN 12.

Andros Compania Maritima, S.A. v. Andre & Cie., S.A.—§ 487, RN 7.

Anonymous v. Anonymous—§ 470, RN 2.

Anti-Defamation League v. Kissinger—§ 470, RN 1.

Application of (see name of party)

Arango v. Guzman Travel Advisors Corp.—§ 458, RN 1.

Arcaya v. Paez—§ 464, RN 1, 16.

Argento v. Horn—§ 333, RN 3.

Argento v. North—§ 333, RN 3.

Aris Gloves, Inc. v. United States—§ 721, RN 8.

Arizti, United States v.—§ 464, RN 1; § 464, RN 15.

Arlington County, Va., United States v.—§ 466, RN 4.

Asahi Metal Industry Co., Ltd. v. Superior Court—§ 403, RN 6; § 421, RN 2, 7; § 453, RN 3; § 712, RN 6.

Asakura v. City of Seattle—§ 111, RN 4, 5; § 711, RN 6; § 713, RN 3.

ASG Industries, Inc. v. United States—§ 806, RN 3.

Ashwander v. Tennessee Valley Authority—§ 114, RN 2.

Aspinall's Club Ltd. v. Aryeh—§ 472, RN 5.

Assarsson, Matter of—§ 475, RN 1; § 476, RN 3.

Association of Data Processing Service Organizations, Inc. v. Camp—§ 302, RN 5.

403

Birch Shipping Corp. v. Embassy of United Republic of Tanzania—§ 456, RN 3; § 460, RN 1.

Bivens v. Six Unknown Named Agents of Federal Bureau of Narcotics—§ 721, RN 13.

Black, United States v.—§ 523, RN 9.

Blackmer v. United States—§ 402, RN 1; § 422, RN 6.

Blagge v. Balch—§ 721, RN 8.

Blaine, United States ex rel. Boynton v.—§ 721, RN 8.

Blake v. McClung—§ 722, RN 13.

Blanchette v. Connecticut General Ins. Corporations—§ 713, RN 3.

Blanco v. United States—§ 326, RN 2.

Bloom v. Illinois—§ 422, RN 6.

Bolanos v. Kiley—§ 722, RN 14.

Bolling v. Sharpe—§ 721, RN 6.

Bors v. Preston—§ 464, RN 16.

Boynton, United States ex rel. v. Blaine—§ 721, RN 8.

Braka v. Bancomer—§ 443, RN 4, 6.

Brandenburg v. Ohio—§ 701, RN 8.

Brauch v. Raiche—§ 476, RN 2.

Bremen, The v. Zapata Off-Shore Co.—§ 421, RN 6; § 482, RN 5.

Brignoni-Ponce, United States v.—§ 721, RN 5.

British Steel Corp. v. United States—§ 806, RN 3.

Broadbent v. Organization of American States—§ 467, RN 4.

Brown v. United States—§ 115, RN 2.

Brulay v. United States—§ 433, RN 1.

Bryant v. International Schools Services, Inc.—§ 721, RN 13.

Buckley v. Valeo—§ 721, RN 6.

Burger King Corp. v. Rudzewicz—§ 421, RN 2; § 453, RN 3.

Burks v. United States—§ 701, RN 8.

Burt, Matter of—§ 478, RN 2.

Burton v. United States—§ 422, Com. c(ii).

C

C. A. B. v. Deutsche Lufthansa Aktiengesellschaft—§ 442, RN 3.

Cabell v. Chavez-Salido—§ 722, RN 5.

Cadena, United States v.—§ 324, RN 1; Pt. III, Intro., n. 2.

Caldwell v. Caldwell—§ 484, RN 3.

Califano v. Aznavorian—§ 721, RN 12.

California v. Superior Court—§ 478, RN 8.

California, United States v. (1947)—§ 512 Com. b; RN 2.

California, United States v. (1965)—§ 511, RN 5.

California, United States v. (1977)—§ 511, RN 2, 3.

Callejo v. Bancomer, S.A.—§ 443, RN 5: § 453, RN 5; § 822, RN 1.

Caltagirone v. Grant—§ 478, RN 1.

Caltex, United States v.—§ 722, RN 16.

Cameron Septic Tank Co. v. City of Knoxville, Iowa—§ 111, RN 5.

Canadian Overseas Ores Ltd. v. Compania de Acero del Pacifico, S.A.—§ 455, RN 1; § 456, RN 4.

Canadian Transport Co. v. United States—§ 512, n. 4.

Caplan v. Vokes—§ 476, RN 3.

Capps, Inc., Guy W., United States v.—§ 115, RN 5; § 303, RN 11; § 803, RN 5.

Carcel, People v.—§ 468, RN 3.

Cardy v. Cardy—§ 481, RN 5.

Carey v. National Oil Corp.—§ 453, RN 5.

Carl Byoir & Associates v. Tsune-Chi Yu—§ 465, RN 4.

Carlson v. Green—§ 702, RN 5; § 721, RN 13.

Carlson v. Landon—§ 722, RN 12.

Carl Zeiss Stiftung v. V.E.B. Carl Zeiss, Jena—§ 205, RN 3.

Carolina Power & Light Co. v. Uranex—§ 487, RN 7.

Carrera v. Carrera—§ 464, RN 1.

Casanova, United States ex rel. v. Fitzpatrick—§ 464, RN 1; § 470, RN 2, 4.

Casey v. Galli—§ 464, RN 16.

Chadha, Immigration and Naturalization Service v.—§ 1, RN 3.

Chandler v. United States—§ 402, RN 1.

Charlton v. Kelly—§ 339, RN 1; § 475, RN 3.

Charming Betsy, The—§ 114, RN 1.

Chase Manhattan Bank, Application of—§ 414, RN 6.

Cherokee Tobacco, The—§ 115, RN 1.

Chew Heong v. United States—§ 111, RN 5; § 114, RN 1.

Chicago, B. & Q. R.R. v. Chicago—§ 721, RN 6.

Chinese Exclusion Case, The—§ 115, RN 1; § 722, RN 1, 15.

Chisholm v. Georgia—§ 111, RN 3.

Church v. Hubbart—§ 513, RN 5.

CIBA Corp., United States v.—§ 403, RN 3.

Cintron v. W & D Machinery Co., Inc.—§ 472, RN 5.

City of (see name of city)

Clark v. Allen—§ 1, RN 5; § 111, RN 5; § 114, RN 1.

Clark v. Uebersee Finanz-Korporation—§ 213, RN 5.

Greater Tampa Chamber of Commerce v. Goldschmidt—§ 302, RN 5.

Green, United States v.—§ 433, RN 4.

Greschler v. Greschler—§ 484, RN 3.

Griffiths, Application of—§ 722, RN 5.

Growe v. Growe—§ 486, RN 3.

Grunenthal GmbH v. Hotz—§ 416, RN 1, 2.

Guaranty Trust Co. of New York v. Virginia—§ 721, RN 6.

Guaranty Trust Co. of New York v. United States—§ 114, RN 1; § 204, RN 1.

Guinness v. Miller—§ 823, RN 1.

Guy W. Capps, Inc., United States v.—§ 115, RN 5; § 303, RN 11; § 803, RN 5.

H

Haig v. Agee—§ 701, RN 8; § 721 Com. i, RN 1, 12.

Haitian Refugee Center, Inc. v. Gracey—§ 433, RN 4; § 513, RN 5; § 712, RN 7.

Haley v. State—§ 464, RN 1.

Hamburg-Amerikanische Packet-Fahrt Actien Gesellschaft, United States v.—§ 415, RN 1.

Hampton v. Mow Sun Wong—§ 721, RN 6; § 722, RN 6.

Hanly v. Kleindienst—§ 601, RN 3.

Hanly v. Mitchell—§ 601, RN 2.

Hanoch Tel-Oren v. Libyan Arab Republic—§ 703, RN 7; § 907, RN 4

Hans v. State of Louisiana—§ 907, RN 2.

Hanson v. Denckla—§ 421, RN 2; § 453, RN 3.

Harisiades v. Shaughnessy—§ 212, RN 2.

Harper v. Virginia State Bd. of Elections—§ 701, RN 8.

Harris v. Rosario—§ 721, RN 3.

Harris v. VAO Intourist, Moscow—§ 453, RN 5; § 454, RN 2.

Harvey, United States v.—§ 502, RN 4.

Hauenstein v. Lynham—§ 111, RN 5; § 722, RN 9.

Hausman v. Buckley—§ 213, RN 5.

Haver v. Yaker—§ 312, RN 4.

Hawaii Housing Authority v. Midkiff—§ 712, RN 4.

Hawaii, Territory of v. Mankichi—§ 721, RN 3.

Hawes, Commonwealth v.—§ 111, RN 5.

Head Money Cases—§ 115, RN 1.

Heaney v. Government of Spain—§ 453, RN 2; § 465, RN 4.

Heath v. Alabama—§ 483, RN 3.

Heim v. McCall—§ 722, RN 5.

Helicopteros Nacionales de Colombia, S.A. v. Hall—§ 453, RN 3; § 721, RN 6.

Hellenic Lines, Ltd. v. Moore—§ 464, RN 9.

Hener v. United States—§ 523, RN 2.

Hensel, United States v.—§ 522, RN 8.

Herbert Harvey, Inc. v. N. L. R. B.—§ 467, RN 2.

Herczog v. Herczog—§ 487, RN 5.

Herrera, United States v.—§ 433, RN 3.

Hicklin v. Orbeck—§ 722, RN 5.

Hilton v. Guyot—§ 101 Com. e; § 481 Com. d, RN 1, 6; § 482 Com. b.

Hines v. Davidowitz—§ 1, RN 5; § 402, RN 5; § 404, RN 2; § 722, RN 1, 2.

Hitai v. Immigration and Naturalization Service—§ 701, RN 5.

Holden v. Joy—§ 111, RN 5.

Holley v. Lavine—§ 722, RN 14.

Holmes v. Laird—§ 422, RN 5.

Hong Kong and Shanghai Banking Corp. v. Com'r of Internal Revenue—§ 442, RN 3.

Hoppe v. Russo-Asiatic Bank—§ 823, RN 2.

Howley, People on Complaint of v. Von Otter—§ 464, RN 8.

Hudson and Goodwin, United States v.—§ 111, RN 6; § 404, RN 1; § 422 Com. a.

Hunt v. BP Exploration Co. (Libya) Ltd.—§ 481, RN 3.

Hunt v. Coastal States Gas Producing Co.—§ 444, RN 4; § 713, RN 8.

Hunt v. Mobil Oil Corp.—§ 443, RN 7; § 461, RN 3.

Huntington v. Attrill—§ 483, RN 4; § 602, RN 3.

Husserl v. Swiss Air Transport Co., Ltd.—Pt. III, Intro., n. 2.

Hu Yau-Leung v. Soscia—§ 476, RN 2.

Hyde v. United States—§ 422 Com. c.

I

Icenogle v. Olympic Airways, S.A.—§ 457, RN 4.

IIT v. Vencap, Ltd.—§ 416, RN 2.

IIT v. Cornfeld—§ 416, RN 1.

Illinois v. City of Milwaukee—§ 111, RN 4; § 601, RN 8.

Illinois Commerce Commission v. Salamie—§ 465, RN 12.

Immigration and Naturalization Service (see opposing party)

Imperial Chemical Industries, United States v.—§ 415, RN 6.

L

412

Mora v. McNamara—§ 1, RN 4.
Morgan v. Lavallee—§ 701, RN 7.
Morgan v. Vance—§ 485, RN 6.
Mormels v. Girofinance, S.A.—§ 416, RN 5.
Morrow, United States v.—§ 433, RN 1.
Mount, United States v.—§ 433, RN 1.
M. Salimoff & Co. v. Standard Oil Co. of New York—§ 205, RN 3.
M/S Bremen v. Zapata Off-Shore Co.— § 421, RN 6; § 482, RN 5.
Mundt, United States v.—§ 433, RN 1.
Murray v. The Charming Betsy—§ 114, RN 1.

N

Nardi v. Segal—§ 486, RN 3.
Narenji v. Civiletti—§ 722, RN 6; § 905, RN 2.
Nashville C. & St. L. R. Co. v. Alabama—§ 422, RN 2.
National Bank of Canada v. Interbank Card Ass'n—§ 415, RN 3.
National City Bank of New York v. Republic of China—§ 456 Com. f.
National Equipment Rental, Ltd. v. Szukhent—§ 421, RN 6.
National Hockey League v. Metropolitan Hockey Club, Inc.—§ 442, RN 8.
National Organization for Reform of Marijuana Laws (NORML) v. United States Dept. of State—§ 601, RN 9.
National S. S. Co. v. Tugman—§ 213, RN 5.
Natural Resources Defense Council, Inc. v. Nuclear Regulatory Commission— § 601, RN 9.
Navios Corp. v. The Ulysses II—§ 113, RN 1.
Neidecker, United States ex rel. v. Valentine—§ 475, RN 3, 4; § 478, RN 7(v).
Neporany v. Kir—§ 482, RN 1.
Nevada v. Hall—§ 452, RN 1.
New England Merchants Nat. Bank v. Iran Power Generation and Transmission Co.—§ 456, RN 1; § 457, RN 2; § 460, RN 2; Pt. IV, ch. 5, Intro., n. 12.
New Rochelle, City of v. Page-Sharp— § 464, RN 8.
New York v. New Jersey—§ 601, RN 1.
New York Life Ins. Co. v. Hendren— § 111, RN 3.
New York Times Co. v. United States— § 721, RN 4.
Nicol v. Tanner—§ 481, RN 1; § 486, RN 4.

Nielsen v. Johnson—§ 111, RN 5; § 114, RN 1.
Nippon Hodo Co. v. United States— § 711, RN 1.
Nissen, People v.—§ 513, RN 5.
Nixon, United States v.—§ 112, RN 1.
Nyquist v. Mauclet—§ 722, RN 5.

O

Occidental of Umm Al Qaywayn, Inc. v. a Certain Cargo of Petroleum—§ 443, RN 7; § 713, RN 3.
Occidental Petroleum Corp. v. Buttes Gas & Oil Co.—§ 443, RN 7.
O'Connell Machinery Co., Inc. v. M.V. Americana—§ 455, RN 3; § 456, RN 1.
O'Dea's Estate, In re—§ 481, RN 5.
O'Donnell, United States v.—§ 209, RN 2.
Oehl v. Oehl—§ 485, RN 4.
Oetjen v. Central Leather Co.—§ 443 Com. a, RN 3.
Ogden v. Ogden—§ 481, RN 1.
Oglala Sioux Tribe of Pine Ridge Indian Reservation v. United States—§ 713, RN 8.
Ohio, State of v. Agler—§ 465, RN 12.
Ohio, State of v. Arthur Andersen & Co.—§ 442, RN 8.
Ohio, State of v. Deckebach—§ 722, RN 5.
Oil Spill by Amoco Cadiz, In re—§ 442, RN 8.
Oliver American Trading Co. v. United States of Mexico—§ 111, RN 3.
Olsen by Sheldon v. Government of Mexico—§ 454, RN 1.
Olson v. United States—§ 712, RN 3.
Oneida Indian Nation v. New York— § 201, RN 9.
Oregon v. Mitchell—§ 701, RN 8.
Orion Shipping & Trading Co. v. Eastern States Petro. Corp. of Panama—§ 456, RN 3.
Ornelas v. Ruiz—§ 476, RN 5; § 478, RN 2.
Ortiz, United States v.—§ 721, RN 5.
Osborn v. Bank of United States—§ 907, RN 2.
Oster v. Dominion of Canada—§ 465, RN 4.
Otherson, United States v.—§ 721, RN 13; § 722, RN 14.
Over the Top, The—§ 115, RN 3.
Owen v. City of Independence, Mo.— § 452, RN 1.
Ozanic v. United States—§ 902, RN 8.

Ramirez de Arellano v. Weinberger—§ 443, RN 3, 5, 7; § 444, RN 4; § 602, RN 3.

Rauscher, United States v.—§ 111, RN 5; § 475, RN 3; § 477, RN 1.

Ray, People ex rel., v. Martin—§ 112, RN 2.

Reading & Bates Corp. v. National Iranian Oil Co.—§ 456, RN 1; § 460, RN 2.

Reasor-Hill Corp. v. Harrison—§ 602, RN 3.

Rediker v. Rediker—§ 484, RN 3.

Reed, United States v.—§ 433, RN 3.

Reeh, United States v.—§ 522, RN 8.

Reeves, Inc. v. Stake—§ 1, RN 5.

Regan v. Wald—§ 721, RN 12.

Regierungspraesident Land Nordrhein-Westfalen v. Rosenthal—§ 481, RN 5.

Reid v. Covert—§ 1, RN 4; § 302, RN 1; § 422, RN 4; § 721, RN 1, 2, 3, 9; § 722, RN 16.

Republic of Argentina v. City of New York—§ 466, RN 4.

Republic of Finland v. Town of Pelham—§ 466, RN 4.

Republic of Iraq v. First Nat. City Bank—§ 443, RN 4.

Republic of Mexico v. Hoffman—§ 1, RN 4; Pt. IV, ch. 5, Intro., n. 8.

Republic of Peru, Ex parte—§ 1, RN 4; Pt. IV, ch. 5, Intro., n. 7.

Republic of Philippines v. Marcos—§ 111, RN 4; § 443, RN 3, 7; § 464, RN 14; § 483, RN 6.

Republic of Vietnam v. Pfizer, Inc.—§ 201, RN 1; § 202, RN 6.

Request for Judicial Assistance from Seoul Dist. Criminal Court, In re—§ 474, RN 2.

Revere Copper & Brass Co. v. Overseas Private Investment Corp.—§ 712, RN 8.

Rex v. _____ (see opposing party)

Reynolds v. Koh—§ 471, RN 4.

Reynolds v. Sims—§ 701, RN 8.

Ricaud v. American Metal Co.—§ 443, RN 3.

Rich v. Naviera Vacuba, S.A.—§ 456, RN 5; Pt. IV, ch. 5, Intro., n. 11.

Rich, Marc & Co., A.G., Matter of—§ 442, RN 11.

Richardson, United States v.—§ 302, RN 5.

Richardson v. Volkswagenwerk, A.G.—§ 471, RN 4.

Ritchie v. McMullen—§ 481, RN 1, 4.

Rivard v. United States—§ 403, RN 8.

Rivers v. Stihl, Inc.—§ 471, RN 4.

Robertson v. General Electric Co.—§ 111, RN 5.

Rocha v. United States—§ 403, RN 8.

Rodriguez Fernandez v. Wilkinson—§ 702, RN 6; § 703, RN 7; § 722, RN 15.

Rogdai, The—§ 205, RN 1.

Rogers v. Bellei—§ 212, RN 4.

Romero v. International Terminal Operating Co.—§ 111, RN 4; § 403, RN 2.

Romero-Galue, United States v.—§ 513, RN 5; § 522, RN 8.

Rosado v. Civiletti—§ 422, RN 5; § 433, RN 1; § 721, RN 11.

Rosenbaum v. Rosenbaum—§ 484, RN 3.

Rosenstiel v. Rosenstiel—§ 484, RN 3.

Roses Inc., United States v.—§ 806, RN 4.

Ross v. McIntyre—§ 422, RN 4; § 721, RN 2.

Ross, United States v.—§ 502, RN 3.

Rostker v. Goldberg—§ 721, RN 6.

Ruckelshaus v. Monsanto Co.—§ 712, RN 6.

Ruggiero v. Compania Peruana de Vapores—§ 457, RN 3.

Rush v. Savchuk—§ 421, RN 2; § 453, RN 3.

Russian Socialist Federated Soviet Republic (RSFSR) v. Cibrario—§ 205, RN 1.

Russian Volunteer Fleet v. United States—§ 205, RN 1; § 722, RN 3.

Rzeszotarski v. Rzeszotarski—§ 485, RN 4.

S

Sabbatino, Banco Nacional de Cuba v.—§ 1, RN 4; § 4; § 111, RN 1, 3; § 204, RN 1; § 205, RN 1; § 326, RN 2; § 443 Com. a, RN 2, 4, 5, 6, 8, 12; § 444 Com. a, RN 1, 2, 4; § 713, RN 9.

Sadat v. Mertes—§ 212, RN 3.

S.A. Empresa de Viacao Aerea Rio Grandense (Varig Airlines), United States v.—§ 454, RN 3.

Samad v. The Etivebank—§ 465, RN 1.

San Antonio Independent School Dist. v. Rodriguez—§ 701, RN 8.

Sanchez-Espinoza v. Reagan—§ 1, RN 4.

Sardino v. Federal Reserve Bank of New York—§ 712, RN 6; § 905, RN 2.

Sarmiento, United States v.—§ 433, RN 4.

Scales v. United States—§ 701, RN 8.

Scherk v. Alberto-Culver Co.—§ 421, RN 6; § 482, RN 5; § 487, RN 8; § 488, RN 1.

Schleiffer v. Meyers—§ 485, RN 6.

Sumitomo Shoji America, Inc. v. Avagliano—§ 213, RN 4; § 326, RN 2; § 711, RN 6.

Svenska Handelsbanken v. Carlson—§ 481, RN 1.

Swearingen v. United States—§ 115, RN 5.

Sweeney v. Woodall—§ 478, RN 8.

Swift v. Tyson—Pt. I, ch. 2, Intro.

T

Tag v. Rogers—§ 115, RN 3.

Tahan v. Hodgson—§ 481, RN 4.

Tamari v. Bache & Co. (Lebanon) S.A.L.—§ 416, RN 5.

Tampimex Oil Limited v. Latina Trading Corp.—§ 487, RN 7.

Taylor v. Taylor—§ 485, RN 4.

Tayyari v. New Mexico State University—§ 722, RN 5.

Tchacosh Co., Ltd. v. Rockwell Int'l Corp.—§ 443, RN 4.

Tel-Oren v. Libyan Arab Republic—§ 703, RN 7; § 907, RN 4.

Tenbergen, The—§ 205, RN 1.

Tennessee Valley Authority, United States ex rel. v. Welch—§ 712, RN 4.

Terlinden v. Ames—§ 208, RN 4; § 210, RN 2.

Terrace v. Thompson—§ 722, RN 5, 9.

Territory of Hawaii v. Mankichi—§ 721, RN 3.

Testa v. Katt—§ 302, RN 3.

Texas v. Louisiana—§ 113, RN 1.

Texas, United States v.—§ 512, RN 2.

Texas Trading & Mill. Corp. v. Federal Republic of Nigeria—§ 453, RN 4; § 457, RN 5.

Theye y Ajuria v. Pan American Life Insurance Co.—§ 822, RN 5.

Thirty Hogsheads of Sugar v. Boyle—§ 112 Com. b.

Thompson, United States v.—§ 433, RN 4.

Thomsen v. Cayser—§ 415, RN 1.

Tickle, State v.—§ 403, RN 5.

Tiede, United States v.—§ 422, RN 4; § 722, RN 16.

Timberlane Lumber Co. v. Bank of America N.T. and S.A.—§ 403, RN 2, 6; § 415, RN 4; § 443, RN 7.

Toll v. Moreno—§ 469, RN 5; § 722, RN 2, 5, 13.

Tomoya Kawakita v. United States—§ 212, RN 3; § 402, RN 1.

Toomer v. Witsell—§ 722, RN 5.

Torao Takahashi v. Fish and Game Com'n—§ 722, RN 2, 5.

Torres v. Com. of Puerto Rico—§ 721, RN 3.

Toscanino, United States v.—§ 433, RN 3.

Toyota Motor Corp., United States v.—§ 442, RN 10.

Tran Qui Than v. Blumenthal—§ 202, RN 6.

Transamerican S.S. Corp. v. Somali Democratic Republic—§ 453, RN 2, 5; § 456, RN 2.

Translinear, Inc. v. Republic of Haiti—§ 458, RN 1.

Trans World Airlines, Inc. v. Franklin Mint Corp.—§ 325, RN 1; § 326, RN 2; § 821, RN 1.

Travis v. Anthes Imperial Ltd.—§ 416, RN 1.

Trop v. Dulles—§ 212, RN 4.

Trost v. Tompkins—§ 464, RN 1.

Truax v. Raich—§ 722, RN 3, 5.

Tsiang v. Tsiang—§ 470, RN 2.

Tsuda Maru, United States v.—§ 722, RN 6.

Tuck v. Pan American Health Organization—§ 467, RN 4.

U

Underhill v. Hernandez—§ 207, RN 1; § 443 Com. a, c, RN 2, 3.

United Mexican States v. Ashley—§ 444, RN 4.

United Nations Korean Reconstruction Agency v. Glass Production Methods, Inc.—§ 223, RN 4.

United Nuclear Corp. v. General Atomic Co.—§ 441, RN 4; § 442, RN 8.

United States v. ____ (see opposing party)

United States ex rel. v. ____ (see opposing party and relator)

United States of Mexico v. Schmuck—§ 464, RN 1.

United States Trust Co. of New York v. New Jersey—§ 712, RN 8.

Upright v. Mercury Business Machines Co.—§ 205, RN 1.

Upton v. Empire of Iran—§ 453, RN 5; § 454, RN 2.

Uranium Antitrust Litigation, In re—§ 403, RN 1, 6; § 441, RN 4; § 442, RN 10.

World-Wide Volkswagen Corp. v. Woodson—§ **421, RN 2**; § **453, RN 1, 3.**
Worthley v. Worthley—§ **486, RN 3.**
Worthy v. Herter—§ **721, RN 12.**
Wright v. Henkel—§ **478, RN 3.**
Wright-Barker, United States v.—§ **403, RN 8.**
Wulfsohn v. Russian Socialist Federated Soviet Republic (RSFSR)—§ **111, RN 3**; § **205, RN 1.**
Wyse, In re—§ **481, RN 2.**

Y

Yamashita, Application of—§ **404, RN 1**; § **722, RN 16.**
Yates v. United States—§ **701, RN 8.**
Yick Wo v. Hopkins—§ **722, RN 3, 4.**
Yiu Sing Chun v. Sava—§ **712, RN 7.**
Yoshida Int'l, Inc., United States v.—§ **803, RN 5**; § **804, RN 6.**
Young, Ex parte—§ **907, RN 2.**
Youngstown Sheet & Tube Co. v. Sawyer—§ **1, RN 3**; § **303, RN 12.**

Z

Zablocki v. Redhail—§ **701, RN 8.**
Zaimi v. United States—§ **466, RN 2.**
Zaubi, Com. *ex rel.* v. Zaubi—§ **485, RN 5.**
Zaubi v. Hoejme—§ **485, RN 6.**
Zeevi and Sons Ltd. v. Grindlays Bank (Uganda) Ltd—§ **822, RN 2.**
Zemel v. Rusk—§ **701, RN 7**; § **721, RN 12.**
Zernicek v. Petroleos Mexicanos (Pemex)—§ **456, RN 2.**
Z. & F. Assets Realization Corp. v. Hull—§ **461, RN 1**; § **721, RN 8.**
Zschernig v. Miller—§ **1, RN 5**; § **208, RN 4**; § **302 Com.** *d*; § **402, RN 5**; § **722 Com.** *b*, **RN 2.**
Zwack v. Kraus Bros. & Co.—§ **443, RN 4.**

2. COURTS OF OTHER COUNTRIES *

---

* Includes decisions of courts of states other than the United States. For mixed claims commissions, European Community cases, and reports of arbitral tribunals, see International Tribunals.

COURTS OF OTHER COUNTRIES

I

In re (see name of party)
India, Gov't of v. Taylor—§ 483, RN 1.
Indyka v. Indyka—§ 484, RN 1.
Interprovincial Co-operatives Ltd. v. The Queen in Right of Manitoba—§ 601, RN 8.

J

Jennings, Government of United States of America v.—§ 476, RN 1.

K

Kahler v. Midland Bank, Ltd.—§ 822, RN 5.
Kavic et al., In re—§ 476, RN 5.
Kelly, Reg. v.—§ 402, RN 1.
Kolczynski and Others, In re—§ 476, RN 5.
Krupp Mak Maschinenbau G.m.b.H. v. Deutsche Bank A.G.—§ 442, RN 10.
Kugele v. Polish State—§ 712, RN 6.

L

Laker Airways Ltd., British Airways Board v.—§ 403, RN 7.
Lessinger v. Mirau—§ 822, RN 2.
Littlejohn, Ex parte, Reg. v. Governor of Winson Green Prison—§ 476 RN 7.
Livingston v. Jefferson—§ 602, RN 3.
Lonrho Ltd. v. Shell Petroleum Co.—§ 442, RN 10.
Luther, A.M. v. James Sagor & Co. (U.K.)—§ 205, RN 3; § 443 RN 12.

M

Mackeson, Ex parte, Reg. v. Bow Street Magistrates—§ 475, RN 6.
Manners v. Pearson & Son—§ 823, RN 6.
Massolombarda, S.p.A. v. Fruchttrunk, G.m.b.H.—§ 488, RN 2.
Matter of (see name of party)
McCaffrey, United States Government v.—§ 475, RN 1; § 476, RN 1.
McGlichey v. Wren—§ 476, RN 7.
Meunier, In re—§ 476, RN 5.
Miliangos v. George Frank (Textiles) Ltd.—§ 481, RN 8; § 823, RN 6.
Molefi v. Principal Legal Adviser—§ 210, RN 3.
Molvan v. Attorney General for Palestine—§ 522, RN 7.
Moojen v. Von Reichert—§ 822, RN 2.
Munzer v. Munzer–Jacoby—§ 481, RN 6.

N

Norway's Application, In re—§ 483, RN 2.

O

Oil Pipelines Case—§ 415, RN 9.
Organic Pigments Case—§ 415, RN 9.

P

Philippine Admiral (Owners) v. Wallem Shipping (Hong Kong), Ltd.—§ 451, RN 1.
Piracy Jure Gentium, In re—§ 522, RN 2.

R

Radio Corporation of America v. Rauland Corporation—§ 442, RN 1; § 473, RN 7.
Radwan v. Radwan—§ 466, RN 2.
Raulin v. Fischer—§ 483, RN 4.
Regina v. ___ (see opposing party)
Rio Tinto Zinc Corp. v. Westinghouse Electric Corp.—§ 403, RN 8; § 442, RN 1; § 473, RN 7.

S

Scott, Ex parte—§ 432, RN 2.
Senembah Maatschappij N.V. v. Republiek Indonesie Bank Indonesia—§ 443, RN 12.
Soc. Cooperative Sidmetal v. Titan International, Ltd.—§ 481, RN 6.
Soc. Eurodif v. Republique Islamique d'Iran—§ 456, RN 3.
Soc. Minera El Teniente, S.A. v. A.G. Norddeutsche Affinerie (German Fed. Republic)—§ 443, RN 12.
Société Filature et Tissage X. Jourdain v. Epoux Heynen–Bintner—§ 822, RN 2.
South Carolina Insurance Co. v. Assurantie Maatschappij "De Zeven Provincien" N.V.—§ 474, RN 9.
Standard Chartered Bank v. International Tin Council—§ 467, RN 6.
St. John, City of v. Fraser–Brace Overseas Corp.—§ 462, RN 1.
Swedish Central Railway Company, Ltd. v. Thompson—§ 411, RN 1.

T

Teh Hu, The—§ 823, RN 6.

3. INTERNATIONAL TRIBUNALS *

A

Aegaen Sea Continental Shelf Case (Greece v. Turkey)—§ 301, RN 1.

Aerial Incident of 27 July 1955, (Israel v. Bulgaria), Case Concerning—§ 903, RN 3.

Air Service Agreement, Case Concerning (U.S./France, 1978)—§ 904, RN 5; § 905, RN 3, 4, 5.

Air Transport Services Argeement between United States and France (1964)—§ 334, RN 2.

Alcan Aluminium Ltd. v. Ircable Corp.— § 213, RN 3.

Ambatielos Case (Greece v. United Kingdom)—§ 713, RN 5; § 902, RN 2; § 904, RN 1.

American Int'l Group v. Islamic Rep. of Iran—§ 712, RN 2.

Anglo-Iranian Oil Co. Case (United Kingdom v. Iran)—§ 301, RN 3; § 713, RN 1; § 903, RN 2, 3, 6.

Asylum Case (Colombia v. Peru)—§ 102, Com. e; § 466, RN 3.

B

Barcelona Traction Case (Belgium v. Spain)—§ 213, RN 2, 3; § 701, RN 2; § 703, RN 2, 3; § 712, RN 1; § 713, RN 1; § 902, RN 1.

Bier v. Mines de Potasse d'Alsace— § 602, RN 4.

British Petroleum v. Libya—§ 901, RN 3.

Brown, Robert E. (United States v. Great Britain)—§ 209, RN 7.

Burkina Faso/Mali, Case Concerning Frontier Dispute—§ 903, RN 6.

C

Cambodia v. Thailand, Case Concerning Temple of Preah Vihear—§ 102, RN 7; § 901, RN 3.

Canevaro Case (Italy-Peru)—§ 713, RN 2.

Casablanca Case (France v. Germany)— § 432, RN 3.

Central Rhodope Forests Case (Greece v. Bulgaria)—§ 901, RN 3.

Certain Norwegian Loans (France v. Norway)—§ 712, RN 10; § 903, RN 3.

Chorzów Factory (Interpretation of Judgments Nos. 7 and 8) (Germany v. Poland)—§ 903, RN 5.

Chorzów Factory (Indemnity) (Germany v. Poland)—§ 713, RN 7; § 901, RN 3.

Competence of the General Assembly for the Admission of a State to the United Nations—§ 222, RN 1; § 325, RN 1.

Conditions of Admission of a State to Membership in the United Nations— § 222, RN 1.

Continental Shelf, Case Concerning (Libyan Arab Jamahiriya/Malta) (Application of Italy for Permission to Intervene)—§ 903, RN 7.

Continental Shelf, Case Concerning (Tunisia/Libyan Arab Jamahiriya) (Application of Malta for Permission to Intervene)—§ 903, RN 7.

Continental Shelf Case (Libya/Malta)— § 903, RN 9.

Continental Shelf Case (Tunisia/Libya)— § 903, RN 9, 10.

Convention of 1902 Governing the Guardianship of Infante (Netherlands v. Sweden), Case Concerning the Application of—§ 485, RN 6.

Cook Case, George W.—§ 902, RN 2.

Corfu Channel Case (United Kingdom v. Albania)—§ 903, RN 2, 10, 11; § 905, RN 1.

D

Delimination of the Continental Shelf (France/United Kingdom)—§ 517, RN 3.

Delimination of the Maritime Boundary, Case Concerning Gulf of Maine Area—§ 517, RN 3.

Dyestuffs Case—§ 402, RN 9; § 414, RN 2; § 415, RN 9.

E

Eastern Carelia—§ 902, RN 3.

Eastern Greenland (Denmark v. Norway)—§ 903, RN 13.

Electric Company of Sofia and Bulgaria Case (Belgium v. Bulgaria)—§ 903, RN 5.

Elefanten Schuh G.m.b.H. v. Jacqmain— § 481, RN 7.

---

* Includes decisions of the International Court of Justice, the European Court of Justice, the European Court of Human Rights, mixed claims tribunals, international arbitral tribunals, and the Iran–United States Claims Tribunal.

TABLE OF STATUTES

(Including references to U.S. Constitution, Executive Orders,
and Federal Rules and Regulations)

UNITED STATES

UNITED STATES CONSTITUTION

Art.	Restatement Sec.
I	412, RN 7
I, § 2	722, Com. *a*
I, § 3	722, Com. *a*
I, § 5	722, Com. *m*
I, § 7	111, Com. *i*
	303, RN 9
I, § 8	1, RN 1
	111, RN 6
	111, RN 8
	339, Com. *a*
	401, Com. *c*
	404, RN 1
	404, RN 2
	412, RN 7
	415, Com. *k*
	721, Com. *a*
	722, RN 1
	722, Com. *e*
	Ch. 1, Pt. I, Intro.
	Ch. 1, Pt. VIII, Intro.
I, § 8, cl. 4	212, Com. *b*
I, § 8, cl. 17	111, RN 6
I, § 8, cl. 18	111, Com. *j*
I, § 9	302, Com. *b*
	Ch. 1, Pt. VIII, Intro.
I, § 10	1, RN 5
	302, Com. *c*
	401, Com. *c*
	402, RN 5
	Ch. 1, Pt. VIII, Intro.
	721, Com. *k*
	722, Com. *a*
I, § 10, cl. 1	302, Com. *f*
I, § 10, cl. 2	201, RN 9
I, § 10, cl. 3	302, Com. *f*
II, § 1	1, RN 2
	303, Com. *g*
II, § 2	1, RN 2
	111, Com. *c*

UNITED STATES CONSTITUTION

Art.	Restatement Sec.
II, § 2 (Cont'd)	204, Com. *a*
	302, Com. *a*
	302, Com. *c*
	303, Com. *a*
	303, Com. *d*
	303, Com. *g*
	311, Com. *b*
	722, Com. *a*
II, § 3	1, RN 3
	115, RN 3
	204, Com. *a*
	303, Com. *g*
	326, Com. *b*
III	111, RN 4
	213, RN 5
	422, Com. *b*
	457, RN 5
III, § 2	Ch. 2, Pt. I, Intro.
	111, RN 4
	111, Com. *e*
	303, Com. *a*
	326, Com. *d*
	422, RN 1
	457, RN 5
	464, RN 16
IV	478, RN 1
IV, § 1	478, RN 8
	481, RN 4
	482, RN 4
	486, RN 1
IV, § 2	213, RN 5
	722, Com. *a*
IV, § 2, cl. 2	478, RN 8
IV, § 3, cl. 2	303, RN 2
IV, § 4	302, RN 3
VI	1, RN 5
	Ch. 2, Pt. I, Intro.
	111, Com. *d*
	111, RN 2
	111, RN 6
	115, RN 1
	302, Com. *c*
	302, RN 1
	303, Com. *a*
	326, Com. *d*

TABLE OF STATUTES

UNITED STATES CODE ANNOTATED

19 U.S.C.A.—Customs Duties

UNITED STATES CODE ANNOTATED

21 U.S.C.A.—Food and Drugs

22 U.S.C.A.—Foreign Relations and Intercourse

UNITED STATES CODE ANNOTATED

31 U.S.C.A.—Money and Finance

Sec.	Restatement Sec.
3725	902, RN 8
5101	823, RN 1

33 U.S.C.A.—Navigation and Navigable Waters

Sec.	Restatement Sec.
131	603, RN 4
381 et seq.	522, RN 2
441	603, RN 7
443–444	603, RN 7
1001–1016	603, RN 4
1221	512, RN 4
1221–1232	603, RN 4
1222	512, RN 4
1228	512, RN 4
1230	512, RN 4
1232	512, RN 4
1251–1376	601, RN 8
	603, RN 7
1320(a)	601, RN 8
1320(c)	601, RN 8
1321(a)(9)	512, RN 4
1321(a)(17)	603, RN 7
1321(b)(1)	512, RN 4
1321(b)(3)	512, RN 4
1321(b)(5)(B)	603, RN 7
1321(b)(6)(A)	603, RN 7
1321(m)	512, RN 4
1365(a)	601, RN 8
1365(g)	601, RN 8
1401–1443	603, RN 7
1401–1473	603, RN 7
1419	603, RN 7
1471(5)	501, RN 1
1471–1487	603, RN 7
1501	511, RN 2
1501 et seq.	514, RN 7
1501–1524	603, RN 7
1502(10)	511, RN 2
1502(19)	501, RN 1
1518(c)	603, RN 7
1521	603, RN 7
1701–1709	603, RN 7
1901	603, RN 5
1901–1911	603, RN 4
	603, RN 5

35 U.S.C.A.—Patents

Sec.	Restatement Sec.
135(d)	488, RN 1
293	421, RN 9
294	488, RN 1

UNITED STATES CODE ANNOTATED

39 U.S.C.A.—The Postal Service

Sec.	Restatement Sec.
407	303, RN 10

41 U.S.C.A.—Public Contracts

Sec.	Restatement Sec.
10a–10d	805, Com. b

42 U.S.C.A.—The Public Health and Welfare

Sec.	Restatement Sec.
402(t)(1)	722, RN 6
411(c)(2)(C)	464, RN 4(c)
1981–1983	702, RN 5
1981 et seq.	721, RN 13
	722, RN 7
1982	722, RN 7
1983	207, RN 4
	452, RN 1
	722, RN 7
1985	702, RN 5
2000a et seq.	722, RN 7
2074 et seq.	812, RN 4
2210(1)	604, RN 1
4321	601, RN 9
4331	601, RN 2
4332(2)(C)	601, RN 3
4332(2)(F)	601, RN 9
4710(a)(2)(E)(i)(I)	601, RN 3
7401–7642	601, RN 8
7415	601, RN 8
7415(a)	601, RN 3
7415(c)	601, RN 8
8011–8012	601, RN 8
8901–8905	601, RN 8
9601	601, RN 8
9601(8)	512, RN 4
9601 et seq.	512, RN 4
9601–9657	603, RN 7
9611(1)	601, RN 8

43 U.S.C.A.—Public Lands

Sec.	Restatement Sec.
1301–1315	512, Com. b
	512, RN 2
	515, RN 3
1312	512, Com. b
1331	Pt. V, Intro., n. 11
1331–1343	515, RN 3
1331–1356	603, RN 7
1333	515, Com. f

TABLE OF STATUTES

TABLE OF STATUTES

TABLE OF STATUTES

STATE STATUTES

COLORADO

Revised Statutes

Sec.	Restatement Sec.
13–1.5.101	602, RN 4

DISTRICT OF COLUMBIA

Code Annotated

Sec.	Restatement Sec.
22–1115	466, RN 2

ILLINOIS

Revised Statutes

Chap.	Restatement Sec.
110, § 16–17	453, RN 4

Code of Civil Procedure

Sec.	Restatement Sec.
2–203	472, RN 5
2–208(b)	472, RN 5

MASSACHUSETTS

General Laws Annotated

Title	Restatement Sec.
235, § 23A	481, RN 1

Acts and Resolves

Year	Restatement Sec.
1966, c. 638	481, RN 1

MONTANA

Code Annotated

Sec.	Restatement Sec.
75–16–101	602, RN 4

NEW JERSEY

Statutes Annotated

Sec.	Restatement Sec.
2A:58A–1	602, RN 4

NEW YORK

Civil Practice Laws and Rules

Art.	Restatement Sec.
302	453, RN 4
302(a)(3)	453, RN 4
308(2)	472, RN 5
313	472, RN 5
328	472, RN 3

Laws

Year	Restatement Sec.
1966, c. 590	453, RN 4

Judiciary Law

Sec.	Restatement Sec.
27	823, Com. b

TEXAS

Vernon's Annotated Revised Civil Statutes

Art.	Restatement Sec.
2328b–6, § 5(7)	481, RN 1

WISCONSIN

Statutes Annotated

Sec.	Restatement Sec.
144.995	602, RN 4

POPULAR NAME ACTS

CIVIL RIGHTS ACT

Title	Restatement Sec.
VII	701, RN 5

CLEAN AIR ACT

Sec.	Restatement Sec.
	601, RN 8

CLEAN WATER ACT

Sec.	Restatement Sec.
	601, RN 8

COMMODITY EXCHANGE ACT

Sec.	Restatement Sec.
8a(9)	461, RN 3

JUDICIARY ACT

Sec.	Restatement Sec.
1	Ch. 2, p. 40
5	111, RN 4
25	Ch. 2, p. 40

POLICY ACT

Sec.	Restatement Sec.
101	601, RN 2
102(2)(C)	601, RN 3

REVENUE ACT

Sec.	Restatement Sec.
222	413, RN 2
238	413, RN 2

SECURITIES EXCHANGE ACT

Sec.	Restatement Sec.
3	416, RN 3
3(9)	416, RN 3
7	416, RN 3
10	416, RN 3
11	416, RN 3
12	416, RN 3
27	421, RN 6
	421, RN 7
	421, RN 9

TARIFF ACT OF 1930

Sec.	Restatement Sec.
3	111, RN 5

TRADE ACT OF 1974

Sec.	Restatement Sec.
122(c)	804, RN 6
203	808, Com. c
	808, RN 5
249	808, RN 4
401–453	805, RN 3
406	808, Com. c
607	808, RN 5

MODEL PENAL CODE

Sec.	Restatement Sec.
1.03(e)–(f)	402, RN 5

UNIFORM COMMERCIAL CODE

Sec.	Restatement Sec.
3–107(2)	823, RN 1

CODE OF FEDERAL REGULATIONS

Title	Restatement Sec.
3, § 2	511, RN 7
3, Pts. 180–182	513, RN 5
3, Pt. 356	512, RN 4
8, § 214.2(a)(2)	464, RN 15
12, § 211.23(h)(3)	461, RN 3(iv)
14, § 99.23	521, RN 2
15, § 369.1	414, RN 4
15, Pts. 386–387	431, RN 3
15, Pt. 388	431, RN 3
	812, RN 3
17, § 3.12	416, RN 5
17, § 17.00	416, RN 5
17, §§ 21.01–03	416, RN 5
17, § 30.02	416, RN 5
17, § 210.3A–02	414, RN 2
17, § 229.101(d)	414, RN 2
17, Pt. 230	461, RN 3
17, § 230.262	431, RN 6
17, Pt. 231	463, Com. b
17, §§ 239.31–239.36	416, RN 4
17, § 249.220F	416, RN 4
19, §§ 148.81–148.90	464, RN 4
19, Pt. 207	442, RN 3
19, Pt. 210	442, RN 3
19, Pt. 353	807, RN 1
22, § 51.27(d)	485, RN 6
22, § 92.85	471, RN 2
22, Pt. 93	457, Com. a
22, § 93.2	457, Com. c
22, §§ 151.1–151.11	464, RN 9
22, Pt. 181	301, RN 4

TABLE OF STATUTES

TABLE OF STATUTES

TABLE OF INTERNATIONAL AGREEMENTS

MULTILATERAL AGREEMENTS *

---

* Agreements are listed alphabetically by key word identifying the agreement, and in some instances also by cities with which they are associated.

444

TABLE OF INTERNATIONAL AGREEMENTS

BILATERAL AGREEMENTS TO WHICH THE UNITED STATES IS PARTY

---

* FCN treaties having slightly different titles, such as "Amity" rather than "Friendship", are nevertheless listed here.

TABLE OF INTERNATIONAL AGREEMENTS

449

TABLE OF INTERNATIONAL AGREEMENTS

OTHER BILATERAL AGREEMENTS

TABLE OF AUTHORITIES

Books and Articles *

Abbott, *Linking Trade to Political Goals: Foreign Policy Export Controls in the 1970's and 1980's,* (1981)—§ **812, RN 5.**

Abecassis, The Law and Practice Relating to Oil Pollution from Ships (1978)—§ **604, RN 1.**

Akehurst, *The Hierarchy of the Sources of International Law,* (1974–75)—§ **102, RN 4.**

——, The Law Governing Employment in International Organizations (1967)—§ **467, RN 7.**

Aksen, *American Arbitration Accession Arrives in the Age of Aquarius: United States Implements United Nations Convention on the Recognition and Enforcement of Foreign Arbitral Awards,* (1971)—§ **487, RN 2.**

Angelo, *Multinational Corporate Enterprises,* (1968)—§ **221, RN 3.**

Anton, *The Hague Convention on International Child Abduction,* (1981)—§ **485, RN 7.**

Areeda and Turner, Antitrust Law (1978)—§ **441, RN 1.**

Atwood and Brewster, Antitrust and American Business Abroad (2d ed. 1981)—§ **415, RN 3;** § **441, RN 1;** § **442, RN 1.**

Baade, *Proving Foreign and International Law in Domestic Tribunals,* (1979)—§ **113, RN 1.**

——, *Proving International Law in a National Forum,* (1976)—§ **113, RN 1.**

——, *The Legal Effects of Codes of Conduct for Multinational Enterprises* (1980)—§ **213, RN 7.**

Badr, State Immunity: An Analytical and Prognostic View (1984)—**Part IV, Ch. 5, Intro. Note, RN 1.**

Baker, *Enforcement of Contracts Violating Foreign Exchange Control Laws,* (1977)—§ **822, RN 2.**

Bankes, *Canada and the Natural Resources of the Polar Regions,* (1985)—§ **602, RN 3.**

Barcelo, *Subsidies, Countervailing Duties and Antidumping after the Tokyo Round,* (1980)—§ **806, RN 3.**

Bassiouni, International Extradition (1983)—**Part IV, Ch. 7, Intro. Note, RN 1;** § **475, RN 1.**

Baxter, *Treaties and Custom,* (1970)—§ **102, RN 5.**

Becker, *A Short Cruise on the Good Ships TOVALOP and CRISTAL,* (1974)—§ **604, RN 1.**

Bello and Holmer, *The Trade and Tariff Act of 1984: Principal Anti-dumping and Countervailing Duty Provisions,* (1985)—§ **806, RN 4.**

Belman, *New Departures in the Law of Sovereign Immunity,* (1969)—**Part IV, Ch. 5, Intro., n. 12.**

Benedick, Transboundary Air Pollution (1985)—§ **601, RN 1.**

Berman, *Excuse for Nonperformance in the Light of Contract Practices in International Trade,* (1963)—§ **336, RN 3.**

Berman and Garson, *United States Export Controls—Past, Present, and Future,* (1967)—§ **431, RN 3;** § **812, RN 5.**

Bernier, International Legal Aspects of Federalism (1973)—§ **302, RN 3.**

Bevans, *Ghana and United States–United Kingdom Agreements,* (1965)—§ **210, RN 3.**

Bishop, *Immunity from Taxation of Foreign State-Owned Property,* (1952)—§ **462, RN 4.**

——, International Law, Cases and Materials (3d ed. 1971)—**Part I, Intro. Note, RN 1;** § **111, RN 8;** § **202, RN 6.**

Block, *Suit against Government Officers and the Sovereign Immunity Doctrine,* (1946)—§ **907, RN 2.**

Boczek, Flags of Convenience (1962)—§ **501, RN 4.**

---

* Books are listed in Roman type, articles and chapters in anthologies are listed in Italics.

451

Bodenheimer, *Interstate Custody: Initial Jurisdiction and Continuing Jurisdiction under the UCCJA,* (1981)— § 485, RN 5.

Boger, *The United States-European Community Agricultural Export Subsidies Dispute,* (1984)—§ 806, RN 2.

Bolintineanu, *Expression of Consent to be Bound by a Treaty in the Light of the 1969 Vienna Convention,* (1974)—§ 312, RN 2.

Borchard, *Shall the Executive Agreement Replace the Treaty?* (1944)— § 303, RN 8.

——, *Treaties and Executive Agreements—A Reply,* (1945)—§ 303, RN 8.

——, The Diplomatic Protection of Citizens Abroad (1915)—§ 211, RN 1; § 901, RN 5.

Born, *Reflections on Judicial Jurisdiction in International Cases,* (1987)— **Part IV, Ch. 2, Intro. n. 1.**

Bowett, *Reservations to Non-Restricted Multilateral Treaties,* (1976–77)— § 313, RN 1.

——, The Law of International Institutions (4th ed. 1982)—**Part II, Intro., RN 1; § 222, RN 3; Part IV, Ch. 6, Subch. B., Intro., RN 1.**

——, Self-Defense in International Law 29 (1958)—§ 905, RN 7.

Bratt, *Issues in Worker Certification and Questions of Future Direction in the Trade Adjustment Assistance Program,* (1982)—§ 808, RN 6.

Brenscheidt, *The Recognition and Enforcement of Foreign Money Judgments in the Federal Republic of Germany,* (1977)—§ 481, RN 6.

Brierly, International Law (6th ed. 1963)—**Part I, Intro. Note, RN 1.**

Briggs, *The Travaux Preparatories of the Vienna Convention on the Law of Treaties,* (1971)—**Part III, Intro. Note, RN 1.**

——, *Unilateral Denunciation of Treaties: The Vienna Convention and the International Court of Justice,* (1974)—§ 335, RN 1.

——, *The International Law Commission* (1965)—§ 904, RN 4.

——, The Law of Nations, Cases, Documents and Notes (2d ed. 1952)—**Part I, Intro. Note, RN 1.**

Brockelbank and Infausto, Interstate Enforcement of Family Support (2d ed. 1971)—§ 486, RN 6.

Brower, *The Future of Foreign Investment—Recent Developments in the International Law of Expropriation and Compensation,* (1976)—§ 713, RN 3.

Brower and Tepe, The Charter of Economic Rights and Duties of States: A Reflection or Rejection of International Law? (1975)—§ 712, RN 1.

Brown, *Marine Oil Pollution Literature: An Annotated Bibliography,* (1982)—§ 603, RN 7.

Brownlie, International Law and the Use of Force by States (1963)—§ 703, RN 8; § 905, RN 7; § 905, RN 8.

——, Principles of Public International Law (3d ed. 1979)—§ 221, RN 2; § 460, RN 1.

Buergenthal, Law–Making in the International Civil Aviation Organization (1969)—**Part II, Intro., RN 1.**

Bullitt, *Deportation as a Denial of Substantive Due Process,* (1953)—§ 722, RN 12.

Caggiano, *The ILC Draft on the Succession of States in Respect of Treaties: A Critical Appraisal,* (1975)—§ 208, RN 4.

Campbell, *The Canada–United States Antitrust Notification and Consultation Procedure,* (1978)—§ 415, RN 9.

Carbonneau, *The Political Offense Exception as Applied in French Cases Dealing with the Extradition of Terrorists* (1983)—§ 476, RN 7.

Cardozo, *Sovereign Immunity: The Plaintiff Deserves a Day in Court,* (1954)—**Part IV, Ch. 5, Intro. Note, n. 9.**

Carlston, The Process of International Arbitration (1946)—**Part IX, Intro. Note, RN 1; § 904, RN 7.**

Carmichael, *At Sea with the Fourth Amendment,* (1977)—§ 433, RN 4.

Casad, *Issue Preclusion and Foreign Country Judgments: Whose Law?,* (1984)—§ 481, RN 3.

Castel, Canadian Conflict of Laws (1975)—§ 481, RN 6.

Cavers, *International Enforcement of Family Support,* (1981)—§ 486, RN 6.

Chayes, Ehrlich and Lowenfeld, International Legal Process (1968)—**Part I, Intro. Note, RN 1; § 312, RN 7; § 803, RN 2; § 809, RN 3.**

Cheng, The Law of International Air Transport (1962)—§ 501, RN 10.

Cheshire and North, Private International Law (10th ed. 1979)—§ 481, RN 6.

TABLE OF AUTHORITIES

TABLE OF AUTHORITIES

Hart, *Relations Between State and Federal Law*, (1954)—§ 112, RN 2.

Hart and Wechsler, The Federal Courts and the Federal System (2d ed. 1973)—§ 111, **Com. d**; § 422, RN 1.

Harvard Research in International Law ——, Extradition (1935)—**Part IV, Ch. 7, Subch. B, Intro. Note, RN 1.**

——, Jurisdiction with Respect to Crime (1935)—§ 502, RN 3.

——, The Law of Territorial Waters (1929)—§ 512, RN 6.

Hay and Walbroeck, European Community Law and Institutions in Perspective (1976)—§ 809, RN 4.

Hazard, *A General Theory of State-Court Jursidiction* (1965)—§ 421, RN 3.

Heininger, *Liability of U.S. Banks for Deposits Placed in their Foreign Branches*, (1979)—§ 414, RN 6.

Henkin, *Act of State Today: Recollections in Tranquility*, (1976)—§ 111, RN 1.

——, *The Constitution and United States Sovereignty: A Century of Chinese Exclusion and its Progeny*, (1987)—§ 115, RN 3; § 703, RN 7; § 722, RN 12.

——, *The Constitution as Compact and as Conscience*, (1985)—§ 722, RN 12.

——, *International Human Rights as 'Rights,'* (1979)—§ 703, RN 5.

——, *International Human Rights and 'Domestic Jurisdiction,'* (1977)—§ 703, RN 2.

——, *International Law in the United States*, (1984)—**Part I, Ch. 2, Intro. Note.**

——, *Is There a 'Political Question' Doctrine?* (1976)—§ 1, RN 4.

——, *Rights: American and Human —* **Part VII, Intro. Note, n. 10.**

——, *The Treaty Makers and the Law Makers: The Law of the Land and Foreign Relations*, (1959)—§ 722, RN 1.

——, *The Treaty Makers and the Law Makers: The Niagara Power Reservation*, (1956)—§ 303, RN 4.

——, Arms Control and Inspection in American Law (1958)—§ 721, RN 9.

——, Foreign Affairs and the Constitution (1972)—§ 1, RN 1; § 111, RN 7; § 115, RN 1, 5; § 302, RN 1; § 303, RN 8, 11; § 712, RN 8; § 721, RN 9.

——, How Nations Behave (2d ed. 1979)—**Part I, Intro. Note**; § 905, RN 7.

——, The International Bill of Rights: The Covenant on Civil and Political Rights (1981)—§ 701, RN 6.

——, The Rights of Man Today (1978)—**Part VII, Intro. Note, RN 1.**

Henkin, Pugh, Schachter, and Smit, eds., International Law (2d ed. 1987)—**Part I, Intro. Note, RN 1**; § 402, RN 1; § 905, RN 7.

Hesse, *The Constitutional Status of the Lawfully Admitted Permanent Resident Alien*, (1959)—§ 722, RN 12.

Higgins, Editorial Comments on Abuse of Diplomatic Privileges (1986)—§ 466, RN 6.

Hoeflich, *Through a Glass Darkly: Reflections upon the History of the International Law of Public Debt in Connection with State Succession* (1982)—§ 209, RN 5.

Hoff, Schulman, Volenik, and O'Daniel, Interstate Child Custody Disputes and Parental Kidnapping: Policy, Practice and Law (1982)—§ 485, RN 2.

Holtzmann, *Settlement of Disputes: the Role of Arbitration in East–West Trade* (1974)—§ 451, RN 1.

Honig, The Legal Status of Aircraft (1956)—§ 501, RN 10.

Horn, ed., Legal Problems of Codes of Conduct for Multinational Enterprises (1980)—§ 213, RN 7; § 301, RN 2.

Horsefield, The International Monetary Fund (1969)—§ 822, RN 4.

Hudec, *GATT Dispute Settlement After the Tokyo Round: An Unfinished Business*, (1980)—§ 806, RN 1; § 902, RN 5.

——, The GATT Legal System and World Trade Diplomacy (1975)—**Part VIII, Intro. Note, RN 1.**

Hudson, The Permanent Court of International Justice (1943)—§ 903, RN 6.

——, The World Court (1938)—§ 903, RN 1.

Hufbauer, Erb and Starr, *The GATT Codes and the Unconditional Most-Favored–Nation Principle*, (1980)—§ 802, RN 1.

Hunnings, *Pirate Broadcasting in European Waters*, (1965)—§ 522, RN 5.

Hyde, International Law Chiefly as Interpreted and Applied by the United States (2d ed. 1945)—**Part I, Intro. Note, RN 1; Part II, Intro. Note, n. 1;** § 210, RN 1; § 501, RN 7; § 512, RN 3; § 711, RN 2; § 722, RN 9; § 905, RN 1, 8.

TABLE OF AUTHORITIES

460

——, *Kidnapping of Fugitives from Justice on Foreign Territory*, (1935)—§ **432, RN 3.**

——, *Settlement of the Jacob Kidnapping Case*, (1936)—§ **432, RN 3.**

Pye, *The Effect of Foreign Criminal Judgments within the United States*, (1965)—§ **483, RN 3.**

Quigley, *Accession by the United States to the United Nations Convention on the Recognition and Enforcement of Foreign Arbitral Awards*, (1961)—§ **487, RN 2.**

Ralston, The Law and Procedure of International Tribunals (1926)—§ **902, RN 2.**

——, Venezuelan Arbitrations of 1903—§ **711, RN 2.**

Ray, Guide to Export Controls (1985)—§ **812, RN 5.**

Re, *The Foreign Claims Settlement Commission and the Lake Ontario Claims Program*, (1965)—§ **601, RN 1.**

Read, *The Trail Smelter Dispute*, (1963)—§ **601, RN 1.**

Reese, *The Status in This Country of Judgments Rendered Abroad*, (1950)—§ **481, RN 1.**

Reeves, *The Act of State—Foreign Decisions cited in the Sabbatino Case: A Rebuttal and Memorandum of Law*, (1965)—§ **443, RN 12.**

Reichert, *Provisional Measures in International Litigation: A Comprehensive Bibliography*, (1985)—§ **903, RN 6.**

Restatement, Conflict of Laws (Second)—**Part VIII, Intro. Note, RN 2; Part IV, Ch. 8, Intro. Note;** § **101, Com. c;** § **421, RN 4, 5;** § **442, Com. d;** § **443, RN 1;** § **481, Com. c;** § **483, RN 2;** § **485, RN 1;** § **486, RN 3, 7.**

Restatement, Judgments (Second)—§ **421, RN 4, 5;** § **481, Com. c;** § **481, RN 4;** § **483, RN 2.**

Restatement (Second) Agency (1958)—§ **207, RN 4.**

Richardson, *Self-Determination, International Law and the South African Bantustan Policy*, (1978)—§ **202, RN 6.**

Rienow, The Test of the Nationality of a Merchant Vessel (1937)—§ **501, RN 6.**

Ristau, International Judicial Assistance in Civil and Commercial Matters (1984)—**Part IV, Ch. 7, Intro. Note, n. 2.**

Robertson, Human Rights in the World (2d ed. 1982)—**Part VII, Intro. Note, RN 1.**

Rosenne, *The Temporal Application of the Vienna Convention on the Law of Treaties*, (1970)—**Part III, Intro. Note, n. 5.**

——, The Law and Practice of the International Court (1965)—**Part IX, Intro. Note, RN 1.**

——, The Law of Treaties: A Guide to the Legislative History of the Vienna Convention (1970)—**Part III, Intro. Note, RN 1.**

——, Procedure in the International Court (1983)—§ **903, RN 6.**

Rossides, U.S. Import Trade Regulation (1986)—**Part VIII, Ch. 1, Intro. Note, RN 1;** § **803, RN 7.**

Roth, Allan, A Guide to Foreign Investment under United States Law (1979)—§ **213, RN 5.**

Roth, Andreas, The Minimum Standard of International Law Applied to Aliens (1949)—§ **711, RN 2.**

Rubin, A., *The International Legal Effects of Unilateral Declarations*, (1977)—§ **301, RN 3.**

——, *Pollution by Analogy: The Trail Smelter Arbitration*, (1971)—§ **601, RN 1.**

Rubin, S., *Most-Favored-Nation Treatment and the Multilateral Trade Negotiations*, (1981)—§ **802, RN 1.**

Ruda, *Reservations to Treaties*, (1975)—§ **313, RN 1.**

Russo, Regulation of the Commodities Futures and Options Markets (1983)—§ **416, RN 5.**

Sadurska, *Soviet Submarines in Swedish Waters*, (1984)—§ **513, RN 2.**

Saltzburg, *The Reach of the Bill of Rights beyond the Terra Firma of the United States*, (1980)—§ **433, RN 2, 4.**

Satow, Guide to Diplomatic Practice (5th ed. Gore-Booth 1979)—**Part IV, Ch. 6, Subch. A., Intro. Note, RN 1.**

Schachor-Landau, *Extraterritorial Penal Jurisdiction and Extradition*, (1980)—§ **475, RN 4.**

Schachter, *Compensation for Expropriation* (1984)—§ **712, RN 1.**

——, *The Crisis of Legitimation in the United Nations*, (1981)—§ **103, RN 2.**

——, *The Twilight Existence of Nonbinding International Agreements*, (1977)—§ **301, RN 2.**

461

Notes

TABLE OF AUTHORITIES

trust Litigation, (Yale L.J.1979)—§ **442, RN 4.**

——, *Foreign Securities: Integration and Disclosure under the Securities and Exchange Acts*, (Notre Dame L.Rev.1983)—§ **416, RN 4.**

——, *High on the Seas: Drug Smuggling, the Fourth Amendment, and Warrantless Searches at Sea*, (Harv. L.Rev.1980)—§ **433, RN 4.**

——, *New York–approved Mexican Divorces: Are They Valid in Other States?*, (U.Pa.L.Rev.1966)—§ **484, RN 4.**

——, *The Act of State Doctrine: Resolving Debt Situs Confusion*, (Colum.L.Rev.1986)—§ **443, RN 4.**

——, *The Alien and the Constitution*, (U.Chi.L.Rev.1953)—§ **722, RN 3.**

——, *The Calvo Clause*, (Int'l L.Forum 1971)—§ **713, RN 6.**

——, *The Court of Claims: Judicial Power and Congressional Review*, (Harv.L.Rev.1933)—§ **907, RN 2.**

——, *The Nonrecognition of Foreign Tax Judgments: International Tax Evasion*, (U.Ill.L.Rev.1981)—§ **483, RN 2.**

——, *Toward Codification of Diplomatic Asylum*, (N.Y.U.J.Int'l L. & Pol.1976)—§ **466, RN 3.**

——, *Towards a More Principled Approach to the Principle of Specialty*, (Cornell Int'l L.J.1979)—§ **477, RN 1.**

——, *United States Recognition of Foreign Nonjudicial Divorces*, (Minn.L. Rev.1969)—§ **484, RN 6.**

Symposia

——, Compelling Discovery in Transnational Litigation, (N.Y.U.J.Int'l L. & Pol.1984)—§ **442, RN 1.**

——, The International Debt Crisis, (N.Y.U.J.Int'l L. & Pol.1985)—§ **821, RN 5.**

——, Unification of International Trade Law: UNCITRAL's First Decade, (Am.J.Comp.L.1979)—§ **805, RN 5.**

——, Transnational Aspects of Criminal Procedure (Mich.Y.B. of Int'l L. 1983)—**Part IV, Ch. 7, Subch. B, Intro. Note, RN 1.**

*

PARALLEL TABLES

OF

RESTATEMENT THIRD SECTION NUMBERS

AND OF

TENTATIVE DRAFT SECTION NUMBERS

Restatement Third, Restatement of the Foreign Relations Law of the United States, was put forth in seven Tentative Drafts between 1980 and 1986 under the Title Restatement of the Law, Foreign Relations Law of the United States (Revised). The order of the Parts was not changed for the Official Text, but section numbers were changed, both to reflect restructuring and to make the numbering system systematic. Because many sections have been discussed in cases, articles, and texts under their Tentative Draft section numbers, the following tables are provided to facilitate conversion.

Table I converts from Official Text section numbers to Tentative Draft section numbers, and Table II does the reverse. Table I shows in the left-hand column the section numbers of the Official Text, and opposite each such number the Tentative Draft and the section number in that Draft in which the material previously appeared. In some cases, two or three Tentative Drafts are involved since the material was presented more than once. (No indication is given of a different numbering when the section was never actually presented under that number, even though the table of contents of a Tentative Draft indicated such renumbering.) Some Parts in the earlier Drafts, and selected sections from other Parts, were republished in Tentative Draft No. 6, in many cases with some changes from the earlier Draft. (The Reporters prepared a Tentative Final Draft in July 1985 and revised it in Spring 1986, but that Draft had limited circulation and is not indexed here.)

One may use Table I also to learn the derivation of a particular section and its history in the Tentative Drafts. To find the Official Text section number of a section referred to by its Tentative Draft section number, one may go directly to Table II.

*

TABLE I

SECTION NUMBERS FROM OFFICIAL TEXT TO TENTATIVE DRAFTS

Official Text Section Number	Tentative Draft
1	TD 1, 1; TD 6, 1
101	TD 1, 101; TD 6, 101
102	TD 1, 102; TD 6, 102
103	TD 1, 103; TD 6, 103
111	TD 1, 131; TD 6, 131
112	TD 1, 132; TD 6, 132
113	TD 1, 133; TD 6, 133
114	TD 1, 134; TD 6, 134
115	TD 1, 135; TD 6, 135
201	TD 2, 201; TD 6, 201
202	TD 2, 202; TD 6, 202
203	TD 2, 203; TD 6, 203
204	TD 2, 204; TD 6, 204
205	TD 2, 205; TD 6, 205
206	TD 2, 206; TD 6, 206
207	TD 2, 207; TD 6, 207
208	TD 2, 208; TD 6, 208
209	TD 2, 209, 210; TD 6, 209
210	TD 2, 211–13; TD 6, 210
211	TD 2, 214; TD 6, 214
212	TD 2, 215; TD 6, 215
213	TD 2, 216; TD 6, 216
221	TD 2, 217; TD 6, 217
222	TD 2, 218; TD 6, 218
223	TD 2, 219; TD 6, 219
301	TD 1, 301–303; TD 6, 301
302	TD 1, 304; TD 6, 302
303	TD 1, 305–308; TD 6, 303
311	TD 1, 309–11; TD 6, 311
312	TD 1, 312–18; TD 6, 312
313	TD 1, 319–22; TD 6, 313
314	TD 1, 323; TD 6, 314
321	TD 1, 324; TD 6, 321
322	TD 1, 325–26; TD 6, 322
323	TD 1, 327; TD 6, 323
324	TD 1, 328; TD 6, 324
325	TD 1, 329–31; TD 6, 325

Official Text Section Number	Tentative Draft
326	TD 1, 332–35; TD 6, 326
331	TD 1, 336–37; 347; TD 6, 331
332	TD 1, 340; TD 6, 332
333	TD 1, 341; TD 6, 333
334	TD 1, 342–44; TD 6, 334
335	TD 1, 345; TD 6, 335
336	TD 1, 346; TD 6, 336
337	TD 1, 348; TD 6, 337
338	TD 1, 349–51; TD 6, 338
339	TD 1, 352; TD 6, 339
401	TD 2, 401; TD 6, 401
402	TD 2, 402; TD 6, 402
403	TD 2, 403; TD 6, 403; TD 7, 403
404	TD 2, 404; TD 6, 404
411	TD 2, 411; TD 6, 411
412	TD 2, 412; TD 6, 412
413	TD 2, 413; TD 6, 413
414	TD 2, 418; TD 6, 414
415	TD 2, 415; TD 6, 415
416	TD 2, 416; TD 6, 416; TD 7, 416
421	TD 2, 441; TD 6, 421
422	TD 2, 442; TD 6, 422
423	TD 2, 443; TD 6, 423
431	TD 3, 431; TD 6, 431
432	TD 3, 432; TD 6, 432
433	TD 3, 433; TD 6, 433
441	TD 3, 419; TD 6, 436
442	TD 3, 420; TD 6, 437; TD 7, 437
443	TD 3, 428; TD 6, 469; TD 7, 469
444	TD 3, 429; TD 6, 470
451	TD 2, 451
452	TD 2, 452
453	TD 2, 453
454	TD 2, 454
455	TD 2, 455
456	TD 2, 456
457	TD 2, 457; TD 6, 457
458	TD 2, 458

PARALLEL TABLES

Official Text Section Number	Tentative Draft
459	TD 2, 459
460	TD 2, 460
461	TD 5, 445
462	TD 5, 446
463	TD 6, 461
464	TD 4, 461
465	TD 4, 462
466	TD 4, 463
467	TD 4, 464
468	TD 4, 465
469	TD 4, 466
470	TD 4, 467
471	TD 5, 481; TD 6, 471
472	TD 5, 482; TD 6, 472
473	TD 5, 483; TD 6, 473
474	TD 5, 484; TD 6, 474
475	TD 5, 486; TD 7, 476
476	TD 5, 487; TD 7, 477
477	TD 5, 488; TD 7, 478
478	TD 5, 489; TD 6, 479; TD 7, 479
481	TD 4, 491
482	TD 4, 492
483	TD 4, 493
484	TD 4, 494
485	TD 4, 495
486	TD 4, 496
487	TD 4, 497
488	TD 4, 498
501	TD 3, 501; TD 6, 501
502	TD 3, 502; TD 6, 502
511	TD 3, 511; TD 6, 511
512	TD 3, 512; TD 6, 512
513	TD 3, 513; TD 6, 513
514	TD 3, 514; TD 5, 514; TD 6, 514
515	TD 3, 515; TD 6, 515
516	TD 3, 516; TD 6, 516
517	TD 3, 517; TD 6, 517
521	TD 3, 521; TD 6, 521

Official Text Section Number	Tentative Draft
522	TD 3, 522; TD 6, 522
523	TD 5, 523; TD 6, 523
601	TD 4, 601
602	TD 4, 602
603	TD 4, 611
604	TD 4, 612
701	TD 3, 701; TD 6, 701
702	TD 3, 702; TD 6, 702
703	TD 3, 703; TD 6, 703
711	TD 3, 711; TD 6, 711
712	TD 3, 712; TD 6, 712; TD 7, 712
713	TD 3, 713; TD 6, 713
721	TD 3, 721; TD 4, 721; TD 6, 721
722	TD 3, 722; TD 4, 722; TD 6, 722
801	TD 4, 801
802	TD 4, 802
803	TD 4, 803
804	TD 4, 804
805	TD 4, 805
806	TD 4, 806
807	TD 4, 807
808	TD 4, 808
809	TD 4, 809
810	TD 4, 810
811	TD 4, 811
812	TD 4, 812
821	TD 5, 851; TD 6, 821
822	TD 5, 852; TD 6, 822
823	TD 5, 853; TD 6, 823
901	TD 5, 901
902	TD 5, 902
903	TD 5, 903; TD 6, 903; TD 7, 903
904	TD 5, 904
905	TD 5, 905; TD 6, 905
906	TD 5, 906
907	TD 5, 907

TABLE II

SECTION NUMBERS FROM TENTATIVE DRAFTS TO OFFICIAL TEXT

Tentative Draft No. 1

Tentative Draft Section Number	Official Text Section Number
1	1
101	101
102	102
103	103
131	111
132	112
133	113
134	114
135	115
301	301
302	301
303	301
304	302
305	303
306	303
307	303
308	303
309	311
310	311
311	311
312	312
313	312
314	312
315	312
316	312
317	312
318	312
319	313
320	313
321	313
322	313
323	314
324	321
325	322
326	322
327	323
328	324
329	325
330	325
331	325
332	326
333	326
334	326
335	326
336	331

Tentative Draft No. 1

Tentative Draft Section Number	Official Text Section Number
337	331
338	331
339	331
340	332
341	333
342	334
343	334
344	334
345	335
346	336
347	331
348	337
349	338
350	338
351	338
352	339

Tentative Draft No. 2

Tentative Draft Section Number	Official Text Section Number
201	201
202	202
203	203
204	204
205	205
206	206
207	207
208	208
209	209
210	209
211	210
212	210
213	210
214	211
215	212
216	213
217	221
218	222
219	223
401	401
402	402
403	403
411	411
412	412
413	413
415	415
416	416

471

PARALLEL TABLES

Tentative Draft No. 2

Tentative Draft Section Number	Official Text Section Number
418	414
441	421
442	422
443	423
451	451
452	452
453	453
454	454
455	455
456	456
457	457
458	458
459	459
460	460

Tentative Draft No. 3

401	401
419	441
420	442
431	431
432	432
433	433
501	501
502	502
511	511
512	512
513	513
514	514
515	515
516	516
517	517
521	521
522	522
701	701
702	702
703	703
711	711
712	712
713	713
721	721
722	722

Tentative Draft No. 4

428	443
429	444
461	464
462	465
463	466
464	467
465	468
466	469
467	470
491	481
492	482
493	483
494	484

Tentative Draft No. 4

Tentative Draft Section Number	Official Text Section Number
495	485
496	486
497	487
498	488
601	601
602	602
611	603
612	604
721	721
722	722
801	801
802	802
803	803
804	804
805	805
806	806
807	807
808	808
809	809
810	810
811	811
812	812

Tentative Draft No. 5

445	461
446	462
481	471
482	472
483	473
484	474
486	475
487	476
488	477
489	478
514	514
523	523
851	821
852	822
853	823
901	901
902	902
903	903
904	904
905	905
906	906
907	907

Tentative Draft No. 6, Volume 1

1	1
101	101
102	102
103	103
131	111
132	112
133	113
134	114

PARALLEL TABLES

*

473

PARALLEL TABLES

OF

RESTATEMENT THIRD SECTION NUMBERS

AND OF

ORIGINAL RESTATEMENT
(RESTATEMENT SECOND)
SECTION NUMBERS

The two tables that follow correlate the present Restatement and the original Restatement (Restatement Second, 1965). Table III shows in the left-hand column the section numbers of the present Restatement, and opposite each such number the corresponding section number of the original Restatement. Table IV shows in the left-hand column the section numbers of the original Restatement and opposite each such number the corresponding section number of the present Restatement.

*

TABLE III

PARALLEL TABLES

Restatement 3rd	Original Restatement (1965)	Restatement 3rd	Original Restatement (1965)
472	—	701	165 Com. *b*
473	—	702	—
474	—	703	—
475	9 Com. *e*	711	178–96
476	—	712	184–96
477	—	713	202–214
478	—	721	—
481	—	722	167 Com. *b*
482	—	801	154 RN 3
483	—	802	154 RN 3
484	—	803	—
485	—	804	—
486	—	805	—
487	—	806	—
488	—	807	—
501	28	808	—
502	28	809	—
511	11, 21, 23	810	—
512	11	811	—
513	45, 46	812	—
514	23, 36	821	—
516	23	822	—
517	23	823	—
521	21	901	164
522	34	902	164, 214
523	—	903	3
601	18 RN 3, 23 RN 3	904	3
602	—	905	200
603	23 RN 3	906	3
604	—	907	3

TABLE IV

SECTION NUMBERS FROM ORIGINAL
RESTATEMENT TO RESTATEMENT THIRD

Original Restatement (1965)	Restatement 3rd	Original Restatement (1965)	Restatement 3rd
1	101, 206	46	513
2	1, 102, 103	47	513
3	901–907	48	512 RN 5
4	201	49	512
5	221	50	512
6	401	51	—
7	401, 403	52	—
8	403	53	—
9	476	54	—
10	402	55	—
11	511,512	56	—
12	—	57	—
13	511	58	—
14	511	59	—
15	511	60	—
16	—	61	—
17	402	62	—
18	402, 415	63	461
19	—	64	461
20	431	65	451, 462
21	521	66	442
22	513 Com. *g*	67	442
23	514, 516	68	451, 455
24	—	69	451, 453
25	—	70	456
26	211, 212	71	—
27	213, 414	72	—
28	501, 502	73	464
29	501 RN 10	74	464
30	402	75	464
31	502	76	464, 465
32	502	77	466
33	402	78	464
34	404, 522	79	464
35	—	80	464
36	514	81	465, 466
37	403	82	464
38	403 Com. *g*	83	467, 468
39	411, 441	84	467, 468
40	403, 431	85	469, 470
41	443	86	470
42	443	87	469
43	443	88	469, 470
44	432	89	469, 470
45	513	90	469, 470

479

Original Restatement (1965)	Restatement 3rd	Original Restatement (1965)	Restatement 3rd
91	470	149	326
92	469	150	326
93	470	151	326
94	202, 203	152	326
95	202, 203	153	336
96	202, 203	154	111
97	202, 203	155	332–34
98	202, 203	156	332–34
99	202, 203	157	336 Com. *d*
100	202, 203	158	335, 337
101	202, 203	159	210
102	202, 203	160	210
103	202, 203	161	210
104	202, 203	162	311
105	202, 203	163	339
106	202, 203	164	207
107	202, 203	165	701
108	202, 203	166	711 Com. *g*
109	202, 203, 207	167	722
110	202, 203	168	206
111	202, 203, 209	169	207
112	202, 203	170	207
113	205, 209	171	211, 713
114	205	172	213, 713
115	301	173	213, 713
116	331 Com. *e*	174	713
117	302	175	906
118	303	176	223
119	302	177	—
120	302	178	711
121	302	179	711
122	312	180	711
123	311	181	711
124	313	182	711
125	313	183	711
126	313	184	712
127	313	185	712
128	313	186	712
129	313	187	712
130	303	188	712
131	312	189	712
132	303	190	712
133	314	191	712
134	314	192	712
135	314	193	712
136	314 Com. *e*	194	712
137	314 Com. *f*	195	712
138	321	196	712
139	324	197	711 Com. *c*
140	321	198	822
141	111	199	711 Com. *c*
142	111	200	905
143	111	201	—
144	111	202	713 Com. *g*
145	115	203	713 Com. *g*
146	325	204	713 Com. *g*
147	325	205	713 Com. *g*
148	325	206	713 Com. *f*

PARALLEL TABLES

Original Restatement (1965)	Restatement 3rd	Original Restatement (1965)	Restatement 3rd
207	713 Com. f	211	713 RN 9
208	713 Com. f	212	713 RN 9
209	713 Com. f	213	713 RN 9
210	713 Com. f	214	713 RN 9

*

TABLE OF CROSS-REFERENCES

TO DIGEST SYSTEM KEY NUMBERS
AND ALR ANNOTATIONS *

Section 1

1. Digest System Key Numbers

International Law ⚷1, 10.18.

Section 101

1. Digest System Key Numbers

International Law ⚷1.

Section 102

1. Digest System Key Numbers

International Law ⚷2; Treaties ⚷1.

Section 103

1. Digest System Key Numbers

International Law ⚷2.

Section 111

1. Digest System Key Numbers

Federal Courts ⚷161, 162; International Law ⚷1; Treaties ⚷11, 12.

2. A.L.R. Annotation

Construction of statute of limitations in Carriage of Goods by Sea Act (46 USC sec. 1303(6)). 2 ALR Fed 347.

Section 112

1. Digest System Key Numbers

Federal Courts ⚷161, 513; International Law ⚷2.

Section 113

1. Digest System Key Numbers

Evidence ⚷38, 39.

Section 114

1. Digest System Key Numbers

Statutes ⚷174; Treaties ⚷11.

Section 115

1. Digest System Key Numbers

International Law ⚷10.18; Treaties ⚷11.

---

* Prepared by West Publishing Company and Lawyers Co-operative Publishing Company.

TABLE OF CROSS-REFERENCES

Section 201

1. Digest System Key Numbers

International Law ⊕3.

Section 202

1. Digest System Key Numbers

International Law ⊕10.2

2. A.L.R. Annotation

Access to federal courts by foreign state, or national thereof, which United States does not recognize or with which United States has no diplomatic relations. 65 ALR Fed 881.

Section 203

1. Digest System Key Numbers

International Law ⊕10, 10.2.

2. A.L.R. Annotation

Access to federal courts by foreign state, or national thereof, which United States does not recognize or with which United States has no diplomatic relations. 65 ALR Fed 881.

Section 204

1. Digest System Key Numbers

International Law ⊕10.2.

2. A.L.R. Annotation

Access to federal courts by foreign state, or national thereof, which United States does not recognize or with which United States has no diplomatic relations. 65 ALR Fed 881.

Section 205

1. Digest System Key Numbers

International Law ⊕10.2, 10.8, 10.27.

2. A.L.R. Annotation

Access to federal courts by foreign state, or national thereof, which United States does not recognize or with which United States has no diplomatic relations. 65 ALR Fed 881.

Section 206

1. Digest System Key Numbers

International Law ⊕8.

2. A.L.R. Annotation

Requirement that agent of foreign principal register with United States Attorney General, under Provisions of Foreign Agents Registration Act of 1938, as amended (22 USC secs. 611 et seq.).. 67 ALR Fed 774.

Access to federal courts by foreign state, or national thereof, which United States does not recognize or with which United States has no diplomatic relations. 65 ALR Fed 881.

Section 207

1. Digest System Key Numbers

International Law ⊕8.

TABLE OF CROSS–REFERENCES

2. A.L.R. Annotation

Requirement that agent of foreign principal register with United States Attorney General, under Provisions of Foreign Agents Registration Act of 1938, as amended (22 USC secs. 611 et seq.). 67 ALR Fed 774.

Section 208

1. Digest System Key Numbers

International Law ☞10.4.

Section 209

1. Digest System Key Numbers

International Law ☞10.4.

Section 210

1. Digest System Key Numbers

Treaties ☞5.

Section 211

1. Digest System Key Numbers

International Law ☞10.3.

2. A.L.R. Annotation

When is a citizen of United States who resides in foreign country a citizen of a particular state for purposes of 28 USC sec. 1332(a)(1), granting Federal District Courts jurisdiction of certain actions between citizens of different states. 54 ALR Fed 422.

Section 212

1. Digest System Key Numbers

Citizens ☞2, 13.

2. A.L.R. Annotation

When is a citizen of United States who resides in foreign country a citizen of a particular state for purposes of 28 USC sec. 1332(a)(1), granting Federal District Courts jurisdiction of certain actions between citizens of different states. 54 ALR Fed 422.

Section 213

1. Digest System Key Numbers

International Law ☞10.3.

Section 221

1. Digest System Key Numbers

International Law ☞10.45.

Section 222

1. Digest System Key Numbers

International Law ☞10.45.

Section 223

1. Digest System Key Numbers

International Law ☞10.45.

485

TABLE OF CROSS-REFERENCES

Section 301

  1. Digest System Key Numbers

    Treaties ☞1.

Section 302

  1. Digest System Key Numbers

    Treaties ☞2, 4.

Section 303

  1. Digest System Key Numbers

    Treaties ☞2.

Section 311

  1. Digest System Key Numbers

    Treaties ☞2.

Section 312

  1. Digest System Key Numbers

    Treaties ☞9.

Section 313

  1. Digest System Key Numbers

    Treaties ☞1.

Section 314

  1. Digest System Key Numbers

    Treaties ☞3.

Section 321

  1. Digest System Key Numbers

    Treaties ☞13.

Section 322

  1. Digest System Key Numbers

    Treaties ☞7, 10.

Section 323

  1. Digest System Key Numbers

    Treaties ☞6.

Section 324

  1. Digest System Key Numbers

    Treaties ☞7.

Section 325

  1. Digest System Key Numbers

    Treaties ☞7.

  2. A.L.R. Annotation

    Treaty or international executive agreement as limiting recovery available to United States citizens or businesses—Supreme Court cases, 80 L Ed 2d 871, sec. 1.

486

TABLE OF CROSS–REFERENCES

Section 326

  1. Digest System Key Numbers

  Treaties ☞7.

Section 331

  1. Digest System Key Numbers

  Treaties ☞4.

Section 332

  1. Digest System Key Numbers

  Treaties ☞5.

Section 333

  1. Digest System Key Numbers

  Treaties ☞5.

Section 334

  1. Digest System Key Numbers

  Treaties ☞6.

Section 335

  1. Digest System Key Numbers

  Treaties ☞14.

Section 336

  1. Digest System Key Numbers

  Treaties ☞5.

Section 337

  1. Digest System Key Numbers

  Treaties ☞4, 5.

Section 338

  1. Digest System Key Numbers

  Treaties ☞5.

Section 339

  1. Digest System Key Numbers

  Treaties ☞5.

Section 401

  1. Digest System Key Numbers

  International Law ☞5, 7.

Section 402

  1. Digest System Key Numbers

  International Law ☞7.

  2. A.L.R. Annotation

  Actionability, under federal and state antidiscrimination legislation, of foreign employer's discriminating in favor of foreign workers in hiring and other employment matters. 84 ALR Fed 114.

487

TABLE OF CROSS–REFERENCES

Propriety of federal court injunction against suit in foreign country. 78 ALR Fed 831.

Extraterritorial application of federal antitrust laws to acts occurring in foreign commerce. 40 ALR Fed 343.

Carriers: applicability to shipments to, destined for, or from foreign countries, of Carmack Amendment to Interstate Commerce Act (49 USC sec. 20(11)). 9 ALR Fed 960.

Section 403

1. Digest System Key Numbers

International Law ⚖7.

2. A.L.R. Annotation

Actionability, under federal and state antidiscrimination legislation, of foreign employer's discriminating in favor of foreign workers in hiring and other employment matters. 84 ALR Fed 114.

Applicability of Jones Act (46 USC sec. 688) to foreign seamen, foreign ships, or other foreign circumstances. 68 ALR Fed 360.

Section 404

1. Digest System Key Numbers

Criminal Law ⚖18.

Section 411

1. Digest System Key Numbers

Taxation ⚖20.

Section 412

1. Digest System Key Numbers

Taxation ⚖20.

Section 413

1. Digest System Key Numbers

Taxation ⚖47(1).

Section 414

1. Digest System Key Numbers

Corporations ⚖636.

Section 415

1. Digest System Key Numbers

Monopolies ⚖24(2, 6).

2. A.L.R. Annotation

Extraterritorial application of federal antitrust laws to acts occurring in foreign commerce. 40 ALR Fed 343.

Section 416

1. Digest System Key Numbers

International Law ⚖10.14; Securities Regulation ⚖1, 67.10.

2. A.L.R. Annotation

Jurisdiction of federal courts over actions arising out of international or foreign banking or financial operations, or banking in a dependency or insular possession of the United States, under sec. 25(b) of the Federal Reserve Act (12 USC sec. 632). 64 ALR Fed 262.

Subject matter jurisdiction of securities fraud action based on foreign transactions, under Securities Exchange Act of 1934. 56 ALR Fed 288.

Extraterritorial application of federal antitrust laws to acts occurring in foreign commerce. 40 ALR Fed 343.

Validity, construction, and effect of provisions of federal securities acts for extraterritorial service of process. 8 ALR Fed 511.

Section 421

1. Digest System Key Numbers

International Law ☞5, 7, 10.29.

2. A.L.R. Annotation

Propriety of federal court injunction against suit in foreign country. 78 ALR Fed 831

Effect of American citizenship or residency of libelant who has alternate forum abroad on applicability of doctrine of forum non conveniens in admiralty action brought in United States District Court. 70 ALR Fed 875.

What constitutes "claim arising in a foreign country" under 28 USC sec. 2680(k), excluding such claims from Federal Tort Claims Act. 57 ALR Fed 275.

Construction and application of 28 USC sec. 1350, giving United States District Courts jurisdiction of action by alien for tort only, committed in violation of law of nations or treaty of United States. 34 ALR Fed 388.

Comment Note.—Admiralty jurisdiction in matters of contract. 29 ALR Fed 325.

Validity or enforceability, under Carriage of Goods by Sea Act (46 USC secs. 1300 et seq.), of clauses in bill of lading or shipping contract as to jurisdiction of foreign courts or applicability of foreign law. 2 ALR Fed 963.

Validity of contractual provision limiting place or court in which action may be brought. 31 ALR4th 404.

Doctrine of forum non conveniens: assumption or denial of jurisdiction of contract action involving foreign elements. 90 ALR2d 1109.

Proper forum and right to maintain action for airplane accident causing death over or in high seas. 66 ALR2d 1002.

Power of court, in action under foreign wrongful death statute, to decline jurisdiction on ground of inconvenience of forum. 48 ALR2d 850.

Discretion of court to refuse to entertain action for non-statutory tort occurring in another state or country. 48 ALR2d 800.

Stay of civil proceedings pending determination of action in another state or country. 19 ALR2d 301.

Section 422

1. Digest System Key Numbers

Criminal Law ☞636(1); International Law ☞10.9.

2. A.L.R. Annotation

Construction and application of 18 USC sec. 3238 relating to venue in cases of federal criminal offenses committed outside jurisdiction of any state or district. 24 ALR Fed 365.

TABLE OF CROSS-REFERENCES

Criminal jurisdiction of courts of foreign nations over American armed forces stationed abroad, 17 ALR Fed 725.

Immunity of nonresident defendant in criminal case from service of process. 20 ALR2d 163 (especially § 9, on residents of foreign country).

Section 423

1. Digest System Key Numbers

Criminal Law ⊕18; International Law ⊕10.9.

2. A.L.R. Annotation

Construction and application of 18 USC sec. 3238 relating to venue in cases of federal criminal offenses committed outside jurisdiction of any state or district. 24 ALR Fed 365.

Section 431

1. Digest System Key Numbers

International Law ⊕7, 8.

2. A.L.R. Annotation

Propriety of federal court injunction against suit in foreign country. 78 ALR Fed 831.

District court jurisdiction over criminal suspect who was abducted in foreign country and returned to United States for trial or sentencing. 64 ALR Fed 292.

Sufficiency of evidence to satisfy "interstate or foreign commerce" requirement of 18 USC sec. 2315, making sale or receipt of stolen goods, securities, moneys, or fraudulent tax stamps criminal offense. 45 ALR Fed 527.

Jurisdiction of federal court to try criminal defendant who alleges that he was brought within United States' jurisdiction illegally or as result of fraud or mistake. 28 ALR Fed 685.

Section 432

1. Digest System Key Numbers

Criminal Law ⊕3.

2. A.L.R. Annotation

District court jurisdiction over criminal suspect who was abducted in foreign country and returned to United States for trial or sentencing. 64 ALR Fed 292.

Sufficiency of evidence to satisfy "interstate or foreign commerce" requirement of 18 USC sec. 2315, making sale or receipt of stolen goods, securities, moneys, or fraudulent tax stamps criminal offense. 45 ALR Fed 527.

Jurisdiction of federal court to try criminal defendant who alleges that he was brought within United States' jurisdiction illegally or as result of fraud or mistake. 28 ALR Fed 685.

Section 433

1. Digest System Key Numbers

Arrest ⊕66(1); Criminal Law ⊕394.2(2, 3); International Law ⊕7.

2. A.L.R. Annotation

District court jurisdiction over criminal suspect who was abducted in foreign country and returned to United States for trial or sentencing. 64 ALR Fed 292.

Sufficiency of evidence to satisfy "interstate or foreign commerce" requirement of 18 USC sec. 2315, making sale or receipt of stolen goods, securities, moneys, or fraudulent tax stamps criminal offense. 45 ALR Fed 527.

Jurisdiction of federal court to try criminal defendant who alleges that he was brought within United States' jurisdiction illegally or as result of fraud or mistake. 28 ALR Fed 685.

Section 441

1. Digest System Key Numbers

International Law ⚮7.

2. A.L.R. Annotation

Propriety of federal court injunction against suit in foreign country. 78 ALR Fed 831.

Section 442

1. Digest System Key Numbers

Administrative Law and Procedure ⚮358; Federal Civil Procedure ⚮1574, 1636.

Section 443

1. Digest System Key Numbers

International Law ⚮10.8.

2. A.L.R. Annotation

Situs of debt or property for purposes of act of state doctrine. 77 ALR Fed 293.

Modern status of the Act of State Doctrine. 12 ALR Fed 707.

Section 444

1. Digest System Key Numbers

International Law ⚮10.12.

2. A.L.R. Annotation

Situs of debt or property for purposes of act of state doctrine. 77 ALR Fed 293.

Modern status of the Act of State Doctrine. 12 ALR Fed 707.

Section 451

1. Digest System Key Numbers

International Law ⚮10.29, 10.33.

2. A.L.R. Annotation

Exceptions to jurisdictional immunity of foreign states and their property under the Foreign Sovereign Immunities Act of 1976 (28 USC secs. 1602 et seq.). 59 ALR Fed 99.

Modern status of the rules as to immunity of foreign sovereign from suit in federal or state courts. 25 ALR3d 322.

Section 452

1. Digest System Key Numbers

International Law ⚮10.34.

2. A.L.R. Annotation

Effect of Foreign Sovereign Immunities Act (28 USC secs. 1330, 1441(d), 1602 et seq.) on right to jury trial in action against foreign state. 56 ALR Fed 679.

TABLE OF CROSS-REFERENCES

Section 454

1. Digest System Key Numbers

International Law ☞10.33.

Section 455

1. Digest System Key Numbers

International Law ☞10.35.

2. A.L.R. Annotation

Exceptions to jurisdictional immunity of foreign states and their property under the Foreign Sovereign Immunities Act of 1976 (28 USC secs. 1602 et seq.). 59 ALR Fed 99.

Section 456

1. Digest System Key Numbers

International Law ☞10.32.

Section 457

1. Digest System Key Numbers

International Law ☞10.42.

2. A.L.R. Annotation

Effect of Foreign Sovereign Immunities Act (28 USC secs. 1330, 1441(d), 1602 et seq.) on right to jury trial in action against foreign state. 56 ALR Fed 679.

Stay of civil proceedings pending determination of action in another state or country. 19 ALR2d 301.

Section 458

1. Digest System Key Numbers

International Law ☞10.42.

2. A.L.R. Annotation

Modern status of the rules as to immunity of foreign sovereign from suit in federal or state courts. 25 ALR3d 322.

Removal to federal court, under 28 USC sec. 1441(d), of civil action brought in state court against foreign state. 63 ALR Fed 808.

Stay of civil proceedings pending determination of action in another state or country. 19 ALR2d 301.

Section 459

1. Digest System Key Numbers

International Law ☞10.42.

Section 460

1. Digest System Key Numbers

International Law ☞10.35.

Section 461

1. Digest System Key Numbers

International Law ☞10.33.

Section 462

1. Digest System Key Numbers

Taxation ☞20.

TABLE OF CROSS–REFERENCES

Section 464

1. Digest System Key Numbers

Ambassadors and Consuls ☞3.

2. A.L.R. Annotation

Requirement that agent of foreign principal register with United States Attorney General, under Provisions of Foreign Agents Registration Act of 1938, as amended (22 USC secs. 611 et seq.). 67 ALR Fed 774.

Section 465

1. Digest System Key Numbers

Ambassadors and Consuls ☞3.

Section 466

1. Digest System Key Numbers

Ambassadors and Consuls ☞3.

Section 467

1. Digest System Key Numbers

International Law ☞10.46.

Section 468

1. Digest System Key Numbers

International Law ☞10.46.

Section 469

1. Digest System Key Numbers

International Law ☞10.46.

Section 470

1. Digest System Key Numbers

International Law ☞10.46.

Section 471

1. Digest System Key Numbers

Federal Civil Procedure ☞461.

2. A.L.R. Annotation

Subpoena, under 28 USC sec. 1783, of persons in foreign countries. 32 ALR Fed 894.

Validity, construction, and effect of provisions of federal securities acts for extraterritorial service of process. 8 ALR Fed 511.

Immunity of nonresident defendant in criminal case from service of process. 20 ALR2d 163 (especially § 9, on residents of foreign country).

Section 472

1. Digest System Key Numbers

Federal Civil Procedure ☞467.

2. A.L.R. Annotation

Subpoena, under 28 USC sec. 1783, of persons in foreign countries. 32 ALR Fed 894.

Validity, construction, and effect of provisions of federal securities acts for extraterritorial service of process. 8 ALR Fed 511.

TABLE OF CROSS-REFERENCES

Immunity of nonresident defendant in criminal case from service of process. 20 ALR2d 163 (especially § 9, on residents of foreign country).

Section 473

1. Digest System Key Numbers

Federal Civil Procedure ⟊1261, 1312.

2. A.L.R. Annotation

Raising and determining issue of foreign law under Rule 44.1 of Federal Rules of Civil Procedure. 62 ALR Fed 521.

What is foreign "tribunal" within 28 USC sec. 1782 (as amended in 1964) for use in which District Court may issue discovery orders in response to letters rogatory. 46 ALR Fed 956.

Sufficiency of evidence to satisfy "interstate or foreign commerce" requirement of 18 USC sec. 2315, making sale or receipt of stolen goods, securities, moneys, or fraudulent tax stamps criminal offense. 45 ALR Fed 527.

Proof of foreign official record under Rule 44(a)(2) of Federal Rules of Civil Procedure. 41 ALR Fed 784.

Comment Note.—Pleading and proof of law of foreign country. 75 ALR3d 177.

Subpoena duces tecum for production of items held by a foreign custodian in another country. 82 ALR2d 1403.

Uniform Judicial Notice of Foreign Law Act. 23 ALR2d 1437.

Section 474

1. Digest System Key Numbers

Federal Civil Procedure ⟊1312.

2. A.L.R. Annotation

Raising and determining issue of foreign law under Rule 44.1 of Federal Rules of Civil Procedure. 62 ALR Fed 521.

What is foreign "tribunal" within 28 USC sec. 1782 (as amended in 1964) for use in which District Court may issue discovery orders in response to letters rogatory. 46 ALR Fed 956.

Sufficiency of evidence to satisfy "interstate or foreign commerce" requirement of 18 USC sec. 2315, making sale or receipt of stolen goods, securities, moneys, or fraudulent tax stamps—criminal offense. 45 ALR Fed 527.

Proof of foreign official record under Rule 44(a)(2) of Federal Rules of Civil Procedure. 41 ALR Fed 784.

Comment Note.—Pleading and proof of law of foreign country. 75 ALR3d 177.

Subpoena duces tecum for production of items held by a foreign custodian in another country. 82 ALR2d 1403.

Uniform Judicial Notice of Foreign Law Act. 23 ALR2d 1437.

Section 475

1. Digest System Key Numbers

Extradition and Detainers ⟊1.

2. A.L.R. Annotation

What is a "political offense" or "offense of political character" within customary law or specific treaty exemption barring international extradition from United States of persons charged with political offenses. 61 ALR Fed 786.

TABLE OF CROSS-REFERENCES

Extradition of federal criminal defendants based on comity of nations. 24 ALR Fed 940.

Necessity that demanding state show probable cause to arrest fugitive in extradition proceedings. 90 ALR3d 1085.

Section 476

1. Digest System Key Numbers

Extradition and Detainers ☞5, 9.

2. A.L.R. Annotation

What is a "political offense" or "offense of political character" within customary law or specific treaty exemption barring international extradition from United States of persons charged with political offenses. 61 ALR Fed 786.

Section 477

1. Digest System Key Numbers

Extradition and Detainers ☞19.

Section 478

1. Digest System Key Numbers

Extradition and Detainers ☞9.

2. A.L.R. Annotation

Extradition of federal criminal defendants based on comity of nations. 24 ALR Fed. 940.

Section 481

1. Digest System Key Numbers

Judgment ☞830.

2. A.L.R. Annotation

Valid judgment of court of foreign country as entitled to extraterritorial effect in Federal District Court. 13 ALR Fed. 208.

Validity, construction, and application of Uniform Enforcement of Foreign Judgments Act. 31 ALR4th 706 (especially § 27 on judgments of foreign countries).

Judgment of court of foreign country as entitled to enforcement or extraterritorial effect in state court. 13 ALR4th 1109.

Construction and application of Uniform Foreign Money–Judgments Recognition Act. 100 ALR3d 792.

Section 482

1. Digest System Key Numbers

Judgment ☞830.

Section 483

1. Digest System Key Numbers

Judgment ☞830.

Section 484

1. Digest System Key Numbers

Divorce ☞351.

TABLE OF CROSS–REFERENCES

2. A.L.R. Annotation

Divorce: what constitutes residence or domicile within state by citizen of another country for purpose of jurisdiction in divorce, 51 ALR3d 223.

Section 485

1. Digest System Key Numbers

Divorce ☞402(1); Parent and Child ☞2(19).

2. A.L.R. Annotation

Extraterritorial effect of valid award of custody of child of divorced parents, in absence of substantial change in circumstances. 35 ALR3d 520 (§§ 9 & 10 on awards by courts of foreign countries).

Section 486

1. Digest System Key Numbers

Divorce ☞389, 392, 403(1).

Section 487

1. Digest System Key Numbers

Arbitration ☞82.5, 83.1.

Section 488

1. Digest System Key Numbers

Arbitration ☞82.5.

Section 501

1. Digest System Key Numbers

Shipping ☞2.

Section 502

1. Digest System Key Numbers

Shipping ☞3, 13.

Section 511

1. Digest System Key Numbers

International Law ☞5, 7.

Section 512

1. Digest System Key Numbers

International Law ☞5.

Section 513

1. Digest System Key Numbers

International Law ☞8.

Section 514

1. Digest System Key Numbers

International Law ☞8; Navigable Waters ☞36(1).

Section 515

1. Digest System Key Numbers

Navigable Waters ☞36.

TABLE OF CROSS-REFERENCES

2. A.L.R. Annotation

Construction and application of sec. 4 of Outer Continental Shelf Lands Act of 1953 (43 USC sec. 1333), relating to laws applicable to subsoil and seabed of Outer Continental Shelf and artificial islands and fixed structures erected thereon. 30 ALR Fed 535, sec. 1.

Section 516

1. Digest System Key Numbers

International Law ⬅5.

Section 517

1. Digest System Key Numbers

International Law ⬅5.

2. A.L.R. Annotation

Construction and application of sec. 4 of Outer Continental Shelf Lands Act of 1953 (43 USC sec. 1333), relating to laws applicable to subsoil and seabed of Outer Continental Shelf and artificial islands and fixed structures erected thereon. 30 ALR Fed 535, sec. 1.

Section 521

1. Digest System Key Numbers

International Law ⬅7.

2. A.L.R. Annotation

Jurisdiction of federal courts over "stateless" vessels on high seas. 73 ALR Fed 162.

Proper forum and right to maintain action for airplane accident causing death over or in high seas. 66 ALR2d 1002.

Section 522

1. Digest System Key Numbers

Piracy ⬅1; Shipping ⬅9.

2. A.L.R. Annotation

Jurisdiction of federal courts over "stateless" vessels on high seas. 73 ALR Fed 162.

Comment Note.—Admiralty jurisdiction in matters of contract. 29 ALR Fed 325.

Proper forum and right to maintain action for airplane accident causing death over or in high seas. 66 ALR2d 1002.

Section 523

1. Digest System Key Numbers

International Law ⬅7.

2. A.L.R. Annotation

Construction and application of sec. 4 of Outer Continental Shelf Lands Act of 1953 (43 USC sec. 1333), relating to laws applicable to subsoil and seabed of Outer Continental Shelf and artificial islands and fixed structures erected thereon. 30 ALR Fed 535, sec. 1.

Section 711

1. Disgest System Key Numbers

International Law ⬅12.

TABLE OF CROSS-REFERENCES

Section 712

1. Digest System Key Numbers

International Law ☞12.

Section 713

1. Digest System Key Numbers

International Law ☞12.

Section 721

1. Digest System Key Numbers

Constitutional Law ☞12.

2. A.L.R. Annotation

Federal constitutional right of international travel. 58 L.Ed.2d 904.

Actionability, under federal and state antidiscrimination legislation, of foreign employer's discriminating in favor of foreign workers in hiring and other employment matters. 84 ALR Fed 114.

Application of Fourth Amendment exclusionary rule to evidence obtained through search conducted by official of foreign government. 33 ALR Fed 342.

Section 722

1. Digest System Key Numbers

Aliens ☞4; Constitutional Law ☞250.5.

2. A.L.R. Annotation

Necessity and sufficiency of notice of claimed refugee's right to apply for asylum under sec. 208 of Immigration and Nationality Act of 1952 (8 USC sec. 1158). 84 ALR Fed 815.

Validity and construction of Department of Labor's "50% Rule," requiring employer hiring seasonal foreign workers to employ qualified domestic workers until fifty percent of period of work contract has lapsed. 81 ALR Fed 531.

Access to federal courts by foreign state, or national thereof, which United States does not recognize or with which United States has no diplomatic relations. 65 ALR Fed 881.

Construction and application of 28 USC sec. 1350, giving United States District Courts jurisdiction of action by alien for tort only, committed in violation of law of nations or treaty of United States. 34 ALR Fed 388.

2. A.L.R. Annotation

Weapons: validity of state statutes restricting right of aliens to bear arms, 28 ALR4th 1096.

State regulation of land ownership by alien corporation. 21 ALR4th 1329.

Section 801

1. Digest System Key Numbers

Customs Duties ☞21.

Section 802

1. Digest System Numbers

Customs Duties ☞21.

TABLE OF CROSS–REFERENCES

Section 803

1. Digest System Key Numbers

Customs Duties ⌖21.

Section 804

1. Digest System Key Numbers

War and National Emergency ⌖505.

Section 805

1. Digest System Key Numbers

Customs Duties ⌖21, 21.5.

Section 806

1. Digest System Key Numbers

Customs Duties ⌖21.5(1).

Section 807

1. Digest System Key Numbers

Customs Duties ⌖21.5(1).

Section 808

1. Digest System Key Numbers

Customs Duties ⌖22; War and National Emergency ⌖505.

Section 812

1. Digest System Key Numbers

War and National Emergency ⌖504.

Section 823

1. Digest System Key Numbers

Damages ⌖226.

Section 901

1. Digest System Key Numbers

International Law ⌖10.

2. A.L.R. Annotation

Construction and application of 28 USC sec. 1350, giving United States District Courts jurisdiction of action by alien for tort only, committed in violation of law of nations or treaty of United States. 34 ALR Fed 388.

Section 902

1. Digest System Key Numbers

International Law ⌖10.29.

Section 906

1. Digest System Key Numbers

International Law ⌖10.29.

2. A.L.R. Annotation

What constitutes "claim arising in a foreign country" under 28 USC sec. 2680(k), excluding such claims from Federal Tort Claims Act. 57 ALR Fed 275.

Construction and application of 28 USC sec. 1350, giving United States District Courts jurisdiction of action by alien for tort only, committed in violation of law of nations or treaty of United States. 34 ALR Fed 388.

TABLE OF CROSS–REFERENCES

Section 907

1. Digest System Key Numbers

International Law ⚷10.29.

2. A.L.R. Annotation

What constitutes "claim arising in a foreign country" under 28 USC sec. 2680(k), excluding such claims from Federal Tort Claims Act. 57 ALR Fed 275.

Construction and application of 28 USC sec. 1350, giving United States District Courts jurisdiction of action by alien for tort only, committed in violation of law of nations or treaty of United States. 34 ALR Fed 388.

INDEX

A

ABDUCTION
Child abduction, § 485; RN 7
Enforcement of criminal law,
  Violation of territorial limits, § 432
    Com. *c*, RN 1-3; § 433 Com. *b*
  International human rights conventions, § 432 RN 1
  International protests against, § 432 RN 3

ACT OF STATE DOCTRINE §§ 443–444
Accounts receivable and, § 443 RN 4
Antitrust cases, § 443 RN 7
Applicability, § 443
  Cases not involving expropriation, § 443 Com. *c*, RN 7
Bernstein letter exception, § 443 RN 8
Certificates of deposit, § 443 RN 4
Commercial transactions, § 443 RN 6
Conflict of laws and act of state, § 443 RN 1
Congress,
  Modification by, § 443(2); § 444
Consent of foreign state to judicial scrutiny, § 443 Com. *e*
Constitutional underpinnings of doctrine, § 443 Coms. *a*, *j*
Counterclaims, § 443 Com. *b*, RN 5, 8, 9; § 444 RN 4
Courts, role of, § 443 Com. *b*, RN 12
Debt situs, § 443 RN 4
Definition, § 443 Com. *a*
Development of, § 443 RN 2
Effect on proceedings in other countries, § 443 Com. *f*
Exceptions, § 443 Com. *b*
Executive Branch,
  Bernstein exception, § 443 RN 8
  Role of, § 443 Com. *h*, RN 8
Expropriation and, § 443 Com. *b*; § 444 Com. *c*

ACT OF STATE DOCTRINE—Cont'd
Cases not involving, § 443 Com. *c*, RN 7
Federal law, § 443 Com. *g*
  State courts bound by, § 443 Com. *g*
Foreign decisions, § 443 RN 12
Foreign law, § 443 RN 12
Form and proof of, § 443 Com. *i*
Formal acts of sovereign authority and, § 443 RN 3
Governmental acts within, § 443 RN 3
Heads of government, application to, § 443 RN 3
Hickenlooper Amendment, § 444
  Aliens, claims by, § 444 RN 6
  Claim to specific property, § 444 Com. *e*, RN 4, 5
  Claims of title to property, § 444 Com. *a*
  Discriminatory taxes by a country, § 444 Com. *c*
  Foreign aid suspension, § 444 Com. *c*
  Foreign Sovereign Immunities Act, § 444 Com. *d*, RN 5; § 455 Com. *c*
  International law and, § 444 Coms. *b*, *c*, RN 2
  Letters of credit, § 444 RN 7
  Presidential determination, § 444 Com. *f*, RN 3
  Rationale of, § 444 RN 1
  Sovereign immunity and, § 444 Com. *d*, RN 5; § 455 Com. *c*
Human rights violations, § 443 Com. *c*
  See also Human Rights
Inapplicability to acts affecting property outside acting state, § 443 RN 4
Injury to foreign nationals, § 712
International law and, § 443 Com. *a*
International law violations, § 444 Coms. *b*, *c*
Just compensation, § 712 Com. *d*, RN 3
Libel, § 443 RN 7

---

* Where reference to section number is followed by a semi-colon, the reference is to the black letter, as well as to the Comment or Note cited.

DOMESTIC LAW
Foreign relations law of United States and, § 1
International law and agreements,
  Inconsistency between law of United States and, § 115
Rules originating in, § 1 Com. *b*
United States and,
  Inconsistency between international law and, § 115

DOMESTIC PERSON
Jurisdiction to tax and,
  Various rules defining, § 411 RN 2

DOMICILE
Corporations, § 412 RN 10
Distinguished from residence and presence, § 412 RN 10
Habitual residence distinguished, § 484 RN 1; § 485 Com. *c*
Jurisdiction to adjudicate, § 421(2)(b)
Jurisdiction to prescribe, § 402 Com. *e*
Jurisdiction to tax, § 411(1)(b); § 412(1)(a)

DONATIVE TRANSFERS
Jurisdiction to tax, § 412 Com. *h*

DOUBLE TAXATION
See also Jurisdiction to Tax
Abstention from taxing to avoid, § 412 RN 3
Bilateral income tax conventions, § 413 RN 2, 3
Conventions on, § 213 RN 4; § 411 RN 2; § 413 RN 3
Exemption of foreign source income and progressive tax rates, § 413 Com. *e*
Foreign tax credit, § 413 Com. *c*
  Controlled entities, § 413 Com. *d*, RN 2
International agreement, § 413 Com. *a*
Limitations on (U.S.), § 413
Overlapping jurisdiction to tax, § 413 RN 1
Wealth transfers, § 413 Com. *b*

DUAL NATIONALITY, § 214 Com. *f*
See also Nationality
Corporations, § 213 RN 9

DUE PROCESS
Foreign affairs and, § 1 RN 6
Jurisdiction to adjudicate foreign offenses, § 422 Com. *a*
United States law on, § 721 Com. *f*, RN 6

DUMPING
See also International Trade
Defined, § 807
Dumping and antidumping duties, § 807
European Economic Community, § 807 RN 4
GATT rules, § 807; Com. *a*, RN 3
  Anti-Dumping Code, § 807 RN 3
  Dumping under, § 807 Com. *a*
Judicial review in the United States, § 807 RN 2
Subsidies distinguished, § 806 Com. *a*
United States procedures, § 807 RN 1
United States rules, § 807(2); Com. *b*

E

ECONOMIC INJURY TO NATIONALS
See also as subhead to Protection of Persons
Nationals of other states, § 712

ECONOMIC SANCTIONS
Foreign branches and subsidiaries,
  Use of by United States to control, § 414 RN 3
Jurisdiction to enforce, § 431 RN 3, 4

EICHMANN CASE, § 432 RN 3

ELLES REPORT, § 711 RN 3

ENEMY ALIENS
Rights of, § 711 Com. *h*, RN 5

ENFORCEMENT
See Jurisdiction to Enforce

ENTRY IN DISTRESS
Passage through waters and, § 513 Com. *a*, RN 1

ENVIRONMENT
Activities that can cause harm, **Intro. Note to Part VI**
Adverse effects defined, § 601 RN 2
Aircraft pollution, § 603 Com. *g*
Antarctica, § 601 RN 5
Clean Air Act, § 601 RN 3, 8
Collisions at sea, § 603 RN 2
Common environment, § 601
Definitions, § 601 RN 2
Discharge of waste, § 603 RN 5
Global commons, impact on, § 601 RN 9
Human environment defined, § 601 RN 2
International Court of Justice and, **Intro. Note to Part VI**

F

H

I

J

JUDGMENTS
Declaratory judgments, § 903 Com. *f*
Default judgment against foreign states, § 459
Enforcement of, § 903 Com. *g*
Foreign judgments and awards, §§ 481–488
See Foreign Judgments

JUDICIAL ASSISTANCE, §§ 471–474
See International Judicial Assistance

JUDICIAL DECREES
Jurisdiction to prescribe and, § 415 Com. *h,* RN 5

JUDICIAL NOTICE
International law, § 113 Com. *b*

JURIDICAL PERSONS
See also Corporations, Protection of Persons
Definitions, § 213 Coms. *a, e;* § 411 RN 2
Jurisdiction to tax, § 412(1)(c)
Nationality, § 211

JURISDICTION
Categories, § 401
Conflicts, §§ 441, 442
  Foreign state compulsion, § 441
  Requests for disclosure and, § 442
Conflicts of jurisdiction, § 403(3); § 441; § 442
  See also Foreign State Compulsion
Different aspects of, § 401 Com. *a*
Foreign branches and subsidiaries, § 414
  See also Foreign Branches and Subsidiaries
International and United States law compared, § 401 Com. *b*
Jurisdiction to adjudicate, §§ 421–423
  See also Jurisdiction to Adjudicate
Jurisdiction to enforce, §§ 431–433
  See also Jurisdiction to Enforce
National and international law, **Intro. Note to Part IV**
Reasonableness, principle of, **Intro. Note to Part IV**
Subject matter jurisdiction, § 401 Com. *c;* § 415 Com. *k;* § 421 Com. *j*
Tax, jurisdiction to, §§ 411–413
  See also Jurisdiction to Tax
United States,
  Limitations on exercise of authority, **Intro. Note to Part IV**
Universal jurisdiction, § 404

JURISDICTION—Cont'd
See also Universal Jurisdiction

JURISDICTION TO ADJUDICATE
Actions based on presence of property, § 421 Com. *i*
Aircraft, § 421(2)(f)
Appearance, § 421(3); Com. *g*
Civil and criminal jurisdiction, § 421 Com. *b*
Consent to jurisdiction of state, § 421(2)(g); RN 6
Constitutional safeguards (U.S.), § 422 Com. *c*
Corporate organized within the state, § 421(2)(e)
Criminal cases (U.S.), § 422
  See also Extradition
Constitutional authority to prescribe, § 422 Com. *c(i)*
Constitutional safeguards, § 422 Com. *c,* RN 2
Consular treaties, § 422 RN 5
Criminal jurisdiction in the United States, § 422 Com. *c*
Criminal trials abroad by United States, § 422 RN 4
Foreign penal trials in United States, § 422 RN 5
Jurisdiction of United States courts, § 422 Com. *b,* RN 1
Military and defense personnel abroad, § 422 RN 4
Place of trial, § 422 Com. *c(ii)*
Presence of accused, § 422 Com. *c(iii)*
Prison facilities and, § 422 Com. *a*
Procedural safeguards, § 422 Com. *c(iv)*
Subpoenas served on United States citizens abroad, § 422 RN 6
Universal and other non-territorial crimes, § 423
  See also Universal and Other Non-territorial Crimes
Defined, § 401(b)
Diversity of citizenship jurisdiction, § 421 RN 7
Doing business, § 421(2)(h)
Domicile, § 421(2)(b)
Effects in state, § 421(2)(j)
Enumerated links discrete, not cumulative, § 421 Com. *c*
Foreign defendants (U.S.), § 421 RN 7
Foreign penal law, § 422 Com. *a*
Forum selection clauses, § 421(2)(g); Com. *h,* RN 6
General and specific jurisdiction, § 421 RN 3

LONG-ARM STATUTES
See also in general, Service of Process
FSIA and, § 453 **RN 4**

LOS CONVENTION (LAW OF THE SEA)
See Law of the Sea Convention

M

MALE CAPTUS, BENE DETENTUS
Criminal law enforcement and, § 432
RN 2
Ker-Frisbie rule, § 433 **Coms. b, c**

MARINE POLLUTION, § 603
Civil liability, § 604 **RN 1**
Wrongful enforcement measures,
§ 604 **Com. f, RN 3**
Ecosystems, protection of fragile, § 603
Com. d, RN 6
Flag state obligations, § 603 **Com. b**
Joint action in emergencies, § 603
Com. f
Joint enforcement by port states, § 604
RN 2
Notification, § 603 **Com. e**
Polluting state, obligations of, § 603
Com. a, RN 1
Remedies for, § 604
Civil liability, § 604 **RN 1**
Coastal state enforcement,
§ 604(3)(a); **Com. d**
Detention of ships, § 604(3)(a)
Flag state, enforcement by, § 604
Com. c
General interstate remedies, § 604
Com. a
Institution of proceedings, § 604(3)
Port states, enforcement by,
§ 604(3)(b), (c); **Com. e**
Private remedies, § 604 **Com. b**
Prompt and adequate compensation,
§ 604(2)
Responsibility for, § 603
Sea-bed mining states, obligations of,
§ 603 **Com. c**
United States legislation on, § 603 **RN
7**

MARITIME
See also High Seas
Special maritime jurisdiction, § 403 **RN
9**

MERCHANT SHIPPING
See Coastal States, Port States, Sea,
Law of

MILITARY FORCES
Immunity from jurisdiction, § 461
Com. f, RN 2
Rights of members of United States
armed forces, § 721 **RN 10**
Securities transactions,
Protection of United States person-
nel, § 416 **RN 2**
Trial of military personnel, § 422 **RN 4**

MILITARY OCCUPATION
Statehood and, § 201 **RN 3**

MINERAL RESOURCES
See also High Seas
Deep sea-bed, § 523

MONETARY LAW
See International Monetary Law

**MONTREAL CONVENTION FOR THE
SUPPRESSION OF UNLAWFUL
ACTS AGAINST THE SAFETY OF
CIVIL AVIATION, § 404 RN 1; 423
RN 1**

**MOST–FAVORED–NATION TREAT-
MENT**
See also International Trade
Defined, § 801(1); **Com. a**
GATT and, § 802(1); **Com. a**
International trade, §§ 801, 802
United States law, § 802(2); **Com. b**

MULTILATERAL AGREEMENTS
International legislation, as, **Intro.
Note to Part III**
Ratification, § 312 **Com. d**
Reservations, § 313; **Com. b**

MULTINATIONAL ENTERPRISES
Domestic law, § 213 **RN 8**
Guidelines as to, § 414 **RN 2**
International law, in, § 213 **RN 7**
Jurisdiction to prescribe, § 414; **Coms.
a, c**
Conduct of subsidiary imputed to par-
ent company, § 414 **RN 2, 3**
Intercorporate affiliation, § 414
Coms. g, h, RN 2
Jurisdiction to tax,
Measurement of income, § 412 **Com.
e**
United States regulation of, § 414 **RN 1**

MULTIPLE NATIONALITY
Protection of persons of, § 713 **Com. d,
RN 2**

N

R

†